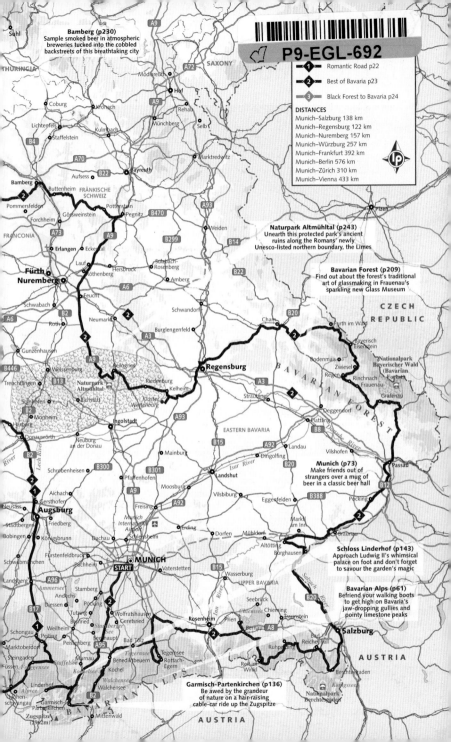

Bamberg (p230)
Sample smoked beer in atmospheric breweries tucked into the cobbled backstreets of this breathtaking city

1 Romantic Road p22
2 Best of Bavaria p23
3 Black Forest to Bavaria p24

DISTANCES
Munich–Salzburg 138 km
Munich–Regensburg 122 km
Munich–Nuremberg 157 km
Munich–Würzburg 257 km
Munich–Frankfurt 392 km
Munich–Berlin 576 km
Munich–Zürich 310 km
Munich–Vienna 433 km

Naturpark Altmühltal (p243)
Unearth this protected park's ancient ruins along the Romans' newly Unesco-listed northern boundary, the Limes

Bavarian Forest (p209)
Find out about the forest's traditional art of glassmaking in Frauenau's sparkling new Glass Museum

Munich (p73)
Make friends out of strangers over a mug of beer in a classic beer hall

Schloss Linderhof (p143)
Approach Ludwig II's whimsical palace on foot and don't forget to savour the garden's magic

Bavarian Alps (p61)
Befriend your walking boots to get high on Bavaria's jaw-dropping gullies and pointy limestone peaks

Garmisch-Partenkirchen (p136)
Be awed by the grandeur of nature on a hair-raising cable-car ride up the Zugspitze

On the Road

Andrea Schulte-Peevers Coordinating Author

This is me (second from right) at the Munich Oktoberfest (p108) displaying my usual quiet dignity, fearlessly confronting the locals on their own turf and enduring their insufferable rituals in my quest to spiritually bond with them and deliver the truth of their ways. Pain, deprivation – but not the lack of anything to drink – such is the harsh life of a Lonely Planet writer.

CATHERINE LE NEVEZ Every time I take in Nuremberg's towering medieval walls, grand hilltop castle and cavernous beer halls (not to mention its beer!) it leaves me awestruck. But I'm most awestruck of all when I'm standing alongside the Way of Human Rights' pillars, contemplating the city's depth of compassion, courage and inspiration.

KERRY WALKER Berchtesgaden National Park is pure drama. I'd joined day-trippers on the early morning boat across the glassy Königssee to St Bartholomä, the trailhead for the **Eiskapelle walk** (p70). The sun shone on the soaring pinnacles of the Watzmann, glacial brooks and fields ablaze with yellow arnica. It was a magnificent start to a short, spectacular hike far from the madding crowd.

See full author bios page 339

MUNICH, BAVARIA & THE BLACK FOREST

Welcome to this land of fairy tales and fast cars, of fanciful castles and flirty dance clubs, a place whose landscapes stir the soul, and where hi tech and tradition are married happily. Picture yourself making friends in a boisterous beer hall, skiing down powdered Alpine slopes or strolling along narrow lanes whose cobblestones have been worn smooth by centuries of carriages and shoe leather. Munich, Bavaria and the Black Forest are every bit as fun, romantic, exciting and charming as you'd imagine.

Spirited

Summer solstice, Lent, a saint's birthday, a historic miracle, or for nothing particular at all – the people in Bavaria and the Black Forest need few excuses to throw a good party. The Oktoberfest drink-a-thon may be the most famous event, but whenever you visit you're sure to find somewhere to join in the revelry.

❶ Oktoberfest

Social barriers dissolve, strangers become friends and everybody sings too loudly, drinks in excess and has waaaay too much fun at the world's biggest beer bash that takes over Munich (p108) for 16 wild and wacky days starting in late September.

❷ Munich Club Scene

Chic party temples, grungy dance halls, house, techno, drum and bass, punk, reggae and ballroom: Munich has plenty of party dens where you can get your nocturnal kicks and dazzle with fancy footwork till sunrise (p121).

❸ Pope Mania

Get into the spirit in Pope Benedict XVI's home town, Marktl am Inn (p209) where you can tour his birth house, touch his baptismal font, bone up on his biography and stock up on Papst Bier labelled with His Beaming Holiness.

❹ Beer Halls & Gardens

Munich's Hofbräuhaus (p119) may be the world's most famous pub, but you'll find lots of cheer and beer throughout Bavaria and the Black Forest. On balmy summer nights, there's nothing quite like clinking mugs below the ancient chestnut trees.

❺ Monastic Brews

In a land where beer is darn near a religious experience, it's no surprise that some of the best hoppy juices are made by monks. Try them for yourself at Kloster Weltenburg (p203) and Kloster Andechs (p129; opposite).

❻ Wine Country

It's not *all* about the beer. Hit the wine taverns or tasting rooms to put some zing in your step with crisp whites and velvety reds from the delightful Franconian Wine Country (p260) and the Black Forest's Kaiserstuhl (p297).

'No matter whether you're a downhill daredevil or just want to glissade gently through the lovely forest, there's a slope or trail with your name on it.'

Adventurous

Spoiled with a virtual pastoral of big-shouldered mountains, gaping canyons, peaceful river valleys, fanning vineyards, crystalline lakes and other equally lyrical landscapes, Bavaria and the Black Forest are dream destinations for outdoorsy types. Trade that couch for the trail and you'll be rewarded with great memories and a toned body.

① Skiing

No matter whether you're a downhill dare-devil or just want to glissade gently through lovely forest, there's a slope or trail with your name on it. Garmisch-Partenkirchen (p137; top left) is the most famous Alpine resort and the Chiemgau (p154) is a cross-country mecca.

② Mountain Biking

Climb into that saddle to zip past the velvety hills and half-timbered villages of the Kinzig-tal (p306), cycle riverside through dramatic gorges in the Naturpark Altmühltal (p243), or go speed-crazy in Berchtesgaden (p157).

③ Hiking

There's no better way to appreciate southern Germany's drop-dead gorgeous scenery than by hitting the trail. Flirt with mountaineer-ing on the Alpspitze Nordwand and descend the sheer Höllentalklamm gorge (p64; top right), or tackle the beer trail in Franconian Switzerland (p236).

④ Windsurfing

Feel the rhythm of the wind and water as you skim across crystal-clear lakes shimmering in shades from turquoise to emerald. Famous spots include the Walchensee (p148) and the virtual inland sea of Lake Constance (accessed via Lindau, p286).

⑤ Snowshoeing

Do the stomp through deep powder and sparkling forests in such top spots as the Black Forest's Feldberg (p301) with giddying views of the Alps, or in the remote National-park Bayerischer Wald (p210; opposite), with its untouched tranquillity.

⑥ Ballooning

For a bird's-eye perspective of this fabled land, drift silently over its woods, valleys and ancient villages, preferably at dawn or sunset. The skies over Rothenburg ob der Tauber (p265) are especially inviting.

10

Fairy Tales

With their thick forests, frilly palaces and rustic traditions, it's no wonder that Bavaria and the Black Forest have spawned such classic fairy tales as *Hänsel and Gretel* and *Snow White and the Seven Dwarfs*. Walt Disney was so impressed, he modelled his Sleeping Beauty's castle on Schloss Neuschwanstein.

'Ramble…past higgledy-piggledy villages, lordly castles and scenery that will have you burning up the pixels in your digicam.'

❶ Ludwig II's Castles

Ludwig II was a king not quite of this world and neither are his palaces. Delve into some of Ludwig's warped fantasies at the theatrical Schloss Neuschwanstein (p283; opposite), the whimsical Schloss Linderhof (p143) or the ostentatious Schloss Herrenchiemsee (p151).

❷ Christmas Markets

Fall under the spell of these gleaming markets sprawled across ancient town squares during the festive season. Baked apples, mulled wine and handmade ornaments are among the irresistible treats in Nuremberg (p223; top), Munich (p111) and Gengenbach (p311).

❸ Puppet Theatres

Take a magic carpet ride into the adorable world of whimsical singing, dancing and talking marionettes. The Augsburger Puppenkiste (p278) and the Figurentheater am Burgtor in Rothenburg ob der Tauber (p267) are among venues sure to delight kids of all ages.

❹ Romantic Road

The name says it all and the reality is even better. This spectacular ribbon of riches (p252) rambles past higgledy-piggledy villages, lordly castles and scenery that'll have you burning up the pixels in your digicam.

❺ Frescoed Façades

In Bavaria even some of the house façades are veritable works of art. Painted in a style called *Lüftlmalerei* (p142), you'll see them all throughout the Tölzer Land (p145) and Werdenfelser Land (p136), but especially in Oberammergau (p141).

❻ Villinger Fasnet

Jingling jesters called *Narro,* straw-stuffed characters called *Wuescht* and cackling witches take the cobbled streets of Villingen's old town (p299) by storm during local carnival celebrations.

❼ Mt Watzmann

Legend has it that the peaks of this lumbering grey massif looming above Berchtesgaden (p72) are in reality King Watzmann, his wife and their seven children, who were turned into stone as punishment for terrorising the land.

The baroque Ramsau church in Berchtesgadener Land (p157)

Contents

Regional Map Contents

Destination Munich, Bavaria & the Black Forest

You must, of course, have endless expectations about what you'll discover on your Bavarian adventure. Palaces straight out of fairy tales, strapping lads in lederhosen, onion-domed churches, beer halls where big-bosomed wenches juggle platters of roast pork, romantic valleys shrouded in fog and backed by the fierce verticality of the Alps. And they're all here, in truth. But they're only part of the mythology.

Bavaria can be as broad-minded as a view from the Zugspitze on a clear day and as narrow as the cobbled lanes threading through Rothenburg ob der Tauber. Its capital, Munich, is sexy, sophisticated and self-confident. It will seduce you with its irresistible *joie de vivre,* a trove of cultural delights and a relaxed flair that's prompted some to call it Italy's northernmost outpost.

Above all, though, Bavaria is successful. Its people earn more than anywhere else in Germany, the unemployment rate is the lowest nationwide, its schools and universities are at the top of the class, and sometimes it seems as though everyone you meet pilots the latest model Mercedes or BMW.

This is a region that cherishes its traditions yet enthusiastically embraces the future. Munich may be celebrating its 850th birthday in 2008, but just outside the city engineers are busy giving birth to the futuristic Galileo Satellite Navigation System. The European Aeronautic Defence & Space Company (EADS) builds Tornado fighter jets near Augsburg and biotech firms are feverishly searching for the cure for cancer. An openness towards innovation, a favourable business climate and a highly qualified workforce are all factors playing key roles in this success story.

Other defining factors are stability and conformity. It's simply not in the Bavarian character to rock the boat. For more than 700 years, one single family – the Wittelsbachs – ruled over the land, and even in democratic times only one party – the Christian Social Union (CSU) – has enjoyed uninterrupted power since WWII. Fiscal and social conservatism go hand in hand here. Same-sex couples may not register at the registry office or adopt children. Immigrants must sign up for integration courses or risk a cut in their welfare payments. Muslim teachers may not wear headscarves in school.

Still, Bavaria is a bewitching land and its people know it. Fortunately, they also know how to enjoy life. Beer gardens and street cafés hum with excited chatter as soon as the last winter storms disappear, and on weekends there's a veritable exodus to either the ski slopes, the hiking trails or the lake-shore beaches. It's a great place for visitors.

So what about the Black Forest? It may not have Bavaria's economic muscle but it, too, suffers from being reduced to a cliché, only it's cuckoo clocks instead of lederhosen. Bookmarked by forever-young Freiburg and stately Baden-Baden, it has more Michelin-starred chefs than any other German region. Its deep valleys, thick forests, Hänsel-and-Gretel houses and quaint traditions seem relics from a simpler past when our lives weren't ruled by laptops, iPods and GPS.

In southern Germany, dreamers and daredevils, romantics and gourmets, explorers and historians will all find ways to connect to this unique part of the world.

FAST FACTS: MUNICH & BAVARIA

Area: 70,549 sq km

Population: 12.5 million

GDP: €357 billion

Per capita income: €2570 per month (blue-collar), €3530 per month (white-collar)

Unemployment rate: 6.2%

Annual per capita beer consumption: 170L

Kilometres of autobahn: 2299

Passenger cars: 7.3 million

Students: 249,000

Overnight stays: 75 million

Museums: 1250

FAST FACTS: BLACK FOREST

Area: 13,000 sq km

Population: 3.43 million

Getting Started

Tourism infrastructure in Bavaria and the Black Forest is outstanding and families, urban nomads and backpackers will all find their needs and expectations met. Room and travel reservations are a good idea between July and August and around major holidays, but otherwise you can keep your advance planning to a minimum.

WHEN TO GO

Most people prefer to visit Bavaria and the Black Forest between May and September when sunny skies and warm temperatures are likely. This is the best time for hiking, cycling, water sports and other outdoor pursuits, hanging out in beer gardens and outdoor cafés, and partying at festivals or alfresco events. For more information, see the Events Calendar, p20. The shoulder seasons (March to May, and October) bring fewer tourists, surprisingly pleasant weather and a riot of colour: wildflowers in spring, foliage in autumn.

With the exception of winter sports, activities between November and February are likely to focus more on culture and city life. Expect short daylight hours, grey skies, low temperatures, and reduced opening times or seasonal closures at museums and other sightseeing venues. Many smaller lodging properties, especially in rural areas, close down through November until early December. The ski season usually kicks off in early to mid-December, moves into full swing after New Year and winds down sometime in March.

See Climate Charts on p315 for more information.

For related information, see Holidays (p316).

TRAVELLING RESPONSIBLY

Since our inception in 1973, Lonely Planet has encouraged readers to tread lightly, travel responsibly and enjoy the magic independent travel affords. International travel is growing at a jaw-dropping rate, and we still firmly believe in the benefits it can bring – but, as always, we encourage you to consider the impact your visit will have on both the global environment and the local economies, cultures and ecosystems.

Fortunately, travelling responsibly within Bavaria and the Black Forest is comparatively easy. Take advantage of the excellent public transport system, use a bicycle and build your itinerary around more than Neuschwanstein,

---

DON'T LEAVE HOME WITHOUT...

- Memorising a few basic words in German (p331)
- Valid travel and health insurance (p317)
- A cholesterol meter (all that meat!)
- Hotel or camping reservations when travelling outside the cities in summer (p312)
- Sturdy and worn-in walking shoes for hiking
- Loose pants to accommodate a potential beer belly
- Good maps or a GPS for finding your way on country roads or in the mountains)
- A raincoat, rainproof shoes and/or umbrella for those days when the sun is a no-show
- Nerves of steel for driving on the autobahns
- A set of smart clothes for hitting big-city clubs, the opera or fancy restaurants
- This book and an open mind

Rothenburg and other impacted hot spots. This book is full of ideas for getting you off the beaten path.

For background on the wider environmental issues facing Bavaria and the Black Forest and how these are being tackled, see the Environment chapter (p52).

Getting There & Away

Travelling to southern Germany by land may be easier and more comfortable than you think. Coming from London, for instance, you could catch the Eurostar train after work, switch to a night train in Paris and be in Munich for breakfast. There are also daytime and overnight trains to Munich and Freiburg from numerous other European cities. See p324 for details.

Although slower and less comfortable, riding the bus is another option, especially if you're headed to a place not served by train. Details are on p323.

If you're driving, consider hiring an efficient car – preferably a hybrid – rather than using your own vehicle, especially if it's older. And decline those 'free' upgrades – that bigger car may be a petrol guzzler. Consider ride-sharing (p327). If you do choose to fly, offset your carbon emissions; see www.climatecare.org, www.terrapass.com or www.sustainabletravelinternational.org for details.

Local Transport

Even if you're travelling by car, consider ditching it at least part of the time. Getting around between towns or to tourist attractions and trailheads by train or bus is usually uncomplicated and inexpensive since timetables are often designed with visitors' needs in mind. In some communities overnight guests get to ride for free. Low-emission or alternative-fuel bus fleets are increasingly common.

Accommodation

Many properties follow simple eco-initiatives, such as offering you the option of reusing your towels and sheets, replacing plastic or Styrofoam cups with glass and dropping prepackaged items from the breakfast buffet. Guests can often borrow bicycles for free or a small fee. Newer hotels are sometimes built using local and/or ecofriendly materials. Recycling is *de rigueur*.

You can help raise awareness among hotel staff by thanking them for any ecofriendly programs they offer; if they don't have any, encourage them to do so and provide a few constructive hints.

Food

Fortunately, chefs in the Black Forest and Bavaria love working with local, seasonal and often organic ingredients, so eating like a 'locavore' shouldn't be a tall order. Farmers markets abound and sometimes local farmers sell their product at roadside stands. Choose restaurants that make use of organic produce whenever possible and only order fish, seafood or meat that's from sustainable sources. If carrying a bottle of water, refill it in bathrooms or at water fountains. Take fast food off the menu.

Responsible Travel Schemes

BayernTour Natur (www.stmugv.bayern.de/aktionen/tournatur/veranstaltungen.htm) Searchable database of more than 2600 eco- and nature-related events – from guided hikes to birdwatching – taking place throughout Bavaria between May and October.

Climate Neutral Travel (www.dasferienland.de/klimaneutral-reisen.asp#rechner, in German) The Schonach/Triberg region in the Black Forest offsets CO_2 emissions caused by its visitors by donating money towards a World Wildlife Fund project in Nepal. Fill out the short form with your name, distance travelled by car and by train, and send it by email.

TOP 10

France   **BLACK FOREST**   **BAVARIA** Czech Republic
                                      • **MUNICH**

BOOKS

Great storytelling opens up a window on a country's culture and the psyche of its people. Get ready for your trip by curling up with these books shining the light on various facets of southern Germany.

1 *Gladius Dei* (1902), Thomas Mann
2 *Caspar Hauser* (1908), Jakob Wassermann
3 *Success* (1930), Lion Feuchtwanger
4 *The Brecht Memoir* (1991), Eric Bentley
5 *Where Ghosts Walked: Munich's Road to the Third Reich* (1996), David Clay Large
6 *Letters Back to Ancient China* (1998), Herbert Rosendorfer

7 *Lola Montez: A Life* (1998), Bruce Seymour
8 *Against the Stream: Growing Up Where Hitler Used to Live* (2002), Anna Rosmus
9 *Massacre in Munich: The Manhunt for the Killers Behind the 1972 Olympics Massacre* (2005), Michael Bar Bar-Zohar and Eitan Haber
10 *Sophie Scholl & the White Rose* (2007), Jud Newborn and Annette Dumbach

MOVIES

Grab a bowl of popcorn and get in the mood for your Bavarian adventure with some of these flicks, made by a cast of top international directors.

1 *Triumph of the Will* (1935) Director: Leni Riefenstahl
2 *Sissi* (1955) Director: Ernst Marischka
3 *Ludwig* (1973) Director: Luchino Visconti
4 *Veronika Voss* (1982) Director: Rainer Werner Fassbinder
5 *Autumn Milk* (1989) Director: Joseph Vilsmaier

6 *The Nasty Girl* (1990) Director: Michael Verhoeven
7 *The Enigma of Kaspar Hauser* (1995) Director: Werner Herzog
8 *Hierankl* (2003, in German) Director: Hans Steinbichler
9 *Munich* (2005) Director: Steven Spielberg
10 *Sophie Scholl – The Final Days* (2005) Director: Marc Rothmund

FESTIVALS

Bavarians are party people, especially during the balmy summer months when the festival season is in full swing. Here's our list of favourites, but also have a look at the Events Calendar on p20 and the Festivals & Events section in the destination chapters.

1 Erlanger Bergkirchweih (p227) – Erlangen, May
2 Zelt-Musik Festival (p289) – Freiburg, June to July
3 Tollwood Festival (p110) – Munich, late June to mid-July
4 Kinderzeche (p269) – Dinkelsbühl, mid-July
5 Salzburger Festspiele (p176) – Salzburg, late July to late August

6 Richard Wagner Festival (p239) – Bayreuth, late July to August
7 Gäubodenfest (p203) – Straubing, August
8 Oktoberfest (p108) – Munich, mid-September to early October
9 Leonhardifahrt (p145) – Bad Tölz, 6 November
10 Nuremberg Christkindlsmarkt (p217) – Nuremberg, late November to 24 December

Umweltsiegel (www.umweltsiegel.de) Ecofriendly hotels and restaurants as certified by the Bavarian state government.
Worldwide Opportunities on Organic Farms (www.wwoof.de) Volunteering on organic farms, including dozens in southern Germany.

COSTS & MONEY

Outside major cities such as Munich and Nuremberg, Bavaria can be quite reasonably priced. You should be able to live comfortably on €120 to €150 per day (per person, travelling as an adult couple). For mere survival you'll need to budget from €40 to €70, but this will have you camping or sleeping in hostels, preparing your own meals or eating snack food, and limiting your entertainment. For ideas on how to stretch your euro further, see p315.

Comfortable midrange accommodation starts at about €80 for a double room with breakfast in cities, and €50 in the countryside. Many hotels and hostels have special 'family rooms' with three or four beds, or will supply sleeping cots for a small fee. For more on travelling with kids, see p314.

A two-course meal in an average restaurant costs between €20 and €30 per person, including a beverage. The bill will be lower if you stick to cafés and casual eateries and skip alcoholic drinks. Kids' menus or dishes are quite common.

Car-hire costs vary widely but you can figure on spending at least €45 per day for a medium-sized car, plus petrol.

TRAVEL LITERATURE

To get in the mood for your trip, consider reading some of the following titles, written by travellers who have visited Bavaria before you.

A Tramp Abroad, by Mark Twain, is a literary classic containing keen and witty observations gathered during his travels in Europe, including a walking tour of the Black Forest and the Alps with his friend Joseph H Twitchell.

Katherine Mansfield's *In a German Pension* is a collection of satirical short stories inspired by her stay in Bavaria as a young woman.

It's a tough slog, but Claudio Magris' *Danube* certainly has its moments. Part travelogue, part meditation, it follows the great river through Bavaria and beyond, reflecting on events that took place along it and the people who've lived here.

Patrick Leigh Fermor's *A Time of Gifts* is a keen and readable account of the author's epic journey on foot from Holland to Turkey, passing through Bavaria along the way, in the years before WWII.

Three Men on a Bummel, by British author Jerome K Jerome, is a delightful comic tale that follows three English gentlemen on their cycling trip through the Black Forest in the 1890s.

INTERNET RESOURCES

Bavarian Government (www.bayern.de) Official Bavarian state government site with good general background information.
Bavarian Tourism Association (www.bayern.by) Official site loaded with useful information on all aspects of travel to and within Bavaria.
Black Forest Tourism (www.blackforest-tourism.com) Loaded with preplanning tips on sights, culture, sport, nature and special events.
Castles in Bavaria (www.schloesser.bayern.de) Overview of all palaces, fortresses, residences and castles in the state.
Expats in Bavaria (www.expats-in-bavaria.com) Especially useful for expats but also with relevant information for visitors.
Lonely Planet (www.lonelyplanet.com) Travel news and summaries, the Thorn Tree bulletin board, and links to more web resources.

HOW MUCH?

Latte macchiato €2.80-3.50

One hour of parking (in a public parking space) €1-2

Cinema ticket €5-9

Pack of 17 cigarettes €4

U-Bahn ticket (Munich) €2.20

See also Lonely Planet index on inside front cover.

Events Calendar

From samba to jazz, historical re-enactments to epic beer drink-ups, Mozart to religious pilgrimages – the party never stops in Bavaria and the Black Forest. Nearly all events highlighted in this short chapter are described in greater detail in the destination chapters, which also list festivals of local importance.

JANUARY–MARCH

HORNSCHLITTENRENNEN   6 Jan
Hilarious celebration in Garmisch-Partenkirchen with locals racing downhill on historical sleds once used for bringing hay and wood to the valleys (p139).

MOZARTWOCHE   Late Jan
Salzburg's Mozart Week (p176) draws an impressive list of internationally renowned conductors, soloists and orchestras.

FASCHING (CARNIVAL)   Jan/Feb
During the six-week pre-Lent period preceding Ash Wednesday, many towns celebrate with costumed street partying, parades, satirical shows and general revelry, especially in Munich (p110). In the Black Forest, the biggest celebration is the Villinger Fasnet (p299).

APRIL–MAY

MAIFEST   30 Apr
On the eve of 1 May, the May Festival celebrates the end of winter with villagers chopping down a tree to make a *Maibaum* (maypole), painting, carving and decorating it, and staging a merry revelry.

INTERNATIONALE JAZZWOCHE   Apr–May
The International Jazz Week (p166) draws the crème de la crème of musicians to Burghausen, near the Austrian border.

NÖRDLINGER PFINGSTMESSE   May
On Pentecost (Whitsuntide) weekend, scores of regional traders exhibit their wares at a huge market (p270) with beer tents, food stalls and entertainment in Nördlingen on the Romantic Road.

AFRICA FESTIVAL   Late May
Bongo drums, hot rhythms and fancy costumes turn the banks of the Main River in Würzburg into Europe's largest festival of black music with international performers (p258).

JUNE–AUGUST

FESTSPIELE EUROPÄISCHE WOCHEN
Mid-Jun–Late Jul
The European 'Festival Weeks' (p206) event is a well-respected international music and cultural festival held in venues in Passau and across the border in Upper Austria and the Czech Republic.

ZELT-MUSIK FESTIVAL   Late Jun–mid-Jul
The Tent Music Festival is a huge three-week festival (p289) held in Freiburg with theatre, cabaret, stand-up comedy acts, concerts, DJs and kids' entertainment.

SONNWENDFEIER   20 Jun
The summer solstice is greeted on the eve of 21 June with big bonfires lit on mountaintops throughout Bavaria.

TOLLWOOD FESTIVAL   Late Jun–mid-Jul
Crowds flock to Munich's Olympiapark for this popular world-culture festival (p110) with concerts, theatre, circus, readings and other fun events. Also in November.

LANDSHUTER HOCHZEIT   Jul
Every four years 2000 townspeople in Landshut dress up in historical costume to re-enact a royal wedding held in 1475 (p215). The next celebration is in 2009.

OPERNFESTSPIELE   Jul
This month-long opera festival (p110) brings international high-calibre talent to the Bavarian State Opera in Munich.

BAVARIAN JAZZ WEEKEND   Mid-Jul
Major jazz festival (p198) brings international top talent and thousands of fans to shake their booties at various stages in the old town of Regensburg.

CHRISTOPHER STREET DAY   Mid-Jul
Gay, lesbian, straight or transgender – everybody comes out to party at Munich's flashy gay parade (p110). Provocative costumes, rainbow flags, techno music and naked torsos guaranteed.

KINDERZECHE   Mid-Jul
Children from Dinkelsbühl re-enact how their city
was saved from devastation during the Thirty
Years' War, along with music and the usual merriment (p269).

SAMBA FESTIVAL   Mid-Jul
This orgy of song and dance draws a quarter of a
million people to Coburg for three days of exotic
and colourful costumes, high-energy music and
sexy dancing (p242).

ST ANNAFEST   Late Jul–early Aug
The enormously popular St Anna Festival (p227)
is a 10-day beer party taking over an 'enchanted'
forest near Forchheim.

RICHARD WAGNER FESTIVAL   Late Jul–Aug
Politicians, blue-bloods, industrialists and other
movers and shakers mingle with actual opera lovers during this prestigious festival (p239) held in
Bayreuth.

SALZBURGER FESTSPIELE   Late Jul–Aug
One of the most important classical-music festivals in Europe, this event (p176) features everything from Mozart to contemporary music, opera
and theatre.

GÄUBODENFEST   Aug
This epic Oktoberfest-style drink-up and occasion
of much revelry draws about a million people to
little Straubing for 11 days starting on the second
Friday of August (p203).

BREISACHER WEINFEST   Aug
This wine festival (p296), held on the last weekend of August, features the coronation of a wine
princess, plus lots of wine tasting, concerts and a
huge fireworks display over the Rhine.

SEPTEMBER–OCTOBER

REICHSSTADT FESTSTAGE   Early Sep
Rothenburg ob der Tauber re-enacts its medieval
history during the Imperial City Festival (p266).

GROSSE WOCHE IFFEZHEIM   Early Sep
Grand Festival Week (p303) is Germany's answer
to Ascot and draws world-class jockeys and famous horses to the Iffezheim racecourse near
Baden-Baden.

OKTOBERFEST   Mid-Sep–early Oct
Millions of people can't be wrong (p108). Enough
said. *Prost!*

NOVEMBER–DECEMBER

LEONHARDIFAHRT   6 Nov
This major procession honours the patron saint
of horses, St Leonard, and features townsfolk
dressed in traditional garments, as well as brass
bands and flower-festooned horse carts. The most
famous version of this is in Bad Tölz (p145).

CHRISTMAS MARKETS   Late Nov–24 Dec
Celebrate the holidays at glittery Christmas markets with mulled wine, gingerbread cookies and
shimmering ornaments. The markets in Munich
(p111), Nuremberg (p223) and Freiburg (p289)
are the most famous, but smaller ones sometimes
have more local flavour.

ADVENTSKALENDAR   Dec
Gengenbach in the northern Black Forest turns
its town hall into a giant advent calendar (p310)
with each of the 24 windows opening one 'door'
at a time to reveal festive scenes painted by well-
known artists.

NIKOLAUSTAG   5 Dec
On the eve of 5 December, children put their
boots outside the door hoping that St Nick will
fill them with sweets and small toys overnight.
Badly behaved children, though, may find only a
prickly rod left behind by St Nick's helper, Knecht
Ruprecht.

SILVESTER   31 Dec
During the German New Year's Eve celebrations,
the new year is greeted with fireworks launched
by thousands of amateur pyromaniacs.

Driving Tours

ROMANTIC ROAD   One week / 450km

After soaking up the vibrant atmosphere of **Würzburg** (p254), carve your way
south through the Tauber Valley to the magnificent palace at **Weikersheim**
(p261) and the astounding Riemenschneider altar in **Creglingen** (p262).
Lose yourself in the tangle of medieval laneways in magical **Rothenburg ob
der Tauber** (p262) and continue southwards, via fetching little **Feuchtwangen**
(p268), to **Dinkelsbühl** (p268) and **Nördlingen** (p270), which are both embraced
by ancient town walls. Set aside some time to check out the storybook
castle guarding the half-timbered village of **Harburg** (p271), and to stroll
along the canalside park at **Donauwörth** (p271) before hitting the energetic
city of **Augsburg** (p272). Countless churches grace the Romantic Road but,
to Augsburg's south, the one packing the mightiest punch is the luminous
Wieskirche (p280). Contemplate King Ludwig II's flights of fancy at his
whimsical castle, **Schloss Neuschwanstein** (p283), and then wind your way west
through the Alps to wrap up your romantic roadtrip on Lake Constance's
idyllic island of **Lindau** (p286). Alternatively, you can kick off your trip in
Lindau and finish in Würzburg.

I can't deny that
I'm a romantic at
heart, but it's the
road tripper in me
that really loves
this route, given
its endless possi-
bilities for detours.
While my main
road highlights
include Rothen-
burg and Harburg,
unplanned side
trips invariably
reveal gems
destined to become
new favourites.

CATHERINE LE NEVEZ

BLACK FOREST TO BAVARIA   Two to three days / 235km

Your adventure begins with a romp through the cobbled alleyways of **Freiburg** (p289), nestled beneath the fiery red-brick Münster. Bid the sunny university city adieu to climb the L124, which corkscrews up through fir forest and affords snapshot vistas of the valley below. If you're driving in winter, make sure you have *Winterreifen* (winter tyres). Pause for knockout views of the Rhine Valley and Alps from **Schauinsland** (p295) before zigzagging north to Kirchzarten and the L127, past deep-green woodlands dappled with purple foxglove in summer. Soon the voluptuous domes of the Benedictine abbey in **St Peter** (p297) slide into view, rivalled in the beauty stakes by the candy-pink pilgrimage church in nearby **St Märgen**. On the B500, **Lachenhäusle** is a great pit-stop for local ham, honey and schnapps. Enjoy your goodies over views of gently rising hills fading off into a watercolour distance. Veer right onto the L180a, a sublime country road that wriggles past meadows of ripening corn, hip-roofed farmhouses and cows grazing the pastures. From the rural village of **Urach**, shadow the gurgling Breg upstream on the L172/L180 to **Vöhrenbach**, picturesquely tucked into the folds of the countryside. The L173 serves up more dreamy scenery on lanes bristling with firs and pines. It's time for a well-deserved break at Ackerloch Grillschopf in **Unterkirnach** (p300) before edging east to explore medieval **Villingen** (p299). To continue onto Bavaria, hop on the A81 towards Singen, an attractive highway traversing the Schwarzwald–Baar plateau. After Engen, you'll snatch your first glimpse of the castle-topped **Hegau volcanoes** and shimmering **Lake Constance** (p286). Skirt the eastern shore on the A98/B31, past vineyards, apple orchards and **Birnau**'s postcard-perfect baroque church. Round out your drive with a few bevvies on the palm-fringed promenade in **Lindau** (p286).

It's hard to cherry-pick the Black Forest, but this offbeat route dishes up some of its juiciest scenery. The winding back-roads bewitch me with their lazy hills and misty vales, fairy-tale woodlands and villages oozing earthy authenticity. Every last crumb is poetry in motion.
KERRY WALKER

BEST OF BAVARIA   Two to three weeks / 1500km

Kick off in **Munich** (p73), where museums, nightlife and brewpubs form a trifecta of treats. Go royal at Ludwig II's **Schloss Linderhof** (p143), then stand on the roof of Germany: Zugspitze above **Garmisch-Partenkirchen** (p136). Head east via the B2, then pick up the scenic lakeside toll road along **Walchensee** (p148) to get to **Bad Tölz** (p145), the heart of the Tölzer Land (p145) and to **Tegernsee** (p149), the playground of the rich and famous. Head east to **Chiemsee** (p150) via the A8 to admire more Ludwig II follies at Schloss Herrenchiemsee, then take a back route along the B305 through the **Chiemgau Alps** (p154) via **Reit im Winkl** (p154), **Ruhpolding** (p154) and **Inzell** (p154). Listen to the famous philharmonic orchestra in **Bad Reichenhall** (p155), then squeeze in a day among the mountains, lakes and intriguing, if dark, history of the **Berchtesgadener Land** (p157) before catching *Sound of Music*–mania in achingly beautiful **Salzburg** (p167). Admire Europe's longest castle in **Burghausen** (p165), combined with side trips to **Altötting** (p163), the 'Lourdes of Germany', or **Marktl am Inn** (p209), Pope Benedict XVI's birthplace. From here head to postcard-pretty **Passau** (p204), an Italianate town at the confluence of three rivers, followed by the **Bavarian Forest** (p209) for hiking and stopping at **Frauenau's** glass museum (p213). Turn your compass towards **Regensburg** (p194), a university town with a nearly impeccably preserved medieval core, then hit Kelheim for the boat ride to **Kloster Weltenburg** (p203) and follow the river through the idyllic **Naturpark Altmühltal** (p243) river valley to Beilngries. From **Nuremberg** (p217), a major draw for history buffs, continue north on the A9 to Pegnitz to pick up the B470 through the dramatically eroded **Fränkische Schweiz** (p236), famous for its pristine Altstadt and breweries, is next. Finish up exploring the **Franconian Wine Country** (p260) before picking up the Romantic Road itinerary (p22) in **Würzburg** (p254).

I always feel like a kid in a candy store when travelling in Bavaria: the selection is vast, everything looks tasty, but my budget is limited and I can't hang around forever. When pushed to make up my mind, these are stops and routes I'd pick.
ANDREA SCHULTE-PEEVERS

History

Bavaria is Germany's largest and southernmost state, as well as one of the oldest in Europe, with origins in the 6th century. Today's territory unites three distinct tribes: the Bajuwaren (Bavarians), the Franken (Franconians) and the Schwaben (Swabians). Each developed quite separately until united by Napoleon as the Kingdom of Bavaria in 1806. Munich was founded in 1158 by Duke Heinrich der Löwe (Henry the Lion) and granted town rights in 1175. It has been capital of Bavaria since 1506. Although never at the centre of power, Bavaria was still a key player in continental politics for centuries. Governed by the same family, the Wittelsbachs, for over 700 years, it was able to form a distinct culture that continues to shape its image and identity to this day. For milestones in the history of the Black Forest region see the boxed text, p33.

For a comprehensive overview of Bavarian history (partly in English) see the website of the government-financed Haus der Bayerischen Geschichte at www.hdbg.de.

TRIBAL MELTING POT

The first inhabitants of Bavaria were Celts, who proved to be an easy pushover for the Romans who began barrelling across the Alps in the 1st century AD. The invaders founded the province of Raetia with Augusta Vindelicorum (Augsburg) as its capital. By the 5th century the tables were turned on the Romans by marauding eastern Germanic tribes pushing up the Danube Valley in search of new *Lebensraum* (living space).

The precise origin of the Bavarian tribe is obscure, but it's widely assumed that it coalesced from the remaining Romans, Romanised Celts and the newcomers from the east. The name 'Bajuwaren' seems to have derived from 'men from Bohemia', a region in today's Czech Republic.

The Franken began forming in the 3rd century AD from several western Germanic tribes who settled along the central and lower Rhine River, on the border with the Roman Empire. The Schwaben, meanwhile, are a subtribe of the population group of the Alemannen (Alemannic tribes) who spread across the southwestern corner of Germany around the 2nd century AD. In the 3rd century they took on the Romans, eventually pushing as far east as the Lech River.

On Bavaria's coat of arms, Old Bavaria is represented by a blue panther, the Franconians by a red-and-white rake, the Swabians by three black lions, and the Upper Palatinate (no longer part of Bavaria today) by a golden lion.

CHURCH DOMINANCE

Religion, especially of the Roman Catholic variety, has shaped all aspects of Bavarian history and culture for nearly two millennia. Following the decline of the Roman Empire, missionaries from Ireland and Scotland swarmed across Europe to spread the gospel. They found open arms and minds among the Agilofinges, the dynasty who had founded the first Bavarian duchy in the 6th century. They adopted the faith eagerly, thereby allowing Christianity

TIMELINE

15 BC	AD 555–788	7th–8th centuries
Nero Claudius Drusus and Tiberius Claudius Nero, stepsons of the Roman emperor Augustus, conquer the Celtic tribes north of the Alps, calling their new colony Raetia, with Augusta Vindelicorum (today's Augsburg) as capital	Members of the Agilofinges dynasty found the first Bavarian duchy with Garibald I (r 555–91) its first-known duke. They remain in power until becoming absorbed into the Frankish Empire in 788 by Charlemagne.	Christianisation takes hold as roving missionaries arrive in Bavaria from Ireland, Scotland and the Frankish Empire. In 738 St Boniface creates the dioceses of Salzburg, Freising, Passau and Regensburg.

WE ARE POPE!

'Habemus papam.' It was a balmy spring evening in Rome when the world – Catholics and non-Catholics – held its collective breath. Who would follow in the footsteps of the charismatic Pope John Paul II who'd led the church for 27 years? That man was Cardinal Joseph Ratzinger, henceforth known as Benedict XVI and born on 16 April 1927 in the Bavarian hamlet of Marktl am Inn. For the first time in nearly 500 years a German had been elected pope. The following day the headline of the sensationalist tabloid German daily *Bild* screamed proudly: 'Wir sind Papst!' (We are Pope).

Ratzinger's election met with a mix of elation and disappointment. Those who had hoped for a more progressive and liberal church leader were stunned to find that the job had gone to this fierce and uncompromising cardinal who for 24 years had been John Paul II's enforcer of church doctrine. He was known as the ultimate hardliner, opposed to abortion, homosexuality and contraception, and ruthless in his crackdowns on dissident priests. 'Panzer cardinal' and 'God's Rottweiler' were just two of his nicknames.

Yet, even his staunchest critics could not deny that Ratzinger was well prepared for the papal post. A distinguished theologian, he speaks seven languages and has written more than 50 books. He looks back on a long career as a university professor, archbishop of Freising and Munich, and 24 years as John Paul II's main man.

As Pope Benedict XVI, he has declared that stemming the tide of secularisation, especially in Europe, and a return to Christian values, is his major priority. He considers interfaith dialogue another important mission but has at times been clumsy in going about accomplishing it. A 2006 speech at Regensburg university in which he quoted a 14th-century Byzantine-Christian emperor as saying that the Prophet Muhammad had only brought evil and inhuman things into the world, launched major protests and ended up with the pope apologising to the Muslim world.

Highroad to the Stake: A Tale of Witchcraft, by Michael Kunze, is a haunting account of the life, arrest, torture and execution of an entire family of paupers in 16th-century Bavaria.

to quickly take root. By 739 there were bishoprics in Regensburg, Passau, Freising and Salzburg, and monasteries had been founded in Tegernsee, Benediktbeuern, Weltenburg and many other places.

For nearly the next 800 years, the Church completely dominated daily life as the only major religion in the land. Until 1517, that is. That's when a spunky monk and theology professor named Martin Luther sparked the Reformation with his 95 theses critiquing papal infallibility, clerical celibacy, selling indulgences and other elements of Catholic doctrine.

Despite the Church's attempt to quash Luther, his teachings resonated widely, especially in Franconia and Swabia, though not in Bavaria proper where local rulers instantly clamped down on anyone toying with conversion. They also encouraged the newly founded Jesuit order to make Ingolstadt the hub of the Counter-Reformation. The religious strife eventually escalated into the Thirty Years' War (1618–48), which left Europe's soil drenched with the blood of millions. During the conflict, Bavaria's Duke Maximilian I (r 1598–1651) fought firmly on the side of Catholic emperor Ferdinand II of Habsburg, who

962	1180	1214
The pope crowns the Saxon King Otto I to Kaiser (emperor), marking the beginning of the Holy Roman Empire, which remained a major force in European history until 1806	The Wittelsbachs' 738-year reign begins with Otto von Wittelsbach's appointment as duke of Bavaria by Emperor Friedrich Barbarossa, marking the transition from tribal duchy to territorial state	Emperor Friedrich II grants the fiefdom of the Palatinate along the Rhine River to Duke Otto II von Wittelsbach, thereby significantly enlarging the family's territory and increasing its power

thanked him by expanding Max's territory and promoting him to *Kurfürst* (prince elector). When calm was restored in 1648 with the signing of the Peace of Westphalia, Bavaria – along with much of the rest of Europe – lay in ruins.

The treaty permitted each local ruler to determine the religion of his territory and essentially put the Catholic and Lutheran churches on equal legal footing. Bavaria, of course, remained staunchly Catholic. In fact, if the baroque church-building boom of the 17th century is any indication, it positively seemed to revel in its religious zeal.

But beyond Bavaria times were a-changing. The Enlightenment spawned reforms throughout Europe, first leading to the French Revolution, then the Napoleonic Wars and ultimately to the demise of the Holy Roman Empire. The ancient Church structure collapsed right along with it, prompting the secularisation of Bavarian monasteries after 1803 and, finally, religious parity. Although Ludwig I restored the monasteries, Protestants have since enjoyed equal rights throughout Bavaria, even though it remains predominantly Catholic to this day.

Much to the delight and pride of the population, Bavarian-born Joseph Cardinal Ratzinger was elected Pope Benedict XVI in 2005. The last German pope in charge of the Catholic Church was Adrian VI who ruled from 1522 to 1523.

In *Jesus of Nazareth* (2007), his first book published as pope, Benedict XVI offers an erudite and scholarly biography of Jesus and examines how his divinity resonates in today's world.

AMBITIOUS RULERS

From 1180 to 1918, a single family held Bavaria in its grip, the House of Wittelsbach. Otto von Wittelsbach was a distant relative of Emperor Friedrich Barbarossa who, in 1180, appointed him duke of Bavaria, which at that time was a fairly small and insignificant territory. Ensuing generations of Wittelsbachs focused on expanding their land – and with it their sphere of influence – through wheeling and dealing, marriage, inheritance and war.

Being granted the fiefdom of the Palatinate, an area along the Rhine River northwest of present-day boundaries, was a good start back in 1214, but the family's fortunes peaked when one of their own, Ludwig the Bavarian, became emperor in 1328. As the first Wittelsbach on the imperial throne, Ludwig used his powerful position to bring various far-flung territories, including the March of Brandenburg (around Berlin), the Tyrol (part of today's Austria) and several Dutch provinces, under Bavarian control.

The Thirty Years' War brought widespread devastation but, by aligning themselves with Catholic emperor Ferdinand II, the Wittelsbachs managed not only to further expand their territory but to score a promotion from duchy to *Kurfürstentum* (electorate), giving them a say in the election of future emperors.

Not all alliances paid off so handsomely. In the 1680s Maximilian II Emanuel (r 1679–1726) – a man of great ambition but poor judgment – battled the Turks alongside the Habsburg Kaiser in an attempt to topple

The most prominent Wittelsbach descendant is Prince Luitpold of Bavaria who runs his own brewery, the Schlossbrauerei Kaltenberg, and hosts a popular jousting tournament, the Kaltenberger Ritterturnier. Learn more at www.kaltenberg.com.

1506	**1516**	**1517**
To further prevent Bavaria from getting split into ever-smaller territories, Duke Albrecht the Wise introduces the law of primogeniture, by which possessions pass to first-born sons instead of being divided between all male children	On 23 April the *Reinheitsgebot* (Purity Law) is passed in Ingolstadt, which limits the ingredients used in the production of beer to water, barley and hops; it remains standard practice until 1993	Martin Luther splits the Christian church by kicking off the Reformation with his 95 theses posted on the door of the cathedral in the eastern German town of Wittenberg

the Ottoman Empire. Much to his dismay, his allegiance did not lead to the rewards (land, titles, power) he had expected. So he tried again, this time switching sides and fighting with France against Austria in the War of the Spanish Succession (1701–14). Again no luck. The conflict ended in a disastrous Franco-Bavarian loss and a 10-year occupation of Bavaria by Habsburg troops. Not only had Max Emanuel failed to achieve his personal goals, his flip-flop policies had also seriously weakened Bavaria's overall political strength.

Max Emanuel's son, Karl Albrecht (r 1726–45), was determined to avenge his father's double humiliation. Through some fancy political manoeuvring, he managed to take advantage of the confusion caused by the War of Succession and, with the backing of Prussia and France, ended up on the imperial throne as Karl VII in 1742. His triumph, however, was short-lived as Bavaria was quickly reoccupied by Austrian troops. Upon Karl Albrecht's death in 1745, his son Maximilian III Joseph (r 1745–77) was forced to renounce the Wittelsbachs' claims to the imperial crown forever.

THE ACCIDENTAL KINGDOM

Modern Bavaria, more or less as we know it today, was established in the early 19th century by a ferocious little Corsican named Napoleon. At the onset of the Napoleonic Wars (1799–1815), Bavaria initially found itself on the losing side against France. Tired of war and spurred on by his powerful minister Maximilian Graf von Montgelas, Maximilian IV Joseph (r 1799–1825) decided to put his territory under Napoleon's protection. Smart move.

In 1803, after victories over Austria and Prussia, Napoleon set about remapping much of Europe. Bavaria fared rather well, nearly doubling its size by receiving control over Franconia and Swabia. In 1806 Napoleon created the kingdom of Bavaria and made Maximilian I his new best friend.

Alas, keeping allegiances had never been Bavaria's strong suit and, in 1813, with Napoleon's fortunes waning, Montgelas shrewdly threw the new kingdom's support behind Austria and Prussia. After France's defeat, the victorious allies again reshaped European boundaries at the Congress of Vienna (1814–15) and Bavaria got to keep most of the territory it had obtained with Napoleon's help.

RELUCTANT REFORMERS

During the 18th century, the ideas of the Enlightenment that had swept through other parts of Europe had largely been ignored in Bavaria. Until Elector Maximilian III Joseph (r 1745–77) arrived on the scene, that is. Tired of waging war like his predecessors, he made peace with Austria and busied himself with reforming his country from within. He updated the legal system, founded the Bavarian Academy of Sciences and made school attendance compulsory. Max Joseph's reign also saw the creation of the Nymphenburg

Bruce Seymour's *Lola Montez: A Life* is a highly entertaining and comprehensive romp through the life of Bavaria's ultimate courtesan, whose affair with Ludwig I changed the course of history.

1555	1618–48	1806
Holy Roman Emperor Karl V signs the Peace of Augsburg agreement allowing each local ruler to decide which religion to adopt in their principality, ending decades of religious struggle and officially recognising Lutherism	The Thirty Years' War involves most European nations, but is fought mainly on German soil, bringing murder, starvation and disease, and decimating Europe's population from 21 million to 13.5 million	Bavaria becomes a kingdom and nearly doubles its size when acquiring Franconia and Swabia. Sweeping reforms result in the passage of the state's first constitution in 1808.

LOLA MONTEZ, FEMME FATALE *Jeremy Gray*

A whip-toting dominatrix and seductress of royalty, Lola Montez (1818–61) showed the prim Victorians what sex scandals were all about. Born as Eliza Gilbert in Limerick, Ireland, to a young British army officer and a 13-year-old Creole chorus girl, Lola claimed to be the illegitimate daughter of poet Lord Byron (or, depending on her mood, of a matador). When her actual father died of cholera in India, her mother remarried and then shipped the seven-year-old Eliza off to Scotland. During her time in Scotland she was occasionally seen running stark naked through the streets. She then finished her schooling in Paris and after an unsuccessful stab at acting, reinvented herself as the Spanish dancer Lola Montez.

She couldn't dance either but her beauty fascinated men, who fell at her feet – sometimes under the lash of her ever-present riding crop. One time she fired her pistol at a lover who'd performed poorly, but he managed to escape with his trousers about his knees.

Those succumbing to her charms included the tsar of Russia, who paid her 1000 roubles for a 'private audience'; novelist Alexandre Dumas; and composer Franz Liszt. Liszt eventually tired of Lola's incendiary temper, locked his sleeping mistress in their hotel room and fled – leaving a deposit for the furniture Lola would demolish when she awoke.

When fired by a Munich theatre manager, Lola took her appeal to the court of Ludwig I himself. As the tale goes, Ludwig asked casually whether her lovely figure was a work of nature or art. The direct gal she was, Lola seized a pair of scissors and slit open the front of her dress, leaving the ageing monarch to judge for himself. Predictably, she was rehired (and the manager sacked).

The king fell head over heels for Lola, giving her a huge allowance, a lavish palace and even the doubtful title of Countess of Landsfeld. Her ladyship virtually began running the country, too, and when Munich students rioted during the 1848 revolution, Lola had Ludwig shut down the university. This was too much for the townsfolk, who joined the students in revolt. Ludwig was forced to abdicate and soon Lola was chased out of town.

Lola cancanned her way around the world; her increasingly lurid show was very popular with gold miners in California and Australia. Next came a book of 'beauty secrets' and a lecture tour featuring topics such as 'Heroines of History and Strong-Minded Women'. She shed her Spanish identity, but in doing so, Lola – who had long publicly denied any link to her alter ego, Eliza – became a schizophrenic wreck. She spent her final two years as a pauper in New York, shuffling through the streets muttering to herself, before dying of pneumonia and a stroke at age 43.

porcelain factory and the construction of the Cuvilliés Theatre (p89), a rococo jewel at the Munich Residenz (p88).

Now that the reform genie was out of the bottle, there was no going back, especially after Bavaria became a kingdom in 1806. The architect of modern Bavaria was a minister of King Maximilian I, Maximilian Graf von Montgelas. He worked feverishly to forge a united state from the mosaic of 'old Bavaria', Franconia and Swabia, by introducing sweeping political, administrative and social changes, including the secularisation of the monasteries. The reforms ultimately led to Bavaria's first constitution in 1808, which was based on

1810 Ludwig I marries Princess Therese von Sachsen-Hildburghausen with a horse race and lavish festivities that mark the beginning of the tradition of the annual Munich Oktoberfest

1835 Drawn by a steam locomotive called *Adler* (Eagle), Germany's first railway commences operations along a 6km route between Nuremberg and Fürth, transporting newspapers, beer and people. It ploughs on until 1922.

1848 A man with a weakness for the arts and beautiful women, King Ludwig I is forced to resign after his affair with the dancer Lola Montez causes a public scandal

rights of freedom, equality and property ownership and the promise of representative government. Ten years later Bavaria got its first *Landtag* (two-chamber parliament).

Under Max I's son, Ludwig I (r 1825–48), Bavaria flourished into an artistic and cultural centre, an 'Athens on the Isar'. Painters, poets and philosophers flocked to Munich, where Leo von Klenze and Friedrich von Gärtner were creating a showcase of neoclassical architecture. Königsplatz with the Glyptothek and Propyläen, flashy Ludwigstrasse with the Siegestor triumphal arch, and the Ludwig Maximilian University were all built under Ludwig I's watch, as was the Alte Pinakothek, one of the world's foremost repositories of art. The king was also keen on new technology and heavily supported the idea of a nationwide railway. The first short line, which ran from Nuremberg to Fürth, opened during his reign in 1835.

Politically though, Ludwig I brought a return to authority from the top as revolutionary rumblings in other parts of Europe coaxed out his reactionary streak. An arch-Catholic, he restored the monasteries, introduced press censorship and authorised arrests of students, journalists and university professors whom he judged to be subversive. Bavaria was becoming restrictive, even as French and American democratic ideas flourished elsewhere in Germany.

On 22 March 1848 Ludwig I abdicated in favour of his son, Maximilian II (r 1848–64), who finally put into place many of the constitutional reforms his father had ignored, such as abolishing censorship and introducing the right to assemble. Further progressive measures passed by his son Ludwig II (r 1864–86) in the early years of his reign included welfare for the poor, liberalised marriage laws and free trade.

THE MYSTIQUE OF LUDWIG II

No other Bavarian king stirs the imagination quite as much as Ludwig II, the fairy-tale king so tragically at odds with a modern world that had no longer any use for an absolutist, if enlightened, monarch. Ludwig was a sensitive soul, fascinated by romantic epics, architecture and the music of Richard Wagner. When he became king at age 18, he was at first a rather enthusiastic leader; however, Bavaria's days as a sovereign state were numbered. After it was absorbed into the Prussian-led German Reich in 1871, Ludwig became little more than a puppet king (albeit one receiving regular hefty allowances from Berlin).

Disillusioned, the king retreated to the Bavarian Alps to drink, draw castle plans, and enjoy private concerts and operas. His obsession with French culture and the Sun King, Louis XIV, inspired the fantastical palaces of Neuschwanstein, Linderhof and Herrenchiemsee – lavish projects that spelt his undoing.

In January 1886 several ministers and relatives arranged a hasty psychiatric test that diagnosed Ludwig as mentally unfit to rule. He was dethroned and taken to Schloss Berg on Lake Starnberg. Then, one evening, the dejected

Margin notes

During secularisation in the early 19th century, even the monk on Munich's coat of arms was banished (it reappeared in 1835, as did many monasteries).

Germany's first stamp was issued in Bavaria in November 1849 and was called the *Schwarze Einser* (Black Penny).

Ludwig, a 1973 flick directed by Luchino Visconti, is a lush, epic and sensitive Oscar-nominated portrayal of the life of Ludwig II, a highly emotional and tormented king out of step with his time.

1886	1914–18	1919
Lifelong dreamer and recluse King Ludwig II is declared mentally unfit and confined to Schloss Berg (Berg Palace) on Lake Starnberg where he drowns under mysterious circumstances in shallow water, alongside his doctor	WWI: Germany, Austria-Hungary and Turkey go to war against Britain, France, Italy and Russia. This ends with Germany's defeat, the overthrow of the monarchy and the declaration of Bavaria as a 'free state'.	Left-leaning intellectuals proclaim the Münchner Räterepublik on 4 April, hoping to create a Soviet-style regime. The movement never spreads beyond Munich and is quashed bloodily by government forces on 3 May.

bachelor and his doctor took a lakeside walk and several hours later were found dead – mysteriously drowned in just a few feet of water.

No-one knows with certainty what happened that night. There was no eyewitness or proper criminal investigation. The circumstantial evidence was conflicting and incomplete. Reports and documents were tampered with, destroyed or lost. Conspiracy theories abound. That summer the authorities opened Neuschwanstein to the public to help pay off Ludwig's huge debts. King Ludwig II was dead, but the myth was just being born.

NAZI LEGACY

If Berlin was the head of the Nazi government, its heart beat in Bavaria. This was the birthplace of the movement, born out of the chaos and volatility of a post-WWI Germany wracked by revolution, crippling reparations and run-away inflation. Right-wing agitation resonated especially among Bavarians who deeply resented losing much of their sovereignty to a centralised national government in Berlin.

In Munich, a failed artist and WWI corporal from Austria – Adolf Hitler – had quickly risen to the top of the extreme right-wing Nationalsozialistische Arbeiterpartei (NSDAP). On 8 November 1923 he led his supporters in a revolt aimed at overthrowing the central government following a political rally in the Bürgerbräukeller near the site of the present-day Gasteig arts centre (p103). The so-called Beer Hall Putsch was an abysmal failure, poorly planned and amateurishly executed. The following day a ragtag bunch of would-be armed revolutionaries marched through Munich streets hoping to pick up further followers along the way. They only got as far as the Feldherrnhalle where a shoot-out with police left 16 Nazis and four policemen dead.

The NSDAP was banned and Hitler was sentenced to five years in prison for high treason. While in Landsberg jail, west of Munich, he began work on *Mein Kampf* (My Struggle), dictated in extended ramblings to his secretary Rudolf Hess. Incredibly, Hitler was released after only nine months in 1924 on grounds of 'good behaviour'.

After Hitler took control of Germany in January 1933, Bavaria was assigned a special status. Munich was declared the 'Capital of the Movement' and Nuremberg became the site of the Nazi party's mass rallies. In 1935 the party brass passed the Nuremberg Laws, which ushered in the systematic repression of the Jews. In Dachau, north of Munich, Germany's first concentration camp was built in 1933. In addition, many Nazi honchos hailed from Bavaria, including *Sturmabteilung* (SA) chief Ernst Röhm (later killed by Hitler); Heinrich Himmler; Hermann Göring; and Franconia's *Gauleiter* (regional chief), Julius Streicher. Hitler himself was born just across the border, in Austria's Braunau. The Alpine resort of Berchtesgaden served as the southern party headquarters and the Winter Olympic Games of 1936 took place in Garmisch-Partenkirchen. The Nazis enjoyed almost universal

In 1923 a postage stamp cost 50 billion marks, a loaf of bread cost 140 billion marks and US\$1 was worth 4.2 trillion marks. In November the new Rentenmark was traded in for one trillion old marks.

The Academy Award–nominated *Sophie Scholl – The Final Days* (2005) re-creates in harrowing detail the last six days in the life of this courageous Nazi resistance fighter, who was executed at age 21.

1923	1933	1939–45
Hitler's failed putsch attempt lands him in jail where he takes just nine months to give birth to his vitriolic rant, *Mein Kampf*. It sells between eight and nine million copies.	Hitler becomes chancellor of Germany and creates a dictatorship, making Munich the 'capital of the movement' and Obersalzberg near Berchtesgaden a second seat of government	WWII: Hitler invades Poland; Britain, France and, in 1941, the US, declare war on Germany; Jews are murdered en masse during the Holocaust. In 1945 Hitler suicides in Berlin while a defeated Germany surrenders.

support in Bavaria, but there were also some pockets of resistance, most famously the Munich-based group Die Weisse Rose (The White Rose; see the boxed text, p95).

Popular Opinion & Political Dissent in the Third Reich: Bavaria 1933–45, by Ian Kershaw, examines everyday attitudes among ordinary people and dispels the perception that practically all were in lockstep behind Nazi policies and their leaders.

In 1938 Hitler's troops met no resistance when they marched into Austria and annexed it to Nazi Germany. The same year, the UK's Neville Chamberlain, Italy's Benito Mussolini and France's Édouard Daladier, in an attempt to avoid another war, continued their policy of appeasement by handing Hitler control over large portions of Czechoslovakia in the Munich Agreement. Chamberlain's naive hope that such a move would bring 'peace for our time' was destroyed on 1 September 1939 when Nazi troops marched into Poland. This kicked off the bloody nightmare of WWII, which left millions dead and countless cities in ruins.

A STATE APART

Modern Bavaria may be integrated thoroughly within the German political construct, but its people take great pride in their distinctiveness. Its history, traditions, attitudes, political priorities and culture are, in many ways, quite different from the rest of Germany. They are uniquely Bavarian.

A Train of Powder (2000), by Rebecca West, ranks as one of the most informative books on the Nuremberg trials, written by a brilliant reporter who was in the courtroom.

After WWII Bavaria became part of the American occupation zone and was allowed to pass its own constitution in December 1946. In 1949 it became the only German state that did not ratify the German constitution because, in its opinion, it put unacceptable limitations on state powers. Bavaria did, however, agree to honour and abide by the federal constitution and has done so to this day. However, to underscore its independent streak it calls itself 'Freistaat' (free state) Bayern, even though this has no political implications.

Since 1946 a single party, the archconservative Christlich-Soziale Union (CSU; Christian Social Union) has dominated Bavarian politics at every level of government, from communal to state. Although peculiar to Bavaria, it is closely aligned with its national sister party, the Christlich-Demokratische Union (CDU; Christian Democratic Union). Long enjoying an absolute majority, the CSU has held an unprecedented two-thirds majority in the state parliament since 2003.

Hitler called his regime the 'Third Reich' because he thought of the Holy Roman Empire and Bismarck's German empire as the first and second Reichs, respectively.

Powerful CSU figures include Franz-Josef Strauss, who served as Bavarian *Ministerpräsident* (minister-president, ie governor) from 1978 until his death in 1988, and his protégé, Edmund Stoiber, who clung to the job from 1999 until 2007. Although hugely popular and successful in Bavaria, both failed in their attempts to become federal chancellor: Strauss when losing to Helmut Schmidt in 1980, and Stoiber when getting outmanoeuvred by Gerhard Schröder in 2002. Since October 2007, Bavaria has been led by Günter Beckstein.

No other German state has been more successful in its postwar economic recovery than Bavaria. Within decades, it transformed from an essentially agrarian society into a progressive, hi-tech state. The upturn was at least in

1943	1945–46	1972
Members of the Nazi resistance group, Die Weisse Rose (The White Rose), are caught distributing anti-Nazi leaflets at Ludwig Maximilian University and executed a few days later, following a sham trial	The victorious Allies hold a series of trials against Nazi leaders accused of crimes against peace and humanity in a courthouse at Nuremberg. Ten of the accused are executed by hanging.	Bavaria shows off its prosperity, friendliness and cutting-edge architecture during the Olympic Games, although the event is overshadowed by the so-called Munich Massacre, a deadly terrorist attack on Israeli athletes

MILESTONES IN BLACK FOREST HISTORY

In the beginning the Black Forest was just that: a huge, dark, dense clump of trees so impenetrable that even the Romans didn't dare colonise it, although they couldn't resist taking advantage of the thermal mineral springs in Baden-Baden on the forest's edge. Around the 7th century, a band of intrepid monks took a stab at taming the area, but it would be another few centuries until the ruling Zähringer clan founded Freiburg in 1120. In order to solidify their claim on the land, they moved farmers into the valleys to clear the trees and create small settlements. This led to the discovery of natural resources and, up until the 15th century, the extraction of iron, zinc, lead and even silver were major industries.

While their feudal lords enjoyed the spoils of subjects' labour, the lot of the miners and farmers got worse and worse. In the 16th century unrest fomenting in the Black Forest eventually grew into the Peasant Rebellion that swept through much of southern Germany. Poorly equipped and haphazardly organised, the farmers were, of course, no match for the authorities who had no qualms in bringing the uprising to a bloody conclusion.

In the following centuries the people of the Black Forest experienced a series of hardships of Biblical proportions. The Thirty Years' War left about 70% of the population dead, and plague and crop failures did much the same for the rest. Unsurprisingly, many of the survivors left for greener pastures in other parts of Europe.

The Black Forest stayed out of the spotlight for well over a century until the Baden Revolution of 1848–9. Inspired by the democratic movement in France and the declaration of the French Republic in February 1848, local radical democratic leaders Friedrich Hecker and Gustav von Struve led an armed rebellion against the archduke of Baden in April 1848, demanding freedom of expression, universal education, popular suffrage and other key democratic ideals. Struve got arrested and Hecker fled into exile, but their struggle inspired people and spilled over into other parts of Germany. Eventually Prussian troops cracked down on the revolutionaries in one final, fiery showdown at Rastatt in July 1849.

Nearly 100 years later, Freudenstadt and Freiburg were among the regional cities that got bombed to bits during WWII. In 1952 the Black Forest became part of the newly formed German state of Baden-Württemberg. Still largely agrarian, tourism is the single biggest source of income to this day. In 1999 Hurricane Lothar blasted through with 200km/h winds, causing widespread damage and denuding large areas of forest.

part fuelled by the arrival of two million ethnic German expellees from the Czech Republic, who brought much-needed work power in the 1950s.

During Stoiber's 14-year reign Bavaria solidified its position as one of Germany's richest states. Unemployment is far below the national average and many of Germany's leading companies, including Allianz, Siemens, BMW and EADS (which owns Airbus), are headquartered here.

Bavaria is also a model pupil when it comes to educational achievement. Although Germany as a whole fared poorly in the 2000 and 2003 international PISA study that compares academic achievement worldwide, Bavaria would take the number five spot if it were an independent country.

In *Massacre in Munich: The Manhunt for the Killers Behind the 1972 Olympics Massacre* (2005) Michael Bar Bar-Zohar and Eitan Haber describe the events in haunting detail and in a style as fastpaced and engrossing as a novel.

1992

The state-of-the-art Munich airport begins operations, quickly becoming the second-busiest in Germany and the seventh-busiest in Europe. It's named for former Bavarian minister-president Franz Josef Strauss, who helped establish Airbus.

2005

Cardinal Joseph Ratzinger, who was born in 1927 in the tiny hamlet of Marktl am Inn near the Austrian border, is elected Pope Benedict XVI

2007

After 14 years, Edmund Stoiber steps down as minister-president of Bavaria and party chairman of the CSU, having seen his leadership skills called into question

The Culture

REGIONAL IDENTITY

Although their histories rarely overlapped, there are strong cultural similarities between Bavaria and the Black Forest. In the rural areas in particular, people have a strong sense of regional identity, cherish family life and tradition, and are more religious (Roman Catholic mostly) than people in other parts of Germany. Many belong to *Heimatverbände* (heritage associations), music or folkloric groups. Village communities are tightly knit and it's still frowned upon if you wash your car on a Sunday, play loud music during the lunch-time break, or don't attend church.

Bavaria is Germany's southernmost state and has always been a crossroads of trading routes to the Mediterranean and Southeast Europe. Since the Alps never formed an impassable barrier, Bavaria early on absorbed the influences of Mediterranean culture. The effect on the Bavarian character? Try an easygoing outlook tempered with a Germanic respect for law and order. Patriotic feeling runs high, and at any hint of an affront, Bavarians close ranks, at least until the next party or festival.

The Black Forest, by contrast, was physically and culturally isolated for a long time, and only in the last century has it opened up to influences from its Swiss and French neighbours. It may take a while to get to know its people, but once you do, you'll find them genuine and warm-hearted. Daily life here is often still linked to the land and it's not uncommon for several generations to share one roof.

But this is not to say that the Black Forest is a provincial backwater filled with hillbillies. Far from it. Educational standards run high, cultural offerings abound and modern technology is embraced here almost as much as in Hamburg or Berlin.

The same is, of course, true of Bavaria, only more so. A popular slogan coined by the state government calls Bavaria the land of lederhosen and laptops, conjuring up images of farmers and computer scientists happily working hand in virtual hand. Modern Bavaria is indeed the land of Oktoberfest, beer and tradition, but it's also about gleaming glass architecture, razzle-dazzle nightlife, hip fashion, sophisticated dining and sport. It's youthful and almost completely without the brooding introspection you may encounter elsewhere in Germany. Its people are open, friendly, polite and – actually – quite happy.

> Indigenous Bavarians still strongly identify with their tribal heritage and call everyone not born in their parts a *Zuagroaste* (newcomer).

LIFESTYLE

So who exactly is the average Bavarian? Statistically speaking, she's 33 years old, white and married, has at least some higher education and lives in a 90-sq-metre rented apartment in a midsized town. She and her husband own a shiny car, but she uses public transport to commute to her workplace in the service industry, where she earns about €2746 per month. About 40% of that disappears in tax and social security deductions. She tends to vote conservative, but would not rule out giving another party the nod. Sorting and recycling her rubbish – of which she produces 512kg per year – is done religiously and, speaking of religion, she is, of course, Roman Catholic, though not a regular churchgoer. She feels comfortable on the hiking trail and ski slopes, but is not fitness obsessed and could actually lose a few pounds. When she and her husband decide to have a family, they will have 1.38 children.

Believe the clichés and you'll have the average Black Forest resident down as someone who dwells in a gingerbready house deep in the woods, where the cupboards are full of cake and Kirsch schnapps. Not so. Statistically, she's 41.7 years old, white, married and has 1.7 children. She's educated to secondary school level and probably works in the manufacturing industry, where she lives comfortably from the €2114 she earns per month. Despite inhabiting a rural corner of Germany, she loves hi-tech gadgets and is particularly fond of her laptop and mobile. She lives in the Freiburg area if she's a student or city slicker, Hochschwarzwald if she's a country gal at heart. She is Christian but, like her Bavarian counterpart, likes a lie-in on Sundays. She zealously recycles her rubbish – of which she produces 345kg annually – into colour-coded bins for glass, paper, organic waste and packaging. If you meet her in the forest, she'll probably be Nordic walking or cross-country skiing. To keep the peace with her neighbours, she is rigorous when it comes to *Kehrwoche* (cleaning the pavement on a rota system) and can often be seen on weekends sweeping the streets till they shine.

Statistically speaking, of course.

Trachten

If the glossy tourist brochures are to be believed, Bavaria is full of happy, smiling people in *Trachten* (folkloric garments); the men in lederhosen and the women in low-cut, aproned dresses called dirndls. Well, if that's what you're expecting, you'll be deeply disappointed when visiting, say, Nuremberg, Rothenburg ob der Tauber, or Bamberg. Travel to the Alpine region, though, and you'll be in cliché heaven. Yes, it's true, even many young, liberal and progressive Munich folks own such traditional outfits, although most only leave the closet for Oktoberfest and special occasions. It's different in the rural areas, especially among older generations. If you want to see *Trachten* on parade, go to any folk festival or even just a Sunday morning church service in Oberammergau or Berchtesgaden.

In the Black Forest, the *Bollenhut,* a hat with a pile of 11 big fluffy pom-poms, has become the trademark for the entire region, even though it's traditionally only worn in Gutach, Wolfach-Kirnbach and Hornberg-Reichenbach. Hats of unmarried women have cheerful red pompoms; married ones wear the black version. Either way, they're only worn on holidays and during festivals.

Conventions

Bavarians and their counterparts in the Black Forest are culturally conservative. When in business mode, at fancy social gatherings or at high-brow cultural events, such as opera and theatre performances, you'll probably feel more comfortable if slightly dressed up. Style and chic clothes are also needed to get into the fancier Munich nightclubs.

Overall, locals are accommodating and fairly helpful towards visitors, and many will volunteer assistance if you look lost. This politeness does not necessarily extend to friendliness, however, and in public, people usually maintain a degree of reserve towards strangers – you won't find many conversations striking up on the bus or in the supermarket checkout line. On the other hand, in younger company it's easy to chat with just about anyone, particularly in student hang-outs (remember German students are generally older than elsewhere, often graduating at 28 rather than 21).

Shaking hands is common among both men and women, as is a hug or a kiss on the cheek, especially among young people. When making a phone call, start by giving your name (eg 'Smith, Grüss Gott'). Not doing so is considered impolite.

Importance is placed on the formal 'Sie' form of address, especially in business situations. Among younger people and in social settings, though,

Heading to Oktoberfest? Ditch the jeans and base-ball hat and dress like a Bavarian. Pick out your favourite lederhosen or dirndl at www.bavarian -superstore.de

people are much more relaxed about using 'Sie' and 'Du'. See the Language chapter (p331) for more on the subject.

ECONOMY

The Bavarian economy generates a gross domestic product of €357 billion, which is about 17% of the German GDP and roughly equivalent to that of Sweden and Ireland combined. Despite international flagship companies like BMW, Audi and Siemens, its success is largely carried by medium-sized businesses. Surprisingly, Bavaria is still among Germany's top agricultural producers, growing a staggering 70% of the entire hop crop in the EU. Dairy farming dominates in the Alpine foothills and the Allgäu. Still, it's manufacturing that's driving the state's economic engine: its vehicles, machines, electrical equipment and chemical products are well-respected and sought-after worldwide. The state's biggest export partner is the USA, followed by Italy, the UK and France. Tourism also adds a 'few' euros to the state's coffers, about €24 billion to be exact. More than half a million Bavarians depend on tourism as the primary source of income.

Tourism is also a major money machine in the historically rather poor Black Forest, where it generates about €5 billion and provides employment for around 140,000 people. Because of its relative remoteness and rural structure, the region has little industry, requiring many people to commute to cities on the forest fringe, such as Pforzheim, Karlsruhe and Rastatt. Agriculture and logging are still major industries, and wine making is big in the Kaiserstuhl area. Another traditional industry, clock making, has suffered tremendously from Asian competition, although there are still some companies making cuckoo clocks and grandfather clocks, mostly for the tourist trade and export.

POPULATION

Bavaria is Germany's second-most populous state with around 12.4 million inhabitants. Most people live in small towns, with only about one-fifth living in cities of 100,000 or more. Munich is Germany's third-largest city, after Berlin and Hamburg.

After WWII the original three tribes of the *Altbayern* ('old' Bavarians), the Franconians and the Swabians, were joined by more than two million expellees from the Czech Sudetenland, the so-called 'fourth tribe'. Another half-million 'guest workers' – primarily from Turkey, Italy, Greece and Spain – arrived in the 1960s and '70s, while the '90s brought a steady influx of people from the former East Germany.

The Black Forest is a subregion of the German state of Baden-Württemberg and was first settled by the Alemannic tribe. Today it has 3.43 million inhabitants, or about one-third of the entire state.

SPORT
Football

Mention *Fussball* (football, soccer) in Bavaria and passions will flare. The FC Bayern München has dominated the national league for the past two decades and has won the German championship 20 times, most recently in 2006. Club president is the legendary Franz Beckenbauer, who led the German side to victory in both the World (1974) and European Cups (1974, 1975, 1976), as both player and manager. The team packs plenty of actual and financial muscle and attracts some of Europe's best players. Lukas Podolski, Miroslav Klose and Philipp Lahm are members of the German national team. The only other Bavarian team in the Bundesliga is the 1 FC Nürnberg, but it hasn't been German champion since 1968.

Driven: Inside BMW, the Most Admired Car Company in the World (2004), by American automotive journalist David Kiley, is a riveting look at the mystique of one of the world's most legendary and successful car makers.

Bundesliga scoreboards, rankings and player profiles are online at www.bundesliga.de.

Munich's secondary team, TSV 1860 München (aka *Die Löwen*, or The Lions), currently play in the '2 Bundesliga' (Second League) along with the SC Freiburg, the FC Augsburg and the SpVgg Greuther Fürth.

Football season runs from September to June, with a winter break from Christmas to mid-February.

Skiing

Bavarian slopes still lure the sport's elite to annual World Cup races held in such resorts as Garmisch-Partenkirchen, Reit im Winkl and Berchtesgaden. On New Year's Day, Garmisch-Partenkirchen is also a stop on the four-part Vierschanzen-Tournee, the World Cup ski-jumping competition. Famous women champions from Bavaria include Rosi Mittermaier, a two-time Olympic gold-medal winner in 1976, and more recently Martina Ertl and Hilde Gerg. In early 2005 Alois Vogl ended the men's drought by snagging the World Cup for slalom. A famous skier from the Black Forest is Georg Thoma, who won a gold medal in the Nordic Combined (cross country and ski jumping) at the 1960 Olympics.

> The strangest game ever won by FC Bayern München (2–1) was against Frankfurt in 1999 when both Bayern goalies got injured and midfielder Michael Tarnet had to save the day.

MULTICULTURALISM

Every 12th resident of Bavaria is of non-German origin, with most of them setting up shop in the bigger cities where economic opportunities are greater and xenophobia less likely. In fact, nearly 24% of people in Munich and 17.4% in Nuremberg are of foreign descent. The largest groups are those from Turkey, the former states of Yugoslavia, Austria and Italy.

Despite a high level of tolerance, few groups mix on a day-to-day basis and racial tensions are increasing, at least in the cities. A new government campaign offers, and sometimes requires, immigrants on welfare payments to participate in so-called 'integration courses' in which they learn German as well as about the country's customs, traditions and history.

Another setback for integration was the passage of the so-called *Kopftuchgesetz*, a law that forbids female Muslim teachers to wear headscarves at school on the grounds that it's a symbol of nonintegration. Both Bavaria and Baden-Württemberg adopted the law in 2004.

Because of lack of economic opportunities, comparatively few non-Germans have settled in the Black Forest, although there is a fair number of French people along the border with the Alsace and Italians in far southwestern Lörrach.

MEDIA

The conservative Christian Social Union (CSU) oversees the media but generally doesn't meddle. The state's combined TV and radio station, Bayerischer Rundfunk (BR), is known for its quality documentaries and cultural fare, including numerous broadcasts of folk music.

> Get in the mood for your trip to Bavaria by listening to authentic Volksmusik via the internet at the commercial-free www.volksmusikanten.de.

Although newspapers claim not to be directly affiliated with any single party, the editorial lines of the *Bayern Kurier* and the *Münchner Merkur* quite clearly lean towards the CSU. The well-respected *Süddeutsche Zeitung* offers a more level-headed approach and is also widely read in other parts of Germany.

The *Badische Zeitung* out of Freiburg and the *Badisches Tagblatt* out of Baden-Baden are the main dailies published in the Black Forest, although both have low circulations and no distribution outside the region.

RELIGION

Southern Germany is overwhelmingly Roman Catholic but pockets of Lutherans can be found in such cities as Munich, Augsburg and Nuremberg, and in the northeastern Black Forest. Munich has a growing Jewish community of 9300 people, most of them recent arrivals from the former Soviet republics. Muslims account for about 2% of the population.

ARTS
Literature

Quite a few German writers of the 18th and 19th centuries, including Jean Paul and ETA Hoffmann, lived in southern Germany, but the golden age of Bavarian literature kicked off in the second half of the 19th century. Some of the finest writers of the time, Thomas Mann and Frank Wedekind (famous for his coming-of-age tale *Spring Awakening,* 1891) among them, contributed to *Simplicissimus,* a satirical magazine founded in 1896 with a cover bearing a trademark red bulldog. A few of its barbs about Emperor Wilhelm II were so biting that the magazine was censored and some of its writers (Wedekind among them) were sent to jail. During his 40 years in Munich, Thomas Mann wrote a pile of acclaimed works and picked up a Nobel prize. His Bavarian gems include the short story *Gladius Dei* (1902), a clever parody of Munich's pretensions to being the Florence of Bavaria.

Catholic Bavaria has produced few Jewish writers of note. A major exception is Jakob Wassermann (1873–1934), a popular novelist of the early 20th century. Many of his works grapple with Jewish identity, but he's best known for his sentimental take on Kaspar Hauser (see the boxed text, p229).

Bavaria's greatest playwright of international stature was the ever-abrasive Bertolt Brecht (1898–1956; see the boxed text, p276). After WWII, writers throughout Germany either dropped out of sight ('inner exile' was the favoured term) or, as Hans Carossa and Ernst Wiechert did, attempted some kind of political and intellectual renewal.

Today's leading literary lights are an eclectic, label-defying bunch. Herbert Rosendorfer (b 1934), a former Munich judge, has a long list of credits, including a legal satire, a history of the Thirty Years' War and travel guides. Anna Rosmus (b 1960) has turned her investigation of the Third Reich period in Passau, her birthplace, into several best-selling novels, including *Against the Stream: Growing Up Where Hitler Used to Live* (2002). Munich-based Patrick Süskind (b 1949) achieved international acclaim with *Das Parfum* (*Perfume;* 1985), his extraordinary tale of a psychotic 18th-century perfumemaker, which was made into a movie by Tom Tykwer in 2006.

Although he lived mostly in Switzerland, Nobel Prize–winner Hermann Hesse (1877–1962) is originally a Black Forest boy whose most famous novels, *Siddhartha* and *Steppenwolf,* became hippie-era favourites. The philosopher Martin Heidegger (1889–1976), author of *Being and Time,* one of the seminal works of German existentialism, also hailed from the Black Forest, as did Hans Jacob Christoffel von Grimmelshausen (1622–76), a 17th-century literary genius and author of the earliest German adventure novel, *Simplicissimus* (Adventures of a Simpleton; 1668), which later inspired the name of the aforementioned satirical magazine.

Cinema & Television

OK, so Germany's most recent high-profile blockbuster, the Oscar-winning *Das Leben der Anderen* (The Lives of Others; 2006), was filmed in Berlin, but Munich's Bavaria Film studio is no slouch in the movie scene either. Recent successes cranked out here include Marc Rothemund's Oscar-nominated *Sophie Scholl – The Final Days* (2005) and Tom Twyker's *Perfume: Story of a Murderer* (2006).

The studio pegs its pedigree back to 1919 and has lured many well-known directors, including Alfred Hitchcock (*The Pleasure Garden;* 1925), Billy

Grimmelshausen's *Simplicissimus* was inspired by the author's experiences and observations during the Thirty Years' War and follows the adventures of an uneducated cattle drover who sets out into the world after soldiers devastate his farm.

In Anna Rosmus' *Against the Stream: Growing Up Where Hitler Used to Live* a teenage girl writes an essay and uncovers shocking crimes in prewar Passau.

Wilder (*Fedora*; 1978), Rainer Werner Fassbinder (*Bolwieser*; 1977) and, most famously, Wolfgang Petersen (*The Boat*; 1979, and *The Neverending Story*; 1984). Many made-for-German-TV features, detective series such as *Polizeiruf 110* and popular soaps such as *Marienhof*, are also produced in Munich. Part of the studio complex is Bavaria Filmstadt (p104), a movie-themed film park with original sets and props from *Das Boot* and other famous flicks.

The Black Forest was put on the media map with one of Germany's most successful ever TV series, the *Schwarzwaldklinik*, a hospital-based prime-time soap that ran from 1985 to 1989. It drew up to 28 million viewers (60% market share in Germany) and was sold to the UK, Spain, Italy and other countries.

Florian von Donnersmarck, director of the Oscar-winning *The Lives of Others* (2006), learned his craft at the Munich film school.

Music
OPERA & CLASSICAL
Ironically, the composer most commonly associated with Bavaria wasn't Bavarian at all. Richard Wagner (1813–83) was born in Leipzig and died in Venice but his career took a dramatic turn when King Ludwig II became his patron in 1864 and financed the *Festspielhaus* (opera house) in Bayreuth, which was completed in 1872. Strongly influenced by Beethoven and Mozart, Wagner is most famous for his operas, many of which dealt with mythological themes (eg *Lohengrin* or *Tristan und Isolde*). His great achievement was a synthesis of visual, musical, poetic and dramatic components into a *Gesamtkunstwerk* (single work of art). Wagner's presence also drew other composers to Bayreuth, most notably Anton Bruckner and Franz Liszt, Wagner's father-in-law.

As the scores for symphonies became more complex, not the least thanks to Wagner, Bavarian composers hastened to join in. Richard Strauss (1864–1949), who hailed from Munich, created such famous symphonies as *Don Juan* and *Macbeth* but later focused on operas, including the successful *Der Rosenkavalier* (The Knight of the Rose).

Last but not least, there's Munich-born Carl Orff (1895–1982), who achieved lasting fame with just one work: his life-embracing 1935 cantata *Carmina Burana* (see the boxed text, p147), a work characterised by simple harmonies, rhythms and hypnotic repetition. Kloster Andechs, where he's buried, holds an annual Orff festival (p130).

First stop for fans of 'serious music' should be Munich where the Münchner Philharmoniker are the chart toppers thanks to music director Christian Thieleman and 'honorary conductor' Zubin Metha. Equally respected is the Bayerische Staatsoper, currently helmed by California wunderkind Kent Nagano. Nuremberg's highbrow scene perked up in 2005 when the Bavarian state government elevated the municipal theatre to the

Bavaria's 'Oscar' is the 'Pierrot', which is handed out to winners of the Bavarian Film Prize. Past recipients include Franka Potente, Michael Verhoeven and Wolfgang Petersen.

THE HEIMATFILM
The gorgeous Alpine landscape helped spawn the *Heimatfilm* (homeland film), the only film genre to have been created in Germany. It reached its zenith of popularity in the 1950s and helped spread many of today's clichés about Bavaria.

Most *Heimatfilms* show a world at peace with itself, focusing on basic themes such as love, family and the joys of village life. An interloper, such as a priest, creates some kind of conflict for the main characters – perhaps a milkmaid and her boyfriend or a poacher fighting local laws – who then invoke traditional values to solve the problem. Stories are set in the mountains of Austria, Bavaria or Switzerland, with predictable plots and schmaltzy film scores.

The Goethe-Institut has created an excellent overview of the *Heimatfilm* and the genre's latest trends, which can be read for free at the Arts section of www.goethe.de under film: dossiers.

Staatstheater Nuremberg (p226), whose opera, concert and ballet productions also get reasonably high marks. One of the most prolific orchestras is the Bad Reichenhaller Philharmonie, which performs almost daily in this lovely Alpine spa town, while the Baden-Badener Philharmonie is the top orchestra in the Black Forest. When in Bamberg, try catching a concert by the Bamberger Symphoniker. The concert series at the monastery in Benediktbeuern also draws sell-out crowds.

Southern Germany keeps a busy festival schedule, but the granddaddy of them all is the Richard Wagner Festival (p239) in Bayreuth. Opened by the maestro himself in 1876 with the *Ring des Nibelungen* opera marathon, it has been run by the composer's grandson, Wolfgang Wagner, since 1951. Although still a major societal and artistic event, the festival has stagnated under his long leadership, and Wolfgang Wagner's age and poor health have fuelled the debate about his successor. Current favourite is his granddaughter Katharina (b 1978), even though her 2007 Bayreuth debut production of *Die Meistersinger* was not met with universal critical acclaim.

VOLKSMUSIK

No other musical genre is as closely associated with Bavaria as *Volksmusik* (folk music). Every village has its own proud brass band or choir, and the state government puts serious euros into preserving this traditional music. More than 600,000 Bavarians, mostly lay musicians, belong to some 11,000 music groups, most of them in the Alpine regions. The basic musical form is the 3/4-time *Landler,* which is also a dance involving plenty of hopping and stomping; men sometimes slap themselves on their knees in what is called *platteln.* Typical instruments are the accordion and the zither and some songs end in a yodel. Popular performers of traditional *Volksmusik* are the Rehm Buam, Sepp Eibl and Ruperti Blech.

In the 1970s and '80s, small stages in Munich such as the Fraunhofer pub (p116) gave birth to a new style of *Volksmusik.* Performers infused the folklore concept with a political edge, freed it from conservative ideology and merged it with folk music from countries as diverse as Ireland and Ghana. Among the pioneers was the Biermösl Blosn, a band known for its satirical and provocative songs. Also keep an ear out for the Fraunhofer Saitenmusik, a chamber folk music ensemble that plays traditional tunes on acoustic instruments and which used to be the Fraunhofer pub's house band.

Since the '90s the scene has gone even further and now champions wacky crossovers of Bavarian folk with pop, rock, punk, hip-hop and techno in what has been dubbed 'Alpine New Wave'. Look for the folk rockers Hundsbuam, or the jazzy Munich trio Die Interpreten. Rudi Zapf uses the hammered dulcimer to take you on a musical journey around the world. The wildest band of them all is the hardcore folk-punk band Attwenger.

Painting & Sculpture
EARLY WORKS

Frescoes and manuscript illumination were early art forms popular between the 9th and 13th centuries. The oldest frescoes in Bavaria are in the crypt of the Benedictine Abbey of St Mang (p285) in Füssen. Stained glass emerged around 1100; the 'Prophets' Windows' in Augsburg's cathedral (p275) are the earliest in Central Europe.

GOTHIC

Portraiture and altar painting hit the artistic stage around 1300. Top dog here was Jan Polack, whose work can be admired in such churches as Munich's Schloss Blutenburg (p104). A famous late work by Martin Schongauer is the

One of the world's most famous violinists, Anne-Sophie Mutter, was born in 1963 in the Black Forest town of Rheinfelden, near the Swiss border.

The Schwarzwald Musikfestival (www .schwarzwald-musik festival.de, in German) celebrates music in all its diversity – from chamber to gospel to jazz – all over the Black Forest from late April to early July.

fresco cycle depicting the Last Judgment in the St Stephansmünster (p296) in Breisach. The same church also has a superb altar painting by an artist known only as 'HL'.

A major Gothic sculptor was Erasmus Grasser, whose masterpieces include the St Peter altar in the St Peterskirche (p77) in Munich and the Morris Dancers in the Munich Stadtmuseum (p87). Another is Veit Stoss, a Franconian who imbued his sculptures with dramatic realism. In 1503 Stoss spent a stint in jail for forgery, but restored his reputation with the main altar in Bamberg's cathedral (p233), his crowning achievement.

The website www.kultur portal-bayern.de is your guide to Bavarian culture, including sections on fine arts, film, museums, traditions and much, much more.

RENAISSANCE

The Renaissance saw the rise of human elements in painting: religious figures were now depicted alongside mere mortals. The heavyweight – quite literally – in Germany was the Nuremberg-born Albrecht Dürer, who excelled both as a painter and graphic artist. His subjects ranged from mythology to religion to animals, all in fantastic anatomical detail, natural perspective and vivid colours. The Alte Pinakothek (p91) in Munich has several famous works, and his house is today a museum in Nuremberg (p220).

Dürer influenced Lucas Cranach the Elder, a main artist of the Reformation. Cranach's approach to landscape painting, though, grew out of the *Donauschule* (Danube School), an artistic movement based in Passau and Regensburg. The amazing details of these landscapes seethed with dark movement, making them the focal point of the painting rather than a mere backdrop. Another Dürer student was Hans Baldung, who fashioned the imposing altar triptych in Freiburg's cathedral (p289).

The brightest star among Renaissance sculptors was Tilman Riemenschneider. His skills were formidable, allowing his stone to mimic wood and featuring compositions playing on light and shadow. Must-sees include the altars in the Jakobskirche (p264) in Rothenburg ob der Tauber and in the Herrgottskirche (p262) in Creglingen, both on the Romantic Road. The Mainfränkisches Museum (p258) in Würzburg also has an outstanding Riemenschneider collection.

BAROQUE & ROCOCO

The sugary styles of these periods left their mark throughout Bavaria, especially in church art. Illusionary effects and contrast between light and shadow are typical features, and surfaces are often bewilderingly ornate.

Arguably the finest and most prolific artists of the period, the brothers Cosmas and Egid Asam were of a generation of Germans educated in Rome in the Italian baroque tradition. Their father, Hans Georg, was a master fresco artist who transformed the Basilika St Benedikt (p146) in Benediktbeuern. Word of their supreme talent, along with the family's connections in the Benedictine order, meant the duo were always swamped with work. Cosmas was primarily a fresco painter while Egid used his considerable talents as an architect and stucco sculptor. Examples of their brilliant collaboration can be found throughout Bavaria, mostly notably in the Asamkirche (p87) in Munich, the Basilika St Emmeram (p197) in Regensburg, the Klosterkirche Weltenburg (p203) near Regensburg and the Asamkirche Maria de Victoria (p249) in Ingolstadt.

Another set of brothers dominating the baroque period was Dominikus and Johann Baptist Zimmermann, whose collaboration reached its pinnacle in the Wieskirche (p280) near Steingaden. Johann Baptist also worked on Munich's St Peterskirche (p77) and Schloss Nymphenburg (p99). Both were members of the so-called Wessobrunner School, which counted architect and stucco artist Josef Schmuzer among its founding members. Schmuzer's work can be admired at Kloster Ettal (p143) and in the Alte St Martinskirche (p137) in Garmisch-Partenkirchen.

Other Wessobrunn artistic hot shots were the Feuchtmayr clan (sometimes spelled Feichtmair), who contributed to the Basilika Vierzehnheiligen (p243) near Coburg and the Benedictine Abbey of St Peter (p297) north of Freiburg.

THE 19TH CENTURY

Heart-on-your-sleeve Romanticism that drew heavily on emotion and a dreamy idealism dominated the 19th century. Austria-born Moritz von Schwind is noted for his moody scenes of German legends and fairy tales. His teacher Peter Cornelius was a follower of the Nazarenes, a group of religious painters who drew from the old masters for inspiration. There's a giant fresco of his in Munich's Ludwigskirche (p94), although for the full survey of Romantic art you should swing by the nearby Schack-Galerie (p102).

Romanticism gradually gave way to the sharp edges of realism and, later on, the meticulous detail of naturalism. Major practitioners were Wilhelm Leibl, who specialised in painting Bavarian country scenes, and Hans Thoma, who joined Leibl in Munich, but favoured the landscapes of his native Black Forest. Look for their works in Munich's Städtische Galerie im Lenbachhaus (p93). The period's most famous Black Forest painter was Franz Xaver Winterhalter who built his reputation on royal portraits, including Queen Victoria. His work hangs in London's National Portrait Gallery and in Munich's Neue Pinakothek (p92).

MUNICH SECESSION & JUGENDSTIL

During the 1890s a group of about 100 artists shook up the art establishment when splitting from Munich's *Künstlergesellschaft* (Artists' Society), a traditionalist organisation led by portrait artist Franz von Lenbach. Secessionists were not linked by a common artistic style, but by a rejection of reactionary attitudes towards the arts that stifled new forms of expression. They preferred scenes from daily life to historical and religious themes, shunned studios in favour of natural outdoor light and were hugely influential in inspiring new styles.

One of them was *Jugendstil* (Art Nouveau), inspired by printmaking and drawing on functional, linear ornamentation partly inspired by Japanese art. The term originated from the weekly trendsetting art-and-literature magazine *Die Jugend,* published in Munich from 1896 until 1940. In Munich you can view some beautiful examples at the Neue Pinakothek (p92) and on building façades along Ainmillerstrasse (p95) and the Erlöserkirche (p97) in Schwabing.

EXPRESSIONISM

'Blue is the male principle, astringent and spiritual. Yellow is the female principle, gentle, gay and spiritual. Red is matter, brutal and heavy and always the colour to be opposed and overcome by the other two.'

FRANZ MARC

In the early 20th century German artists looked for a purer, freer approach to painting through abstraction, vivid colours and expression. In Bavaria the trailblazer was the artist group *Der Blaue Reiter* (The Blue Rider), founded by Wassily Kandinsky and Franz Marc in 1911, and joined later by Paul Klee, Gabriele Münter and other top artists. The Städtische Galerie im Lenbachhaus (p93) has the most comprehensive collection, much of it donated by Münter, who managed to hide her colleagues' paintings from the Nazis. A good selection of Münter's own paintings is on view at the Schlossmuseum Murnau (p144). Expressionists are also in the spotlight at the Franz-Marc-Museum in Kochel (p147). At the Buchheim Museum (p129) on Lake Starnberg, the focus is on the equally avant-garde artist group called *Die Brücke* (The Bridge), founded in 1905 in Dresden by Ernst Ludwig Kirchner, Erich Heckel and Karl Schmidt-Rottluff.

NAZI ERA

After the creative surge in the 1920s, the big chill of Nazi conformity sent Germany into an artistic deep freeze in the 1930s and '40s. Many internationally famous artists, including Paul Klee and Max Beckmann, were classified as 'degenerate' and their paintings confiscated, sold off or burned (see the boxed text, p102).

MODERN & CONTEMPORARY

Post-1945 creativity revived the influence of Nolde, Kandinsky and Schmidt-Rottluff, but also spawned a new abstract expressionism in the work of Willi Baumeister. The completely revamped and enlarged Franz Marc Museum (p147) in Kochel am See traces the evolution of pre- and post-WWII expressionism.

An edgy genre that has found major representation in Bavaria is concrete art, which emerged in the 1950s and takes abstract art to its extreme, rejecting any natural form and using only planes and colours. See what this is all about at the Museum für Konkrete Kunst (p249) in Ingolstadt and the Museum im Kulturspeicher (p257) in Würzburg.

The Bavarian photorealist Florian Thomas is among the influential artists whose work is now in the Museum Frieder Burda (p304) in Baden-Baden. Other good spots to plug into the contemporary art scene are the Neues Museum (p222) in Nuremberg, the Pinakothek der Moderne (p91) and the upcoming Museum Brandhorst (p93) in Munich.

'The best thing about Augsburg is the train to Munich.'

BERTOLT BRECHT, 1898–1956

Theatre

Theatre in its various forms enjoys a wide following in Bavaria, especially in Munich, which has the famous Münchner Kammerspiele (p124), but also in Nuremberg, Regensburg and Bamberg. Bavaria's longest-running drama is the *Passionsspiele* (Passion Play; p141), which has been performed in Oberammergau once every decade since the 17th century.

For a dose of local colour, head to a *Bauerntheater* (literally, 'peasant theatre'), which usually presents silly and rustic tales in dialect so thick that it's basically incomprehensible to all non-Bavarians. But never mind, because the story lines are so simplistic, you'll probably be able to follow the plot anyway. The oldest Bauerntheater (p140) is in Garmisch-Partenkirchen.

If you're travelling with kids, don't miss one of the many excellent marionette theatres starring endearing and often handmade puppets. The most famous is the Augsburger Puppenkiste (p278) in Augsburg, but the Figurentheater am Burgtor (p267) in Rothenburg ob der Tauber, the Marionettentheater Bad Tölz (p145) and the Münchner Marionettentheater (p108) will also take you on a magic carpet ride.

The ultimate portal with links to hundreds of theatre stages throughout the German-speaking world is www.theaterparadies -deutschland.de (in German).

44

Food & Drink

Traditionally, food in Bavaria and the Black Forest has a hearty, carnivorous bent and many dishes only give a passing nod to the vegetable kingdom. Thankfully, things are changing as bright young chefs modernise classic dishes by making them lighter, healthier, more creative and, frankly, more interesting. The best ones use local, seasonal and organic ingredients. Additionally, in Munich, Nuremberg, Freiburg and the other bigger cities, an international potpourri of eateries is bringing the world's food to the two regions. Asian food especially has become immensely popular and even sushi has developed a loyal fan base.

STAPLES & SPECIALITIES
Main Dishes

The Chinese say you can eat every part of the pig bar the 'oink', and Bavarian chefs seem to be in full agreement. No part of the animal is spared their attention as they cook up its *Schweinshaxe* (knuckles), *Rippchen* (ribs), *Züngerl* (tongue) and *Wammerl* (belly). Pork also appears as *Schweinebraten* (roast pork) and the misleadingly named *Leberkäse* (liver cheese), a savoury meatloaf that actually contains neither liver nor cheese. The Black Forest contributes the famous *Schwarzwälder Schinken* – ham that's been salted, seasoned and cured for around two weeks.

Non-pork-based dishes include *Hendl* (roast chicken) and *Fleischpflanzerl*, the Bavarian spin on the hamburger. Fish is often caught fresh from the lakes. *Forelle* (trout) is especially popular in the Black Forest and served either *Forelle Müllerin* (baked), *Forelle Blau* (boiled) or *Räucherforelle* (smoked). In Bavarian beer gardens, you'll often find *Steckerlfisch* – skewers of grilled mackerel.

Originating in Swabia but now served throughout southern Germany are *Maultaschen*, which are ravioli-like stuffed pasta pockets, and *Kässpätzle*, the local take on macaroni and cheese.

Sausages

Wurst (sausage) is traditionally served with *süsser Senf* (sweet mustard) alongside sauerkraut or potato salad and a slice of bread. Bavaria's flagship link is the *Weisswurst* (see boxed text, opposite). In Eastern Bavaria and Franconia the mildly spicy *Bratwurst* rules. Nuremberg and Regensburg make the most famous versions: finger-sized and eaten by the half dozen or dozen. Other sausages you may encounter include the spicy *Krakauer* and the hot dog–like *Wiener*.

Vegetables & Side Dishes

The *Kartoffel* (potato) is 'Vegetable *Nummer Eins*' in any meat-and-three-veg dish and can be served as *Salzkartoffeln* (boiled), *Bratkartoffeln* (fried), *Kartoffelpüree* (mashed) or shaped into *Knödel* (dumplings). Dumplings can be made of bread *(Semmelknödel)* and there's also a meaty version made with liver *(Leberknödel)*. Pickled cabbage is another common vegetable companion and comes as either sauerkraut (white) or *Rotkohl* and *Blaukraut* (red).

May is peak season for *Spargel* (white asparagus), which is classically paired with boiled potatoes, hollandaise sauce and sometimes *Schinken* (smoked or cooked ham). In spring, look for *Bärlauch*, a wild-growing garlic that is often turned into a delicious pesto sauce. Wild mushrooms peak in late summer and early autumn when you find many dishes revolving around *Pfifferlinge* (chanterelles) and *Steinpilze* (cep or porcini). Around the same time, *Zwiebelkuchen* (onion tart) makes an appearance, especially in the Kaiserstuhl wine region, where it is paired with sweet *Neuer Süsser* (new wine).

Black Forest Cuisine, by Walter Staib, is like a well-crafted meal: inspired, fresh, creative, finely nuanced and beautifully presented. More than just recipes.

Bavarians like to 'pig out' and the numbers prove it: of the 60kg of meat consumed by the average resident each year, about two-thirds are pork. Oink!

If you want to train your tummy for your trip to Bavaria, try any of the recipes – roast pork to liver dumplings – detailed on www.bavarian-online.de.

WEISSWURST ETIQUETTE

Bavarians love sausage and there is no sausage more Bavarian than the *Weisswurst*. It's so Bavarian, in fact, that there's even an imaginary boundary – the *Weisswurst* equator – beyond which it is no longer served (ie, roughly north of Frankfurt). Unlike most sausages, which are pork-based, this one's made from veal and, before refrigeration, had to be eaten before noon to prevent spoilage. Now they're available all day. They're brought to the table still swimming in hot water. Discard the skin and eat only with fresh pretzels, sweet mustard and, preferably, paired with a mug of Helles. Enjoy!

Sweets & Dessert

The most famous German cake is, of course, the *Schwarzwälder Kirschtorte* (Black Forest cake), a three-layered chocolate sponge cake filled with cream, morello cherries and Kirsch (cherry brandy). Read our interview with the man who invented this delicious hip-expander p184. Usually served with a dollop of ice cream is *Apfelstrudel* (apple strudel), which actually originated in Austria but is now eaten all over southern Germany. A tasty alternative is *Dampfnudeln,* steamed doughy dumplings drenched in custard sauce.

DRINKS
Beer

Bavarians have made beer-making a science, and not just since the passage of the *Reinheitsgebot* (Purity Law) in Ingolstadt in 1516, which stipulates brewers may use only four ingredients – malt, yeast, hops and water. It stopped being a legal requirement in 1987 when the EU struck it down as uncompetitive, but many Bavarian brewers still conform to it anyway, making local brews among the best in the world. Many traditional family-run concerns have been swallowed up by the big brewers, but some smaller operations have survived, including those set up in monasteries. Kloster Weltenburg (p203) in the Altmühltal and Kloster Andechs (p129) near Munich are especially famous.

Beer aficionados face a bewildering choice of labels. The following is a small glossary of the most commonly encountered varieties. Note that most Bavarian beer has an alcohol content between 5% and 5.5%, although some can be as strong as 8%.

BEER GLOSSARY

Alkoholfreies Bier – nonalcoholic beer
Bockbier/Doppelbock – strong beer (*doppel* meaning even more so), either pale, amber or dark in colour with a bittersweet flavour
Dampfbier (steam beer) – originating from Bayreuth, it's top-fermented (this means the yeast rises to the top during the fermentation process) and has a fruity flavour
Dunkles Lagerbier (dark lager) – a reddish-brown, full-bodied lager, malty and lightly hopped
Helles Lagerbier (pale lager) – a lightly hopped lager with strong malt aromas and a slightly sweet taste
Hofbräu – type of brewery belonging to a royal court
Klosterbräu – type of brewery belonging to a monastery
Malzbier – sweet, aromatic, full-bodied malt beer
Märzen – full bodied with strong malt aromas and traditionally brewed in March; today associated with Oktoberfest.
Pils (pilsener) – a bottom-fermented lager with strong hop flavour
Rauchbier (smoke beer) – dark beer with a fresh, spicy or 'smoky' flavour
Weissbier/Weizenbier (wheat beer) – made with wheat instead of barley malt, comes as *Helles Weissbier* (pale), *Dunkles Weissbier* (dark), *Kristallweizen* (clear) and *Hefeweizen* (cloudy; with a layer of still-fermenting yeast on the bottom of the bottle)

With roughly 14,000 distillers, the Black Forest has the highest density of schnapps makers in the world.

In Bavaria beer is officially defined not as alcohol but as a staple food, just like bread.

For an in-depth study of what's pouring at Munich's beer halls and gardens, Larry Hawthorne's *The Beer Drinker's Guide to Munich* is an indispensable tool that will take you far beyond the Hofbräuhaus.

BEER GARDEN GRUB

In beer gardens tables laid with a cloth and utensils are reserved for people ordering food. If you're only planning to down a mug of beer, or have brought along a picnic, don't sit there.

If you do decide to order food, you'll find very similar menus at all beer gardens. Typical dishes include roast chicken, spare ribs, *Schweinebraten* (roast pork) and schnitzel.

Radi is a huge, mild radish that's eaten with beer; you can buy prepared radish or buy a radish at the market and a *Radimesser* at any department store; stick it down in the centre and twist the handle round and round, creating a radish spiral. If you do it yourself, smother the cut end of the radish with salt until it weeps to reduce the bitterness (and increase your thirst!).

Obatzda (oh-batsdah) is Bavarian for 'mixed up'. This cream cheese–like speciality is made of butter, ripe Camembert, onion and caraway. Spread it on *Brezn* (a pretzel) or bread.

If you want to go easy on the booze, order a sweetish *Radler*, which comes in half or full litres and mixes *Helles Lagerbier* and lemonade. A *Russe* (Russian) is generally a litre-sized concoction of *Helles Weissbier* and lemonade.

Prost! (with beer) or *Zum Wohl!* (with wine) are typical drinking toasts.

Wine

Bavaria's only wine-growing region is located in Franconia (p260) in and around Würzburg. Growers here produce some exceptional dry white wines, which are bottled in distinctive green flagons called *Bocksbeutel*. If *Silvaner* is the king of the grape here, then *Müller-Thurgau* is the prince and Riesling, *Weissburgunder* (Pinot Grigio) and *Bacchus* the courtiers. The latter three thrive especially on the steep slopes flanking the Main River. Red wines play merely a supporting role. Nearly 80% of all wine produced is consumed within the region.

Kaiserstuhl is the major wine-growing area in the Black Forest. It produces mainly *Spätburgunder* (Pinot Noir) and *Grauburgunder* (Pinot Gris).

Nonalcoholic Drinks

Tap water is fine to drink, but asking for a glass at a restaurant will raise brows at best and may be refused altogether. Instead most people order *Mineralwasser* (mineral water), which usually comes loaded *mit Kohlensäure* (with bubbles). If you don't like this, ask for *stilles Wasser*. *Eiswürfel* (ice cubes) are usually served only on request.

For more information about German grape varieties, growing regions, wine festivals and courses, check out the pages of the German Wine Institute at www .deutscheweine.de.

Carbonated soft drinks are widely available, although the diet versions are not. A popular and refreshing alternative is *Apfelschorle* or *Johannisbeerschorle*, which is apple juice or black currant juice mixed with sparkling mineral water.

Coffee is another popular drink and many locals, especially the blue-haired set, still gather for afternoon *Kaffee und Kuchen* (coffee and cake) in traditional cafés. In the cities, though, these are being supplanted by stylish, modern coffee-bars, including Bavaria-based Black Bean (p120). Coffee is usually brewed fresh and all the usual varieties are on offer, including cappuccinos, cafe lattes and French-style bowls of milky coffee called *Milchkaffee*.

Except in better cafés, tea is usually a teabag in a glass or pot of hot water and served with a slice of lemon. If you want milk, ask for *Tee mit Milch*.

CELEBRATIONS

Major holidays are feast days and usually spent at home with family, gorging and guzzling way more than everyone knows is good for them. At Easter roast lamb is often the star of the show. Easter is preceded by Lent, a period of fasting when sweet dishes such as *Rohrnudeln* (browned yeasty buns served with plum compote and vanilla sauce) are enjoyed and fish replaces meat in Catholic households. Carp, served boiled, baked or fried, is popular at Christmas time, although more people roast up a goose or a turkey as the main event. *Lebkuchen* (gingerbread) and *Spekulatius* (spicy cookies) are both sweet staples of *Advent* (the pre-Christmas season). For drinks, gluhwein (spicy mulled wine), best consumed at a Christmas market, is a favoured seasonal indulgence.

WHERE TO EAT & DRINK

Restaurants are often formal places with uniformed servers, full menus, crisp white linen and high prices. A *Gaststätte* is generally a more relaxed and local place to eat, with daily specials and perhaps a beer garden or terrace. Cafés tend to serve both coffee and alcohol as well as light meals, although ordering food is usually not obligatory. Beer halls are essentially large pubs serving hearty dishes that wash down well with the local brew. Once the last winter storms are gone, the action moves outdoors into the beer gardens.

Most restaurants are open for lunch and dinner only, but more casual places tend to be open all day, serving a limited menu, often called *Brotzeit*, in the afternoon. If you're looking for authenticity, avoid restaurants near major tourist attractions, in the *Ratskeller* (basement of the town hall), or those posting menus in multiple languages.

German fast-food places are called *Imbiss* or *Schnellimbiss*. Sausage kiosks are ubiquitous and many bakeries serve sandwiches alongside pastries. A tasty and filling alternative, especially in the cities, is the *döner* (doner kebab), a pita stuffed with meat slices, salad and doused with garlicky yogurt sauce. Pizza, sold by the slice, is also popular.

Pick up three Michelin stars' worth of tips and tricks at a cooking seminar run by fabled chef Heinz Winkler (p154) in Aschau. See www .residenz-heinz-winkler .de for details.

VEGETARIANS & VEGANS

While vegetarians and vegans will have fewer tummy grumbles in Munich and other big cities, they'll have a bit of a tough go in the countryside, although even there awareness is increasing. Most menus now feature a few meat-free dishes, although these may not be terribly inspired, and unenlightened chefs may see nothing wrong with cooking vegetables in meat stock. Fish is also often considered a 'meatless' dish, and salads may be dressed in mayonnaise and have eggs and ham mixed in with the lettuce and tomatoes. Indian, Thai, Vietnamese and other Asian eateries are your best bet for tofu- or vegetable-based mains. A delicious snack is the Turkish speciality called *börek* or *pide,* pastry stuffed or topped with different fillings, including vegetarian-friendly ones; it's sold wherever *döner* are sold.

EATING WITH KIDS

Dining with kids is by no means difficult in Germany. High chairs are a permanent fixture in restaurants and many restaurants have special kids' menus or will try to meet any special small-appetite requirements. Nappy- (diaper-) changing facilities are rare, although some quick-eat places have a fold-down changing table in the women's bathroom. Baby food, soy- and dairy-based infant formulas, organic fruit juices and teas and the like are widely available in supermarkets and drugstores. Also see p314.

HABITS & CUSTOMS

Most Bavarians eat three meals a day. *Frühstück* (breakfast) usually consists of bread, cheese, cold cuts and jam, and maybe a boiled egg. Hotel buffets usually add cereals, fruit and yogurt.

Traditionally, *Mittagessen* (lunch) has been the main meal of the day, but modern working practices have changed this considerably, at least in the cities. However, many restaurants still tout lunch-time dishes or a fixed *Gedeck* or *Tagesmenü* (lunch menu).

OUR TOP EATING EXPERIENCES

Bavaria

- **Auberge Moar-Alm near Bad Tölz** (p146) Possibly the best French cuisine north of the Alps in a romantic pasture setting with a view of the mountains.
- **Augustiner Bräustuben in Munich** (p119) Rub elbows and toast with locals and visitors at the long wooden tables of this authentic beer hall with superb *Schweinshaxe* (roast pork) and other hearty meals.
- **Residenz Heinz Winkler in Aschau** (p154) With three Michelin stars to his credit, Winkler truly is a magician in the kitchen.
- **Heilig-Geist-Stift-Schenke in Passau** (p207) Home-made wine, jam and schnapps team up with spirited cooking in this haunt dripping with historic ambience.
- **Stadtmarkt in Augsburg** (p278) A snacker's paradise with a United Nations of choices.
- **Bratwursthäusle in Nuremberg** (p225) Possibly Bavaria's best sausage kitchen.

Black Forest

- **Café Schäfer in Triberg** (p298) The quintessential Black Forest cake – a heavenly combination of light sponge cake, fresh cream and morello cherries with a subtle Kirsch kick.
- **Osteria & Enoteca de' Messeri in Villingen** (p300) Gnocchi with hand-picked porcini or pigeon in truffle cream? Fabio Vallini rustles up Tuscan specialities with passion and prowess.
- **Höhengasthaus Kolmenhof near Freiburg** (p299) Perched above the valley, this rustic haunt serves the freshest trout in the forest with the source of the Danube right in the backyard.

Abendbrot (supper) at home is normally served between 5pm and 7pm and doesn't involve cooked food. Going out to *Abendessen* (dinner) tends to be a relaxed and social event that starts between 7pm and 8pm and can easily last two or three hours. Restaurants are busiest on Friday to Sunday nights, although reservations are recommended any night.

Some Bavarians also indulge in a fourth meal, the *Brotzeit* (literally 'bread time'), typically an afternoon snack featuring bread with various cold cuts, cheeses or sausages. Traditional restaurants often have a special *Brotzeit* menu. Those with a sweet tooth may opt for *Kaffee und Kuchen* (coffee and cakes), served in cafés, instead.

From *Allerseelenzopf* (a sweet bread loaf) to *Zwickelbier* (unfiltered beer), all of the mysteries behind Bavaria's regional culinary secrets are revealed on www.food-from-bavaria.com.

EAT YOUR WORDS

For pronunciation guidelines and other useful phrases, see the Language chapter on p331.

Useful Phrases

I'd like to reserve a table.
Ich möchte einen Tisch reservieren.   ikh *merkh*·te *ai*·nen tish re·zer·*vee*·ren

Do you have a menu in English?
Haben Sie eine englische Speisekarte?   *ha*·ben zee *ai*·ne *eng*·li·she *shpai*·ze·kar·te?

What would you recommend?
Was empfehlen Sie?   vas emp·*fay*·len zee?

I'd like a local speciality.
Ich möchte etwas Typisches aus der Region. ikh *merkh*·te et·vas *tü*·pi·shes ows dair re·*gyawn*

I'm a vegetarian.
Ich bin Vegetarier/Vegetarierin. (m/f)   ikh bin ve·ge·*tah*·ri·er/ve·ge·*tah*·ri·er·in

That was delicious!
Das war köstlich!   das var *kerst*·likh!

DOS & DON'TS AT DINNER

▪ Do bring a small gift – flowers or a bottle of wine – when invited to a meal.

▪ Do say *Guten Appetit*! (*bon appetit!*) before starting to eat.

▪ Do offer to help with the dishes afterwards.

▪ Don't start eating until everyone has been served.

▪ Don't expect to get a glass of tap water at a restaurant.

▪ Don't assume you can pay by credit card when eating out.

The bill, please.
  Die Rechnung, bitte.   dee rekh·nung bi·te

Food Glossary
BASICS

Brot	brawt	bread
Butter	*bu*·ter	butter
Ei(er)	*ai*·(er)	egg
Käse	*kay*·ze	cheese
Milch	milkh	milk
Nudeln	*noo*·deln	noodles
Pfeffer	*pfe*·ffer	pepper
Reis	rais	rice
Salz	zalts	salt
Semmel	*tse*·mel	bread roll
Zucker	*tsu*·ker	sugar

MEAT & MEATY DISHES

Ente	*en*·te	duck
Fasan	fa·*zahn*	pheasant
Flammekuchen	*fla*·me·koo·khen	Alsatian-style pizza topped with cream and bacon
Fleischpflanzerl	*flaish*·pflan·tserl	meatballs
Gans	gans	goose
Hackfleisch	*hak*·flaish	chopped or minced meat
Hähnchen/Huhn	*hayn*·khen/hoon	chicken
Herz	herts	heart
Kalbfleisch	*kalp*·flaish	veal
Kalbsgeschnetzeltes	*kalps*·ge·shnet·tsel·tes	sautéed veal in cream sauce
Krustenbraten	*kroos*·ten·brah·ten	roast pork with crackling crust
Lammbraten	*lam*·brah·ten	roast lamb
Lammfleisch	*lam*·flaish	lamb
Lammkotelett	lam·kot·*let*	lamb chop
Leber	*lay*·ber	liver
Leberkäs	*lay*·ber·kay·ze	pork and beef meatloaf
Leberknödel	*lay*·ber·kner·del	chopped liver dumpling
Lende	*len*·de	loin
Niere	*nee*·re	kidney
Pressack	*pray*·sak	sausagelike spiced pork served sliced with bread
Pute	*pu*·te	turkey
Putenbrust	*pu*·ten·broost	turkey breast
Rehbraten	*ray*·brah·ten	roast venison

Rinderbraten	*rin*-de-*brah*-ten	roast beef
Rindfleisch	*rint*-flaish	beef
Roulade	roo-*lah*-de	thin-sliced beef rolled up and braised with spices
Sauerbraten	*zow*-er-*brah*-ten	beef marinated in vinegar, then braised
Saure Lungen	*zow*-re-*lung*-en	soup made with lungs marinated in vinegar
Saure Zipfel	*zow*-re-*tsee*-pfel	sausages boiled in vinegar and spices until blue
Schinken	*shing*-ken	ham
Schlachtteller/Schlachtplatte	*shlakh*-te-le/*shlakh*-pla-te	platter of various cold meats and sausages
Schweinebraten	*shvai*-ne brah-ten	roast pork
Schweinefleisch	*shvai*-ne-flaish	pork
Spanferkel	*shpan*-fer-kel	suckling pig
Wachtel	*vakh*-tel	quail
Wild	vilt	game
Wildschwein	*vilt*-shvain	wild boar
Zunge/Züngerl	*tsung*-e/*tsoong*-erl	tongue

FISH

Dorsch	dorsh	cod
Forelle	fo-*re*-le	trout
Garnele	gar-*nay*-le	prawn
Hering	*hay*-ring	herring
Karpfen	*karp*-fen	carp
Lachs	laks	salmon
Seezunge	see-*tsung*-e	sole

VEGETABLES & MEATLESS DISHES

Artischocke	ar-ti-*sho*-ke	artichoke
Auflauf	*owf*-lowf	casserole
Blumenkohl	*bloo*-men-kawl	cauliflower
Bohnen	*baw*-nen	beans
Gemüse	ge-*moo*-ze	vegetables
Gurke	*gur*-ke	cucumber; gherkin
Kartoffel	kar-*to*-fel	potato
Kässpätzle	kays-*shpez*-le	type of pasta drenched in cheese
Knoblauch	*knawp*-lowkh	garlic
Kohl	kawl	cabbage
Krautsalat	*krowt*-sa-lat	coleslaw
Linsen	*lin*-sen	lentils
Radieschen	ra-*dees*-khen	radish
Rosenkohl	*raw*-zen-kawl	Brussels sprouts
Rotkohl	*rawt*-kawl	red cabbage
Schupfnudeln	*shupf*-noo-deln	finger-shaped fried dumplings
Schwammerl	*shwam*-erl	mushroom
Spargel	*shpar*-gel	white asparagus
Zwiebel	*tswee*-bel	onion

FRUIT

Apfel	*ap*-fel	apple
Apfelsine	*ap*-fel-zee-ne	orange
Birne	*bir*-ne	pear

Dattel	*da*·tel	date
Erdbeere	*ert*·bair·re	strawberry
Feige	*fai*·ge	fig
Holunderbeere	*ho*·lund·er bair·re	elderberry
Kirsche	*kir*·she	cherry
Pfirsich	*pfir*·zikh	peach
Rote/Schwarze Johannisbeere	*ro*·te/*shvar* tse yo·*ha*·nis·bair re	red/blackcurrant
Weintraube	*vain*·trow·be	grape
Zitrone	tsi·*traw*·ne	lemon

Environment

THE LAND

In Bavaria and the Black Forest nature has been as prolific and creative as Picasso in his prime. The most dramatic region is the Bavarian Alps, a phalanx of craggy peaks created by tectonic uplift some 770 million years ago and chiselled and gouged by glaciers and erosion ever since. Several ranges stand sentinel above the rest of the land, including, west to east, the Allgäuer Alps, the Wetterstein/Karwendel Alps (with Germany's highest mountain, the Zugspitze at 2962m) and the Berchtesgadener Alps. Many peaks are well above 2000m.

North of here, the Alpine Foothills – a wedge of land between the Danube and the Alps – are a lush mosaic of moorland, rolling hills, gravel plains and pine forests dappled with glacial lakes, including the vast Chiemsee, Lake Starnberg and the Ammersee. The foothills are book-ended by Lake Constance in the west and the Inn and Salzach Rivers in the east.

The Bavarian Forest along the Czech border in eastern Bavaria is a classic *Mittelgebirge,* a midsize mountain range whose highest peak, the Grosse Arber (1456m), juts out like the tall kid in your third-grade class picture. Much of it is blanketed by dark, dense forests that fade into the thinly populated Frankenwald and Fichtelgebirge areas further north.

The Black Forest, west of Bavaria in Germany's southwestern corner, is another *Mittelgebirge*, a storied quilt that enwraps enigmatic waterfalls, rolling hills, sparkling lakes, lush vineyards, and oak, pine and beech forests into one mystique-laden package. The little Kinzig River divides the north from the much higher south, where the Feldberg is the highest elevation at 1493m.

Much of Franconia and Swabia is a complex patchwork of low ranges, rifts and deep meandering valleys. A Jurassic limestone range is responsible for bizarre rock formations, such as those in the Franconian Switzerland region north of Nuremberg.

Southern Germany is traversed by several major rivers, of which the Danube, which originates in the Black Forest, and the Main are the longest. The Inn and the Isar flow down from the Alps into the Danube, the former at Passau, the latter near Deggendorf on the edge of the Bavarian Forest. Germany's main south–north river, the mighty Rhine, divides the Black Forest from France and Switzerland.

WILDLIFE

Keep your peepers open and you'll be amazed by how many critters you'll encounter as you traipse around Bavaria and the Black Forest, especially in the national and nature parks. Centuries of human impact have taken their toll, of course, causing many animals – including certain reptiles, beetles and butterflies – as well as plants, to limp onto the endangered species list.

Animals

The most common large forest mammal throughout Southern Germany is the red deer, a quick-footed fellow with skinny legs supporting a chunky body. Encounters with wild boar, a type of wild pig with a keen sense of smell but poor eyesight, are also possible, especially in the Bavarian Forest.

Beavers faced extinction in the 19th century not only because they were coveted for their precious pelts (beaver hats were all the rage), but also because they were cooked up in strict Catholic households each Friday since the good people considered them to be 'fish'. Reintroduced in the

---

Bavaria sprawls over 70,550 sq km, making it bigger than Ireland, Portugal or Denmark. The Black Forest is comparatively small at only 13,500 sq km.

The first recorded ascent of the Zugspitze was on 27 August 1820 by a trio of land surveyors led by Josef Naus.

The Black Forest is part of the Continental Divide. Water either drains into the north-flowing Rhine, which empties into the Atlantic Ocean, or into the east-flowing Danube, which empties into the Black Sea.

mid-1960s, beavers are thriving once again, especially along the Danube, between Ingolstadt and Kelheim, and its tributaries.

Lynxes actually died out in Germany in the 19th century but in the 1980s Czech authorities released 17 lynxes in the Bohemian Forest, and a small group of brave souls have since tried their luck again in the Bavarian Forest right across the border. There have even been rare sightings around the Feldberg in the southern Black Forest.

In the Alps, the Alpine marmot, a sociable chap that looks like a fat squirrel, lives in burrows below the tree line, while wild goats make their home in the upper mountains. The snow hare, whose fur is white in winter, is also a common Alpine denizen as is the elusive chamois, a goatlike creature that likes to hang out in steep and rocky terrain, and is also found around the Feldberg. The endangered *Auerhuhn* (capercaillie), a grouselike bird, also makes its home here and in the Bavarian Forest. Lizards, praying mantids and European bee-eaters live in the sunny Kaiserstuhl area.

Owls of the World: Their Lives, Behaviour and Survival, by James R Duncan, makes the ideal companion for wildlife enthusiasts out to spot the eagle-owl, Eurasian pygmy owl and other owl species.

Local skies are home to over 400 bird species, from white-backed woodpeckers and pygmy owls to sparrowhawks, grey herons, jays and black redstarts. The Wutach Gorge in the Black Forest is a unique habitat that supports such rare birds as treecreepers and kingfishers, as well as many species of butterflies, beetles and lizards.

The true king of the skies, though, is the golden eagle. If you're lucky, you might spot one patrolling the mountain peaks in Nationalpark Berchtesgaden.

Plants

Despite environmental pressures, southern German forests remain beautiful places to escape the crowds. At lower altitudes, they usually consist of a potpourri of beech, oak, birch, chestnut, lime, maple and ash that erupt into a kaleidoscope of colour in autumn. Up in the higher elevations, fir, pine, spruce and other conifers are more prevalent. Canopies often shade low-growing ferns, heather, clover and foxglove.

Gustav Hegi's *Alpenflora* is an illustrated field guide (in German) to major Alpine plant life in Bavaria, Austria and Switzerland.

In spring, Alpine regions especially burst with wildflowers – orchid, cyclamen, gentian, pulsatilla, Alpine roses, edelweiss and buttercups – which brighten meadows and hillsides. Minimise your impact by sticking to trails.

In summer, wild berries add splashes of colour to the forest. Many of them are perfectly edible, from blueberries to raspberries to blackberries. In late summer and early autumn, mushroom hunters swarm the forests in search of *Pfifferlinge* (chanterelles), *Steinpilze* (porcini) and other delicacies.

NATIONAL & NATURE PARKS

Bavaria is home to Germany's oldest national park, the Nationalpark Bayerischer Wald, which was founded in 1970. There is only one more of

---

WORLD HERITAGE SITES IN BAVARIA

For more information see Unesco's website: whc.unesco.org.

- Residenz and Hofgarten in Würzburg (p255; declared 1981) – splendid art and opulence courtesy of the local prince-bishops.

- Wieskirche (p280; declared 1983) – richly decorated rococo pilgrimage church in the middle of a meadow.

- Altstadt (old town) of Bamberg (p231; declared 1993) – immaculately preserved historic town centre.

- Altstadt of Regensburg (p195; declared 2006) – medieval town centre with Roman, Romanesque and Gothic buildings.

NATIONAL & NATURE PARKS IN BAVARIA & THE BLACK FOREST

Park	Features	Activities	Best time to visit	Page
Nationalpark Bayerischer Wald	mountain forest, bogs, streams (243 sq km); deer, hazel grouse, fox, otter, pygmy owl, three-toe woodpecker	hiking, mountain biking, cross-country skiing	year-round	p210
Nationalpark Berchtesgaden	lakes, mixed forest, cliffs, meadows (210 sq km); eagle, chamois, marmot, blue hare, salamander	hiking, skiing, wildlife-watching	year-round	p68
Naturpark Altmühltal	mixed forest, streams, rock formations, Roman ruins (2962 sq km)	hiking, cycling, canoeing, kayaking, rock climbing, cross-country skiing, fossil digging	late spring to autumn	p243
Naturpark Bayerischer Wald	largest continuous forest in Germany (includes the smaller Nationalpark Bayerischer Wald), moorland, meadows, rolling hills (3077 sq km)	hiking, cycling, cross-country skiing, Nordic walking	May–Oct	p209
Naturpark Frankenwald	low mountains, dense coniferous forest, streams (1020 sq km)	hiking, cycling, mountain biking, cross-country skiing	spring, summer, autumn	p241
Naturpark Fränkische Schweiz	forest, valleys, caves (2346 sq km)	hiking, cycling, canoeing	late spring to autumn	p236
Naturpark Schwarzwald Mitte/Nord	mixed forest, deep valleys, lakes (3750 sq km); deer, wild boar, raven, capercaillie	hiking, Nordic walking, mountain biking	late spring to autumn	p288
Naturpark Steigerwald	rolling hills, mixed forest, ponds, vineyards (1200 sq km)	hiking, cycling, swimming, canoeing	late spring to autumn	p236
Naturpark Südschwarzwald	mixed forest, pastures, vineyards, lake, moorland (3700 sq km); capercaillie, deer, lynx	hiking, Nordic walking, snowshoeing, mountain biking	year-round	p288

Germany's 15 national parks in Bavaria but it's a good one: the Nationalpark Berchtesgaden on the Austrian border. Both parks have been relatively untouched by human impact, and preserve places of outstanding natural beauty and rare geographical features. They also protect various species of wildlife and act as natural laboratories for researchers and scientists.

The Black Forest has no national parks but it does have two nature parks, which enjoy a lower degree of environmental protection and are essentially outdoor playgrounds. Don't picture them as traditional 'parks' either: these are sprawling rural landscapes crisscrossed by roads and dotted with villages. Logging and agricultural use is possible here, although done in a controlled and environmentally friendly fashion. See the table (above) for an overview of the parks described in this book.

Bavaria's two national and 16 nature parks occupy about 30% of the state's total area.

Those interested in German nature parks can download a comprehensive English-language document from www .naturparke.de.

ENVIRONMENTAL ISSUES

Bavaria has an impressive conservation record that goes back to 1970 when it became the first German state to appoint a minister of the environment, some 16 years before such a position was created on the federal level. In 1984 the protection of nature was made part of the Bavarian state constitution.

Policy has largely focused on decreasing pollution and waste; investing in clean technologies and renewable energies; educating people and industry; and cleaning up existing problems. A key goal is to bring greenhouse gas emissions down to Kyoto Protocol levels. And indeed, Bavarian carbon-dioxide levels are one-third below the German average, largely through heavy reliance on nuclear power. Fully two-thirds of energy in Bavaria (vs 30% nationwide) is generated in this fashion. However, while this method keeps emissions low, it also ignores the still unresolved issue of nuclear waste disposal.

Paradoxically, Bavaria has also managed to attract investors in renewable energies, such as hydroelectric, wind and solar energy. In fact, photovoltaic power stations are sprouting all over the state. In 2005 and 2006, respectively, the world's two largest solar plants, Bavaria Solarpark near Regensburg and Pocking near Passau, started generating power. And the Walchensee hydro-power station south of Munich is one of the largest in Germany. All in all, Bavaria generates about 8% of its energy through ecofriendly methods.

In doing its part in slowing down global warming, Bavaria is at least partly motivated by enlightened self-interest. Ski tourism in the Alps generates millions of euros each winter, but the warmest succession of winters on record has brought unreliable snow levels and melting glaciers. A 2006 OECD study predicts the death of scores of low-lying German ski resorts by 2020. For now, communities try to fight missing snow with snow cannons, but these only work in sub-zero temps and consume a heck of a lot of water and energy, to say nothing of the damage done to the landscape and the mountain ecology.

Snow levels are already quite low in the Black Forest, whose highest elevation is below 1500m. One of the major success stories in the region has been the cleaning up of the Rhine River. Declared dead by 1970, the Upper Rhine was spawning salmon and sea trout again by 1997 – for the first time in 50 years.

Forestry is fundamental to the Black Forest's economy. The *Forstamt* (Forestry Office) is responsible for managing the forest, for instance through selective logging, which is largely done in a sustainable way (no clear-cutting) to minimise impact on the environment. Selected trees (usually marked with a luminous paint splash) are felled, opening up the canopy and allowing other trees and vegetation to grow. The *Forstamt* is creating paths (30m apart) through the forest, so logging machines can pass through without damaging flora and fauna. Forest regeneration is taking place in some nature reserves. Helicopters have recently been applying lime to restore the balance of the soil.

Another priority has been given to protecting natural spaces. Bavaria has two national parks, 16 nature parks and over 1200 protected nature areas totalling about 45,000 sq km.

From 1850 to 1980, Alpine glaciers lost about 40% of their area and since then another 20% has melted.

For details about Bavaria's environment policy, check out the website of the Bavarian Environmental Protection Agency at www.bayern.de/lfu (partly in English).

Bavaria & the Black Forest Outdoors

Bavaria and the Black Forest live up to their reputation as splendid outdoor playgrounds. There's plenty to do year-round, with each season offering its own special delights, be it hiking among a painter's palette worth of spring wildflowers, swimming in an Alpine lake warmed by the summer sun, biking among a kaleidoscope of autumn foliage or celebrating winter by skiing through deep powder.

HIKING & WALKING

Got wanderlust? With scenery to die for, Bavaria and the Black Forest are perfect for exploring on foot. Ramble through romantic river valleys, hike among fragrant pines, bag Alpine peaks or simply go for a walk by the lake. Some of the finest treks in the Berchtesgaden and Zugspitze areas are detailed in the Walking in the Bavarian Alps chapter, p61, which also includes a boxed text with route suggestions in other regions (p71). The destination chapters also steer you towards shorter, local hikes.

Trails are usually well signposted, sometimes with symbols quaintly painted on tree trunks. To find a route matching your fitness level and time frame, pick the brains of local tourist office staff, who can also supply you with maps and tips. Many also offer multiday 'hiking without luggage' packages that include accommodation and luggage transfer between hotels.

For details, including maps and satellite images, about the 24,000km of hiking trails lacing the Black Forest, check out the www.wanderservice-schwarzwald.de (in German), an interactive portal maintained by the Schwarzwaldverein.

MOUNTAINEERING

'Climb every mountain…' the Mother Superior belted out in the *Sound of Music*, and the Bavarian Alps – the centre of mountaineering in Germany – will give you plenty of opportunities to do just that. You can venture out on day treks or plan multiday clambers from hut to hut, as long as you keep in mind that hiking in the Alps is no walk in the park. You need to be in reasonable condition and come equipped with the right shoes, gear, topographic maps or GPS. Trails can be narrow, steep and have icy patches, even in summer.

Garmisch-Partenkirchen (p136), Mittenwald (p140) and Berchtesgaden (p157) are good gateways to your mountain adventure.

Before heading out, seek local advice on trails, equipment and weather and take all precautions concerning clothing and provisions. And always let someone know where you're going. If you're inexperienced, ask at the tourist offices about local outfitters offering instruction, equipment rental and guided tours. These are usually run by young, energetic and English-speaking folks with an infectious love for and deep knowledge of the mountains. For potential problems and how to deal with hypothermia, see p330.

Before heading out into the mountains in winter, check the avalanche danger level at www.lawinenwarndienst-bayern.de (in German).

The **Deutscher Alpenverein** (DAV; www.alpenverein.de, in German) is a good resource for information on hiking and mountaineering, and has local chapters in practically every German town. For details see p62.

CYCLING & MOUNTAIN BIKING

Strap on your helmet! Bavaria and the Black Forest are superb cycling territories, no matter whether you're off on a leisurely lakeside spin, an adrenaline-fuelled mountain exploration or a multiday bike touring adventure.

Practically every town and region has a network of signposted bike routes. For day tours, staff at the local tourist offices can supply you with ideas, maps

---

TOP FIVE BIKE TOURING TRAILS

- **Altmühltal Radweg** (p245; 241km) Rothenburg ob der Tauber (p262) to Kelheim – this trail follows the Altmühl River through the Naturpark Altmühltal (p243).

- **Benediktweg** (p164; 248km) Altötting to Altötting – easy loop trail in the footsteps of Pope Benedikt XVI with stops including Marktl am Inn (p209), Wasserburg (p151) and Burghausen (p165).

- **Bodensee–Königssee Radweg** (414km) Lindau (p286) to Berchtesgaden (p157) – this moderate route runs along the foot of the Alps with magnificent views of the mountains, charming lakes and forests.

- **Donauradweg** (434km) Neu-Ulm to Passau (p204) – a delightful, easy- to moderate-level riverside trip that travels along the Danube, one of Europe's great streams.

- **Romantic Road** (p253; 359km) Würzburg (p254) to Füssen (p281) – this easy to moderate trail is one of the nicest ways to explore Germany's most famous holiday route, although it can get busy.

---

and advice. Most towns have at least one bike-hire station (often at or near the train station); many are listed throughout this book. Depending on the model, you'll pay between €8 to €40 per day or €50 to €120 per week, plus a deposit. The folks at bike shops are also great for getting the inside scoop on the local scene.

Mountain biking is hugely popular in the Black Forest and in the Alpine region, especially in Ruhpolding (p154) in the Chiemgau, and also around Garmisch-Partenkirchen (p136), Bad Reichenhall (p155), Berchtesgaden (p157) and Freudenstadt (p306). The Bavarian Forest (p209) is another top destination for mountain bikers with more than 450km of challenging routes and climbs.

Southern Germany is crisscrossed by dozens of long-distance trails, making it ideal for *Radwandern* (bike touring). Routes are well signposted and typically are a combination of lightly travelled back roads, forestry tracks and paved highways with dedicated bike lanes. Many traverse nature reserves, meander along rivers or venture into steep mountain terrain.

For inspiration and route planning, check out www.germany-tourism.de/cycling, which provides (in English) an overview of routes, helpful planning tips, a route finder and free downloads of route maps and descriptions. For more detailed route descriptions German readers can consult www.schwarzwald-bike.de, www.blackforest-tourism.com and www.bayernbike.de. The **Galli Verlag** (www.galli-verlag.de) publishes a variety of bike guides sold in bookshops and by the publisher.

For basic route maps, order or download the free *Bayernnetz für Radler* (Bavarian Cycling Network) from www.bayerninfo.de. For on-the-road navigating the best maps are those published by the national cycling organisation **Allgemeiner Deutscher Fahrrad Club** (ADFC; www.adfc.de). Regional maps for day and weekend tours and cycle tour maps for longer excursions are available in bookshops, at tourist offices and online. They indicate inclines, track condition and how busy the tracks are, and the location of repair shops. GPS users should find the UTM grid coordinates useful.

ADFC also publishes useful online directories called **Bett & Bike** (www.bettundbike.de, in German) that lists hundreds of bicycle-friendly hotels, inns and hostels. Bookshops carry the printed version for Bavaria and Baden-Württemberg (€6.50 each).

For an overview of transporting your bike within Bavaria and the Black Forest, see p324.

For the inside scoop on healthy holidays in Germany, plus a full list of spa resorts, point the cursor towards www.heilklima.de (partly in English).

To learn the secrets about restoring physical and mental strength by dipping into the 'fountain of youth' at a spa, pick up Nathaniel Altman's *Healing Springs: The Ultimate Guide to Taking the Waters*.

WATER SPORTS

Southern Germany's lakes and rivers are popular playgrounds for water-based pursuits. The water quality is usually very good, especially in the Alpine lakes, but the swimming season is relatively short (June to September) since water temperatures rarely climb above 21°C. The warmest lakes are the Staffelsee

---

SKIING & SNOWBOARDING

Modern lifts, trails from 'Sesame Street' to 'Death Wish', breathtaking scenery, cosy mountain huts, steaming mulled wine, hearty dinners by a crackling fireplace – all these are the hallmarks of a German skiing holiday.

The Bavarian Alps, only an hour's drive south of Munich, offer the best slopes and most reliable ski conditions. The most famous resort town here is, of course, Garmisch-Partenkirchen, which hosted the 1936 Olympic Games and is popular with the international set. It's also a stop on the Vierschanzen-Tournee ski-jumping competition circuit.

There's also plenty of skiing and snowboarding to be done in the Bayerischer Wald, where mountains may not soar as high as in the Alps but snow conditions are still surprisingly reliable. Smaller crowds and a more low-key atmosphere make this area especially well suited to families. The downhill action centres on the Grosser Arber mountain, while the Bretterschachten is a major draw for cross-country skiing aficionados. The best cross-country skiing, though, is done in the Chiemgau, especially in Ruhpolding and Reit im Winkl, but many towns throughout southern Bavaria offer their own network of groomed tracks.

The Black Forest is too low-lying to offer dependable snow levels with the exception of the Feldberg area, which often gets snow as early as November. Otherwise, it's mostly cross-country skiing, including some particularly scenic trails at Martinskapelle (p298) and around Titisee (p301).

The skiing season generally runs from late November/early December to March but thanks to global warming, snow levels are becoming less reliable, especially in the lower-lying resorts. Most try to trick Mother Nature by installing efficient snow-making equipment, which works up to a point but gobbles up tons of water and energy. All resorts have equipment-hire facilities. Rates for downhill gear start at about €10 per day, with discounts for longer rental periods. Cross-country equipment costs slightly less. Daily ski-lift passes start at around €20.

We've picked out a few of the best resorts in Bavaria and the Black Forest. For details follow the cross-references to the destination chapters. An excellent source for additional resorts not covered in this book is www.bergfex.com.

Garmisch-Partenkirchen

Few ski hounds can resist the siren call of Germany's winter sports capital, which hosted the 1936 Olympic Games. Its 118km of downhill runs spread across three ski fields (Zugspitze, Alpspitze-Hausberg-Kreuzeck and Eckbauer) are accessed by 30 cable cars and chairlifts. There are some runs for beginners and intermediates but hardcore expert skiers will have plenty of white-knuckle cornices, chutes and bowls to play with. Boarders can jib down the mountain in a terrain park up on top. The kicker and rail areas have separate lines for beginners and advanced. Kids, meanwhile, can take it easy in the new Kinderland at the Hausberg.

- Nearest town: Garmisch-Partenkirchen (p136)
- One-day adult lift ticket: Zugspitze €37.50, Classic Ski Area (Alpspitze, Hausberg, Kreuzeck) €31.50, Eckbauer €18
- Information: ☎ 08821-7970; www.zugspitze.de

Winklmoos-Alm/Steinplatte

This gem proves that bigger isn't always better. The top skiing area in the Chiemgau ranges in elevation from 1100m to 1900m and has sunny skies and a surprisingly reliable snow pack. The terrain is crisscrossed by 14 runs, the longest being 2.6km, with vertical drops up to 870m. Snowboarders have a half-pipe to play in.

near Murnau (p144) and the Titisee (p300). The Walchensee (p148) in the Tölzer Land enjoys peculiar wind conditions that make it a mecca for windsurfers. Diving is also a possibility here. The Forggensee (p285) near the royal castles in the Allgäu also offers great surfing in lovely surroundings, as do the Starnberger See (p127), Lindau on Lake Constance (p286) and the

- Nearest town: Reit im Winkl (p154)
- One-day adult lift ticket: €36.50
- Information: ☎ 08640-8002; www.winklmoosalm.com, in German

Jenner

Locals and visitors cherish the truly royal vistas of the emerald Königssee from the Jenner, the most demanding of the five ski fields in the Berchtesgadener Land with vertical drops up to 600m; the longest run is 3.1km.

- Nearest town: Berchtesgaden (p157)
- One-day adult lift ticket: €25
- Information: ☎ 08652-958 10; www.jennerbahn.de

Götschen

Also in the Berchtesgadener Land, this compact ski field is set in a stunningly beautiful Alpine landscape near the village of Bischofswiesen. It enjoys a huge fan base among snowboarders and pistes are illuminated for night skiing every Tuesday and Friday.

- Nearest town: Berchtesgaden (p157)
- One-day adult lift ticket: €21
- Information: ☎ 08652-7656; www.goetschen.com, in German

Grosser Arber

The highest mountain in the Bayerischer Wald, Grosser Arber (1456m) has mostly easy to moderate runs and a kickin' snowboard park. It's especially popular with families but has also hosted World Cup ski races. There's also access to 90km of cross-country skiing.

- Nearest town: Bodenmais (p212)
- One-day adult lift ticket: €24
- Information: ☎ 09925-941 40; www.arber.de

Kranzberg

Mittenwald's local ski mountain is the family-friendly Kranzberg (1391m), which has only 15km of pistes with superb views of the Karwendel and Wetterstein ranges. There's night skiing, a 1.6km-long toboggan run and a Kinderpark for children.

- Nearest town: Mittenwald (p140)
- One-day adult lift ticket: €21.50
- Information: ☎ 08823-1553; www.skiparadies-kranzberg.de, in German

Feldberg

The highest mountain in the Black Forest, the Feldberg (1493m) has 28 lifts to access 50km of runs, with 15km each for beginners and advanced and 20km for intermediate piste hounds. Cross-country skiers can work up a sweat on 60km of cross-country trails, including a 14km skating track.

- Nearest town: Feldberg (p301)
- One-day adult lift ticket: €25
- Information: ☎ 07655-8019; www.liftverbund-feldberg.de

SOAKIN' & SWEATIN'

If the road has left you frazzled and achy, a trip to a day spa may just be what the doctor ordered. Every place has its own treatment menu of massages (shiatsu, deep tissue, Swedish, tandem – ie for two people, hot stone, etc) and beauty treatments (facials, wraps, botanical baths, mud baths etc). Many hotels, especially in the countryside, have so-called 'wellness areas' with a sauna, perhaps a whirlpool, a steam room or even a swimming pool. Massage services are often available on request.

'Taking a cure', ie booking a multiweek regimen of sauna, bath, massage and exercise in a *Kurort* (spa resort), has been a German tradition for more than 100 years. Visitors can pick and choose from treatments offered through the local spa centres *(Kurzentrum)* or spa administrations *(Kurverwaltung)*. Bookings can usually be made at short notice.

Water parks, which seem to be proliferating faster than rabbits on Viagra, are also good for getting pummelled into a state of bliss. Most have several indoor and outdoor pools (often filled with thermal water from local mineral springs), Jacuzzis, surge channels, massage jets and waterfalls, multiple saunas plus a big menu of pampering options. Good spots include the Königliche Kristall-Therme in Schwangau (p285), Alpamare in Bad Tölz (p145), Vita Alpina in Ruhpolding (p154), Prienavera (p152) in Prien on the Chiemsee, the Rupertustherme (p156) in Bad Reichenhall, the Watzmann Therme (p162) in Berchtesgaden, and the Caracalla-Therme and Friedrichsbad in Baden-Baden (p304).

Most *Stadtbäder* (municipal baths) also have sauna facilities, usually with fixed hours for men and women as well as mixed sessions. Note that not a stitch of clothing is worn in any German sauna, so leave your modesty in the locker but bring a towel or two.

The mountain-bike elite comes to the Black Forest to test their mettle in several international MTB races, including the Black Forest Ultra Bike Marathon, the Vaude Trans and the Worldclass MTB Challenge.

For a big bag of tips and tricks on how to minimise your impact on the environment while traipsing through the forest, visit the Leave No Trace Center website at www.lnt.org.

Schluchsee (p302). Sailors will also feel at home on the latter as well as on the Starnberger See and the Chiemsee (p150).

Few water-based sports are as accessible and fun for the whole gang as kayaking and most people manage to get paddling quickly and with minimal instruction. The most popular area for this kind of pursuit is the Naturpark Altmühltal (p243), where the mellow Altmühl River meanders past steep cliffs, willow-fringed banks and little beaches. A similarly dreamy landscape awaits in the Fränkische Schweiz (p236). Here, the diminutive Wiesent River carves its course past villages, medieval castles and eroded rock faces. If you're up for a rollicking rafting trip, head to Lenggries (p146) at the foot of the Bavarian Alps for a wild ride on the Isar River, which gushes northward all the way to Munich.

ROCK CLIMBING

Clambering around steep rock faces chiselled and carved by time and the elements is a popular pursuit in southern Germany. Rock hounds – from beginner to expert – test their mettle on the Jurassic limestone cliffs in the Naturpark Altmühltal (p243) and the Fränkische Schweiz (p236), both in Bavaria. Wherever you go, there are local outfitters that can set you up with equipment and advice.

Walking in the Bavarian Alps

Lederhosen, beer halls and King Ludwig's fantastical castles are synonymous with Bavaria, but the best way to immerse yourself in its rich scenery and culture is to get out and stride. While the Bavarian Alps cannot rival those of Switzerland or Austria in height, they are every bit as dramatic; perpendicular turrets of limestone rising abruptly above rolling hills that stretch from Allgäu to the Austrian border. Walking here reaps sensational rewards: from spotting ibex clambering over the crags to waking up in a cosy hut perched on the mountainside.

The Bavarian Alps offer a kaleidoscope of landscapes that shift from the deep gullies of Partnachklamm and Höllental to Berchtesgaden's lonely karst plateau and the wrinkled faces of Zugspitze and Watzmann, Germany's highest peaks. Lakes that glitter sapphire and emerald are strung like necklaces along the heights and ringed by thick forests and Alpine pastures. After a long day's march, the storybook villages down in the valleys welcome weary walkers with shady gardens perfect for guzzling homebrews and enjoying the view.

If there's one thing that motivates hikers more than the marvellous scenery or promise of beer, it's the down-to-earth locals whose passion for *wandern* is contagious. Learning to love your walking boots is as much a rite of passage here as being able to drink from a stein or eat *Weisswurst* without grimacing. The trails are dutifully waymarked, and everywhere you trudge fellow walkers bid you a cheery *Grüss Gott*. This zeal for trekking may come as a surprise in the birthplace of fast BMWs and the speed limit–free autobahn. But even Bavarians are prepared to admit that the wild places are best appreciated on foot – in beautiful slow motion.

HIGHLIGHTS

- Traversing ledges across the vertiginous north face of the **Alpspitze** (p64)
- Pinballing down the wild **Höllentalklamm gully** (p64) past thundering falls and rivers
- Enjoying vistas of the Northern Limestone Alps on the star trek from Germany's highest peak, **Zugspitze** (p64)
- Scaling **Schneibstein** (p68) for knockout views of the Watzmann and Hagengebirge karst plateau
- Feeling the glacial blast of a 200m-high ice cavern at the **Eiskapelle** (p70)

Schneibstein (2276m)

Eiskapelle ★

Höllentalklamm
★ ★ Alpspitze (2628m)

Zugspitze (2962m)

INFORMATION
Maps
The Bavarian Alps are extremely well mapped and paths are usually waymarked. The standard references at a 1:50,000 scale are produced by Landesvermessungsamt and Kompass. The latter includes a nifty little booklet in German with each map that lists contact details for mountains huts and gives some background information. If you prefer larger-scale walking maps, use the clear yet detailed DAV 1:25,000 series. Maps are widely available from bookshops and outdoor-equipment shops locally. See each section for specific map requirements.

Books
The Cicerone (UK) title *Walking in the Bavarian Alps,* by Grant Bourne and Sabine Kröner-Bourne, describes 57 walks from the Allgäu to Berchtesgadener Land. All but one are day walks and many are graded as fairly easy. German publisher Rother prints *Around the Zugspitze,* by Dieter Seibert, in English. It briefly describes some 50 mostly shorter walks around Oberammergau, Garmisch-Partenkirchen, Mittenwald, Ehrwald and Leutasch, including some on the Austrian side of the border.

Websites
The website of the **German National Tourist Office** (www.germany-tourism.de) should be your first port of call, with inspirational information in English on walking in regions such as the Bavarian Alps, Bavarian Forest and Black Forest. Other excellent hiking websites include www.tourentipp.de (in German), with mountain weather forecasts, mapping information and walks searchable by region, and www.wanderbares-deutschland.de (in German), featuring comprehensive information on 92 walking trails throughout Germany.

Deutscher Alpenverein (DAV)
If you're planning multiday treks in the Bavarian Alps, consider becoming a member of the **Deutscher Alpenverein** (DAV; German Alpine Club; www.alpenverein.de, in German) for a 30% to 50% discount on Alpine huts and other benefits, including insurance. Annual membership fees depend on the region and range from €44 to €88. The Deutscher Alpenverein owns 2000 huts in the Alps and many provide food and accommodation. Beds cost €12 to €22 in *Zimmerlager* (rooms) and €9 to €16 in *Matrazenlager* (dorms).

The DAV website is a mine of information on walking and mountaineering. Brochures, membership forms, web forecasts and hut details are available online.

WHEN TO WALK
The summer months (June to September) are the best for walking in the Alps, when snow retreats to the highest peaks, and wildflowers such as purple gentian, yellow arnica and dainty Alpine rose carpet the slopes. Rush hour is from July to August when you'll need to book hut accommodation well in

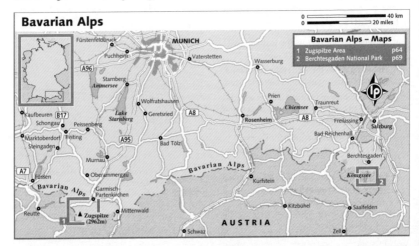

RESPONSIBLE WALKING

Follow these tips to tread lightly and minimise your impact on the fragile Alpine environment.

Trail Etiquette

- On narrow paths, ascending walkers have right of way over those descending.
- Always leave farm gates as you find them.
- Moving too close unnerves wild animals, distracting them from their vital summer activity of fattening up for the long winter.

Rubbish

- Carry out all rubbish (including cigarette butts, tin foil, plastic wrappers and sanitary pads).
- Burying rubbish disturbs soil and ground cover and encourages erosion. It may be dug up by animals (potentially harming them).
- Take reusable containers or stuff sacks. Avoid plastic bags and bottles.

Human Waste Disposal

- Make an effort to use toilets in huts and refuges where provided.
- Where there is no toilet, bury your waste. Dig a small hole 15cm deep and at least 100m from any watercourse. Cover the waste with soil and a rock. Use toilet paper sparingly and bury that, too. In snow, dig down beneath the soil.

Erosion

- Stick to existing tracks and avoid short cuts that bypass a switchback. If you blaze a new trail straight down a slope, it will turn into a watercourse with the next heavy rainfall.
- Avoid removing the plant life that keeps topsoils in place.

---

advance. Autumn has its own charm, with fewer crowds and a riot of colour in deciduous forests. Walking opportunities are more limited during the rest of the year, as snow makes it impossible to undertake high-altitude walks. Many of the big resorts, however, are crisscrossed with winter walking trails, and crunching through snow with a crisp blue sky overhead can be quite magical.

WHAT TO TAKE

Bavaria's superb network of Alpine huts removes the need to lug a heavy pack and gives walkers complete freedom and flexibility. It's worth taking the essentials, though, which include lightweight layers, waterproofs and a sturdy pair of boots. Pack high-energy foods and at least 1L of water per person to keep you going between pit stops. Sunblock, shades and a hat to protect against strong Alpine rays are also recommended. On more difficult treks at higher elevations, consider bringing walking sticks, a compass and a first-aid kit for emergencies.

SAFETY & EMERGENCIES

Most walker deaths are directly attributable to fatigue, heat exhaustion and inadequate clothing. A fall resulting from sliding on grass, scree or iced-over paths is a common hazard. In high Alpine routes avalanches and rockfall can be a problem. Study the forecast before you go and remember that weather patterns change dramatically in the mountains.

Where possible don't walk in the mountains alone. Two is the minimum number for safe mountain walking. Inform a responsible person of your plans, and let them know when you return. Under no circumstances should you leave marked trails in foggy conditions.

The standard Alpine distress signal is six whistles, six calls, six smoke puffs – that is, six of whatever sign you can make – followed by a pause equalling the length of time taken by the calls before repeating the signal again. Mountain rescue (☎ 140) in the Alps is efficient but extremely expensive, so make sure you have insurance that includes mountain rescue costs, such as helicopter evacuation.

ZUGSPITZE AREA

The Zugspitze (2962m) is the highest summit in Germany, though half the mountain is shared with Austria. It is the best-known peak of the Wettersteingebirge, a range in the Northern Limestone Alps. The pale limestone pinnacles, walls and ridges of this mountain range rise abruptly from meadows and wide valleys, home to picture-book villages and towns, including the main year-round resort, Garmisch-Partenkirchen.

The very detailed Bayerisches Landesvermessungsamt 1:50,000 topographic map *Werdenfelser Land* covers all walks described for the Zugspitze area. Available from the tourist office, a much simpler walking trail map (1:25,000) is *Garmisch-Partenkirchen Grainau-Farchant,* which also covers both walks.

ALPSPITZE NORDWAND & HÖLLENTALKLAMM
Duration 4¾ to 6¼ hours
Distance 13km
Difficulty moderate to demanding
Nearest Town Garmisch-Partenkirchen (p136)

Summary Climb past a mountain tarn to traverse the north face of the Alpspitze pyramid, then descend via a spectacular valley and gorge.

The pyramid-shaped Alpspitze (2628m) is arguably the most distinctive peak in the Wettersteingebirge, rising sharply above Garmisch-Partenkirchen. The famous Höllentalklamm (Hell Valley Gorge), a wild and steep gorge, was made accessible by a series of galleries and tunnels hewn from the walls in 1905. The trek, a semicircle involving a 650m ascent and 1400m descent, links these two features in a varied and spectacular outing.

There is an extensive network of trails in the basin above Kreuzeck. The route described aims to maximise scenic variety while avoiding ski-field development as much as possible. However, if you have less time, the weather is inhospitable or you wish to avoid the Alpspitze's north face, other routes are possible, as a glance at the map will reveal. The hike should be undertaken in clear, dry weather; the former to maximise the views, the latter because damp limestone on the *Klettersteig* can be quite slippery.

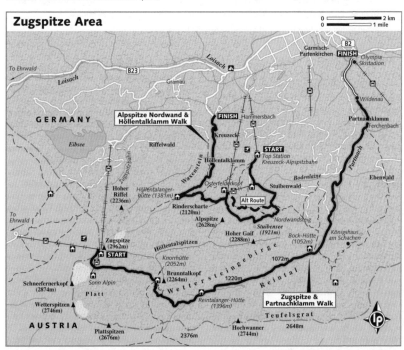

The route across the Alpspitze Nordwand (north face) involves a *Klettersteig* section, a descending traverse of a series of ledges secured by cable handrails and iron foot pegs where necessary. While the descent is technically straightforward, you'll need to be sure-footed and have a good head for heights as it is extremely steep. It is possible to bypass this section by following other trails (as outlined in the walk description), but this would also avoid the Stuibensee basin and views from the east shoulder of Alpspitze, both highlights of the walk.

Getting to/from the Walk

Take local bus 2 (Kreuzeck–Alpspitzbahn) from Garmisch-Partenkirchen to the Kreuzeckbahn gondola lift station (€2, 10 minutes, hourly). Alternatively, the Bayerische Zugspitzbahn train from Garmisch will also stop at the Kreuzeckbahn gondola lift station (€1.40, 10 minutes, hourly). Take a gondola to the upper station (€13.50) at 1651m. The lift operates from 8.30am.

At the end of the walk, the Grainau–Eibsee bus passes through the tiny settlement of Hammersbach en route to Garmisch-Partenkirchen (€3.20, 30 minutes, usually hourly but times may vary). The Zugspitzbahn train also passes through Hammersbach. If you arrive by car, it is a 20- to 30-minute walk back to the Kreuzeckbahn car park from Hammersbach

The Walk

Follow the wide gravel path south from the upper station towards the bare grey pyramid of the **Alpspitze**. This precipitous wall is the north face, which you will traverse later. After about five minutes, the path forks just below a small hut; bear left (southeast). About 100m later sidle left again onto a foot trail signed Stuiben (among other things), which descends below the road and contours southeast. After rounding a spur and entering forest, the trail heads south into the next valley and reaches a junction with a grey limestone cliff rearing above. Continue straight ahead here (signed to Stuiben, Alpspitze) and within five minutes reach a second junction (1520m), where you should turn right uphill.

To avoid the vertiginous *Klettersteig* traverse of the north face, turn right uphill at the first junction described, below the grey cliff. This leads up into the basin below the

Alpspitze's north face, where a trail climbs to Rinderscharte via the Osterfelderbahn top station.

The route to the Alpspitze north face ascends via **Stuibensee**, and most of the day's ascent is undertaken on this section. From the second junction described previously, head uphill (south) through forest. The trail soon winds up through grass and shrubs to a basin surrounded by grey crags. Within it sits the little green Stuibensee, at 1921m (up to one hour from the second trail junction). You are likely to sight chamois grazing the slopes around here. The trail climbs north above the lake, rising across grey scree and then through small bluffs before heading west across grassy slopes up to the crest of the northeast spur of the Alpspitze (2120m; 20 minutes from Stuibensee). Enjoy the fantastic view across the north face and up to the summit.

Head southwest towards the Alpspitze, rising soon to traverse rock and scree. There is a trail junction immediately below the bluffs of the Alpspitze's east ridge. The route climbing scree to the left goes to the summit and is quite challenging; your route to the **Nordwandsteig** (north-face path) continues straight ahead (west). Walk up a short, steep gully then around a rocky spur and out onto the north face. The onward route is obvious, descending across the north face. While the route requires a degree of surefootedness, it is not difficult. The exposed trail follows ledges and benches with a couple of short scramble sections, protected where necessary with a steel cable handrail. The Nordwandsteig culminates in a tunnel section and, after 30 minutes, the really exciting bit is over.

Just beyond the tunnel, pass a junction with the Alpspitze-Ferrata route (much more challenging) and continue northwest, rising slightly to cross a grassy shoulder. Head towards the Osterfelderkopf cable-car station but, after 10 minutes and before you reach it, branch left uphill (signed Höllental etc). A few minutes of climbing leads to **Rinderscharte** (2120m), a notch in the ridge. The quick scramble up the knob to the right (north) is worthwhile for a spectacular view into the upper Höllental and up to the Zugspitze.

The onward route heads west into the cleft below. Descend wooden steps over scree before a near-endless series of switchbacks lead steeply into the **Höllental**, with good views across to the Waxenstein wall and up-valley to the Zugspitze all the way. The trail eventually enters forest and, soon after, reaches a junction; bear left (signed to Höllentalangerhütte) here. Descend a little further, then contour up-valley to the popular 1381m-high **Höllentalangerhütte** (☎ 088-218 811; ☉ late May–mid-Oct) probably surrounded by other walkers enjoying liquid refreshments and taking in the view. The descent to the hut will take one to 1½ hours.

The U-shaped valley above the hut is clearly of glacial origin and a tiny remnant is visible below the Zugspitze: the **Höllentalferner** snowfield. Below the hut the narrow valley culminates in the deep and dramatic Höllentalklamm, which was cut by meltwaters from the Ice Age glacier.

Follow a gravel path downstream past the hut, initially on the true right (east) bank. The stream is crossed several times as high grey walls close in on either side. After descending several switchbacks, the trail enters the **Höllentalklamm**. The breathtakingly beautiful gorge is 1km long; along it the river drops some 200m in a series of falls and canyons. The path traverses a series of short, damp tunnels and galleries hacked from the shadowed rock walls, with the river cascading right beside you. The €2.50 fee is payable at the kiosk as you exit the gorge (1045m), up to one hour from the hut. From the kiosk, continue through forest for 35 to 45 minutes to Hammersbach (760m).

ZUGSPITZE & PARTNACHKLAMM

Duration 5½ to 7 hours
Distance 19km
Difficulty moderate
Nearest Town Garmisch-Partenkirchen (p136)
Summary Descend from the summit of Germany's highest peak to cross a barren plateau, enter a lush mountain valley and exit through a stunning limestone gorge.

This hike descends 2200m through varied terrain, including a barren karst plateau, the steep-walled Reintal valley, moss-floored forest and the slotlike gorge of Partnachklamm. Ground access routes to the Zugspitze summit from the Garmisch-Partenkirchen side are for mountaineers only; however a cable car provides easy access for walkers and maximises the opportunity to enjoy the long descent. Though walking downhill may sound like a breeze, the dramatic change in elevation means the trek is hardly a walk in the park

and you'll certainly feel your leg muscles the next day.

The initial descent from the Zugspitze summit is a straightforward *Klettersteig* (climbing path protected by fixed ropes and ladders) followed by the descent of a steep scree slope. If you don't fancy this, after enjoying the summit views take the Gletscherbahn cable car down to Sonn Alpin (four minutes) and start the walk there. You could undertake the walk in the opposite direction to that described, but the very long ascent would require a night at either Reintalanger-Hütte or Knorrhütte. The walk traverses a stark limestone plateau and there is no surface water until the Reintal valley floor, though drinks can be purchased at Knorrhütte.

Getting to/from the Walk

Catch the Grainau–Eibsee bus from Garmisch-Partenkirchen to Eibsee (€3.80, 40 minutes), then take the Eibsee–Seilbahn cable car (€26.50), which whisks you up almost 2000m in 10 minutes. The last section is only metres from the summit cliffs. The first cable car departs at 8am. A cheaper, but rather longer, option for starting the walk is to take the funicular railway to Sonn Alpin from Eibsee (40 minutes) or all the way from Garmisch-Partenkirchen (1¼ hours), though you then miss the Zugspitze summit views. The train spirals up a tunnel within the Zugspitze. Local bus 1 will get you from the Olympia Skistadion back into town at the end of the walk (€1, every 45 minutes to one hour).

The Walk

Straddling the Austrian–German border, **Zugspitze** (2962m) affords sweeping views across undulating wooded slopes and the Northern Limestone Alps. The peak has been developed and features a complex that includes the cable-car station, a panoramic restaurant, souvenir shops and a weather station to gather meteorological data for the Global Atmosphere Watch. The first task is to find your way out of this complex onto the viewing terrace.

For peak baggers, the lofty Zugspitze summit, marked with a large yellow cross, can be gained via a metal ladder and a steep scramble protected with a cable handrail. While the trail is well trodden, it is also exposed and the rock is well polished, so care is required. At the top you are rewarded with an incredible vista of the sheer Höllental valley and the bright **Eibsee** lake, twinkling like a sapphire surrounded by dark forest far below.

After admiring the view, walk to the southwest side of the lookout terrace (near the telecommunication towers), descend the metal staircase to the ridge crest below and follow it southwest. The ridge is exposed in places and sometimes loose underfoot, but there are sections of cable handrail to safeguard the route where necessary. After passing a ridge-crest seat, the route drops left (south) off the crest and zigzags down steeply, then descends a very steep and loose scree slope towards Sonn Alpin, the Gletscherbahn cable-car station at 2600m (20 to 30 minutes from Zugspitze summit). The small **Schneeferner** snowfield nearby is virtually the sole remaining remnant of the glacier that once scoured the Platt basin and Reintal; it is shrinking dramatically and reports suggest it could disappear entirely by 2030.

From near Sonn Alpin, walk east along the well-trodden trail across stony hummocks below the cliffs of the Zugspitze; the route is marked by metal snow poles that make it easy to follow even when weather conditions are poor. There are great views across the barren Platt basin to the limestone peaks that enclose it and into Austria beyond. Within 20 minutes start descending steadily towards the deep cleft of the Reintal. Situated at 2052m, the **Knorrhütte** (☎ 088-212 905; ☷ late May-Oct) below eventually slides into view. The trail zigzags down below Brunntalkopf to this hut (one to 1½ hours from Sonn Alpin), where refreshments are available.

Your trail continues south from the hut (another branches right, southwest) and plunges into the Reintal, where there are superb views of **Königshaus am Schachen**, the whimsical hunting lodge of King Ludwig II. Despite the drop, the trail is well graded, though occasionally loose underfoot, and it switchbacks down into a tributary valley. Follow the trail southeast to the valley floor. Skirting debris from an old rockfall, the trail meanders across the grassy valley floor to enter pine forest, then crosses to the left (north) bank of the milky blue Partnach stream to **Reintalanger-Hütte** (☎ 088-212 903; ☷ late May-Oct) at 1369m. Colourful Tibetan prayer flags are strung across the water in front of the hut; it's run by climbing

guru Charly Wehrle, who has climbed the eight-thousanders of Nepal and is something of a local celebrity. Take a break from your hike to relax in the beer garden.

The route down the beautiful **Reintal** follows an easy gravel path on the north side of the rushing stream. The valley is a complete contrast to the barren Platt basin; the walk traverses Arolla pine forest and grassy openings, with the serrated limestone cliffs of the Hochwanner (the crest of which is the Austria border) and Teufelsgrat (Devil's Ridge) towering above. About 40 minutes from the hut, the valley becomes strangely silent, the stream having disappeared beneath debris from a massive ancient rockfall. The karst cliffs lining the south side of the valley are pockmarked with holes. Many of them are round caves long abandoned by the subterranean streams that once flowed through here before eons of glacier and river erosion lowered the valley floor.

Bock-Hütte (1052m) offers yet another refreshment stop about 1¼ to 1½ hours down the valley. Beyond here the valley rapidly opens out and there are several trail junctions; follow signs to Partnachklamm, usually the main path. The path crosses a wooden bridge from Bock-Hütte, crossing back 10 minutes later. Soon after, the river enters a narrow gorge and the path rises above it, then becomes a narrow gravel road. Continue along the road as it winds north through forest. Just after the road crosses a small stream, bear right downhill at a junction. Also bear right at two subsequent road junctions, despite confusing signs.

After one to 1¼ hours of walking, the road crosses the main river. At a right-hand bend 150m later (just above the confluence of the Partnach and Ferchenbach streams), several trails diverge from the road. Take the trail that heads north, straight ahead across the Ferchenbach stream on a small footbridge. Soon after the footbridge, bear right and follow a wide path along the true right (east) of the frothing Partnach River. The path almost immediately enters a series of tunnels and galleries, just above river level, through the **Partnachklamm**. This stunning 750m-long, 80m-deep limestone slot canyon is one of the day's highlights. The path ducks behind waterfalls and torrents that thunder into deep blue pools. There is a €2 toll for this constructed trail that will be collected at the kiosk as you exit the gorge (note that the gorge gates close at 6pm in summer and 5pm in winter).

Beyond the gorge kiosk, walk five minutes along the footpath to Wildenau, a collection of restaurants and souvenir shops, and the start of the paved road to Partenkirchen. Walk north along the road for 15 to 20 minutes to the Olympia Skistadion (740m).

BERCHTESGADEN NATIONAL PARK

Enclosed by the Austrian–German border on three sides, Berchtesgadener Land is a self-contained universe of wooded hilltops and valleys framed by formidable mountains. Germany's second-highest mountain and the highest peak in the Watzmann Range is Mittelspitze (2713m), which towers above crystalline lakes, rushing streams and slender church steeples. While Watzmann is often referred to in the singular, it is a mountain range that includes the 2307m-high Watzmannfrau (Watzmann's Wife) and the seven not-so-little Watzmannkinder (Watzmann's Children).

About half of the terrain is protected as the 210-sq-km Berchtesgaden National Park (see boxed text, below), the centrepiece of which is the fjordlike Königssee, 8km long and 190m deep. With 230km of walking paths and climbing trails and a number of mountain huts, the national park offers fabulous walking and other outdoor opportunities.

Camping is not permitted within Berchtesgaden National Park. The quite detailed Bayerisches Landesvermessungsamt 1:50,000 topographic map *Berchtesgadener Alpen* covers

both walks described for Berchtesgaden National Park. For more detail, pick up the Deutsche Alpenverein 1:25,000 map *UK 25-1 Nationalpark Berchtesgaden*.

SCHNEIBSTEIN & HAGENGEBIRGE

Duration 6 to 7 hours
Distance 16km
Difficulty moderate
Nearest Town Berchtesgaden (p157)
Summary Traverse a mountain ridge with sublime Alpine scenery and prime views of Königssee and the Watzmann, descending through forest and alm pastures.

The grassy Schneibstein (2276m) summit sits astride the Austrian–German border and offers far-reaching vistas over the steep valleys and jagged limestone peaks of Berchtesgaden National Park and east into Austria. The rolling Hagengebirge, to the south, is a starkly beautiful limestone plateau that also straddles the border. Catching the Jennerbahn gondola lift certainly eases the day's efforts but it is still a 600m uphill trudge to the summit. Thereafter it is essentially downhill all the way, though the 1700m of steady descent should not be underestimated.

The exhilarating ridge traverse beyond Schneibstein is not recommended in poor visibility, when conditions can become dangerous and there would be no views anyway. There is no surface water on the ridge section of this walk until you reach Seeleinsee, so be sure to carry enough water to keep you going for the day.

Getting to/from the Walk

Königssee is situated 5km from Berchtesgaden and RVO bus 841 departs from outside the

---

EXPLORING BERCHTESGADEN NATIONAL PARK

The campaign for a national park in Berchtesgadener Land was generated by opposition to a cable car up the Watzmann in the early 1970s. This proposal was defeated and the Berchtesgaden National Park was eventually declared in 1978. Featuring high mountain landscapes, steep rock faces and extensive forests, the park is part of a Unesco Biosphere Reserve. In addition to the Königssee, the park boasts the highest rock face in the Eastern Alps (the east face of the Watzmann), the longest and deepest caves in Germany and the northernmost glacier in the Alps.

The national park is divided into an activity zone and a remote, largely natural core zone left for nature to take its own course. The activity zone includes provision for summer cattle grazing, a fishery, limited forestry and boat traffic on the Königssee lake. There are 25 summer pastures within the park, most east of the Königssee. These remain in state ownership, but grazing rights go back centuries. These days it is usually just young cows that are grazed at the *alm* (Alpine pasture) and it is rare for butter and cheese to still be made there.

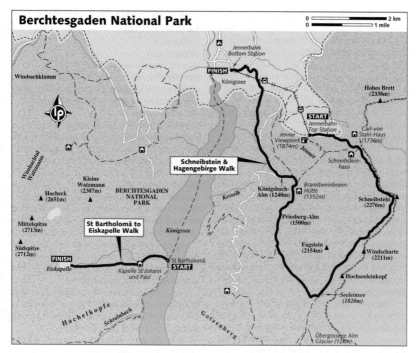

The Walk

Hauptbahnhof roughly hourly (€2.30, 13 minutes). The Jennerbahn gondola lift lower station is a couple of minutes' walk east from the Königssee bus stop. Take a gondola to the top station (1802m) to start the walk (€14.90, 25 minutes). The lift starts running from 9am.

The Walk

From the Jenner top station, the five-minute ascent to the **Jenner viewpoint** (1874m) is worthwhile for the incredible 360-degree views; the Königssee glitters emerald-green at the foot of the mighty Watzmann (2713m) to the west, while the craggy summit of Hoher Göll (2522m) rises to the east. Shimmering to the south is the Übergossene Alm glacier that caps the Hochkönig massif. The famous German explorer Alexander von Humboldt described this as one of the most beautiful places in the world and it's certainly difficult to drag yourself away from the panorama at the rocky peak.

Leading southeast, the trail takes the wide gravel path downhill, signed to Schneibstein and Schneibsteinhaus. Pass several junctions, continuing to follow the

signs for Schneibsteinhaus until, after 20 to 30 minutes, you reach a fork signed 'Carl-von-Stahl-Haus 10 minutes'. Bear left here, contouring above Schneibsteinhaus to reach **Carl-von-Stahl-Haus** (☎ 08652-2752; ☺ year-round) at 1736m; this wooden hut is scenically situated in a saddle on the main ridge crest and the Austrian border.

Veering right (southeast) from the hut, the steepish climb up to **Schneibstein** (2276m) soon begins. It's 1¼ to 1¾ hours up a trail waymarked with paint to the broad grassy summit, marked by a cross. Surefootedness is needed on this section, particularly as the limestone underfoot can be very slippery when wet. The summit is a fine balcony over the Northern Limestone Alps and commands rewarding views of the nearby wall of Hohes Brett (2338m), the soaring Watzmann massif to the west, and east into Austria. To the south lies the vast and rolling Hagengebirge karst plateau, its barren-looking surface dotted with copses of dwarf pines and shrubs.

Head south then southwest from the summit, following the undulating ridge crest to **Windscharte** saddle at 2100m (35 to 45 minutes from Schneibstein). This is a good place to spot ibex. Ignore the turn-off left at this saddle (which descends to Hinterschlum-Alm in Austria) and continue southwest, sidling across the northeast slope of Windschartenkopf (2211m). The route then steadily descends a verdant valley on the west side of the main ridge to **Seeleinsee** at 1820m (1¼ hours), an aquamarine tarn nestled beneath rugged grey cliffs and scree.

Leaving the Seeleinsee basin you shortly come to another junction. Turn right (west) here and descend a valley trending northwest. Initially stony, the trail soon enters shady forest beneath cliffs. Contour northwards through grassy openings, dotted with pink Alpine roses in summer, which afford fine views of the Watzmann. After about an hour, the melodic clanging of cow bells welcomes you to **Priesberg-Alm** (1500m), the first of several pastures. Beautifully set above the alm, the hut here is a great spot to snack on home-made cheese and ham with a glass of creamy buttermilk.

The trail now gets wider to form a narrow gravel road and this road is followed for about 15 to 20 minutes down and across some moorland to the **Branntweinbrenn-Hütte** (1352m), a small log hut where gentian schnapps is still distilled according to 400-year-old methods. During the week it's possible to taste the fiery liqueur, which will surely put a spring in your step for the final descent. Soon after the hut, swing left at the fork and continue downhill more steeply. At another junction appearing a few minutes later, ignore the path leading north across a wooden bridge and again bear left downhill. Follow the narrow gravel road westwards to **Königsbach-Alm** (1240m), then northwest, taking the downhill option at any junctions. The road descends into pleasant forest above the gurgling Königsbach stream.

About 15 minutes' walk further past Königsbach-Alm, just before the road rises slightly, a wide footpath descends left downhill below the road. Take this and follow it down and around north through forest, with snapshot views of Königssee through the trees. After passing beneath the Jennerbahn gondola lift, descend past a few houses and out onto a sealed road just above the Jennerbahn bottom station and car park (630m; one to 1¼ hours from Königsbach-Alm to the car park).

ST BARTHOLOMÄ TO EISKAPELLE

Duration 2 to 2½ hours
Distance 6km
Difficulty easy
Nearest Town Berchtesgaden (p157)
Summary Cruise the jade waters of fjordlike Königssee and ascend gently through forest to the Eiskapelle, all the while overlooked by the towering east face of the Watzmann

This short amble takes in the gorgeous scenery of the Berchtesgaden National Park with minimal effort and is suitable for young children. The vista is instantly spectacular on the boat ride across Königssee (sit on the right for the best views), an Alpine lake that sparkles an exquisite shade of green and is ringed by sheer cliffs thrusting skywards. Leaving behind the bulbous domes of St Bartholomä pilgrimage church, the walk begins with a gradual ascent along a well-graded forest trail, crosses a babbling stream and emerges at the Eiskapelle (Ice Chapel), an ice cavern that changes size and shape according to season.

The walk is accessible from May to October and is popular both with locals and tourists, so it's worth getting here early to beat the crowds and appreciate the lake at its finest; first thing in the morning it's like gliding across a sheet of bottle-green glass. Spring and early summer are ideal for admiring the sculpted Eiskapelle, while in autumn the forest creates a rich tapestry of colour set against the steely backdrop of the Watzmann. On the approach to the Eiskapelle, signs warn walkers not to step onto the ice or enter the cavern because of the danger should it collapse.

Getting to/from the Walk

Königssee is situated 5km from Berchtesgaden and RVO bus 841 departs from outside the Hauptbahnhof roughly hourly (€2.30, 13 minutes). Boats to St Bartholomä operate from 8.30am to 6pm in summer; return tickets cost €11.50 for adults and €5.80 for children. Hours vary at other times of the year, see www.seen schifffahrt.de for timetable details.

The Walk

At the start of your walk, you'll be drawn to the iconic pilgrimage chapel of **St Bartholomä**, set on a promontory on the western shore of Königssee. With its trio of red shingled cupolas, the 12th-century chapel is extremely photogenic. Just behind is a log chalet that shelters a national park visitor centre, where you can pick up information on the region and learn about its unique flora and fauna. Continue on the path that leads past the chapel, and note the former hunting lodge that is now a Bavarian restaurant and the cluster of farmhouses to the left. A weather-worn sign points the way to the Eiskapelle (one hour).

Moving west and away from the lake, the path weaves gently through maple and beech woodlands, where ferns, clover and purple cornflowers carpet the forest floor. Through the trees, you are rewarded with fleeting glimpses of the chiselled east face of the Watzmann.

About 15 minutes into the walk, the trail reaches a glade where pebbly beaches flank a glacially cold **stream** fed by the melting ice; pause to dangle your toes in the tingling water. The stream is traversed by a wooden bridge and on the opposite side lies the chalk-white **Kapelle St Johann und Paul** chapel, its shingled roof and tiny belltower peeping above the greenery. Veering right from the stream, a narrow path commences a gradual but gentle climb through lichen-clad forest and there are plenty of benches where the weary can rest and enjoy the calm.

At the fork in the path, stick to the right and continue along the track past boulders sprouting ferns and trees. There soon comes a wooden **memorial** commemorating those who have lost their lives on Watzmann East Face. Around 30 minutes from the stream, you'll cross another bridge over a dried-up riverbed; to the left (south) are incredibly sheer and crumbling cliffs, while to the right (north) the Watzmann looms large. The trail now makes its final ascent, winding steadily up through the forest until it reaches the **Eisgraben** river valley.

The valley is wildly beautiful and feels light years away from the holiday crowds at St Bartholomä. A flat path crosses piles of scree and meanders alongside a series of streams that flow swiftly over the rocks. The banks here are perfect for a picnic, commanding wonderful vistas of stone pinnacles, waterfalls streaking jagged limestone cliffs and up ahead the magnificent **Eiskapelle**. As snow gathers in the corner of the rocks, a dome emerges that reaches heights of over 200m. In summer, as the ice melts, the water digs tunnels and creates a huge opening in the solid ice. On the approach to the edge of the ice cavern, the

---

FOOTLOOSE IN THE FOREST

The spiky peaks of the Alps never fail to mesmerise hikers, but the Black and Bavarian forests are equally enchanting, with trails crisscrossing silent woodlands and undulating hills. The Black Forest alone offers 23,000km of footpaths managed by the Schwarzwaldverein (www.schwarzwaldverein .de). Each season reveals its own beauty here: from the spongy moss blanketing the spruce forests in summer to the snow flurries creating a monochrome backdrop in winter. Whether you're planning a gentle amble or a multiday trek, here are five of the best walks.

Almühltal Panoramaweg (medium-difficult; p246) Starring among Bavaria's finest multiday treks, this trail stretches 200km from Gunzenhausen to Kelheim. Shadowing the Altmühl river, the path slices through beech forest and deep gorges. Particularly striking are the Zwölf Apostel (Twelve Apostles), granite rock formations rising dramatically above Solnhofen. For further details, see www.naturpark-almuehltal.de.

Baden-Baden Panoramaweg (medium; p305) Expect the kind of postcard-worthy scenery able to convince the spa-going masses to exchange fluffy bathrobes for muddy walking boots on this 40km hike. The circular trail rambles through the surrounding woody wonderland, taking in waterfalls, orchards and panoramic views of Baden-Baden.

Feldberg-Steig (easy-medium; p302) This 12km walk traverses a nature reserve that's home to chamois and wildflowers. The track orbits Feldberg (1493m), the Black Forest's highest peak, affording tremendous views of Zugspitze and Mont Blanc.

Westweg (medium-difficult) Up for an adventure? This famous long-distance trail, marked with a red diamond, stretches 280km from Pforzheim in the Northern Black Forest to Basel, Switzerland. Highlights feature the steep Murgtal valley, the bottle-green waters of Titisee and hilltop Martinskapelle. Download maps and brochures at www.westweg.de.

Zwiesel to Kleiner Arbersee (easy; p212) This 15km trudge reveals one of the Bavarian Forest's three forest-fringed lakes sculpted during the last Ice Age. Ascending through woods, the track emerges at Kleiner Arbersee (keep an eye out for resident otters and beavers). The lake itself is well known for its remarkable *Schwimmende Insel* (Floating Islands).

THE WATZMANN LEGEND

The sheer rock faces of the Watzmann massif are steeped in legend. A myth recounts how a barbaric king named Watzmann once ruled Berchtesgadener Land together with his wife and seven children. He loved nothing more than to terrorise his subjects and torture their animals. Bloodthirsty and cruel, the family would embark on wild hunts high in the hills, unleashing their savage hounds upon innocent victims.

One day, they came across a humble farm where an old lady sat with her grandchild. The king trampled them down with his horses, then set his hunting dogs on the grief-stricken farmer and his wife. As the blood flowed freely, the dying grandmother put a curse upon the king and his family, asking God to punish them for having stony hearts by turning them to stone. Immediately the heavens opened, fire raged and the earth swallowed up Watzmann, his wife and their seven children; they're now immortalised in the rocks that reign above Königssee.

temperature suddenly plummets and a blast of frosty air hits you; listen carefully and you'll hear the ice squeak and crack.

Retrace your steps back along the valley and descend through the forest to **Königssee** where, if the sun's out, you might want to finish up with a refreshing dip in the lake, or a cool beer on the restaurant terrace to drink in some more of that striking scenery before boarding the boat back.

Munich

Pulsing with prosperity and Bavarian *Gemütlichkeit* (cosiness), Munich loves to revel in its own contradictions. This sophisticated modern metropolis draws as much inspiration from *nouvelle cuisine* and Hugo Boss as sausages and thick leather shorts. Munich may be a high-minded fellow but pop a keg and he'll be out there tearing up the dance floor.

Polls of wistful Germans confirm Munich is the most popular place to live – and in a blink you'll see why. Balmy summer evenings at one of its street-side cafés make the city feel like a Florence or a Milan. Thrilling Alpine landscapes, crystal-clear lakes and fairy-tale castles lie at its doorstep. It is a haven for all sorts of culture. And at Oktoberfest the entire planet converges to toast the town.

Parts of Germany may have fallen on hard times but Munich shakes it off like magic. A forest of construction cranes dots the landscape, planting hi-tech office towers and sharp, ecofriendly residences where highways once stood.

Bavaria never grew much heavy industry, so Munich's centre retains a small-town feel. Global players such as Siemens and BMW hug the outskirts and their influence lends the city a cosmopolitan flair and a good chunk of its wealth. In the beer gardens you may hear more English than German, and almost as much Italian or Japanese.

Forget the Teutonic clichés about grim workaholics – Münchners have plenty to smile about and any time of year the mood is infectious, be it during the tourist-packed summer or the cold stillness of a February afternoon.

HIGHLIGHTS

- Hoisting a mug of Helles at an authentic beer hall, such as the **Augustiner Bräustuben** (p119)
- Watching the daredevil surfers negotiate the dangerous wave in the **English Garden** (p105)
- Getting unusual perspectives – and an incredible adrenaline rush – while clambering around the roof of the Olympic Stadium, **Olympiapark** (p96)
- Feeling your spirits soar among the fantastic art of the **Alte Pinakothek** (p91)
- Hitting the bars and clubs of the **Gärtnerplatzviertel** (p120) for a night of fun

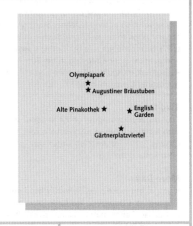

Olympiapark
★
★ Augustiner Bräustuben

Alte Pinakothek ★   ★ English
                              Garden

★
Gärtnerplatzviertel

- TELEPHONE CODE: 089   - POPULATION: 1.26 MILLION   - AREA: 310 SQ KM

MUNICH

HISTORY

It was the Benedictine monks, drawn by fertile farmland and the closeness to Catholic Italy, who first settled present-day Munich. They also gave the city its name, for München is medieval German for monk.

In 1240 the city passed to the Wittelsbach dynasty who would run Munich (as well as Bavaria) until the 20th century. Munich prospered as a centre for the salt trade but was hit hard by the outbreak of plague in 1349. When the epidemic finally subsided 150 years later, the *Schäffler* (coopers) began a ritualistic dance to remind burghers of their good fortune. The *Schäfflertanz* is reenacted daily by the little figures on the city's glockenspiel (carillon) on Marienplatz.

By the early 19th century, furious monument building gave Munich its spectacular architecture and wide Italianate avenues. Culture and the arts flourished, but when Ludwig II ascended the throne his grandiose projects, his numerous lavish palaces for example, bankrupted the royal house and threatened the government. Ironically, today they are the biggest money-spinners of Bavaria's tourism industry.

Munich has seen many turbulent times but last century was particularly rough. WWI practically starved the city; the Nazis first rose to prominence here and the next world war nearly wiped the city off the map. The 1972 Olympic Games ended in tragedy when 17 people were killed in a terrorist hostage-taking incident. In 2006 the city won a brighter place in sporting history when it hosted the opening game of soccer's World Cup.

Today Munich's claim to being 'secret capital' of Germany is alive and well. The city is recognised for its high living standards, the most millionaires per capita after Hamburg and for an appreciation of the good life.

ORIENTATION

The heart of Munich beats in the Altstadt, the historic centre, where you'll find such blockbuster sights as Marienplatz, Viktualienmarkt, the Residenz and the Hofbräuhaus. North of here are the student and museum quarter of Maxvorstadt and bustling Schwabing with its see-and-be-seen Leopoldstrasse boulevard and the vast English Garden. Keep going north and you'll eventually arrive at the Olympiapark, while further west, Schloss Nymphenburg lords it over Neuhausen, an unprepossessing residential quarter with great pub life. To the south, Neuhausen segues smoothly into multicultural Westend,

---

MUNICH IN...

One Day

Spend your first day exploring Munich's historic Altstadt. Get your bearings from the St Peterskirche tower (p77), peruse the colourful bounty at the Viktualienmarkt (p77), then keep a tab on the city's evolution at the Münchner Stadtmuseum (p87), whose Third Reich exhibit makes a poignant transition to the nearby Jüdisches Museum (p87). Duck into the lavishly baroque Asamkirche (p87), then compare it to the Gothic starkness of the landmark Frauenkirche (p90). Time for lunch and perhaps some shopping in the Fünf Höfe arcade (p90). In the afternoon, pick your favourite Pinakothek museum (p91), then cap the day with a classic Bavarian meal, for instance in the Augustiner Bräustuben (p119).

Two Days

Tour the royal splendour of the Residenz (p88), then relax in the English Garden (p96). Follow up with a coffee break in a Schwabing café, then treat your ears to a concert at the Kulturzentrum Gasteig (p103) or Jazzclub Unterfahrt (p122) and finish the night with a bar hop around the Gärtnerplatzviertel (p120).

More Days

If you've got more time, definitely head out to Schloss Nymphenburg (p99), visit the Deutsches Museum (p101), browse the funky boutiques in the Gärtnerplatzviertel and confront the ghosts of Dachau Concentration Camp (p131). If you need a break from urbanity, head to the Fünf-Seen-Land (p127).

whose still affordable rents are drawing a growing contingent of artists and scenesters. It's also not far from the Oktoberfest grounds on Theresienwiese. East of the Wiesn, Ludwigvorstadt has a split personality with lovely, villa-studded residential streets around Beethovenplatz and a slightly seedy vibe just south of the Hauptbahnhof. Past the Sendlinger Tor, the Glockenbachviertel is Munich's lesbigay HQ and, along with the adjacent Gärtnerplatzviertel, the current hipster zone with alt-flavoured bars, interesting restaurants and the best clubs in town. East of here, on the right (south) Isar bank, Haidhausen is a district in transition that mixes high-brow culture with a down-and-dirty party scene and progressive restaurants. Across the river, peaceful Lehel brims with stylish Art Deco apartment houses and key museums along Prinzregentenstrasse.

Maps

Falk's foldout concertina maps of Munich are the handiest to use. Allgemeiner Deutscher Automobil Club's (ADAC) large-format map is good but is tricky to use while driving.

INFORMATION
Bookshops

Geobuch (Map pp82-3; ☎ 265 030; Rosental 6, Altstadt; ☽ 9am-7pm Mon-Fri, 9am-6pm Sat) Best travel bookshop in town.

Hugendubel (www.hugendubel.de) Karlsplatz (Map pp82-3; ☎ 484 484; Karlsplatz 11-12); Marienplatz (Map pp82-3; ☎ 484 484; Marienplatz 22) Excellent all-purpose chain with reading corners, a café, and plenty of travel guides and English books.

Hugendubel English Bookshop (Map pp82-3; ☎ 01801-484 484; Salvatorplatz 2, Altstadt) Huge selection of novels, guidebooks and nonfiction in the original Hugendubel branch.

Sussmann Presse & Buch (Map pp82-3; ☎ 551 170; Hauptbahnhof) Major English-language publications and books for reading between train stops.

Words' Worth Books (Map p81; ☎ 280 9141; Schellingstrasse 3, Maxvorstadt) Academic tomes and literature in English near the university.

Discount Cards

City Tour Card (www.citytourcard.com; 1/3 days €9.80/18.80) Includes transport and discounts of between 10% and 50% for about 30 attractions, including the Residenz, the zoo and Bier- und Oktoberfestmuseum. It's available at some hotels, Munich public transport authority (MVV) offices, and U-Bahn and S-Bahn vending machines.

Emergency

Ambulance (☎ 192 22)
Fire (☎ 112)
Lost & Found (Map pp78-9; ☎ 01805-386 328; Ötztaler Strasse 17, Untersendling; ☽ 8.30am-noon Mon-Thu, 7am-noon Fri, 2-6.30pm Tue) Take U6 to Partnachplatz.
Police (☎ 110) Nonemergencies (Map pp82-3; ☎ 545 8290; Arnulfstrasse 1, Ludwigvorstadt)
Rape Crisis Hotline (☎ 763 737; ☽ 10am-11pm Mon-Fri, 6pm-2am Sat & Sun)

Internet Access

Most public libraries offer internet access for €0.50 per 30 minutes; see www.muenchner-stadtbibliothek.de (in German).

Cyberice-Café (Map p81; ☎ 3407 6955; Feilitzschstrasse 15, Schwabing; per 30/60 min €1.50/2.50; ☽ 10am-1am) In an ice-cream parlour near the English Garden.

easyInternetCafe (Map pp82-3; Bahnhofplatz 1; per hr €1-3.80; ☽ 7.30am-11.45pm) Rude staff and confusing price scheme but easy to find and with 600 terminals.

MISC-24 (Map pp82-3; ☎ 2371 2672; Weinstrasse 6/cnr Sporergasse; per 30min €1; ☽ 24hr) With extra services such as printing and CD burning. A second branch is in the passageway at Sonnenstrasse 8 near Karlsplatz (Map pp82–3).

Internet Resources

www.muenchen-tourist.de Munich's official website.
www.munichfound.de Munich's expat magazine.
www.toytowngermany.com English-language community website with specialised Munich pages.

Left Luggage

Gepäckaufbewahrung (staffed storage room; ☎ 1308 6664; main hall, Hauptbahnhof; per 24hr per piece €4; ☽ 8am-8pm Mon-Sat, 8am-6pm Sun)
Lockers (Hauptbahnhof main hall & opposite tracks 16, 24 & 28-36; per 24hr €2-4; ☽ 4am-12.30am)

Libraries

Bayerische Staatsbibliothek (see p94)
Stadtbücherei Haidhausen (city library; Map p85; ☎ 4809 8316; Rosenheimer Strasse 5); Schwabing (Map p81; ☎ 336 013; Hohenzollernstrasse 16); Westend (Map pp82-3; ☎ 507 109; Schrenkstrasse 8)

Media

Abendzeitung Light broadsheet that, despite the name, has a morning delivery.
Münchner Merkur The city's archconservative daily.
Süddeutsche Zeitung Widely read regional paper with a liberal streak. Monday's edition has a *New York Times* supplement in English.
tz Daily local tabloid.

Medical Services

The US and UK consulates (p316) can provide lists of English-speaking doctors.

Bereitschaftsdienst der Münchner Ärzte (Map pp82-3; ☎ 01805-191 212; Elisenhof; ☼ 24hr) Non-emergency medical services with English-speaking doctors.

Chirurgische Klinik (Map pp82-3; ☎ 5160 2611; Nussbaumstrasse 20; ☼ 24hr) Emergency room.

Emergency Dentist (☎ 723 3093; ☼ 10am-11pm)

Emergency Pharmacy (☎ 594 475; www.apotheken .de, in German) Referrals to the nearest open pharmacy.

Most pharmacies have employees who speak passable English, but there are several designated 'international' pharmacies with staff fluent in English.

Bahnhof-Apotheke (Map pp82-3; ☎ 598 119; Bahnhofplatz 2, Ludwigsvorstadt)

Internationale Ludwigs-Apotheke (Map pp82-3; ☎ 550 5070; Neuhauser Strasse 11, Altstadt)

Metropolitan Pharmacy (☎ 9759 2950; central area, 3rd fl; ☼ 6.30am-9pm) At the airport.

Money

Reisebank (Map pp82-3; ☎ 551 080; Bahnhofplatz; ☼ 7am-10pm) At the Hauptbahnhof. EurAide's newsletter the *Inside Track* gets you a 50% reduction on commissions at this branch.

Travelex (Map pp82-3; ☎ 235 0920; Petersplatz 10; ☼ 9.30am-6pm Mon-Fri, 9.30am-2pm Sat)

Post

For additional branches, see the tourist office map, search www.deutschepost.de or call ☎ 01802-3333.

Post office (Map pp82-3; Bahnhofplatz 1; ☼ 7.30am-8pm Mon-Fri, 9am-4pm Sat)

Tourist Information

ADAC (Map pp82-3; ☎ 5491 7231; Sonnenstrasse 23; ☼ 9am-7pm Mon-Fri, 9am-2pm Sat)

EurAide (Map pp82-3; ☎ 593 889; www.euraide .de; Hauptbahnhof; ☼ 8am-12.30pm & 2-6pm May-Sep, 8am-noon & 2-5pm Oct-Apr) The office makes reservations, sells tickets for DB trains and a variety of tours, such as the 'Two Castles in a Day' tour to Neuschwanstein and Hohenschwangau, and finds rooms (€3 per booking). EurAide's free newsletter, the *Inside Track,* is packed with practical info about the city and surroundings, and gives discounts on moneychanging. The office is next to the Reisezentrum, between the U-Bahn and the Subway sandwich shop.

Infopoint Museums & Castles (Map pp82-3; ☎ 2101 4050; www.infopoint-museen-bayern.de; Alter Hof 1; ☼ 10am-6pm Mon-Fri, 10am-11pm Sat) Information central for museums and palaces throughout Bavaria.

Tourist Office (☎ 2339 6500; www.muenchen .de) Hauptbahnhof (Map pp82-3; Bahnhofplatz 2; ☼ 9.30am-6.30pm Mon-Sat, 10am-6pm Sun); Marienplatz (Map pp82-3; Neues Rathaus, Marienplatz 8; ☼ 10am-8pm Mon-Fri, 10am-4pm Sat) Opens longer in summer and during holidays

DANGERS & ANNOYANCES

During Oktoberfest crime and staggering drunks are major problems, especially around the Hauptbahnhof. It's no joke: drunks in a crowd trying to get home can get violent, and there are about 100 cases of assault every year. Leave early or stay very cautious, if not sober, yourself.

Strong and unpredictable currents make cooling off in the Eisbach creek in the English Garden more dangerous than it looks. Exercise extreme caution: there have been several deaths.

SIGHTS

Each of Munich's districts has its own appeal, but must-sees concentrate in the Altstadt, and north of here in the Maxvorstadt museum quarter and Schwabing with the English Garden. Schloss Nymphenburg and the Olympia Park are a bit further afield, but well worth the effort.

Altstadt
MARIENPLATZ & AROUND

The heart and soul of the Altstadt, Marienplatz is a popular gathering spot and packs a lot of personality into its relatively small frame. It's anchored by the **Mariensäule** (Map pp82–3; Mary's Column), built in 1638 to celebrate victory over Swedish forces during the Thirty Years' War; it's topped by a golden statue of the Virgin Mary balancing on a crescent moon. At 11am and noon (also 5pm March to October), the square jams up with tourists craning their necks to take in the animated **Glockenspiel** (carillon) in the **Neues Rathaus** (New Town Hall), a neo-Gothic fantasy festooned with gargoyles, statues and a dragon scaling the turrets; the tourist office is on the ground floor. For pinpointing Munich's landmarks without losing your breath, catch the lift up the 85m-tall **tower** (adult/child €2/1; ☼ 9am-7pm Mon-Fri, 10am-7pm Sat & Sun).

The **carillon** has 43 bells and 32 figures that perform two actual historic events. The top half tells the story of a knight's tournament held in 1568 to celebrate the marriage of Duke

adult/child €1.50/0.30; church 7.30am-7pm Thu-Tue, 7.30am-2pm Wed, tower 9am-6pm Mon-Sat, 10am-6pm Sun), Munich's oldest church (1180). Also known as 'Alter Peter' (Old Peter), it's a virtual textbook of art through the centuries, from the Gothic St-Martin-Altar to Johann Baptist Zimmermann's baroque ceiling fresco and Ignaz Günther's rococo sculptures, plus some really creepy relics of an obscure saint named Munditia.

VIKTUALIENMARKT & AROUND

Fresh fruits and vegetables, piles of artisan cheeses, tubs of exotic olives, hams and jams, chanterelles and truffles – **Viktualienmarkt** (Map pp82-3; varies, generally 10am-6pm Mon-Fri, 10am-3pm Sat) is a feast of flavours and one of Europe's finest gourmet markets. Prices are high, naturally, but so is the quality and many items sold here are hard to find elsewhere. Generally speaking, stalls along the main walkways are more expensive than those a little off to the side. A fun thing to do is to lug your treats to the market's beer garden (p118) for a picnic with a brew and view of the market action.

Stalls – many of them family-run for generations – were first set up here in 1807 after the market had outgrown its original spot on Marienplatz. To make room for it, the medieval hospice attached to the still extant **Heiliggeistkirche** (Church of the Holy Spirit; Map pp82-3; 224 402; Im Tal 77; 7am-6pm) had been levelled a year earlier. Gothic at its core, the church has fantastic ceiling frescos depicting the hospice foundation in 1720, courtesy of the Asam brothers.

A few paces southwest of the stalls is the **Schrannenhalle** (Map pp82-3; 518 1818; Viktualienmarkt 15; admission free; 24hr), a 19th-century grain market hall reconstructed in 2005. The 400m-long glass-and-iron structure itself is quite impressive but the overpriced and often tacky shops and cafés inside are not.

East of the Viktualienmarkt is the **Bier- und Oktoberfestmuseum** (Beer- & Oktoberfestmuseum; Map pp82-3; 2423 1607; www.bier-und-oktoberfestmuseum .de, in German; Sterneckerstrasse 2; adult/child/family €4/2.50/6; 1-5pm Tue-Sat), where you can learn all about the golden nectar and the world's favourite drink-up. Think four floors of old brewing vats, historic photos and some of the earliest Oktoberfest regalia. The building itself, a sensitively restored survivor from 1340,

---

TOP FIVE VIEWS OF MUNICH

- **Bavaria** – see the Oktoberfest through her eyes (p100)
- **Frauenkirche** – put the Alps and Altstadt at your feet (p90)
- **Monopteros** – survey the charms of the English Garden (p96)
- **Olympiaturm** – ogle panoramic views of up to 100km (p97)
- **St Peterskirche** – survey all of Munich's major landmarks (below)

Wilhelm V to Renata of Lothringen, while the bottom half portrays the Schäfflertanz (p74). If you want to see the show at eye level, head to the top floor of the Hugendubel book shop (p75) or snag a table at the Café Glockenspiel (p120).

Altes Rathaus

The eastern side of Marienplatz is dominated by the **Altes Rathaus** (Map pp82-3; old town hall). Lightning got the better of the medieval original in 1460 and WWII bombs levelled its successor, so what you see is really the third incarnation of the building designed by Jörg von Halspach of Frauenkirche fame. On 9 November 1938 Joseph Goebbels gave a hate-filled speech here that launched the nationwide *Kristallnacht* pogroms.

Today it houses the adorable **Spielzeugmuseum** (Toy Museum; Map pp82-3; 294 001; Alter Rathausturm, Marienplatz 15; adult/child €3/1; 10am-5.30pm), with its huge collection of rare and precious toys from throughout Europe and the US. The oldest ones – made of paper, tin and wood – are on the top floor and from the 3rd you have a neat view of Marienplatz and Tal street.

Lovesick? Head to the old town hall's south side and pay your respects to Romeo's heartthrob Juliet, a beautiful **bronze sculpture** that was a gift from Munich's sister city, Verona. Leave her some flowers and your love life will improve…

St Peterskirche

It requires a little effort (306 steps, to be precise), but for our money the best view of central Munich is from the 92m-tall tower of the **St Peterskirche** (Church of St Peter; Map pp82-3; 260 4828; Rindermarkt 1; church admission free, tower

(Continued on page 87)

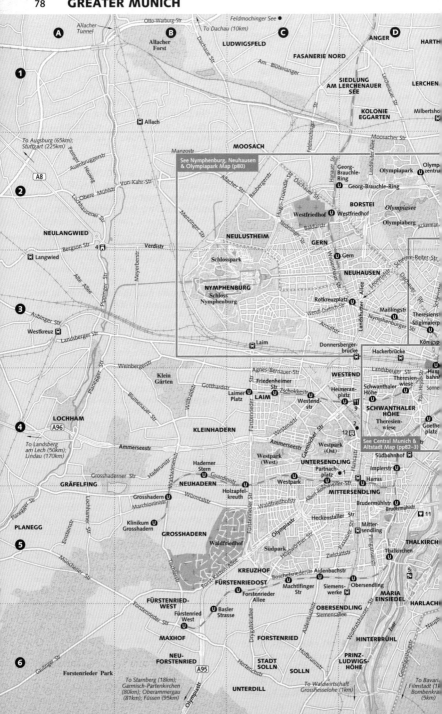

Allacher Tunnel

Otto-Warburg-Str

Feldmochinger See ●

To Dachau (10km)

ANGER

HARTH

Ⓐ   Ⓑ   Ⓒ   Ⓓ

Allacher Forst

LUDWIGSFELD

FASANERIE NORD

❶

Am Blütenanger

SIEDLUNG AM LERCHENAUER SEE

LERCHEN

🚉 Allach

KOLONIE EGGARTEN

Milbertsho

To Augsburg (65km); Stuttgart (225km)

Manzostr

MOOSACH

Moosacher Str

A8

Auenbruggerstr

Georg-Brauchle-Ring

Olympiapark

Olymp zentru

See Nymphenburg, Neuhausen & Olympiapark Map (p80)

Georg-Brauchle-Ring

Ⓤ

❷

Von-Kahr-Str

BORSTEI

Olympiasee

Westfriedhof

Ⓤ Westfriedhof

Olympiaberg

NEULANGWIED

Ackerman

NEULUSTHEIM

GERN

🚉 Langwied

Bergson Str

4 🚉

Verdistr

Schlosspark

Ⓤ Gern

NEUHAUSEN

❸

Aubinger Str

NYMPHENBURG

Schloss Nymphenburg

Rotkreuzplatz Ⓤ

Maillingstr Ⓤ

Theresien

Westkreuz 🚉

Arnulfstr

Stiglmaierp

Landsberger Str

🚉 Laim

Donnersberger-brücke

Königsp

Weinbergerstr

Agnes-Bernauer-Str

WESTEND

Hackerbrücke

Ⓤ

Klein Gärten

Friedenheimer Str

Landsberger Str

Hauf bahn

Gotthardstr

Zschokestr

Heimeran-platz

Theresien-wiese

Sonne

Laimer Platz

LAIM

Westend-str

Ⓤ

Schwanthaler Höhe Ⓤ

❹

LOCHHAM

Westenrieder

1 9

SCHWANTHALER HÖHE

A96

KLEINHADERN

Ammerseestr

Garmischer Str

2

Theresien-wiese

Goethe platz

To Landsberg am Lech (50km); Lindau (170km)

12 🏛

See Central Munich & Altstadt Map (pp82–3)

GRÄFELFING

Ammerseestr

Westpark (Ost)

UNTERSENDLING

Südbahnhof Ⓤ

Haderner Stern Ⓤ

Guardinistr

Westpark (West)

Partnach-platz Ⓤ

Implerstr Ⓤ

PLANEGG

NEUHADERN

Westpark Ⓤ

Harras Ⓤ

Grosshadern Ⓤ

Holzapfel-kreuth Ⓤ

MITTERSENDLING

Marchioninistr

Waldfriedhofstr

Heckenstaller Str

Brudermühlstr Ⓤ

Brudermühlstr

Klinikum Grosshadern Ⓤ

Mitter-sending 🚉

11

GROSSHADERN

Olympiastr

THALKIRCH

❺

Waldfriedhof

Südpark

Zielstattstr

Thalkirchen Ⓤ

KREUZHOF

Hofbrunnstr

Aidenbachstr

Obersendling Ⓤ

MARIA EINSIEDEL

FÜRSTENRIEDOST

Machtlfinger Str

Siemens-werke 🚉

OBERSENDLING

HARLACH

FÜRSTENRIED-WEST

Forstenrieder Allee Ⓤ

Siemensallee

HINTERBRÜHL

Fürstenried West Ⓤ

Basler Strasse Ⓤ

Drygalskiallee

PRINZ-LUDWIGS-HÖHE

MAXHOF

FORSTENRIED

NEU-FORSTENRIED

STADT SOLLN

To Bavaria Filmstadt (1 Bombenkra (5km)

❻

A95

SOLLN

Forstenrieder Park

To Starnberg (18km); Garmisch-Partenkirchen (80km); Oberammergau (81km); Füssen (95km)

Olympiastr

UNTERDILL

To Waldwirtschaft Grosshesselohe (1km)

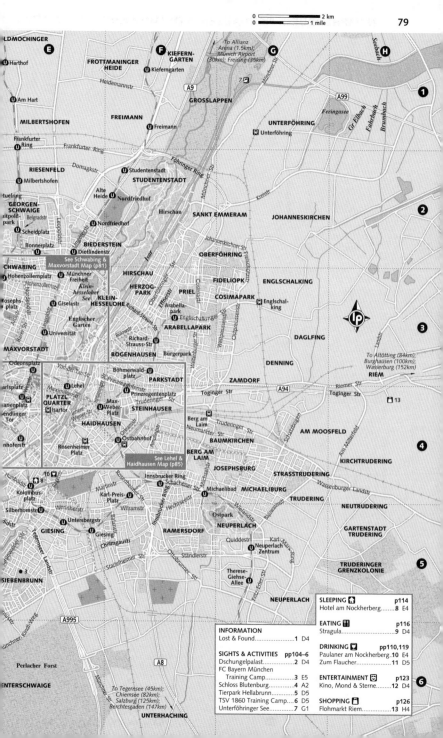

0 |===| 2 km
0 |===| 1 mile

INFORMATION
Lost & Found......................1 D4

SIGHTS & ACTIVITIES   pp104–6
Dschungelpalast....................2 D4
FC Bayern München
    Training Camp...............3 E5
Schloss Blutenburg..............4 A2
Tierpark Hellabrunn.............5 D5
TSV 1860 Training Camp....6 D5
Unterföhringer See.............7 G1

SLEEPING 🏠   **p114**
Hotel am Nockherberg........8 E4

EATING 🍴   **p116**
Stragula.............................9 D4

DRINKING 🍷   **pp110,119**
Paulaner am Nockherberg.10 E4
Zum Flaucher....................11 D5

ENTERTAINMENT 🎭   **p123**
Kino, Mond & Sterne........12 D4

SHOPPING 🛍   **p126**
Flohmarkt Riem..............13 H4

0 ——— 500 m
0 ——— 0.3 miles

INFORMATION	
Chinese Consulate	1 B3
Info-Pavilon	2 F1

SIGHTS & ACTIVITIES	pp97–100
Amalienburg	3 B3
Badenburg	4 A3
Bikram Yoga München	5 D3
BMW Headquarters	6 F1
BMW Museum	7 F1
BMW Welt	8 F1
Herz-Jesu-Kirche	9 D3
Magdalenenklause	10 B3
Marstallmuseum	11 B3
Museum Mensch und Natur	12 B3
Neuer Botanischer Garten	13 B3
Olympia Schwimmhalle	14 E1
Olympia-Eissportzentrum	15 F1
Olympiahalle	16 E1
Olympiastadion	17 E1
Olympiaturm	18 F1
Pagodenburg	19 A3
Rock Museum	(see 18)
Schloss Nymphenburg	20 B3
Sea Life München	21 F1
Theatron	22 E1

SLEEPING	p112
Hotel Laimer Hof	23 B3

EATING	p116
Eiscafé Sarcletti	24 D4
Ruffini	25 D3
Zapata	26 D4
Zauberberg	27 E3

DRINKING	p119
Hirschgarten	28 C4

ENTERTAINMENT	p122
Backstage	29 E4
Hide-Out	30 D4

SHOPPING	pp109, 126
Brauseschwein	31 D3
Porzellan Manufaktur Nymphenburg	32 B3

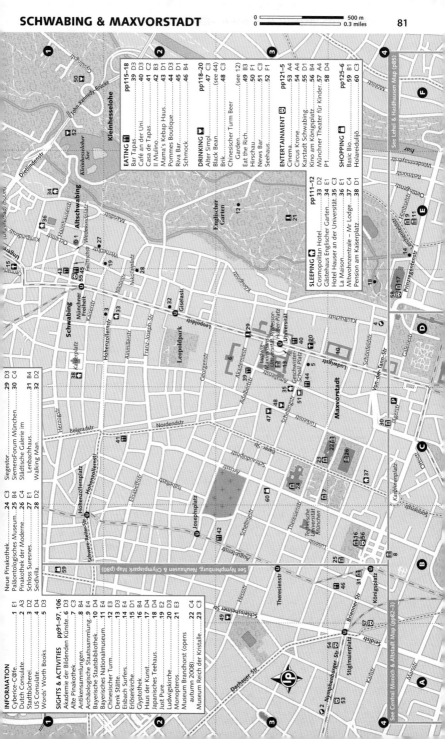

INFORMATION
Cyberc@c@fe	1 E1
Dutch Consulate	2 A3
Stadtbücherei	3 D2
US Consulate	4 D4
Words' Worth Books	5 D3

SIGHTS & ACTIVITIES   pp91–97, 106
Akademie der Bildenden Künste	6 D3
Alte Pinakothek	7 C3
Antikensammlungen	8 B4
Archäologische Staatssammlung	9 E4
Bayerische Staatsbibliothek	10 D4
Bayerisches Nationalmuseum	11 E4
Chinesischer Turm	12 E3
Denk Stätte	13 D3
Eisbach Surfers	14 E4
Erlöserkirche	15 D1
Glyptothek	16 B4
Haus der Kunst	17 D4
Japanisches Teehaus	18 D4
Just Pure	19 E2
Ludwigskirche	20 D3
Monopteros	21 E3
Museum Brandhorst (opens autumn 2008)	22 C4
Museum Reich der Kristale	23 C3
Neue Pinakothek	24 C3
Paläontologisches Museum	25 B4
Pinakothek der Moderne	26 C4
Schloss Suresnes	27 E1
Seidlvilla	28 D2
Siegestor	29 D3
SiemensForum München	30 C4
Städtische Galerie im Lenbachhaus	31 B4
Walking Man	32 D2

EATING 🍴   pp115–18
Bar Tapas	39 D3
Café an der Uni	40 D3
Casa de Tapas	41 C2
Il Mulino	42 B3
Mama's Kebap Haus	43 D1
Pommes Boutique	44 D3
Riva Bar	45 D1
Schmock	46 B4

DRINKING 🍷   pp118–20
Alter Simpl	47 C3
Black Bean	(see 44)
Brik	48 C3
Chinesischer Turm Beer Garten	(see 12)
Eat the Rich	49 B3
Hirschau	50 F1
News Bar	51 C3
Seehaus	52 F1

ENTERTAINMENT 🎭   pp121–5
Cinema	53 A4
Circus Krone	54 A4
Karstadt Schwabing	55 D1
Kino am Königsplatz	56 B4
Münchner Theater für Kinder	57 A4
P1	58 D4

SHOPPING 🛍   pp125–6
Basic Bio	59 B1
Holareidulijö	60 C3

SLEEPING 🛏   pp111–12
Cosmopolitan Hotel	33 D2
Gästehaus Englischer Garten	34 E1
Hotel Hauser an der Universität	35 C3
La Maison	36 E1
Mitwohnzentrale – Mr Lodge	37 C4
Pension am Kaiserplatz	38 D1

See Nymphenburg, Neuhausen & Olympiapark Map (p80)

See Central Munich & Altstadt Map (pp82–3)

See Lehel & Haidhausen Map (p85)

0 | 500 m
0 | 0.3 miles

E **F** **G** **H**

Karolinenplatz

Jägerstr

52

139

40

Hofgarten

41

32

Von-der-Tann-Str

Galeriestr

1

Bayer Str

Ottostr

Brienner Str

167

Odeonsplatz

Hofgartenstr

Franz-Josef-Straße

Altstadt

Karlstr

Sophienstr

88

Maximiliansplatz

70

157

Lenbachplatz

Alter Botanischer Garten

61

Prannerstr

10

72

53

Residenz

36

Residenzstr

42

Max-Joseph-Platz

156

160

2

48

Karlsplatz

Maxburgstr

Promenadeplatz

34

Kardinal-Faulhaber-Str

Salvatorstr

44

Maffeistr

Theatinerstr

65

68

Schrammerstr

143

Maximilianstr

75

Karlsplatz

57

51

11

66 35

Neuhauser Str

55

39

Frauenplatz

43

17

Kaufinger Str

62

25

121

102

13

60

Hofgraben

Alter Hof

27

Perusastr

Am Kosttor

131

63

146

Münzstr

87

152

154

101

Hildegardstr

151

Adolf-Kolping-Str

18

47 145

Herzogspitalstr

Altheimer Eck

Damenstift

14

108

45

165

54

172

12

Marienplatz

129

58

Burgstr

Sparkassenstr

Ledererstr

Orlandostr

77

119

Neuturmstr

Hochbrückenstr

3

144

128

Josephspitalstr

37

105

115

Brunnstr

81

171

Petersplatz

67

169

26

29

100

46

Im Tal

4

Dreifaltigkeits Platz

112

56

116

161 33

Isartor

110

Sonnenstr

30

Sendlinger Str

Oberanger

103

St.-Jakobs-Platz

59

9

Rosental

73

120

69 Viktualienmarkt

134

Westenriederstr

Frauenstr

126

Thomas-Wimmer-Str

4

162

5

Nussbaumstr

111

Sendlinger Tor

Sendlinger Tor-Platz

Pettenkoferstr

49

50 71

83

82

150

Rumfordstr

80

78

Buttermelcherstr

125

106

Kohlstr

79

1

149

153

15

127

117

Gärtnerplatz

158

132

142

Corneliusstr

Reichenbachstr

Reichenbachplatz

148

Unterer Anger

Blumenstr

Müllerstr

93

124

138

114

104

99

94

135

137

5

Klenzestr

Baaderstr

89

140

166

16

170

109

130

118

Hans-Sachs-Str

Jahnstr

141

123

Fraunhoferstr

Fraunhoferstr

Ickstattstr

168

163

Isar

Gebsattel

Glockenbach-Viertel

28

Pestalozzistr

Westermühlstr

Thalkirchner Str

Lindwurmstr

Mathildenstr

Auenstr

Wittelsbacherstr

Ohlmüllerstr

6

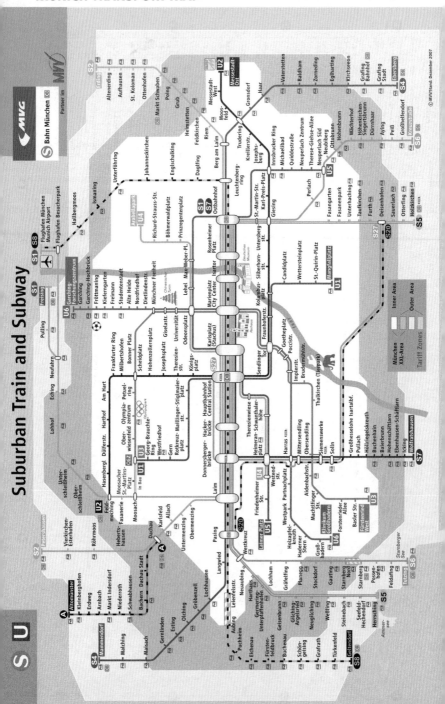

(Continued from page 77)

has some great medieval features, including painted ceilings and a kitchen with an open fire. The earthy pub is open 5pm to midnight (closed Monday).

JÜDISCHES MUSEUM & AROUND

Coming to terms with its Nazi past has not exactly been a priority in Munich, which is why the opening of the **Jüdisches Museum** (Jewish Museum; Map pp82-3; ☎ 2339 6096; www.juedisches -museum.muenchen.de; St-Jakobs-Platz 16; adult/concession €6/3; ☯ 10am-6pm Tue-Sun) in early 2007 was hailed as a major milestone. Relatively small and as yet without much of its own collection, its permanent exhibit in the basement offers insight into Jewish history, life and culture in Munich, creatively presented in seven installations. The Holocaust is dealt with, but the accent is clearly on contemporary Jewish culture, especially in the changing exhibits on the two upper floors.

The museum is part of the new Jewish complex on St-Jakobs-Platz that also includes a community centre with a restaurant and a synagogue that's rarely open to the public. The ensemble reflects the burgeoning renaissance of Munich's Jewish population, which numbers around 9300, making it the second largest in Germany after Berlin.

Münchner Stadtmuseum

You could spend hours roaming through the collections of the rambling **Münchner Stadtmuseum** (City Museum; Map pp82-3; ☎ 2332 2370; www.stadtmuseum-online.de, in German; St-Jakobs-Platz 1; adult/concession/family €4/2/6, free Sun; ☯ 10am-6pm Tue-Sun), making it a perfect rainy day destination.

Historical exhibits help you understand how the royal residence evolved into today's modern metropolis, but the main artistic draw is the ensemble of Erasmus Grasser's 10 sprite-like **Morris Dancers** (1480), medieval travelling entertainers who performed at court and on market squares. The late Gothic figures originally adorned the ballroom of the Altes Rathaus.

Also of special note is the small but powerful section on **Munich during the Third Reich** that forms an enlightening complement to the nearby Jüdisches Museum (Jewish Museum). Set in a windowless hall among riveted steel plates, it reveals the city as the birthplace and

spiritual centre of Nazism through excellent visuals – photographs to propaganda posters, Gestapo uniforms to flags, underground resistance papers to letters from concentration camp victims.

The upper floors house the speciality collections. A delightful diversion, not only for tots, is the **Puppentheater-Museum**, a fantasy world inhabited by an international cast of hand puppets, marionettes, shadow puppets, stick figures, and all manner of dolls, dragons and devils. Call for upcoming shows.

The **Musikinstrumenten-Museum** is packed with fun, precious and rare sound machines from around the world, including Indonesian ceremonial gongs and mechanical musical instruments. Some of them are cranked up regularly during concerts. The **Foto Museum** (Photography Museum) focuses on the early years of the medium, beginning around 1840.

The **Filmmuseum** keeps things dynamic with well-curated screenings of tributes, retrospectives, foreign films, both old and new. Directors, actors and film historians often swing by for pre-show presentations.

Asamkirche

Though pocket-sized, the late baroque **Asamkirche** (Map pp82-3; Sendlinger Strasse 62; admission free; ☯ 8am-5.30pm), built in 1746, is as rich and epic as a giant's treasure chest. Its creators, the brothers Cosmas Damian and Egid Quirin, dipped deeply into their considerable talent box to swathe every inch of wall space with paintings, *putti* (cherubs), gold leaf and stucco flourishes. The crowning glory is the ceiling fresco illustrating the life of St John Nepomuk to whom the church is dedicated (lie down on your back in a pew to fully appreciate the complicated perspective). The brothers lived next door and this was originally their private chapel. One neat trick was that the main altar could be seen through a window from their home.

More of Cosmas' masterful frescoes can be viewed in the ornate **Damenstiftskirche** (Map pp82-3; Damenstiftstrasse 1) just north of Sendlinger Strasse.

HOFBRÄUHAUS & AROUND

No visit to Munich would be complete without a stop at the **Hofbräuhaus** (p119), Bavaria's most celebrated beer hall. The writhing hordes of tourists tend to overshadow the sterling interior, where dainty twirled flowers and Bavarian flags adorn the medieval vaults. The swirl of flags underneath the chandeliers recently got a paint job to minimise their resemblance to Nazi swastikas. The ballroom upstairs was the site of the first large meeting of the National Socialist Party on 20 February 1920.

Northwest of here is the central courtyard of the **Alter Hof** (Map pp82–3; Burgstrasse 8), the oldest Wittelsbach residence with origins in the 12th century and 1282 birthplace of Holy Roman Emperor Ludwig the Bavarian. The bay window on the southern façade was nicknamed 'Monkey Tower' in honour of a monkey that saved the infant ruler from the clutches of a ferocious market pig. Local lore at its finest.

Exit the courtyard at its northern end and continue north on Hofgraben, past the former **Münzhof** (mint; Map pp82–3). This historic courtyard is remarkable for its three-storey arcades dating from 1567. An inscription on the western side of the building reads *Moneta Regis* (Money Rules).

RESIDENZ

The **Residenz** (Map pp82–3) is a suitably grand palace that reflects the splendour and power of the Wittelsbach clan, the Bavarian rulers who lived here from 1385 to 1918. The edifice dwarfs Max-Joseph-Platz along with the grandiose **Nationaltheater**, home to the Bavarian State Opera (p123). Its museums are among the jewels in Munich's cultural crown.

A quadriga of giant bronze lion plaques guards the entrance to the palace on Residenzstrasse, supported by pedestals festooned with a half-human, half-animal face. Note the creatures' remarkably shiny noses. If you wait a moment, you'll see the reason for the sheen: scores of people walk by and casually rub one or all four noses. It's supposed to bring you wealth and good luck.

Residenzmuseum

The Wittelsbach's amazing treasures, as well as all the trappings of their lifestyles, are on display at the **Residenzmuseum** (Map pp82–3; ☎ 290 671; www.residenz-muenchen.de; enter from Max-Joseph-Platz; adult/under 18/concession incl audioguide €6/free/5; ☽ 9am-6pm Apr–mid-Oct, 10am-5pm mid-Oct–Mar), which takes up 130 rooms or about half of the palace. It's so large that it's divided into

two sections, one open until 12.30pm, the other in the afternoon, although the most important sections overlap. You can see it all on guided tours or on your own with an audioguide. If you only have time for one tour, come in the morning.

Both tours soon take you to the **Grottenhof** (grotto court), home of the wonderful **Perseusbrunnen** (Perseus Fountain), with its namesake holding the dripping head of Medusa. Next door is the famous **Antiquarium**, a barrel-vaulted hall smothered in frescoes and built to house the Wittelsbachs' enormous antique collection. This leads to the **Schlachtensäle** (Battle Halls) decorated with scenes from the Napoleonic campaigns, some of which Ludwig himself participated in.

Upstairs and only accessible in the morning are the **Kurfürstenzimmer** (Elector's Rooms), with some stunning Italian portraits and a passage lined with two dozen views of Italy, painted by local romantic artist Carl Rottmann. Also up here, and accessible all day, are François Cuvilliés' **Reiche Zimmer** (Rich Rooms), a six-room extravaganza of exuberant rococo carried out by the top stucco and fresco artists of the day; they're a definite museum highlight. Both tours also take you through the downstairs **Ahnengallery** (Ancestors' Gallery), a riot in rococo with 121 portraits of the rulers of Bavaria in chronological order.

Only open in the afternoon are two chapels: the **Hofkapelle**, which was reserved for the ruler and his family; and the **Reichekapelle** for the other court residents. Another highlight is the **Steinzimmer** (Stone Room), awash in intricately patterned and coloured marble, which was where the emperor stayed during his Munich visits.

Even without a museum ticket, you're free to visit the **Nibelungensäle** (Halls of the Nibelungs) off the Königsbauhof courtyard to marvel at an exhibit depicting the near total destruction of the Residenz in WWII and the miraculous restoration in subsequent decades.

A combination ticket with the Schatzkammer is €9/8.

Schatzkammer der Residenz

The Residenzmuseum entrance also leads to the **Schatzkammer der Residenz** (Residence Treasury; Map pp82–3; ☎ 290 671; www.residenz-muenchen.de; enter from Max-Joseph-Platz; adult/under 18/concession €6/free/5; ☽ 9am-6pm Apr–mid-Oct, 10am-5pm mid-Oct–Mar). It's an Aladdin's cave worth of jewel-encrusted crowns, sceptres and royal accoutrements. Included among the mind-boggling treasures are portable altars, the ruby jewellery of Queen Therese, amazing pocket watches, and 'exotic handicrafts' from Turkey, Iran, Mexico and India. It's well worth the entry price.

Cuvilliés Theater
One of Europe's finest rococo theatres, the Cuvilliés Theatre (Map pp82–3; ☎ 290 671; adult/under 18 /concession €3/free/2; ⏰ 9am-6pm Apr–mid-Oct, 10am-5pm mid-Oct–Mar) hosted the premiere of Mozart's opera *Idomeneo*. The sumptuous interior is expected to emerge from major restoration by this book's publication. To get there, enter the court on Residenzstrasse, walk through the Kapellenhof to the Brunnenhof and the entrance will be on your left.

Staatliches Museum Ägyptischer Kunst
Late 19th-century archaeologists dug up some excellent finds, some of which made their way into the Staatliches Museum Ägyptischer Kunst (Egyptian Art Museum; Map pp82–3; ☎ 298 546; www .aegyptisches-museum-muenchen.de, in German; enter from Hofgartenstrasse 1; adult/concession/child under 16 €5/4/free, Sun €1; ⏰ 9am-9pm Tue, 9am-5pm Wed-Fri, 10am-5pm Sat & Sun). It's in the northwestern wing of the Residenz (look for the obelisk) and has a small but choice collection of sculpture, jewellery, vases and other objects from 5000 years of art in ancient Egypt. Highlights include the gilded coffin mask of Queen Sat-dejhutji (1650 BC) and a rare double statue of King Niuserre (2390 BC) showing him both as a young and an old man.

Hofgarten
Office workers catching some rays during their lunch break, stylish mothers pushing prams, seniors on bikes, a gaggle of chatty nuns – *every*body comes to the Hofgarten (Map pp82–3). The formal court gardens with fountains, radiant flower beds, lime tree-lined gravel paths and benches galore sits just north of the Residenz. Paths converge at the Dianatempel (Map pp82–3), a striking octagonal pavilion honouring the Roman goddess of the hunt. In summer it's a favourite spot for classical music recitals.

Boules players gather by the arcades on the park's north side, where the Deutsches Theatermuseum (German Theatre Museum; Map pp82–3; ☎ 210 6910; Galeriestrasse 4a; admission free; ⏰ 10am-4pm Tue-Sun) trains the spotlight on theatre in German-speaking countries with sets, props, costumes, masks and programmes in changing themed exhibits.

Bavaria's governor keeps his office in the humongous Bayerische Staatskanzlei (Bavarian Chancellery; Map pp82–3; ☎ 216 50; Franz-Josef-Strauss-Ring 1), which takes up the entire eastern flank of the Hofgarten. It's a strikingly modern glass palace built around the restored centre section of the Army Museum that for years stood as a ruined antiwar memorial.

MAXIMILIANSTRASSE
It's pricey and pretentious, but no trip to Munich would be complete without a saunter down Maximilianstrasse, one of the city's grandest boulevards. Starting at Max-Joseph-Platz, it's a 1km-long ribbon of style where sample-size fembots browse for Escada and Prada, and suits sip champagne in pavement cafés, with nary a hair out of place. Several of Munich's finest theatrical venues, including the Nationaltheater, the Kammerspiele and the Kleine Komödie am Max II, are also here.

Built between 1852 and 1875, Maximilianstrasse was essentially an ego trip of King Max II. He harnessed the skills of architect Friedrich von Bürklein to create a unique stylistic hotchpotch ranging from Bavarian rustic to Italian Renaissance and English Gothic. It even became known as the 'Maximilianic Style'. That's the king gazing down upon 'his' boulevard – engulfed by roaring traffic – from his perch at the centre of the strip. Clinging to the base are four rather stern-looking 'children' holding the coats of arms of Bavaria, Franconia, Swabia and the Palatinate.

ODEONSPLATZ & AROUND
Odeonsplatz marks the beginning of the Maxvorstadt, a 19th-century quarter built to link central Munich with Schwabing to the north. Leo von Klenze masterminded its overall design and several of the buildings, including the Leuchtenberg-Palais (Map pp82–3; ☎ 230 60; Odeonsplatz 4; ⏰ 8am-5pm Mon-Fri), a stately town palace modelled after a Roman palazzo and now home of the Bavarian Finance Ministry. There are several nice, if pricey, cafés, including Schumann's Bar (p119) as well as the plushly furnished Café Tambosi, which has a pedigree going back more than 200 years and used to be popular with Munich's high society.

MUNICH

Theatinerkirche

The mustard-yellow **Theatinerkirche** (Map pp82-3; ☎ 210 6960; Theatinerstrasse 22), built to commemorate the 1662 birth of Prince Max Emanuel, was dreamed up by Swiss architect Enrico Zuccalli. Also known at St Kajetan, it's a voluptuous design with two massive twin towers flanking a giant cupola. Inside, an intensely ornate dome lords over the *Fürstengruft* (royal crypt), the final destination of several Wittelsbach rulers, including King Maximilian II.

Feldherrnhalle

Corking up Odeonsplatz's south side is the **Feldherrnhalle** (Field Marshall's Hall; Map pp82-3; Residenzstrasse 1), built by Klenze's main rival Friedrich von Gärnter and modelled on the Loggia dei Lanzi in Florence. Sombre and chunky, it honours the valour of the Bavarian army and positively drips with testosterone; just check out the statues of General Johann Tilly, who kicked the Swedes out of Munich during the Thirty Years' War; and Karl Phillip von Wrede, who first fought with, then against Napoleon in the early 19th century.

It was here on 9 November 1923 that police stopped the so-called Beer Hall Putsch, Hitler's attempt to bring down the Weimar Republic. A fierce skirmish left 20 people, including 16 Nazis, dead. A plaque in the pavement of the square's eastern side commemorates the police officers who perished in the incident.

Hitler was tried and sentenced to five years in jail, but ended up serving a mere nine months, which he used to give birth to his hate-filled manifesto *Mein Kampf.*

Fünf Höfe

Munich usually feels more cosy than cosmopolitan, but one exception is the **Fünf Höfe** (Map pp82-3), a ritzy shopping arcade whose modernist design is as interesting as the fancy flagship and concept stores lining its passageways. There's plenty of steel and glass, fountains and public art, as well as a great 'hanging garden' with real vines dangling from the ceiling. Shopping options include Armani, Alessi, D&G and even a branch of the Japanese department store Muji. Cafés invite refuelling and people-watching, and there's also the **Kunsthalle der Hypo-Kulturstiftung** (Map pp82-3; ☎ 224 412; www .hypo-kunsthalle.de; Theatinerstrasse 8; admission varies, usually adult/concession €8/4, half-price Mon; ☯ 10am-8pm), an art space with high-calibre changing exhibits. Entrances to the Fünf Höfe are on Theatinerstrasse, Salvatorstrasse, Maffeistrasse and Kardinal-Faulhaber-Strasse.

FRAUENKIRCHE & AROUND

The landmark **Frauenkirche** (Cathedral of Our Lady; Map pp82-3; ☎ 290 0820; Frauenplatz 1; admission free; ☯ 7am-7pm Sat-Wed, 7am-8.30pm Thu, 7am-6pm Fri), built 1468–88, is Munich's spiritual heart and the 'Mt Everest' among its churches. No other building in the central city may stand taller than its onion-domed twin towers, which reach a lofty 99m. From April to October, you can enjoy panoramic city views from the **south tower** (adult/concession €3/1.50; ☯ 10am-5pm Mon-Sat).

Bombed to bits in WWII, the reconstruction is a soaring passage of light but otherwise fairly spartan. Of note is the epic cenotaph (empty tomb) of Ludwig the Bavarian just past the entrance and the bronze plaques of Pope Benedict XVI and his predecessor John Paul II affixed to nearby pillars.

Deutsches Jagd- und Fischereimuseum

Pose with a bronze boar, admire a rococo hunting sledge or examine prehistoric fishing tackle at the old-school **Deutsches Jagd- und Fischereimuseum** (Map pp82-3; ☎ 220 522; www .jagd-fischerei-museum.de, in German; Neuhauser Strasse 2; adult/concession/family €3.50/2.50/7; ♱ 9.30am-5pm, to 9pm Thu), spread across three floors of a former Augustinian church. There are plenty of stuffed critters and dioramas alongside trophies, weapons, paintings and porcelain embellished with hunting motifs. Creepy or captivating? Up to you.

Michaelskirche

It stands quiet and dignified amid the commercialism engulfing Kaufingerstrasse, but to fans of Ludwig II the **Michaelskirche** (Church of St Michael; Map pp82-3; Kaufingerstrasse 52) is the ultimate place of pilgrimage. Its dank **crypt** (♱ 9.30am-4.30pm Mon-Fri, 9.30am-2.30pm Sat & Sun; admission €2) is the final resting place of the 'Mad King', whose humble tomb is usually drowned in flowers.

Completed in 1597, St Michael was the largest Renaissance church north of the Alps and boasts an impressive unsupported barrel-vaulted ceiling. The massive bronze statue between the two entrances shows the Archangel finishing off a dragonlike creature, a classic Counter Reformation–era symbol of Catholicism triumphing over Protestantism.

A little further west, the early 18th-century **Bürgersaalkirche** (Map pp82-3; Neuhauser Strasse 14) contains the tomb of Rupert Mayer, a Jesuit priest and noted Nazi opponent who was beatified in 1987. The modern **fountain** near this church commemorates the composer Richard Strauss, who was born in Munich in 1864. It's decorated with scenes from Strauss' most famous opera *Salomé*.

Neuhauser Strasse culminates in Karlsplatz, punctuated by the medieval **Karlstor**, one of Munich's remaining medieval town gates.

Maxvorstadt

'Museums and universities' pretty much sums up Maxvorstadt, meaning that you'll likely be spending some time in this delightful district. The Pinakothek art museums are here and so are the Glyptothek with its precious antiquities, the hallowed **Ludwig-Maximilians-Universität** and the venerable **Kunstakademie** (Art Academy). The area has been a hotbed of culture since the early 20th century. The painters Franz Marc and Wassily Kandinsky had their studios here and Thomas Mann used to talk literature with kindred colleagues in smoky coffeehouses. Today students shape the district's vibe, and café-, bar- and boutique-lined streets such as Türkenstrasse and Schellingstrasse invite exploration and soaking up the boho spirit.

Maxvorstadt was the first city expansion, conceived by Maximilian I around 1805 but not really taking shape until his son, Ludwig I, put his mind – and money – to it some 20 years later. Flashy Ludwigstrasse is just one reminder of the legacy of this king who dreamed of turning Munich into a city of art and culture, an 'Athens on the Isar'. The grand boulevard links Odeonsplatz with the Siegestor, where Maxvorstadt spills over into Schwabing. The remarkably uniform and well-proportioned row of neoclassical piles is a credit to court architects Klenze and Gärtner.

ALTE PINAKOTHEK

Munich's main repository of Old European Masters, the **Alte Pinakothek** (Map p81; ☎ 2380 5216; www.pinakothek.de/alte-pinakothek; Barer Strasse 27, enter from Theresienstrasse; adult/concession/under 18 incl audioguide €5.50/4/free, Sun €1; ♱ 10am-8pm Tue, 10am-6pm Wed-Sun) is stuffed with all the major players that decorated canvases between the 14th and 18th centuries. It's in a neoclassical temple masterminded by Leo von Klenze and is a delicacy even if you can't tell your Rembrandt from your Rubens. Nearly all the paintings were collected or commissioned by Wittelsbach rulers and mirror their eclectic tastes over the centuries. It fell to Ludwig I to unite the bunch in a single museum

The collection is world famous for its exceptional quality and depth, especially when it comes to German masters. The oldest works are altar paintings, of which the *Four Church Fathers* by Michael Pacher and Lucas Cranach the Elder's *Crucifixion* (1503), an emotional rendition of the suffering Jesus, stand out.

A key room is the **Dürersaal** upstairs. Here hangs Albrecht Dürer's famous Christlike *Self-Portrait* (1500), showing the gaze of an artist brimming with self-confidence. His final major work, *The Four Apostles,* depicts John, Peter, Paul and Mark as rather humble men in keeping with post-Reformation ideas. Compare this to Matthias Grünewald's *Sts Erasmus and Maurice,* which shows the saints dressed in rich robes like kings.

For a secular theme, inspect Albrecht Altdorfer's *Battle of Alexander the Great* (1529), which captures in dizzying detail a 6th-century war pitting Greeks against Persians.

There's a choice bunch of **Dutch masters**, including an altarpiece by Rogier van der Weyden called *The Adoration of the Magi,* plus *The Seven Joys of Mary* by Hans Memling, *Danae* by Jan Gossaert and *The Land of Cockayne* by Pieter Bruegel the Elder. Rubens fans also have reason to rejoice. At 6m in height, his epic *Last Judgment* is so big that Klenze custom-designed the hall for it. A memorable portrait is *Hélène Fourment* (1631), a youthful beauty who was the ageing Rubens' second wife.

The Italians are represented by Botticelli, Rafael, Titian and many others, while the French collection includes paintings by Nicolas Poussin, Claude Lorrain and François Boucher. The Spaniards field such heavy hitters as El Greco, Murillo and Velázquez.

Budget at least two hours for a visit.

NEUE PINAKOTHEK

Picking up where the Alte Pinakothek leaves off, the **Neue Pinakothek** (Map p81; ☎ 2380 5195; www.pinakothek.de/neue-pinakothek; Barer Strasse 29, enter from Theresienstrasse; adult/concession/under 18 incl audioguide €5.50/4/free, Sun €1; ☼ 10am-5pm, to 8pm Wed, closed Tue) harbours a well-respected collection of 19th- and early 20-century paintings and sculpture, from rococo to *Jugendstil* (Art Nouveau). Its imposing original structure by Friedrich von Gärtner was destroyed during WWII and not rebuilt; since 1981 works are housed in a modernist structure by Alexander von Branca.

All the world-famous household names get coverage here, including crowd-pleasing French impressionists such as Monet, Cézanne and Degas as well as Van Gogh, whose bold pigmented *Sunflowers* (1888) radiates cheer. There are also several works by Gauguin, including *Breton Peasant Women* (1894); and by Manet, including *Breakfast in the Studio* (1869).

Perhaps the most memorable canvases, though, are by Romantic painter Caspar David Friedrich, who specialised in emotionally charged, brooding landscapes such as *Riesengebirge Landscape with Rising Mist.*

Locals painters getting a shot at wall space include Carl Spitzweg and Wilhelm von Kobell of the so-called Dachau School; and Munich society painters such as Wilhelm von Kaulbach, Franz Lenbach and Karl von Piloty. Another focus is on the works by the *Deutschrömer* (German Romans), a group of neoclassicists centred around Johann Koch, who stuck mainly to Italian landscapes.

PINAKOTHEK DER MODERNE

Germany's largest modern art museum, the **Pinakothek der Moderne** (Map p81; ☎ 2380 5360; www.pinakothek.de/pinakothek-der-moderne; Barer Strasse 40, enter from Theresienstrasse; adult/concession/under 18 €8/5/free, Sun €1; ☼ 10am-6pm Tue-Wed & Fri-Sun, 10am-8pm Thu) opened in 2002 in an extravagant building by Stephan Braunfels that's a perfect setting for artists that dominated the art world throughout the last century. The spectacular four-storey interior centres on a vast eye-like dome, which spreads soft natural light throughout blanched white galleries. Many walls are curved, gently leading the viewer from one discovery to the next, and right angles are disrupted by diagonals.

The museum unites four significant collections under a single roof. The **State Gallery of Modern Art** has some exemplary modern classics by Picasso, Klee, Magritte, Kandinsky and many lesser-known works that will be new to many visitors. More recent big shots include Georg Baselitz, Andy Warhol, Cy Twombly and the late *enfant terrible* Joseph Beuys. His signature piece is the large-scale installation *The End of the 20th Century* (1983), a pile of prone basalt columns scattered throughout a blank chamber.

The **New Collection** in the basement lasers in on applied design from the industrial revolution via Art Nouveau and Bauhaus to today. VW Beetles, Eames chairs and early Apple Macs stand alongside more obscure items, such as AEG's electric kettles from 1909.

The **State Graphics Collection** boasts a collection of 400,000 pieces of art on paper, including drawings, prints and engravings by such craftsmen as Leonardo da Vinci and Paul Cézanne. Because of the light-sensitive nature of these works, only a tiny fraction of the collection is shown at any given time.

Finally, there's the **Architecture Museum**, with oodles of drawings, blueprints, photographs and models by such top practitioners as baroque architect Balthasar Neumann, Bauhaus maven Le Corbusier and 1920s expressionist Erich Mendelsohn.

MUSEUM BRANDHORST

Yet another museum dedicated to postmodern masters is scheduled to open by this book's publication in a new building at the corner of Theresienstrasse and Türkenstrasse (Map p81). Andy Warhol and American abstract expressionist Cy Twombly will get plenty of wall space; and there will also be entire rooms exploring the provocative art of Damien Hirst, Robert Gober and Mike Kelley.

MUSEUM REICH DER KRISTALLE

If diamonds are your best friends, head to the **Museum Reich der Kristalle** (Museum of the Crystal Realm; Map p81; ☎ 2180 4312; Theresienstrasse 41, enter from Barer Strasse; adult/child €1.50/1; ⏰ 1-5pm Tue-Sun), with its Fort Knox–worthy collection of gemstones and crystals, including a giant Russian emerald and meteorite fragments from Kansas.

KÖNIGSPLATZ

Nothing less than the Acropolis in Athens provided the inspiration for Leo von Klenze's imposing **Königsplatz** (Map p81), commissioned by Ludwig I and anchored by a Doric-columned **Propyläen** gateway and two temple-like museums. The Nazis added a few buildings of their own and abused the square with their mass parades. Only the foundations of these structures remain at the east end of the square, rendered unrecognisable by foliage. Peaceful and green today, the square comes alive in summer during concerts and open-air cinema.

BEST MUSEUM FOR...

- **Curious kids** – KinderReich at the Deutsches Museum (p107)
- **Car fetishists** – BMW Welt & Museum (p98)
- **Dino divas** – Paläontologisches Museum (p94)
- **Art-ficionados** – Alte Pinakothek (p91)
- **History groupies** – Bayerisches Nationalmuseum (p101)
- **Tech heads** – Deutsches Museum (p101)

GLYPTOTHEK

If you're a fan of classical art or simply enjoy the sight of naked guys without noses (or other pertinent body parts), make a beeline to the **Glyptothek** (Map p81; ☎ 286 100; www.antike-am-koenigsplatz.mwn.de, in German; Königsplatz 3; adult/concession €3.50/2.50, Sun €1, combined with Antikensammlungen €5.50/3.50; ⏰ 10am-5pm Tue-Wed & Fri-Sun, 10am-8pm Thu). One of Munich's oldest museums, it's a feast of art and sculpture from ancient Greece and Rome amassed by Ludwig I between 1806 and 1830, and opens a surprisingly naughty window onto the ancient world.

An undisputed highlight is the marble Barberini Faun (220 BC), a sleeping satyr rendered in meticulous anatomical detail and striking a pose usually assumed by *Playgirl* centrefolds. Rooms X to XII contain superb busts, including one of a youthful Alexander the Great and several of Emperor Augustus. Also of note is the tomb relief of Mnesarete, a Greek courtesan. Don't miss the sculptures from the Aphaia Temple in Aegina with extensive supportive displays to lend context.

The inner courtyard has a calm and pleasant café where, in summer, classical theatre takes place under the stars.

ANTIKENSAMMLUNGEN

Complementing the Glyptothek, the **Antikensammlungen** (Antiquities Collection; Map p81; ☎ 5998 8830; www.antike-am-koenigsplatz.mwn.de, in German; Königsplatz 1; adult/under 18/concession €3.50/free/2.50, Sun €1, combined with Glyptothek €5.50/3.50; ⏰ 10am-5pm Tue & Thu-Sun, 10am-8pm Wed) is an engaging showcase of exquisite Greek, Roman and Etruscan antiquities. The collection of Greek vases, each artistically decorated with gods and heroes, wars and weddings, is particularly outstanding. Other galleries present gold and silver jewellery and ornaments; figurines made from terracotta and more precious bronze; and super-fragile drinking vessels made from glass.

STÄDTISCHE GALERIE IM LENBACHHAUS

Leading late 19th-century portraitist Franz von Lenbach used his considerable fortune to build a fabulous Tuscan-style home, which his widow later sold to the city for a pittance but with the proviso that it be used as a museum. To get things going, she also threw in a bunch of hubbie's works. Today's **Städtische Galerie im Lenbachhaus** (Municipal Gallery; Map p81; ☎ 2333 2000; www.lenbachhaus.de; Luisenstrasse 33; adult/concession/family incl Kunstbau €6/3/9, more for special exhibits; ⏰ 10am-6pm

Tue-Sun) is swarmed by fans of the expressionist Blauer Reiter (Blue Rider) artist group founded by Wassily Kandinsky and Franz Marc in 1911. Soon joined by August Macke, Gabriele Münter, Alexej von Jawlensky and others, they rebelled against traditional academy art and instead pursued ground-breaking visions and themes. Ironically, Lenbach's portraits seem comparatively staid and retro.

Contemporary art is another focal point. The acquisition of Joseph Beuys' installation *Show Your Wound* nearly caused a riot in the conservative city council, but the collection took off anyway. All the big names are here: Gerhard Richter, Sigmar Polke, Anselm Kiefer, Andy Warhol, Dan Flavin, Richard Serra and Jenny Holzer among them.

Works are also shown in the nearby **Kunstbau**, a 120m-long underground tunnel above the U-Bahn station Königsplatz.

Both spaces are scheduled to close in 2009 for a top-to-bottom renovation directed by British star architect Lord Norman Foster. A reopening date has not been set.

PALÄONTOLOGISCHES MUSEUM

The curatorial concept of the **Paläontologisches Museum** (Palaeontological Museum; Map p81; ☎ 2180 6630; www.palmuc.de; Richard-Wagner-Strasse 10; admission free; ⏰ 8am-4pm Mon-Thu, to 2pm Fri) could use a little dusting up but otherwise this archaeological trove of prehistoric skulls and bones is anything but stuffy. The most famous resident is a fossilised archaeopteryx, the creature that forms the evolutionary link between reptile and bird. Dino fans can check out the wicked horns on a triceratops skull or the delicate bone structure of a plateosaurus. Admission is free, so why not pop in for your Jurassic fix?

SIEMENSFORUM MÜNCHEN

If you need a break from all that art, amble over to the **SiemensForum** (Map p81; ☎ 6363 2660; www.siemens.de/siemensforum; Oskar-von-Miller-Ring 20; admission free; ⏰ 9am-5pm Mon-Fri). It's a fun, hands-on kind of place with five floors of promotional exhibits on electronics and microelectronics, ranging from the first Morse telegraph to the PC, chewing through 140 years of company history in the process. The changing special exhibits are usually more interesting.

SIEGESTOR

Munich's massive **Siegestor** (Victory Gate; Map p81) was modelled on Constantine's arch in Rome and looks like a miniature version of Paris' Arc de Triomphe. Built to honour the Bavarian army for kicking out Napoleon, it's crowned by a triumphant Bavaria piloting a lion-drawn chariot. Severely damaged in WWII, the arch was turned into a peace memorial. The inscription on the upper section reads: *Dem Sieg geweiht, vom Kriege zerstört, zum Frieden mahnend* (Dedicated to victory, destroyed by war, calling for peace).

LUDWIG-MAXIMILIANS-UNIVERSITÄT

Bavaria's oldest university, the **Ludwig-Maximilians-Universität** (LMU; Map p81; ☎ 218 00; www.uni-muenchen.de; Geschwister-Scholl-Platz 1) started out as political football for its rulers. Founded in Ingolstadt in 1472, it moved to Landshut in 1800 before being lassoed to Munich in 1826 by newly crowned King Ludwig I. It has produced more than a dozen Nobel Prize winners, including Wilhelm Röntgen in 1901 and Theodor Hiersch in 2005.

The main building, by Gärtner of course, has cathedral-like dimensions and is accented with sculpture and other art work. A flight of stairs leads to a light court with a memorial to *Die Weisse Rose*, the Nazi resistance group founded by Hans and Sophie Scholl. The boxed text, opposite, has more details, but to get the full story visit the exhibit called **Denk Stätte** (Map p81; ☎ 2180 3053; Geschwister-Scholl-Platz 1; admission free; ⏰ 10am-4pm Mon-Fri) behind the memorial.

LUDWIGSKIRCHE

The twin-towered **Ludwigskirche** (Church of St Ludwig; Map p81; ☎ 288 334; Ludwigstrasse 20; ⏰ 8am-8pm), built by Friedrich von Gärtner between 1829 and 1844, is a sombre affair with a major showpiece: the *Last Judgment* fresco by the Nazarene painter Peter Cornelius in the choir. It's one of the largest in the world and an immodest – and thoroughly unsuccessful – attempt to outdo Michelangelo's version. Even King Ludwig I was none too impressed, which prompted Cornelius to beat a hasty retreat to Berlin.

BAYERISCHE STAATSBIBLIOTHEK

A Gutenberg Bible, the original Carmina Burana (p147) and 1000-year-old prayer books are part of the amazing archive of the **Bayerische Staatsbibliothek** (Bavarian State Library; Map p81; ☎ 286 382 322; www.bsb-muenchen.de; Ludwigstrasse 16; ⏰ main reading room 8am-midnight).

THE WHITE ROSE

Open resistance to the Nazis was rare during the Third Reich, where arbitrary terror meted out by the SA and Gestapo served as powerful disincentives. In 1942, however, a group of medical students, led by Hans and Sophie Scholl, formed Die Weisse Rose (The White Rose), which aimed to encourage Germans to wake up and smell the crematory.

Members acted cautiously at first, creeping through the streets of Munich and smearing slogans such as 'Freedom!' or 'Down With Hitler!' on walls. Growing bolder, they printed and distributed anti-Nazi leaflets, reporting on the mass extermination of the Jews and other Nazi atrocities. One read: 'We shall not be silent – we are your guilty conscience. The White Rose will not leave you in peace.'

In February 1943 Hans and Sophie were caught distributing leaflets at the university. Together with their best friend, Christian Probst, the Scholls were arrested and charged with treason. After a summary trial, all three were found guilty and beheaded the same afternoon. Their extraordinary courage inspired the award-winning film *Sophie Scholl – Die Letzten Tage* (The Last Days of Sophie Scholl; 2005).

Founded in 1558 by Duke Albrecht V, it's in another Gärtner building and brims with 9.1 million volumes, nearly 400,000 maps and subscriptions to over 42,000 periodicals. Yup, that would make it one of the largest in the German-speaking world. Check it out, if only for the free art exhibits.

KARLSPLATZ

Karlsplatz and the medieval **Karlstor** (Map pp82–3) form the western gateway to the Altstadt and the pedestrianised shopping precinct along Neuhauser Strasse and Kaufinger Strasse. The busy square was laid out in 1791 as an ego project of the highly unpopular Elector Karl Theodor. When he named it for himself, locals were even less impressed and insisted on referring to the square as 'Stachus', possibly in memory of a pub that had been displaced by its construction. The huge fountain in the centre is a favoured meeting spot, but Karlsplatz is really at its most magic in winter when a Rockefeller Center–style outdoor ice-skating rink brings out young and old.

Just west of Karlsplatz, the 1890s **Justizpalast** (Palace of Justice; Map pp82-3; Prielmayerstrasse 7; admission free; 9am-4pm Dec–mid-Apr & May–mid-Oct) looms like a pompous presence with neobaroque and neo-Renaissance flourishes. 'Justice' was not exactly meted out here on 22 February 1943 when Hans Scholl, Sophie Scholl and Christoph Probst were condemned to death by the notorious judge Roland Freisler. The verdict was read at 1pm. Four hours later they were dead. There's a permanent exhibit about the sham trial in the very courtroom in room 253. Also see the boxed text, above. A second

courthouse, the **Neuer Justizpalast** (New Palace of Justice) was built just a few years later and is more of a neo-Gothic confection.

Behind the courthouses, the **Alter Botanischer Garten** (Old Botanical Garden; Map pp82–3) is a nice place to cool your heels after an Altstadt shopping spree. Created under King Maximilian in 1814, the tender specimens were moved after WWII to a clean-air spot behind Schloss Nymphenburg. All remaining 'foreign' plants were removed under the Nazis in 1935, who turned it into a pleasant, if rather generic, park. The ferocious **Neptunbrunnen** (Neptune Fountain; Map pp82–3), on the south side, dates back to the same year. The neoclassical entrance gate is called the Kleine Propyläen and is a leftover from the original gardens.

Schwabing

Take the U-Bahn to Münchner Freiheit, grab a table in a street-side café on Leopoldstrasse and watch the world on parade. What do you see? Bronzed lotharios in deep-buttoned white shirts. Faux blondes in tiny tees. Teens in tight premium jeans. Chic mamas walking designer dogs. Yup, no matter what you've heard or read, Schwabing's reputation as a boho stronghold of artists and students is a thing of the past. Fact is, Schwabing is thoroughly gentrified, has some of the highest rents in town, and is populated by lawyers, editors, professors and trust-fund babies in beemers. Some live in beautifully restored *Jugendstil* (Art Nouveau) buildings along such streets as Ainmillerstrasse and Gedonstrasse. Through it all runs urban Leopoldstrasse with

UP ON THE ROOF

Don't have time to make it to the Alps for climbing around lofty heights? No sweat. Just head to the Olympic Stadium for a **walk on the roof** (adult/student & child €35/25; ☉ 2.30pm daily Apr-Oct). Yup, the roof; that famously contorted steel and plexiglass confection is ready for its close-up. Just like on the mountains, you'll be roped and hooked up to a steel cable as you clamber around under the eagle-eyed supervision of an experienced guide showering you with fascinating details about the stadium's architecture and construction. Unusual perspectives are guaranteed, but the vertigo-prone might want to take a pass on this one. Minimum age is 10 and expeditions last two hours. Wear rubber-soled shoes.

True daredevils might also be tempted by the **abseiling tour** (adult/student & child €45/35; ☉ 4pm Fri, Sat & Sun Apr-Oct), which has you scaling up the stadium north side to a height of 50m, then heading straight back down in a free rappel. For details and reservations on either tour, call ☎ 3067 2414.

its wide footpaths, poplar trees and cafés, and bars aplenty. Best of all, the English Garden is only a quick stroll away. The student quarter, meanwhile, is actually south of Schwabing, in Maxvorstadt. But don't worry; even locals get the two confused.

LEOPOLDSTRASSE
Like all grand boulevards, **Leopoldstrasse** is a catwalk for the masses, a wide and shady promenade in full view of passing traffic and perfect for showing off the goods – a new car, a new woman, a new outfit – especially on warm summer evenings. The task is made easier by the rows of street-side café tables packed with aspirants and *arrivés*. The tallest eye-catcher along here, though, is Jonathan Borofsky's **Walking Man** (Map p81), a white 17m-high alien captured in mid-stride.

The **Akademie der Bildenden Künste** (Academy of Fine Arts; Map p81; ☎ 385 20; Akademiestrasse 2-4) is housed in a three-storey neo-Renaissance building. Founded in 1808 by Maximilian I, it advanced to become one of Europe's leading arts schools in the second half of the 19th century and still has a fine reputation today. Famous students included Max Slevogt, Franz von Lenbach and Wilhelm Leibl; and, in the early 20th century, Lovis Corinth, Paul Klee, Wassily Kandinsky, Franz Marc and others who went on to become modern-art pioneers.

ENGLISCHER GARTEN
The sprawling **Englischer Garten** (English Garden; Map p81) is among Europe's biggest city parks – bigger than even London's Hyde Park and New York's Central Park and a favourite playground for locals and visitors alike.

It stretches north from Prinzregentenstrasse for about 5km and was conceived in 1789 – coincidentally (or perhaps not) the year of the French Revolution – as a 'garden for the people' by Elector Karl Theodor. The design job went to Benjamin Thompson, an American-born scientist working as an advisor to the Bavarian government and at one time as its war minister.

Paths piddle around in dark stands of mature oak and maple before emerging into sunlit meadows of lush grass. Locals are mindful of its popularity and tolerate the close quarters of bicyclists, walkers and joggers. Street musicians dodge balls kicked by frolicking children, and students sprawl on the grass to chat about missed lectures.

Sooner or later you'll find your way to the **Kleinhesseloher See**, a lovely lake at the centre of the park. Work up a little sweat while taking your sweetie on a spin around three little islands, then quaff a well-earned foamy one at the **Seehaus beer garden** (p119).

When the sun's out, many Münchners love to get naked and work on their tan, even during their lunch break when they stack their coats, ties and dresses neatly beside them. It's all perfectly legal and socially acceptable, so leave your modesty at home.

Several follies lend the park a playful charm. The **Chinesischer Turm** (Map p81), now at the heart of Munich's oldest beer garden (p119), was built during an oriental craze in the 18th century. Further south, at the top of a gentle hill, is the **Monopteros** (1838; Map p81), a small Greek temple whose ledges are often knee-to-knee with dangling legs belonging to people admiring the view of the Munich skyline.

Another hint of Asia awaits further south at the **Japanisches Teehaus** (Japanese Teahouse; Map p81; ☎ 224 319; ☒ tea ceremony 3pm, 4pm, 5pm Sat & Sun Apr-Oct) right by an idyllic duck pond. The best time to come is for an authentic tea ceremony celebrated by a Japanese tea master.

Don't even think about spending the night in the park! Muggers, drug fiends and proselytisers often keep the cops busy till dawn.

ALT-SCHWABING

The tangle of quiet streets east of the Münchner Freiheit U-Bahn station offers a glimpse of pre-yuppification Schwabing. The heart of Alt-Schwabing (Old Schwabing) – **Wedekindplatz** – still preserves a boho touch thanks to nearby small shops, gritty bars and alternative theatres. While living here from 1899 to 1901, Thomas Mann penned his famous novel *Buddenbrooks*. Beatniks and hippies invaded in the '60s, fuelling a minor spin on the 1968 revolution.

South of the square is the baroque **Schloss Suresnes** (Map p81; Werneckstrasse 1), a petite palace built in 1718 for one of Elector Max's government officials. Paul Klee had a studio here from 1919 to 1922, and it now houses a Catholic academy. Nearby is another gorgeous residence, the **Seidlvilla** (Map p81; ☎ 333 139; www.seidlvilla.de, in German; Nikolaiplatz 1B; admission free; ☒ noon-7pm), now a community centre and art gallery. Ring the buzzer: if a show's on someone should let you in.

The church with the bold clock face on the north side of the Münchner Freiheit U-Bahn station is the **Erlöserkirche** (Map p81; ☎ 3837 7140; Germaniastrasse 4). Built at the turn of the 20th century, it's filled with Art Nouveau flourishes and a popular concert venue thanks to superior acoustics.

Olympiapark & Around

The huge area in the northern city where soldiers once paraded and the world's first Zeppelin landed in 1909 found a new destiny in the 1960s as the **Olympiapark** (Olympic Park; Map p80; www.olympiapark-muenchen.de). Built for the 1972 Olympic Summer Games, it hasn't lost any of its magic and draws people year-round with concerts, festivals, fireworks and sporting events. The swimming hall (p106) and the ice-skating rink (p105) are open to the public as well.

A good first stop is the **Info-Pavilion** (☎ 3067 2414; ☒ 10am-6pm Mon-Fri, 10am-3pm Sat), which has information, maps, tour tickets and a neat model that will have you marvel at the vastness of the complex. Staff also rent MP3 players for a self-guided **Audio-Tour** (€7, plus €50 refundable deposit). Tickets to the 90-minute guided **Adventure Tour** (adult/concession €8/5.50) that covers the entire Olympiapark on foot and by toy train are available, too.

Olympiapark has two world-famous eye-catchers: the 290m **Olympiaturm** and the warped **Olympiastadion** (Olympic Stadium; Map p80; ☎ 3067 2707; enter via 'Kasse Nord'; adult/child/family €2/1/5; ☒ 8.30am-6pm mid-Apr–mid-Oct, 9am-4.30pm mid-Oct–mid-Apr, closed on events days). Germans have a soft spot for the latter because it was on this hallowed grass in 1974 that the national soccer team – led by the 'Kaiser' Franz Beckenbauer – won the FIFA World Cup. Older people on the guided one-hour **Stadium-Tour** (adult/concession €6/4; ☒ 11am Apr-Oct) often wax nostalgic when setting foot in the old locker rooms or seeing the VIP lounges.

When the sky is clear, you'll quite literally have Munich at your feet against the breathtaking backdrop of the Alps from the top of the **Olympiaturm** (Map p80; ☎ 3067 2750; adult

---

OLYMPIAN SOUNDS

Munich summers simply would not be the same without free concerts in the Olympiapark. All through August, the **Theatron MusikSommer Festival** (www.theatron.de) brings international bands from hip-hop to gospel, pop to punk to the amphitheatre next to the Olympic Lake. Kids won't get bored at the **Lilalu Umsonst und Draussen Festival** (www.lilalu.org), which features circus acts, music from mostly local and regional bands, and readings for about two weeks late in the month.

Can't get (or afford) a concert ticket to the Rolling Stones, U2 or Robbie Williams at the Olympic Stadium? No sweat, don't fret – you can hear them for free (!) simply by climbing up the **Olympiaberg**. At 564m high, it's a so-called *Trümmerberg*, meaning a pile of war debris that's been greened over. It happens to be right across from the open-air Olympic Stadium, with the sound travelling neatly across the little lake. How handy is that? Bring a blanket and beverage and join the local throngs for a free concert with, and under, the stars.

MUNICH'S OLYMPIC TRAGEDY

The 1972 Summer Olympics presented Munich with a historic chance. It was the first time since 1936 that the Olympic Games would be held in the country. The motto was the 'Happy Games', the emblem a blue solar 'Bright Sun'. The city built a shiny Olympic Park, including buildings with striking plexiglass tents that, at the time, were revolutionary in design. It was the opportunity to present a new, democratic Germany full of pride and optimism.

In the final week of the Olympics, members of the Palestinian terrorist group 'Black September' killed two Israeli athletes and took nine others hostage at the Olympic Village, demanding the release of political prisoners and escape aircraft. During a failed rescue attempt by German security forces at Fürstenfeldbruck, a military base west of Munich, all the hostages and most of the terrorists were killed. The competition was suspended briefly before Avery Brundage, the International Olympic Committee president, famously declared 'the Games must go on'. The bloody incident cast a pall over the entire Olympics and sporting events in Germany for years to follow.

The events are chronicled in an Oscar-winning documentary *One Day in September* (2000), by Kevin McDonald, and also inspired Steven Spielberg's searing *Munich* (2005). The killings prompted German security to rethink its methods and create the country's elite counter-terrorist unit, GSG 9.

/concession €4/2.50; 9am-midnight, last trip 11.30pm). Your lift ticket also buys access to the small if quirky **Rock Museum** (Map p80; same hours), also up on top. Ozzie Osbourne's signed guitar, a poem penned by Jim Morrison and Britney Spears' glitter jeans jostle for space with letters, photos and concert tickets, all the result of three decades of collecting by a pair of rock fans.

The **Olympiahalle**, meanwhile, is getting a complete overhaul, which is expected to last through 2009.

SEA LIFE MÜNCHEN

Meet Nemo the clownfish and learn that seahorse males get pregnant at **Sea Life München** (Map p80; 450 000; www.sealifeeurope.com; Willi-Daume-Platz 1; adult/child/concession €13.50/8.75/11.50; 10am-6pm Mon-Fri, 10am-7pm Sat & Sun), a walk-through aquarium that takes you on a virtual journey along the Isar and Danube Rivers to the Black Sea and the Mediterranean. Along the way you'll meet aquatic denizens living in various habitats, which have been re-created in 30 tanks. The biggest of them teems with sharks and rays, which dart around you as you walk through a 10m-long underwater tunnel. Kids can test their knowledge by answering quiz questions throughout. All labelling is in English and German. See the website for discount coupons.

BMW-WELT, MUSEUM & PLANT

Next to the Olympiapark, where Lerchenauer Strasse meets Petuelring, a glass and steel double-cone 'tornado' spirals skyward. It's arrested only by a roof the size of an aircraft carrier yet imbued with the lightness of a cloud. Open since October 2007, the **BMW Welt** (Map p80; www.bmw-welt.de; admission free, tours adult/child/family €6/3/12; 9am-8pm) is an architectural showstopper, a cathedral to cars, a place of pilgrimage for those who worship at the altar of the auto. The lucky ones get to drive away with their dream car, for BMW Welt is first and foremost a car pick-up centre. Everyone else can admire the latest models, straddle a powerful motorbike, browse the 'lifestyle shop' or take a guided 80-minute tour. On the Junior Campus, kids learn about mobility, fancy themselves car engineers and even get to design their own vehicle in workshops. Classical and jazz concerts, many of them free, take place year-round. Sure, it's all a brilliant PR ploy, but let's not get too cynical…

The BMW Welt is linked via a bridge to the **BMW Headquarters** (Map p80), another stunning building of four gleaming cylinders, and to the silver-bowl-shaped **BMW Museum** (Map p80; www.bmw-museum.de), due to emerge from a complete revamp by this book's publication. Channel your inner Michael Schumacher in an avant-garde exhibition space merging art, history and design. Check the website for details.

With some planning, you can also tour the belly of the beast, the adjacent **BMW Plant** (Map p80; 01802-118 822; www.bmw-werk-muenchen.de; tours adult/child/family €6/3/12). Reservations are required and can be made up to six months in advance. Tours (also in English) last 2½ hours, and children under four are not allowed.

Neuhausen & Nymphenburg

One of Munich's oldest districts, Neuhausen has an air of relaxed confidence, Europe's largest beer garden (the Hirschgarten; p119) and pretty good nightlife and dining. It also has a long and cosy association with the royal family since becoming the servants' quarter for the newly built Schloss Nymphenburg in the 17th century. A couple of hundred years later, Neuhausen was revamped as a residential pad for the well heeled, with the villas along the Nymphenburg Canal resembling second-string royal residences. The canal, by the way, often freezes over in winter, luring skaters and curlers onto the ice.

The commercial heart of Neuhausen – bustling Rotkreuzplatz (nicknamed 'Stachus of Neuhausen') – may be an aesthetically challenged product of the 1960s, but at least it's home to Munich's best ice-cream parlour, the Eiscafé Sarcletti (p117). The square is also the gateway to low-key and tourist-free bars and restaurants in radiating side streets. On Thursday a farmers market brings out the locals from 10am to 7pm.

En route to Schloss Nymphenburg, swing by the **Herz-Jesu-Kirche** (Map p80; ☎ 130 6750; Lachnerstrasse 8; admission free; ☉ 8am-7pm except Tue 8am-noon), a stunning modernist church crafted from glass, concrete, steel and wood that shimmers blue like a magic crystal, especially at night.

SCHLOSS NYMPHENBURG
Adelaide of Savoy certainly married well. After she gave birth to her son Max Emanuel, her husband, Elector Ferdinand Maria, was so overjoyed that he rewarded her with her own palace, **Schloss Nymphenburg** (Nymphenburg Palace; Map p80; ☎ 179 080; combination ticket except Museum Mensch und Natur adult/concession €10/8 Apr–mid-Oct, €8/6 mid-Oct –Mar; ☉ 9am-6pm Apr–mid-Oct, 10am-4pm mid-Oct–Mar). Later rulers dabbled with the place until it grew into the lavish edifice you see today.

Schloss Nymphenburg is about 5km north-west of the Altstadt and easily reached by tram 17 or 41. It's backed by a lavish park sprinkled with outbuildings. The combination ticket entitles you to one-time admission to any of the buildings and is good for multiple days. Admission to all the buildings is free to anyone under 18. Note that the Badenburg, the Pagodenburg and the Magdalenenklause are closed from mid-October until March.

Schloss
The primary **palace** (adult/concession €5/4) consists of a central villa and two wings. The self-

guided tour begins upstairs in the **Steinerner Saal** (Stone Hall), a two-storey dining hall with fantastic stucco and frescoes by Johann Baptist Zimmermann. The **Gobelinzimmer**, with stunning detailed tapestries, is almost as good. The tour also takes in the **Wappenzimmer** (Heraldic Room) and the **Chinesisches Lackkabinett** (Chinese Lacquer Room), but do take time out to see the cute chapel in the western wing.

The most famous room, though, is the **Schönheitengalerie** (Gallery of Beauties), in the southern wing, a portrait gallery of 38 'beauties' from all walks of life and parts of the world hand selected by Ludwig I.

In the south wing are the coaches and riding gear of the royal family, suitably displayed in the **Marstallmuseum** (Map p80; adult/concession €4/3). It's worth checking out if only to see Ludwig II's fairy tale–like rococo sleigh, ingeniously fitted with oil lamps for his crazed nocturnal outings. Upstairs is the world's largest collection of old **porcelain** made by the famous Nymphenburger Manufaktur. Also known as the Sammlung Bäuml, it presents the entire product palette from the company's founding in 1747 until 1930.

Museum Mensch und Natur
Kids will have plenty of 'ooh and aah' moments in the **Museum Mensch und Natur** (Museum of Humankind & Nature; Map p80; ☎ 179 5890; www .musmn.de; adult/concession/under 18 €2.50/1.50/free, Sun €1; ☉ 9am-5pm Tue-Sun), in the palace north wing. Anything but old school, it puts a premium on interactive displays, models, audiovisual presentations and attractive animal dioramas.

Gardens & Outbuildings
The sprawling park behind Schloss Nymphenburg is a favourite spot with Münchners and visitors for strolling, jogging or whiling away a lazy afternoon. It's laid out in grand English style and accented with water features, including a large lake, a cascade and a canal popular for feeding swans, and ice-skating and ice-curling when it freezes over in winter.

The park is at its most magical without the masses, ie early in the morning and an hour before closing. But even in the daytime, you can usually commune in solitude with water-lilies and singing frogs at the **Kugelweiher** pond in the far northern corner.

The park's chief folly – and quite frilly to boot – the **Amalienburg** (Map p80; adult

/concession €2/1) – is a small hunting lodge dripping with crystal and gilt decoration; don't miss the amazing Spiegelsaal (Mirror Hall). The two-storey **Pagodenburg** (Map p80; adult/concession €2/1) was built in the early 18th century as a Chinese teahouse and is swathed in ceramic tiles depicting landscapes, figures and floral ornamentation. The **Badenburg** (Map p80; adult/concession €2/1) is a sauna and bathing house that still has its original heating system. Finally, the **Magdalenenklause** (Map p80; adult/concession €2/1) was built as a mock hermitage in faux 'ruined' style. A combination ticket to all four park buildings is €4/3 per adult/concession.

Neuer Botanischer Garten

Munich's vivacious **Neuer Botanischer Garten** (New Botanical Garden; Map p80; ☎ 1786 1350; www.botmuc.de; Menzinger Strasse 65; adult/concession/under 12 €3/1/free; ☽ 9am-7pm May-Aug, 9am-6pm Apr & Sep, 9am-5pm Feb-Mar & Oct, 9am-4.30pm Nov-Jan) segues smoothly from the north side of the palace park and ranks among the most important in Europe. About a century old, it boasts some 14,000 plant species from around the world. Highlights include the Victorian-style *Palmenhaus* (palm pavilion) with its famous collection of tropical and subtropical plants. Other greenhouses shelter cacti, orchids, ferns, carnivorous plants and other leafy treasures.

Ludwigsvorstadt & Westend

Once a neglected working-class backwater perfumed by the hoppy aroma wafting over from its breweries, the Westend is gradually finding its groove and evolving into one of Munich's most vibrant and intriguing neighbourhoods. There are no major sights, which is just fine because its charms reveal themselves in subtler, often unexpected, ways: on leafy Gollierplatz, for instance, or in hip cafés and pubs. Or in the growing number of artists' studios and indie boutiques, and the Turkish corner store with its artfully piled produce.

For contrast, head west of the Theresienwiese Oktoberfest grounds, where Ludwigsvorstadt basks in an air of bourgeois smugness, its leafy streets lined with grand old mansions looking as impeccable now as they did a century ago. However, the district's face changes drastically the further north, and closer to the Hauptbahnhof, you get: strip clubs, sex shops and cheesy import stores dominate.

THERESIENWIESE

The **Theresienwiese** (Theresa Meadow; Map pp82–3), better known as 'Wiesn', just southwest of the Altstadt is the site of the Oktoberfest. At the western end of the meadow is the **Ruhmeshalle** (Hall of Fame) guarding solemn statues of Bavarian leaders, as well as the **statue of Bavaria** (☎ 290 671; adult/ under 18/concession €3/free/2; ☽ 9am-6pm Apr–mid-Oct, to 8pm during Oktoberfest), an 18m-high Amazon in the Statue of Liberty tradition, oak wreath in hand and lion at her feet. This iron lady has a cunning design that makes her seem solid, but actually you can climb via the knee joint up to the head for a great view of the Oktoberfest. At other times, views are not particularly inspiring.

CIRCUS KRONE

No matter how you feel about circuses, the venerable **Circus Krone** (Map p81; ☎ 01805-247 28; www.circus-krone.de; Zirkus-Krone-Strasse 1-6; ☽ Dec-Mar) is not like any other. A Munich fixture for decades, its tent is vast and the shows are dazzling. After three months of performances, the circus goes on tour, leaving the city in a grand procession with elephants and camels driven along Arnulfstrasse towards the Hauptbahnhof. The hall is left to host rock concerts and other events the rest of the year.

Gärtnerplatzviertel & Glockenbachviertel

Southeast of the Altstadt, the Gärtnerplatzviertel and Glockenbachviertel pack more personality into a fairly compact frame than most other Munich neighbourhoods. The trendiest bars, cafés and clubs are here; pretty streets teem with local designer boutiques and lifestyle stores; and creatives of all stripes peck away on their iMacs in stylish offices. After dark, this is a hipster haven, not as student-y as Maxvorstadt, not as snooty as Schwabing, not as multicultural as Haidhausen. The epicentre of lesbigay life is here as well, with rainbow flags flying especially proudly along Müllerstrasse and Hans-Sachs-Strasse. Further south is the up-and-coming Schlachthofviertel, an area where the slaughterhouses used to be located. The official name for all three quarters is Isarvorstadt.

Everyone gravitates towards the circular Gärtnerplatz, lorded over by the splendid **Staatstheater am Gärtnerplatz** (p123). Founded by citizens in 1865, the theatre was taken over by Ludwig I after the owners went bankrupt.

The Glockenbachviertel (Bell Brook Quarter) derives its name from a foundry once located on a stream nearby. Many of the city's carvers and woodworkers lived here, giving rise to street names such as Baumstrasse (Tree St) and Holzstrasse (Wood St). A lovely spot for a walk is along the babbling Glockenbach creek, which runs south along Pestalozzistrasse. It's the sole survivor of a network of brooks that once crisscrossed Munich; the rest have been rerouted or paved over. This one parallels the **Alter Südlicher Friedhof** (Map pp82–3), a cemetery that's a favourite 'Six-Feet-Under' destination for the posh crowd. Famous residents include the painter Carl Spitzweg, the physicist Joseph von Fraunhofer and the architect Friedrich von Gärtner. Look for a plaque with names and grave locations near the entrance.

DEUTSCHES MUSEUM

Even if memories of school science make you groan, a visit to **Deutsches Museum** (German Museum; Map p85; ☎ 217 91; www.deutsches-museum .de; Museumsinsel 1; adult/child 6-15/concession/family €8.50/3/7/17; ☒ 9am-5pm) should convince you that, gee, science *can* be fun. Spending a few hours in this temple of technology is an eye-opening journey of discovery that takes you from the future back to the Stone Age. There are loads of interactive displays (including glass blowing and paper making), live demonstrations and experiments, model coal and salt mines, and engaging sections on cave paintings, geodesy, microelectronics and astronomy. In fact, it can be pretty overwhelming after a while, so it's best to prioritise what you want to see, especially if you're here with attention-span-challenged kids. In fact, little ones probably have the most fun in the **KinderReich** (Children's Kingdom; see p107).

The museum's collection is so huge that some sections have been moved to separate locations. Vehicles are now in the **Verkehrszentrum** (p103), while aircraft are at the **Flugwerft Schleissheim** (p133). Combination tickets to all three museums cost €15 and may be used on separate days.

Lehel

Just east of the Altstadt proper, Lehel (lay-hl) has the second-highest concentration of museums after the art nexus in Maxvorstadt.

It's the oldest Munich suburb, having been absorbed into the city in 1724, and a charismatic warren of quiet streets lined with late-19th-century buildings.

BAYERISCHES NATIONALMUSEUM

A highlight of Munich's museum scene, the **Bayerisches Nationalmuseum** (Bavarian National Museum; Map p81; ☎ 211 2401; www.bayerisches-national museum.de; Prinzregentenstrasse 3; adult/concession/under 18 €5/4/free, Sun €1; ☒ 10am-5pm Tue-Sun, 10am-8pm Thu) is chock-full of items illustrating the art, folklore and cultural history of southern Germany between the Middle Ages and the early 20th century. The ground floor yields new treasures and surprises in every room, from suits of armour to oil paintings, town models to altars and emotionally charged sculpture by Tilman Riemenschneider. Upstairs there are specialised collections of historic board games, musical instruments, porcelain and a ridiculously ostentatious rococo silver table setting. By contrast, the basement shows the ways of life of the simple peasant folk through a series of period rooms.

HAUS DER KUNST

It was built in 1937 to showcase Nazi art, but now the **Haus der Kunst** (House of Art; Map p81; ☎ 2112 7113; www.hausderkunst.de; Prinzregentenstrasse 1; admission varies; ☒ 10am-8pm Fri-Wed, 10am-10pm Thu) presents works by exactly the artists whom the Nazis rejected and deemed degenerate (see boxed text, p102). Another focus is on contemporary art and design supplemented by hip events, including an after-work party that includes a tour, nibbles snacks and drinks.

STAATLICHES MUSEUM FÜR VÖLKERKUNDE

A bonanza of art and objects from Africa, India, the Americas, the Middle East and Polynesia, the **Staatliches Museum für Völkerkunde** (State Museum of Ethnology; Map p85; ☎ 210 136 100; www.voelker kundemuseum-muenchen.de; Maximilianstrasse 42; adult/under 18/concession €3.50/free/2.50, Sun €1; ☒ 9.30am-5.30pm Tue-Sun) has one of the most prestigious and complete ethnological collections anywhere. Sculpture from West and Central Africa is particularly impressive, as are Peruvian ceramics, Indian jewellery, mummy parts, and artefacts from the days of Captain Cook.

ARCHÄOLOGISCHE STAATSSAMMLUNG

Turns out Bavaria has been a popular place of residence for 120,000 years. Prehistoric Stone

Age people came first, then the Romans, the Celts and finally various Germanic tribes. The **Archäologische Staatssammlung** (Archaeological Collection; Map p81; ☎ 211 2402; www.archaeologie -bayern.de; Lerchenfeldstrasse 2; adult/concession €3/2, Sun €1; ☺ 9.30-5pm Tue-Sun) opens up a window on these long-gone civilisations with cult objects, floor mosaics, jewellery, medical equipment and scores of other items. This could be pretty dry stuff, but curators do their best to keep things as dynamic as possible with special themed exhibits and activities for children. Some sections may be under renovation.

SCHACK-GALERIE

Count Adolf Friedrich von Schack (1815–94) was a great fan of 19th-century Romantic painters such as Böcklin, Feuerbach and Moritz von Schwind. His collection is housed in the former Prussian embassy, now the **Schack-Galerie** (Map p85; ☎ 2380 5224; www.pinakothek .de/schack-galerie; Prinzregentenstrasse 9; adult/concession €3/2.50; ☺ 10am-6pm Wed-Mon). A tour of this intimate space is like an escape into the idealised fantasy worlds created by these artists.

PRATERINSEL

In the middle of the Isar, below Maximilians-brücke, **Praterinsel** (Prater Island) is a popular bathing spot in summer and also home to the **Aktionsforum Praterinsel** (Map p85; ☎ 2123 830; www .praterinsel.org; Praterinsel 3-4). It's an art and cultural centre in a former schnapps distillery with artists studios, exhibits, open-air performances and parties.

In a deceptively beautiful building on the island's southern tip, the **Alpines Museum** (Map p85; ☎ 211 2240; www.alpines-museum.de, in German;

Praterinsel 5; adult/concession/child €3/2/1; ☺ 1-6pm Tue-Fri, 11am-6pm Sat & Sun) could deliver a fascinating exhibit about the Alps but is actually a pretty dry and predictable presentation. Paintings, photographs, scientific instruments and graphics illustrate the history of the mountain range, its settlement, expeditions and the popularity of Alpinism. Sadly it avoids the debate over the mountains' touristic exploitation and environmental problems resulting from global warming.

ST-ANNA-PLATZ

The Asamkirche may be more sumptuous, but the **Klosterkirche St Anna im Lehel** (Map p85; ☎ 211 260; St-Anna-Platz 21; ☺ 6am-7pm) is actually a collaboration of the top dogs of the rococo. Johann Michael Fischer designed the building, and Cosmas Damian Asam painted the stunning ceiling fresco and altar. So there.

Pompous by comparison, the neo-Romanesque **Pfarrkirche St Anna im Lehel** (Map p85; ☎ 212 1820; St-Anna-Platz 5; ☺ 8am-6pm) across the square arrived on the scene in the 1890s after the Klosterkirche had become too small. Conceived by Gabriel von Seidl, it's worth a spin for its huge altar and impressive nave paintings.

Haidhausen

Haidhausen is hip, eclectic and leagues away from its 19th-century working-class roots. Major gentrification since the late 1970s has made the district desirable for artsy professionals, professional artists and all urban types, although there are still plenty of upwardly hopeful immigrants, artists and students and ageing lefties left. For visitors, the main draw

---

'DEGENERATE' ART

Expressionism, surrealism, Dadaism…modern art of all stripes was anathema to Hitler and his honchos, who even devised their own 'final solution' for the offensive art work. Internationally renowned artists like Klee, Beckmann and Schlemmer were forced into exile, their work was removed from museums and confiscated from private collections. The Nazis then sold them off to rake in foreign currency; about 4000 of them were publicly burned in Berlin.

In July 1937, though, Goebbels gathered about 650 paintings, sculptures and prints in the crammed and poorly lit Galerie am Hofgarten, calling it an exhibit of Entartete Kunst (Degenerate Art). Organised into such themes as Mockery of God and Insult to German Womanhood, it was intended to portray modern art as debauched and decadent. The propaganda show opened on 19 July 1937, just one day after the 'Great German Art Exhibition' of Nazi-approved works premiered in the nearby, custom-built Haus der Deutschen Kunst. Ironically, the Nazi art was largely reviled by the public, while over two million people came to see the Entartete Kunst, more than any other modern art show in history.

is a congenial mix of sceney bars and boundary-pushing restaurants, the Gasteig Culture Centre, fun streets like Metzstrasse and gorgeously restored late-19th-century buildings in the French quarter around Pariser Platz. Unfortunately, there's also quite a bit of druggie action going on around Orleansplatz and the party zone near Ostbahnhof (Kunstpark and Optimolwerke; see p121).

DEUTSCHES MUSEUM – VERKEHRSZENTRUM

An ode to mobility, the **Verkehrszentrum** (Transportation Centre; Map p85; ☎ 500 806 500; www .deutsches-museum.de/verkehrszentrum; Theresienhöhe 14a; adult/concession/child under 6/family €5/3/free/10; ☻ 9am-5pm) is all about the ingenious ways humans have devised to transport things and each other. From the earliest automobiles to famous race cars and the high-speed ICE trains, the collection is a virtual trip through transport history. The exhibit is spread over three historic trade fair halls near Theresienwiese, each with its own theme – Public Transportation, Travel and Mobility & Technology – and is a fun place even if you can't tell your piston from your carburettor. There's even a special kiddie corner where little ones can build their own fantasy vehicles.

KULTURZENTRUM GASTEIG & AROUND

Haidhausen is home to one of Munich's finest cultural venues, the **Kulturzentrum Gasteig** (Gasteig Culture Centre; Map p85; ☎ 480 980; www.gasteig .de; Rosenheimer Strasse 5), whose postmodern, boxy, glass-and-brick design caused quite a controversy back a generation ago. The name is derived from the Bavarian term 'gaacher Steig', meaning 'steep trail'. The complex harbours four concert halls, including the 2400-seat Philharmonie, which is the permanent home of the Münchner Philharmoniker (p123) and also hosts renowned international orchestras. The Carl-Orff-Saal and the Kleiner Konzertsaal (Small Concert Hall) are more intimate, as is the Black Box, which is primarily used for experimental theatre and dance. Free 45-minute concerts by students from the onsite Richard Strauss Conservatory often take place in the Kleiner Konzertsaal at 1.15pm, 6.15pm and 10.30pm. And for good measure, there's a huge municipal library with internet access as well.

Right on the Isar, west of the Gasteig, is the **Müller'sches Volksbad** (p106), a richly detailed Art Nouveau indoor swimming pool. Nearby, the **Muffathalle** culture centre was converted from an old power plant.

The prim church ensemble north of here is the **St Nikolai & Lorettokapelle** (Map p85). St Nikolai was first built in 1315 in Gothic style only to go for baroque three centuries later. The design of the little Loreto Chapel emulates the *Gnadenkapelle* in Altötting (p164). Outside, the covered walkway protects some pretty nifty 'Stations of the Cross' made of Nymphenburg porcelain.

MUSEUM VILLA STUCK

Franz von Stuck was a leading light in Munich's art scene around the turn of the 20th century and his residence is one of the finest *Jugendstil* homes you'll ever see. Stuck himself came up with the intricate design, which forges tapestries, patterned floors, coffered ceilings and other elements into a harmonious work of art. His furniture even earned a gold medal at the Paris World Fair in 1900. Today his pad is open as the **Museum Villa Stuck** (Map p85; ☎ 455 5510; www.villastuck.de in German; Prinzregentenstrasse 60; adult/concession/family €9/4.50/13.50; ☻ 11am-6pm Wed-Sun) and presents changing exhibits, usually starring Stuck's contemporaries but also later 20th-century avant-gardists such as Nam June Paik and Cindy Sherman. The most famous Stuck painting is *Die Sünde* (Sin; 1893), infused with an unabashed eroticism that caused quite a stir back in the old days. Naturally.

MAXIMILIANEUM

Maximilianstrasse culminates in the glorious **Maximilianeum** (Map p85; ☎ 412 60; Max-Planck-Strasse 1), completed in 1874, a decade after Max II's sudden death. It's an imposing structure, drawn like a theatre curtain across a hilltop, bedecked with mosaics, paintings and other artistic objects. There's a free exhibit about the Bavarian parliament, which moved here in 1949. It's framed by an undulating park called the **Maximilliananlagen**, which is a haven for cyclists in summer and tobogganists in winter.

Bogenhausen

Bogenhausen is not shy about flaunting its wealth. Elegant villas sprang up here from the 1870s onwards and the area is peppered with gilded Art Nouveau buildings. Just take a wander along Möhlstrasse (Map p85), a chic avenue branching northeast from the

Europa-Platz near the Friedensengel, which is lined with mansions for the super-rich, foreign consulates and law offices. East of here (via Siebertstrasse and Ismaninger Strasse), Holbeinstrasse is a treasure chest of listed Art Nouveau houses, with the one at No 7 (Map p85) being an especially fine specimen. Prinzregentenstrasse, the main artery, divides Bogenhausen from Haidhausen to the south.

FRIEDENSENGEL

Just east of the Isar River, the **Friedensengel** (Angel of Peace; Map p85) statue stands guard from its perch atop a 23m-high column. It commemorates the 1871 Treaty of Versailles, which ended the Franco-Prussian War, and the base contains some shimmering golden frescoes. On New Year's Eve the steps around the monument are party central.

PRINZREGENTENTHEATER

One of Bogenhausen's main landmarks is the **Prinzregententheater** (Map p85; ☎ 2185 2899; Prinzregentenplatz 12). Its dramatic mix of Art Nouveau and neoclassical styles was conceived under Prince-Regent Luitpold as a festival house for Richard Wagner operas. After WWII it became the temporary home of the Bavarian State Opera for a couple of decades, but then was left to crumble for a quarter-century to the point where it almost had a date with the wrecking ball. A theatre director named August Everding eventually rode to the rescue and raised the funds for its renovation. In 1996 it reopened to the strains of Wagner's *Tristan und Isolde*. Today the beautiful venue is used for drama, concerts and other events, and is also the seat of the Bavarian Theatre Academy.

Outer Districts

ALLIANZ ARENA

Sporting and architecture fans alike should take a side trip to the northern Munich suburb of Fröttmaning to see the ultraslick €340 million **Allianz Arena** (off Map pp78–9; ☎ 01805-555 101; www.allianz-arena.com; Werner-Heisenberg-Allee 25; adult/child 7-12 years €8/4; ☒ daily tours in German 10.15am, 11am, 1pm, 3pm, 4.30pm, in English 1pm), Munich's dramatic new football stadium. Nicknamed the 'life belt' and 'rubber boat', it has walls made of inflatable cushions that can be individually lit to match the team colours of the host team (red for 1 FC Bayern, blue for TSV 1860 and white for the national soccer team). The 75-minute stadium tours are hugely popular (no

tours on game days); tickets are sold in the shop inside the Markenwelt on the 3rd floor. To get there take U6 to Fröttmaning.

SCHLOSS BLUTENBURG

Idyllically encircled by the little Würm River, **Schloss Blutenburg** (Map pp78–9; ☎ 891 2110; cnr Pippinger Strasse & Verdistrasse) creates the illusion of a moated castle. It was here where Duke Albrecht III retreated with his commoner wife Agnes Bernauer before his dad had her bumped off (see p203 for details). The trio of three tall green grass blades rising from the water are leftovers from the 2005 Bundesgartenschau (Federal Garden Show).

The palace is now state owned and houses the **Internationale Jugendbibliothek** (International Youth Library; ☎ 891 2110; www.ijb.de; ☒ 10am-4pm Mon-Fri), a unique research and lending library with about half a million children's books in 130 languages. It has reading rooms, runs exhibits and activities, and also has a small **museum** (☒ 2-5pm Wed-Sun) dedicated to Michael Ende, author of *The Neverending Story*.

The **palace church** (admission free; ☒ 9am-5pm Apr-Sep, 10am-4pm Oct-Mar) is a rare Gothic jewel that wasn't drenched in baroque frilliness in the 17th century. The three altars by Jan Polack are outstanding examples of late-Gothic panel painting.

Schloss Blutenburg is about 11km northwest of the Altstadt. Take the S-Bahn to Pasing, then bus 73, 75 or 76 to 'Schloss Blutenburg'.

TIERPARK HELLABRUNN

Some 6km south of the city centre, **Tierpark Hellabrunn** (Hellabrunn Zoo; Map pp78–9; ☎ 625 080; www.tierpark-hellabrunn.de; Tierparkstrasse 30; adult/concession/child €9/6.50/4.50; ☒ 8am-6pm Apr-Sep, 9am-5pm Oct-Mar) has 5000 furry, feathered and finned friends that rarely fail to enthral the little ones. It was one of the first to be set up like a 'geo-zoo' with spacious natural habitats dividing animals by continent. A baby giant panda (born in July 2007) is a current squeeze of the preteen set, as is the large petting zoo where tots get to feed deer and goats. Other crowd-pleasers include the 'Villa Dracula' (inhabited by bats, what else?), the penguins and polar bears in the 'Polarium', and the 'Orang-utan paradise'. To get here take the U-Bahn to Thalkirchen or bus 52.

BAVARIA FILMSTADT

Movie magic made in Munich is the draw of the **Bavaria Filmstadt** (off Map pp78–9; ☎ 6499 2304;

Bavariafilmplatz 7; www.bavaria-filmtour.de; adult/child/concession/family €11/8/10/34, with stunt show & 4D cinema €20/17/19/64; ☺ 9am-4pm Mar-Oct, 10am-3pm Nov-Feb), a theme park built around Bavaria Film, one of Germany's oldest studios founded in 1919. The top-grossing German film of all time, *Das Boot*, was among the classics shot here but today's German audience is more interested in sets of the family soap *Marienhof*. Films and TV are still produced today, and who knows, you might see a star during the guided 90-minute tours. The 1pm tour is in English.

The crash-and-burn **Stunt Show** (show only €8.50) is a runaway hit as well, while kids are particularly fond of the wacky **4D cinema** (tickets €4.50), with seats that lurch and other special effects from silly to spooky. The Filmstadt is in the southern suburb of Geiselgasteig, about 14km from the Altstadt. Take the S2 Silberhornstrasse, then tram 25 to Bavariafilmplatz. Admission is free on your birthday (ID required).

ACTIVITIES
Boating

A lovely spot to take your sweetheart for a spin is on the Kleinhesseloher See in the English Garden. Rowing or pedal boats cost around €7 per half-hour for up to four people. Boats may also be hired at the Olympiapark.

Cycling

Munich is an excellent place for cycling, particularly along the Isar River. The holy grail for mountain- and downhill bikers is the **Bombenkrater** (off Map pp78-9; www.bombenkrater.de, in German), a unique terrain of hillocks, dips, roots, ridges, holes and ramps created by WWII bombs. It's in a woody area on the southern city edge, right on the Isar River. Take the S7 to Höllriegelskreuth.

Hiking

For information about hiking and climbing as well as gear rental, swing by the Munich chapter of the **Deutscher Alpenverein** (German Alpine Club; Map pp82-3; ☎ 551 7000; Bayerstrasse 21; ☺ 8am-6pm Mon, 10am-6pm Tue, Wed & Fri, 10am-7pm Thu), near the Hauptbahnhof. For buying gear and equipment, it's hard to beat **Sport Scheck** (Map pp82-3; ☎ 216 60; Sendlinger Strasse 6), which has multiple floors of everything from camping equipment to expedition wear, plus lots of books. **Sport Schuster** (Map pp82-3; ☎ 237 070; Rosenstrasse 1-5) is just as good.

Skating

From May to August, thousands of skaters take to Munich streets every Monday during **Blade Night** (www.muenchenerbladenight.com; per person €2) an organised roll through town that starts and ends with a big street party on Wredestrasse near Circus Krone (Map p81). The refreshment stands open at 7pm and thousands of bladers hit the streets at 9pm for a leisurely 10km to 20km tour around various neighbourhoods. Check the website for details. The Olympiapark and the English Garden are both popular blader destinations as well.

Ice-skaters can glide alongside future medallists in the **Olympia-Eissportzentrum** (Map p80; ☎ 306 70; Spiridon-Louis-Ring 21; adult/child per session €3.50/2.50; ☺ sessions 10am-noon & 1.30-4pm daily, 8-10.30pm Wed-Sun), hit the frozen canals in Nymphenburg (free) or twirl around at the **Münchner Eiszauber**

A TOTALLY AWESOME WAVE, DUDE

Munich is famous for beer, sausages and surfing. Yep, you read that right. Just go to the southern tip of the English Garden at Prinzregentenstrasse and you'll see scores of people leaning over a bridge to cheer on wetsuit-clad daredevils as they 'hang 10' on an artificially created wave in the Eisbach. It's only a single wave, but it's a damn fine one. In fact, the surfers are such an attraction, the tourist office even includes them in its brochures. But if park director Thomas Köster gets his way, the fun will soon be a thing of the past. You see, surfing or even swimming in the Eisbach is actually *verboten*. And for good reason. It looks pretty harmless, but the little river is quite a raging torrent with dangerous currents and undertows. Numerous people – though none of the surfers – have drowned in the chilly waters, including a 27-year-old Australian traveller on a Munich holiday whose body has never been found. Signs warning about its dangers are widely ignored, usually with the tacit approval of park wardens and the police. Köster wants this to change, and he also wants to get rid of the wave. Surfers are up in arms and have even started a petition (www.rettet-die-eisbachwelle.de) to ensure their playground's survival.

MUNICH

(Map pp82–3; www.muenchnereiszauber.de; per person €4; Nov-Jan) ice rink on Karlsplatz.

Swimming

Bathing in the Isar River isn't advisable because of strong and unpredictable currents (especially in the English Garden), though many locals do. Better to head out of town to one of the many nearby swimming lakes, including the popular **Feringasee** (S8 to Unterföhring, then follow signs), where the party never stops on hot summer days; the pretty **Feldmochinger See** (Map pp78–9), which is framed by gentle mounds and has a special area for wheelchair-bound bathers (S1 to Feldmoching); and the **Unterföhringer See** (Map pp78–9), which has warm water and is easily reached by bicycle via the Isarradweg or by the S8 to Unterföhring.

The best public swimming pool options, both indoors, are the **Olympia Schwimmhalle** (Map p80; ☎ 01801 796 223; Olympiapark, Coubertinplatz 1; adult/concession/family €3.60/2.60/9.20; 7am-11pm), where Mark Spitz famously won seven gold medals in 1972; and the spectacular **Müller'sches Volksbad** (Map p85; ☎ 01801 796 223; Rosenheimer Strasse 1, Haidhausen; adult/concession swimming €3.40/2.70, sauna €13.20; 7.30am-11pm), where you can swim in Art Nouveau splendour, then sweat it out in the Roman-Irish bath.

Yoga & Spas

Bikram Yoga München (Map p80; ☎ 1301 1218; Leonrodstrasse 6, Neuhausen; session €16) At the hottest yoga temple in town, you'll do the downward dog in a studio heated to 38°C (bring a bath towel).

Blue Spa (Map pp82–3; ☎ 212 0992; Promenadeplatz 2-6, Altstadt; per day €28) Get your stressed-out self over to the rooftop of the ultraposh Bayerischer Hof hotel to luxuriate in the deep-blue designer pool and steam room or have the jet lag kinks worked out with a massage.

Just Pure (Map p81; ☎ 3835 6999; Siegesstrasse 13, Schwabing) A session at German beauty queen Gabriela Just's posh but pleasant day spa will leave your skin quenched, radiant and ready for your close-up. Products and treatments are calibrated to the phases of the moon.

WALKING TOUR

This circuit covers the highlights within Munich's historic centre and the English Garden. Kick-off is at Marienplatz, the heart and soul of Munich. The glockenspiel springs into action at the **Neues Rathaus** (**1**; p76), the impressive Gothic town hall with six courtyards and multiple towers. The steeple of the **St Peterskirche** (**2**; p77) affords a great vista of the old town, including the **Altes Rathaus** (**3**; p77), now home to a toy museum. Turn left as you leave St Peter's and walk down Petersplatz to the **Viktualienmarkt** (**4**; p77), a tantalising array of colours and aromas from around the globe, with a beer garden to boot. Exiting the market to the south takes you to Sebastiansplatz with the resurrected **Schrannenhalle** (**5**; p77) on your left. Turn into Sebastiansplatz to reach the **Münchner Stadtmuseum** (**6**; p87), home not only to historic city exhibits but also to a prestigious film museum and other collections. The big cube looming opposite on St-Jakobs-Platz is Munich's spanking new synagogue, which is flanked by the **Jüdisches Museum** (**7**; p87) and a Jewish community centre.

From here follow Unterer Anger, turn right on Klosterhofstrasse, which continues as Schmidstrasse and reaches Sendlinger Strasse. Turn right, then take a quick peek inside the pocket-sized **Asamkirche** (**8**; p87), the city's most ornate baroque church. Backtrack a few steps on Sendlinger Strasse, turn left on Hackenstrasse, right on Hotterstrasse, past the tiny and quirky **Hundskugel** (**9**; p115) restaurant, left on Altheimer Eck and immediately right on Färbergraben. This takes you to Kaufinger Strasse, the Altstadt's pedestrianised main shopping strip. The shiny spot opposite invites you to visit the **Deutsches Jagd- und Fischereimuseum** (**10**; p91). Rub the boar for good luck but skip the museum and continue on Augustinerstrasse to the distinctively twin-onion-domed **Frauenkirche** (**11**; p90) with more great views from the top. Pick one of the little lanes behind the church to reach Weinstrasse, turn left and continue on Theatinerstrasse, taking a few minutes to marvel at the postmodern **Fünf Höfe** (**12**; p90) shopping arcade or checking out the latest exhibit at the Kunsthalle der Hypo-Kulturstiftung gallery. Backtrack a few steps on Theatinerstrasse, then turn left on tiny Perusastrasse, which delivers you to Max-Joseph-Platz and the grand **Residenz** (**13**; p88), home of the Wittelsbach rulers for four centuries. A tour of the place will give you an eyeful of the family's lifestyle and penchant for collecting great art and other fancy treasure.

Continue north on Residenzstrasse to reach Odeonsplatz, site of the Nazis' first

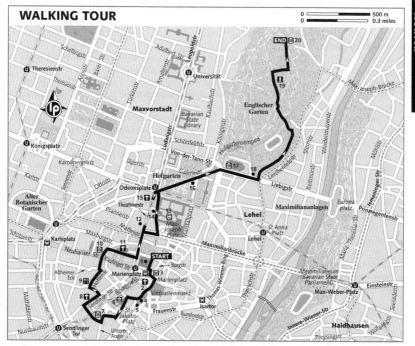

WALKING TOUR

WALK FACTS	
Start Marienplatz	
Finish Chinesischer Turm, English Garden	
Distance 6km	
Duration Minimum 2 hours, with museums all day or more	

lunge at power. Here looms the **Feldherrnhalle** (**14**; p90), a hulking shrine to war heroes. The bombastic, mustard-yellow **Theatinerkirche** (**15**; p90) contains the Wittelsbachs' family crypt. The tour heads into green territory from here, starting with the neoclassical **Hofgarten** (**16**; p89). Cross it diagonally and go through the underpass, then turn right on Prinzregentenstrasse and proceed past the **Haus der Kunst** (**17**; p101), a gallery and one-time forum for Nazi art propaganda. Just beyond, from the little bridge, don't miss the **surfers** (**18**; p105) riding the artificially created wave of the gushing Eisbach creek. Past the bridge, turn left into the English Garden and follow the creek to a vast meadow popular with Frisbee experts and nude sunbathers. A

little hill with a classical folly, the **Monopteros** (**19**; p96), completes the leisurely scene. At the end of the tour you can plop down in the beer garden alongside the curious, multitiered **Chinesischer Turm** (**20**; p96), where an oompah band belts out traditional tunes.

MUNICH FOR CHILDREN

(Tiny) hands down, Munich is a great city for children with plenty of activities to please even the most attention-span challenged rug rats. There are plenty of parks for romping around, swimming pools and lakes for cooling off and beer gardens with children's playgrounds for making new friends. Many museums have special kid-oriented programs, but the highly interactive **KinderReich** (Children's Kingdom; ☺ 9am-4.30pm) at the Deutsches Museum (p101) specifically lures the single-digit set. Here tots ages three to eight can climb all over a fire engine, build things with giant Lego, construct a waterway with canals and locks, or bang on the drum all day in a – thankfully – sound-proof instrument room.

Kids love animals, of course, making the zoo **Tierpark Hellabrunn** (p104) a sure bet.

OKTOBERFEST

'Mass' Hysteria

Blame it all on the 'Mass'; that towering mug holding a full litre of golden nectar that sets you back about €8 – and right back on your heels. Oktoberfest is indeed the world's largest drink-a-thon, where normally prim and sober citizens from every country in the world lurch around like drunken rats. 'Tradition' may be everything at the Oktoberfest, but 'convention' gets thrown right out the window.

The sky is a classic Bavarian blue when we fight for a spot to see the fantastic Brewer's Parade. Horses the size of small elephants pull flower-festooned wagons piled high with beer barrels around town and to the Wiesn. It's all eerily disciplined, even quiet, until – at the stroke of noon – the Munich mayor opens the first keg with a mallet, great pomp and ceremony. As the beer flows forth, the crowd cheers and the mayor exclaims: *'Ozapft ist's!'* (It's tapped!). Let the 'games' begin!

Other 'traditions' are less pleasant. Scores of revellers have raised their abilities at projectile vomiting to an art form and creatively, if disgustingly, decorate the streets around the Wiesn. And though portable potties are ubiquitous, the time-honoured performance of 'wildes Bieseln' (wild pissing) is still the preferred form of relief (at least among men).

Then there are the mating rituals. Dark patches of shadow just off the midway become cluttered with writhing bodies, while in the tents you'll encounter pairs of blottoed faces doing their level best to mutually suck themselves out of existence. The faint of heart should cling to well-lit areas.

After a few days of this Dionysian assault on the senses – and our livers – verbal skills, memory and other mental functions quickly become impaired. Kind of like arriving at the 'Death Zone' on Everest. We somehow start developing fond feelings for Betty Ford. Oh, the horror! The horror…

History

The world's biggest party had its origins in a simple horse race. In 1810 Bavarian Crown Prince Ludwig – later King Ludwig I – married Princess Therese of Saxe-Hildburghausen, and following the wedding a horse race was held at the city gates. The six-day celebration was such a rip-roaring success that it became an annual event, was extended and moved forward to start in September so that visitors would enjoy warmer weather. Faced with all those fine suds, the horse race became little more than a sideshow and was finally dropped in 1938.

Parades

Starting at 10.45am on the first day of Oktoberfest, the Brewer's Parade travels through the city centre from Sonnenstrasse to the fairgrounds via Schwanthalerstrasse. By noon it's all over. The next day, the even more colourful Costume Procession is led by a young girl on horseback dressed as the Münchner Kindl, the child monk from the city's coat of arms. She's followed by an endless

---

Petting baby goats, feeding pelicans, watching falcons and hawks 'perform', or even riding a camel should make for some unforgettable memories. For a 'fishy' immersion head to the new **Sea Life München** (p98) in the Olympic Park. Dino fans gravitate to **Paläontologisches Museum** (p94), while budding scientists will find plenty to marvel at in the **Museum Mensch und Natur** (p99) in Schloss Nymphenburg. The **Spielzeugmuseum** (toy museum; p77) is of the 'look but don't touch' variety, but tots might still get a kick out of seeing what toys grandma used to play with. Bookworms will be in heaven in the **International Youth Library** (p104) at Schloss Blutenburg.

The adorable singing and dancing marionettes performing at the **Münchner Marionettentheater** (Map pp82-3; ☎ 265 712; www .muenchner-marionettentheater.de; Blumenstrasse 32, Altstadt; tickets €6-15; ☽ 3pm Wed-Sun, 8pm Sat) have enthralled generations of wee ones. At the **Münchner Theater für Kinder** (Map p81; ☎ 593 858; Dachauer Strasse 46, Neuhausen; tickets €7-9) budding thespians can enjoy fairy tales and children's classics à la *Max & Moritz* and *Pinocchio*. In winter, a show at the venerable **Circus Krone** (p100) is a magical experience.

For hands-on fun head to the **Dschungelpalast** (Map pp78-9; ☎ 7248 8441; www.dschungelpalast.de, in German; Hansastrasse 41, Westend), which organises

stream of marching folklore clubs, oompah bands, riflemen clubs, and other groups from Bavarian villages and beyond in a two-hour procession starting at 10am at the Max II Monument.

Nostalgic Favourites

On the midway, amid the hi-tech roar, a few nostalgic favourites have survived. Among these are the magic shows at **Schicht'l Tent**, where beheadings are a speciality. Generations have gasped at this bloody sleight of hand, which is no mean feat. Even master illusionist David Copperfield has paid his respects by losing his head.

Oktoberfest also has Germany's last remaining **flea circus** – a fixture since the 19th century – where trained pests provide the oomph for miniature chariots that outweigh them a thousandfold.

Top 10 Tips, Facts & Figures

- Oktoberfest runs from mid-September to early October at the Theresienwiese, a 15-minute walk southwest of the Hauptbahnhof.
- More than 6.2 million people guzzled 6.7 million litres of beer during Oktoberfest 2007.
- Oktoberfest employs about 12,000 people and has its own police force, lost and found office, childcare centre, fire brigade, baggage checkroom, post office and first-aid station.
- The 14 tents are open between 10am and 11.30pm (9am on Sunday), with last call at 10.30pm. Only Käfers Wiesnschenke and the Wein- und Sektzelt are licensed until 1am. Leave no later than 10pm to avoid unruly masses staggering to the stations.
- Beer tents are elbow-to-elbow all day on Saturday and Sunday, but for lighter traffic try a weekday afternoon. Until Friday of the first week the evenings aren't swamped either.
- An Oktoberfest brew is big but not cheap: a 1L *Mass* (tankard) costs around €8, payable with special tokens sold by the tents. Half a roast chicken costs about the same.
- You may bring snacks with you to the outdoor terraces of the beer tents, but not inside.
- Many beer tents and food stalls are certified as ecofriendly and serve only regional quality meats, sausages, sweets, waffles, toasted almonds and other delicacies.
- Married women tie their dirndl apron on the right, others on the left. Women who've been harassed can seek assistance from the **Aktion Sichere Wiesn** (☎ 5022 2366; www.sicherewiesn .de) right on the Oktoberfest grounds.
- Chances of scoring a room in town if arriving without a booking during Oktoberfest are next to nil, and even the crummiest ones command sky-high prices. You might have better luck in Augsburg, Garmisch-Partenkirchen, Bad Tölz or another nearby town. Tenters could try **Wiesn Camp** (www.munich-oktoberfest.com in German).

low-cost arts and crafts workshops and a Sunday family brunch.

At **Jogoli's Fantastic Kinderworld** (Map p85; ☎ 9972 0920; www.jogolis.de; Friedenstrasse 22b, Haidhausen; 2hr /3½hr/5hr/all day €8/13/20/32; ☺ 2-7pm Mon-Fri, 10am-7pm Sat & Sun), a supervised indoor/outdoor playground, kids up to age 10 can get as creative, messy and interactive as they wish. Another toy-filled refuge is **Münchner Kindl** (Map pp82-3; ☎ 2423 1600; Burgstrasse 6, Altstadt; per hr €4.50; ☺ 9am-6pm Mon-Fri, 10am-4pm Sat), which welcomes kids aged 18 months to 10 years old.

If you happen to be in Neuhausen, near Schloss Nymphenburg, swing by **Brauseschwein** (Map p80; ☎ 1395 8112; Frundsbergstrasse 52), a wacky toy shop selling everything from penny candy to joke articles and wooden trains.

German readers can find lots more tips and useful information at www.pomki.de and www.spiellandschaft.de.

TOURS

New Munich Free Tour (www.newmunich.com; tours free; ☺ 10.45am & 11.45am) These English-language walking tours tick off all of Munich's central landmarks and historical milestones (kings to Nazis) in three hours. Guides are well-informed, sharp-witted and fun, and they do work only for tips, so give what you can. Tours depart from Marienplatz (Map pp82–3). New

Munich's (in)famous **Pub Crawl** (€12; ⏰ 8.30pm Tue–Sun) makes stops in five bars and clubs, includes free vodka shots and meets at the corner of Münzstrasse and Orlandostrasse. The **Beer Tour** (€16; ⏰ 2.30pm) takes a more, ahem, academic approach, but includes a free litre of beer and entry to the Pub Crawl…

Radius Tours (Map pp82–3; ☎ 5502 9374; www .radiusmunich.com, Hauptbahnhof, opposite track 32) Get the nitty gritty on city sights, history and architecture on these entertaining and informative English-language tours. Options include the two-hour **Munich Highlights Walk** (adult/student €10/9; ⏰ 10am daily Apr–mid-Oct, 10am Mon, Thu, Sat mid-Oct–Mar); the fascinating 2½-hour **Hitler & The Third Reich Tour** (adult/student €10/9; ⏰ 3pm Apr–mid-Oct, 11.30am Tue, Fri & Sun mid-Oct–Mar); and the three-hour **Prost! Beer & Food tour** (adult/student €22/20; ⏰ 6pm selected days). The latter is an introduction to Bavarian drinking culture but not a pub crawl. Tours leave from Marienplatz.

Hop-On Hop-Off Tour (Map pp82–3; ☎ 5490 7560; www .msr-muc.de; Schützenstrasse 9; adult/child €13/7; ⏰ every 20min) It's your basic predictably cheesy sightseeing bus tour but not a bad way for first timers to get oriented. The circuit starts outside the Karstadt department store at the Hauptbahnhof and then loops around the Pinakothek museums, the Residenz, Marienplatz and Karlsplatz in one hour, although you're free to get on and off as often as you like. An extended route taking in Schloss Nymphenburg and the Olympic Park costs €18/9 for one day or €23/11 for two days.

Mike's Bike Tours (Map pp82–3; ☎ 2554 3988, 0172-852 0660; www.mikesbiketours.com; 4hr/all-day tour €24/39; ⏰ mid-Mar–Oct) This outfit runs guided bike tours of the city from the Altes Rathaus on Marienplatz. The standard tour covers about 6.4km in four hours (with a 45-minute beer garden break); the extended tour goes for seven hours and covers 16km.

Munich Walk Tours (☎ 2423 1767; www.munich walktours.de) In addition to running an almost identical roster of tours (see website for times and prices) this outfit also rents bicycles (€15 per 24 hours) and offers internet access at Thomas-Wimmer-Ring 1 (Map pp82–3; €1 per 35 minutes).

FESTIVALS & EVENTS

Beer to opera, film to Christmas, Munich keeps a year-round calendar of fun goings-on. We've picked through the pile for our faves, but www.muenchen-tourist.de has the full run-down. Check individual websites for line-ups and ticket information. For Oktoberfest details, see p108.

January–March

Fasching (Carnival; www.munich-tourist.de) Pre-Lent celebration with concerts, fancy-dress balls and costume parades starting 7 January and ending on Ash Wednesday.

Starkbierzeit (Stout Season) Salvator, Optimator, Unimator, Maximator and Triumphator are not the names of gladiators but potent *doppelbock* brews poured only from 19 March to early April. Monks allegedly invented them to ease hunger pangs during Lent. The tapping of the first keg on 19 March at the Paulaner am Nockherberg (Map pp78–9; ☎ 459 9130; Hochstrasse 77) is even broadcast on TV.

April–June

Frühlingsfest (Spring Festival; www.muenchner-volks feste.de, in German; Theresienwiese) This miniature Oktoberfest kicks off the outdoor festival season with three weeks of beer tents and midway attractions starting around 20 April. Highlight: the giant flea market on the first Saturday.

Maidult (www.auerdult.de, in German; Mariahilfplatz) The first of three traditional 'dult' fairs held for nine days with crafts, carousels, drinking, toasted almonds and roast chicken. Local colour at its most authentic. Starts on the Saturday preceding 1 May.

Stustaculum (www.stustaculum.de, in German) Giant open-air festival in Europe's largest student quarter, the Studentenstadt Freimann in northern Schwabing brings four days of theatre, music and general merriment, usually in late May. Take U6 to Studentenstadt.

Filmfest München (Munich Film Festival; www.film fest-muenchen.de) Not as glamorous as Cannes or Venice, this flick festival presents intriguing and often high-calibre fare by newbies and masters from around the world in the last week of June.

Tollwood Festival (www.tollwood.de, in German; Olympiapark Süd) Major world-culture festival with concerts, theatre, circus, readings and other fun events held from late June to mid-July. Also in November.

July–September

Christopher Street Day (www.csd-munich.de, in German) Gay festival and parade culminating in a big street party on Marienplatz. Usually held on the second weekend in July.

Jakobidult See Maidult. The second 'dult' starts on the Saturday following 25 July.

Opernfestspiele (Opera Festival; www.muenchner -opern-festspiele.de) The Bavarian State Opera brings in top-notch talent from around the world for this month-long festival concluding on 31 July with Wagner's *Meistersinger von Nürnberg*.

Tanzwerkstatt Europa (www.jointadventures.net) Performances and workshops for modern dance, drama and readings held over 10 days in early August.

October–December

Oktoberfest (www.oktoberfest.de) Legendary beer-swilling party running from mid-September to the first Sunday in October. See p108 for the low-down.
Kirchweihdult See Maidult, opposite. Opens on the third Saturday in October.
Munich Marathon (www.muenchenmarathon.de, in German) More than 10,000 runners from around the world take to the streets in mid-October, finishing after nearly 42km at the Olympic Stadium.
Christkindlmarkt (www.christkindlmarkt.de, in German) Traditional Christmas market on Marienplatz and a visual stunner.

SLEEPING

Munich's excellent public transport system puts you within easy reach of everything. If you prefer being steps from the trophy sights, find a place in the Altstadt, although you'll pay a premium for the privilege. Choices are greater and rates more reasonable in Ludwigsvorstadt near the Hauptbahnhof and the Oktoberfest grounds. Party people will enjoy Schwabing, Maxvorstadt and the Gärtnerplatzviertel–Glockenbachviertel area. Lodging options are thinner on the ground in slower-paced residential neighbourhoods such as Haidhausen and Lehel, but are often the most charming and authentic.

Room rates skyrocket during Oktoberfest and other major events and trade shows. Book well ahead to avoid disappointment. The tourist office operates a free **room reservation service** (☎ 2339 6500; www.muenchen.de/hotels; ◷ 8am-7pm Mon-Fri, 9am-5pm Sat).

Altstadt
BUDGET
Hotel Alcron (Map pp82-3; ☎ 228 3511; Ledererstrasse 13; www.hotel-alcron.de, in German; s €60-70, d €80-95, tr €90-105; ✕ ▢) Within stumbling distance of the Hofbräuhaus, this quaint hotel has a dizzying spiral staircase leading up to traditionally furnished rooms that don't spoil you with space. Beds, though, are comfortable enough to sleep off any excesses.

MIDRANGE
Hotel Blauer Bock (Map pp82-3; ☎ 231 780; www .hotelblauerbock.de; Sebastiansplatz 9; s €64-72, d €100-120; ℗ ✕) A whiff of roasted almonds away from

the Viktualienmarkt, this no-nonsense hotel once provided shelter for Benedictine monks and has a location that's the envy of more prestigious abodes. It's comfy, familiar and spacious, but if you also want a bit of style request one of the recently updated rooms. Cheaper ones share bathrooms.

Hotel am Viktualienmarkt (Map pp82-3; ☎ 231 1090; www.hotel-am-viktualienmarkt.de; Utzschneiderstrasse 14; s/d/tr/f €48/98/115/135; ✕) Owners Elke and her daughter Stephanie run this good-value property with panache and a sunny attitude. A steep staircase (no lift) leads to rooms, the nicest of which have wooden floors and framed poster art. Prices drop 20% Friday to Sunday.

TOP END
Cortiina (Map pp82-3; ☎ 242 2490; www.cortiina.com; Ledererstrasse 8; s/d €146-196, d €186-206; ℗ ✕ ✕ ▢) Tiptoeing between hip and haute, this hotel scores best with trendy, design-minded travellers. The street-level lounge usually buzzes with cocktail-swilling belles and beaus, but all traces of hustle evaporate the moment you step into your minimalist, Feng Shui–inspired room. Breakfast is best enjoyed in the little garden.

Hotel Mandarin Oriental Munich (Map pp82-3; ☎ 200 980; www.mandarinoriental.com; Neuturmstrasse 1; s €325-440, d €375-490; ℗ ✕ ▢ ▣) This luxe neo-Renaissance villa woos presidents, diplomats, stars and the merely rich with top-notch rooms and off-the-charts service. Paul McCartney, Bill Clinton and Prince Charles have all spent the night. Service is polite almost to a fault, but breakfast will set you back an additional €19.

Schwabing & Maxvorstadt
Pension am Kaiserplatz (Map p81; ☎ 349 190; fax 339 316; Kaiserplatz 12, Schwabing; s with shared bathroom €31-47, d €49-59; ✕) This sweet and unhurried B&B in a *Jugendstil* building has just 10 rooms, lovingly decorated in a hodgepodge of styles, from modern to rococo. Nice touch: breakfast is delivered to your door by the congenial host herself.

Gästehaus Englischer Garten (Map p81; ☎ 383 9410; www.hotelenglischergarten.de; Liebergesellstrasse 8, Schwabing; s/d from €97/158, s/d with shared bathroom from €70/90; ℗) This bastion of warmth and hospitality occupies a 200-year-old ivy-clad mill whose idyllic terrace abuts the English Garden. It's quite popular despite the fact that six of the 12 rooms must share one toilet per floor, plus one full bathroom in the basement (robes are provided).

Hotel Hauser an der Universität (Map p81; ☎ 286 6750; www.hotel-hauser.de; Schellingstrasse 11, Maxvorstadt; s €80-135, d €105-190, tr €125-230; **P** ✖) This student-quarter property delivers a lot more comfort than first meets the eye. Each of the 34 updated rooms come with air-con, special noise-proof windows and crisply blonde furniture. Sightseeing fatigue quickly fades in the impeccable sauna and steam room.

Hotel Marienbad (Map pp82-3; ☎ 595 585; www.hotelmarienbad.de; Barer Strasse 11, Maxvorstadt; s €80-100, d €110-135; **P**) Back in the 19th century, Wagner, Puccini and Rilke shacked up in what once ranked among Munich's finest hotels. Still friendly and well maintained, it now flaunts an endearing alchemy of styles, from playful Art Nouveau to floral country Bavarian to campy 1960s utilitarian. Amenities, fortunately, are of more recent vintage.

Cosmopolitan Hotel (Map p81; ☎ 383 810; www.cosmopolitan-hotel.de; Hohenzollernstrasse 5, Schwabing; s €115-170, d €125-180; **P**) This heart-of-Schwabing property focuses on delivering amenities and services people actually want and need. Rooms have balconies and a crisp contemporary look thanks to chic Ligne Roset furniture; those in the back wing are better for light sleepers. Breakfasts are lavish.

La Maison (Map p81; ☎ 3303 5550; www.hotel-la-maison.com; Occamstrasse 24; s/d €140/175; **P** ✖ ✖ 🖳) It didn't take long for this sassy designer hotel to score points with chic, style-minded international travellers. The décor is cutting edge but with a sensuous vibe stemming from rich materials like heated oak floors, extravagant design touches and a love for shades of purple. The restaurant gets high marks, and wi-fi is free.

Nymphenburg, Neuhausen & Olympiapark

Hotel Laimer Hof (Map p80; ☎ 178 0380; www.laimerhof.de; Laimer Strasse 40; s €70-155, d €90-175; **P** ✖) Run by a lovely couple, this charismatic respite from the big-city bustle has a relaxed country feel and is only a five-minute walk from Schloss Nymphenburg. No two of the 23 rooms are alike, but all get a timeless elegance from antique furniture, oriental carpets and cosy beds.

Ludwigsvorstadt & Westend
BUDGET

Wombat's City Hostel (Map pp82-3; ☎ 5998 9180; www.wombats-hostels.com; Senefelderstrasse 1; dm €12-24, s/d

€68; **P** 🖳) This hostel-hotel combo gets top marks for style, comfort and location. You'll sleep well in pine beds with real mattresses (free linen) and reading lamps in doubles and dorms with private bathrooms. A welcome drink is thrown in at the in-house bar but optional breakfast is an extra €4.

our pick Meininger City Hostels & Hotel (Map pp82-3; ☎ 030-6663 6100; www.meininger-hostels.de; Landsbergerstrasse 20; dm/s/d from €16.50/43/62; **P** ✖ 🖳) Run with smiles and aplomb, this hotel-hostel scores points with wallet-watching global nomads for three reasons: location, amenities and service. Just west of the Hauptbahnhof, it has 380 beds in 95 cheerful rooms ranging in size from singles to 12-bed dorms, each with clean private shower and toilet. Rates include a generous buffet breakfast, security is tops and the bar is great for making friends. Best of all: it's right across from the Augustiner brewery, which operates one of the city's best beer halls, the Augustiner Bräustuben (p119).

Other budget abodes:

Hotel Eder (Map pp82-3; ☎ 554 660; www.hotel-eder.de; Zweigstrasse 8; s €45-95, d €60-150, tr €87-180, q €97-200; ✖) Expect local colour galore at this traditional, rustic hotel with unevenly sized rooms, including some for families.

Pension Westfalia (Map pp82-3; ☎ 530 377; www.pension-westfalia.de; Mozartstrasse 23; s €50-70, d €70-95, s/d shared bathroom from €37/50; ✖) Near the Oktoberfest meadow, this cosy, family-run *Pension* has comfy, modern rooms reached by a lift.

Hotel Jedermann (off Map pp82-3; ☎ 543 240; www.hotel-jedermann.de; Bayerstrasse 95; s €50-135, d €70-185; **P** ✖ ✖ 🖳) Friendly and progressive family hotel with attractive black-and-blonde furniture and modern bathrooms.

MIDRANGE

Hotel Uhland (Map pp82-3; ☎ 543 350; www.hotel-uhland.de; Uhlandstrasse 1; s €75-140, d €85-185; **P** ✖ 🖳) The Uhland is an enduring favourite with regulars who expect their hotel to feel like a home away from home. Three generations of family members are constantly finding ways to improve their guests' experience, be it with wi-fi, bathroom phones, ice cubes, bike rentals or mix-your-own breakfast muesli.

Belle Blue Hotel Garni (Map pp82-3; ☎ 550 6260; www.hotel-belleblue.com; Schillerstrasse 21; s €80-220, d €90-250; **P** ✖ ✖ 🖳) This chic little hotel employs a tried-and-true design formula to great effect. Snazzy bath fixtures, tailor-made furniture and walls splashed in various hues of blue – cool cobalt to spunky turquoise to soft lavender – compensate for the comparatively snug size of the rooms. Other perks include a gargantuan breakfast buffet and kind hosts.

Hotel-Pension Mariandl (Map pp82-3; ☎ 534 108; www.hotelmariandl.com; Goethestrasse 51; s €60-90, d €95-145) If you like quirkiness and history, you'll find both aplenty in this rambling neo-Gothic mansion. It's an utterly charming place where rooms convincingly capture the *Jugendstil* period with hand-selected antiques and ornamented ceilings. Breakfast is served until 4pm in the Vienna-style downstairs café, which also has live music nightly.

Hotel Hotelissimo Haberstock (Map pp82-3; ☎ 557 855; www.hotelissimo.com; Schillerstrasse 4; s €70-200, d €100-200; ✕) The cheery décor at this value-for-money pick reflects the vision of the owners, a husband-and-wife team with a knack for colour, fabrics and design. Easy-on-the-eye gold, brown and cream tones dominate the good-sized rooms on the lower floors, while upper ones radiate a bolder, Mediterranean palette.

Alpen Hotel (Map pp82-3; ☎ 559 330; www.alpenhotel-muenchen.de, in German; Adolf-Kolping-Strasse 14; s/d from €110/140; ✕ ▣) Keeping up with the times has been a credo of the Bauer family for four generations. The latest makeover has resulted in a winsome blend of rustic and modern design with a bevy of amenities. In fine weather, sip your morning coffee in the snug, flower-filled garden, while the clubby fireplace salon is a cosy retreat on rainy afternoons.

Schiller 5 (Map pp82-3; ☎ 515 040; www.schiller5.com; Schillerstrasse 5; s €117-177, d €140-200, ste €250-300, breakfast €14; ▣ ✕ ✕) You won't miss many comforts of home in these breezy boarding house units where a kitchenette and sound system are as much a part of the inventory as the direct-dial phone with voicemail, the extra-large beds and free wi-fi. Rates drop for stays of more than five days.

TOP END

Sofitel Munich Bayerpost (Map pp82-3; ☎ 599 480; www.sofitel.com; Bayerstrasse 12; s €160-400, d €185-420; ▣ ✕ ✕ ▣ ▣) The restored Renaissance façade of a former post office hides this high-concept jewel that wraps all that's great about Munich – history, innovation, elegance, the art of living – into one neat and appealing package. Be sure to make time for the luxurious spa whose grotto-like pool juts into the atrium lobby lidded by a tinted glass roof.

ourpick **anna hotel** (Map pp82-3; ☎ 599 940; www.geisel-privathotels.de; Schützenstrasse 1; s €170-215, d €190-235; ✕ ✕ ▣) Urban sophisticates love this designer den where you can retire to rooms dressed in sensuous Donghia furniture and regal colours, or others with a more minimalist feel tempered by teakwood, marble and mosaics. The swanky restaurant-bar is a 24/7 beehive of activity.

Gärtnerplatzviertel & Glockenbachviertel

BUDGET & MIDRANGE

Pension Gärtnerplatz (Map pp82-3; ☎ 202 5170; www.pension-gaertnerplatztheater.de; Klenzestrasse 45; s/d from €70/95; ▣) Escape the tourist rabble, or reality altogether, in this eccentric establishment where rooms are a stylish interpretation of Alpine pomp. The one named 'Sisi' will have you sleeping in a canopy bed guarded by a giant porcelain mastiff. Quality bedding and free wi-fi are nice touches.

Pension Eulenspiegel (Map pp82-3; ☎ 266 678; www.pensioneulenspiegel.de; Müllerstrasse 43a; s €50-70, d €80-100; ▣ ✕) Completely nonsmoking, this little guesthouse has undergone a major face-lift and now features rooms with sparkling wooden floors, phones and showers (toilets are down the hall). Wi-fi is free.

Deutsche Eiche (Map pp82-3; ☎ 231 1660; www.deutsche-eiche.com; Reichenbachstrasse 13; s €70-90, d €95-245; ▣ ✕) If the walls of this legendary restaurant-hotel combo could talk, the stories would make you laugh, blush, cry and cringe. It's traditionally been a gay outpost but style junkies of all sexual persuasions should enjoy the plushly designed rooms. Older rooms downstairs are cheaper. Also on the premises: a gay sauna.

Hotel Olympic (Map pp82-3; ☎ 231 890; www.hotel-olympic.de; Hans-Sachs-Strasse 4; s €90-150, d €140-180; ▣ ✕ ✕) If you're into designer décor, Frette linens and chocolate on your pillow, go elsewhere. But if you like a hip location, public areas doubling as an art gallery and spacious rooms, give this one a try. Rooms facing the inner courtyard are quieter.

TOP END

Hotel Advokat (Map pp82-3; ☎ 216 310; www.hotel-advokat.de; Baaderstrasse 1; s €120-140, d €140-160; ▣ ✕) At Munich's first boutique hotel, minimalist '60s décor meets maximum service. Rooms won't fit a tonne of luggage but are nicely dressed in creamy hues, tactile fabrics and subtle lighting. Guests rave about the breakfast; a smorgasbord of fresh fruit, deli salads, smoked salmon and organic cheeses.

Hotel Admiral (Map pp82-3; ☎ 216 350; www .hotel-admiral.de; Kohlstrasse 9; s €120-270, d €150-300; Ⓟ ✗) Checking into this hotel feels a bit like arriving at your rich uncle's manor in the English countryside. Fine woven tapestries, oil paintings and richly polished woods smoothly blend into a refined atmosphere. Start days with breakfast in the rose garden, then wind down with free port in the bar before retiring to mostly good-sized rooms.

Lehel

Hotel Splendid-Dollmann (Map p85; ☎ 238 080; www .hotel-splendid-dollmann.de; Thierschstrasse 49; s €133-163, d €175-215; ✗) This small but posh player delivers old-world charm by the bucket and is sure to delight romantics. The mood is set at check-in where fresh orchids, classical music and friendly staff welcome you. Retire to antique-furnished rooms, the idyllic terraced garden or the regally furnished lounge. Rooms in front must deal with tram noise.

Hotel Opéra (Map p85; ☎ 210 4940; www.hotel-opera .de; St-Anna-Strasse 10; s €185-235, d €210-265; ✗ 💻) Like the gates to heaven, a white double door opens at the touch of a tiny brass button. Beyond awaits a posh and petite cocoon of quiet sophistication with peaches-and-cream marble floors, a chandelier scavenged from the Vatican and uniquely decorated rooms. In summer, the serene arcaded courtyard is perfect for alfresco breakfast, served à la carte.

Haidhausen

Hotel Ritzi (Map p85; ☎ 419 5030; www.hotel-ritzi .de; Maria-Theresia-Strasse 2a; s/d from €100/155) Rooms are like fantasies transporting you to the Caribbean, Africa, Morocco and other exotic lands at this charming art hotel next to a little park perfect for a stress-busting jog. All 25 are outfitted with modern gadgets and amenities, including wi-fi. The Art Deco bar-lounge is a great launch pad for a night on the town.

Hotel am Nockherberg (Map pp78-9; ☎ 623 0010; www.nockherberg.de; Nockherstrasse 38a; s €87-110, d €110-125; Ⓟ ✗) This charming base of operation south of the Isar puts you close to the Deutsches Museum, the bar- and restaurant-filled Gärtnerplatzviertel and the Gasteig cultural centre. The room décor is pleasing in a generic kind of way but all major mod-cons,

including free wi-fi, are accounted for, and there's a sauna to boot.

Long-Term Rentals

If you're staying in Munich for a week or longer, it might work out cheaper to rent a room, flat or apartment. Rooms start at €180 per week and €350 per month, while studio flats will set you back about €300 per week and €600 per month, all excluding the 25% commission and 19% VAT. Places to try:

Mitwohnzentrale – Mr Lodge (Map p81; ☎ 340 8230; www.mrlodge.de; Barer Strasse 32)

Statthotel (☎ 08709-926 00; www.statthotel.de)

EATING

Munich has Bavaria's most exciting cuisine scene. Sure, plenty of eating still goes on in traditional beer halls and restaurants where the menu rarely ventures beyond the roast pork and sausage routine. But there's also lots of innovation in Munich kitchens, where the best dishes make use of fresh regional, seasonal and organic ingredients. The most adventurous chefs flirt with foreign influences, be they Middle Eastern spices, Asian cooking techniques or Mediterranean flavour pairings. There's something for every palate, and generally, for every wallet. Dinner reservations are always a good idea, even in casual places.

Restaurants
ALTSTADT

Bratwurstherzl (Map pp82-3; ☎ 295 113; Dreifaltigkeitsplatz 1; mains €6-10; ⊗ 10am-11pm) Cosy panelling and an ancient vaulted brick ceiling set the tone of this Old Munich chow house with a Franconian focus, awarded an *Umweltsiegel* (ecoseal) by the Bavarian government. Home-made organic sausages are grilled to perfection on an open beechwood fire, served on heart-shaped tin plates and best enjoyed with a cold beer straight from the wooden keg.

Yum2Take (Map pp82-3; ☎ 6606 3613; Sebastiansplatz 8; mains €7-9; ⊗ 11am-11pm Mon-Sat, 3-11pm Sun) Thai gets a contemporary, healthy twist (all meats are organic) at this stylish lunchtime favourite of cubicle slaves and sales clerks. Luscious dishes like coconut-based *tom kha* soup, *pad thai* or a fragrant curry perfectly capture the mood of Siam. Skip the salads – the sickly sweet dressing needs fine-tuning.

Weisses Brauhaus (Map pp82-3; ☎ 299 875; Tal 7; mains €7-15; ⊗ 8am-midnight) Graduates of the sausage-

and-pork-knuckle school of Bavarian cooking can mount their own *Survivor* challenge at this uberauthentic Munich pub, awarded an ecoseal for ecofriendly management. Sour pork kidney, baked udder and fried cow's head anyone? Wash it down with the Schneider Weisse house *hefeweizen*.

Riva (Map pp82-3; ☎ 220 240; Tal 44, Altstadt; mains €7-15; ☻ 8am-1am) Watch the pizza acrobats toss and twirl the dough into submission before tickling it with wood fire just long enough to produce perfectly crispy thin crusts. For toppings you can go classic with tomato, basil and mozzarella or adventurous with veal slices, tuna creme and capers. Also has a branch in Schwabing (p116).

Prinz Myschkin (Map pp82-3; ☎ 265 596; www .prinzmyschkin.com; Hackenstrasse 2; mains €7-17; ☻ 11am-12.30am; Ⓥ) Herbivore or meathead, your tastebuds will be doing somersaults at what many hail as Munich's best vegetarian restaurant. The high-ceilinged hall can get noisy but the menu is an intriguing mosaic of international flavours with special kudos going to the *crespelle al forno* (spinach-ricotta filled crepes).

Hundskugel (Map pp82-3; ☎ 264 272; Hotterstrasse 18; mains €8-20; ☻ 10.30am-midnight) Munich's oldest tavern, founded in 1440, has only 40 seats and is so intimate that it feels like sitting inside a cutesy doll house. The food's honest-to-goodness Bavarian home cooking, and the roast suckling pig with dark beer sauce (€14.50) is the undisputed speciality.

Lamm's (Map pp82-3; ☎ 359 1963; Sendlinger-Tor-Platz 11; mains €9-18; ☻ 24hr) It's old school, the music is terrible and the service challenged, but after a night of partying, a pile of Lamm's spare ribs is simply the perfect hangover antidote. On weekdays, tourists invade for the €5 lunches (served until 5pm). Awarded an ecoseal from the Bavarian government for minimising packaging, using local and seasonal produce and recycling.

Conviva (Map pp82-3; ☎ 2333 6977; Hildegardstrasse 1; 3-course lunch €8-10, dinner mains €10-15; ☻ 11am-1am Mon-Sat Oct-Mar, 5pm-1am Sat & Sun Apr-Sep; Ⓥ) Great food in a theatre restaurant? The Conviva folks show it can be done. Clever but unfussy dishes like carrot-lime-ginger soup, goat cheese flan or rabbit with porcini are prepared day by day by a kitchen staff that integrates people with learning disabilities.

Zerwirk (Map pp82-3; ☎ 2323 9191; Ledererstrasse 3; mains €10-18; ☻ 11am-1am Mon-Sat, 6pm-1am Sun; Ⓥ) A vegan haven inside an 800-year-old former meat factory? Kind of a sick twist, but who cares when the chef is a genius at coaxing flavour out of even the humblest vegetable. Swiss chard roulade or spinach bulgur strudel taste delicious in the airy, minimalist dining room. Deli dabblers enjoy healthy soups or salads in the organic food store in the basement.

SCHWABING & MAXVORSTADT

Café an der Uni (Map p81; ☎ 2898 6600; Ludwigstrasse 24, Maxvorstadt; snacks from €3.50, mains €8-11; ☻ 8am-2am; Ⓥ) Anytime is a good time to be at charismatic CADU. Enjoy breakfast (served until a hangover-friendly 11.30pm!), a cuppa Java or a Helles in the lovely garden hidden by a wall from busy Ludwigstrasse.

Bar Tapas (Map p81; ☎ 390 919; Amalienstrasse 97, Maxvorstadt; tapas €3.90 each; ☻ 4pm-1am; Ⓥ) A phalanx of 30 tapas – *boquerones* (anchovies) to octopus salad to garlic chicken – reports to duty behind glass along the bar of this convivial Iberian outpost. Write down the numbers, then sit back with a jug of sangria and wait for your tasty morsels to arrive.

Il Mulino (Map p81; ☎ 523 3335; Görresstrasse 1, Schwabing; mains €5-10; ☻ 10am-1am; Ⓥ) It's got a new owner but the food is as sharp as ever at this neighbourhood classic that's been feeding Italophiles for three decades. All the expected pastas and pizzas are accounted for, although the daily specials will likely tickle the palate of more curious eaters.

Casa de Tapas (Map p81; ☎ 2731 2288; Bauerstrasse 2, Schwabing; tapas €2.50-6, mains €9.50-15; ☻ 4pm-1am; Ⓥ) The painted ceiling and rustic elegance of this buzzy bodega transport you straight to the Iberian Peninsula. There's a fine menu of meat and fish mains, but it's also a top spot for such tapas as Serrano ham, marinated squid, garlic prawns and other tastebud ticklers.

Schmock (Map p81; ☎ 5235 0535; Augustenstrasse 52, Schwabing; mains €14-22; ☻ 6pm-1am; Ⓥ) Kosher

---

TOP FIVE RESTAURANTS FOR VEGETARIANS

- **Prinz Myschkin** (left)
- **Zewirk** (left)
- **Maoz** (p117)
- **Kao Kao** (p116)
- **Café an der Uni** (above)

food gets a gourmet twist at this elegant restaurant with its stucco ornamented ceiling, fresh flowers and complexion-friendly Art Nouveau lamps. The goat cheese in filo is a great overture for such flavour symphonies as venison with chestnut puree.

Riva Bar (Map p81; ☎ 309-051 808; Feilitzschstrasse 4; mains €7-15; ⏱ 11.30am-1am) The sexier sister pizzeria of the original Altstadt branch (p115).

NEUHAUSEN

Ruffini (Map p80; ☎ 161 160; Orffstrasse 22; meals €7-10; ⏱ 10am-midnight Tue-Sun; **V**) This been-there-forever café is a fun place to be no matter where the hands of the clock are. On sunny days, the self-service rooftop terrace gets a steady stream of tattooed scenesters, hip families and wallet-watching students. Organic ingredients are used, wherever possible.

Zapata (Map p80; ☎ 166 5822; Wilderich-Lang-Strasse 4; mains €8-18; ⏱ 5pm-1am) It's always fiesta time at Munich's most authentic Mexican cantina where one stiff margarita may be all it takes to drown your sorrows. To stay stable, load up on sizzling fajitas, ginormous burritos and other delicious south-of-the-border staples.

Zauberberg (Map p80; ☎ 1899 9178; Hedwigstrasse 14; lunch €7-9; dinner menu 3/4/5 courses €38/48/55, with wine €52/65/72; ⏱ noon-2am Tue-Thu, 7pm-1am daily; ✗) Far off the tourist track, this 40-seat locals' favourite will put your tummy into a state of contentment with its elegant, well-composed international creations. Single plates are available but in order to truly sample the chef's talents, you should order a multicourse menu.

WESTEND & LUDWIGSVORSTADT

Müller & Söhne (Map pp82-3; ☎ 4523 7867; Kazmairstrasse 28, Westend; mains €6-12; ⏱ 9am-11pm Mon-Fri, 9am-6pm Sat; **V**) In a former bakery, this sweet, unhurried café fits as comfortably as a well-worn shoe. Everyone from young mothers to office folks and local artists gathers behind the big windows for breakfast, strong Java or tasty, Italian-flavoured sustenance.

Marais (Map pp82-3; ☎ 5009 4552; Parkstrasse 2, Westend; dishes €4-9; ⏱ 8am-8pm; **V**) Conversation never seem to flag at this dusty haberdasher turned ultracosy coffeehouse. The old shelves, glass cases and creaky cash register from the 1930s are still there and everything – from buttons to bio-cosmetics and the antique chair you're sitting on – is for sale.

Stragula (Map pp78-9; ☎ 507 743; Bergmannstrasse 66, Westend; mains €7-12; ⏱ 11.30am-2.30pm & 5.30pm-1am Mon-Thu, 6pm-1am Fri-Sun) This Westend institution has been feeding friendly locals for nearly a quarter-century. It maintains a relaxed, living-room–like feel, holds regular literary readings, and serves Bavarian and Italian food.

Kao Kao (Map pp82-3; ☎ 505 400; Tulbeckstrasse 9, Westend; mains €12-19; ⏱ noon-2pm Mon-Thu, 5pm-1am daily; **V**) A tantalising aroma of lemongrass, curry and coconut will perk up even the most jaded proboscis at this top Thai parlour with zero kitsch factor. The menu hopscotches from classic *pad thai* to red shrimp curry with lychees and Barbary duck in whisky sauce, usually with palate-pleasing results. The lunch buffet is a steal at €7.50.

La Vecchia Masseria (Map pp82-3; ☎ 550 9090; Mathildenstrasse 3, Ludwigsvorstadt; mains €6-15; ⏱ 11.30am-midnight) The ambience here is indelibly Italian: loud, good value but somehow still romantic. Earthy wood tables, antique tin buckets, baskets and clothing irons conjure up the ambience of a Tuscan farmhouse. The chef comes out to greet customers in his trademark straw hat.

GÄRTNERPLATZVIERTEL & GLOCKENBACHVIERTEL

our pick Fraunhofer (Map pp82-3; ☎ 266 460; Fraunhoferstrasse 9, Gärtnerplatzviertel; mains €5-14; ⏱ 4.30pm-1am) This classic brewpub brings tradition into the 21st century. The olde-worlde atmosphere (mounted animal heads and a portrait of Ludwig II) contrasts with the clued-in, intergenerational crowd and a menu that offers progressive takes on classical fare. The tiny theatre at the back has some great shows and was among the venues that pioneered a modern style of *Volksmusik* (folk music) back in the '70s and '80s.

Sushi + Soul (Map pp82-3; ☎ 201 0992; Klenzestrasse 71, Glockenbachviertel; mains €8-18; ⏱ 6pm-1am) The sushi is good, other dishes can be hit or miss but the scene is fun anyway with hipsters washing down piscine morsels with creative cocktails (Tokyopolitan anyone?) while getting showered with Japanese pop. A flirty *Sex & the City* vibe rules, especially during happy hour (6pm to 8pm and after 11pm) when drinks are half-price.

Joe Peña's (Map pp82-3; ☎ 226 463; Buttermelcherstrasse 17, Gärtnerplatzviertel; mains €10-17; ⏱ 5pm-1am) This festive cantina-style restaurant is regarded as Munich's best Tex-Mex place and can get very crowded, especially during happy hour (5pm to 8pm). The food is tasty and as authentic as you'd expect this side of the Atlantic.

La Bouche (Map pp82-3; ☎ 265 626; Jahnstrasse 30, enter on Westermühlstrasse, Glockenbachviertel; mains €12.50-17.50; ☺ noon-3pm Mon-Fri, 6-10pm Mon-Sat) It's good vibes all around at this French-inspired port of call where tables are squished as tight as lovers and the accent is on imaginative but gimmick-free fare. We loved the truffle ravioli. By the way, it's much bigger than first meets the eye – there's a second room at the back.

Also recommended:

MC Müller (Map pp82-3; ☎ 1891 0039; cnr Müllerstrasse & Fraunhoferstrasse, Gärtnerplatzviertel; burger from €5; ☺ 6pm-2am Sun-Wed, 6pm-4am Thu-Sat) Sixties looks and triple duty as bar, DJ lounge and burger joint until the wee hours.

Sevenfish (Map pp82-3; ☎ 2300 0219; Gärtnerplatz 6; mains lunch €8.50-13.50, dinner €14-23, menu €40; ☺ 10am-1am) Great and innovative fish dishes, albeit served with a side of trendy aloofness. Get real!

LEHEL & HAIDHAUSEN

Nage & Sauge (Map p85; ☎ 298 803; Mariannenstrasse 2; mains €7.50-13; ☺ 5.15pm-1am) Candles, Chianti and a table for two are the hallmarks of a romantic night out. Even if your date doesn't make you swoon, the delicious Italian food will ensure an unforgettable evening. The signature dish is Ente Elvis, starring duck flambéed with cassis (black current liqueur).

Wirtshaus in der Au (Map p85; ☎ 448 1400; Lilienstrasse 51; mains €9-18; ☺ 5pm-1am Mon-Fri, 10am-1am Sat & Sun) A traditional Bavarian restaurant with a solid 21st-century vibe – how refreshing is that? Dumplings are the speciality at this top pick near the Deutsches Museum (try the trio with cheese, red beet and spinach variations) but other favourites, updated of course, also keep regulars coming back. Beer garden in summer, crackling fireplace in winter.

No MiYa (Map p85; ☎ 448 4095; Wörthstrasse 7; à la carte €1.20-7.60, platters €15-27; ☺ 6pm-1am) Antlers and sushi? Weissbier and *yakitori* (grilled chicken on skewers)? This Bavarian-Japanese tavern definitely takes fusion to new heights. If the packed tables are any indication, Ferdinand Schuster's concept is a winner, and not only with the fickle in-crowd.

Paros (Map p85; ☎ 470 2995; Kirchenstrasse 21; mains €8-18; ☺ 5pm-1am) You'll kick up your heels like Zorba himself after filling your tummy with Greek soul food at this simple yet sophisticated nosh spot. The menu features all the usual suspects (gyros, moussaka, *avgolemono* soup) but daily specials like veal cutlet grilled on lava rock are worth exploring as well. *Opa!*

Showroom (Map p85; ☎ 444 290; Lilienstrasse 6; mains €17-25, menu €55; ☺ 5pm-1am Mon-Sat) Andreas Schweiger's crossover creations strike just the right balance between adventure and comfort, which is why his restaurant is among the hottest in town. Foie gras spiced with *lebkuchen* or quail and shrimp with pear-lentil salad pack plenty of substance to please even demanding palates.

Nektar (Map p85; ☎ 4591 1311; Stubenvollstrasse 1; dinner menu €49; ☺ 7pm-2am Tue-Sun) With its dramatic mood-lighting, drag queen performers and sexy crowd, this big-city spot delivers so much eye candy, it's hard to focus on the flavour-intense fusion food. Eating is done Roman style: lying down (but without the buckets…). Wear nice socks.

Also recommended:

L'Angolo della Pizza (Map p85; ☎ 448 8979; Breisacher Strasse 30; pizza €3-10; ☺ 11.30am-2pm & 5.30pm-12.30am Mon-Fri & Sun, 4pm-12.30am Sat) Modern, uncluttered pizzeria with delicious, thin-crust pies plus daily blackboard specials.

Quick Eats

Bergwolf (Map pp82-3; ☎ 2325 9858; Fraunhoferstrasse 17, Glockenbachviertel; sausage €2.80; ☺ noon-2am Mon-Thu, noon-4am Fri & Sat, noon-10pm Sun, closed 3-6pm Sun-Fri) At this favourite pit stop for night owls, the poison of choice is *Currywurst*, a sliced spicy sausage provocatively dressed in a curried ketchup and best paired with a pile of steamy fries. Hangover prevention at its finest.

Eiscafé Sarcletti (Map p80; ☎ 155 314; Nymphenburger Strasse 155, Neuhausen; ☺ 8.30am-11pm) Addicts brave rock-star-worthy lines to get their gelato fix at this Munich institution that has been working its frozen magic since 1879. Choose from more than 50 mouthwatering flavours, from not-so-plain vanilla to honey-yogurt or caramel.

Maoz (Map pp82-3; ☎ Lueg Ins Land 1, Altstadt; sandwich €2.50-3.50; ☺ 10am-10pm; Ⓥ) One bite and you're hooked by Maoz' crunchy falafels tucked into a wholemeal or white pita pocket. Get as creative as you want when loading up on crisp salads and tasty sauces at the DIY bar. A healthy, meat-free snack.

Pommes Boutique (Map p81; ☎ 9547 3312; Amalienstrasse 46, Maxvorstadt; fries €2.20; ☺ 10am-10pm Mon-Sat, noon-8pm Sun) At Bergwolf's classier

MUNICH

TOP FIVE LATE-NIGHT NOSH SPOTS

▪ **Alter Simpl** (p120)
▪ **Bergwolf** (p117)
▪ **Eat the Rich** (p120)
▪ **Lamm's** (p114)
▪ **MC Müller** (p117)

cousin the walls are mod green and purple, the sausage gourmet and the fries organic. Pair them with 20 different dips, most of them fingerlickin' delish.

Dönertier (Map pp82-3; Sendlinger Strasse 31; döner €3.60-4.20; 🕑 10.30am-8.30pm Mon-Fri, 11am-8pm Sat) This spacey *döner* (doner kebab) bar takes the humble snack to new heights. Go classic or try the 'deluxe' version with *rucola* (rocket) and mozzarella, and definitely top it off with the refreshing mango yogurt.

Mama's Kebap Haus (Map p81; ☎ 392 642; Feilitzschstrasse 7, Schwabing; döner €3.50, mains around €10; 🕑 11am-1am) A döner institution popular with night owls.

Self-Catering

The dominant supermarket chains are Aldi, Penny, Tengelmann, Lidl and Plus, with multiple branches scattered throughout the city. For a better, more upscale (and pricier) selection, head to the supermarket in the basement of the **Kaufhof** (Map pp82-3; ☎ 512 50; Karlsplatz 21-24, Altstadt) department store or the **Viktualienmarkt** (p77). Deep-pocketed gourmets have a couple of venerable destinations to look forward to: **Dallmayr** (Map pp82-3; ☎ 213 50; Dienerstrasse 14, Altstadt; 🕑 9.30am-7pm Mon-Sat) is famous for its coffee but has so much more, including cheeses, ham, truffles, wine, caviar and exotic foods from every corner of the earth. **Käfer** (Map p85; ☎ 416 8255; Prinzregentenstrasse 73, Haidhausen; 🕑 9.30am-8pm Mon-Fri, 8.30am-4pm Sat) is just as good.

For organic anything, steer towards **Basic Bio** (🕑 8am-8pm; **V**) Altstadt (Map pp82-3; ☎ 242 0890; Westenriederstrasse 35); Schwabing (Map p81; ☎ 323 8470; Schleissheimer Strasse 158) or Zerwirk (p114).

Need a bottle of wine, dog food or toilet paper at 5am in the morning? You'll find all of this and then some at **Kiosk Reichenbachbrücke** (Map pp82-3; ☎ 201 5297; Fraunhoferstrasse 46, Gärtnerplatzviertel; 🕑 24hr), a kiosk with cult status among clued-in Münchners.

DRINKING

Munich is a great place for boozers. Raucous beer halls, snazzy hotel lounges, chestnut-canopied beer gardens, hipster DJ bars, designer cocktail temples – the variety is so huge that finding a party pen to match your mood is not exactly a tall order. Generally speaking, student-flavoured places abound in Maxvorstadt and Schwabing, while traditional beer halls and taverns cluster in the Altstadt; Haidhausen goes for trendy types and the Gärtnerplatzviertel and Glockenbachviertel is a haven for gays and hipsters.

No matter where you are, you won't be far from an enticing café to get a Java-infused pick-me-up. Many also serve light fare and delicious cakes (often home-made) and are great places to linger, chat, write postcards or simply watch people on parade. See the boxed text (opposite) and the reviews under Bars & Cafés (opposite) for suggestions.

Beer Halls & Gardens

Bavaria's brews are best sampled in a venerable old *Bierkeller* (beer hall) and *Biergarten* (beer garden). People come here primarily to drink, and although food may be served, it is generally an afterthought. In beer gardens you are usually allowed to bring your own picnic as long as you sit at tables without tablecloths and order something to drink. Sometimes there's a resident brass band showering you with oompah music. And don't even think about sitting at a *Stammtisch*, a table reserved for regulars (look for a brass plaque, a shingle or some other sign)!

Beer costs €6 to €7.50 per litre. A deposit of €2 or so may be charged for the glass.

ALTSTADT

Viktualienmarkt (Map pp82-3; ☎ 297 545; Viktualienmarkt 6; 🕑 9am-10pm) After a day of sightseeing or shopping stock up on tasty nibbles at the Viktualienmarkt, then lug your loot a few steps further to this chestnut-shaded beer garden, a Munich institution since 1807. The breweries take turns serving here, so you never know what's on tap.

Braunauer Hof (Map pp82-3; ☎ 223 613; Frauenstrasse 42; 🕑 9am-midnight Mon-Sat) Near the Isartor, this pleasingly twisted beer garden is centred on a snug courtyard. There's a hedge maze, a fresco with a bizarre bunch of historical figures and a golden bull that's illuminated at night.

Hofbräuhaus (Map pp82-3; ☎ 221 676; Am Platzl 9)
Definitely the mecca of beer halls. We can't
stop you from making the pilgrimage but we
bet that after witnessing the drunken shenani-
gans, you'll agree that there are more civilised
imbibing options in town. The beer garden
offers some sensory relief.

SCHWABING
Chinesischer Turm (Map p81; ☎ 383 8730; Englischer
Garten 3) This one's hard to ignore because of
its English Garden location and pedigree as
Munich's oldest beer garden (since 1791).
Tourists and trendoids clump around the
wooden pagoda, showered by the strained
sounds of possibly the world's drunkest
oompah band.

Hirschau (Map p81; ☎ 322 1080; Gysslingstrasse 15)
This beer garden for 1700 people has live
jazz almost daily in summer, and Spaten and
Franziskaner on tap. Kids get their kicks on
the playground and adjacent minigolf course.
Take the U6 to Dietlindenstrasse, then it's a
15-minute walk.

Seehaus (Map p81; ☎ 381 6130; Kleinhesselohe 3)
A drinks station for the posh set, right on
the Kleinhesseloher See, with dreamy views
of the lake and the park. Paulaner is the
featured brew.

NEUHAUSEN & NYMPHENBURG
Hirschgarten (Map p80; ☎ 172 591; Hirschgartenallee
1, Nymphenburg; ☯ 9am-midnight) The 'Everest' of
Munich gardens can accommodate up to 8000
Augustiner lovers, but still manages to feel
airy and uncluttered. It's in a lovely spot in
a former royal hunting preserve and rubs up
against a deer enclosure and a carousel. Steer
here after visiting Schloss Nymphenburg – it's
only a short walk south of the palace.

Augustiner Keller (off Map pp82-3; ☎ 594 393;
Arnulfstrasse 52, Neuhausen; ☯ 10am-midnight) A bell
chimes every time a new keg is tapped and at
this handsome leafy beer garden with space

for 5000 thirsty revellers it rarely stops. The
ancient chestnuts are thick enough to seek refuge under when it rains, or else lug your mug
to the actual beer cellar. Small playground.

WESTEND
our pick **Augustiner Bräustuben** (Map pp82-3; ☎ 507
047; Landsberger Strasse 19, Westend; ☯ 10am-midnight)
Depending on the wind, an aroma of hops
envelops you as you approach this ultra-
authentic beer hall inside the actual Augustiner
brewery, popular with the brewmeisters themselves (there's an entire table reserved just
for them). The Bavarian grub here is superb,
especially the *Schweinshaxe*. Giant black draft
horses are stabled behind glass on your way
to the loo.

HAIDHAUSEN
Biergarten Muffatwerk (Map p85; ☎ 4587 5073;
Zellstrasse 4; ☯ 5pm-1am Mon-Thu, noon-1am Fri & Sat)
Think of this one as a progressive beer garden
with reggae instead of oompah, civilised imbibing instead of brainless guzzling, organic
meats, fish and vegetables on the grill, and
the option of chilling in lounge chairs. Plus
it's open late.

BEYOND THE INNER CITY
Zum Flaucher (Map pp78-9; ☎ 723 2677; Isarauen 8,
Sendling; ☯ 11.30am-10pm Tue-Sun) This congenial
restaurant-cum-beer garden in the Isar River
meadows feels a like a microvacation from
the city bustle. The spare ribs are fall-off-the-
bone tender, kids can wear themselves out on
the imaginative playground and soccer fans
descend for big matches beamed onto a giant
screen. Take the U3 to Brudermühlstrasse.

Waldwirtschaft Grosshesselohe (off Map pp78-9;
☎ 795 088; Georg-Kalb-Strasse 3, Grosshesselohe; ☯ 11am-
11pm) One of Munich's nicest beer garden
oases, this one delivers Spaten beer, 2500
seats under shady chestnuts, idyllic views of
the Isar valley and live jazz nightly in good
weather from Easter through September. Kids
can frolic in the big playground. Take the S7
to Grosshesselohe/Isartalbahnhof.

Bars & Cafés
Cafés listed here can be considered child-
friendly during the day.

ALTSTADT
Schumann's Bar (Map pp82-3; ☎ 229 060; Odeonsplatz
6-7) Urbane and sophisticated, Schumann's

TOP FIVE PLACES FOR COFFEE

- **Black Bean** (p120)
- **Café an der Uni** (p115)
- **Götterspeise** (p121)
- **Marais** (p116)
- **Zappeforster** (p121)

has been shaking up Munich's nightlife with libational flights of fancy in an impressive range of more than 220 concoctions. Great for a first date.

Master's Home (Map pp82-3; ☎ 229 909; Frauenstrasse 11) This is a wonderfully quirky cellar just east of the Viktualienmarkt. The off-centre décor time warps you back to the colonial era – antique furnishings, plenty of knickknacks and oddities such as a room built around a bathtub.

Café Cord (Map pp82-3; ☎ 5454 0780; Sonnenstrasse 19; 11am-at least 1am) A good stop for breakfast (served to 4pm), a light lunch or coffee, Cord also makes for an ideal first pit stop for a long night ahead on the club circuit. In summer, the super-delicious global fare tastes best on the romantic, twinkle-lit courtyard.

Café Glockenspiel (Map pp82-3; ☎ 264 256; Marienplatz 28; 10am-1am Mon-Sat, 10am-7pm Sun) Not exactly an insider tip but still much beloved for eye-level views of the Neues Rathaus glockenspiel (p76), ideally from the rooftop terrace.

MAXVORSTADT & SCHWABING

Alter Simpl (Map p81; ☎ 272 3083; Türkenstrasse 57, Maxvorstadt, mains €5-13; 11am-3am Mon-Thu, 6pm-4am Fri & Sat) Thomas Mann and Hermann Hesse used to knock 'em back at this legendary thirst parlour, which is also a good place to satisfy midnight munchies as bar bites are available until one hour before closing time. The curious name, by the way, is an abbreviation of the satirical magazine *Simplicissimus*.

Eat the Rich (Map p81; ☎ 185 982; Hessstrasse 90, Maxvorstadt; 7pm-3am Tue-Sat) Strong cocktails served in half-litre glasses quickly loosen inhibitions at this sizzling 'meet' market where wrinkle-free hotties mix it up with banker types halfway up the career ladder. A great spot to crash when the party's winding down everywhere else. Food is served till 2.30am.

News Bar (Map p81; ☎ 281 787; Amalienstrasse 55, Maxvorstadt; breakfast €3-10; 7.30am-2am) From tousled students to young managers and greying professors, everybody loves their news, especially at this stylish café that also sells international papers and mags. It's an ideal breakfast spot before embarking on a day of Pinakothek museum hopping.

Brik (Map p81; ☎ 2899 6630; Schellingstrasse 24, Schwabing; sushi €5-10) This slick Japanese-style café, bar and lounge is a temple of minimalism and draws a hip crowd as much for the

delicious sushi snacks as for the drinks. From Thursday to Sunday, DJs usually play a wicked mix of indie, techno and top 40.

Black Bean (Map p81; ☎ 2867 5088; Amalienstrasse 44, Maxvorstadt; 7.30am-8pm Mon-Fri, 9am-6.30pm Sat, 10am-6.30pm Sun) If you think the only decent 'brew' Bavarians made is beer, train your Java radar to this regional retort to Starbucks. The organic coffee gets tops marks and so do the muffins.

GÄRTNERPLATZVIERTEL & GLOCKENBACHVIERTEL

Trachtenvogl (☎ 201 5160; Reichenbachstrasse 47, Gärtnerplatzviertel; 10am-1am) At night you'll have to shoehorn your way into this buzzy lair favoured by a chatty, boozy crowd of scenesters, artists and students. Daytimes are mellower, all the better to slurp its hot chocolate menu and check out the cuckoo clocks and antlers, left over from the days when this was a folkoric garment shop.

Netzer & Overrath (Map pp82-3; ☎ 2023 2840; Baaderstrasse 33, Gärtnerplatzviertel; Overrath 9am-11pm Sun-Wed, Netzer 8pm-3am Thu-Sat) This alt-flavoured double pub is named for two members of the German national soccer team that won the FIFA World Cup in 1974. Overrath is the quieter one, more a daytime place for reading, sipping coffee or snacking. After dark Netzer puts 'fun' in 'funky' with loud rock, Britpop, cold beer and a *Fussball* table.

Baader Café (Map pp82-3; ☎ 201 0638; Baaderstrasse 47, Gärtnerplatzviertel; 9.30am-1am) This literary think-and-drink place gets everyone from short skirts to tweed jackets to mingle beneath the conversation-fuelling map of the world. Lines for the awesome Sunday brunch are longer than for the clubs that got everyone hungover the night before.

Café am Hochhaus (Map pp82-3; ☎ 8905 8152; Blumenstrasse 29; 8pm-3am Mon-Sat) Once a stodgy café only grandmas could love, this tiny joint now heaves with libidinous hipsters decades away from retirement. Cool photo wallpaper and handpicked live DJs keep the sizzle on until the wee hours. Gay tea-dance on Sundays.

K&K (☎ 2020 7463; Reichenbachstrasse 22; 8pm-2am) Only the name and some of the furnishings recall the days when this was a stuffy Austrian gourmet restaurant and not an upbeat DJ-and-drinks den. Creative lighting gives even pasty-faced hipsters a healthy glow.

Zappeforster (Map pp82-3; ☎ 2024 5250; Corneliusstrasse 50, Glockenbachviertel; ☑ 9am-1am) This relaxed hang-out is known for its creamy cappuccino, perky ice teas and warm home-made waffles served beneath groovy mountain wallpaper or on the sunny terrace.

Götterspeise (Map pp82-3; ☎ 2388 7374; Jahnstrasse 30, Glockenbachviertel; ☑ 8am-7pm Mon-Fri, 9am-6pm Sat) If the Aztecs thought of chocolate as the elixir of the gods, then this shop-cum-café must be heaven. Cocoa addicts satisfy their cravings with rave-worthy French chocolate cake, thick hot drinking chocolate, handmade *ganache* and even chocolate-flavoured 'body paint' for those wishing to double their sins.

WESTEND

Kilombo (Map pp82-3; Gollierstrasse 14a) Having been kicked out of its Haidhausen outpost, Christian Blau reopened his cult pub in September 2007 in multicultural Westend, which he considers Munich's most 'urban' area. Check your attitude at the door and make new friends over reasonably priced drinks and at occasional literary readings.

ENTERTAINMENT

Munich's entertainment scene is lively and multifaceted, if not particularly edgy. You can hobnob with high society at the opera or the chic P1 disco, hang with the kool kids at an indie club, catch a flick alfresco or watch one of the world's best soccer teams triumph in a futuristic stadium.

Listings

E-zines useful for plugging into the local scene include www.munig.com, www.munichx .de, http://muenchen.nachtagenten.de and www.ganz-muenchen.de. All are in German only but not too hard to navigate with basic language skills.

In München (www.in-muenchen.de, in German; free) Freebie mag available at bars, restaurants and shops is the most clued-in print source for what's on in Munich.

München im… Free A-to-Z pocket-sized booklet of almost everything the city has to offer.

Munich Found (www.munichfound.de; €3) English-language magazine geared towards expats and visitors.

Prinz München (http://muenchen.prinz.de; €1) Weekly lifestyle and entertainment glossy.

Tickets & Reservations

Tickets to cultural and sporting events are available at venue box offices and official ticket outlets, such as **Karstadt Schwabing** (Map p81; ☎ 336 659; Leopoldstrasse 82). For online bookings, try **München Ticket** (Map pp82-3; ☎ 5481 8181; www .muenchenticket.de, in German; Marienplatz, Altstadt), which shares premises with the tourist office.

Clubbing

Munich has a thriving club scene, so no matter whether your musical tastes run to disco or dancehall, house or punk, noise pop or punk-folk, you'll find some place to get those feet moving. To get the latest from the scene, peruse the listings mags or sift through the myriad flyers in shops, cafés and bars. This being Munich, expect pretty strict doors at most venues. Dress to kill to get into the fanciest clubs. Dance floors rarely heat up before 1am, so showing up early may increase your chances of getting in without suffering the indignities of a ridiculous wait and possible rejection. If you look under 30, bring ID. Cover charges rarely exceed €15.

Kultfabrik (Map p85; www.kultfabrik.info; Grafingerstrasse 6, Haidhausen) If you've been to Munich before, you may remember this 'fun ghetto' near the Ostbahnhof as Kunstpark Ost. Now the former dumpling factory has a different name but it's still the same party mecca for libidinous kids and has more than a dozen, mostly mainstream, venues. Electro and house beats charge up the crowd at the loungy **apartment 11**, the Asian-themed **Koi** and at the small and red cocktail cantina called **Die Bar**. Hard rock hounds mash it up at **Titty Twister**, metals freaks bang on at **Refugium**, and nostalgic types can become disco queens at such '70s and '80s emporia as **Noa**, **Rafael** and **Q Club**. For the latest line-ups, happy hours and other useful info, check the website or look around for KuFa's own listings mag, the free *Das K-Magazin*.

Optimolwerke (Map p85; www.optimolwerke.de; Friedenstrasse 10, Haidhausen) Just behind KuFa, Optimol is another clubbers' nirvana with about 15 different venues after dark. Favourites include **Harry Klein** (p122) and **Milch & Bar**, which is open daily until 6am (weekends till 9am) and the place to go when the action winds down elsewhere. Latin lovers flock to **Do Brasil**, while **Choice-Club** heats up the dance floor with black beats, chart music and house.

P1 (Map p81; ☎ 211 1140; Prinzregentenstrasse 1, Lehel; ☑ from 9pm daily) Is a Munich guide definitive without a nod to this playground of playboys, tabloid regulars and trust-fund babies? Not yet, perhaps. If you make it past the notorious bouncers, you'll find the crowd too busy seeing and being seen than to actually have a good time, but the décor, summer terrace and great pizza still have their appeal.

Atomic Café (Map pp82-3; ☎ 228 3054; www.atomic .de; Neuturmstrasse 5, Altstadt; ⏰ 10pm-4am, 9pm on concert nights Tue-Sun) This bastion of indie sounds with funky '60s décor is known for bookers with a knack for catching upwardly hopeful bands before their big break. Otherwise it's party time; long-running 'Britwoch' is the hottest Wednesday club in town. Also check out the in-house label Panatomic (www.panatomic.de).

Backstage (Map p80; ☎ 126 6100; www.backstage089 .de; Helmholzstrasse 18, Neuhausen; ⏰ 7pm-3am Mon-Wed, 8pm Thu, 10pm Fri & Sat) Refreshingly nonmainstream, this groovetastic *boîte* has a chill night beer garden and a shape-shifting line-up of punk, nu metal, hip-hop, dance hall and other alt sounds, both canned and live. The Free & Easy festival (bands, movies and comedy) in August and September enjoys cult status among clued-in locals.

Erste Liga (Map pp82-3; ☎ 260 8403; www.ersteliga .com; Thalkirchner Strasse 2, Glockenbachviertel; ⏰ 11pm-5am Thu-Sat) You better be a top-rated 'player' to make it into hot 'n' heavy 'Premier League'. Beyond the velvet rope awaits a stylish basement club dressed in shock green where high-profile DJs whip the crowd into a frenzy with sassy electro. The cool dance floor lights up with LEDs.

Harry Klein (Map p85; ☎ 4028 7400; www.harryklein club.de; Friedenstrasse 10, Haidhausen; ⏰ 11pm-7am Fri & Sat) An amazing alchemy of electro sound and visuals, this party palace gets a punky-funky crowd fired up for extended dance-a-thons. Great place to crash in the wee hours. Major cool factor: live video art mixes projected onto the walls.

Rote Sonne (Map pp82-3; ☎ 5526 3330; www.rote -sonne.com; Maximiliansplatz 5, Altstadt; ⏰ 11pm Thu-Sun) Named for a 1969 Munich cult movie starring 'It-Girl' Uschi Obermaier, the Red Sun is a fiery nirvana for fans of electronic sounds. An international roster of DJs from the US, Berlin, Paris, Glasgow and elsewhere keeps the wooden dance floor packed and sweaty until the sun rises.

Substanz (Map pp82-3; ☎ 721 2749; www.substanz -club.org; Ruppertstrasse 28, Ludwigsvorstadt; ⏰ 8pm-2am Sun-Thu, 8pm-3am Fri & Sat) About as alternative as things get in Munich, this low-key, beery lair gets feet moving with house to indie to

soul, tickles your funny bones during the English Comedy Club (first Sunday of the month) and brings out edgy wordsmiths for the SRO (standing-room-only) Poetry Slam (second Sunday).

8 Seasons (Map pp82-3; ☎ 2429 4444; www.8-sea sons.com; Maximilianstrasse 2, Altstadt; ⏰ 6pm-4am Tue, 7pm-4am Thu, 10pm-6am Fri & Sat) This flirty dancing den has a famous after-work party on Tuesdays (one free drink and a buffet), a chill rooftop terrace, a sensuous designer look and changing DJs that spin *Happy Feet*–inducing house and electro beats.

Jazz & Blues

Jazzclub Unterfahrt (Map p85; ☎ 448 2794; www .unterfahrt.de; Einsteinstrasse 42, Haidhausen; ⏰ 7.30pm-1am Sun-Thu, 7.30pm-3am Fri & Sat) Like a fine wine, Unterfahrt only gets better with age. The crowd defines the word 'eclectic' and so do the acts, which range from old bebop to edgy experimental. The Sunday open jam sessions are legendary. A must for Blue Note fans.

Jazzbar Vogler (Map pp82-3; ☎ 294 662; Rumfordstrasse 17, Gärtnerplatzviertel; ⏰ 7pm-1am Mon-Sat) This intimate watering hole brings some of Munich's baddest cats to the stage. You never know who'll show up for Monday's blues-jazz-Latin jam session. Cover (none to €7) is added to your final bill, allowing you to listen in for a bit before committing to staying.

Café am Beethovenplatz (Map pp82-3; ☎ 5440 4348; Goethestrasse 51, Ludwigsvorstadt) Downstairs at the Hotel Mariandl, this is Munich's oldest music café with an eclectic menu of sounds ranging from bossa nova to piano to Italian *canzoni* (songs). Reservations advised, especially for the Sunday jazz brunch.

Hide-Out (Map p80; ☎ 169 668; Rotkreuzplatz 2a, Neuhausen; ⏰ 8pm-3am Tue-Sat) This blues joint draws national and international talent but keeps cover charges wallet friendly (free to

---

MUNICH'S MONTY PYTHONS

Amid all the culture, need a little comic relief? If you happen to be in town on the first Sunday or Monday of the month, head to Substanz (left), where stand-up (and often stand-out) comics imported from the UK spin everyday material into comedic gold. Tickets cost €18 and shows usually sell out, so score yours online at www.english comedyclub.de.

MOVIES UNDER THE STARS

Screenings under the stars have become a popular summer tradition with classic and contemporary flicks spooling off in various locations around town. Come early to stake out a good spot and bring pillows, blankets and snacks.

- **Kino am Königsplatz** (Map p81; www.kinoopenair.de; Königsplatz, Maxvorstadt) In late July, cineastes gather in front of the majestic neoclassical setting of this central square to take in the latest blockbusters.

- **Kino am Pool** (off Map p81; www.kinoampool.de; Traubestrasse 3, Schwabing) Splash around in the municipal Ungererbad swimming pool, then stay around for the latest flick screened poolside throughout July and August.

- **Kino, Mond & Sterne** (Map pp78-9; www.kino-mond-sterne.de; Seebühne im Westpark, Am Westpark, Sendling) The repertory at this heavenly alfresco amphitheatre runs mostly towards Hollywood classics, including several in English. Take the U6 to 'Westpark'.

€15). It's fun any day, but Thursday's jam sessions are legendary.

Classical Music & Opera

Münchner Philharmoniker (☎ 480 980; www.mphil.de; Rosenheimer Strasse 5, Haidhausen) Munich's premier orchestra regularly performs at the Gasteig cultural centre (p103). Book tickets early as performances usually sell out. Check the website for upcoming public rehearsals costing just €8 (free for students, tickets available one hour before the concert).

Bayerische Staatsoper (Map pp82-3; ☎ 2185 1920; www.bayerische.staatsoper.de; Max-Joseph-Platz 2, Altstadt) Considered one of the best opera companies in the world, the Bavarian State Opera puts the emphasis on Mozart, Strauss and Wagner but doesn't shy away from early baroque pieces by Monteverdi and others of the period. In summer it hosts the prestigious Opernfestspiele (p110). Performances are at the Nationaltheater in the Residenz and often sell out. The opera's 'house band' is the **Bayerisches Staatsorchester** (Map pp82–3), in business since 1523 and thus Munich's oldest orchestra. It's currently under the capable helm of Kent Nagano, who occasionally shakes up the tried-and-true repertory with contemporary and avant-garde works.

BR-Symphonieorchester (☎ 5900 4545; www.br -online.de/kultur-szene/klassik/pages/so) Charismatic Lithuanian maestro Mariss Jansons has rejuvenated this orchestra's play list and often performs with its choir at such venues as the Gasteig (Map p85) and the Prinzregententheater (Map p85).

Staatstheater am Gärtnerplatz (Map pp82-3; ☎ 2185 1960; www.staatstheater-am-gaertnerplatz.de; Gärtnerplatz 3, Gärtnerplatzviertel) Munich's 'other' opera house takes a more populist approach and also presents musicals and light opera, usually in German.

Cinemas

For show information check any of the listings publications. Admission usually ranges from €6.50 to €8.50, though one day a week, usually Monday or Tuesday, is *Kinotag* (cinema day) with reduced prices. Movies presented in their original language are denoted in listings by the acronym 'OF' (*Originalfassung*) or 'OV' (*Originalversion*); those with German subtitles are marked 'OmU' (*Original mit Untertiteln*). The following theatres all show English-language movies.

Atelier (Map pp82-3; ☎ 591 918; Sonnenstrasse 12, Ludwigsvorstadt) Art-house cinema in a backyard; Monday is 'MonGay' with homo-themed releases.

Atlantis (Map pp82-3; ☎ 555 152; Schwanthalerstrasse 2, Ludwigsvorstadt)

SNEAK A PEEK AT A PREVIEW

If you want to be the first to see tomorrow's blockbuster, head to these theatres for a sneak preview, which is when studios gauge a movie's popularity before its general release. You won't know which film you'll see, but the cheaper tickets, cool short films, lack of advertising and general suspense make sneaks a super-popular night out. Cinema has them Friday at 11pm, Atlantis Wednesday at 9pm and Mathäser that night at 10.30pm. For more, see www .sneak-muenchen.de (in German).

'OUT' & ABOUT IN MUNICH

Munich's gay and lesbian scene is the liveliest in Bavaria but tame if compared to Berlin, Cologne or Amsterdam. The rainbow flag flies especially proudly along Müllerstrasse and the adjoining Glockenbachviertel and Gärtnerplatzviertel. To plug into the scene, keep an eye out for the freebie mags *Our Munich* and *Sergej*, which contain up-to-date listings and news about the community and gay-friendly establishments around town. Another source is www.gaymunich.de, which has a small section in English. For help with lodging, check out www.gaytouristoffice.com.

Max & Milian (Map pp82-3; ☎ 260 3320; Ickstattstrasse 2; ⌚ 10.30am-8pm Mon-Fri, 11am-4pm Sat) is Munich's bastion for queer lit, nonfiction and mags. **Sub** (Map pp82-3; ☎ 260 3056; Müllerstrasse 43, Glockenbachviertel; ⌚ 7-11pm) is a one-stop service and information agency; lesbians can also turn to **Lesbenberatungsstelle** (Map pp82-3; ☎ 725 4272; Angertorstrasse 3, Gärtnerplatzviertel; ⌚ 2.30-5pm Mon & Wed, 10.30am-1pm Tue).

The festival season kicks off in April with the **Verzaubert** (www.verzaubertfilmfest.com) film series featuring the best of international queer cinema at Atelier (p123). The main street parties are **Christopher Street Day** (p110) and the **Schwules Strassenfest** (www.schwules-strassenfest.de) held in mid-August along Hans-Sachs-Strasse in the Glockenbachviertel. During **Oktoberfest** (p108), lesbigay folks invade the Bräurosl beer tent on the first Sunday and Fischer-Vroni on the second Monday.

Regular gay fun events include **MonGay** cinema at Atelier (p123) and the **Gay Tea-Dance** on the second Sunday of the month at the Café im Hochhaus (p120).

Bars & Clubs

- **Morizz** (Map pp82-3; ☎ 201 6776; Klenzestrasse 43) This mod Art Deco–style lounge with red-leather armchairs and mirrors for posing and preening goes for a more moneyed clientele and even gets the occasional local celebrity drop in. The service is impeccable, the food's good, and the wine and whisky list keeps everyone happily pickled. Packed on weekends.

Mathäser Filmpalast (Map pp82-3; ☎ 515 651; www .mathaeser.de; Bayerstrasse 5, Altstadt) Modern 14-screen multiplex in a former beer hall.

Museum-Lichtspiele (Map p85; ☎ 482 403; www .museum-lichtspiele.de; Lilienstrasse 2, Haidhausen) Cult cinema with wacky interior and weekly screenings of *Rocky Horror Picture Show* (Saturday nights) and Luchino Visconti's *Death in Venice* (Sunday mornings)

Cinema (Map p81; ☎ 555 255; www.cinema-muenchen .de; Nymphenburger Strasse 31, Neuhausen) Cult cinema with all films in English, all the time.

Theatre

Bayerisches Staatsschauspiel (☎ 218 501; www .bayerischesstaatsschauspiel.de; Max-Joseph-Platz 1, Altstadt) This leading ensemble has a bit of a conservative streak but still manages to find relevance for today's mad mad world in works by Shakespeare, Schiller and other tried-and-true playwrights. Performances are in the Residenztheater (Map pp82-3), the Theater im Marstall (Marstallstrasse, Map pp82-3) and the theatre in the Haus der Kunst (Map p81).

Münchner Kammerspiele (Map pp82-3; ☎ 2333 7000; www.muenchner-kammerspiele.de; Maximilianstrasse 26-28, Altstadt) Just as venerable as the Staats-schauspiel, this stage has an edgier, more populist bent and delivers provocative interpretations of the classics as well as works by contemporary playwrights. Performances are in a beautifully refurbished Art Nouveau theatre at Maximilianstrasse and in the Neues Haus (Map pp82–3), a new glass cube at Falckenbergstrasse 1.

Touring Broadway productions and shows like Stomp or Blue Man Group find a temporary home at the **Deutsches Theater** (Map pp82-3; ☎ 5523 4444; Schwanthalerstrasse 13, Ludwigsvorstadt), while the **Komödie am Max II** (Map p85; ☎ 221 859; Maximilianstrasse 47, Lehel) is the place to catch lightweight comedies, often starring German TV actors.

Spectator Sports

FC Bayern München (☎ 6993 1333; www.fcbayern. de) This is one of the most successful soccer clubs in history and has won the German cup and other championships more often than any other team. Home games are at the Allianz Arena (p104) and usually sell out far in advance. Tickets can be ordered online. Watch the team training for free at Säbener Strasse 51 (Map pp78–9) in Harlaching.

- **Nil** (Map pp82-3; ☎ 265 545; Hans-Sachs-Strasse 2) A construct in wood and marble, this chill café-bar is open till 3am and a good place to crash after the party has stopped elsewhere. If you need a reality check, a plate of its kick-ass goulash soup should do the trick.

- **NY Club** (Map pp82-3; ☎ 6223 2152; Sonnenstrasse 25; ☟ Fri & Sat) After a complete revamp, it's again 'Raining Men' at Munich's hottest gay dance temple where you can party away with Ibiza-style abandon on the cool, back-lit main floor.

- **Die Carmens** (Map pp82-3; ☎ 2300 0496; Theklastrasse 1; ☟ Fri & Sat) This sizzling venue for dancing, cruising and drinking attracts the entire GLBT community with quirky décor and an upbeat music mix of '80s, charts and club sounds. Transgendered folks get in for free.

- **Teddy Bar** (Map pp82-3; ☎ 260 3359; Hans-Sachs-Strasse 1) Presided over by cuddly Fridl, this is a friendly, been-there-forever kind of bar for 'bears' and friends that still manages to stay current and cool. The crowd is generally older and you can actually hear yourself talk. Happy hour till 9pm Monday to Thursday.

- **Bau** (Map pp82-3; ☎ 269 208; Müllerstrasse 41) Bilevel bar that's party central for manly men with nary a twink in sight but plenty of leather, Levis and uniforms. The foam parties in the small cellar darkroom are legendary.

- **Deutsche Eiche** (Map pp82-3; ☎ 231 1660; Reichenbachstrasse 13) A Munich institution, this was once filmmaker Rainer Werner Fassbinder's favourite hang-out. It's still a popular spot and packs in a mixed crowd for its comfort food and fast service.

- **Bei Carla** (Map pp82-3; ☎ 227 901; Baaderstrasse 16) This energised scene staple behind the drab façade has been keeping lesbians happy since, well, like forever. It's a popular spot with a good mixed-age crowd, lots of regulars and snack foods if you're feeling peckish.

Take the U1 to Mangfallplatz, then bus 139 to Säbener Strasse.

The Allianz Arena is also home turf for Munich's 'other' soccer team, the perennial underdogs **TSV 1860** (☎ 01805-601 860; www.tsv1860.de). They only play in Germany's second league but still have an enormously loyal fan base. The team trains at Grünwalder Strasse 114 (Map pp78–9), also in Harlaching (take tram 25 to Südtiroler Strasse).

Call ahead for training times.

SHOPPING

Munich is a fun and sophisticated place to shop that goes far beyond chains and department stores. If you want those, head to Neuhauser Strasse and Kaufingerstrasse. East of there, Sendlinger Strasse has smaller and somewhat more individualistic stores, including a few resale and vintage emporia.

To truly 'unchain' yourself, though, you need to hit the Gärtnerplatzviertel and Glockenbachviertel, the bastion of well-edited indie stores and local designer boutiques. Hans-Sachs-Strasse and Reichenbachstrasse are especially promising. Maxvorstadt, especially Türkenstrasse, also has an interesting line-up of stores with stuff you won't find on the high street back home. Shoe fetishistas can indulge their lusts on Hohenzollernstrasse in Schwabing.

Maximilianstrasse, meanwhile, is the catwalk for the Prada and Escada brigade, especially in the new, minimalist Maximilianhöfe in the Bürkleinbau just past the Nationaltheater. Snob shoppers will also be happy on Theatinerstrasse (home of the Fünf Höfe arcade), on Residenzstrasse and Brienner Strasse.

Here's a quick and dirty selection of shops you might find of interest:

Beauty & Nature (Map pp82-3; ☎ 2423 1233; 1st fl, Westenrieder Strasse 35, Altstadt; ☟ 8am-8pm Mon-Sat) All natural, all the time, is the motto at this drugstore that stocks only top-performing products by Dr Hauschka, Logona, Lavera and other Euro brands, usually at much lower prices than found overseas. Ask about its manicures and beauty treatments.

Servus Heimat (Map pp82-3; ☎ 2429 4780; Brunnstrasse 3, Altstadt) Everything a gift shop should be – fun, happy to see you and stocked with unique souvenirs that play with Bavarian symbols like tees emblazoned with Empress

Sisi or the Olympic Stadium outline. Campy, tongue-in-cheek chic.

Sebastian Wesely (Map pp82-3; ☎ 264 519; Rindermarkt 1, Altstadt; ☺ 9am-6.30pm Mon-Sat) If you're in the market for traditional souvenirs, this little shop (in business since 1557) has floor-to-ceiling shelves of carved angels, pewter tankards, beer steins, carved figurines and handmade candles. The saleswomen are quick with a smile and happy to help.

Siebter Himmel (Map pp82-3; ☎ 267 053; Hans-Sachs-Strasse 17, Glockenbachviertel; ☺ 11am-7pm Mon-Fri, 10am-6pm Sat) Cool hunters will be in seventh heaven when browsing the assortment of fashions and accessories by hip indie labels like Pussy de Luxe, Indian Rose and Religion, all sold at surprisingly reasonable prices. Complement your new outfit with shoes from Schuhhimmel across the street.

Flohmarkt Riem (Map pp78-9; ☎ 9605 1632; Willy-Brandt-Platz, Riem; ☺ 6am-4pm Sat) Like urban archaeologists, you have to sift through trash and detritus to unearth treasure at Bavaria's largest flea market, far out of town by the trade fair grounds in Riem. Take the U2 to Messestadt-Ost.

Loden-Frey (Map pp82-3; ☎ 210 390; Maffeistrasse 5-7, Altstadt) Stocks a wide range of Bavarian wear. Expect to pay at least €300 for a good leather jacket, pair of lederhosen or dirndl dress.

Holareidulijö (Map p81; ☎ 271 7745; Schellingstrasse 81, Maxvorstadt; ☺ noon-6.30pm Tue-Fri, 10am-1pm Sat) If Loden-Frey's price tags are too steep, check this out. The name is a phonetic yodel, appropriate for a store that carries preloved lederhosen and other folkwear in good condition.

Click, click, click... is the sound of customers flipping through the well-edited selection of new and used CDs and vinyl at **Optimal** (Map pp82-3; ☎ 268 185; Kolosseumstrasse 6, Glockenbachviertel; ☺ 11am-8pm Mon-Fri, 11am-4pm Sat) and **Resonanz** (Map pp82-3; ☎ 2020 5205; Auenstrasse 4, ☺ 11am-8pm Mon-Fri, 11am-4pm Sat), Munich's best purveyors of indie sounds with handy listening stations. For classical music and jazz recordings there's no better selection – and more knowledgeable staff – than at **Ludwig Beck** (Map pp82-3; ☎ 2369 1441; Marienplatz 11) on the 4th floor of the eponymous department store.

Other shops:

Foto-Video-Media Sauter (Map pp82-3; ☎ 5515 0450; Sonnenstrasse 26, Altstadt) The largest camera and video shop in town.

Porzellan Manufaktur Nymphenburg Altstadt (Map pp82-3; ☎ 282 428; Odeonsplatz 1, Altstadt; ☺ 10am-6.30pm Mon-Fri, 10am-4pm Sat); Schloss Nymphenburg (Map p80; ☎ 179 1970; Nördliches Schlossrondell 8, Nymphenburg; ☺ 10am-5pm Mon-Fri) Traditional and contemporary porcelain masterpieces by the royal manufacturer.

GETTING THERE & AWAY
Air
Munich's sparkling **Flughafen München** (Munich International Airport; ☎ 975 00, flight inquiries 9752 1313; www.munich-airport.de) is easy to navigate and – within Germany – second in importance only to Frankfurt for international and domestic flights. The main carrier is Lufthansa, but other international airlines serving Munich include Air France, British Airways, Delta, easyJet, El Al, Scandinavian Airlines (SAS) and United Airlines. For contact and flight information see p321.

Bus
The Busabout (p323) hop-on hop-off bus service comes through Munich on the Northern Loop and the Southern Loop with pickup and dropoff at Wombat's City Hostel (Map pp82-3).

Europabus (p325) links Munich to the Romantic Road. For details of fares and timetables inquire at EurAide (p76) or **Deutsche Touring** (Map pp82-3; ☎ 8898 9513; www.touring.com; Hirtenallee 14) near the Hauptbahnhof.

BEX BerlinLinienBus (☎ 01801-546 436; www.berlin linienbus.de) runs daily buses between Berlin and Munich (one way/return €45/84, 8½ hours), via Ingolstadt, Nuremberg, Bayreuth and Leipzig. Buses depart from bus platform 5 on Arnulfstrasse, north of the Hauptbahnhof.

In spring 2009 a new central bus station is expected to open near Hackerbrücke.

Car & Motorcycle
Munich has autobahns radiating in all directions. Take the A9 to Nuremberg, the A8 to Salzburg, the A95 to Garmisch-Partenkirchen and the A8 to Ulm or Stuttgart.

All major car-hire companies have offices at the airport. Sixt (Budget), Hertz, Avis and Europcar have counters on the 2nd level of the Hauptbahnhof.

Train
Train services from Munich are excellent. There are swift direct connections to such key destinations in Bavaria as Nuremberg (€45, one hour), Regensburg (€22, 1½ hours) and Würzburg (€59, two hours). Going to

Freiburg (€78, 4½ hours) or Baden-Baden (€72, four hours) requires a change, usually in Mannheim. There are also frequent direct services to Berlin (€105, 5¾ hours), Frankfurt (€81, three hours) and Cologne (€119, 4½ hours); and to other European cities, such as Vienna (€72, 4¼ hours), Prague (€52, six hours) and Zürich (€61, 4¼ hours). There's also a night train to Paris (price varies, 10 hours).

GETTING AROUND
Central Munich is compact enough to explore on foot. To get to the outlying suburbs make use of the public transport network, which is extensive and efficient.

To/From the Airport
Munich's airport is about 30km northeast of the city and linked by S-Bahn (S1 and S8) to the Hauptbahnhof. The trip costs €8.80, takes about 40 minutes and runs every 20 minutes from 3am until around 12.30am.

The **Lufthansa Airport Bus** (☎ 323 040) shuttles at 20-minute intervals between the airport and Arnulfstrasse at the Hauptbahnhof between 5.10am and 9.40pm. The trip takes about 45 minutes and costs €10 (return €16). A taxi from the airport to the Altstadt costs about €55.

Car & Motorcycle
Driving in central Munich can be a nightmare; many streets are one way or pedestrian only, ticket enforcement is Orwellian and parking is a nightmare. Car parks (indicated on the tourist office map) charge about €1.50 to €2 per hour.

Public Transport
Munich's excellent public transport system is composed of buses, trams, the U-Bahn and the S-Bahn. It's operated by MVV, which maintains offices in the U-Bahn stations at Marienplatz, Hauptbahnhof, Sendlinger Tor, Odeonsplatz, Olympiazentrum, Karlsplatz and Münchner Freiheit. Staff hand out free network maps and timetables, sell tickets and answer questions. Automated trip planning is available by phone (☎ 4142 4344) and online (www.mvv-muenchen.de).

The U-Bahn and S-Bahn cease operation at around 12.30am Monday to Friday and 1.30am on weekends when night buses (*Nachtbusse*) ferry home night owls and shift workers.

TICKETS & FARES
The Munich region is divided into four zones with most places of visitor interest (except Dachau and the airport) conveniently clustering within the 'white' *Innenraum* (inner zone). Short rides (*Kurzstrecke*; four bus or tram stops; or two U-Bahn or S-Bahn stops) cost €1.10, longer trips cost €2.20. Children aged between six and 14 pay a flat €1.10 regardless of the length of the trip.

Cut down costs by buying a strip card (*Streifenkarte*) of 10 tickets for €10.50, then stamp one strip for short trips or two strips for longer ones. Day passes are €5 for individuals and €9 for up to five people travelling together. Three-day passes are €12.30/21. There's also a weekly pass called IsarCard, which costs €15.80 but is only valid from Monday to Sunday – if you buy on Wednesday, it's still only good until Sunday. For details about the Bayern-Ticket, see p328.

Bikes costs €2.50 and may only be taken aboard U-Bahn and S-Bahn trains, but not during the 6am to 9am and 4pm to 6pm rush hours.

BUYING & USING TICKETS
Bus drivers sell single tickets and day passes but tickets for the U- /S-Bahn and other passes must be purchased from vending machine at stations or MVV offices. Tram tickets are available from vending machines aboard. Tickets must be stamped (validated) at station platform entrances and aboard buses and trams before use. The fine for getting caught without a valid ticket is €40.

Taxi
Taxis cost €2.70 at flag fall (€3.70 if ordered by phone), plus €1.25 to €1.60 per kilometre and are not much more convenient than public transport. Luggage is charged at €0.50 per piece. Ring a taxi on ☎ 216 10 or ☎ 194 10. Taxi ranks are indicated on the city's tourist map.

AROUND MUNICH

STARNBERGER FÜNF-SEEN-LAND
pop 85,000 / elev 584m
Once a royal retreat and still a popular place of residence with the rich and famous, the Fünf-Seen-Land (Five Lakes District) is set in a glacial plane and makes a fast and easy escape from the urban bustle of Munich.

The largest lake is the narrow 21km-long **Starnberger See**, nicknamed 'Munich's bathtub' and ringed by a necklace of resorts, including Starnberg, Berg, Pöcking-Possenhofen, Feldafing, Tutzing, Bernried and Seeshaupt. The road linking all these communities can get terribly clogged, especially on summer weekends. It also rarely skirts the lake shore, much of which is privately owned. There is, however, a paved trail dedicated to biking and walking along the shore. Circumnavigating the entire lake (50km) takes about 12 hours on foot and four hours by bike.

The other lakes – Ammersee, Pilsensee, Wörthsee and Wesslinger See – are smaller and offer more secluded charm. Swimming, boating and windsurfing are popular activities on all lakes, and the district is also crisscrossed by a 250km network of bike paths and 185km of hiking trails.

This area has long been a favourite with the Bavarian nobility. The 19th-century 'fairytale' king Ludwig II – 'Kini' to his adoring fans – had a soft spot for the Starnberger See. That is until he mysteriously drowned in the lake on the eastern shore. Ludwig's bosom

buddy, Empress Sisi of Austria (1837–98), spent many a summer staying in Possenhofen on the western shore; her descendent Otto von Habsburg – head of the Austrian royal family – still lives in nearby Pöcking.

The present head of the Wittelsbach family, the art-loving Duke Franz, still uses Ludwig's former palace in Berg.

Information

Tourist Information Starnberger Fünf-Seen-Land (☎ 08151-906 00; www.sta5.de, in German; Wittelsbacherstrasse 2c, Starnberg; ✆ 8am-6pm Mon-Fri Nov-May, also 9am-1pm Sat May-Oct) Regional tourist office just north of Bahnhofsplatz, with a free room-finding service and trip planning to other lake towns. The website has links to all tourist offices in the local communities.

Sights
STARNBERG

The town of Starnberg is the northern gateway to the lake district but lacks any lasting allure, so most people head straight on to the other towns. The train station is just steps from the cruise-boat landing docks, pedal-boat hire, the regional tourist office and the **Museum Starnberger See** (☎ 08151-772 132; www.museum-starnberger-see.de, in German; Possenhofener Strasse 5, enter on Bahnhofsplatz; adult/child €1.50/0.50; ✆ 10am-noon & 2-5pm Tue-Sun). You may have to duck your head when touring this 400-year-old farmhouse that offers a glimpse into yesteryear's life on the lake and also boasts a precious Ignaz Günther sculpture in the little chapel. By the time you're reading this, a modern extension showcasing a fancy royal barge and an exhibit on its construction, use and purpose should have opened.

Starnberg is just 30 minutes by S6 from Munich (€4.40 or four strips on the *Streifenkarte*).

BERG

It's about an hour's walk (4km) from Starnberg to Berg on the northeastern lake shore, where King Ludwig II spent summers on **Schloss Berg** and where he and his doctor died in 1886 under mysterious circumstances. The palace and its lovely gardens still belong to the Wittelsbach family and are closed to prying eyes, but you're free to walk through its wooded park to the **Votivkapelle** (Votive Chapel; ☎ 08151-5276; admission free; ✆ 9am-5pm Apr-Oct). Built in honour of Ludwig and shrouded by mature trees, this neo-Romanesque memorial chapel overlooks the spot in the lake – marked by a simple cross,

AROUND MUNICH

0   10 km
0   6 miles

Scheyern
Aichach
Petershausen
Altomünster
Freising
Markt Indersdorf
Munich International Airport
Dachau
Schleissheim
Fürstenfeldbruck
Puchheim
MUNICH
Vaterstetten
Wesslinger See
Wörthsee
Gauting
Pilsensee
Seefeld
Oberhaching
Herrsching
Starnberg
Ammersee
Pöcking
Sauerlach
Andechs
Berg
Diessen
Feldafing
Possenhofen
Tutzing
Münsing
Wolfratshausen
Ilkahöhe
Starnberger See
Holzkirchen
Bernried
Oberambach
Geretsried
Ambach
Weilheim
Seeshaupt
Peissenberg
Penzberg   Bad Tölz
Waakirchen
Tegernsee

erected years later by his mother – where Ludwig's dead body was supposedly found.

POSSENHOFEN & FELDAFING

Austrian empress Sisi, cousin of Ludwig II, spent her childhood summers at **Schloss Possenhofen**, a chunky cream-coloured palace on the western shore of Lake Starnberg. It's since been converted into condos but the grounds are now a huge leisure park with lake access, volleyball nets and barbecue pits that's swarmed with stressed-out city folk on hot summer weekends. To learn a bit more about the Sisi mystique, swing by the new **Kaiserin-Elisabeth-Museum** (☎ 08151-164 79; Schlossbergstrasse 2; admission free; ☉ 2-6pm Fri-Sun Jun–early Oct or by appointment). It's a small exhibit in the grand surroundings of the former royal waiting rooms of the historic *Bahnhof* Possenhofen, now the S-Bahn station.

Sisi was so taken with the lake's beauty that she returned as an adult to summer in what is now the **Hotel Kaiserin Elisabeth** (☎ 08157-930 90; Tutzinger Strasse 2), in the hamlet of Feldafing a couple of kilometres south. A larger-than-life sculpture in the garden shows her with a book in relaxed repose, gazing back at the hotel. You can eat in the rustic Ludwigstüberl (p131) or the silver-service restaurant where aproned waiters serve the 'Sisi Menu'.

Fans of Art Nouveau villas should take a spin around Feldafing, which also has a popular swimming beach, the **Strandbad Feldafing** (☎ 08157-8200; adult/child/student €4.50/2.50/3.50; ☉ 10am-10pm daily mid-Mar–mid-Oct, 10am-10pm Thu-Sun mid-Oct–mid-Mar).

From the Strandbad, it's an easy 10-minute walk to the Glockensteg, the place to catch a historical ferry called **Plette** (☎ 0171-722 2266; adult/child/student €4/1/3; ☉ May–mid-Oct in good weather) to the **Roseninsel**. Sisi and Ludwig frequently rendezvoused on this romantic island, where Ludwig also received other luminaries, Richard Wagner among them. Neglected for a century after the king's death, the island, rose garden and his summerhouse, called the **Casino** (adult/under 18 yr/child €3/free/2; ☉ noon-6pm Tue-Sun May–mid-Oct), have been restored and are now open to the public. A small exhibit in the garden house (same hours, included in admission) has displays of about 6000 years of the island's history.

Possenhofen and Feldafing are both stops on the S6 from Munich (€6.60 or six strips of a *Streifenkarte*, 40 minutes).

BUCHHEIM MUSEUM

A bronze statue of a BMW sprouting octopus-like tentacles is the mind-teasing overture to the full symphony of art and objects at the amazing **Buchheim Museum** (☎ 08158-997 00; www .buchheimmuseum.de; Am Hirschgarten 1, Bernried; adult/ child/student/family €8.50/3.50/3.50/18, combined boat & museum ticket €16; ☉ 10am-6pm Tue-Sun Apr-Oct, 10am-5pm Tue-Sun Nov-Mar), right on the Starnberger See about 1km north of the town of Bernried. The modernist structure by Olympia Stadium architect Günter Behnisch houses the private collection of Lothar-Günther Buchheim, author of *Das Boot*, the novel that inspired the famous film. The heart and soul of the museum are German Expressionist works by members of Die Brücke (The Bridge), an artist group founded in Dresden in 1905. The bright, emotionally coloured canvasses by Ludwig Kirchner, Emil Nolde, Max Beckmann, Otto Dix and Karl Schmidt-Rottluff marked the beginning of modern art in Germany.

Other galleries present a fascinating hotchpotch of global arts and crafts, which justifies the museum's subtitle 'Museum of the Imagination'. You'll see handsome Art Nouveau vases, African masks, Japanese woodcuts, jewellery from India and a stunning collection of some 3000 paperweights.

The most scenic approach to the museum is by an hour-long **boat trip** (combination ticket with museum €17, no concessions; ☉ 3 sailings daily except Mon May-Oct) from Starnberg. Alternatively, take the RegionalBahn (RB) to Tutzing, then take either bus 9614 to the 'LVA Höhenried' stop near the museum (weekday only) or another RB train to Bernried, then walk north for about 15 minutes.

ANDECHS

Founded in the 10th century, the hilltop **Kloster Andechs** (Andechs Monastery; ☎ 08152-3760; www.andechs.de; Bergstrasse 2, Andechs; admission free) has long been a place of pilgrimage, although these days more visitors come to quaff the Benedictine monks' fabled brews, which rank among Bavaria's finest.

Religious pilgrims are drawn by several relics in the monastery's possessions, including a piece said to have come from Christ's crown-of-thorns. Some of the offertory candles in the holy chapel stand over 1m tall and are among Germany's oldest. The church itself boasts a rococo riot of frescoes, sculptures and a sophisticated altar designed by Munich court architect François Cuvilliés. In June and July the **Carl Orff Festival** celebrates the Bavarian composer of *Carmina Burana* (see the boxed text on p147) with a series of concerts; he's buried inside the church.

Most visitors to the 'Holy Mountain', as Andechs is known, really come to worship at the **Braustüberl**, the monastery's beer hall and garden. The resident monks have been brewing beer for over 500 years and serve a deliciously sudsy Helles, a rich and velvety Doppelbock Dunkel and fresh, unfiltered Weissbier. Summer weekends are so insanely busy it's easy to forget that you're in a religious institution, pious as your love for the brew may be…

For a behind-the-scenes look at the monks' operations, take a guided tour of the **brewery** (adult/child €4/2; ☽ 11am Tue-Thu May–mid-Oct) or the **church** (admission free; ☽ noon Mon-Sat May–mid-Oct).

Andechs is served three times daily (twice on Sunday) by bus 951 from the S-Bahn station in Starnberg Nord (S6; 27 minutes) and the one in Herrsching (S5; 10 minutes).

DIESSEN

To see one of the area's most magnificent baroque churches, you must travel to Diessen, some 11km west of Andechs, which is home to the **Marienmünster** (☎ 08807-948 940; ☽ 8am-noon & 2-6pm). Part of a monastery complex, this festive symphony in white stucco, red marble and gold leaf involved some of the most accomplished artists of the 18th century, including the architect Johann Michael Fischer; François Cuvilliés, who designed a high altar; and Giovanni Battista Tiepolo, who was responsible for an altar painting.

Diessen also has the small **Carl-Orff-Museum** (☎ 08807-919 81; Hofmark 3; adult/concession €2/1; ☽ 2-5pm Sat, Sun & holidays), with a biographical exhibit, a cabinet of instruments and a video room where you can watch performances of his work.

Activities

From Easter to mid-October, **Bayerische-Seen-Schifffahrt** (BSS; ☎ 01851-8061; www.seenschiff fahrt.de) runs scheduled boat services on the Starnberger See and the Ammersee – a leisurely way to explore the region. In Starnberg, boats leave from the landing docks just south of the main station. For the Ammersee, Herrsching is the most convenient starting point. BSS also offers narrated tours of both

lakes, varying from one to four hours and costing from €8 to €15.

If cruises are too tame, consider taking a spin around the lake under your own steam. Boat hire is available on the Starnberger See, the Ammersee and the Wörthsee. In Starnberg, **Paul Dechant** (☎ 08151-121 06; Hauptstrasse 20), near the train station, has rowing, pedal and electric-powered boats for €13 per hour. In Herrsching, near Andechs on the Ammersee, **Alfred Schlamp** (☎ 08152-969 533; Summerstrasse 30) charges €7 per hour for his pedal and rowing boats.

If the weather plays along, there's no better way to explore the area than by bicycle. **Radhaus Starnberg** (☎ 08151-167 14; Wittelsbacherstrasse 20; per day €10) in Starnberg and **Fahrradgeschäft Nandlinger** (☎ 08152-1266; Mühlfelder Strasse 5; per day €10) in Herrsching have a decent selection of two wheelers. **Bike It** (☎ 08151-746 430; Bahnhofstrasse 1) in Starnberg runs guided bike tours from €25. There's a famous in-line skating stretch on the eastern shore between Berg and Ambach.

There's plenty of good hiking as well. A delightful half-day trip starts in Tutzing and goes via a moderate ascent to the Ilkahöhe, which is a 730m hill with a restaurant (opposite), beer garden and panoramic lake views.

Sleeping

DJH Hostel Possenhofen (☎ 08157-996 611; www.pos senhofen.jugendherberge.de, in German; Kurt-Stieler-Strasse 18, Pöcking-Possenhofen; dm €21, s/d €29/50; P 🖳) A jewel among DJH hostels, this modern, spacious and well-run contender sits next to Schloss Possenhofen and a popular swimming beach.

Hotel Alte Linde (☎ 08157-933 180; www.linde -wieling.de, in German; Wieling 5, Feldafing; s €55-88, d €80-110; P ✖) Run with panache and personality, this congenial inn welcomes guests with modern country-style elegance. The nicest rooms have unique features such as sleeping alcove or four-poster beds below a painted ceiling. Enjoy a cold one in the beer garden, then savour delicious modern, organic twists on classic Bavarian in the restaurant, where mains cost about €10 to €18.

Schlossgut Oberambach (☎ 08177-9323; www .schlossgut.de; Oberambach 1, Münsing; s/d €120/240; P ✖ ✖ 🖳 🐾) Dreams will be sweet in the ecofriendly and charmingly Mediterranean rooms of this certified 'biohotel' with private lake access. Renewable sources provide all the energy and there's also a wonderful Ayurveda spa to recharge your own batteries before feeding stomach and soul with big-flavoured, contemporary country cooking (mains €12-24).

Eating

Ludwigstüberl (☎ 08157-930 90; Tutzinger Strasse 2, Feldafing; Brotzeit €6-9, mains €10-20; ☻ dinner Wed-Mon, lunch Sun) On cold nights it's a treat to sit near the fireplace in this cosy tavern, digging into a soulful menu ranging from salads to roast beef. Bookings are recommended. It's part of the Kaiserin Elisabeth Hotel; don't confuse this place with the stuffy hotel restaurant.

Forsthaus Ilkahöhe (☎ 08158-8242; Auf der Ilkahöhe, Tutzing; mains €16-23; ☻ Wed-Sun) It's hard to tell what's more appealing: the gourmet regional cuisine or the idyllic hilltop setting, with spectacular views of the Starnberger See and the Alps. Come for a full meal or just a foamy *Mass* in the beer garden, open daily in fine weather.

Braustüberl (☎ 08152-376 261; Bergstrasse 2, Andechs; mains €3-15; ☻ 10am-8pm) Food may seem an afterthought here, but the hearty roast pork, *leberkäse* and home-made cheeses actually go a long way to keeping your balance.

Klostergasthof (☎ 08152-930 90; Bergstrasse 9; mains €7.50-17; ☻ 10am-11pm) For a more sophisticated experience, make reservations here.

Dechant's Fischladen (☎ 08151-121 06; Hauptstrasse 20, Starnberg; mains €8-12; ☻ 10am-7pm Tue-Thu, 10am-midnight Fri) Clued-in fish fans book a table in the tiny restaurant attached to this place to enjoy the day's catch.

Getting There & Away

Starnberg lies 25km southwest of central Munich – a half-hour's journey by car or S-Bahn. The S6 links Munich with Starnberg and Possenhofen, Feldafing and Tutzing on the western lake shore. The S5 goes from Munich to Herrsching am Ammersee in about 45 minutes.

DACHAU

☎ 08131 / pop 40,100 / elev 508

Mention Dachau and most people shudder at the thought of the atrocities committed in the infamous Nazi concentration camp, now visited by more than 800,000 people each year. Few of them realise that there was a town of Dachau some 1100 years before the camp was built. Fewer still ever make it to the town's little Altstadt with its historic buildings, a pretty Renaissance palace and garden. And hardly anyone knows that in the late 19th to

the early 20th century, Dachau had a thriving artists colony, whose leading lights included Carl Spitzweg and Max Liebermann. Even today, about 100 artists live in Dachau.

Orientation & Information

Dachau's *Bahnhof* is about 3.5km southwest of the concentration camp memorial and about 1km southeast of the Altstadt, where you'll find the **tourist office** (☎ 752 86; www.dachau.info; Konrad-Adenauer-Strasse 1, Dachau; ☻ 9am-1pm Mon-Wed & Fri, 2-6pm Thu). Aside from dispensing maps, brochures and information, staff at the office also rent out audioguides (€2.50) for self-guided Altstadt tours taking about 90 minutes.

Sights

DACHAU CONCENTRATION CAMP MEMORIAL

> The way to freedom is to follow one's orders; exhibit honesty, orderliness, cleanliness, sobriety, truthfulness, the ability to sacrifice and love of the Fatherland.
>
> *Inscription from the roof of the concentration camp at Dachau*

Dachau was the Nazis' first concentration camp; it was built by Heinrich Himmler in March 1933 and became the prototype for all other camps. Originally meant to corral political prisoners, it also held thousands of Jews after the 1938 pogroms. All in all, some 32,000 people died at the camp, but it was not specifically designed as a 'death camp' such as Auschwitz. Instead it was a 'slave labour camp', where most deaths resulted from disease, exhaustion and starvation. Budget two to three hours to fully absorb the haunting exhibits. Children under 12 may find the experience too disturbing.

Information

The **memorial** (☎ 669 970; www.kz-gedenkstaette-dachau.de; Alte Römerstrasse 75, Dachau; admission free; ☻ 9am-5pm Tue-Sun) is in the northeastern corner of Dachau. Map pamphlets in about a dozen languages are available for €0.50. For more in-depth descriptions, pick up the brochure *Dachau Concentration Camp* (€2) or the detailed catalogue (€15). A 22-minute English-language documentary runs at 11.30am and 3.30pm. No refreshments are available at the memorial, so bring at least something to drink, especially in summer.

The Memorial

You enter the compound through the **Jourhaus**, originally the only entrance. Set in wrought iron, the chilling slogan '*Arbeit Macht Frei*' (Work Sets You Free) hits you at the gate. Beyond here is the former **roll-call square**, where the prisoners were counted every morning and evening and assigned to their work details.

On your right is the former utility building, now the main **documentation centre**, which details what happened to prisoners at the camp. Newcomers were registered in the **shunt room**, where they also had to surrender all their personal clothes and belongings. The '**baths**' were indeed initially used to disinfect the new inmates and shave their heads. After 1941, though, the SS converted the room into a torture and execution chamber; the whipping block is still there. Executions also took place in the **bunker courtyard** behind the exhibit building. The **bunker** itself was the notorious camp prison where inmates were tortured to extort 'confessions'; some of the cells are too small for prisoners to even sit.

Inmates were housed in large **barracks**, now demolished, which used to line the main road north of the roll-call square. Two have been reconstructed; of the other 32 you can only see the outlines. Built for 6000 prisoners, they housed more than 30,000 at the time of liberation in 1945.

At the end of the central camp road, behind the former barracks, is a cluster of **religious memorials** that includes a Catholic chapel, a Protestant church and a Jewish memorial. A Russian Orthodox chapel is a little off to the side, en route to perhaps the camp's most haunting site: the **crematorium** in the northwest corner, outside of the camp boundaries. Also here is a **gas chamber**, disguised as a shower room, but never used. Instead, prisoners marked for gassing were sent to other camps.

Tours

To maximise your educational experience, we highly recommend taking a guided tour, but be absolutely sure to join tours authorised by the memorial staff, such as those listed below.

Dachauer Forum (☎ 996 880; ticket €3; ⏰ 1.30pm Tue-Sun, noon Sat & Sun May-Sep 1.30pm Tue, Sat & Sun Oct-Apr; duration 2½hr) Volunteer-run English-language tours. Buy tickets at white containers along the entranceway. Also available are half-hour introductions for €1.50. These are held at 12.30pm Tuesday to Sunday and 11am Saturday and Sunday from May to September, and 12.30pm Thursday, Saturday and Sunday October to April.

Self-guided audio tour (adult/child €3/2; duration up to 2hr) If you prefer to go at your own pace, pick up one of these, also available at the containers.

Radius Tours & Bikes (☎ 5502 9374; www.radius munich.com; adult/child under 14 €21/10.50; ⏰ 9.15am & 12.30pm Tue-Sun Apr–mid-Oct, 11am Jun, Jul & mid-Oct–Mar) English-language tours leaving from opposite track 32 in the Hauptbahnhof. Tickets include public transport from Munich; bookings are advised.

New Munich Tours (adult/student €19/15; duration 3hr; ⏰ noon Fri, Sat & Sun) English-language tours departing from Marienplatz. Tickets include public transport.

SCHLOSS DACHAU

First built as a medieval castle for local nobles, **Schloss Dachau** (☎ 879 23; Schlossstrasse 7, Dachau; adult/under 18 yr/concession €2/free/1; ⏰ 9am-6pm Tue-Sun Apr-Sep, 10am-4pm Tue-Sun Oct-Mar) was transformed into a monolithic complex in the 16th century for the Wittelsbach dukes, who in turn made it their summer palace. The residence then fell into disrepair and just one of its four wings survived, namely the baroque number you see today. Behind its creamy façade is a festival hall with a magnificent wooden Renaissance ceiling that glorifies the Wittelsbach rulers. This is also the delightful setting of the Dachauer Schlosskonzerte, which is a classical concert series (tickets about €17 to €28).

Behind the Schloss, the baroque **Hofgarten** (admission free; ⏰ 8am-dusk, latest 8pm) harbours an orchard, a rose garden and lovers' paths sheltered by a leafy canopy. The terrace of the Schlosscafé overlooks this oasis of calm.

GEMÄLDEGALERIE DACHAU

The work of Carl Spitzweg, Max Liebermann and other Dachau School artists can be seen in the **Gemäldegalerie Dachau** (☎ 567 50; www.dachauer -galerien-museen.de; Konrad-Adenauer-Str 3; adult/concession €3.50/2; ⏰ 11am-5pm Tue-Fri, 1-5pm Sat & Sun), next to the tourist office. Climb up to the roof terrace for a view of the city and the landscape that inspired them.

Getting There & Around

Dachau is about 16km northwest of central Munich. The S2 makes the trip from Munich Hauptbahnhof to the station in Dachau in 22 minutes. You'll need a two-zone ticket (€4.40) or four strips of a *Streifenkarte*, including the bus connection. Here change to bus 720/722 to get to the Altstadt and the Schloss and bus 726 (direction 'Saubachsiedlung') to get to the camp. Show your stamped ticket to the driver. By car, follow Dachauer Strasse straight out to Dachau and follow the Altstadt or KZ-Gedenkstätte signs.

SCHLEISSHEIM

☎ 089 / pop 5700 / elev 486m

The northern Munich suburb of Schleissheim is renowned for its three palaces and an aviation museum. A combination ticket to the palaces is €6/5 adult/concession. Children under 18 years are free.

The crown jewel of the palatial trio is the **Neues Schloss Schleissheim** (New Palace; ☎ 315 8720; www.schloesser-schleissheim.de; Max-Emanuel-Platz 1, Schleissheim; adult/concession €4/3; ☺ 9am-6pm Apr-Sep, 10am-4pm Oct-Mar, closed Mon). This pompous pile was dreamed up by Prince-Elector Max Emanuel in 1701 in anticipation of his promotion to emperor. It never came. Instead he was forced into exile for over a decade and didn't get back to building until 1715. Cash flow problems required the scaling back of the original plans, but given the palace's huge dimensions (the façade is 330m long) and opulent interior, it's hard to imagine where exactly they cut back. Some of the finest artists of the baroque era were called in to create such eye-candy sights as the ceremonial staircase, the Victory Hall and the Grand Gallery. There are outstanding pieces of period furniture, including the elector's four-poster bed, amazing intricately inlaid tables, and a particularly impressive ceiling fresco by Cosmas Damian Asam.

The palace is home to the **Staatsgalerie** (State Gallery), a selection of European baroque art drawn from the Bavarian State Collection, including works by such masters as Peter Paul Rubens, Antonis van Dyck and Carlo Saraceni. The most impressive room here is the Grand Galerie.

While construction was ongoing, the elector resided in the fanciful hunting palace of **Schloss Lustheim** (☎ 315 8720; adult/concession €3/2; ☺ 9am-6pm Apr-Sep, 10am-4pm Oct-Mar, closed Mon), on a little island in the eastern Schlosspark, providing an elegant setting for porcelain masterpieces from Meissen.

Nearby, the **Altes Schloss Schleissheim** (☎ 315 8720; Maximilianshof 1; adult/concession €2.50/1.50; ☺ 9am-6pm Apr-Sep, 10am-4pm Oct-Mar, closed Mon) is a mere shadow of its Renaissance self. It houses paintings and sculpture on religious culture and

festivals all over the world, including an impressive collection of more than 100 crèches.

Only a short walk away, the **Flugwerft Schleissheim** (☎ 315 7140; www.deutsches-museum .de/flugwerft; Effnerstrasse 18; adult/concession/family €5/3/10; ☺ 9am-5pm), the aviation branch of the Deutsches Museum (p101), makes for a nice change of pace and aesthetics. Spirits will soar at the sight of the lethal Soviet MiG-21 fighter jet, the Vietnam-era F-4E Phantom and a replica of Otto Lilienthal's 1894 glider, with a revolutionary wing shaped like Batman's cape. Another highlight is the open workshop where you can observe the restoration of historical flying machines. Kids can climb into an original cockpit, land a plane and even get their 'pilot's license'.

To get to Schleissheim, take the S1 (direction: Freising) to Oberschleissheim, then walk along Mittenheimer Strasse for about 15 minutes towards the palaces. On weekdays only, bus 292 goes to the 'Schloss Lustheim' stop.

By car, take Leopoldstrasse north until it becomes Ingolstädter Strasse. Then take the A99 to the Neuherberg exit, at the south end of the airstrip.

FREISING

☎ 08161 / pop 43,000 / elev 448m

For a thousand years Freising was the spiritual and cultural centre of southern Bavaria. Now near the airport, it is a bedroom community for Munich but retains the feel of a traditional market town. In 1821 the bishop bowed to the inevitable and moved his seat to Munich. Freising sank in the ecclesiastical ranking but hung onto its religious gems, the main reasons to visit today. The town was a major way station in the life of Pope Benedict, who studied and taught at the university, was ordained as a priest and later even became archbishop here.

Orientation & Information

The bulk of Freising's sights are in the Altstadt on or around the Lehrberg, site of the cathedral complex and more popularly known as the Domberg. For information, visit the **tourist office** (☎ 541 22; www.freising.de, in German; Marienplatz 7; tours per adult/concession/family €6.50/4/12; ☺ 9am-6pm Mon-Fri, 9am-1pm Sat & Sun). Staff run several guided tours in English, including one that follows in the steps of the Pope. Check for specific times.

Sights

Freising's charming **Altstadt** is crisscrossed by a tangle of lanes lined by baroque and Renaissance town houses, immaculately restored and clean almost to a fault.

Looming over the old town is the Domberg, a hub of religious power with the twin-towered **Dom St Maria und St Korbinian** (☎ 1810; 8am-noon & 2-5pm, to 6pm May-Oct) as its focal point. The restored church interior is a head-turning masterpiece by the Asam brother megastars, whose baroque frescoes grace the most pious ceilings of Bavaria. Remnants from the Gothic era include the choir stalls and a *Lamentation of Christ* painting in the left aisle. The altar painting by Rubens is a copy of the original in the Alte Pinakothek museum in Munich.

Don't miss the crypt, not so much to view Korbinian's mortal remains as to admire the forest of pillars, no two of which are carved alike. The famous Bestiensäule (Beast Pillar) features an epic allegory of Christianity fighting the crocodile-like monsters of evil.

East of the Dom are the cloisters, whose halls drip with fancy stucco and a thousand years' homage in marble plaques to the bishops of Freising. The baroque hall of the **cathedral library** (2-3pm Mon-Fri mid-May–Oct) shines with the gold-and-white fantasies of François Cuvilliés, designer of the magnificent Cuvilliés Theatre in Munich.

At the western end of the hill is the **Dom Museum Freising** (☎ 487 90; Domberg 21; adult/child €2/1; 10am-5pm Tue-Sun). The largest ecclesiastical museum in Germany, it has a Fort Knox–worthy collection of bejewelled gold vessels, reliquaries and ceremonial regalia as well as some exquisite nativity scenes. Pride of place goes to the *Lukasbild,* a 12th-century Byzantine icon set in its own diminutive silver altar. Upstairs you'll discover works by Rubens and other masters.

Southwest of the Domberg, a former Benedictine monastery hosts, among other university faculties, a respected college of beer brewing. Also here is the **Staatsbrauerei Weihenstephan**, (☎ 5360; www.weihenstephaner.de; Alte Akademie 2; tours 60/120min €6/9; 10am Mon-Wed, 1.30pm Wed), a brewery founded in 1040, making it the world's oldest that's still in operation. Guided tours trace 1000 years of brewery history in the museum, which is followed by a behind-the-scenes spin around the 'hallowed halls' and concluded with a beer tasting (you get to keep the glass). Bookings are advised. Tours include a pretzl and a €2 voucher good for souvenirs or another brew served in the beer garden and the vaulted cellar of the Bräustüberl.

Getting There & Away

Freising is about 35km northeast of Munich at the northern terminus of the S1 (€6.60, 40 minutes) and is also frequently served by faster regional trains (€6.60, 25 minutes). The Domberg and Altstadt are a 10-minute walk from the train station. By car, take Leopoldstrasse north and turn right on Schenkendorfstrasse. Then take the A9 north and the A92 to the Freising-Mitte exit.

Bavarian Alps

Quaint, invigorating and absurdly beautiful, the Bavarian Alps captivate with equal drama and grace, and embrace with a gusto that leaves city dwellers gasping. The air is bracing, the skies blow a cobalt blue and the lakes shimmer in a myriad of shades. It's enough to convert the most dedicated couch potato to the great outdoors.

You'll also find clichés in spades: the thigh-slapping lederhosen lads, the foaming mugs of beer and platters groaning beneath portions of pork roast with sauerkraut. An admirable job is done in exploiting these popular images, but the story is presented with such sincerity that you can't resist playing along.

Much of the region is rural, endowed with the kind of scenery that is the stuff of post-cards. Nature and architecture blend harmoniously just about everywhere you look. Overall, people here are patriotic, politically conservative, overwhelmingly Roman Catholic and proud of their traditions.

The region is a paradise for outdoor activities, offering everything from leisurely dips and Alpine hikes to thrilling swooshes through some of Europe's most alluring ski areas. Although in many villages time seems to stand still, the tourism industry is state of the art. Every place has a helpful tourist office, there's good public transport and finding accommodation to suit every budget is rarely a problem.

BAVARIAN ALPS

HIGHLIGHTS

- Exorcising Nazi ghosts in the **Eagle's Nest** (p158) near Berchtesgaden
- Marvelling at the fantastical riches in Ludwig II's **Schloss Linderhof** (p143)
- Riding a pulse-quickening cable car to the top of the **Zugspitze** (p136), Germany's highest mountain
- Splashing, surfing and taking a sauna in the **Alpamare** (p145) fun pool in Bad Tölz
- Spending the night on the idyllic **Frauen-insel** (p152) in the Chiemsee

WERDENFELSER LAND

GARMISCH-PARTENKIRCHEN

☎ 08821 / pop 26,200 / elev 708m

A favourite haunt for outdoor enthusiasts and
moneyed socialites, Garmisch-Partenkirchen
is blessed with a fabled setting and some of
the best skiing in the land, including runs
on Germany's highest peak, the Zugspitze
(2962m). To say you were 'skiing in Garmisch'
has a fashionable ring, but it's really a superb
destination in any season. The towns of
Garmisch and Partenkirchen were merged on
the occasion of the 1936 Winter Olympics and
to this day host international skiing events.
Each retains its own distinct flair: Garmisch
feels more cosmopolitan; Partenkirchen flaunts
an old-world Alpine village vibe.

Orientation

The train tracks that divide the two towns
culminate at the Hauptbahnhof. From here,
turn west on St-Martin-Strasse to get to
Garmisch and east on Bahnhofstrasse to get
to Partenkirchen.

Information

HypoVereinsbank (Am Kurpark 13 & Rathausplatz 11)

Internet Café (☎ 2727; Zugspitzstrasse 2, Garmisch;
per 15min €1; ☼ 6am-6pm) Fast connections inside a
bakery.

Klinikum (☎ 770; Auenstrasse 6, Partenkirchen) Full-
service hospital with emergency room.

Post office (Bahnhofstrasse, Partenkirchen)

Presse & Buch (☎ 4400; Hauptbahnhof, Partenkirchen)
International papers and mags.

Tourist office (☎ 180 700; www.garmisch-parten
kirchen.de; Richard-Strauss-Platz 1, Garmisch; ☼ 8am-
6pm Mon-Sat, 10am-noon Sun) Also sells the Zugspitzcard
(www.zugspitzcard.de, in German), which includes
cable-car rides, admission to museums and fun pools, and
other activities in Garmisch-Partenkirchen and surrounding
villages. The three-day version costs €39/24 per adult/child.

Sights

ZUGSPITZE

Views from Germany's rooftop (www.zugs
pitze.de) are quite literally breathtaking and,
on good days, extend into four countries.
Skiing and hiking are the main activities here.
For a detailed description of the hike descending from the summit via the Partnachklamm,
see p66.

The trip to the Zugspitze summit is as
memorable as it is popular; beat the crowds
by starting early in the day and, if possible,
skip weekends altogether. In Garmisch, board
the **Zahnradbahn** (cogwheel train) at its own
station behind the Hauptbahnhof. Trains first
chug along the mountain base to the Eibsee,
a forest lake, then wind their way through
a mountain tunnel up to the Schneeferner
Glacier (2600m). Here, you'll switch to the
Gletscherbahn cable car for the final ascent to
the summit. When you're done soaking in the
panorama, board the **Eibsee-Seilbahn**, a steep
cable car, that sways and swings its way back
down to the Eibsee in about 10 minutes. It's

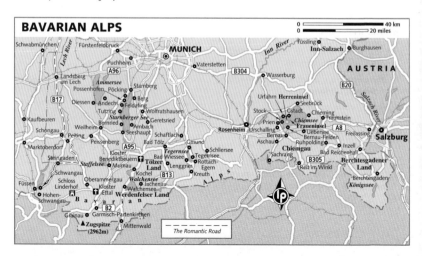

BAVARIAN ALPS

0 ——— 40 km
0 ——— 20 miles

The Romantic Road

not for vertigo sufferers, but the views surely are tremendous.

Most people come up on the train and take the cable car back down, but it works just as well the other way around. Either way, the entire trip costs €37.50/22.50 per adult/child in winter and €47/27.50 in summer. Winter rates include a day ski pass.

TOWN CENTRES

The heart of Garmisch is the Kurpark, just north of Richard-Strauss-Platz and the tourist office. A pedestrian zone lined with touristy shops and cafés leads west to Marienplatz and the richly stuccoed 18th-century **Alte St Martinskirche**, a work by the prolific Joseph Schmuzer, whose name you'll inevitably encounter again and again in this part of Bavaria. North of the church, across the little Loisach River, is Garmisch's most idyllic street, the **Frühlingstrasse**, which is flanked by proud houses frescoed in a style called *Lüftlmalerei* (see the boxed text, p142).

More magnificent houses are along **Ludwigstrasse**, a former trading route and still Partenkirchen's main commercial drag. Local arts and crafts are a focal point of the **Werdenfels Museum** (☎ 2134; Ludwigstrasse 47, Partenkirchen; adult/child €1.50/0.50; ⏲ 10am-5pm Tue-Sun), where the prized possessions include some pretty scary local carnival masks. The tangle of rooms also showcases Oberammergau woodcarvings, an 18th-century silver crib and delicate glass paintings.

KÖNIGSHAUS AM SCHACHEN

High in the mountains above Garmisch-Partenkirchen, at a lofty 1866m, the **Königshaus am Schachen** (☎ 929 30; adult/concession €4/3; ⏲ tours 11am, 1pm, 2pm & 3pm Jun-early Oct) was Ludwig II's little-known mountain retreat. What looks like a rather plain wooden hut actually has some surprisingly magnificent rooms, including the over-the-top Turkish Room. A fantasy of fine carpets, peacock feathers, a fountain and boldly coloured glass windows, it could easily have been dreamed up by Scheherazade herself. Picture the king in its midst, smoking water pipes and surrounded by turban-wearing servants. Downstairs is more functional, with a dining room, study, bedroom and chapel.

If you'd like to spend the night, check for availability in the **Schachenhaus** (☎ 0172-876 868; www.schachenhaus.de; dm/r with shared bathroom per person

€9.50/14.50; ⏲ Jun-early Oct), where accommodations are anything but royal. The inn also serves refreshments and hot meals.

Getting up here involves a gruelling three- to four-hour hike via the Partnachklamm (below) or Schloss Elmau.

Activities

SKIING

Garmisch-Partenkirchen's ski season runs from late November to early May in the higher elevations, making it the longest in Bavaria. See the boxed text on p58 for details. **Skischule Alpin** (☎ 945 676; www.skischulealpin.de; Reintalstrasse 8, Partenkirchen; 1-day group lessons €30, ski gear €18) and **Skischule Garmisch-Partenkirchen** (☎ 4931, 74260; www.skischule-gap.de; Am Hausberg 8, Garmisch; 1-day group lessons €35, ski gear €25) are both outfitters with good reputations.

Cross-country ski trails run along the main valleys, including a long section from Garmisch to Mittenwald.

HIKING

Garmisch-Partenkirchen is the gateway to superb hikes, two of which are detailed on p64. Tourist-office staff will happily supply you with additional ideas, tips and maps.

One of the most popular destinations that's easily accessed from the valley is the magnificent **Partnachklamm** (☎ 3167; adult/child €2/1), a narrow 750m-long gorge with walls rising up to 80m. It's especially magical in winter when you can walk beneath curtains of icicles the size of swords, and waterfalls frozen in mid-splash. Call ahead to make sure it's open. The entrance is about a 15-minute walk south of the Olympia Skistadion.

OTHER ACTIVITIES

Built for the 1936 Olympics, the **Olympia-Eissportzentrum** (☎ 753 291; www.gw-gap.de; Am Eisstadion, Garmisch; adult/child €4/2.30) has three indoor and two outdoor rinks (winter only) for skating, ice hockey and curling. It's open daily, but skating times vary.

The **Alpspitz-Wellenbad** (☎ 753 313; Klammstrasse 47, Garmisch; adult/child per 3hr €4.80/2.70, all day €6.50/3.70; ⏲ 9am-9pm Mon-Sat, 9am-7pm Sun) is a fun indoor wave pool with multiple saunas.

Festivals & Events

Garmisch-Partenkirchen hosts international skiing and ski-jumping competitions, but on

BAVARIAN ALPS

GARMISCH-PARTENKIRCHEN

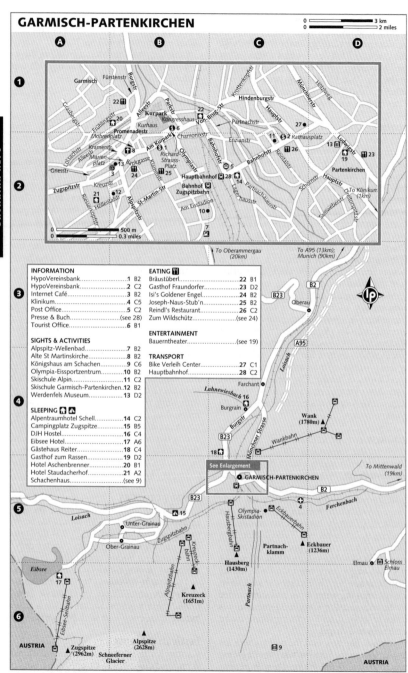

6 January thousands of spectators invade for the quirky **Hornschlittenrennen** (www.hornschlitten .de, in German). About 100 teams of four daredevils each race down a 1200m-long narrow ice track, clinging to historic wooden sledges, with the winners crowned Bavarian champions.

Top international musical talent comes to town in early June for the **Richard-Strauss-Festival** (tickets ☎ 730 1995; www.muenchenticket.de, www.richard-strauss-tage.de, in German), which honours the composer who lived in Garmisch from 1908 until his death in 1949. It's a highlight on the year's cultural calendar.

Sleeping

There is an electronic room-reservation board outside the tourist office and a 24-hour **reservation hotline** (☎ 194 12).

DJH hostel (☎ 967 050; www.garmisch.jugendher berge.de; Jochstrasse 10; dm €20.50-26.50; P X 🖳) Amenities at this smartly revamped hostel in a gorgeous creekside spot are as good as at basic chain hotels. It has 205 beds in brightly pigmented rooms with IKEA-type furnishings, including 21 four-bed family rooms with private bathroom and toilet. Diversions include a climbing wall.

Gasthof zum Rassen (☎ 2089; www.gasthof-rassen.de; Ludwigstrasse 45, Partenkirchen; s €32-53, d €52-90; P X) The modern rooms in this beautifully frescoed 14th-century building are a welcome respite from the frilly traditional décor of the lobby and restaurant. The Bauerntheater (p140) performs in the former barn.

Alpentraumhotel Schell (☎ 957 50; www.hotel -schell.de; Partnachauenstrasse 3, Partenkirchen; s from €45, d €75-100, tr €90-115; P) Sick of heavy retro furniture and bad oil paintings? Then book a 'dream room' in this small, family-run hotel where lovebirds can share their fantasies in the sensuous 'Life is for Love' room, and teens might get a kick out of 'Fire on Ice' with its ice-hockey theme. It's close to the Hauptbahnhof but very quiet, with a big garden for playing and relaxing.

Hotel Staudacherhof (☎ 9290; www.staudacher hof.de; Höllentalstrasse 48, Garmisch; s €46-96, d €118-142; P X 🖳 🛋) This elegant country inn is a top-flight address for class and personal service. Rooms are dressed in cheerfully elegant vanilla and cherry hues and come with balconies and a bevy of 21st-century amenities. Head to the spa for an extended relaxation session or go active with yoga, pilates or aqua-fitness.

Hotel Aschenbrenner (☎ 959 70; www.hotel-aschen brenner.de; Loisachstrasse 46, Garmisch; s €55-70, d €90-120; P X) Small but beautiful, this hotel is a class act all around and has bright and airy rooms, mostly in a peaches-and-cream colour palette with mountain-view balconies. Breakfast is a bonanza served under the stern gaze of carved apostles.

Eibsee Hotel (☎ 988 10; www.eibsee-hotel.de; Am Eibsee 1-3, Grainau/Eibsee; s €111, d €125-175; P X 🖳 🛋) Take a dream location, mix with a gourmet restaurant, stir in a lake-view sauna and private beach and you'll get one killer cocktail of a hotel. Choose from luxe rooms facing either the lake, the Zugspitze or the forest. In winter, a beginner's ski lift is right outside the hotel.

Other places you might consider:

Campingplatz Zugspitze (☎ 3180; www.zugspitz camping.de, in German; Griesener Strasse 4, Grainau; per tent/person/vehicle €3/5/3) Well-kept year-round campsite with heated bathrooms, all hemmed in by craggy mountains.

Gästehaus Reiter (☎ 2223; www.reiter-gap.com; Burgstrasse 55, Garmisch; s €20-30, d €40-60; P X) Chalet-style guesthouse with modern rooms and garden.

Eating & Drinking

Bräustüberl (☎ 2312; Fürstenstrasse 23, Garmisch; mains €6-17; ⏲ 9.30am-midnight Thu-Tue) Conversation flows as freely as the beer at this quintessential Bavarian brew-pub, complete with enormous enamel coal-burning stove and dirndl-clad waitresses. In summer, locals and tourists share tables beneath the chestnuts in the beer garden; the beer hall oozes the charms of yesteryear.

Gasthof Fraundorfer (☎ 9270; Ludwigstrasse 24, Partenkirchen; mains €7-17; ⏲ 7am-1am Thu-Mon, 5pm-1am Wed) The Fraundorfers have been in the hospitality business since 1820, so they know what people want: big mugs of beer, gigantic portions of some part of the pig, and yodelling, knee-slapping and dancing locals in lederhosen. It's kitsch, it's camp, and, after a beer or two, it's a rollicking good time.

Isi's Goldener Engel (☎ 948 757; Bankgasse 5, Garmisch; mains €9-18; ⏲ 11am-2.30pm & 5-11pm, closed Nov-Christmas) The 'Golden Angel' is a rococo riot, complete with wacky frescoes and gold-leaf-sheathed ceilings that wouldn't look out of place in a church. It's family run, neighbourhood adored and delivers classic Bavarian cooking, including a mean pork knuckle with the crust done just so.

Reindl's Restaurant (☎ 943 870; Bahnhofstrasse 15, Garmisch; mains €12-24; ✆ noon-2.30pm & 6.30-11pm) Empty tables are rare in this art- and antique-stuffed bulwark of tradition. Regulars keep such classics as rack of venison in juniper cream sauce on the menu, but the chef's talent truly shines with lighter, more inspired flavour bombs, such as lamb filet with date balsamico jus.

Joseph-Naus-Stub'n (☎ 9010; Klammstrasse 19, Garmisch; mains €14-20, menu €25-55; ✆ 6-11pm Tue-Sun, noon-3pm Sat & Sun) The creative, light and contemporary comfort food with ingenious Bavarian and Mediterranean accents has vaulted this charmer to the top of many a local's fave list. It's in the Zugspitze hotel.

Zum Wildschütz (☎ 3290; Bankgasse 9, Garmisch; mains €6-17; ✆ 10am-midnight) The best place in town for fresh venison, rabbit and other seasonal game dishes, this place is, not surprisingly, popular with hunters.

Entertainment

Bauerntheater (peasants' theatre; ☎ 562 24; tickets €6-8) Bavaria's oldest theatre of this sort, this place has been staging folk plays ranging from ribald to religious (or both) since 1892. Performances take place once a week, normally on Saturday, at the Gasthof zum Rassen in Partenkirchen (p139). Even native German speakers have trouble understanding the strong dialect, but the traditional costumes are fun and the silly stories easy to grasp.

Getting There & Around

Garmisch is serviced twice hourly by trains from Munich (€16.40, 1½ hours). RVO bus 9606 travels to Füssen via the Wieskirche, Neuschwanstein and Oberammergau, while bus 9608 goes as far as Kochel via Mittenwald. If you're driving, the A95 from Munich is the direct road route.

Bus tickets cost €1.50 for journeys within town. For a big selection of reliable touring and mountain bikes try **Bike Verleih Center** (☎ 549 46, 0151-1222 4466; Ludwigstrasse 90, Garmisch; per day €12-25; ✆ 9am-6.30pm).

MITTENWALD
☎ 08823 / pop 7865 / elev 913m
Mittenwald is about tradition not trendiness, family not flings – it's an authentic getaway from the urban bustle. Goethe described it as 'a living picture book' and he wasn't just talk-

ing about the gorgeous setting or unhurried village flair. No, he meant it quite literally, for nearly every façade here is festooned with colourful and intricate frescoes in a style called *Lüftlmalerei* (see the boxed text, p142).

Information
HypoVereinsbank (Obermarkt 30)
Post office (Bahnhofsplatz 1) Opposite the train station.
Tourist office (☎ 339 81; www.mittenwald.de; Dammkarstrasse 3; ✆ 8.30am-6pm Mon-Fri, 9am-noon Sat, 10am-noon Sun May-Sep, 8.30am-5pm Mon-Fri Oct-Apr)

Sights
Competing with the Karwendel (2384m) for prominence is the baroque tower of the **Pfarrkirche St Peter und Paul** (Church of St Peter and Paul), standing at the eastern end of the pedestrianised Obermarkt like the dot in an exclamation point. It's an especially successful collaboration by stucco master Josef Schmuzer and Matthäus Günther, who created the elaborate frescoes inside and on the tower starring the church's patron saints, Peter and Paul.

The memorial outside the church honours **Matthias Klotz** (1653–1743), the man credited with turning Mittenwald into an internationally renowned centre of violin making. Learn more about him, the craft and the instrument itself in the engagingly organised **Geigenbaumuseum** (Violinmaking Museum; ☎ 2511; Ballenhausgasse 3; adult/child/concession €4/2/3; ✆ 10am-5pm Tue-Sun Feb–mid-Mar, mid-May–mid-Oct & mid-Dec–early Jan, other months 11am-4pm Tue-Sun). There's still a violin-making school in town today and the film showing the many steps required in fashioning the instrument is truly fascinating.

Obermarkt itself is a parade of *Lüftlmalerei* beauties, most notably the **Gasthaus Alpenrose** (Obermarkt 1), which uses secular themes to convey a religious message: at the bottom are the four virtues, in the middle the five senses and on top the Virgin Mary ringed by angels and saints. The **Neunerhaus** (Obermarkt 24) is another eye-catcher. The oldest frescoes, though, are west of the church, on Im Gries. Today this ancient tradition is still kept alive by local artist Stephan Pfeffer.

Activities
HIKING
Mittenwald is an excellent place for hiking. Popular local hikes with cable-car access go to

BAVARIAN ALPS

the Alpspitze (2628m), the Wank (1780m), Mt Karwendel (2384m) and the Wettersteinspitze (2297m). The **Karwendelbahn cable car** (☎ 8480; adult/child one way €13.50/9.50, return €22/12; ☒ 8.30am–5pm) goes to Germany's second-highest mountain station at 2244m, the gateway to a number of strenuous hikes.

An exciting walk, especially for kids, runs through the **Leutascher Geisterklamm** (Leutasch Ghost Gorge; admission free; ☒ 9am-6pm mid-May–late Oct), a series of metal walkways and bridges built into or suspended above the steep-sided rocky canyon. Along the way, you'll have several encounters with an imaginary 'ghost' living at the bottom of the gorge who reveals secrets about the area's geology, history and mythology. Hokey, but fun. Views can be rather dizzying, so don't attempt if you're afraid of heights. Parking is €5.

SKIING

For details about the Kranzberg, Mittenwald's local ski mountain, see the boxed text on p58. A special treat for advanced skiers is surfing the powder of the 7km **Dammkar** (☎ 8480; day pass adult/child €27/18; ☒ 9am-4.30pm), a spectacular free ride area reached via a 400m tunnel from the Karwendelbahn mountain station.

For equipment hire and ski or snowboard instruction, contact the **Erste Skischule Mittenwald** (☎ 3582; Bahnhofsplatz). A three-hour ski or snowboard lesson costs €30, while complete ski gear goes for €20.

Sleeping & Eating

The tourist office website (www.mittenwald .de) has a room-booking function.

Gästehaus Sonnenbichl (☎ 922 30; www.sonnen bichl-tourismus.de; Klausnerweg 32; s €34-43, d €68-82; ☐) At this hillside charmer, about a five-minute saunter from town, you'll sleep like a log in bright, well-kept rooms that skimp neither on space nor country-style charisma. We also like the soul-restoring Karwendel views from the balcony or the pretty garden, and the free bike and toboggan rentals.

Hotel Post (☎ 938 2333; www.posthotel-mittenwald .de; Obermarkt 9, enter via Karwendelstrasse 14; s €50-75, d €86-136; ☐ ☒) Mittenwald's premier in-town hotel is a classic outpost of charm and tradition. Rooms, many with balconies, come in three styles and categories; we recommend the bright and spacious *Jugendstilzimmer* that face away from the street. The restaurant does interesting things with local rabbit and deer.

Gröblalm (☎ 9110; www.groeblalm.de, in German; Gröblalm 1-2; s €54, d €83-89; ☐) This family-run mountain lodge on a sunny slope embraces you with warmth, peace and quiet and delivers fabulous views. Rooms, while comfortable, are not of the latest vintage but the sauna area has been redone in a neat Alpine mountain-hut look. Restaurant dishes show off local farm and field products.

Restaurant Arnspitze (☎ 2425; Innsbrucker Strasse 68; mains €17-23; ☒ Thu-Mon, closed Apr) Regional cooking goes gourmet at Herbert Wipfelder's critically acclaimed restaurant, about 1km south of town. Dishes such as rabbit paired with goat cheese or olive-encrusted lamb spotlight both the quality ingredients and the chef's know-how.

Getting There & Away

Mittenwald is served by hourly trains from Munich (€19.10, two hours), Garmisch-Partenkirchen (€3.50, 20 minutes) and Innsbruck (€9.70, one hour).

RVO bus 9608 links Mittenwald with Garmisch-Partenkirchen (30 minutes) frequently and Kochel (50 minutes) twice daily.

Mittenwald is about 20km southeast of Garmisch-Partenkirchen on the B2.

OBERAMMERGAU

☎ 08822 / pop 5400 / elev 850m

A blend of genuine piety, religious kitsch and commercial greed of Disney proportions, Oberammergau sometimes seems to sink under the weight of day-trippers. Sadly, the crush of humanity may distract from the town's triple charms: its gorgeous valley setting below the jagged Kofel peak, a 500-year-old woodcarving tradition and a wealth of houses painted with *Lüftlmalerei*. About 20km north of Garmisch-Partenkirchen, Oberammergau is known worldwide for hosting the famous **Passion Play**, acted out by hundreds of townspeople every 10 years since 1634 to give thanks for being spared from the plague. The next one is in 2010.

For information, stop by the **tourist office** (☎ 923 10; www.oberammergau.de; Eugen-Papst-Strasse 9a; ☒ 9am-6pm Mon-Fri, 9am-noon Sat year-round, plus 10am-noon Sun Jun-Oct). Internet access is available at **Hotel Alte Post** (☎ 9100; Dorfstrasse 19).

Sights & Activities

It's hard to escape the hordes, but one place that's usually pretty quiet is the church of **St**

Peter and Paul (Herkulan-Schwaiger-Gasse 5), another fine collaboration by local master artists Joseph Schmuzer (design and stucco) and Matthäus Günther (frescoes). The churchyard has some moody headstones and crosses.

But ultimately it's the eye-popping *Lüftlmalerei* frescoes that give Oberammergau its special appeal. Some even have endearing fairy-tale themes, such as the **Hänsel & Gretel House** (Ettaler Strasse 41) and the **Little Red Riding Hood House** (Ettaler Strasse 48). The most accomplished, though, is the **Pilatushaus** (☎ 923 10; Ludwig-Thoma-Strasse 10; admission free; ☺ 1-6pm Tue-Sat May-Oct), which depicts the scene of Jesus being handed his death sentence. Inside, local woodcarvers are busy carving and chiselling everything from saints to devils. This local tradition is also a main focus of the **Oberammergaumuseum** (☎ 941 36; Dorfstrasse 8; adult/child/concession €4/1/3.50; ☺ 10am-5pm Tue-Sun Dec-Jan & Apr-Oct), although the historic crib collection on the ground floor is even more impressive.

The Passion Play is performed at the **Passionstheater** (☎ 923 10; Passionswiese 1; tour adult/child/concession €4/1/3.50; ☺ tours 9.30am-5pm Mar-Oct & Dec). The 45-minute tour provides ample background on the play's history and also lets you peek at the costumes and sets. Museum/theatre combo tickets are €6/1/5. Ask at the tourist office about performances.

About 1.5km east of town, the **Laber-Bergbahn** (☎ 4770; www.laber-bergbahn.de; Ludwig-Lang-Strasse 59; one way/return adult/child €8.50/13.50; ☺ 9am-4.30pm Sep-Jun, 9am-5.30pm Jul & Aug) ferries hikers, skiers and sightseers to the peak of Mt Laber (1684m), which also has a restaurant and sweeping views of the valley and Alps. Day ski passes per adult/child cost €21.50/14.50.

Another fun place to frolic around is the **WellenBerg** (☎ 923 60; www.wellenberg-oberammergau.de; Himmelsreich 52; adult/child per 4hr €9/6, with sauna €14/9; ☺ 10am-9pm) indoor/outdoor swimming pool and sauna complex, where highlights include a sandy beach and a circular wave pool.

Sleeping & Eating

Oberammergau has plenty of private rooms, small *Pensionen* and holiday flats. Otherwise, your best budget bet is the **DJH hostel** (☎ 4114; www.jugendherberge.de/jh/oberammergau, in German; Malensteinweg 10; dm €18-22; ☺ closed mid-Nov–late Dec; ✗), a 132-bed facility with modern bunks and baths. It's about a 15-minute walk south of the train station.

Hotel Alte Post (☎ 9100; www.ogau.de; Dorfstrasse 19; s €42-48, d €63-84; ✗ ▣) This frescoed hotel has a pedigree going back to 1612 but is also solidly rooted in the here and now. Thumbs up for rooms sparkling in a frill-free country look, wi-fi and the on-site internet café. It has an *Umweltsiegel* (ecoseal) from the Bavarian government for operating ecoconsciously. The restaurant (mains €8 to €16) is OK but nothing special.

Hotel Turmwirt (☎ 926 00; www.turmwirt.de; Ettalerstrasse 2; s €67, d €94-108; ✗) This homey inn (restaurant mains €9 to €18) has 22 spotless rooms done up in fine-looking Bavarian style and outfitted with all major amenities; many have balconies. It's run by the well-travelled and personable Glas family, who speak fluent English. Light sleepers may be bothered by the church bells next door.

Hotel Antonia (☎ 920 10; www.hotel-antonia.com; Freikorpsstrasse 5; s/d/tr €68/89/98) Another fine place to sleep. It has bright and modern rooms and free wi-fi.

Landgasthaus Café Beim Kargl (☎ 640; Im Kirchfeld 9, Saulgrub; mains €12-24; ☺ 11am-midnight) It's worth the quick drive north of town to savour Anton Kargl's exquisite Old Bavarian cooking made almost exclusively with locally sourced organic meats and vegetables. He does magical things with *Bärlauch*, a wild-growing leafy herb with a garlicky taste, which he turns into pastas, pestos, soups, even schnapps.

Getting There & Around

Hourly trains connect Munich with Oberammergau with a change at Murnau (€15.60, 1¾ hours). RVO bus 9606 links Oberammergau with Füssen and the Wieskirche as well as Garmisch-Partenkirchen almost hourly. For bike rental, **Sportzentrale Papistock** (☎ 4178; Bahnhofstrasse 6a) charges €10 per day.

ETTAL

☎ 08822 / pop 810 / elev 877m
Ettal would be another turn in the road were it not for its famous monastery **Kloster Ettal** (☎ 740; www.kloster-ettal.de; admission free; 8am-6pm). Ludwig der Bayer founded the place in 1330 after returning from a quarrel with the Pope in Rome. In his pocket he carried a marble Madonna, now the monastery's prized possession and displayed as part of the basilica's high altar. A fire devastated most of the old Gothic structure, which was rebuilt in the sugary rococo style you see today. Enrico Zuccalli and Joseph Schmuzer pulled out all the stops to create this imposing complex with its vast courtyard, weighty dome and a façade sporting larger-than-life statues of the apostles.

In the basilica all eyes are drawn to Johann Jakob Zeiller's dome fresco, which shows a hearty celebration of the Trinity by St Benedict and his followers, with (count them) 431 individual figures. Elaborate stucco ornamentation smoothly frames the painting.

Today's monastery still has about 55 Benedictine monks, an enterprising bunch who manage not only a prestigious boarding school but also a publishing business, a hotel-restaurant, a brewery and a distillery churning out the famous Ettaler Klosterlikör, a sweet herbal digestif.

Check with the **tourist office** (☎ 3534; www .ettal.de; Ammergauer Strasse 8; 8am-noon Mon-Fri) about hotel options or try **Blaue Gams** (☎ 6449; www.blaue-gams.de; Vogelherdweg 12; s/d €42/80; ✕), a bastion of warmth and hospitality with modern rooms, dream views of the monastery complex and a well-respected restaurant (mains €10 to €18).

Ettal is about 5km south of Oberammergau on the B23 and served by RVO bus 9606 from Garmisch-Partenkirchen and Oberammergau and bus 9622 from Linderhof and Oberammergau.

SCHLOSS LINDERHOF

The pocket-sized palace of **Schloss Linderhof** (☎ 08822-920 30; www.schlosslinderhof.de; adult/under 18yr/concession Apr-Sep €7/free/6, Oct-Mar €6/free/5; 9am-6pm Apr-Sep, 10am-4pm Oct-Mar) is Ludwig II's most irresistibly charming whimsy. Embedded in an idyllic valley about 13km southwest of Oberammergau, it hugs the hillside in a romantic setting of French gardens, fountains and follies. Ludwig used the palace as a retreat and hardly ever received visitors here. Like Herrenchiemsee (p151), Linderhof was inspired by Versailles and dedicated to Louis XIV, Ludwig's idol.

Linderhof is full of fanciful treasures and myth-laden frescoes, evidence of the king's creativity as well as his ostentatious taste. The largest room is the heavily ornamented **bedroom** with its enormous crystal chandelier. An artificial waterfall, built to cool the room in summer, cascades just outside the window. The **dining room** reflects both the king's passion for privacy and for newfangled gadgets: its central fixture is a 'magic table' that sinks through the floor to the kitchen. No need to see the servants.

Ludwig also poured enormous effort and imagination into the gardens and outbuildings, which are only open April to October. In the **Moorish Kiosk** he used to hang out pasha style, dressed in exotic costumes and

LUDWIG'S BEST FOR...

The myth and mystique of King Ludwig II is one of Bavaria's most endearing attractions. Here's our list of favourite places to soak up his enigma.

- Over-the-top frilliness – **Schloss Linderhof** (above)
- Romantic getaway – **Roseninsel** (p129)
- Least overrun – **Königshaus am Schachen** (p137)
- Bragging rights back home – **Schloss Neuschwanstein** (p283)
- Unbridled opulence – **Schloss Herrenchiemsee** (p151)
- Final resting place – **Michaelskirche** (p91)
- Sad remembrance – **Berg on Lake Starnberg** (p128)

enjoying late-night entertainment from his flashy peacock throne. Just as kooky is the **Venus Grotto**, a fake stalactite cave with an illuminated lake and a conch-shaped boat with cherub prow.

Bus 9622 makes the trip out to Linderhof from Oberammergau nine times on weekdays and four times on weekends, while RVO bus 9606 comes in from Garmisch-Partenkirchen (1½ hours). By car, turn off the B23 and onto ST2060 between Oberau and Oberammergau. To avoid the worst crowds, come early or after 4pm in summer.

Schloss Linderhof is about a one-hour drive east of Schloss Neuschwanstein (p283) via Reutte (Austria).

MURNAU
☎ 08841 / pop 12,000 / elev 700m

What is it about Murnau that has inspired so many artists? Is it the backdrop of the muscular mountains, the majesty of the lake, the crispness of the sky, the higgledy-piggledy village, the ethereal quality of light? 'All of the above', the painters of Der Blaue Reiter (The Blue Rider) might say. Two of the founders of this seminal early-20th-century artist group, Gabriele Münter and Wassily Kandinsky, first fell in love with Murnau in 1908. They continued spending their summers here until the outbreak of WWI in 1914, often joined by fellow Blaue Reiter members Alex Jawlensky, August Macke, Franz Marc and other avant-gardists. Marc bought a house at the nearby Kochelsee (p147), while Münter stayed in Murnau until her death in 1962. During the Nazi years, she fiercely safeguarded a vast trove of paintings, especially Kandinsky's, that had been deemed 'degenerate' by the regime. In 1957, she donated her entire private collection to the Städtische Galerie im Lenbachhaus (p93) in Munich.

Orientation & Information
Murnau's *Bahnhof* and main bus station are about 700m northwest of the town centre. Take Bahnhofweg to Bahnhofstrasse south, which gets you to Gabriele-Münter-Platz and the tourist office. One block east is Obermarkt, the main artery, with the Schlossmuseum up on a low hill. The Staffelsee is about 1km west of Obermarkt. For information, stop by the **tourist office** (☎ 614 10; www.murnau.de; Kohlgruber Strasse 1; ⏰ 9am-noon Mon-Sat & 2-6pm Mon-Fri May-Jul & Sep-Oct, 9am-noon Mon-Sat & 2-5pm Mon-Fri Nov-Apr).

The website www.dasblaueland.de also has some good info.

Sights & Activities
The **Münter-Haus** (☎ 628 880; Kottmüllerallee 6; adult/under 18yr €2.50/free; ⏰ 2-5pm Tue-Sun), also known as the Russian House, has been faithfully restored to its original state when Münter lived here with Kandinsky. Highlights include the furniture the two of them painted, as well as an amazing staircase decorated by Kandinsky. Two rooms focus on the book *The Blue Rider Almanac*, a collection of essays and illustrations considered a groundbreaking manifesto on avant-garde art.

Münter's art spanning the entire arc of her creative life is on view at the **Schlossmuseum Murnau** (☎ 476 207; www.schlossmuseum-murnau.de; Schlosshof 4-5; adult/child/concession €4.50/2/3; ⏰ 10am-5pm Tue-Sun Oct-Jun, 10am-6pm Sat & Sun Jul-Sep). Other rooms focus on the Blaue Reiter, the writer Ödon von Horváth, the history of the palace, Murnau landscapes and painted glass. The **Münter-Brunnen**, a modern fountain on Gabriele-Münter-Platz, re-creates the floor plan of the Münter-Haus.

One much-painted motif is the **Staffelsee** and its seven islands. Warmer than most Alpine lakes, it's ideal for swimming. You can also cycle or walk around its 18km circumference or hire rowing or paddle boats. From May to October, boats shuttle between the three lake communities (Murnau, Seehausen and Uffing, the latter with beer gardens near the landing) four times daily. The entire loop costs €7/3.50 per adult/child.

Sleeping & Eating
Lodging is bookable via www.murnau.de, or swing by the tourist office for referrals.

Griesbräu (☎ 1422; www.griesbraeu.de; Obermarkt 37; s €50-65, d €80-95; ⏰ 10am-1am; ✗) Right in town, rooms here have dark furniture and a lot of ambience. Some are wi-fi enabled (for a fee). The traditional brew-pub (meals €6 to €12) with beer garden and hotel makes sudsy amber Weissbier that goes exceptionally well with the roast piglet and crispy chicken.

Am Eichholz Galerie & Art-Hotel (☎ 5863; www .ameichholz.de; Am Eichholz 21; d €95-140; ✗) Artist Gina Feder (www.feder-art.de) has infused her quiet four-unit Art Nouveau retreat with a delightful marriage of tradition and modern designer flair. Splashes of colour, original art throughout and great mountain views make for a romantic and/or inspiring getaway. Ask about art workshops.

Alpenhof Murnau (☎ 4910; www.alpenhof-murnau
.de; Ramsachstrasse 8; s €140-195, d €190-290; ✗) An urge to splurge is well directed towards this Relais & Chateaux charmer that makes a virtue out of sophisticated chic while maintaining a laid-back vibe. Spacious rooms lack no comforts and rates include spa access.

For succulent pork knuckle and superb Weissbier, head to the **Karg's Bräustüberl**
(☎ 8272; Untermarkt 27; mains €5-13; ☯ 11am-11pm Tue-Sun) brew-pub.

Getting There & Away

Direct RB trains go hourly to Munich (€12.40, one hour), Garmisch-Partenkirchen (€4.80, 30 minutes) and Oberammergau (€4.80, 40 minutes). RVO bus 9611 makes at least hourly trips to Kochel (30 to 40 minutes). Murnau is on the B2, about 25km north of Garmisch-Partenkirchen and 36km southwest of Bad Tölz.

TÖLZER LAND

BAD TÖLZ
☎ 08041 / pop 17,700 / elev 659m
The picture-book-pretty spa town of Bad Tölz is a popular getaway for city-weary Münchners and it's easy to see why. The location on the Isar River is gorgeous, the old town quaint and the family-friendly attractions numerous.

Orientation & Information

The Isar separates the spa quarter in the west from the Altstadt in the east. The *Bahnhof* is near the eastern edge of town, about a 20-minute walk from the river. The **tourist office** (☎ 786 70; www.bad-toelz.de; Max-Höfler-Platz 1; ☯ 9am-6pm Mon-Fri, 9am-noon Sat) has a public internet terminal.

Sights & Activities

Cobblestoned and car free, the **Marktstrasse** gently slopes through the Altstadt, flanked by statuesque town houses with painted façades and overhanging eaves. Have a closer look at the Sporerhaus at No 45 and the Pflegerhaus at No 59. The old town hall now houses the **Stadtmuseum** (☎ 504 688; Marktstrasse 48; adult/child €2/1; ☯ 10am-4pm Tue-Sun), which touches on practically all aspects of local culture and history. It has an especially good col-lection of painted armoires (the so-called Tölzer Kisten) along with the usual assortment of beer steins, folkloric garments and religious objects.

Paralleling Marktstrasse is Säggasse, which leads up to the 707m-high Kalvarienberg where the twin-towered baroque **Kalvarienbergkirche** (Cavalry Church) dwarfs the tiny adjacent **Leonhardikapelle** (Leonhardi Chapel; 1718), the destination of the Leonhardi pilgrimage (below).

In the spa section of town, **Alpamare** (☎ 509 999; www.alpamare.de; Ludwigstrasse 14; all-day weekday pass adult/child €23/19, weekend pass €32/23; ☯ 9am-10pm) is one of the oldest fun pools in Europe but it's by no means old-fashioned. Rainy days evaporate as you splash around in the indoor and outdoor mineral pools, compete for waves in the surfing pool and chase each other down breakneck waterslides. Afterwards, saunas and steam rooms invite unwinding. Take bus 9570 (from the *Bahnhof*) to the Kurviertel/Alpamare stop.

Southwest of town, the **Blomberg** (1248m) is a family-friendly mountain with a wicked **Alpine slide**. This fibreglass track snakes 1.3km downhill through 17 hairpin bends, with you crouched on wheeled bobsleds and controlling the speed with a joystick. You can go as fast as 50km/h but be careful not to ram anyone or to fly off the track, and wear a long-sleeved shirt and jeans. Getting up the hill involves a chairlift ride aboard the **Blombergbahn** (☎ 3726; adult/child return top station €8/3.50; ☯ 9am-6pm May-Oct, 9am-4pm Nov-Apr weather permitting). Riding to the midway station and sliding down costs €4/3.50 per adult/child, with discounts for multiple trips. In winter there's skiing, but the real kick is the 5.5km **toboggan track**; half-day passes are €11/9 per adult/child and sledges cost an extra €6.50.

Back in town, the traditional **Marionetten-theater Bad Tölz** (☎ 741 46: Schlossplatz 1) has delighted young and old since 1908 with fanciful tales acted out by endearing, handcrafted puppets on a string.

Festivals & Events

Every year on 6 November the town celebrates the patron saint of horses, Leonhard, with the famous **Leonhardifahrt**, a pilgrimage up to the Leonhardi chapel on Kalvarienberg. Townsfolk dress up in their finest traditional costume for the occasion and ride in garlanded horse-drawn carts to the strains of brass bands.

Sleeping & Eating

For a casual meal, try **Solo** (☎ 730 923; Königsdorfer Strasse 2; mains €7-10; ☺ 9am-midnight), in town and right on the Isar, which draws an all-ages crowd with global bistro favourites (pasta, curries, enchiladas, salads).

Altes Fährhaus (☎ 6030; An der Isarlust 1; mains €13-28; ☺ 11.30am-2pm & 6-9.30pm Wed-Sun) Elly Reisser-Kluge helms this romantic riverside inn, where she orchestrates choice ingredients into such tastebud stunners as dove breast with foie gras tortellini. Rooms (singles/doubles from €70/100) are just as classy and overlook the Isar.

For additional lodging options, contact the tourist office (p145) or test-drive its online room search and booking function.

our pick Auberge Moar-Alm (☎ 08021-5520; www .moar-alm.de; Holzkirchner Strasse 14, Sachsenkam; mains €21-26, 3-course meal €29-48; ☺ noon-2pm & 6pm-midnight Wed-Fri, noon-midnight Sat & Sun) At this handsome chalet cum art gallery the kitchen swings between Mediterranean brio (excellent fish and seafood dishes) and heart-warming dishes from northern France. The warm, congenial hosts also offer cooking courses and baby-sitting for guests. It's about 10km north of Bad Tölz, just off the main B13, and well worth the drive.

Getting There & Away

Bad Tölz has hourly train connections with Munich on the private Bayerische Oberlandbahn (BOB; €9.60, 50 minutes). Bus 9612 goes to Kochel via Benediktbeuern, bus 9557 to Tegernsee and bus 9564 to Lenggries.

LENGGRIES

☎ 08045 / pop 9500 / elev 700m

Outdoorsy day trippers from Munich often deluge this tiny village, the gateway to hiking and skiing on the Brauneck (1555m). The recently modernised **Brauneckbahn** (☎ 08042-503 940; www.brauneck-bergbahn.de; one way/return €9/15, day ski pass adult/child €26/14.50; ☺ 8.30am-4.30pm) ferries people up the mountain. Snow levels can be unreliable, but on good days skiing here is pure joy.

Lenggries is also a popular departure point for white-water canoeing, kayaking and rafting trips on the Isar River. **Kajakschule Oberland** (☎ 916 916; www.viactiva.de, in German; Ganghoferstrasse 7) is an experienced outfitter offering courses (from €119) and rafting tours (four hours from €44, including equipment).

DETOUR: LENGGRIES TO WALCHENSEE

This leisurely drive, 34km in total, links Lenggries with Walchensee, taking you past velvety meadows dotted with traditional Alpine barns. From Lenggries, take Wegscheider Strasse 2km south and turn right on the road marked Jachenau. Well off the busy highways, the soundtrack is of burbling brooks and tinkling cowbells. You'll pass through a clutch of hamlets until you reach pretty **Jachenau** village, with bucolic *Lüftlmalerei* paintings along Dorfstrasse. Continuing west, pay the road toll (€3) and carry on till you reach the **Walchensee**. The road skirts the south shore of this emerald-green lake with numerous spots for pulling over for a swim or a picnic. At the end of the road, turn right and reach Walchensee village, about 3km away.

The **tourist office** (☎ 501 80; www.lenggries.de; Rathausplatz 2; ☺ 8am-6pm Mon-Fri, 10am-noon Sat & Sun, shorter hours in low season) can help you find accommodation, or try **Hotel Gasthof Der Altwirt** (☎ 8085; www.altwirt-lenggries.de; Marktstrasse 13; s/d €43/70; P ☒), a massive inn from 1469 with cosy, traditional rooms, a small sauna and a good restaurant (mains €7 to €15). It has the Bavarian state ecoseal for its thorough approach to ecofriendly hotel management.

Dorfschänke Lenggries (☎ 2108; Bachmairgasse 3; mains €8-20; ☺ 10am-10pm Fri-Tue, 5-10pm Thu), a locals' favourite nicknamed 'Bunker', welcomes you with the irresistible aroma of ribs, steaks and sausages tickled by an open fire. The home-made, unfiltered Kellerbier is the perfect complement.

Open late and good for a beer and a snack is the earthy **Hirschbach Stüberl** (☎ 8312; Karwendelstrasse 50; dishes €5-9; ☺ 5pm-1am Mon-Sat, noon-1am Sun), home of the famous *Hirschisemmeln* – giant sandwiches with delicious fillings.

Lenggries is the southern terminus of the private BOB railway from Munich (€12.40, one hour) and is linked to Bad Tölz by buses 9564 and 9553.

KLOSTER BENEDIKTBEUERN

One of the oldest monasteries in Bavaria (c 739), the venerable **Kloster Benediktbeuern** (☎ 08857-880; www.kloster-benediktbeuern.de, in German; Don-Bosco-Strasse 1; admission free; ☺ 9am-5.30pm) is run by Salesian monks who operate a school of theology, environmental education centre, restaurant, youth hostel and guesthouse, and high-calibre cultural programme. The *Benediktbeurer Konzerte,* a classical concert series held in summer, is renowned throughout Bavaria.

Concerts take place in the **Basilika St Benedikt**, a baroque confection heavily stuccoed with flowers, fruit and vegetables in praise of creation. The ceiling fresco shows pivotal moments from the life of Jesus and is an early work by Hans Georg Asam, father of the famous brothers Cosmas and Damian Asam.

The small rococo **Anastasiakapelle** (Anastasia Chapel), the collaborative effort of top talent from the era, seems almost playful by comparison. It's dedicated to a 4th-century martyr whose bones came to Benediktbeuern in 1053 but who didn't get her own magnificent chapel until performing a miracle in the 18th century. When the monks and villagers found themselves under attack, with enemy forces about to cross the frozen Kochelsee, everyone prayed fervently to Anastasia for help. Lo and behold – a warm wind came up, melted the ice and drove away the marauders (who apparently were too lazy to go around the lake).

If that's too much hocus-pocus for you, return to earth in the **Fraunhofer-Glashütte**, which harbours the re-created workshop of, and exhibits about, Joseph von Fraunhofer (1787–1826). It was here in the early 19th century that the famed physicist discovered the 'Fraunhofer lines' (the dark lines in the sun's spectrum) and produced optical lenses that paved the way for spectral analysis. The exhibit was getting a revamp at the time of research but should have reopened by now.

From Munich, regional trains travel hourly to Benediktbeuern (€10.60, one hour). The monastery is just off the B11, about 14km southwest of Bad Tölz and served several times daily by bus 9612 (30 minutes).

KOCHEL AM SEE

☎ 08851 / pop 4200

Charismatic Kochel, with its rich and sensuous palette of colours and lake motifs, greatly inspired one of the most influential early-20th-century German painters Franz Marc (1880–1916). Along with Wassily Kandinsky and Gabriele Münter, who spent their summers in nearby Murnau (p144), Marc was a co-founder of the artists' group *Der Blaue Reiter* (The Blue Rider; 1911). Marc first fell in love with Kochel in 1908 while still a student at the Munich Arts Academy, finally buying a house here in 1914. Two years later he died on the battlefields of Verdun. He's buried in Kochel cemetery and best remembered for his paintings featuring animals, horses in particular.

For information, stop by the **tourist office** (☎ 338; www.kochel.de; Kalmbachstrasse 11; 8am-noon Mon-Fri year-round, plus 1-4pm Apr-Sep) in the tiny town centre.

Sights

Kochel's main cultural draw is the **Franz Marc Museum** (☎ 7114; www.franz-marc-museum.de; Herzogstandweg 43; adult/child/student/family €7.50/3.50/5/18; 10am-6pm Tue-Sun Apr-Oct, 10am-5pm Tue-Sun Nov-Mar). At research time a modern, natural-stone-clad extension was being docked to the original hillside villa. Set to open by this book's publication, it will showcase not only oils and works on paper

BAVARIAN ALPS

CARMINA BURANA

Medieval love poems in a dead language don't usually make it into film soundtracks. But through composer Carl Orff (1895–1982), the rants of a hedonistic band of Germans have survived to titillate, amuse and inspire movie scores for a host of films, including *The Omen, Excalibur* and *The Doors.*

Carmina Burana (literally, 'Songs of Beuern') is a collection of about 250 raging, erotic and humorous poems composed by goliards (defrocked monks, minstrels and wastrels). The 13th-century manuscript was found, by accident, in the monastery of Benediktbeuern in 1803.

Early in his career, Orff was mainly a music educator whose life was forever changed after he wrote his famous secular cantata, which disregards the notation of the Latin originals. The epic premiered in Frankfurt in 1937 to immediate acclaim. In treating these celebrations of eroticism, gluttony, drinking and gambling, his choral and instrumental arrangements were light-hearted, inspirational and downright frightening. Through the driving strains of the *Carmina Burana,* one fact about the 13th century is made abundantly clear: they sure knew how to party.

by Marc and fellow Blue Riders but also by other expressionist artists, including Brücke members Karl Schmidt-Rottluff and Ernst Kirchner. A third focus is on abstract post-WWII painters, such as Willy Baumeister, who were influenced by these early-20th-century avant-gardists.

At the southern end of the Kochelsee, you can learn how water is turned into electricity at the multimedia **Informationszentrum Walchensee** (☎ 770; Altjoch 21; admission free; ☽ 9am-5pm), attached to the Walchenseekraftwerk, a 1924 hydroelectric power plant. It produces about 300 million kWh of clean energy per year by channelling water from the higher Walchensee via six giant tubes to the Kochelsee, some 200m below. The exhibit explains the process through models, turbines and other techno displays. Labelling is in German, but free English-language brochures are available. Sponsored by the energy concern E.ON, the centre is easy to dismiss as a propaganda ploy, but it's actually quite well done. Just ignore the third room where the company presents itself.

Sleeping & Eating

Campingplatz Renken (☎ 615 505; www.campingplatz-renken.de; Mittenwalder Strasse 106; per adult/car/tent €6/2.50/3; ☽ Apr-Sep) New owners have breathed new life into this place. It's in a pretty spot right on the lake, but has little shade and can get cramped.

Landhotel Herzogstand (☎ 324; www.herzogstand.de; Herzogstandweg 3; s €44-55, d €70-100; P ✗) King Ludwig II once kept his horses at this traditional hotel, which counts country-style rooms, a huge garden and a convivial restaurant among its assets. It has the Bavarian ecoseal and has Viabono (green hotel association) accreditation.

Alpenhof Postillion (☎ 1820; www.alpenhofpostillion.de; Kalmbachstr 1; s/d from €50/100; P ✗ ⌨ ⌾) At this good-value inn rooms come in soothing colours and with free wi-fi, and dishes (mains €10 to €16) starring fresh lake fish or home-grown *Bärlauch* (wild garlic) are the kitchen's best ambassadors. This hotel also minimises energy consumption and uses ecofriendly technology. Kids will love splashing around in the grotto-like minipool.

Getting There & Away

Kochel is about 22km southwest of Bad Tölz and is served several times daily by bus 9612 from Bad Tölz via Benediktbeuern (40 minutes). Trains from Munich connect with Kochel hourly; change in Tutzing (€12.40, one hour).

WALCHENSEE

☎ 08858 / pop 580

A Harley rider's dream road, the **Kesselbergstrasse** twists and turns between the Kochelsee and the much larger Walchensee, at 194m Germany's deepest Alpine lake and a water-sports mecca. In summer, when water temperatures may reach a tolerable 23°C, swimmers and sun worshippers crowd the pebbly beaches; the inlets along the southern shore are the prettiest. Want to catch your dinner? Enquire about fishing permits at the **Walchensee tourist office** (☎ 411; Ringstr 1; ☽ 9am-noon Mon-Fri, 1-4pm Mon-Thu); the Walchensee is one of the few lakes allowing foreign visitors to pull out pike and lake trout.

Rumours of Nazi treasure buried in the depths of the lake continue to captivate divers, but the Walchensee's real fame is as a hot spot of the windsurfing scene. A peculiar microclimate generating strong breezes during fine-weather days lures experienced surfers and even the sport's elite, such as Robbie Naish of Hawaii. On weekends, the water can get crowded. **Windsurf & Bike-Center** (☎ 261; Seestrasse 10), on the western shore right next to the Herzogstandbahn gondola, rents gear and runs courses.

A particularly rewarding day hike with superb views takes you to the peak of the 1731m Herzogstand, one of King Ludwig's favourite mountains. You can start either near Urfeld on the northern shore of the Walchensee or in Schlehdorf/Raut on the Kochelsee. If you want to enjoy the views without breaking a sweat, catch a gondola ride on the **Herzogstandbahn** (☎ 236; Am Tanneneck 6; adult/child one way €7.50/4.25, return €12.50/6.75; ☽ 8.30am-5.45pm Apr-Oct, 9am-4.15pm Nov-Mar). Those not prone to vertigo could extend this tour via the craggy, cable-lined ridge walk from Mt Herzogstand to Mt Heimgarten (1790m). From here, you could either double back or work your way downhill to Walchensee. All local tourist offices sell hiking maps.

Walchensee is about 35km southwest of Bad Tölz. Bus 9608 makes several stops along the western shore on its route between Kochel and Garmisch-Partenkirchen, via Mittenwald.

TEGERNSEER LAND

Set against an Alpine stage and surrounded by forests, the Tegernseer Land is about 50km south of Munich and embraces the Tegernsee, one of Bavaria's most beautiful lakes. This fact has not gone unnoticed by Germany's money elite – celebs, industrialists and blue-bloods – many of whom keep weekend villas here (which has inspired the nickname Lago di Prozzo, or Braggers' Lake). But as supermodels know, being blessed with great beauty can also be a curse. Here, this is especially true on sunny summer weekends when the only road linking the four lakeside communities gets as clogged as a Los Angeles freeway. Better to get out of the car and onto a trail or a boat.

The lake is usually warm enough for swimming from May to September. Point, a sandy beach on a small peninsula between Tegernsee and Rottach-Egern, offers the nicest shore access, although it can get crowded on weekends.

A leisurely way to explore the lake communities is by **boat**. You can travel between towns, make a full loop (€12) or a southern loop (€8) that stops everywhere except Gmund.

Getting There & Around

Gmund and the town of Tegernsee (€9.60, one hour) are both stops on the private BOB railway from Munich (€9.60, 53 minutes).

RVO bus 9551 stop in all lake communities before continuing on to Munich (1¾ hours). Bus 9557 goes to Bad Tölz from Tegernsee via Gmund and Bad Wiessee, although it's faster to take the BOB and change in Schaftlach (€3.50, about one hour, depending on connection).

Bus 9559 makes a sweep of the lake communities every 30 to 60 minutes.

TEGERNSEE

On the eastern lakeshore, the lake and region's namesake town is also the most historical and once had considerable pull on the monastic scene. Founded in 746 by Benedictine monks, Tegernsee monastery had a library that, for a while, was the envy of even the Vatican. In 1817, the Wittelsbach ruling family bought the place, used it as a summer residence and took over the monastery brewery, which descendants still operate today. Sample the suds in the famous **Bräustüberl** (☎ 4141; Schlossplatz 1; dishes €3.50-10; ☻ 9am-11pm), where grizzled locals mingle with noisy tour groups under the vaults of this historic beer hall. The beverage of choice is the delicious Tegernseer beer, known for its mild, malty taste. The menu has all the usual brew-pub eats, but *Weisswurst* (veal sausage) with potato salad is recommended.

Next door, **Pfarrkirche St Quirinus** (Church of St Quirin; ☻ 9am-7pm Apr-Oct, 9am-4.30pm Nov-Mar), with frescoes by Johann Georg Asam, completes the 'Bavarian Trinity' of palace, brewery and church. The complex also houses a grammar school.

Fans of biting caricature should check out the **Olaf-Gulbransson-Museum** (☎ 3338; Im Kurgarten; adult/child €4/1; ☻ 10am-5pm Tue-Sun). The Norwegian-born artist (1873–1958) worked for the Munich-based satirical magazine *Simplicissimus*, but spent much of his adult life in Tegernsee. The museum shows the entire range of his work, from cartoons to oils and drawings. His caricatures of Kaiser Wilhelm are world famous.

For general information, stop by the **tourist office** (☎ 180 140; www.tegernsee.de; Hauptstrasse 2), where staff can also make lodging referrals. For a killer hilltop location with postcard views, head to **Leeberghof** (☎ 188 090; www.leeberghof.de; Ellingerstrasse 10; s €78-180, d €200-320; Ⓟ Ⓧ), a first-class boutique hotel with 15 individually decorated rooms. Even if you can't afford the steep tab, come up here for a meal (mains €16 to €25) or a drink with a view from the terrace or a cocktail in the stylish Sassa Bar. To get there, make a sharp turn on Leebergstrasse and follow the signs.

ROTTACH-EGERN

The two-part town of Rottach-Egern, on the southern shore, is the most glamorous of the lakeside communities. Its streets are lined by beautiful old houses with painted shutters and façades. Many more houses with overhanging eaves and wooden balconies cling to the slopes of nearby hills.

Rottach-Egern is the departure point of the **Wallbergbahn** (☎ 705 370; Am Höhenrain 5-7, Rottach-Egern; one way/return €15/9 Apr-Oct, €4.50/7 Nov-Mar; ☻ 8.45am-5pm Apr-Oct, 8.45am-4.30pm Nov-Mar), a cable car up Mt Wallberg (1722m) where there's a restaurant, trailheads and predictably superb views. In winter you can head back down on the exhilarating 6.5m-long toboggan run – the longest in Germany!

If you have your own vehicle, a drive up the mountain on the panoramic **Wallbergstrasse** (toll €3) to the **Berggasthof Wallbergmoos** (☎ 5638; ☻ 10am-6pm Wed-Mon), is another fun thing to do. From here, it's a one-hour hike to the Wallberg summit through lovely Alpine terrain dotted with edelweiss and gentian. Also keep an eye out for snow hens and chamois.

BAVARIAN ALPS

Back in town, a lovely overnight option is **Hotel Garni Reiffenstuel** (☎ 927 350; www.reiffenstuel .de; Seestrasse 67; s €69, d €76-102; **P**). This friendly lakeside hotel has its own swimming beach, boat hire and a vast back garden for taking in the rays. Its countrified rooms are spacious and comfy, most with views of the lake and the Alps beyond.

If they're full, stop by the **tourist office** (☎ 671 341; www.rottach-egern.de; Nördliche Hauptstrasse 9) for more ideas.

For eats, locals' favourite **Beim Zotz'n** (☎ 2999; Wolfgrubstrasse 6; mains €6.50-12; ⏲ from 5pm Tue-Sat, from 11.30am Sun) scores a perfect 10 on our charm meter for its three woodsy chambers, its jovial host Herr Bogner and, of course, the perfectly executed Bavarian-Tyrolean food (the *Krustenbraten* pork roast is a speciality). It's a bit hard to find but worth the effort.

Also good is **Weinhaus Moschner** (☎ 5522; Kisslinger Strasse 2; mains €9-20; ⏲ from 6pm Wed-Sun, bar from 9.30pm), where you can warm up with rustic food in the wine bar downstairs, then indulge in libational flights of fancy in the upstairs cocktail bar.

OTHER LAKE COMMUNITIES

Tegernsee's two other lakeside towns are family-oriented **Gmund** in the north and the spa town of **Bad Wiessee**, well known for its curative iodine springs and lavish new casino, in the west. Bad Wiessee has a **tourist office** (☎ 860 30; www.bad-wiessee.de) at Adrian-Stoop-Strasse 20, while **Gmund's** (☎ 750 527; www.gmund.de) is at Kirchenweg 6.

A few kilometres south of the lakeshore is tradition-minded **Kreuth**, whose beautiful 15th-century church is the destination of Bavaria's oldest Leonhardifahrt, a pilgrimage honouring the patron saint of horses (the biggest celebration is in Bad Tölz, see p145). Cross-country skiers have a scenic 23km trail to explore from Kreuth, which does not have its own tourist office.

Feng shui meets classy Bavarian country style at Bad Wiessee's ourpick **Romantik Hotel Landhaus Wilhelmy** (☎ 986 80; www.romantikhotels .com/bad-wiessee; Freihausstrasse 15; s €80-95, d €140-170; **P** ✕), which puts a premium on an eco-friendly approach to hospitality. The organic bath amenities, the plush robes, and the sauna and steam room in the small but exclusive spa are all thoughtful touches.

Gourmets should book early for a table at ourpick **Gasthaus zum Hirschberg** (☎ 08029-315;

Nördliche Hauptstrasse 89; mains €10-25; ⏲ 11.30am-11pm Wed-Mon) in Kreuth. The region's star chef, Alex Winkelmann, is a wizard when it comes to giving Bavarian home cooking the gourmet treatment. Trout, venison, veal and other ingredients are all organic, locally sourced and paired with seasonal treats like white asparagus or porcini mushrooms. From 2pm to 6pm, snacks and home-made cakes are served. Dinner reservations are de rigueur.

CHIEMGAU

The Chiemgau is the kind of holiday region that will have you storing memories by the gigabyte. Nature has been especially prolific here, creating a rich pastiche of landscapes from rolling foothills to the rugged peaks of the Chiemgau Alps, rippling mountain streams to romantic river valleys and moody moorland to majestic lakes, most notably the giant Chiemsee. Bordered by the Inn River in the west and the Salzach River on the Austrian border, the Chiemgau is perfect for outdoor pursuits of all stripes. Swimming, boating, windsurfing, cycling and hiking are all popular, while in winter the snow makes the higher elevations suitable for snowboarding and downhill and cross-country skiing. Toss in a few ancient monasteries and Ludwig II's grandest palace for cultural appeal and you'll have one potent cocktail of experiences.

CHIEMSEE

Shimmering softly in umpteen shades of blue, the Chiemsee is backed by the Chiemgau Alps and is rich in trout, pike and other fish. Affectionately known as the 'Bavarian Sea', it's a haven for water rats, stressed-out city dwellers and anyone on the grand palace tour. Ludwig II liked it so much, he chose to build his homage to Versailles – Schloss Herrenchiemsee – on one of its islands. On summer weekends, ferries to the palace quite literally spill over with day-trippers, so come during the week or in the low season in order to understand the region's true magic.

Though not the prettiest lake towns, **Prien** and **Bernau**, about 5km south, are the most convenient bases for exploring the region. Both are stops on the Munich–Salzburg rail line. Of the two, Prien is the larger and more commercial.

Information

Chiemsee Infocenter (☎ 08051-965 550; www
.chiemsee.de; Felden 10, Bernau; ☒ 9am-6pm Mon-Fri,
10am-3pm Sat & Sun; ☐) General information for the
entire area; it's on the southern lakeshore, just off the
autobahn exit Bernau-Felden.

Prien tourist office (☎ 08051-690 50; www.tourismus
.prien.de; Alte Rathausstrasse 11, Prien; ☒ 8.30am-6pm
Mon-Fri, 8.30am-4pm Sat, 8.30am-noon Sun May-Sep,
8.30am-5pm Mon-Fri Oct-Apr; ☐)

Sights

SCHLOSS HERRENCHIEMSEE

Ludwig II's worship of French king Louis
XIV reached its pinnacle with the building
of **Schloss Herrenchiemsee** (☎ 08051-688 70; www
.herren-chiemsee.de; adult/under 18yr/concession €7/free/6;
☒ tours 9am-5.15pm Apr–mid-Oct, 9.40am-3.40pm mid-
Oct–Mar) on its own island (the Herreninsel) in
the Chiemsee. Ludwig truly pulled out all the

stops for his 'Bavarian Versailles', spending
more money here than on Neuschwanstein
and Linderhof combined. When cash ran out
in 1885, one year before his death, 50 rooms
remained unfinished.

The vast **Prunktreppenhaus**, a double staircase leading to a frescoed gallery and topped
by a glass roof, is the first visual knockout
on the 30-minute guided tour. But even this
fades in comparison with the dizzying **Grosse
Spiegelgalerie** (Great Hall of Mirrors), which is
10m longer than that in Versailles.

Just as gaspworthy are the chapel-like
Paradeschlafzimmer (State Bedroom), where
morning and evening audiences were held, and
the king's **private bedroom**, encrusted with gilded
stucco and wildly extravagant carvings.

For insight into the man, his warped brain
and intriguing predilections, take a spin around
the **König Ludwig II Museum** in the south wing

BAVARIAN ALPS

DETOUR: WASSERBURG AM INN

Utterly enchanting **Wasserburg** (population 12,000, elevation 419m) hangs like a teardrop in a
spectacular hairpin loop of the Inn River. It's a tiny, quiet spot with an almost completely intact
medieval old town of turrets, towers, gables and steeples that's enlivened by a dynamic contemporary arts scene. The driving force here is the **Arbeitskreis 68** (www.arbeitskreis68.de), an artist group
whose work can be seen along the 1.5km-long **Skulpturenweg** (Sculpture Path). It follows the
river starting at Brucktor, a massive bridge gate at the end of the Rote Brücke (Red Bridge).

On the left past the Brucktor is the Heilig-Geist-Spital, a medieval hospital that now harbours
the **Imaginäres Museum** (☎ 08071-4358; adult/child €2.50/1; ☒ 1-5pm Tue-Sun May-Sep, 1-4pm Oct-Dec,
Feb-Apr), which shows eerily perfect reproductions of famous paintings – from Monet to Hundert-
wasser – created by a special screen technique developed by the late artist Günter Dietz.

Strolling around the old town, you'll eventually arrive at the central square, Marienplatz, lorded
over by the imposing **Rathaus** (☎ 1050; tours adult/child €2.50/1; ☒ tours 10am & 11am Tue-Sun, 2pm,
3pm & 4pm Tue-Fri), the Gothic town hall that also survived a stint as a bakery. Join a tour to see
the stunning 16th-century murals in the wood-panelled council chamber. The **tourist office**
(☎ 08071-105 22; www.wasserburg.de; ☒ 9am-5pm Mon-Fri, 10am-2pm Sat May-Sep, 9am-3pm Mon-Fri, 10am-
1pm Sat Oct-Apr) is downstairs.

Boat trips (☎ 08071-4793; adult/child €6/3; ☒ Apr-Oct) depart from the south end of the Rote
Brücke. Call or check locally for current departure times. To truly appreciate Wasserburg's scenic
setting, though, head up to the **Schöne Aussicht** viewpoint on the Kellerberg, reached in a 15-
minute walk via Salzburger Strasse from the south side of the Rote Brücke.

If hunger strikes, you'll eat sensationally well and cheaply in the **Wasserburger Markthallen**
(☎ 08071-3838; Salzsenderzeile 4; mains around €4), famous for its Saturday all-you-can-eat buffet breakfast (€7.50; served to 11am). Or stock up on crusty bread, cheese and cold cuts here and find a
picnic spot by the inn. For lunch or dinner (preferably on the terrace) prepared with local, seasonal
and organic ingredients, there are few finer destinations than the 'Weisses Rössl' (☎ 08071-502
91; Herrengasse 1; menu lunch €12.50, dinner €23-34; ☒ 11.30am-2pm & 6pm-midnight Tue-Sat). If you'd like
to spend the night, check out the romantic **Hotel Fletzinger** (☎ 08071-908 90; www.hotel-fletzinger
.de; Fletzingergasse 1; s €66-78, d €88-128; ☒), with its modern designer rooms, stylish bar and plenty
of thoughtful perks like fresh fruit and wi-fi.

Wasserburg is about 28km north of the Chiemsee, near the crossroads of the B15 and the B304.
RVO bus 9414 makes the trip from Prien am Chiemsee several times daily in 50 minutes.

DETOUR: URSCHALLING

God depicted as a woman? Nope, it's not the work of Damien Hirst or some other 'art heretic' but of an unknown 15th-century artist who decorated the walls of the **St Jacobuskirche** in the hamlet of Urschalling with this 'offensive' imagery. The Church was so incensed that the frescoes were swiftly painted over and remained hidden until a cleaning lady accidentally rediscovered them in 1923. In fact, this unusual take on the Holy Trinity (located on the altar ceiling) continues to stir debate today.

To get to the church from Prien am Chiemsee, take Bernauer Strasse south for 2km, turn right into Urschallinger Strasse and drive half a kilometre. If you find the doors locked, get a key from the sexton (☎ 5886).

---

of the palace. The broad collection includes his christening and coronation robes, displays on his Wagner obsession, blueprints for more manic architectural projects and his death mask, but nothing about his controversial death.

Ferries to Herreninsel leave from Prien-Stock (€6.20 return, 15 minutes), Bernau-Felden (€6.70 return, 25 minutes, May to September only) and Gstadt via Fraueninsel (€6.20 return, 20 minutes). Prien gets busiest, so board in Gstadt if possible.

It's about a 20-minute walk from the landing to the palace through lovely gardens.

FRAUENINSEL

From Herrenchiemsee boats continue on to the romantic Fraueninsel, the southern section of which is taken up by the **Frauenwörth Abbey** (☎ 08054-9070; admission free; 🕑 8am-noon & 1-6pm), a nunnery active since the late 8th century. Its ancient **basilica** has a Romanesque core, Gothic net-vaulted ceiling and fabulous baroque altars. Replicas of its Romanesque frescoes are in the nearby **Torhalle**, a gatehouse that's another century older still. It presents artistic or historical exhibits in summer.

Return ferry fare, including a stop at Herreninsel, is €7.30 from Prien-Stock, €7.80 from Bernau-Felden and €4 from Gstadt.

Activities

The most easily accessible **swimming** beaches are at Chieming and Gstadt (both free) on

the lake's east and north shores, respectively. The small beach at Urfahrn, about 5km west of Gstadt, is particularly nice. **Boats**, available for hire all around the lake, range from €5 to €20 per hour, depending on the type.

Rainy days are best spent in **Prienavera** (☎ 08051-609 570; Seestrasse 120, Prien; adult/child 4hr pass €10/5.50, day pass €12/6.50, sauna extra €3; 🕑 10am-9pm Mon-Fri, 9am-9pm Sat & Sun), an enormous pool complex with sauna, steam baths, slides, Jacuzzi and fitness area in Prien-Stock. The **beach** (admission €2.50; 🕑 9am-8pm) opens from May to September.

Reasonably fit cyclists can cover the lake's 65km circumference in a day. Rent bikes from **Radlverleih Chiemsee** (☎ 964 789; Prien-Stock), right by the minigolf course in Prien harbour. Touring bikes cost €5 per day and mountain bikes range from €10 to €18.

Festivals & Events

For three hot days in late August, the world's reggae elite and some 25,000 of their fans come together for the open-air **Chiemsee Reggae Summer** (www.chiemsee-reggae.de), one of Europe's largest such festivals in Uebersee, close to the lake's southern shore.

Sleeping

Panorama Camping Harras (☎ 08051-904 613; www.camping-harras.de; Harrasser Strasse 135, Prien; per person/tent/car €5.50/3.60/1.70; 🕑 Apr-Nov) In a scenic location on a peninsula, this modern campground has top-notch bathrooms, a private beach, catamaran and windsurfing gear rentals and a restaurant with lakeview terrace. Prices are 15% higher for stays under four days.

DJH hostel (☎ 08051-687 70; www.prien.jugendherberge.de, in German; Carl-Braun-Strasse 66, Prien; dm €18.50-22.50; 🕑 closed Dec–mid-Feb; ✗) Often deluged with school groups, Prien's modernised hostel doubles as an environmental study centre and is about a 15-minute walk from the Hauptbahnhof.

Gästehaus Lechner (☎ 08051-7373; www.gaestehaus-lechner.de; Aschauerstrasse 85, Bernau; s €37.50, d €52-62, apt €53-66) This renovated farmhouse on the quiet outskirts of Bernau offers quite literally a breath of fresh air. You'll be charmed by the owner, the modern country-look rooms and the redolent garden with private pond. There's a surcharge for stays of under three days.

Hotel Bonnschlössl (☎ 08051-965 6990; www.bonnschloessl.de; Ferdinand-Bonn-Strasse 2, Bernau; s €42-72, d €70-97; ✗) Fancy yourself knight and damsel in this turreted 1477 palace with rooms of considerably more modern vintage. The integrated spa has a long menu of relaxation options (massages from €21) and breakfast on the terrace overlooking the rambling garden is just as blissful.

Inselhotel zur Linde (☎ 08054-903 66; www.linde -frauenchiemsee.de; Fraueninsel; s/d €70/120; ✗) Once the last ferry boat leaves the Fraueninsel, the ambience goes from frantic to romantic in no time. Take a deep breath: a dinner in the cosy restaurant (great fish plucked fresh from the lake; mains €6.50 to €16.50) and a night in this 600-year-old hotel await.

Eating

Hacienda (☎ 4448; Seestrasse 7, Prien; tapas €2-3.50, mains €7-16; ✹ 6pm-1am Mon-Sat) This sassy little number is often mobbed by hip and youthful locals lusting after tapas, paella, mojitos and sangria, and making it an ideal place to take a break from the schnitzel and *Schweinshaxe* (pork knuckles) routine.

Der Alte Wirt (☎ 890 11; Kirchplatz 9, Bernau; Brotzeit €4-9, mains €7-16; ✹ 11am-11pm Tue-Sun) In a massive half-timbered inn with five centuries of history, this place is an ambience-laden port of call for dependable Bavarian cuisine. The *Leberkäse* is the star of the menu but – thanks to an in-house butcher – all meat dishes are uniformly excellent. The waitresses dart around as if on roller blades.

Badehaus (☎ 970 300; Rasthausstrasse 11, Bernau; mains €6-15; ✹ 10am-1am) Near the Chiemsee Infocenter and the lakeshore, this contemporary beer hall has quirky décor and upscale fare enjoyed by a mix of locals and coach tourists. The Sunday brunch is popular; don't even think about showing up without reservations.

Mühlberger Restaurant (☎ 08051-966 888; Bernauer Strasse 40, Prien; mains €18-23; ✹ 11.30am-2pm & 6-10pm Thu-Mon) The shooting star in Chiemsee's culinary firmament; Thomas Mühlberger's cooking is all about substance, not smoke and mirrors. Only fresh and carefully edited ingredients find their destiny in such dishes as turbot with poached tomato, foie gras with apple compote and a swoonworthy *mousse au chocolat*.

Getting There & Around

Prien and Bernau are served by hourly trains from Munich (€14.20, one hour). Hourly bus 9505 connects the two lake towns (10 minutes) before going on to Reit im Winkl (p154). Local buses operate between Prien *Bahnhof*

and the harbour in Stock or go the nostalgic route aboard the historic **Chiemseebahn** (one way/return €2/3; daily late May-Sep, Sat & Sun Oct–mid-May), the world's oldest steam tram from 1887. Also from May to September, the **Chiemseeringlinie** 'hike and bike bus' loops around the lake, stopping in all communities.

Chiemsee-Schifffahrt (☎ 6090; www.chiemsee -schifffahrt.de; Seestrasse 108, Prien) operates ferries between Herreninsel, Fraueninsel, Bernau, Gstadt, Seebruck and Chieming on a seasonally changing schedule. You can circumnavigate the entire lake and make all these stops with or without getting off for €10.20. Children aged six to 15 get a 50% discount, and family tickets are also available.

ASCHAU IM CHIEMGAU
☎ 08052 / pop 5600 / elev 615m

Cradled by the craggy Kampenwand (1669m), tiny Aschau sits prettily in the forested Prien Valley, a mere 5km south of the Chiemsee lakeshore. It's not a bad town to base yourself in as long as you don't mind the sight of big-city boomers in beemers flocking to Heinz Winkler's Michelin-starred gourmet temple. Otherwise, Aschau keeps a pretty low profile and has some of the best hiking in the area.

Aschau's **tourist office** (☎ 904 937; www.aschau .de, in German; Kampenwandstrasse 38; ✹ 8am-6pm Mon-Fri, 9am-noon Sat, 10am-noon Sun May–mid-Oct, 8am-noon & 1.30-5pm Mon-Fri mid-Oct–Apr) is on the main drag.

Sights & Activities

The Gothic parish church is worth a look, but Aschau's main sight is the hilltop **Schloss Hohenaschau** (☎ 904 937; Schlossbergstrasse; tour & museum adult/child €3/2; ✹ tours 9.30am, 10.30am, 11.30am Tue-Fri May-Sep, Thu only Apr & Oct). It has 12th-century origins and still looks quite imposing despite now being a government-owned holiday retreat. Guided tours let you peek inside the baroque chapel, the prison and the ornately stuccoed Preysingsäle. Also inside is the rather lame **Prientalmuseum** (✹ 9.30-noon Tue-Fri May-Sep, Thu only Apr & Oct), with exhibits about local rulers and the valley's industrial heritage.

No matter if you just want to soak in the dramatic Alpine panorama or are planning an all-day mountain trek, be sure to head up the Kampenwand aboard the **Kampenwandbahn** (☎ 4411; An der Bergbahn 8; adult/5-15yr one way €11/5.50, return €15.50/8; ✹ 9am-5pm May-Jun & Sep-Oct, 9am-6pm Jul & Aug, 9am-4.30pm Dec-Apr). In less than 15 minutes, gondolas whisk you to the mountain station at 1500m and a nearby restaurant. From up here you'll have access to one of the most extensive trail networks in the Bavarian Alps, including a 1.5km groomed trail in winter. Skiers have 12km of pistes to play with, including the 5km valley run; all-day ski passes cost €22.50/13.50 per adult/child.

Sleeping & Eating

Prillerhof (☎ 906 370; www.prillerhof.de; Höhenbergstrasse 1; s €33, d €64-72; ✗) Run by an award-winning young hotelier, Prillerhof is both a feel-good and good-value place. The generously sized, modern rooms have pantry kitchens, balconies, fluffy bathrobes and other amenities more typical of pricier properties. The sparkling spa with sauna, Jacuzzi, steam room and such unusual relaxation devices as a 'body-swing' (only sounds naughty) is a perfect spot for reliving the day's exploits.

Residenz Heinz Winkler (☎ 179 90; www.residenz-heinz-winkler.de; Kirchplatz 1; á la carte from €48, 5-/8-course menus from €120-150; ☿ noon-3pm & 6.30pm-midnight) Make reservations early if you hope to join a Rolls-Royce crowd of diners for triple-Michelin-starred Heinz Winkler's complex, elegant and supremely satisfying gourmet creations. The dining room is part of the historic hotel that Winkler modernised in 1989. The elegant rooms (singles/doubles from €205/250) have the full gamut of creature comforts. Check the website for upcoming cooking seminars (packages from €510).

SonnenAlm (☎ 4411; dm incl breakfast €29.50 May-Oct, €34.50 Nov-Apr) For an unforgettable mountaintop sunrise, book a bed in this simple and family-friendly lodge near the mountain station of the Kampenwandbahn.

Café Pauli (☎ 907 40; Höhenweg 3; dishes €3-10; ☿ Apr-Oct & late Dec/early Jan) A good eatery for the tot-brigade is this charismatic place, which has home-made cakes, hearty snacks, a chestnut-shaded beer garden, and a petting zoo with goats and rabbits.

Getting There & Away

Regional trains link Prien with Aschau hourly (€1.90, 15 minutes). Trains also stop in Urschalling.

CHIEMGAU ALPS

South of the Chiemsee, the gentle foothills gradually rise up to an elevation of 1800m, forming the so-called Chiemgau Alps. The three key resort towns are Ruhpolding, Inzell

and Reit im Winkl, all top winter-sports resorts in Bavaria. **Ruhpolding** is a cross-country skiing mecca and hosts the annual Biathlon World Cup. **Inzell** is best known for its ice-skating rink where lightning-fast speed skaters compete in national and international events. **Reit im Winkl** has the largest Alpine ski area and is also the birthplace of Rosi Mittermaier and Eva Sachenbacher, both multiple Olympic medal winners in downhill and cross-country skiing, respectively.

In summer, the area is premier hiking terrain with trails suitable for everyone from stroller-strapped families to rock hounds. The main cultural draw is the rare and precious Romanesque Madonna (c 1200) in the church of St Georg in Ruhpolding.

Information

Inzell tourist office (☎ 08665-988 50; www.inzell.de; Rathausplatz 5)
Reit im Winkl tourist office (☎ 08640-800 27; www.reit-im-winkl.de; Dorfstrasse 38)
Ruhpolding tourist office (☎ 08663-880 60; www.ruhpolding.de; Hauptstrasse 60)

Activities

SKIING

The Chiemgau's top ski area is the **Winklmoos-Alm**; see the boxed text on p58 for details.

Cross-country skiers can go wild on 60km of groomed trails in Ruhpolding, 30km in Inzell and 90km in Reit im Winkl. A nice and easy terrain is the 'Drei Seen' area between Ruhpolding and Reit im Winkl. Fitter types should find the 40km sunny 'Chiemgau-Marathon-Loipe', which links all three communities and runs past several lakes, a scenic challenge.

All three resort towns have ski schools, which also hire out boots, skis and poles, as well as snowboards.

CYCLING

Beautiful scenery and routes from easy to demanding give the Chiemgau Alps an edge among pedal freaks. The most ambitious route is the **Chiemgau MTB Marathon Trail**, with both a 65km and a 130km version starting in Ruhpolding. The 50km **Reit im Winkl-Unken** tour is for moderate to advanced riders, while less athletic types may prefer the **Chiemgau Radweg**, which connects the three communities via a 34km route along the valley floor. Bicycles may be hired in all communities, or check out **Radl**

Sepp (☎ 08663-5607; St Valentin 19, Ruhpolding), who charges between €7.50 and €18 and can also show his favourite spots on guided bike tours.

OTHER ACTIVITIES

From Ruhpolding, cable cars go up the **Unternberg** (1450m) and the **Rauschberg** (1672m), where the imaginative playground is a big hit with kids. The hike up either is quite strenuous but can be done in two to three hours.

If you need to soothe sore muscles or just want to splash around, head to the **Vita Alpina** (☎ 08663-419 90; Brander Strasse 1; indoor 3hr without/with sauna €9.50/13, outdoor 3hr €3.20; ☼ indoor 9am-9pm year-round, outdoor 9am-7pm Jun-Aug) indoor and outdoor adventure pool. Frolicking stations include a saltwater wave pool, a steam bath, saunas, massage jets and a 76m waterslide.

Sleeping & Eating

Landhotel Maiergschwendt (☎ 08663-881 50; www .landhotel-maiergschwendt.de; s/d from €39/78; P ✗) This low-key country inn on a quiet meadow outside Ruhpolding is a hit with families and a youthful, sporty clientele. Roomwise you can go traditional in the Alpine-style Stammhaus or cutting-edge in the ecofriendly and smoke-free Biohaus. All rooms have balconies.

Steinbach-Hotel (☎ 08663-5440; www.steinbach-hotel.de; Maiergschwendter Strasse 8-10a; s €47-64, d €84-130; P ✗ ⬛) The moment you enter the lobby with its lusty fireplace, thick oriental carpets and open-beam ceiling, you know this lodge is all about relaxation. Wrap up your day by unwinding in the sauna or pool, then dream softly knowing that the breakfast buffet will be there until a sleep-friendly 11am.

Klauser's Café & Restaurant (☎ 08640-8424; Birn-bacher Strasse 8, Reit im Winkl; mains €18-35) Wolfgang Klauser learned his craft in some of Germany's top kitchens and now treats demanding diners to contemporary spins on Bavarian cuisine. Veal filet with chanterelles mushrooms or monkfish with saffron sauce are typical menu items.

Getting There & Around

Trains travel to Ruhpolding from Munich with a change in Traunstein (€20.30, two hours). Ruhpolding, Inzell and Reit im Winkl are all connected by RVO bus 9506 with several departures throughout the day. Bus 9505 goes from Prien am Chiemsee to Reit im Winkl via Bernau. Bus 9526 goes to Bad Reichenhall from Inzell.

BAD REICHENHALL
☎ 08651 / pop 17,200 / elev 471m

Bad Reichenhall, on the River Saalach, sits serenely at the foot of the Berchtesgadener and Chiemgauer Alps. Its history and prosperity has quite literally been built on salt, which has been hauled from the underground mines since Roman days. To this day, Bad Reichenhall – meaning a spa 'rich in salt' – remains the largest supplier of table salt in Germany.

It's also a famous spa town thanks to its richly concentrated briny springs. Prominent guests such as King Maximilian II took the waters here. Spas aren't quite the rage they used to be, however, and a charming air of faded elegance now hangs over the town.

Bad Reichenhall is equidistant (about 20km) to Berchtesgaden and Salzburg, and makes a good alternative base for outdoor and cultural explorations.

Orientation

Bad Reichenhall's compact Altstadt is custom-made for strolling, but otherwise the town is rather sprawling. The Hauptbahnhof is a short walk east of the historic centre, with the pedestrianised Ludwigstrasse as the main drag.

Information

Café Amadeo (☎ 6404; Poststrasse 29; per hr €2; ☼ 8am-1am) Internet access.
Post office (☎ 778 150; Bahnhofstrasse 35) At the train station.
Sparkasse (Bahnhofstrasse 17) Bank with ATM and money-changing counter.
Tourist office (☎ 6060; www.bad-reichenhall.de; Wittelsbacher Strasse 15; ☼ 8am-5.30pm Mon-Fri, 9am-noon Sat Apr-Oct, 8am-5pm Mon-Fri, 9am-noon Sat Nov-Mar, 9am-noon Sun May-Sep)

Sights

KURPARK

Plenty of signs lead you to the **Kurpark** (admission free; ☼ 7am-10pm Apr-Oct, 7am-6pm Nov-Mar), the town's historic spa gardens and a nice spot to break a busy day with a relaxing stroll. Folded into the groomed paths and mature trees is the neo-baroque **Kurhaus**, where blue-haired foxes often do the foxtrot to schmaltzy evergreens played by a home-town band. The bizarre structure opposite the Kurhaus is an open-air inhalation facility – the so-called **Gradierwerk** – built in 1912 and as quaint as it is big. From

---

WAGNERIAN CREAM PUFFS

For a unique treat, brave the tourist throngs at the **Windbeutelgräfin** (☎ 08663-1683; Brander Strasse 23, Ruhpolding; ☽ 10am-6pm), an endearing farmhouse café famous for its Lohengrin-Windbeutel – giant profiteroles generously stuffed with layers of berries, cream and ice cream. Inspired by the Wagner opera *Lohengrin*, each is decorated with a cardboard swan neck with a number on it that tells how many have been served thus far (more than 2.2 million, and counting). If you manage to eat three, you get the fourth one for free (the record, held by a guy from Berlin, is eight).

April to November about 100,000 blackthorn twigs are constantly drizzled with salty spring water, creating a fine mist eagerly gulped by those sedately pacing the ambulatory. To further improve your health, also stop by the Art Nouveau **Wandelhalle** to guzzle cups of saline mineral water from a marble fountain.

ALTE SALINE & SALZMUSEUM

A treat for tech heads, the red-brick industrial 'cathedral' housing the **Alte Saline & Salzmuseum** (Old Salt Works & Salt Museum; ☎ 700 2146; Salinenstrasse; adult/child €5.90/3.90; ☽ 10am-11.30pm & 2-4pm May-Oct, 2-4pm Tue & Thu Nov-Apr) is essentially a 3D text book on salt production through the ages. A fire destroyed the original 16th-century salt works in 1834, giving King Ludwig I an excuse to rebuild in fanciful neo-Romanesque style and with machinery still in use today. Guided one-hour tours (in German) thread through a network of tunnels and bring you face to face with mighty water wheels and pumps (bring a jumper, the temperature is a steady 12°C). Afterwards you're free to bone up on 'white gold' (ie salt) in the museum.

ST ZENO

Church and architecture fans should make a quick detour to **St Zeno** (☎ 714 290; Salzburger Strasse 30), the largest basilica in Bavaria with Romanesque origins. Alas, only the original west portal survived a 1512 fire, but it's a looker: two types of marble, pillars propped up by lions and a top decorated with sculptures of Mary, St Zeno and St Rupert. The church itself was rebuilt in Gothic style and later got the obligatory barococo update. There are some fine altars inside, but it's usually closed.

Activities

Bad Reichenhall offers the full monty of outdoor activities. Many easy hiking trails start right in town, but for a more challenging foray, head up Hochstaufen mountain (1771m) north of town. Climbing to the top takes about three hours from the Padinger Alm (Nonner Strasse 79), a mountain restaurant at 667m.

Lazy types can still reach lofty heights via a steep ascent aboard Germany's oldest original cable car still in existence, the 1928 **Predigtstuhlbahn** (☎ 2127; Südtirolerplatz 1; one way/return €10/17; ☽ 8.30am-7pm mid-Apr–mid-Oct, 9am-5pm mid-Oct–mid-Apr). It goes up the 1613m Predigtstuhl mountain, where you can enjoy the views in the comfort of a hotel-restaurant or on several trails. The valley station is in the southern suburb of Kirchberg, which is served by bus 1.

Club Aktiv (☎ 672 38; Frühlingstrasse 61) and **Sport Müller** (☎ 3776; Spitalgasse 3) are outfitters that can organise various outdoor activities, including mountain biking, canyoning, skiing and mountain climbing.

A perfect rainy-day destination, the luxe **Rupertustherme** (☎ 01805-606 706; Friedrich-Ebert-Allee 21; 4hr ticket €14, incl sauna €19; ☽ 9am-10pm) is a natural saline-spring day spa and sauna complex that's just the ticket to get rid of those aches. Its wraparound panoramic windows make you feel like you're swimming through the Alps, and some of the heated salt pools are outside in the fresh mountain air.

Sleeping

Hotel Bergfried & Schönblick (☎ 780 60; www.fuchs-ho tels.de; Adolf-Schmid-Strasse 8; s €35-44, d €64-76, tr €72-87; P ☒ ☐) Rather than rest on its laurels, this popular twin property has recently been linked with a modern addition and treats you to a lavish breakfast buffet (€4.50) with garden views and a small library and big sauna perfect for playing back the day's adventures. Rooms are spacious and inoffensively neutral-toned.

Hotel-Pension Erika (☎ 953 60; www.hotel-pension-erika.de, in German; Adolf-Schmid-Strasse 3; s €38-58, d €64-96; P ☒ ☐) This delightful 50-room palazzo-style hotel combines old-style elegance in the public areas with snappy modern rooms where lines are clean and linens crisp. The garden is fantastic for lolling about with the Alps in your lap. Closed November to February.

Bio und Nichtraucherhotel Hansi (☎ 983 10; www .hotel-hansi.de; Rinckstrasse 3; s/d/tr/q €44/88/105/124; P ⊠) Smoking is a no no and ecoprinciples are heartily embraced at this family-run charmer near the Kurpark. Retreat to cheerfully decorated rooms with wooden floors and energy-saving devices. Days begin with an extra-lavish organic spread that will spoil you with choices.

Hotel Neu-Meran (☎ 4078; www.hotel-neu-meran .de; Nonn 94; s €58, d €116-128; P ⊠ ⊠) If you don't fall in love with the mountain panorama, you will develop a hankering for the exquisite cuisine (mains €10 to €16) at this uphill and upmarket contender. Rooms blend traditional and modern country style and the nicest have a balcony perfect for serenading the sunset, cold beer in hand. Afterwards, work out the kinks in the basement spa with pool, sauna, steam room and small gym.

Eating

Wieninger Schwabenbräu (☎ 969 50; Salzburger Strasse 22; Brotzeit €3-10, mains €8-11, dinner buffet €7) For a cold snack or casual meal (from salads to roasts), come to this convivial place with a young clientele and a small beer garden. It's about 2km north of the spa district.

Café Reber (☎ 600 3174; Ludwigstrasse 10; mains €6-10; ☼ 9am-6pm) This coffee-and-cake shop and café is famous for its *Mozartkugeln* (a round chocolate confection with a nougat and pistachio centre) and also serves a few hot dishes at lunchtime. Piano music is piped onto the terrace.

Bürgerbräu (☎ 6089; Waaggasse 1-2; mains €6-12) Next to the Rathaus, this traditional beer hall serves some interesting brews, including a rare Bavarian pilsner and a low-alcohol Weissbier that's a great thirst quencher. Traditional fare comes in belt-loosening portions, so bring an appetite. Each of the rooms has a different ceiling, including a vaulted one that looks like an upside-down egg carton.

Piccolino (☎ 984 343; Schachtstrasse 2; mains €9-20; ☼ closed Sat lunch & Sun) This pint-sized Tuscan-style bistro is run by a delightful couple (he cooks, she serves) and offers a small menu of freshly prepared, seasonal cuisine. Standards are frighteningly high and as the sign says, pizza is not served.

Kirchberg Schlössl (☎ 2760; Thumseestrasse 11; mains €14-22; ☼ 11am-3pm & 6pm-midnight Thu-Tue) At this upscale indulgence you can stick with feel-good Bavarian food (eg suckling pig in beer sauce) or go contemporary with lighter and more international creations. Reservations advised.

Entertainment

Bad Reichenhaller Philharmonie (☎ 762 8080; www .bad-reichenhaller-philharmonie.de, in German) Whenever you're in town, chances are that this well-respected 40-member orchestra will be playing somewhere, either in the Kurhaus, the Wandelhalle, the modern Kurgastzentrum (spa guest centre) or alfresco in the Kurpark summer pavilion. Check with the tourist office for the schedule.

Magazin 4 (☎ 965 360; www.magazin4.de, in German; Alte Saline 12) The old salt works gets a contemporary edge at this music, cabaret and party pen. Completely oompah free, it's a great spot for plugging into the Bavarian music scene – rock to jazz, reggae to pop.

Getting There & Around

Regional trains to Berchtesgaden depart at least hourly (€3.50, 30 minutes). Coming from Munich requires a change in Freilassing (€24.60, 2½ hours). To get to Salzburg, either take the train (€4.80, 30 minutes) or RVO bus 180, which goes straight to Mirabellplatz in about one hour. Bus 839 travels to the Königssee in Berchtesgaden.

BERCHTESGADEN & BERCHTESGADENER LAND

☎ 08652 / pop 7750 / elev 550

Steeped in myth and legend, the Berchtesgadener Land enjoys a natural beauty so abundant that it's almost preternatural. A tale has it that angels, charged with handing out Earth's wonders, were startled by God's order to hurry up and dropped them all here. Framed by six formidable mountain ranges and home to Germany's second-highest mountain, the Watzmann (2713m), the dreamy, fir-lined valleys are filled with gurgling streams and peaceful Alpine villages.

Much of the terrain is protected by law as the Nationalpark Berchtesgaden, which embraces the pristine Königssee, one of Germany's most photogenic lakes. Outdoor activities, notably hiking, are plentiful. Yet Berchtesgaden's history is also indelibly entwined with the Nazi period as chronicled at the Dokumentation Obersalzberg. The Eagle's Nest, a mountaintop lodge built for Hitler, is now a major tourist attraction.

ORIENTATION

The main town in Berchtesgadener Land is Berchtesgaden, home to the Hauptbahnhof, which doubles as the central bus station, as well as most hotels, restaurants and the main tourist-office branch. About 5km south of town is the Königssee community of Schönau, while the Obersalzberg is about 3km east, Marktschellenberg is some 9km north, Ramsau is about 9km west and Bischofswiesen is 5km northwest.

INFORMATION

HypoVereinsbank (Weihnachtsschützenplatz 2½, Berchtesgaden)

Internet Café (☎ 0160-9721 7399; Königsseer Strasse 17, Berchtesgaden; per 15min €1.50; ☙ 9am-8pm) Coin-operated, high-speed internet access.

Nationalpark-Haus (☎ 643 43; www.nationalpark -berchtesgaden.de; Franziskanerplatz 7, Berchtesgaden; ☙ 9am-5pm Mon-Sat) Hiking and environmental information galore.

Post office (Franziskanerplatz 2½, Berchtesgaden)

Tourist office (☎ 9670; www.berchtesgadener-land .com; Königsseer Strasse 2, Berchtesgaden; ☙ 8.30am-6pm Mon-Fri, 9am-5pm Sat, 9am-3pm Sun May–mid-Oct, 8.30am-5pm Mon-Fri, 9am-noon Sat mid-Oct–Apr) Has a public internet terminal.

SIGHTS

Dokumentation Obersalzberg

In 1933, the quiet mountain retreat of Obersalzberg (some 3km from Berchtesgaden) became the southern headquarters of Hitler's government, a dark period that's given the full historical treatment at the **Dokumentation Obersalzberg** (☎ 947 960; www.obersalzberg.de; Salzbergstrasse 41, Obersalzberg; adult €3, child & student free; ☙ 9am-5pm daily Apr-Oct, 10am-3pm Tue-Sun Nov-Apr). It's a fascinating exhibit that will probably make you queasy and uneasy, but seeing it is an essential experience. You'll learn about the forced takeover of the area, the construction of the compound and the daily life of the Nazi

elite. All facets of Nazi terror are illuminated, including Hitler's near-mythical appeal, his racial politics, the resistance movement, foreign policy and the death camps. A section of the underground bunker network is open for touring. To get there take bus 838 from the Hauptbahnhof in Berchtesgaden.

Eagle's Nest

Berchtesgaden's creepiest – yet impressive – draw is the Eagle's Nest atop Mt Kehlstein, a sheer-sided peak at Obersalzberg. Martin Bormann, one of Hitler's leading henchmen, got 3000 workers to carve the steep road in only 13 months and to build this lofty retreat for the Führer's 50th birthday. Perched at 1834m, the innocent-looking lodge (called Kehlsteinhaus in German) is in an achingly scenic spot with sweeping views across the mountains and down into the valley where the Königssee shimmers like an emerald jewel. Ironically, Hitler is said to have suffered from vertigo and rarely enjoyed the spectacular views himself.

The Kehlsteinhaus opens to visitors from mid-May to October. It's both a splendid and a disturbing spot, but frankly, even just getting up there is a lot of fun. Drive or take bus 849 from the Berchtesgaden Hauptbahnhof to the Kehlstein stop, where you board a special **bus** (www.kehlsteinhaus.de; adult/child €13/12) that drives you up the mountain. It runs between 7.20am and 4pm, and takes 35 minutes. The final 124m stretch to the summit is in a luxurious, brass-clad lift. The Kehlsteinhaus now contains a **restaurant** (☎ 2969; mains €6-13; ☙ 8.20am-5pm) that donates profits to charity.

Salzbergwerk

Once a major producer of 'white gold', Berchtesgaden has thrown open its **salt mines** (☎ 600 20; adult/child €14/9, combination ticket with Alte Saline in Bad Reichenhall €17.50/11.50; ☙ 9am-5pm May-Oct, 11.30am-3.30pm Nov-Apr) for fun-filled 90-minute tours. Kids especially love donning miners' garb and whooshing down a wooden slide into the depth of the mine. Down below, highlights include mysteriously glowing salt grottoes and the crossing of a 100m-long subterranean salt lake on a wooden raft.

Königssee

Crossing the beautiful, emerald-green **Königssee** makes for some unforgettable memories. Framed by steep mountain walls some

BERCHTESGADENER LAND

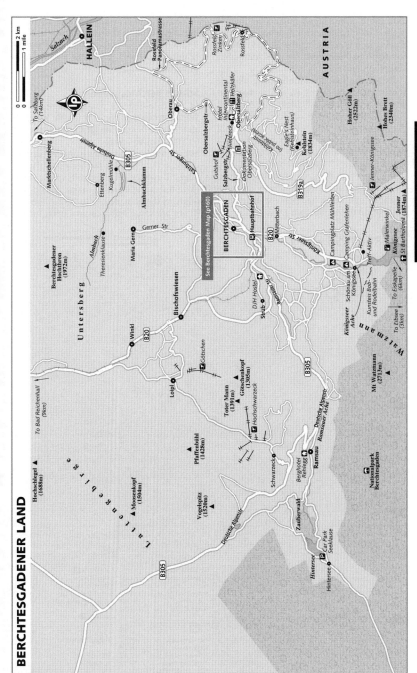

BAVARIAN ALPS

0   2 km
0   1 mile

To Salzburg (14km)

Salzach

HALLEIN

Rossfeld Panoramastrasse

Rossfeld Zinken

Rossfeld

AUSTRIA

Oberau

Hotel Intercontinental

Hintereck

Obersalzberg

Deutsche Alpenstr

Marktschellenberg

B305

Oberau

Obersalzbergstr

Hoher Göll (2522m)

Hohes Brett (2340m)

Ettenberg

Kugelmühle

Almbachklamm

Salzburger Str

Gutshof

Salzbergstr

Hölzkäfer

Kehlstein (1834m)

Eagle's Nest (Kehlsteinhaus)

Jenner-Königssee

B319a

Almbach

Maria Gern

Gerner Str

Dokumentation Obersalzberg

Berchtesgadener Hochthron (1972m)

Theresienklause

BERCHTESGADEN

Hauptbahnhof

Mitterbach

B20

Königsseer Str

Campingplatz Mühlleiten

Camping Grafenlehen

Treff-Aktiv

Jenner (1874m)

Malerwinkel

Königssee

St Bartholomä

U n t e r s b e r g

Bischofswiesen

See Berchtesgaden Map (p160)

Winkl

B20

DJH Hostel

Strub

Deutsche Alpenstr

Schönau am Königssee

Kunstels Bob und Rodelbahn

Königsseer Ache

To Eiskapelle (6km)

To Elbsee (3km)

Götschen

Loipl

Gölschenkopf (1305m)

Toter Mann (1391m)

Hochschwarzeck

B305

Mt Watzmann (2713m)

W a t z m a n n

To Bad Reichenhall (9km)

Pfaffenbühl (1428m)

Schwarzeck

Bergbotel Rehlegg

Deutsche Alpenstr

Ramauer Ache

Ramsau

Nationalpark Berchtesgaden

Hochschlegel (1688m)

Moosenkopf (1504m)

Vogelspitz (1520m)

L a t t e n g e b i r g e

B305

Zauberwald

Car Park Seeklause

Hintersee

Hintersee

5km south of Berchtesgaden, it's Germany's highest lake (603m), with clear waters shimmering into fjordlike depths. Bus 841 makes the trip out here from the Berchtesgaden Hauptbahnhof roughly every hour.

Escape the hubbub of the bustling lakeside tourist village by taking an electric **boat tour** (www.seenschifffahrt.de; adult/child €11.50/5.80) to St Bartholomä, a quaint onion-domed chapel on the western shore. At some point, the boat will stop while the captain plays a horn towards the Echo Wall – the sound will bounce seven times. Pure magic! The effect only fails during heavy fog. From the dock at St Bartholomä, an easy trail leads to the wondrous **Eiskapelle** in about one hour. See p70 for a detailed description of this fabulous ramble.

You can also skip the crowds by meandering along the lake shore. It's a nice and easy 3.5km return walk to the secluded **Malerwinkel** (Painter's Corner), a lookout famed for its picturesque vantage point.

Schloss Berchtesgaden

In Berchtesgaden's main square, **Schloss Berchtesgaden** (Royal Palace; ☎ 947 980; Schlossplatz; adult/child €7/3; ☼ tours 10am–1pm & 2–4pm mid-May–Oct, 11am & 2pm mid-Oct–mid-May) used to be a monastery and shows off items from the personal collection of Bavaria's former ruling family, who still own the place. Exhibits spread across three floors and cover all major artistic periods from the Romanesque to the Biedermeier. There are some real treasures here, includ-

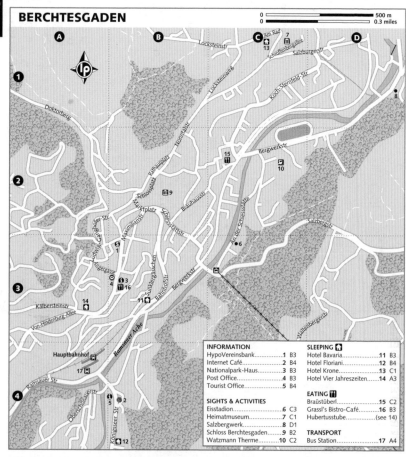

BERCHTESGADEN

INFORMATION		SLEEPING	
HypoVereinsbank.............1 B3		Hotel Bavaria.....................11 B3	
Internet Café...................2 B4		Hotel Floriani....................12 B4	
Nationalpark-Haus...........3 B3		Hotel Krone......................13 C1	
Post Office.......................4 B3		Hotel Vier Jahreszeiten......14 A3	
Tourist Office...................5 B4			
		EATING	
SIGHTS & ACTIVITIES		Braüstüberl.......................15 C2	
Eisstadion.......................6 C3		Grassl's Bistro-Café............16 B3	
Heimatmuseum................7 C1		Hubertusstube................(see 14)	
Salzbergwerk...................8 D1			
Schloss Berchtesgaden......9 B2		TRANSPORT	
Watzmann Therme...........10 C2		Bus Station.......................17 A4	

HITLER'S MOUNTAIN EYRIE

Of all the German towns tainted by the Third Reich, Berchtesgaden has a burden heavier than most. Hitler fell in love with nearby Obersalzberg in the 1920s and bought a small country home here, later enlarged into the imposing Berghof.

After seizing power in 1933, Hitler turned the sweet area into a second seat of government after Berlin, bringing much of the party brass, including Hermann Göring, Martin Bormann and Albert Speer with him. They bought or confiscated large tracts of land and tore down ancient farmhouses to build a 2m-high barbed-wire fence and guardhouses along the three access roads. There were special barracks for SS members, a bunker system inside the mountain and, at a lofty 1834m, the Eagle's Nest.

Little is left of Hitler's 'Alpine Fortress' today. In the final days of WWII, the Royal Air Force and American long-distance bombers levelled much of the Obersalzberg, though the Eagle's Nest was left strangely unscathed. In 1952, the Bavarian government destroyed the remaining ruins and the American military used it as recreational zone, kept off limits by the general public. After troops left in 1996, the area was returned to the Bavarian government, which decided to build a commemorative exhibit. The Dokumentation Obersalzberg opened in 1999.

Yet, despite this effort of coming to terms with the past, the area's wartime legacy is never far below the surface, as demonstrated by the vituperative debate over the unseemliness of building the ultraluxurious Hotel Intercontinental near the site of the Platterhof, a Nazi-era hotel. In the end, the prospect of drawing more luxury cash to the area outweighed the local council's qualms and the new hotel complex was unveiled in 2005.

---

ing sculpture by Tilman Riemenschneider, baroque hunting rifles, a giant stag trophy weighing more than 18kg and porcelain from Nymphenburg. In the rose garden, you'll want to bring out your digicam to snap awesome views of the Watzmann.

Heimatmuseum

Local crafts and history take centre stage at the **Heimatmuseum** (Local History Museum; ☎ 4410; www.heimatmuseum-berchtesgaden.de; Schroffenbergallee 6; adult/child/student €2.50/free/1; ☼ 10am-4pm Tue-Sun Dec-Oct), one of the Alps' most interesting folk museums inside the petite Adelsheim palace. One exhibit traces the tradition of Berchtesgaden's hand-crafted boxes made from thin strips of pine, then painted and decorated with flowers and traditional designs. Other rooms display altars and dollhouses carved from ivory or cow bones, religious art, gingerbread moulds, toys and a vintage marionette theatre.

ACTIVITIES
Hiking

The wilds of the Nationalpark Berchtesgaden unquestionably offer some of the best hiking in Germany. Trails weave along placid lake shores, past lush mountains meadows, through dark forests and into sunny valleys, all beneath a phalanx of horned Alpine peaks. We've outlined a couple of hikes here, but p68 provides great detail on two more.

ZAUBERWALD

This family-friendly 1.5km hike starts at the car park Seeklause and skirts the shores of the idyllic **Hintersee**, just west of Ramsau, where rowing boats share the water with ducks. The trail continues through the 'Magic Forest', where massive boulders pile up haphazardly along the creek. May to July are the best months.

ALMBACHKLAMM

The hearts of romantics will beat faster when traipsing through the **Almbach gorge** (Almbachklamm; ☎ 08650-461; adult/child €2.50/1.30; ☼ 7.30am-7pm May-Oct), a dramatic wonderland of steep cliffs flanking a rushing stream with waterfalls tumbling into clear pools. The trail picks up about 4km northeast of Berchtesgaden at the **Kugelmühle**, Germany's oldest functioning marble mill (1683) and climbs up to the dam at Theresienklause. From here, it spills out into a lovely valley leading to the village of Ettenberg with its pilgrimage church. This is a good spot for a picnic or a *Brotzeit* (snack) before heading down a steepish trail back to Marktschellenberg. The hike has an elevation gain of 320m and takes about three hours (walking time only).

The best time of year is between May and October. To get to the trailhead, take bus 840 from Berchtesgaden.

Skiing

The Berchtesgadener Land has five ski areas with almost 60km of downhill slopes, 80km of groomed cross-country tracks, and plenty of ski schools and outfitters. Skiing conditions, however, are not as reliable as in other Alpine resorts such as Garmisch-Partenkirchen, or across the Austrian border. On the plus side there are cheaper lift tickets and less crowded slopes. For snow conditions, call ☎ 967 297 (recording in German).

For details on the two main ski areas – the Götschen and the Jenner – see the boxed text on p58. Good family playgrounds:

Gutshof (www.obersalzbergbahn.de, in German; adult/child one-day lift ticket €16/9) In the Obersalzberg area; attractions include a 4km tobogganing track.

Rossfeld-Zinken (www.rossfeld.info; adult/child one-day lift ticket €14.50/11) The most snow reliable, with a separate area for boarders.

Hochschwarzeck, (www.hochschwarzeck.info; adult/child one-day lift ticket €19/12.50) Has a tobogganing track and other attractions.

For equipment hire and courses, try **Treff-Aktiv** (☎ 667 10; www.treffaktiv.de, in German; Jennerbahnstrasse 19, Königssee), a full-service outfitter that also organises hikes, mountaineering and rafting trips and other outdoor adventures.

Other Winter Sports

Speed freaks will love the **Kunsteis Bob- und Rodelbahn** (☎ 9670, 1760; Schönau). It's a 1.2km-long ice canal with an 11% incline and 14 curves, including a full loop. You can go down in a regular guest bobsleigh but if that's too tame, whiz down at up to 120km/h with a professional racer in a four-person racing bob (per person €85).

There's ice-skating at the **Eisstadion** (☎ 614 05; An der Schiessstätte 7, Berchtesgaden; adult/child/family €3/1.70/7), or you could head out to the Hintersee, which is usually frozen in winter.

Watzmann Therme

Berchtesgaden's thermal wellness and fun activity pool complex, **Watzmann Therme** (☎ 946 40; www.watzmann-therme.de; Bergwerkstrasse 54, Berchtesgaden; tickets 2hr/4hr/day €8.30/10.80/15.30; ⏱ 10am-10pm) has several indoor and outdoor pools with various hydrotherapeutic treatment stations, a sauna and fabulous Alpine views.

Rossfeld Panoramastrasse

Memorable views are guaranteed on a drive along the Rossfeld Panoramastrasse, which corkscrews up to an elevation of 1600m and at times crosses over into Austrian territory. There's some excellent hiking up here, for instance to the Purtscheller Haus at 1692m or the Eagle's Nest at 1834m. The toll is €4.30 for the car and driver, plus €1.70/1.10 for each additional adult/child.

TOURS

An excellent way to experience the creepy legacy of the Obersalzberg area, including the Eagle's Nest and the underground bunker system, is by taking a four-hour tour with **Eagle's Nest Tours** (☎ 649 71; www.eagles-nest-tours.com; adult/6-12yr €45/30; ⏱ 1.30pm mid-May–Oct). Buses depart from the tourist office and reservations are advised.

SLEEPING

DJH hostel (☎ 943 70; www.berchtesgaden.jugendher berge.de, in German; Struberweg 6, Bischofswiesen; dm €16-20, s/d from €24/40; ⏱ closed Nov-late Dec; ✗) This 274-bed hostel has great views of Mt Watzmann but can't quite shake that institutional feel. For an adrenaline jolt, swing up the new high-rope course. The hostel is a 25-minute walk from the Hauptbahnhof.

Hotel Floriani (☎ 660 11; www.hotel-floriani.de; Königsseer Strasse 37, Berchtesgaden; s €29-46, d €58-86; Ⓟ) The framed mountain-scene prints and plastic flowers won't land this place in *Architectural Digest* but who cares when the price is right, beds are comfortable, and your hosts are incredibly friendly and English speaking. It's just past the tourist office and within walking distance of the station.

Hotel Krone (☎ 946 00; Am Rad 5; www.hotel-krone -berchtesgaden.de; s €37-42, d €68-104; Ⓟ ▣) In a quiet spot, yet close to the town centre, this family-run property offers great extras (including wi-fi, a sauna and steam room) at very reasonable prices. The cosiest rooms are the lodge-style ones, which are clad in knotty pine. TVs are small but you'll be more than entertained by the stunning mountain panorama outside your balcony, provided you've invested a few extra euros for a south-facing room.

Hotel Bavaria (☎ 966 10; www.hotelbavaria.net; Sunklergässchen 11, Berchtesgaden; s €46-61, d €64-170; Ⓟ ✗) Owned by the same family for 100 years, this place has been seriously slicked up and now has delightful 'romantic' rooms and suites, the latter with canopy beds and private whirlpool. Breakfast is a gourmet affair with sparkling wine and both hot and cold items. The cheapest rooms are rather ordinary.

Hotel Vier Jahreszeiten (☎ 9520; www.hotel -vierjahreszeiten-berchtesgaden.de; Maximilianstrasse 20, Berchtesgaden; s €50-72, d €76-100; P 🔊) For a glimpse of Berchtesgaden's storied past, stay at this traditional in-town lodge where Bavarian royalty once entertained. Rooms are a bit long in the tooth but the spectacular mountain views (only from south-facing rooms) more than compensate. Don't miss dinner in the atmospheric Hubertusstube restaurant (right).

Berghotel Rehlegg (☎ 988 40; www.rehlegg.de; Holzengasse 16, Ramsau; s €70, d €120-160; P ✗ 🔊) This 17th-century farmhouse delivers 21st-century comforts and a mountain-cool vibe in its rooms with ministereo, sunny dining room with modern German cuisine and especially the bar-lounge, where you can plan the next day's adventure, cocktail in hand, next to an open fireplace. Active types have several saunas and two pools – one indoor, one outdoor – to look forward to.

Hotel Intercontinental (☎ 975 50; www.inter continental.com; Hintereck 1; r €205-295, ste €281-678; P ✗ 🔊 🖥 🔊) An upscale palace in the clouds (1000m), the Interconti has luxuries such as all-season terraces, a library with fireplace, 24-hour fitness centre and state-of-the-art rooms – if you can accept its controversial location on the Obersalzberg (see the boxed text on p161).

The nicest campgrounds are near the Königssee in Schönau and include **Camping-platz Mühlleiten** (☎ 4584; www.camping-muehlleiten.de; Königsseer Strasse 70, Königssee; per site/person €6.50/5.50) and **Camping Grafenlehen** (☎ 4140; www.camping-grafenlehen.de; Königsseerfussweg 71, Schönau; per site/person €6.50/5.50).

EATING & DRINKING

Grassl's Bistro-Café (☎ 2524; Maximilianstrasse 11, Berchtesgaden; mains €3-9; 🕑 9am-6pm Mon-Sat) This cosy café with the porcelain knick-knacks is an ideal lunch spot, not least for the breathtaking terrace. Besides its array of soups, sandwiches and daily specials, try its snow-capped Mt Watzmann chocolates.

Holzkäfer (☎ 621 07; Buchenhöhe 40; dishes €4-9; 🕑 2pm-1am Wed-Mon) This funky log cabin in the Obersalzberg hills is a great spot for a night out with fun-loving locals. Cluttered with antlers, carvings and backwoods oddities, it's known for its tender pork roasts, dark beer and Franconian wines.

Bräustüberl (☎ 876 724; Bräuhausstrasse 13, Berchtesgaden; Brotzeit €4-9, mains €8-13; 🕑 10am-1am Mon-Sat, 11am-10pm Sun) One of the few places in town that's open late (food until midnight), this venerable brew-pub pegs its inception back to 1645 but has a menu that's very much in the now. The beer hall drips with quaintness but the courtyard is the spot to be on balmy nights.

Hubertusstube (☎ 9520; Maximilianstrasse 20; mains €15-25; V) Peter Miller, the owner of the Hotel Vier Jahreszeiten, also works his magic in the kitchen with imaginatively prepared German and Austrian classics. Game is locally shot, the trout is still alive when you order it and the warm apple strudel is worth the hip-expanding indulgence. Fine views of the mountains are served on the side.

Le Ciel (☎ 975 50; Hintereck 1; mains €29-39; 🕑 6.30pm-10pm) Don't let the Hotel InterConti location turn you off: Le Ciel really is as heavenly as its French name suggests and it has the Michelin star to prove it. Testers were especially impressed by Ulrich Heimann's knack for spinning regional ingredients into such inspired gourmet compositions as fried lobster with apple sweet-pea salad and coconut foam. Service is smooth and the circular dining room is magical.

GETTING THERE & AROUND

For the quickest train connections to Berchtesgaden, it's usually best to take a Munich–Salzburg train and change at Freilassing (€32, 2½ hours). There are direct trains from Salzburg (€7.90, 1¼ hours), although RVO bus 840 makes the trip in about 45 minutes and has more departures. Berchtesgaden is south of the Munich–Salzburg A8 autobahn.

Berchtesgadener Land towns are well linked by local RVO buses. Pick up a detailed schedule at the tourist office. For a taxi call ☎ 4041.

INN-SALZACH

ALTÖTTING

☎ 08671 / pop 12,800 / elev 403m

What Lourdes is to France, Altötting is to Bavaria. Every year more than a million

Roman Catholic pilgrims deluge this innocuous little town to pay their respects to a limewood sculpture of Mary. She arrived here about 1330, worked a few miracles and soon became everybody's favourite gal. Kings, dukes and popes, including current pope, Benedict XVI, who was born in nearby Marktl am Inn (p209), have stopped by.

Mostly, though, it's nuns in habits, frocked priests and robed monks mingling with the mainly elderly pilgrims. Unsurprisingly, the pope connection has further intensified the stream of the faithful, turning Altötting ever more into a Disneyland for the devout. Commercialisation is rampant: images of an awkwardly smiling Benedict grace everything from beer steins to tea cosies. And, this being Bavaria, there's even a Papst-Bier. Altötting is also the starting point of the Benediktweg, a 248km cycling route taking in major Pope-related places, including Marktl am Inn, Wasserburg and the Chiemsee. For more information, see www.benediktweg.info.

Note that Altötting all but shuts down from mid-November to early March.

Orientation & Information

Altötting's compact centre is anchored by Kapellplatz, a short walk north of the *Bahnhof*. For information, stop by the **tourist and pilgrimage office** (☎ 506 219; www.altoetting.de; Kapellplatz 2a; ☺ 8am-5pm Mon, 8am-noon & 2-5pm Tue-Fri, 9am-4pm Sat, 10am-1pm Sun).

Sights

Like moths to the flame, pilgrims flutter towards the **Gnadenkapelle**, a tiny 8th-century octagonal chapel right on Kapellplatz, where miraculous Mary perches amid silver and gold, clad in festive robes and blackened from centuries of exposure to candle soot. The chapel wall is lined with silver urns containing the hearts of various Wittelsbach rulers, including Ludwig II. Creepy! Everywhere you look, *ex voto* tablets have been put up in gratitude, indicating that Mary is still quite busy in the miracle department. Some of them are really quite beautiful examples of folk art. In a further show of devotion, super-pilgrims schlepp heavy crosses around the chapel, sometimes crawling on their knees and reciting the rosary in religious ecstasy.

Kapellplatz is ringed by half a dozen other churches, most notably the big twin-towered late-Gothic **Stiftskirche**, built in 1511 to accommodate the burgeoning throng. Inside is an oversized grandfather clock topped by a scythe-wielding silver skeleton mercilessly signalling someone's death with each swing. Known as the *Tod von Eding* (Death of Eding), the fellow was created during the 1634 black plague. If that's not macabre enough, descend down into the **Tilly-Gruft** (Crypt, enter via cloister; admission free; ☺ 7.30am-5pm) to view the bony remains of Catholic Thirty Years' War general Count von Tilly.

The church's **Schatzkammer** (Treasury; ☎ 5166; adult/child/senior €3/free/2; ☺ 10am-noon & 1-4pm Tue-Sun Apr-Nov) has plenty of precious baubles, most famously the exquisite Goldenes Rössl (Golden Horse) from 15th-century Paris, a small silver-and-gold altar smothered with pearls and jewels.

More impressive still is the rare **Jerusalem Panorama** (☎ 6934; www.panorama-altoetting.de; Gebhard-Fugel-Weg 10; adult/child/concession/family €4.50/1/3.50/6; ☺ 9am-5pm Mar-Oct, 11am-2pm Sat & Sun Nov-Feb), an accomplished monumental 360-degree painting of Jerusalem at the time of Jesus' crucifixion created in 1903 by Gebhard Fugel. A 30-minute surround-sound narration (in German) vividly narrates the events leading up to this fateful day.

Across the street, the **Mechanische Krippe** (Mechanical Creche; ☎ 6653; Kreszentiaheimstrasse 18; adult/child €2/0.50; ☺ 9am-5pm Mar-Dec) is a dizzying setup of 130 wooden figurines carved by Oberammergau's masters in the 1920s.

Sleeping & Eating

Landgasthof Bauernsepp (☎ 08633-8940; www.bauernsepp.de; Kiefering 42, Tüssling; s €40-48, d €65-72) In an idyllic spot about 7km southwest of Altötting, this family-run ex-farmhouse is modern in attitude and even has a lovely *wintergarten* (a glass-enclosed, plant-filled terrace) with palm trees. The cuisine gets top marks, especially the game dishes, often personally shot by dad or son. Rooms are charming and individually decorated.

Hotel-Café Plankl (☎ 928 480; www.hotel-altoetting.de; Schlotthamerstrasse 4; s/d from €45/79; P ⊠ ☂) Bored with rustic Bavarian décor? Then let your fantasies go wild in the Oriental, the Circus, the Egyptian or any of the 15 other themed rooms, many with private Jacuzzi, steam bath, a solarium above the bed and other sexy features, in a building that's won a state award for its sustainability and eco-sensitivity. 'Normal' rooms also available (but why bother?).

Hotel Zur Post (☎ 5040; www.zurpostaltoetting .de; Kapellplatz 2; s €52-93, d €108-150; ☐P) Drenched in tradition, this venerable hotel has bedded Mozart, Ludwig III, the Pope and other famous folk in rooms that lack no modern comforts, even though some are a bit modest in size. The integrated 'Roman' spa and sauna complex is a snazzy refuge from the pilgrim hordes outside. Free wi-fi in the restaurant.

Getting There & Away

Coming from Munich by train requires a change in Mühldorf (€15.60, 1½ hours). Trains to Burghausen leave at least hourly (€3.50, 20 minutes). Altötting is just off the B12, about 93km due east of Munich.

BURGHAUSEN

☎ 08677 / pop 18,250 / elev 350m
Burghausen was once a mover and shaker in Europe, a flourishing centre of the salt trade and a regional seat of government. Decline set in, as it tends to do, and by the 17th century Burghausen's star had dimmed. Looking on the bright side, the old town preserved its medieval appearance for posterity.

The lovely Altstadt hugs a gentle bend of the Salzach River – which separates it from Austria – and is lorded over by Europe's longest castle complex, draped grandly across a mountain ridge. North of the Altstadt – and feeling like a separate universe – is the modern part of Burghausen, which developed with the arrival of the chemical industry in the early 20th century. There's little reason to go here, unless you're arriving at the train station; from there bus 1 quickly whisks you to the Stadtplatz, the old town hub and site of the **tourist office** (☎ 887 140; www.tourismus.burghausen.de; Stadtplatz 112; ❦ 9am-5pm Mon-Fri, 9am-1pm Sat).

The best views of the castle and the Altstadt are from the Austrian side. Cross the bridge over the Salzach and either drive or walk uphill to the signposted viewpoint.

Sights
BURG ZU BURGHAUSEN

Stretching out for 1034m, and visible from anywhere in the Altstadt, Burghausen's namesake **Burg** (castle) consists of several groups of buildings wrapped around six courtyards. The dukes lived in the lap of luxury, although there was a fair amount of discord as the nobles tended to keep their ex-wives cooped up in the same complex. The main castle at the

southern end has an inner core dating back to 1255 and now houses several museums. A combination pass is €5.50. Tickets are sold in the information office past the last gate and on your left near the big staircase.

The **Stadtmuseum** (☎ 651 98; adult/under 18yr/concession €2/free/1; ❦ 9am-6pm May-Sep, 10am-4pm mid-Mar–Apr & Oct, closed Oct–mid-Mar) opens a window onto Burghausen's illustrious and turbulent past in the ambience-laden rooms of the Gothic *Kemenate*, the former ladies' wing. The assortment is predictably eclectic, with religious folk art, nifty guns and, somewhat incongruously, a huge collection of mounted butterflies and stuffed birds all competing for your attention.

The **Staatsgalerie** (State Gallery; ☎ 4659; adult/under 18yr/concession €3/free/2; ❦ 9am-6pm Apr-Sep, 10am-4pm Oct-Mar) is a collection of paintings, sculptures, furniture and Gobelins (tapestries) produced by Bavarian and Austrian artists in the 15th and 16th centuries. Don't miss the view over town and river from the rooftop terrace.

Finally, there's the **Haus der Fotografie** (House of Photography; ☎ 4734; adult/child/concession €2/free/1; ❦ 10am-6pm Wed-Sun mid-Mar–Oct), which has lots of old cameras – including a Hasselblad that took pictures on the moon in 1968 – plus changing exhibits by contemporary photographers to keep things dynamic.

There are several ways to get to the castle. If you're driving, you'll find a car park at its northern end near Curaplatz. Trails leading to the Altstadt are in the second and sixth courtyards, while another, via the Georgstor, heads down the other side to the Wöhrsee, a large recreational lake.

ALTSTADT

Sights in the old town frame the pretty **Stadtplatz**, an elongated, Italianate square hemmed in by candy-coloured town houses. Edifices worth closer inspection include the magnificent **Tauffkirchenpalais** (Stadtplatz 97), where Napoleon stayed briefly in 1809; the exotically blue **Regierungsgebäude** (Government Building; Stadtplatz 108), bearing some elaborate coats of arms and topped by a trio of copper-domed turrets; and the **Rathaus** (Stadtplatz 112), which now houses the main tourist office. The southern end of the square is punctuated by the **Pfarrkirche St Jakob**, from where a painted arch leads to the pedestrianised In den Grüben, the former craftsmen's quarter. The ancient Gothic buildings along this lane now teem with charming boutiques, wine taverns, pubs and restaurants. It ends in the **Mautnerschloss**, the former toll-collector's home and now home to **Jazzkeller** (☎ 2741; In den Grüben 193), a general culture centre, despite the name.

Tours

From March to October, Altstadt and castle tours (in German; €4), leave from Curaplatz on weekends and holidays at 11am and 2pm.

Festivals & Events

Burghausen is famous for its jazz festivals, especially the **Internationale Jazzwoche** (International Jazz Week; www.b-jazz.com, in German) in April and May, which draws an international line-up.

Sleeping & Eating

DJH hostel (☎ 4187; www.burghausen.jugendherberge .de, in German; Kapuzinergasse 235; dm incl breakfast €16.30-22.30; ☺ closed Dec; ✗) None of the rooms inside this former monastery sleep more than four people, but all are cheerfully painted, furnished in pine and sport a locker for each person.

Altstadt Pension (☎ 878 686; In den Grüben 138/142; s/d €42/59; **P**) This *Pension* with bright flowers and solid pine furniture is tucked away in an alley south of the main square. You can have breakfast in the riverside beer garden at the rear, or just watch the rowers plying the Salzach.

Reisingers Bayerische Alm (☎ 9820; www.bayer ischealm.de; Robert-Koch-Strasse 211; s/d €78/105; **P** ✗) Time seems to slow down at this progressive port of call. Watch the sun set over the castle from the leafy beer garden or the comfort of your room, where the abstract canvases of a local artist add splashes of colour. Accolades have also been heaped on the restaurant (mains €10 to €20), where regional farm-fresh ingredients steer the seasonal, organic menu. Rooms without castle views are a bit cheaper, but wi-fi is free for all.

In den Grüben is lined with cafés full of character that draw the young and young at heart. **Café Uhu** (☎ 650 68; 40 In den Grüben) and **Café am Bichl** (☎ 913 993; 162 In den Grüben) are recommended.

Getting There & Away

Trains from Altötting make the trip to Burghausen at least hourly (€3.30, 25 minutes). Burghausen is on the B20, about 15km southeast of Altötting.

Salzburg

A shrine to Mozart's melodies? A stage for *The Sound of Music*? A Disneyfied city with scrumptious cakes, sugar-coated mountains and one helluva fortress? Yep, Salzburg is undeniably touristy and theatrical, yet still it's a composition that takes some beating: from Festung Hohensalzburg atop Mönchsberg to the baroque splendour of Residenzplatz and the slender spires that crowd the skyline.

This is a city where kitsch and class walk hand in hand. If Maria is just itching to get out, take her on a warble-as-you-pedal tour of the sights; if Wolfgang is more your cup of tea, join the well-heeled crowd at Schloss Mirabell to hear the maestro's symphonies. Whether it's to be a shopping spree on Getreidegasse to find lederhosen that fit, or a horse-drawn carriage ride through the cobbled city centre, in Salzburg embracing the clichés is positively encouraged. And why not? It's fun.

When the overload of Mozart and Miss Andrews gets too much to handle, Salzburg's lesser-known corners offer blissful respite. The contemporary contours of Museum der Moderne, the chilled bars lining the right bank and the solitude of Kapuzinerberg are the perfect remedy for an overkill of the obvious. Sitting on the banks of the fast-flowing Salzach as the sun sinks over the city, it becomes clear that this place still rocks. Even without Amadeus.

SALZBURG

HIGHLIGHTS

- ▣ Roaming the clifftop ramparts of **Festung Hohensalzburg** (p173) to see Salzburg spread out beneath you

- ▣ Giving Maria a run for her money with a rendition of 'Do-Re-Mi' by the Pegasus statue in **Mirabellgarten** (p172)

- ▣ Squeezing into tiny **Scio's Specereyen** (p180) to indulge in the naughtily decadent Venusbrüstchen (chocolate Venus breasts)

- ▣ Hearing the glockenspiel's tuneful chime and the clip-clop of horse-drawn carriages on **Residenzplatz** (p174)

- ▣ Discovering your inner child as marionettes dance to Mozart at the enchanting **Salzburger Marionettentheater** (p190)

★ Mirabellgarten

Salzburger ★ Marionettentheater

Salzach River

Scio's ★ Specereyen

Residenzplatz ★

Festung Hohensalzburg ★

▣ TELEPHONE CODE: 0662 ▣ POPULATION: 150,000 ▣ AREA: 66 SQ KM

HISTORY

Salzburg has had a tight grip on the region as far back as Roman times, when the town Juvavum stood on the site of the present-day city. This Roman stronghold came under constant attack from warlike Celtic tribes and was ultimately destroyed by them or abandoned due to disease.

St Rupert established the first Christian kingdom in this part of Austria in about 696. As centuries passed, the successive archbishops of Salzburg gradually increased their power and eventually were given the grandiose titles of princes of the Holy Roman Empire.

Wolf Dietrich von Raitenau (1587–1612), one of Salzburg's most influential archbishops, instigated the baroque reconstruction of the city, commissioning many of its most beautiful buildings. He fell from power after losing a dispute over salt with the powerful rulers of Bavaria and died a prisoner.

Another of the city's archbishops, Paris Lodron (1619–53), managed to keep the principality out of the Europe-wide Thirty Years' War. Salzburg also remained neutral during the War of the Austrian Succession a century later, but bit by bit the province's power gradually waned; during the Napoleonic Wars Salzburg came under the thumb of France and Bavaria. It became part of Austria in 1816.

CLIMATE

Average temperatures in Salzburg range from 23°C in July and August to -1°C in January. In the mountains winter brings heavy snowfalls and much lower temperatures, with cooler but sunny days in summer. Spring is the wettest time, with an average of 13 rainy days per month.

ORIENTATION

Salzburg is split in two by the snaking Salzach River. The compact, pedestrianised Altstadt (old town) is on the left bank. Rising above the city, Festung Hohensalzburg clings to cliffs of Mönchsberg. Stepping over the river, the right bank is home to Schloss Mirabell, Kapuzinerberg, and numerous entertainment venues, hotels and restaurants. About 10 minutes' walk further north is the Hauptbahnhof and bus station.

Maps

The tourist office and most hotels hand out free maps of the city centre. Many bookshops and souvenir kiosks also sell city maps.

INFORMATION
Bookshops

Motzko (Map p169; ☎ 88 33 11; Elisabethstrasse 1) Stocks English-language books.

Motzko Reise (Map p169; ☎ 88 33 11-55; Rainerstrasse 24) Across the road from Motzko; sells maps and guidebooks.

News & Books (Map p169; Hauptbahnhof platform 2a) International newspapers and magazines.

Emergency

Ambulance (☎ 144)

Hospital (Landeskrankenhaus; Map p170; ☎ 44 82; Müllner Hauptstrasse 48) Just north of the Mönchsberg.

Police headquarters (Map p169; ☎ 63 83; Alpenstrasse 90)

Internet Access

Internet cafés are scattered all over Salzburg; those near the train station are much cheaper than those in the Altstadt.

International Telephone Discount (Map p169; ☎ 88 31 99; Kaiserschützenstrasse 8; per hr €2; ☾ 8.30am-10pm Mon-Sat) Also has cheap international telephone calls.

Salzburg Internet Café (Map p172; ☎ 84 20 63-0; Gstättengasse 3; per hr €2; ☾ 10am-10pm) Skype and discount international calls available.

Laundry

Norge Exquisit (Map p172; ☎ 87 63 81; Paris-Lodron-Strasse 16; self-service wash €10; ☾ 7.30am-6pm Mon-Fri, 8am-12pm Sat).

Money

Bankomats (ATMs) are all over the place.

Amex (Map p172; ☎ 84 38 400; Mozartplatz 5; ☾ 9am-5.30pm Mon-Fri, 9am-12pm Sat & Sun) Next to the tourist office. Amex travellers cheques are cashed free of charge.

Western Union (Map p169; ☎ 93 00 03-162; ☾ 8.30am-7pm Mon-Fri, 8.30am-4.30pm Sat) Changes money at its branch in the Hauptbahnhof. Exchange booths are open all day every day at the airport. There are also plenty of exchange offices in the city centre, but beware of high commission rates.

Post

Main post office (Map p172; Residenzplatz 9; ☾ 7am-6.30pm Mon-Fri, 8am-10am Sat)

Station post office (Map p169; Südtiroler Platz 1; ☾ 8am-6pm Mon-Fri)

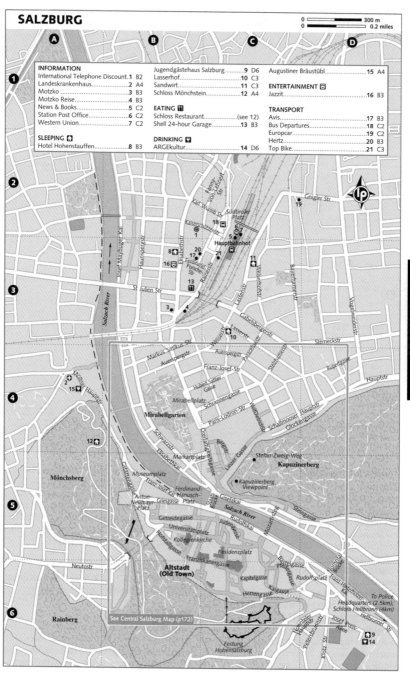

SALZBURG

0 _____ 300 m
0 _____ 0.2 miles

INFORMATION
International Telephone Discount.**1** B2
Landeskrankenhaus......................**2** A4
Motzko **3** B3
Motzko Reise...............................**4** B3
News & Books..............................**5** C2
Station Post Office.......................**6** C2
Western Union.............................**7** C2

SLEEPING
Hotel Hohenstauffen.....................**8** B3

Jugendgästehaus Salzburg............**9** D6
Lasserhof...................................**10** C3
Sandwirt....................................**11** C3
Schloss Mönchstein.....................**12** A4

EATING
Schloss Restaurant...................(see 12)
Shell 24-hour Garage..................**13** B3

DRINKING
ARGEkultur................................**14** D6

Augustiner Bräustübl...................**15** A4

ENTERTAINMENT
Jazzit...**16** B3

TRANSPORT
Avis...**17** B3
Bus Departures...........................**18** C2
Europcar....................................**19** C2
Hertz...**20** B3
Top Bike....................................**21** C3

SALZBURG

SALZBURG

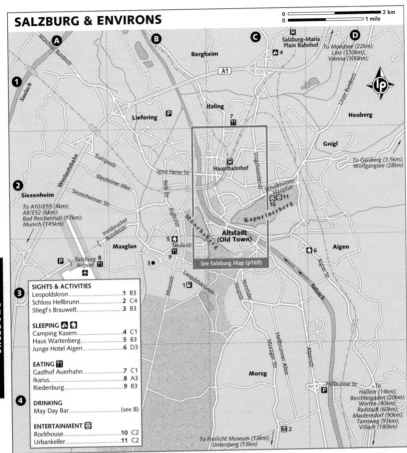

SALZBURG & ENVIRONS

Tourist Information

The main **tourist office** (Map p172; ☎ 889 87-330; www.salzburg.info; Mozartplatz 5; ⏰ 9am-6pm Mon-Sat Jan-Apr & mid-Oct–Nov, 9am-7pm May–mid-Oct & Dec) has plenty of information about the city and its immediate surrounds. There's a ticket booking agency in the same building. For information on the rest of the province, contact **Salzburgerland Tourismus** (☎ 66 88-0; www.salzburg erland.com).

Salzburg Information (☎ 88 98 70; www.salzburginfo .at) is the head tourism office for the region. Advance **hotel reservations** (☎ 88 98 73 14) placed through this office are free. The office also deals with marketing inquiries and sends out tourist brochures; however, for in-person inquiries go to the Mozartplatz office.

It's worth investing in the **Salzburg Card** (low /high season 24hr card €21/23, 48hr €29/31, 72hr €34/36) for free entry to all major sights and reduced entry to a further 24 attractions, plus free public transport for the duration. The free Salzburg Card booklet details opening hours and entry fees for important sights.

Travel Agencies

STA Travel (Map p172; ☎ 45 87 33-0; www.statravel.at; Rainerstrasse 2) Student and budget travel agency.

SIGHTS

Salzburg's star attractions cluster around the Altstadt, a Unesco World Heritage site dominated by the hilltop Festung Hohensalzburg on Mönchsberg. Many sights extend their opening hours during the Salzburger Festspiele (p176) in August. The hours given here are for nonfestival times.

Salzburg Museum

Salzburg's new flagship attraction is **Salzburg Museum** (Map p172; ☎ 62 08 08-700; Mozartplatz 1; www .smca.at; adult/student/child €7/6/3; ⊙ 9am-5pm Tue-Sun, to 8pm Thu). Housed in the sublime Neue Residenz palace, the museum sheds light on Salzburg's rich heritage with its hands-on exhibits. A visit starts beneath the cobbled courtyard in the impressively illuminated **Kunsthalle**, which presents rotating exhibitions of contemporary art. On the 1st floor, **Salzburg Persönlich** offers fascinating insight into the characters that have shaped the city's history, including the alchemist Paracelsus and performer Richard Mayr; kids love to watch the birdie-style camera that takes nostalgic portrait shots you can send home by email. Upstairs, prince-archbishops glower down from the walls at **Mythos Salzburg**, which celebrates the city as a source of artistic and poetic inspiration over the ages. Be sure to glimpse Carl Spitzweg's renowned Sonntagsspaziergang (Sunday Stroll) painting and the home videos of Asian tourists giving their unique take on Salzburg.

Residenz State Rooms & Gallery

The **Residenz** (Map p172; ☎ 80 42-26 90; Residenzplatz 1; adult/child €8.20/2.60; ⊙ 10am-5pm Tue-Sun) was the not-so-humble dwelling of the archbishops until the 19th century. An audioguide tour takes in the unashamedly opulent state rooms, festooned with tapestries and frescoes by Johann Michael Rottmayr, and the Konferenz Saal, where Mozart gave his first public performance (Violin Concerto No 5 in A Major) at the ripe old age of six.

The admission covers the **Residenz Galerie** (☎ 84 04 51; www.residenzgalerie.at; Residenzplatz 1; ⊙ 10am-5pm Tue-Sun), which features a superb collection of Dutch and Flemish works, including a clutch of masterpieces from the likes of Rembrandt and Rubens.

Mozart's Houses

Mozart fans won't want to miss out on the two museums dedicated to the great man. Both cover similar ground, displaying musical instruments, sheet music and memorabilia.

Mozarts Geburtshaus (Mozart's Birthplace; Map p172; ☎ 84 43 13; www.mozarteum.at; Getreidegasse 9; adult/child €6/1.50; ⊙ 9am-7pm Jul & Aug, 9am-6pm Sep-Jun) is where Mozart spent the first 17 years of his life. In the first room, the holy Wolfgang is shown as a babe beneath a fluorescent blue halo. Other curiosities include the minivolin that Amadeus played as a toddler, plus a lock of his hair and buttons from his jacket.

The **Mozart-Wohnhaus** (Mozart's Residence; Map p172; ☎ 87 42 27-40; www.mozarteum.at; Makartplatz 8;

SALZBURG

FAR FROM THE MADDING CROWD

The crowds on Getreidegasse and the zillionth souvenir shop selling Mozart paraphernalia are part and parcel of Salzburg. Yet this city has plenty of lesser-known, quiet nooks off the well-trodden tourist track. Here is a rundown of peaceful retreats to help you keep your cool:

- The narrow, cobblestoned **Steingasse** was first a Roman road, then home to tanners and potters during the Middle Ages. It's particularly beautiful in the late morning sun when diffused light casts soft shadows across its medieval façades.

- Take a breather by kicking back with a picnic or beer on the banks of the meandering **Salzach River**. Grab a spot to admire the city's skyline from a different angle on tree-lined promenades such as Elisabethkai and Josef-Mayburger-Kai.

- Festung Hohensalzburg is not the only highlight on **Mönchsberg**; wander a little further at the top to find crumbling, overgrown fortifications and snatch glimpses of Salzburg's rooftops through the trees.

- A few paces from the hubbub of Linzer Gasse, the cloisters of **Friedhof St Sebastian** (Map p172) are an oasis of calm. Amid the sea of iron and stone crosses, pick out the graves of Mozart's wife (Constanze) and father (Leopold). At the centre of the cemetery stands Gabrielskapelle, Archbishop Wolf Dietrich von Raitenau's elaborate mausoleum.

- Stefan-Zweig-Weg climbs up towards the peace of **Kapuzinerberg**, passing through shady beech forest and emerging at a viewpoint with wide-screen views of Salzburg. It's a great vantage point to take photos of the dramatic fortress, Hohensalzburg.

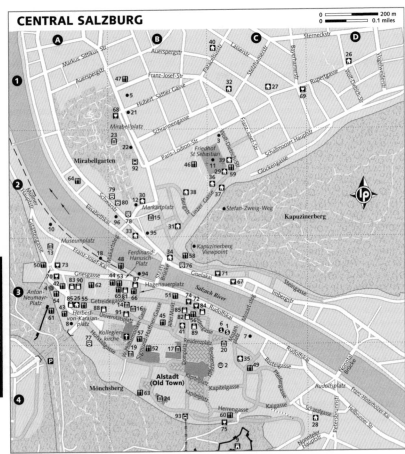

CENTRAL SALZBURG

adult/child €6/2; 🕓 9am-7pm Jul & Aug, 9am-6pm Sep-Jun)
takes a more hi-tech approach, with an audioguide giving the low-down on the Mozart
family and serenading you with opera ex-
cerpts. Under the same roof is the **Mozart Ton-
und Filmmuseum** (Map p172), a film and music
archive of interest to the ultra-enthusiast.

Rupertinum

The sister gallery of the Museum der Moderne
(opposite), the **Rupertinum** (Map p172; ☎ 84 22
20-451; Wiener-Philharmoniker-Gasse 9; adult/child €6/4;
🕓 10am-6pm Tue-Sun, 10am-9pm Wed) is devoted to
rotating exhibitions of modern art, with a
strong emphasis on graphic works and photography. See www.museumdermoderne.at for
up-to-date listings of exhibitions.

Schloss Mirabell

The 17th-century **Schloss Mirabell** (Map p172)
was built by Prince-Archbishop Wolf Dietrich
for his mistress Salome Alt, who bore the
archbishop at least 10 children (sources disagree on the exact number – poor Wolf was
presumably too distracted by spiritual mat-
ters to keep count himself). The best way to
experience the Mirabell magic is to attend
a lunchtime or evening concert (p189) in
the palace's magnificent Marble Hall, which
boasts chandeliers and wall reliefs.

If you fancy skipping through gardens
von Trapp style, there's no better place to
act out those fantasies than the manicured
Mirabellgarten, where the young scallywags
practised singing 'Do-Re-Mi' around the

Pegasus statue. The neat lawns, rose gardens and tree-fringed avenues are less overrun first thing in the morning and early evening. The Tanzerin sculpture is a great spot to photograph the gardens with the fortress as a backdrop.

Festung Hohensalzburg

Rising like a vision above Salzburg, this mighty 900-year-old **fortress** (Map p172; ☎ 84 24 30-11; Mönchsberg; adult/child €10/5.70; ⏱ 9.30am-5pm Jan-Apr & Oct-Dec, 9am-6pm May-Jun & Sep, 9am-7pm Jul-Aug) is one of the biggest and best preserved in Europe. It's easy to spend a half a day up here, roaming the ramparts for far-reaching views over the city's spires, the Salzach and surrounding Alps. The fortress is a steep 15-minute jaunt from the city centre, or a speedy ride in the glass **Festungsbahn funicular** (included in the ticket price).

The imposing fortress bears witness to the power of the prince-archbishops. As you stroll around, keep your eyes peeled for turnips (there are 58 in total). Rumour has it that Leonard von Keutschach, archbishop of Salzburg from 1495 to 1519, used to squander money, so his uncle flung a turnip at his head to (literally) knock some sense into him. Ironically, the turnip became a symbol for Leonard's new-found wisdom. Other highlights include the **Golden Hall** with its gold-studded ceiling imitating a starry night sky; the **Eiserner Wehrmann** soldier encrusted with 328,000 iron nails (a creative means of raising money for war victims); and the spine-tingling **torture chamber**.

Museum der Moderne

Perched atop Mönchsberg, the white-marble, oblong-shaped **museum** (Map p172; ☎ 84 22 20-403; adult/child €8/6; ⏱ 10am-6pm Tue-Sun, 10am-9pm Wed) stands in stark contrast to the fortress. The futuristic glass-and-concrete reels in art aficionados with its rotating exhibitions of 20th- and 21st-century works. While you're up here, enjoy an espresso and fabulous views

ROCK ME AMADEUS

- Aged two, Mozart identified a pig's squeal as G sharp. He gave his first public recital aged five.

- Aged 23 Mozart fell in love with the soprano Aloysia Weber. When she rebuffed him, he promptly married her sister.

- When not composing, Mozart enjoyed billiards, heavy drinking sessions and teaching his pet starling to sing operettas.

- A boy once asked Mozart how to write a symphony. He replied that a symphony was too difficult at such a young age. 'You wrote symphonies at my age!' exclaimed the boy. 'But I didn't have to ask how,' replied Mozart.

- Modern psychologists believe that Mozart suffered from Tourette's Syndrome, a disorder leading to uncontrolled outbursts of swearing and obscene behaviour.

on the panoramic terrace of **M32** (☼ 9am-1am Tue-Sat, 9am-6pm Sun), or nip into James Turrell's cylindrical **Sky Space** to while away the hours gazing up at the sky.

Stiegl's Brauwelt
Beer lovers should check out Austria's largest private **brewery** (Map p170; ☎ 83 87-14 92; Bräuhausstrasse 9; adult/child €9/4; ☼ 10am-5pm Wed-Sun Jun-Sep), where a tour runs through the different stages of the brewing process and includes a peek at the world's tallest beer tower. For those who would rather quaff brews than learn about them, a free Stiegl beer and pretzel are thrown in for the price of a ticket. Take bus 1 or 2 to Bräuhausstrasse.

ACTIVITIES
The old town is squeezed between Kapuzinerberg and Mönchsberg, both of which are crisscrossed with excellent **walking** trails. There is a **viewpoint** (Map p172) at the western end of the Kapuzinerberg, with ramparts built during the Thirty Years' War; the climb up from Linzer Gasse takes 10 minutes. On Mönchsberg, the stroll from Festung Hohensalzburg to Augustiner Bräustübl (p189) is scenic. There is also a great network of **cycling routes**; bikes are available for hire in various places in Salzburg (p191).

The incredibly popular **River Cruises** (Map p172; ☎ 82 58 58; www.salzburgschifffahrt.at; adult/child €12/7, to Schloss Hellbrunn €15/10; ☼ Apr-Oct) are a leisurely way to see the sights. Cruises depart from Makart bridge and take about an hour, with some of them chugging on to **Schloss Hellbrunn** (Map p170; ☎ 82 03 72-0; www.hellbrunn.at; Fürstenweg 37; adult/child/family €8.50/3.80/21.50; ☼ 9am-4.30pm Apr & Oct, 9am-5.30pm May & Jun, 9am-10pm Jul & Aug); the ticket price does not cover entry to the palace.

WALKING TOUR
Start this leisurely two- to three-hour walk by absorbing the bustle of **Domplatz (1)** and the adjoining **Kapitelplatz (2)** and **Residenzplatz (3)**. The hubbub from the market stalls lining these broad squares competes with the clip-clop of horses' hooves and the backbeat of buskers. On Residenzplatz, listen out for the chime of the **Glockenspiel (4)** at 7am, 11am and 6pm.

Soaring skywards, the 15th-century **Dom (5**; cathedral; Domplatz) features three bronze doors symbolising – left to right as you face them – faith, hope and charity. Its striking cupola was rebuilt after being destroyed by a bomb in 1944. Step inside to see the dome and the Romanesque font where Mozart was baptised. The adjacent **Dommuseum** (☎ 84 41 89; adult/child €5/1.50; ☼ 10am-5pm Mon-Sat, 11am-6pm Sun) is a treasure-trove of baroque art, lavish goldwork and tapestries.

Turning left at the first courtyard off Franziskanergasse brings you to the marvellously ornate **Stiftskirche St Peter (6**; St Peter Bezirk). Beneath a green stuccoed ceiling lit by chandeliers, the walls are smothered with religious art and baroque swirls. Look out for the dramatic statue of the archangel Michael shoving a crucifix through the throat of a goaty demon. The graveyard is home to the so-called **catacombs (7**; Katakomben; ☎ 84 45 78-0; adult/child €1/0.60; ☼ 10.30am-5pm daily May-Sep, 10.30am-3.30pm Wed & Thu, 10.30am-4pm Fri-Sun Oct-Apr), cave-like chapels and crypts hewn out of the cliff face.

Back on Franziskanergasse, your gaze is drawn to the slender spires of the **Franziskanerkirche (8**; ☎ 84 36 29-0; Franziskanergasse 5; ☼ daylight), housing a baroque altar surrounded by five pillars.

The western end of Franziskanergasse opens into Max-Reinhardt-Platz, where you'll see the back of Fischer von Erlach's baroque **Kollegienkirche (9**; Universitätsplatz; ☼ daylight).

Stroll left to reach Herbert-von-Karajan-Platz and the **Pferdeschwemme (10**; horse trough),

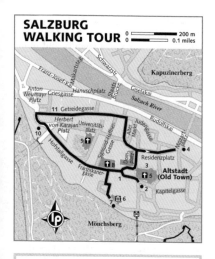

SALZBURG WALKING TOUR

0 ————— 200 m
0 ————— 0.1 miles

WALK FACTS

Start Domplatz
Finish Residenzplatz
Distance 1.5km
Duration Two to three hours, including stops

a rather elaborate drinking spot for the arch-bishops' mounts. Created in 1700, this is a horse-lover's delight, with rearing equine pin-ups surrounding Michael Bernhard Mandl's statue of a horse tamer.

Head right around the corner and you'll join the bustling crowds beneath the wrought-iron shop signs along **Getreidegasse (11)**. Turning right down Alter Markt brings you back to Residenzplatz.

SALZBURG FOR CHILDREN

With marionettes galore, sticky chocolate balls and a big fairy tale–like fortress, Salzburg is truly a kid-oriented city. If the crowds prove unbearable with tots in tow, take them to let off steam at the city's adventure **playgrounds** (there are 80 to pick from); a great choice is the one on Franz-Josef-Kai (Map p172). In summer, little 'uns love to splash in shallow pools and whiz down the slides at Austria's largest outdoor pool, **Leopoldskron** (Map p170; ☎ 82 92 65; Leopoldskronstrasse 50; adult/child €3.80/1.80; ⏰ 7am-7pm May-Sep), just south of the city centre.

Salzburg's sights are usually half-price for children and many are free for under six year

olds. Plenty of galleries, museums and theatres also have dedicated programmes for kids and families. These include the **Museum der Moderne** (p173), which has Saturday art workshops for over fives and guided tours for over 10s (€2), and the matinée performances at the enchant-ing **Salzburger Marionettentheater** (p190). The **Salzburg Museum** (p171) has plenty of hands-on displays, from coin rubbings and puzzles to a practice *barre* for budding ballerinas.

Aside from the above, the **Haus der Natur** (Map p172; ☎ 84 26 53; www.hausdernatur.at; Museumsplatz 5; adult/child €5/3; ⏰ 9am-5pm) has a massive aquarium with Nemo-style clown fish and coral reefs, and a reptile enclosure teeming with snakes and crocs. Shark feeding time is 10.30am on Mondays. Near Untersberg, the open-air **Freilicht Museum** (Map p170; ☎ 85 00 11; Hasenweg; adult/child €7/3.50; ⏰ 9am-6pm Tue-Sun Mar-Nov) steps back in time and back to nature. There are 60 traditional Austrian farmhouses to explore, tractors to clamber over, goats to feed and a huge adventure playground to run around in.

TOURS

The following companies offer *The Sound of Music* tours that are broadly the same; all last from three to four hours and cost around €40. They take in major landmarks featured in the film and include a visit out into the Salzkammergut countryside for more movie locations. You'll see the Nonnberg Abbey, the church in Mondsee used for the wedding scenes, and Liesl's gazebo, now relocated to the gardens of Schloss Hellbrunn (opposite). The soundtrack to the film is played in the buses as they bowl merrily along. It can be a real scream if you're with a lively crowd who are prepared to get into the whole thing by singing along and acting out scenes from the film.

Bob's Special Tours (Map p172; ☎ 84 95 11; www .bobstours.com; Rudolfskai 38) Also offers *The Sound of Music* tour in a light aircraft.

Salzburg Panorama Tours (Map p172; ☎ 87 40 29; www.panoramatours.com; Mirabellplatz) Boasts the 'original *Sound of Music* Tour' with letters from Maria von Trapp to prove it. Tours booked through YOHO youth hostel are 10% cheaper.

Salzburg Sightseeing Tours (Map p172; ☎ 88 16 16; www.salzburg-sightseeingtours.at; Mirabellplatz 2) This company claims one of its buses was used in the film.

If you'd rather pedal around town warbling songs from the film, opt for **Fräulein Maria's Cycling Tours** (Map p172; ☎ 342 62 97; incl bike hire €22; ⏰ 9.30am

May-Sep). These freewheeling tours last a leisurely three hours and take in the main film locations along the route. No advance booking is necessary, so you can just turn up at the meeting point at the entrance to Mirabellgarten.

FESTIVALS & EVENTS

The **Salzburger Festspiele** (Salzburg Festival; www.salzburg festival.at) is the annual summer bash, which brings world-class opera, classical music and drama to stages across the city from late July to August. This is the zenith of Salzburg's cultural calendar, a time when the city takes on a new vitality, and a few thousand extra tourists, too.

Prices stretch from €5 to €250; the cheapest prices are for standing-room tickets. Under-26-year-olds are eligible for reduced-price deals for two or more events (€15 to €22). Most tickets sell out months in advance but try checking for cancellations – inquire at the **ticket office** (Map p172; ☎ 80 45-500; info@salzburgfes tival.at; Herbert-von-Karajan-Platz 11; ☼ 9am-start of last performance of the day). You can see the programme as early as the previous November on the festival's website.

Held in late January, the **Mozartwoche** (Mozart Week; www.mozarteum.at) is a nod to Salzburg's most famous son, while Easter is yet another excuse for a mammoth music festival, the **Osterfestspiele** (www.osterfestspiele-salzburg.at). Salzburg leaps back into the 21st century at the **Sommerszene** (www.sommerszene.at), hosting cutting-edge dance, theatre and music performances from mid-June to mid-July. In the city where 'Silent Night' was composed, it's little wonder that Advent is a big deal; the **Christmas Market** on Domplatz is a festive highlight, with carol singers and the obligatory stalls offering gingerbread and mulled wine.

SLEEPING

Salzburg has long been known for its pricey accommodation, but that's starting to change. Spearheading the city's style revolution, sleeping spots are revamping the old and ringing in the new: from boutique hotels with baroque finery to funky backpacker digs. If you're on a budget, the right bank is probably your best bet. Prices skyrocket during the Festspiele, when you'll need to book well ahead. For a list of private rooms, check www.salzburg.info or inquire at the tourist office.

Budget

Camping Kasern (Map p170; ☎ 45 05 76; www.camping -kasern-salzburg.com; Carl-Zuckmayer-Strasse 3; campsites per adult/child/tent €6/3.50/3; P ☐) Just north of the A1 Nord exit, this tree-shaded campsite offers internet access, a laundry and mini-market. Hop on bus 21 from Paris-Lodron-Strasse to Jägerwirt.

YOHO Salzburg (Map p169; ☎ 87 96 49; www.yoho .at; Paracelsusstrasse 9; 8-/6-bed dm €17/18, per person s/d/ tr/q €29/22/20/19; ☼ reception 24hr; ☐) If you just wanna have fun, this hip hostel is the place to meet like-minded backpackers. There's a daily happy hour at the bar and *The Sound of Music* is blasted out at 10.30am (bring your earplugs or join in the singsong). Other perks include free wi-fi and lockers, plus a 10% discount on Panorama tours. You can book adventure sports here such as rafting (€40) and canyoning (€49).

Junge Hotel Aigen (Map p170; ☎ 62 32 48; www.lbsh -aigen.at; Aignerstrasse 34; per person dm/s/d/q €15/31/23/19; P) Set in parkland, this HI hostel south of Kapuzinerberg in Aigen offers excellent facilities, including a common room, table tennis and dining hall. Family rooms are also available. It's 15 minutes' walk from the old town or take bus 49.

Jugendgästehaus Salzburg (Map p169; ☎ 84 26 70; www.jgh.at; Josef-Preis-Allee 18; per person dm/q/d €15.50/20/37.50; P ☐) Head to this popular hostel for prime views of the fortress, bike rental and discounts on Salzburg Sightseeing Tours. Half and full board are also available.

Institut St Sebastian (Map p172; ☎ 87 13 86; www .st-sebastian-salzburg.at; Linzer Gasse 41; dm/s/d €19/38/62) Tucked behind Sebastianskirche, this peaceful hostel oozes monastic charm with its high vaults, polished stone floors and roof terrace. The dorms are clean and well kept. Ring the bell if reception is unstaffed.

Sandwirt (Map p169; ☎ 87 43 51; Lastenstrasse 6a; s/d/tr €23/44/57; P) Facing the train tracks, the location of this guesthouse is hardly picturesque, but it's handy if you need to be near the station and like gnomes – the garden is full of 'em! Rooms are crying out for a lick of paint, but still offer good value. The chirpy landlady will let you use her washing machine and kitchen.

Junger Fuchs (Map p172; ☎ 87 54 96; Linzer Gasse 54; s/ d/tr without bathroom €28/44/55) Despite being above a kebab shop (handy for late-night munchies), the wood-floored rooms in this conveniently located *Pension* on the right bank are clean and spacious.

Hinterbrühl (Map p172; ☎ 84 67 98; hinterbruehl@ aon.at; Schanzlgasse 12; s/d without bathroom €42/54) Part of the original city walls, this 14th-century guesthouse is a bargain given its old-town location. The '70s-style rooms are basic but clean. Try to get room 14 – it's the biggest and has a balcony, private bathroom and lounge area.

Midrange

Trumer Stube (Map p172; ☎ 87 47 76; www.trumer-stube .at; Bergstrasse 6; s €56-89, d €89-103; 🖳) Silvia and Giovanni will make you feel at home at this pretty little *Pension*. Its rooms have an old-world feel – think pastel shades, squishy beds and flouncy fabrics.

Bergland Hotel (Map p169; ☎ 87 23 18; www.berg landhotel.at; Rupertgasse 15; s/d/ste €63/93/135; 🅿 🖳) This peach-fronted hotel attracts creative souls who appreciate Mr Kuhn's brushwork – his fabulous paintings are hung all over the walls. The homey rooms in warm hues display – you guessed it – more art, while the suite is festooned with Austrian straw bonnets. Other pluses include free parking and wi-fi. Bike hire costs €6 per day.

Lasserhof (Map p169; ☎ 87 33 88; www.lasserhof.com; Lasserstrasse 47; s/d €69/109; 🅿) Smack between Mirabellgarten and the train station, this family-run hotel is not a bad deal, but choose your room wisely. The nicer ones have Venetian chandeliers and ceramic stoves, but others are plain and on the poky side.

Hotel Hohenstauffen (Map p169; ☎ 87 21 93; www .hotel-hohenstauffen.at; Elisabethstrasse 19; s/d €80/109; 🅿 🖳) It may not be in the swishest part of town, but this friendly hotel near the train station is well set up for cyclists with a garage for repairing punctures – ring the bicycle bell at reception for service. The rooms are a tad dated, but comfy and quiet.

Hotel Wolf (Map p172; ☎ 84 34 53-0; www.hotelwolf .com; Kaigasse 9; s/d €80/110; 🖳) Pass through a Hobbitlike door into this lovingly converted town house in a quiet corner of the old town. The 15th-century hotel exudes an historic feel with its uneven stone staircases and antique furnishings. The light, parquet-floored rooms range from modern to rustic.

Hotel Mozart (Map p169; ☎ 87 22 74; www.hotel -mozart.at; Franz-Josef-Strasse 27; s/d €90/110; 🅿 🖳) Just like Amadeus, this central hotel rocks. The antique-filled lobby gives way to tidy rooms with mod cons, such as wi-fi, gleaming bathrooms, and plump beds that will have you creating a snoring symphony. If you want breakfast, though, you'll have to shell out an extra €10.

our pick **Haus Wartenberg** (Map p170; ☎ 84 84 00; www.hauswartenberg.com; Riedenburgerstrasse 2; s/d €55/128; 🅿 🖳) Hemmed in by trees, this gorgeous 400-year-old country cottage just minutes from the old town is a real find. Bedecked with geranium-filled flowerboxes and family heirlooms, the green-shuttered cottage borders a shady garden. Smooth stone steps lead up to light-flooded rooms, which are befitting of this rustic hideaway with their chunky pinewood furniture, floral curtains and stripy bedspreads.

Zur Goldenen Ente (Map p172; ☎ 84 56 22; www.ente .at; Goldgasse 10; s €75-82, d €125-150) Bang in the heart of the Altstadt, this 700-year-old town house has oodles of charm – some rooms have four-poster beds, while Emperor Franz Josef guards over others. The sunny terrace overlooks the rooftops of the old town.

Wolf Dietrich (Map p172; ☎ 87 12 75; www.salzburg -hotel.at; Wolf-Dietrich-Strasse 7; s/d €81/129; 🖳 🐾) Central and friendly, this hotel's fabulous facilities include a pool, sauna and solarium. The swanky rooms are heavy on the floral fabrics and chandeliers and the breakfast buffet is 100% organic. There's also a fabulously over-the-top suite based on Mozart's *Magic Flute*, featuring a star-studded ceiling and freestanding bathtub.

Hotel Amadeus (Map p172; ☎ 87 14 01; www.hotel amadeus.at; Linzer Gasse 43-45; s/d €88/170; 🖳) Situated on the right bank, this three-star hotel has a boutiquey feel, with personal touches such as free afternoon tea. The airy rooms are decorated in vibrant colours; some are kitted out with wrought-iron four-poster beds and chandeliers.

Top End

Arthotel Blaue Gans (Map p172; ☎ 84 24 91-50; www .blauegans.at; Getreidegasse 43; s €99-119, d €135-185; 🖳) An extreme face-lift has propelled this 650-year-old hotel into the 21st century. The revamped inn now brims with abstract artworks and modernist furnishings. Clean lines, wood floors and flat-screen TVs spruce up the whiter-than-white rooms. The centuries-old vaults harbour the excellent Blaue Gans Restaurant (p179)

Hotel Stein (Map p172; ☎ 87 43 46-0; www.hotelstein .at; Giselakai 3-5; s €99-155, d €140-165, ste €220-275; 🅿 🖳) This funky design hotel on the banks of the Salzach is no wallflower. The rooms are jazzed up with splashes of purple or ruby red, black leather chairs and zebra-print bedspreads; many also feature marble bathrooms.

Das Auersperg (Map p169; ☎ 88 94 40; www.auersperg.at; Auerspergstrasse 61; s €95-105, d €145-185, ste 205; Ⓟ 🖳 🖳) This charismatic villa fuses late-19th-century elegance with contemporary design. The modern rooms have free wi-fi and guests can kick back in the serene garden, centred on a lily pond, or in the rooftop sauna. Free bike hire is an added bonus.

Hotel Gablerbräu (Map p172; ☎ 889 65; www.gablerbrau.com; Linzer Gasse 9; s/d €102/148; 🖳) This swish hotel has been around since 1429. Expect contemporary, high-ceilinged rooms with parquet floors, comfy beds and spotless bathrooms. The vaulted restaurant (mains €8 to €15) has a seasonal menu with vegetarian options.

Hotel Sacher (Map p172; ☎ 88 97 70; www.sacher.com; Schwarzstrasse 5-7; s €149-265, d €220-390; Ⓟ 🖳) Down by the river, this turn-of-the-century hotel is pure class with its glittering chandeliers and posh piano bar. The opulent rooms feature antiques, oil paintings and shiny marble bathrooms. Tom Hanks, the Dalai Lama and Maria herself (Julie Andrews) have all snoozed here.

Goldener Hirsch (Map p172; ☎ 80 84-0; Getreidegasse 37; s €204-376, d €274-538; 🖳) A skylight illuminates the arcaded inner courtyard of this 600-year-old hotel in the Altstadt. The rustic, low-ceilinged rooms are pretty plush with lots of polished wood and sparkly pink-marble bathrooms. Queen Elizabeth and Pavarotti top the list of famous guests. Downstairs are two award-winning restaurants: S'Herzl (opposite) and Restaurant Goldener Hirsch (opposite).

Hotel Bristol (Map p172; ☎ 87 35 57; www.bristol-salzburg.at; Makartplatz 4; s/d/ste €289/340/581; Ⓟ 🖳) Emperor Franz Josef and Sigmund Freud felt at home in this elegant hotel on the square, just around the corner from Mirabellgarten. The plush pad has palatial rooms with five-star luxuries that come with their hefty price tag.

Schloss Mönchstein (Map p169; ☎ 84 85 55-0; www.monchstein.at; Mönchsberg Park 26; d €335-445, ste €475-1195; Ⓟ 🖳) Nestled in acres of grounds, this gabled medieval castle on Mönchsberg is fairy-tale stuff. The sumptuous rooms have all the trimmings: Persian rugs, antiques, oil paintings and Calcutta-marble bathrooms are standard. If you have money to burn, you can even rent the whole castle.

EATING

Schnitzel with noodles and crisp apple strudel may have been Maria's favourites, but there's a whole lot more to Salzburg's gastro scene, ranging from African restaurants with attitude to nice-and-spicy vegetarian places. If you're seeking classics – and let's face it, they taste pretty good – the wall-to-wall Gasthöfe (inns) in the old town won't disappoint.

Restaurants
BUDGET
Mensa Toscana (Map p172; ☎ 80 44 69 09; Sigmund-Haffner-Gasse 11; lunch €4-4.70; 🕑 lunch Mon-Fri) With its old town location, sunny terrace and (surprisingly) good food, the Toscana is no cookie-cutter Mensa (university restaurant).

Fisch-Krieg (Map p172; ☎ 84 37 32; Ferdinand-Hanusch-Platz 4; mains €4-7; 🕑 8.30am-6.30pm Mon-Fri, 8.30am-1pm Sat) The fish that lands on your plate at this cheap-and-cheerful place is as fresh as it comes. Take a seat on the riverside terrace to chomp on fish kebabs, octopus and paella.

Il Sole (Map p172; ☎ 84 32 84; Gstättengasse 15; mains €5.50-8.50; 🕑 lunch & dinner) The wood-fired pizza at this authentic trattoria is delicious. The smiley Italian owner starred on the German TV series *Das Traumschiff* (Love Boat), and the evidence is plastered all over the walls in the entrance.

SKS Spicy Spices (Map p172; ☎ 87 07 12; Wolf-Dietrich-Strasse 1; mains €6; 🕑 lunch & dinner) 'Healthy heart, lovely soul' is the philosophy of this Indian vegetarian restaurant with an ethnic atmosphere and cheerful staff. A few euro buys you a slap-up samosa feast or fiery curry. The organic juices and lassis pack a vitamin punch.

Wilder Mann (Map p172; ☎ 84 17 87; Getreidegasse 20; mains €6.50-8.50; 🕑 lunch & dinner Mon-Sat) Creaking with age, this cosy Austrian tavern in the Altstadt dishes up dumplings, fried sausages and other light and airy fare at rock-bottom prices.

Stadtalm (Map p172; ☎ 84 17 29; Mönchsberg 19; mains €7-12.50; 🕑 lunch & dinner mid-May–mid-Sep) Affording sweeping views over Salzburg, the cosy Stadtalm on Mönchsberg has a hearty menu with lashings of goulash and Tafelspitz (boiled beef with apple and horseradish sauce).

St Paul's Stub'n (Map p172; ☎ 84 32 20; Herrengasse 16; mains €7-14; 🕑 5pm-1am Mon-Sat) Set in a quiet corner of town, this small, wood-panelled restaurant has a good-value menu stretching from *risotto nero* (risotto made with cuttlefish ink) to roast suckling pig. There's a lovely garden for warm evenings.

Shrimps Bar (Map p172; ☎ 87 44 84; Steingasse 5; mains €7-18; 🕑 dinner) Luminous butterflies, tangerine walls and modern art give this bar a funky twist. The shrimps baguette slathered in cocktail sauce is a lip-smacking speciality (both hands required), but you can also sink your jaws into a shark steak.

Sternbräu (Map p172; ☎ 84 21 40; Griesgasse 23; mains €8-16, set menu €16.50-18.50; ⊙ lunch & dinner) The tree-shaded courtyard is the big draw at this rustic restaurant. House specials such as venison stew and trout are accompanied by copious amounts of Sternbräu beer. *The Sound of Music* dinner show takes place here (see p189).

Saran Essbar (Map p172; ☎ 84 66 28; Judengasse 10; mains €9-13; ⊙ lunch & dinner) Super-friendly Mr Saran uses the freshest ingredients in his tasty Indian dishes. Savour a Bengali fish curry or wok-fried vegetables beneath medieval vaults or on the pavement terrace. If you've room, finish off with a slice of Zaga's home-made strudel.

MIDRANGE

ᴏᴜʀ ᴘɪᴄᴋ Afro Café (Map p172; ☎ 84 48 88; Bürgerspitalplatz 5; mains €10-20; ⊙ 9am-midnight Mon-Sat) This eye-catching African café ventures into Salzburg's wackier waters. The retro design is pure genius: a blend of hot-pink walls, butterfly-shaped chairs, plastic palms and artworks sculpted from junk gathered on the beach. The menu takes some beating, too – try the sticky ostrich kebabs or coconutty Zanzibar salad with Algiers ginger punch.

Alt Salzburg (Map p172; ☎ 84 14 76; Bürgerspitalgasse 2; mains €10.20-25.80; ⊙ lunch & dinner Tue-Sat, dinner Mon) Tucked into a cobblestone courtyard at the base of the Mönchsberg, this cosy restaurant has prim-and-proper service and a meaty menu featuring specials such as venison and veal knuckle.

Nagano (Map p172; ☎ 84 94 88; Griesgasse 19; mains €10-18; ⊙ lunch & dinner) Hidden in the cobbled Artis Hof courtyard, this unassuming Japanese restaurant pushes the right buttons with fresh sushi, tempura and sashimi.

S'Herzl (Map p172; ☎ 8084-0; Getreidegasse 37; mains €11-19; ⊙ lunch & dinner) Dark wood beams, arched windows and low lighting create a cosy feel in this tavern, housed in the Goldener Hirsch (opposite). It's a fine place to snuggle up in winter over calorie-rich treats, such as sausages and sauerkraut or scrumptious puddings.

Stiftskeller St Peter (Map p172; ☎ 84 12 68-0; St Peter's Bezirk 1-4; mains €11-21.50; ⊙ lunch & dinner) Set around a vine-clad courtyard by Stiftskirche St Peter, this restaurant comprises a string of wood-panelled rooms that roll out Austrian fare, such as wild boar and roast pork with sauerkraut. It's well known for its Mozart dinner concerts (see p189).

Zum Eulenspiegel (Map p172; ☎ 84 31 80; Hagenauerplatz 2; mains €11-23; ⊙ lunch & dinner) There's a gingerbready feel about this restaurant, with its fairy lights, wonky walls and low beams. Stone steps twist up to intimate cubbyholes (some just big enough for four people), where you can savour 650 years of history, prime views of the square, and flavours such as stroganoff and sander fillet.

Gasthof Auerhahn (Map p170; ☎ 45 10 52; Bahnhofstrasse 15; mains €13-22; ⊙ lunch & dinner Tue-Sat, lunch Sun) It's off the beaten track, but that doesn't stop foodies from making the pilgrimage to Auerhahn. This award-winning restaurant serves specialities such as clams in lime froth and fluffy *Topfenknödel* (sweet dumplings). The chestnut-tree-shaded garden is popular when the sun's out.

Pan e Vin (Map p172; ☎ 844 666; Gstättengasse 1; mains €15-30; ⊙ lunch & dinner Mon-Sat, trattoria closed Mon) This cheery place comprises a smart trattoria and Mediterranean restaurant. As well as antipasti and pasta just like mamma used to make, the chef excels in the art of preparing shellfish.

Blaue Gans Restaurant (Map p172; ☎ 84 13 17-54; www.blauegans.at; Getreidegasse 43; mains €16-20; ⊙ lunch & dinner Wed-Mon) In the historic vaults of Arthotel Blaue Gans (p177), this smart restaurant is prized for fresh, locally sourced fare like tender Pinzgauer lamb. Dwarfed by the cliffs of Mönchsberg, the palm-shaded terrace is wonderful when the sun's out.

TOP END

Schloss Restaurant (Map p169; ☎ 84 85 55-0; Mönchsberg Park 26; mains €20-30; ⊙ lunch & dinner) This grand restaurant in Schloss Mönchstein dishes up a right royal feast, from tender loin of lamb to herb-crusted sole. Service is (as befits a castle) impeccable.

Restaurant Goldener Hirsch (Map p172; ☎ 8084-0; Getreidegasse 37; mains €21-27; ⊙ lunch & dinner, closed Sun in winter) Vaulting and polished wood set the scene for gourmet flavours at this well-heeled restaurant in the Goldener Hirsch (opposite). The chef has won awards for signature dishes, such as venison saddle with cabbage and dumplings.

SALZBURG

Riedenburg (Map p170; ☎ 83 08 15; www.riedenburg.at; Neutorstrasse 31; lunch €18, mains €26-35; ◷ lunch & dinner Tue-Sat) Pop art adds a splash of colour to this sleek Michelin-starred restaurant. The chef presents delicacies such as crayfish on Riesling risotto, with a razor-sharp eye for detail. The pavilion in the garden is a romantic hideaway in summer.

Ikarus (Map p170; ☎ 21 97-77; www.hangar-7.com; set menu €85-110; ◷ lunch & dinner) Hangar-7, the spacey complex at Salzburg airport, shelters this exclusive restaurant, where each month different celebrity chefs are invited to put their creative stamp on the menu. Be sure to head for some after-dinner drinks in the Hangar-7's hi-tech May Day Bar (p189).

Quick Eats

Icezeit (Map p172; ☎ 84 33 73; www.icezeit.at; Chiemseegasse 1; scoop €1-1.30; ◷ 11am-9pm) The snaking queue speaks for the quality of the homemade ice cream at this hole-in-the-wall gelateria. Refresh with zingy varieties, such as choco-chilli, ginger and lemon pepper.

Indigo (Map p169; ☎ 87 08 62; Auerspergstrasse 10; light meals €2.50-6; ◷ 10am-10pm Mon-Fri, 10am-6pm Sat) Salads by the scoopful, sushi and vegetarian curries feature on the healthy menu at this gallery-style café, decked out with wicker chairs and vibrant art.

Capp&ccino (Map p172; ☎ 87 55 45; Linzer Gasse 39; snacks €3-9, lunch €6.90; ◷ 8am-11pm) Capp&ccino is the right bank's coolest café with its high ceilings, laid-back terrace and lounge music. The moreish *tramezzini* (small Italian tea sandwiches) and free wi-fi access add to its popularity.

Coffee Shop (Map p169; ☎ 89 07 73; Franz-Josef-Strasse 3; bagels €3; ◷ breakfast, lunch & dinner) Based on Ayurvedic principles, this Zenlike café is a temple of calm and healthy living. The all-vegetarian menu includes a superb selection of bagels, salads and freshly squeezed juices.

Café Tomaselli (Map p172; ☎ 84 44 88; Alter Markt 9; pastries €4; ◷ breakfast & lunch) If you like your service with a dollop of Viennese grumpiness and strudel with a dollop of cream, this grand, wood-panelled coffee house in the city centre is just the ticket.

Scio's Specereyen (Map p172; ☎ 84 16 38; Sigmund-Haffner-Gasse 16; mains €5.50-11, snacks €2.20-4.90; ◷ 10am-8pm) Breathe in as you enter this pint-sized bistro, which bursts at the seams on weekends. No wonder, with a menu starring tasty morsels such as blinis with trout caviar. Don't leave without sampling the divine chestnut-and-nougat Venusbrüstchen (Venus breasts).

Vegy Vollwertimbiss (Map p172; ☎ 87 57 46; Schwarzstrasse 21; lunch €8; ◷ lunch Mon-Fri) Helga has been dishing up wholesome vegetarian food to Salzburg for more than 25 years. Try the tasty soups and honey-sweetened cake.

Self-Catering

If a picnic on the banks of the Salzach appeals, stock up on cheese, bread and honey at the **market** (Map p172) on Universitätsplatz.

There are several supermarkets for self-caterers, including **Billa** (Map p172; Griesgasse 19). The **Shell** (Map p169; St Julien Strasse 33) garage has a shop open 24 hours, with snacks, provisions and alcohol.

DRINKING

Salzburg is starting to shake off its purely traditional image with some trendy bars sprouting up by the Salzach. You'll still find the beer-and-pretzel type places that have been around for donkey's years, but they are making space for a new generation of lounge bars and clubs that keep partygoers on their toes till the sun rises.

Humboldt Stub'n (Map p172; ☎ 84 31 71; Gstättengasse 4-6; ◷ 12pm-4am) This bar has an upbeat, pre-clubbing vibe. Cartoons deck the walls and a nail-studded Mozart punk guards the bar. Speaking of Mozart, there's even a cocktail dedicated to the virtuoso here (a sickly sweet composition of liqueur, cherry juice, cream and chocolate). Wednesday is student night, with beers a snip at €2.50.

Republic (Map p172; ☎ 84 16 13; Anton-Neumayr-Platz 2; ◷ 8am-1am Sun-Thu, 8am-3am Fri & Sat) Opposite Humboldt Stub'n, this café is defined by high ceilings and neon lighting. By night it morphs into one of the city's trendiest haunts when DJs spinning house, salsa and electro attract a 20-something, daiquiri-sipping crowd.

Die Weisse (Map p169; ☎ 87 22 46; Rupertgasse 10; ◷ 10.30am-midnight Mon-Sat) The cavernous brew-pub belonging to the Salzburger Weissbierbrauerei is the place to guzzle cloudy wheat beers beside shiny copper vats. Choose from the wood-floored pub, the industrial-style bar or the shady beer garden out the back.

(Continued on page 189)

Meeting the Locals

Riding the chairoplane at Munich's Oktoberfest (p108).

LUDGER VORFELD

Basstscho Brews

NAME	Georg Schroll
AGE	37
OCCUPATION	Brewer, Brauerei Schroll (p236)
RESIDENCE	Nankendorf, Franconia

'Until recently Franconian breweries were dying – the other brewery in my village closed – but that's reversing now. Beer is becoming like wine: something connoisseurs appreciate for the taste.'

My great-great grandfather started brewing here in 1848. When I was 16 I planned to go abroad, but my father wanted me to stay and continue the business, so I've never left.

I brew 300,000 litres of beer each year. It's small, but enough to live on. I could produce three times as much and I thought about getting employees, but as soon as you employ people it's not less work, it's more.

For me there's no typical day – I might be brewing, or cleaning, or filling bottles or kegs, or doing deliveries in the area. I also slaughter pigs to make *Pressack* (sausages) that I serve here at the brewery.

Technology has improved; I now use a closed-water cooling system, so it's easier to control the quality consistently, but I haven't changed anything essential since my great-great grandfather's time.

I'm always thinking about the brewery – I can never switch off. It can be a lonely job and I'd like to meet someone and get married, but it's hard because it's a small village and I don't get much time to socialise.

The best thing about brewing is that it's an important Franconian tradition. It's an honourable job.

AS RELATED TO CATHERINE LE NEVEZ

Hi tech meets tradition: the operator console in a Bavarian brewery.
MEDIACOLOR'S / ALAMY

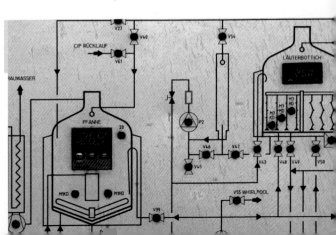

Brass beer boilers gleam inside Mahrs-Bräu-Keller (p235) in Bamberg, Franconia.

PAT BEHNKE / ALAMY

GEORG'S FAVOURITE FRANCONIAN BREWERIES

Brauerei Reichold, Aufsess (p237) It's difficult for Franconians to explain; the best I can say is *basstscho* ('it fits'). It's a perfectly 'round' beer with no faults: no dry aftertaste, not too bitter; just a good beer.

Spezial-Keller (p235) and **Schlenkerla** (p235), **Bamberg** I really like *Rauchbier* (smoked beer) and these two have strong traditions. Spezial comes from the Franconian *Spezl*, meaning 'mate'; and Schlenkerla comes from the Franconian *Schlenkert*, meaning 'limp', because a horse-and-carriage drove over the former brewmaster's foot.

Krug, Breitenlesau (p236) This beer is darker than mine and sweeter than Reichold; again, *basstscho*!

The *Reinheitsgebot* (Purity Law; p45) stipulates brewers use only four ingredients – malt, yeast, hops (left) and water.

LOUISE MURRAY / ALAMY

The Perfect Black Forest Cake

NAME	Claus Schäfer
AGE	64
OCCUPATION	Confectioner, Café Schäfer (p298)
RESIDENCE	Triberg

'I don't want to be some kind of *Kirschtorte* pope, but I will say this: you can't hurry a good Black Forest cake and the proof is in the eating.'

Baking a great Black Forest cake isn't rocket science, but it involves time, practice and fresh ingredients. Josef Keller invented *Schwarzwälder Kirschtorte* in 1905 and my father passed his original recipe onto me. It's important not to cut corners. I make the short pastry myself with a hint of marzipan. The chocolate sponge is better if it's home-made too; the bottom layer needs to be twice as thick as the others to support the Morello cherries.

I lightly whip the cream until soft and silky – beat it too hard and it'll turn out like cement. And here's the secret: the Kirsch (cherry brandy) is added to the cream, not the sponge, so the aroma isn't overly intense. After a couple of minutes when it's firmed up, I can spoon on the cherries without fear of the whole thing collapsing. Finishing touches are also important: carefully smoothing the edges, adding dark chocolate shavings and a dusting of icing sugar. *Kirschtorte* is like a beautiful woman – when it looks good, it gives you an appetite!

Yes, I've seen some Black Forest cake disasters in my time. The worst culprits are those mass-produced gateaux frozen at -45°C, which lose their entire Kirsch aroma. Black Forest cake really needs to be eaten on the same day. I make mine fresh every morning, just two or three at a time. Many customers say that the *Kirschtorte* here is so light, they could eat another slice. And they usually do. Once you've tried the real thing, there's no going back.

AS RELATED TO KERRY WALKER

Chocolate shavings: the finishing touch to the perfect Black Forest cake.

ANDY CHRISTIANI

Home-made Black
Forest cake using
Josef Keller's original
1905 recipe: an
authentic Black
Forest experience.

ANDY CHRISTIANI

BLACK FOREST FLAVOURS

**Höhengasthaus
Kolmenhof** (p299)
Franz and Karin serve
the freshest *Forelle*
(trout) at this snug
farmhouse by the
spring of the Breg.

Ackerloch Grillschopf
(p300) A rickety barn
selling home-smoked
Black Forest ham that's
air-dried over pine and
fir to achieve its intense
aroma.

Kaiserstuhl (p297)
Pick a random winery
to quaff spicy Pinot
Noir and fragrant Pinot
Gris wines.

Chocolate cherries on
display in the Black
Forest (p288).

ANDY CHRISTIANI

The Munich Club Scene

NAME	Gerhard Maier
AGE	30
OCCUPATION	Film & music journalist, hobby DJ
RESIDENCE	Munich

'Know which club you want to end up in, adapt your style accordingly and never arrive wasted – at least not when you're male.'

My plan to go partying at the rock-indie cellar Liberty at age 15 fell to pieces when the bouncer took one look at my ID and pointed to the exit. Of course I eventually earned the privilege to party in Liberty's run-down catacombs, but even now – all those years later – the role of the bouncer in Munich's clubscape never fails to amaze me.

As supreme ruler over the gates to clubworld he has the power to end any meticulously planned party night with one dismissive flick of his hand. It's a phenomenon I've yet to see anywhere else in the world. In Berlin, New York or Buenos Aires maybe there's a call for such harsh profiling in high-class venues but not here, in slightly provincial Munich, where even the tiniest electro club has strict rules about who's allowed in.

Just hang outside Atomic Café or Erste Liga on a Friday night and witness the minidramas playing out between mighty enforcer and snubbed clubbers. The variables of who gets in range from coherent to cryptic, depending on the event or the bouncer's mood. Too many boys, too drunk, wrong shoes, wrong overall style – all possible reasons for denying entrance. If there was a comprehensive philosophy behind all this, one could at least adapt. But in the words of one bouncer: 'Just deal with it.'

AS RELATED TO ANDREA SCHULTE-PEEVERS

Party mecca: Kultfabrik (p121) in Haidhausen, Munich, houses more than a dozen nightclubs.

PAT BEHNKE

A night out in Munich's thriving club scene (p121).

JAN GREUNE

GERHARD'S FAVOURITE PARTY DENS

Atomic Café (p122) Be sure to catch Henning's Britwoch, the Rare Groove parties or one of the intimate club-concerts of Britain and Scandinavia's up-and-coming acts. Tip: come early, dress indie-hip.

Erste Liga (p122) The hottest international DJs and local heroes like Jay Scarlett and the Gomma Gang infect clubgoers with tunes in all shades of danceable. Tip: dress snappy, don't be too drunk.

Substanz (p122) Caters to all musical needs, from indie to funk, house to hip-hop. Tip: none, just have fun.

Sunset over the Alpsee
near Füssen (p281):
part of the view from
Ludwig II's fairy-tale
castle Schloss Neusch-
wanstein (pp283) on the
Romantic Road (p252).

THOMAS WINZ

(Continued from page 180)

Living Room (Map p172; ☎ 87 73 61; Imbergstrasse 2a; ☒ 10am–2am Sun–Thu, 10am–4am Fri & Sat) Hugging the banks of the Salzach, this avant-garde newcomer combines a lounge-style bar with a decked terrace. Sink into a wicker armchair to admire the illuminated fortress and listen to mellow grooves. Meals are also served (€8.90 to €11.80).

Baboon Bar (Map p172; ☎ 88 59 32; Imbergstrasse 11; ☒ 7pm–4am Mon–Sat) Look out for the funky monkey at this hip riverside bar, playing '70s and '80s classics and acid jazz. The garden is popular on warm summer evenings.

Augustiner Bräustübl (Map p169; ☎ 43 12 46; Augustinergasse 4-6; ☒ 3-11pm Mon-Fri, 2.30-11pm Sat & Sun) With swinging steins and pretzels aplenty, this monk-run brewery proves that quaffing clerics can enjoy themselves. Fill your huge stone mug from the pump in the foyer, visit the snack stands and take a pew beneath the chestnut trees in the 1000-seat beer garden.

Bellini's (Map p172; ☎ 87 13 85; Mirabellplatz 4; ☒ 9am-1am Mon-Fri, 11am-1am Sat & Sun) This Italian job next to Mirabellgarten is a cool, lively bar with a cobbled terrace, great cocktails and tasty tramezzini.

Stiegl Keller (Map p172; ☎ 84 26 81; Festungsgasse 10; ☒ 11am-11pm) Beneath the fortress, this Munich-style beer hall (it shares the same architect as the Hofbräuhaus) has an enormous garden above the city's rooftops. Beer is cheapest from the self-service taps outside.

Shamrock (Map p172; ☎ 84 16 10; Rudolfskai 12; ☒ noon-2am Sun, 3pm-2am Mon, 3pm-3am Tue & Wed, 3pm-4am Thu, noon-4am Fri & Sat) This spit-and-sawdust Irish pub screens all the big sport events, plus there's live music daily from 9pm and Guinness on tap.

O'Malley's (Map p172; ☎ 84 92 65; Rudolfskai 16; ☒ 6pm-2am Mon-Thur & Sun, 6pm-4am Fri & Sat) Shamrock's more laid-back twin is run by the same people and centres on a bar built from the timber of a 300-year-old Irish church.

ARGEkultur (Map p169; ☎ 84 87 84-0; www.argekultur .at; Josef-Preis-Allee 16; ☒ 9.30am-1am Mon-Fri, 6pm-1am Sat) Students and arty types hang out at this alterative haunt, which is a bar, a bistro and a small-scale performing arts venue rolled into one. Expect an eclectic line-up of concerts and parties.

May Day Bar (Map p170; ☎ 2197; www.hangar-7.com; ☒ 5.30pm-2am Sun-Thu, 5.30pm-3am Fri & Sat) After-dinner drinks are served at this bar in the hi-tech Hangar-7 complex, where Flying Bulls aircraft zip around the glasses and virtual bar staff interact with guests.

ENTERTAINMENT
Classical Music & Musicals

Schloss Mirabell's baroque Marble Hall (p172) sets the scene for **Schlosskonzerte** (☎ 84 85 86; www.salzburger-schlosskonzerte.at; tickets €8-31), Mozart recitals given by international soloists and chamber musicians.

The **Mozarteum** (Map p172; ☎ 87 31 54; Schwarzstrasse 26-28; tickets €15-60) stages the works of Mozart and other classical composers. More light-hearted are the **Mozart dinner concerts** (☎ 84 12 68-0; tickets €45; ☒ dinner) held by candlelight and starring performers dressed in period costume at Stiftskeller St Peter (p179). **Mozart concerts** (www.mozartfestival.at), some with dinner, are also held at the Festung Hohensalzburg (p173).

If you're lucky enough to be in Salzburg during the Festspiele, try to get tickets for concerts, operas and plays at the **Festspielhaus** (Map p172; ☎ 84 45-579; Hofstallgasse 1), which is built into the sheer sides of the Mönchsberg.

If the above options sound too highbrow, **The Sound of Music Show** (☎ 82 66 17; with/without dinner €45/29; ☒ nightly May-Oct) at the Sternbräu (p179) might appeal. You'll feast on Maria's favourite things as performers bash out much-loved hits from the musical.

Rock & Jazz

Rockhouse (Map p170; ☎ 88 49 14; www.rockhouse.at, in German; Schallmooser Hauptstrasse 46; admission €10-20; ☒ 6pm-2am Mon-Sat) Playing to a young crowd, the Rockhouse is Salzburg's premier venue for rock and pop bands – check the website for details of what's on. There's also a tunnel-shaped bar that has DJs (usually free) and live bands.

Szene (Map p172; ☎ 84 34 48; www.szene-salzburg .net; Anton-Neumayr-Platz 2; tickets €10-45) Next to Republic, this venue hosts everything from DJs to cutting-edge dance productions and jam sessions. Visit the website for details of the line-up.

For live jazz, check out **Jazzit** (Map p169; ☎ 87 68 91; www.jazzit.at, in German; Elisabethstrasse 11), which stages regular gigs, or **Urbankeller** (Map p170; ☎ 87 08 94; Schallmooser Hauptstrasse 50; ☒ 5pm-1am), host to live jazz, blues, rock and funk.

SALZBURG

Theatre & Cinema

Das Kino (Map p172; ☎ 87 31 00; www.daskino.at, in German; Giselakai 11; tickets €8) Independent and art-house films are screened in their original language at this small cinema. It's also a good place to pick up fliers for clubs and happenings around town. The Latin American Film Festival takes place here in March.

Landestheater (Map p172; ☎ 87 15 12-0; www.theater.co.at, in German; Schwarzstrasse 22; tickets €5-42) This leading performing-arts venue offers a varied programme of musicals, ballets, plays and operas (mostly in German).

Salzburger Marionettentheater (Map p172; ☎ 87 24 06-0; www.marionetten.at; Schwarzstrasse 24; tickets €18-35; ☺ May-Sep, Christmas, Easter & Mozart Week in Jan) Who says puppetry is just for kids? This traditional marionette theatre stages a repertoire of well-known operas – from *Bastien and Bastienne* to *The Magic Flute* – in a gorgeous baroque auditorium. The talented puppeteers perform with grace and gusto to create the illusion of life-sized performers on a miniature stage.

SHOPPING

You can souvenir shop for everything from tight-fitting dirndls to cuckoo clocks in the Altstadt, particularly on bustling Getreidegasse and Judengasse, but be prepared to pay over the odds – this is firmly tourist territory. Design divas with bulging bank balances head for boutique-lined Linzer Gasse and Griesgasse.

Salzkontor (Map p172; Waagplatz 6) The shelves in this tiny shop are stocked with mineral-rich Salzkammergut salt, ranging from herby concoctions to bath crystals scented with lavender and citrus.

Kaslöchl (Map p172; ☎ 84 41 00; Hagenauerplatz 2) There's no room to swing a cat in Salzburg's smallest cheese shop. Squeeze in to buy delicious organic, locally sourced cheeses, such as creamy Vorarlberger or fresh cheese with basil.

Stiftsbäckerei St Peter (Map p172; Mühlenhof; ☺ 10am-5pm Mon-Fri, 10am-12pm Sat) Right next to the monastery, this 900-year-old bakery still bakes tasty loaves in a wood-fired oven.

Drechslerei Lackner (Map p172; ☎ 84 23 85; Badergasse 2) The hand-carved nutcrackers, nativity figurines and filigree Christmas stars are the real deal in this traditional craft shop.

Fürst (Map p172; ☎ 84 37 59; Getreidegasse 47) The Mozartkugeln (Mozart balls) at this speciality chocolate shop are based on Paul Fürst's original 1890 recipe. The chocolate-coated nougat and marzipan treats cost €0.90 per mouthful.

Easter in Salzburg (Map p172; ☎ 84 17 94; Judengasse 13) It's impossible to pass this shop without gawping: an incredible 150,000 real, hand-painted eggs are spread over two glittering floors. Prices range from €2 for a modestly painted hen's egg to €146 for an ostrich egg bearing a portrait of Mozart.

Christmas in Salzburg (Map p172; ☎ 84 67 84; Judengasse 10) Just opposite Easter in Salzburg, this five-floor shop puts Santa's grotto to shame. Here, gold cherubs, stockings and delicate baubles replace the eggs. Just, for goodness' sake, don't trip…

GETTING THERE & AWAY

Air

Salzburg airport (Map p170; ☎ 85 80-0; www.salzburg-airport.com), roughly half an hour by bus from the city centre, has regular scheduled flights to destinations all over Austria and Europe. Low-cost flights from the UK are provided by **Ryanair** (☎ 0900 210 240; www.ryanair.com). Other airlines flying into Salzburg include **British Airways** (☎ 0179 567 567; www.britishairways.com) and **KLM** (☎ 858 09 69; www.klm.com).

Bus

Buses depart from just outside the Hauptbahnhof (Map p169) on Südtiroler Platz, where timetables are displayed. Bus information and tickets are available from the information points on the main concourse.

Hourly buses leave for the Salzkammergut between 6.30am and 8pm – destinations include Bad Ischl (€8.70, 1¾ hours), Mondsee (€5.40, 50 minutes), St Wolfgang (€7.90, 1¾ hours) and St Gilgen (€5.20, 50 minutes). All prices are one way. Return tickets include travel on the local city-bus network. For information on bus travel further afield and an online timetable, see www.postbus.at.

Train

Salzburg is well served by InterCity (IC) and EuroCity (EC) services. For train information call ☎ 05-1717 (8am to 8pm daily), or visit the office in the Hauptbahnhof. Tickets (no commission) and train information are also available from **Salzburger Landesreisebüro** (Map p172; ☎ 87 34 03; Schwarzstrasse 11).

Fast trains leave from the Hauptbahnhof hourly for Vienna's Westbahnhof (€43.40, 3½ hours), travelling via Linz (€19.90, 1½ hours).

TOP TEMPLES OF KITSCH

- **Miracle's Wax Museum** (Map p172; Getreidegasse 7) is the place to sniff out Mozart eau de toilette (€15), pocket a pair of yodeller's lederhosen (€13) or snap up a gorgeous Sissi bust (€10) to grace your mantelpiece.

- **Residenzplatz** (Map p172) brims with high-quality kitsch – is it to be that sexy feathered Alpine hat (€19.90), the stylish edelweiss neckerchief (€5) or child prodigy Mozart captured forever in a snow globe (€5.50)?

- **Gifts & Things** (Map p172; Judengasse 6) isn't cheap, but who can resist the gem-encrusted Fabergé egg playing 'The Blue Danube' (€65) or the won't-stop-whistling marmot (€8)?

- **Candela** (Map p172; Getreidegasse 24) is a must if you've always wanted a metallic German Christmas pickle (€3.50 to €10) to hang on your tree. Glittering papayas and gaudy carrots complete your festive fruit-and-veg collection.

- **Perfect** (Map p172; Universitätsplatz 4) has the solution to carry your kitsch home. Whatever your favourite pet – poodle, Pekinese or Siamese puss – this boutique has a bejewelled purse (€12) or bag (€40) to suit.

The two-hourly express service to Klagenfurt (€31.70, 3¼ hours) runs via Villach.

The quickest way to Innsbruck is by the 'corridor' train through Germany; trains depart at least every two hours (€33.80, two hours) and stop at Kufstein. Trains to Munich take about two hours and run every 30 to 60 minutes (€27); some of these continue to Karlsruhe via Stuttgart.

If you hop on the train in Salzburg, you can also hop off in Berlin (€119, eight hours), Budapest (€70.60, seven hours), Prague (€55.40, seven hours), Rome (€90, 10½ hours) or Venice (€50, 6½ hours).

Car & Motorcycle

Three motorways meet in Salzburg to form a loop around the city: the A1 from Linz, Vienna and the east; the A8/E52 from Munich and the west; and the A10/E55 from Villach and the south. The quickest way to Tyrol is to take the Bad Reichenhall road in Germany and continue to Lofer (Hwy 312) and St Johann in Tyrol.

GETTING AROUND
To/From the Airport

Salzburg airport is less than 4km west of the city centre at Innsbrucker Bundesstrasse 95. Bus 2 (€1.80, 25 minutes) departs from outside the terminal roughly every 10 minutes and terminates at the Hauptbahnhof. This service operates from 5.30am to 11pm and doesn't go via the old town, so you'll have to take a local bus from the Hauptbahnhof once you arrive, or walk (15 to 20 minutes). A taxi between the airport and the centre costs about €15.

Bicycle

Salzburg has an excellent cycling network and hiring your own set of wheels is a carbon-neutral, hassle-free way of exploring the city and its surrounds. Next to the Hauptbahnhof, **Top Bike** (☎ 06272-4656; www.topbike.at; Südtiroler Platz 1; ⏰ 10am-5pm Apr-Oct, 9am-5pm Jul & Aug) rents bikes for around €15 per day (half-price for kids). The Salzburg Card (see p170) offers a 20% discount off these rates.

Bus

Bus drivers sell single (€1.80), 24-hour (adult/child €4.20/2.10) and weekly tickets (€11.70). Single tickets bought in advance from *Tabak* (tobacconist) shops are cheaper (€1.60 each) and are sold in units of five. Children under six years travel free.

Bus routes are shown at bus stops and on some city maps; buses 1 and 4 start from the Hauptbahnhof and skirt the pedestrian-only old town.

Bus Taxi

'Bus taxis' operate from 11.30pm to 1.30am (3am on weekends) on fixed routes, dropping off and picking up along the way, for a cost of €3.50. Ferdinand-Hanusch-Platz is the departure point for suburban routes on the left bank, and Theatergasse for routes to the right bank.

Car & Motorcycle

Parking places are limited and much of the old town is only accessible by foot, so it may be better to avoid taking your car in – there are three park-and-ride points to the west, north and south of the city. The largest car park in the city centre is the Altstadt Garage under the Mönchsberg. Expect to pay around €14 per day; some restaurants in the centre will stamp your ticket for a reduction. Rates are lower on streets with automatic ticket machines (blue zones); a three-hour maximum applies (€3 or €0.50 for 30 minutes) 9am to 7pm on weekdays.

Car rental offices:

Avis (Map p169; ☎ 87 72 78; Ferdinand-Porsche-Strasse 7)

Europcar (Map p170; ☎ 87 16 16; Gniglerstrasse 12)

Hertz (Map p169; ☎ 87 66 74; Ferdinand-Porsche-Strasse 7)

Fiacre

A *Fiacre* (horse-drawn carriage) for up to four people costs €33 for 25 minutes. The drivers line up on Residenzplatz. Not all speak English, so don't expect a guided tour.

Taxi

Taxi fares start at €3 plus around €2 per kilometre. To book a radio taxi, call ☎ 8111 or ☎ 1715. There's a huge taxi rank outside the main train station.

Regensburg, Eastern Bavaria & the Bavarian Forest

Threading through Eastern Bavaria's patchwork of bleached gold and green fields, white-washed red-roofed villages, dense forests and vibrant cities is one of the world's most celebrated waterways, the Danube. This epic river has captured the imagination of poets, painters and composers, and delivered the region power and prosperity.

For over two millennia, the Danube has lured Celts, Romans, missionaries, kings, Kaisers, merchants, and, more recently, international cruise goers, to Eastern Bavaria. Even so, its charms remain far removed from the theme-park feel of Neuschwanstein or the see-and-be-seen slopes of Garmisch-Partenkirchen. Life is unhurried, the locals are welcoming and genuinely glad to see you, and their traditions haven't been hijacked by Hollywood or kitsch promoters.

The region's centrepiece, the Unesco-listed city of Regensburg, is a vibrant blend of medieval architecture and 21st-century verve, and an ideal starting point for your explorations: Landshut's proud castle, Straubing's treasure-packed churches and Passau's riverside Altstadt (old town) are all easily reached from here. Blanketing the far-eastern edge, the mountains and valleys of the Bavarian Forest shelter a centuries-old tradition of glass-making and pristine hiking and skiing, along with Germany's oldest national park, the Nationalpark Bayerischer Wald. Combine this with some of the country's lowest-priced quality lodging, and Bavaria's east makes an affordable, active and unforgettable getaway.

REGENSBURG, EASTERN BAVARIA & THE BAVARIAN FOREST

HIGHLIGHTS

- Scaling the sheer marble staircase to encounter a pantheon of Germany's greatest minds and achievers at the opulent temple **Walhalla** (p202)

- Forging through the heart of the **Bavarian Forest** (p209) on its single-track railway as spruce branches smack the carriage windows on either side

- Savouring local brews in river-front **beer gardens** (p200) with the romantic skyline of Regensburg as a backdrop

- Dining beneath the vines or in the candlelit cellar of Passau's historic **Heilig-Geist-Stift-Schenke** (p207)

- Taking a pilgrimage to the pope's hometown, the little village of **Marktl am Inn** (boxed text, p209)

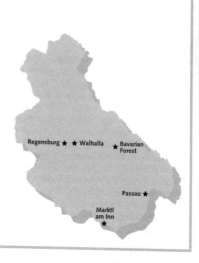

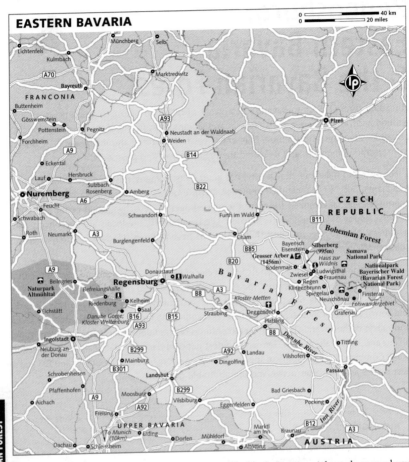

EASTERN BAVARIA

REGENSBURG

☎ 0941 / pop 150,000 / elev 330m

At once ancient and vibrant, Regensburg is one of Bavaria's most beautiful cities and among the best-preserved medieval towns in Europe. Its magic reveals itself in countless, often surprising, places. You'll find it in a leafy beer garden on the banks of the Danube, in the Altstadt's honeycomb of laneways and beneath the soaring spires of the Dom (cathedral). This is a city where you can eat pasta in a former Gothic chapel, lean against a wall erected by the Romans and prowl the corridors of a royal residence bigger than Buckingham Palace. You'll also find spirited nightlife (thanks to 25,000 university students), no fewer than three local breweries

and enough engaging sights to keep you busy for at least a couple of days.

History

'Regensburg is so beautifully situated, someone had to settle here,' rhapsodised Goethe. And indeed, that's what's happened: the Romans built a fortress housing a 6000-strong legion here in 179 AD, marking their northern boundary; St Boniface founded a bishopric; and the Bavarian dukes made the town their capital.

Regensburg's prominence rose steadily through the Middle Ages, and so did its fortunes, especially after the completion of the Steinerne Brücke (Stone Bridge), which put the city at the crossroads of both the east–west and north–south trade routes, turning it into a medieval trading metropolis. By 1200, it had a population of 20,000 – one of the largest in Europe. The Altstadt's pastel-shaded patrician town houses, with their tall, square towers, date back to Regensburg's heyday as a Free Imperial City from 1245 to the end of the 15th century.

Competition from Augsburg and Nuremberg led to Regensburg's decline, although it regained some prestige as the seat of the Perpetual Diet (permanent parliament) of the Holy Roman Empire from 1663 to 1806. That competition, however, largely spared Regensburg from destruction come WWII, when a mere 13% of the city was destroyed. Oskar Schindler lived in Regensburg for years; his house at Watmarkt 5 bears a plaque.

Today, this thriving capital of the Oberpfalz (Upper Palatinate) boasts an acclaimed university (where Joseph Ratzinger – now Pope Benedict XVI – taught theology), modern industries (notably Siemens and BMW) and a proud heritage. City pride hit an all-time high when Regensburg's medieval Alstadt was recently proclaimed a Unesco World Heritage site.

Orientation

Regensburg's major sights cluster in the Altstadt, which is hemmed in by the Danube on the northern edge and is almost entirely closed to private-vehicle traffic (driving to your hotel is OK). The Hauptbahnhof (central train station) is about a 10-minute walk south of the heart of the Altstadt, ie the area around the Dom.

Information
BOOKSHOPS
Bücher Pustet (☎ 569 70; Gesandtenstrasse 6-8) Good selection of maps, English-language travel guides and novels.
Presse + Buch (☎ 585 750; inside Hauptbahnhof) English books and magazines.

EMERGENCY
Ambulance (☎ 192 22)
Police (☎ 110, nonemergencies 5060; Minoritenweg 1)

INTERNET ACCESS
Acom Center (☎ 599 8318; Fröhliche-Türken-Strasse 5, entry via Grasgasse; per hr €1; ☼ 10am-10pm) Online computers plus broadband access for laptops.

Dali (Speirchergasse 1; per hr €3.50; ☼ 6am-2am) Cavernous internet hall with roomy workstations and licensed bar.

MEDICAL SERVICES
Evangelisches Krankenhaus (Hospital; ☎ 504 00; Emmeramsplatz 10)

MONEY
Sparkasse City Center (Neupfarrplatz 10; ☼ 24hr) Automated foreign-exchange machine and English-enabled ATMs.

POST
Post office Altstadt (Domplatz 3); Hauptbahnhof (Bahnhofstrasse 16) The Hauptbahnhof branch also changes money.

TOURIST INFORMATION
Tourist office (☎ 507 4410; www.regensburg.de; Altes Rathaus; ☼ 9.15am-6pm Mon-Fri, 9.15am-4pm Sat, 9.30am-4pm Sun & holidays)

Sights
DOM ST PETER & AROUND
Lording over Regensburg, **Dom St Peter** (St Peter's Cathedral; ☎ 597 1002; Domplatz; admission free, 75min tours in German €3; ☼ 6.30am-6pm Apr-Oct, 6.30am-5pm Nov-Mar, tours 10.30am & 2pm Mon-Sat, 2pm Sun) ranks among Bavaria's grandest Gothic cathedrals. Construction of this twin-spired landmark began in the late 13th century, mostly to flaunt the city's prosperity. The cavernous interior's prized possessions include kaleidoscopic stained-glass windows and a pair of animated sculptures attached to pillars just west of the altar: the Angel of the Annunciation beams at the Virgin on the opposite pillar as he delivers the news of her pregnancy.

If that whets your appetite, the attached former bishop's residence, the **Domschatzmuseum** (Cathedral Treasury; ☎ 576 45; adult/under 14yr €2/1; ☼ 10am-5pm Tue-Sat, noon-5pm Sun Apr-Oct, 10am-4pm Fri & Sat, noon-4pm Sun Dec-Mar) brims with vestments, monstrances, tapestries and other riches. Still more religious treasures await at the nearby **Diözesanmuseum St Ulrich** (☎ 516 88; Domplatz 2; adult/concession €2/1; ☼ 10am-5pm Tue-Sun Apr-Oct), inside a medieval church.

Just north of the Dom, the arched gate called **Porta Praetoria** (Unter den Schwibbögen) is the most impressive reminder of Regensburg's Roman heritage. It was built in AD 179 by Emperor Marcus Aurelius as part of the Castra Regina fortress. To see more remains of the Roman wall, stroll along Unter den Schwibbögen.

REGENSBURG, EASTERN BAVARIA & THE BAVARIAN FOREST

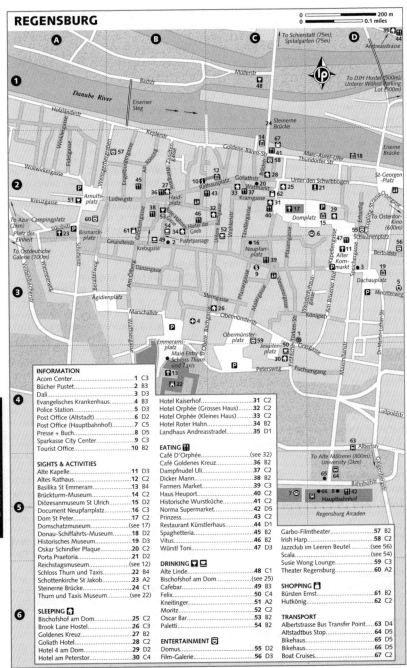

South of the Dom, the graceful **Alte Kapelle** (Old Chapel; Alter Kornmarkt 8) wows visitors with rich and harmonious rococo decorations, but at its core it's actually about 1000 years old. The church is only open during services, but peering through the wrought-iron gate will give you at least partial views.

HISTORISCHES MUSEUM

A medieval monastery provides a suitably atmospheric backdrop for the city's **Historisches Museum** (Historical Museum; ☎ 507 2448; Dachauplatz 2-4; adult/concession/family €2.20/1.10/4.40; ☺ 10am-4pm Tue, Wed, Fri-Sun, 10am-8pm Thu). The collections trace through the region's history from the Stone Age to the 19th century, with special emphasis on the Roman period and Regensburg's medieval glory days.

ALONG THE DANUBE

A veritable miracle of engineering in its time, the **Steinerne Brücke** (Stone Bridge) was cobbled together between 1135 and 1146. For centuries it remained the only solid crossing along the entire Danube. An artificial canal now allows larger rivercraft to bypass its low arches.

According to legend, the bridge's crafty builder promised the devil the first soul to cross it if he let him beat the cathedral-builder who had bet on completing his church first. The bridge-builder won and hoodwinked Satan, too, for the first to cross the bridge were a dog, a cat and a chicken.

Ensconced in its southern tower is the **Brückturm-Museum** (Bridge Tower Museum; ☎ 567 6015; Weisse-Lamm-Gasse 1; adult/concession/family €2/1.50/4; ☺ 10am-5pm Apr-Oct), which houses a small historical exhibit about this unique bridge, although most people come for the bird's-eye river views from the top. (You need to stretch your imagination to conjure up the colour of Schubert's famous musical composition – the title was inspired by its rhyming German title, 'Blaue Donau', not by the green-tinged water.)

A short walk east along the Danube, the **Donau-Schiffahrts-Museum** (Danube Navigation Museum; ☎ 507 5888; Marc-Aurel-Ufer; adult/concession/family €2/1.50/4; ☺ 10am-5pm Apr-Oct) is a historic paddle-wheel steam tugboat with exhibits on the history of navigation on the river.

ALTES RATHAUS & REICHSTAGSMUSEUM

The seat of the *Reichstag* (parliament) from 1663 to 1803, the **Altes Rathaus** (old town hall) is now home to Regensburg's three mayors, the tourist office and the **Reichstagsmuseum** (☎ 507 4411; adult/concession/family €6/3/15; ☺ tours in English 3pm Apr-Oct, 2pm Nov, Dec & Mar). Tours take in not only the richly decorated **Reichssaal** (Imperial Hall), where the delegates convened, but also the stomach-turning torture chamber in the basement. Walk into the old holding cell and look down to the dungeon before entering the interrogation room, which bristles with scary tools of the trade. Kids will either love it or freak out.

DOCUMENT NEUPFARRPLATZ

Excavations in the mid-1990s revealed remains of Regensburg's once-thriving 16th-century Jewish quarter, along with Roman buildings, gold coins and a Nazi bunker. The subterranean **document Neupfarrplatz** (☎ 507 3454; Neupfarrplatz; adult/concession €5/2.50; ☺ tours 2.30pm Thu-Sat Sep-Jun, Thu-Mon Jul & Aug) only provides access to a small portion of the excavated area, but tours feature a nifty multimedia presentation (in German) about the square's history. Back up above, on the square itself, a work by renowned Israeli artist Dani Karavan graces the site of the former synagogue.

SCHLOSS THURN UND TAXIS & MUSEUMS

In the 15th century, an Italian entrepreneur who adopted the name Franz von Taxis (1459–1517) was bestowed with nobility after establishing Europe's first postal system. It remained a family monopoly until the 19th century, and to compensate for its loss, the family was given the former Benedictine monastery of St Emmeram. Henceforth known as **Schloss Thurn und Taxis** (☎ 504 8133; www.thurnund taxis.de; Emmeramsplatz 5; tours adult/concession €11.50/9; ☺ tours in English 1.30pm daily Jul-Sep, tours in German 11am, 2pm, 3pm & 4pm daily plus extra tour 10am Sat, Sun & holidays Apr-Sep, 10am, 11am, 2pm & 3pm Sat, Sun & holidays Nov-Mar), it became state of the art for its time (with running water, central heating and a labyrinth of concealed servants' passageways and secret doors), and outranks London's Buckingham Palace in size.

The palace is still the primary residence of Franz's current heirs, and the only way to visit is by tour (free English audioguides are available to take on German-language tours). These 90-minute tours take you through a succession of colour-themed rooms (such as the ornate 'silver room'), the former cloisters and the 100-sq-m dining room with a one-tonne chandelier. Also included is a peek at the cloister of the **Basilika St Emmeram** (☎ 510 30; Emmeramsplatz 3; ☺ 10am-4.30pm, 10am-1pm Fri & noon Sun), a masterpiece by the Asam brothers.

Porcelain, glass, furniture and other items from the family's private collection are displayed at the onsite **Thurn und Taxis museum** (☎ 504 8133; www.thurnundtaxis.de; adult/concession €4.50/3.50; ☺ 11am-5pm Mon-Fri, 10am-5pm Sat & Sun).

Cloaking the palace are luxuriant gardens, which only open to the public during special events. The gardens' limited access allows them to form an important biotope for birdlife.

SCHOTTENKIRCHE ST JAKOB

In the western Altstadt, the 12th-century main north portal of the **Schottenkirche St Jakob** (Scottish Church of St Jacob; Jakobstrasse 3) is considered one of the supreme examples of Romanesque architecture in Germany. Its numerous reliefs and sculptures form an incredibly complicated iconography, the meaning of which continues to baffle even the experts. The church's blackened façade makes it look like it's suffered a fire, but the discolouration is due to centuries of pollution.

OSTDEUTSCHE GALERIE

The **Ostdeutsche Galerie** (East German Gallery; ☎ 297 140; Dr Johann Maier Strasse; adult/child €4/2; ☺ 10am-5pm Tue-Sun) opened in 1966 as a way to maintain a connection with Regensburg's neighbours behind the iron curtain. Today it celebrates wildly diverse contemporary art by artists from former Eastern Bloc communist countries. The museum backs onto the sprawling Stadtpark (City Park) – perfect for combining a visit with a picnic.

Tours

English-Language Walking Tours (☎ 507 4410; www.regensburg.de; Altes Rathaus; adult/concession/family €6/3/10; ☺ 1.30pm Wed & Sat May-Sep & Dec) Tours last 90 minutes and depart from the tourist office. German tours are offered several times daily year-round.

Personenschifffahrt Klinger (☎ 521 04; adult/child/student €7/3/4.50; ☺ 10am-4pm May-Sep, 11am-3pm Apr & Oct, tour departure times vary) Operates 50-minute Danube cruises from the Steinerne Brücke landing docks. For boat cruises to Walhalla, see p202.

Festivals & Events

Bavarian Jazz Weekend (☎ 562 244; www.bayer isches-jazzweekend.de, in German) Venues throughout the Altstadt in early or mid-July.

Christmas markets Regensburg hosts a traditional market (Neupfarrplatz; admission free), a torch-lit medieval market (Schloss Thurn und Taxis; admission €3 to €5 depending on time of day) and a handcraft market (Haidplatz; admission free), all in December.

Dult (Dultplatz) Oktoberfest-style party with beer tents, carousel rides and entertainment in Pentecost and late Aug.

Schlossfestspiele (www.thurnundtaxis.de; Schloss Thurn und Taxis) Opera and classical music at the palace in mid-July.

Sleeping

Reserve ahead during festivals and special events when Regensburg's accommodation books up completely. The tourist office has a list of self-catering holiday apartments. Lonely Planet's Hotels & Hostels (http://hotels.lonely planet.com) reviews properties in all price ranges that can be booked online.

BUDGET

Azur-Campingplatz (☎ 270 025; www.azur-camping .de/regensburg, in German; Weinweg 40; per person €5.50-7, campsites €6-8, family €25) Campers can swim at this beautifully sited riverside spot about 2km west of the Altstadt.

Brook Lane Hostel (☎ 690 0966; www.hostel-regens burg.de, in German; Obere Bachgasse 21; dm €15, d with shared bathroom €35, linen €2) This ever-expanding indie hostel in the heart of town has a full kitchen, colourful dorms with timber bunks and even a small supermarket downstairs. Reception hours are restricted to shopping hours at the time of writing (though it's anticipated this will loosen up), but checking in any time is no problem if you call ahead.

DJH hostel (☎ 574 02; jhregensburg@djh-bayern .de; Wöhrdstrasse 60; dm incl breakfast & linen from €18.85; ☒) Occupying a meticulously renovated old building on a river island, Regensburg's DJH hostel is an easy 10-minute walk east of the Altstadt.

Spitalgarten (☎ 847 74; www.spitalgarten.de; St Katharinenplatz 1; s/d with shared bathroom €30/54) A stumble upstairs from this legendary brewery and beer garden (p200) are 11 clean, sunlit rooms (all with shared bathroom; towels are provided). Herringbone parquet floors and timber furnishings add to the old-fashioned atmosphere, and kids' beds are available on request.

Hotel am Peterstor (☎ 545 45; www.hotel-am-pe
terstor.de; Fröhliche-Türken-Strasse 12; s/d €38/48; ☺ reception 7-11am & 4-10.30pm) Am Peterstor's pale-grey
décor might be nondescript, but its rooms are
spacious and sparkling clean, the location is
great and staff go out of their way to assist.
Breakfast is an optional €5 extra; otherwise
hit the nearby cafés.

MIDRANGE
Hotel Kaiserhof (☎ 585 350; www.kaiserhof-am-dom.de;
Kramgasse 10-12; s €62-75, d €92-130) Seven of the 33
rooms inside this landmark pistachio-green
hotel have front-and-centre views of the
Dom's forestry of stone spires, which can also
be seen from the upper-level breakfast room.
Brocade curtains and bedspreads give the
comfortable rooms an air of faded grandeur.
You can log onto wi-fi using your credit card,
and discounted parking is available nearby.

Goldenes Kreuz (☎ 558 12; www.hotel-goldeneskreuz
.de; Haidplatz 7; s €75-105, d €95-125; P) Dating back
to at least 1531, and frequented by emperors,
nobles and other luminaries, this ancient inn
has been painstakingly renovated to house a
choice little hotel. Each of its nine rooms is
inspired by a former guest: Napoleon III's
has crimson velvet armchairs and a canopied
bed, while Gustav Wasa from Sweden's has
half-timbered internal walls. Wi-fi is available, and one room is wheelchair accessible.
Parking's free.

Hotel Roter Hahn (☎ 595 090; www.roter-hahn.com;
Rote-Hahnen-Gasse 10; s/d from €85/105; P) A hefty
beamed ceiling and a glassed-in Roman
stone well greet you in the lobby of the 'Red
Rooster', contrasting with streamlined rooms
offering up-to-date amenities. Breakfast is
truly a gourmet spread – sparkling wine
anyone? – and the mezzanine restaurant
(mains €15.50 to €19) serves succulent fish
and meat dishes. Parking costs €12; request a room on the 2nd floor to access the
free wi-fi.

Hotel Orphée (☎ 596 020; www.hotel-orphee.de;
Untere Bachgasse 8; Grosses Haus s €90-120, d €110-140,
Kleines Haus s with shared bathroom €30-60, with private
bathroom €80-105, d with shared bathroom €70, with private
bathroom €85-115) Exquisite rooms in both the
Orphée's Grosses Haus ('big house', where
reception for both is located) and its Kleines
Haus ('small house'; Wahlenstrasse 1) incorporate details like antique basins, four-poster
beds, and a bathroom hidden behind a cupboard door. Rates include in-room water and

wine; the Kleines Haus has a communal TV
lounge but no in-room TVs.

ourpick Landhaus Andreasstradel (☎ 5960 2300;
www.hotel-orphee.de; Andreasstrasse 26; s €100-120, d €120-
140; ☺ reception 6am-2pm & 5-8pm; P) Occupying
a medieval salt warehouse on the northern
banks of the Danube, this rambling country
manor has six rooms that face the riverside
park, each with a private patio screened by
greenery. All 10 rooms feature furnishings
imported from India, DVD players, honey
soap, and kitchenettes with fridges and hotplates (breakfast – at Café D'Orphée – costs
extra). Parking (€6) and free broadband are
available; contact Hotel Orphée if reception
is closed.

Hotel 4am Dom (www.4amdom-hotel.de; Alter Kornmarkt 3) Look out for this artist-designed hotel.
Each of its four rooms (inspired by the four
elements: water, earth, air, fire) occupies an
entire floor of a tower, and are due to be open
by the time you read this.

TOP END
Bischofshof am Dom (☎ 584 60; www.hotel-bischofshof
.de; Krautermarkt 3; s €76-107, d €132-146, ste €195; P ☒)
The rambling residence of generations of
bishops is now a romantic hotel where grand
rooms wraparound a flower-filled courtyard
(plus brewery and summer beer garden – see
p201), and some rooms incorporate original
Roman walls. The restaurant (mains €14.40 to
€19.80) serves gourmet Bavarian cuisine.

Goliath Hotel (☎ 200 0900; www.hotel-goliath
.de; Goliathstrasse 10; s/d from €99/140; P ☒ ☒)
Regensburg's newest and funkiest hotel fuses
fuchsia-and-lime-green rooms carpeted in
short-pile tortoiseshell with fresh flowers and
silk-screen prints. Two floors have communal timber decks, and room 305 has its own
private terrace. Wi-fi and broadband are free;
parking costs €12.

Eating
Regensburg claims more restaurants, cafés
and bars per capita than anywhere else in
Germany, with some 700-odd venues for
drinking and/or dining. Like all good student
cities, it has many places that serve breakfast
until 6pm.

RESTAURANTS
ourpick Spaghetteria (☎ 563 695; Am Römling 12;
mains €5-7.50, small antipasti buffet €6.90, large antipasti buffet €9.60; Ⓥ) Lit by huge candelabras

suspended from its cross-vaulted ceiling, this one-time Gothic chapel cooks up mix-and-match pastas and tangy sauces (the broccoli-hazelnut is divine). Its antipasti buffet is as colourful as a Michelangelo painting, and its young, hip staff can tip you off about places to kick on after your meal.

Restaurant Künstlerhaus (☎ 830 5998; Andreasstrasse 28; mains €8-18; ☺ 10am-midnight Tue-Sun; **V**) This striking open-plan space over-looking the river is filled with contemporary art produced by artists occupying the atelier above. Fresh, seasonal and locally sourced produce is prepared in creative ways – from sheep's cheese salad to a sweet mustard and chocolate soufflé for dessert.

Dicker Mann (☎ 573 70; Krebsgasse 6; dishes €9-15.50; ☺ 10am-1am; **V**) Within its uneven cobblestone floors and dark timber furni-ture scattered in multiple dining rooms and a leafy walled beer garden, this traditional restaurant serves rib-sticking breakfasts in-cluding a 'Good Morning Bavaria' version of white and liver sausages with mustard, wheat beer and pretzels. Every salad con-tains meat (occasionally fish), but a hand-ful of vegetarian options are flagged on the menu.

Vitus (☎ 526 46; Hinter der Grieb 8; daily set menu €9, mains €13.90-18.50; ☺ 9am-1am) Colourful can-vasses mix with ancient beamed ceilings at this bustling place serving provincial French food, including delicious *Flammekuche* (Alsatian-style pizza). Sit in the rustic bar area, the restaurant with linen-draped tables or the child-friendly café section.

Haus Heuport (☎ 599 8297; Domplatz 7; mains €9.50-25.90; ☺ 9am-1am Mon-Fri, 9am-2am Sat & Sun; **V**) Enter an internal courtyard (flanked by stone blocks where medieval torches were once extinguished) and climb up the grand old wooden staircase to this Gothic dining hall for front-row views of the Dom and culinary celebrations from sautéed tofu to raw minced smoked salmon. Reservations are advised for weekend breakfast, while in summer tables spilling out onto the square offer a less pricey bistro menu.

CAFÉS & BISTROS
Café Goldenes Kreuz (☎ 558 12; Haidplatz 7; breakfast €4-7.50, cakes €1.50-3; ☺ 7am-7pm Mon-Sat, 9am-7pm Sun) This classic Viennese-style coffeehouse is an elegant spot for breakfast or afternoon coffee and cake.

Prinzess (☎ 595 310; Rathausplatz 2; dishes €2.50-6.50; ☺ 9.30am-6.30pm) Enjoy a civilised cuppa at this refined café situated above Germany's oldest chocolatier, which has been making pralines since 1676.

Café D'Orphée (☎ 529 77; Untere Bachgasse 8; mains €13.80-20.80; ☺ 7.30am-1am; **V**) Ensconced in tim-ber panelling, red-velvet banquettes, framed posters and gilded mirrors, this *belle époque* brasserie has fabulous French fare, includ-ing paté, quiche and crêpes along with baked treats like *clafoutis aux cerises* (cherry flan).

QUICK EATS & SELF-CATERING
Historische Wurstküche (☎ 466 210; Thundorfer Strasse 3; meals €6.30-12.60, roll with 2 sausages €1.90; ☺ 8am-7pm) Regensburg's finger-sized sausages have been grilled over beechwood and dished up with sauerkraut and sweet grainy mustard in this spot since 1135, purportedly making it the world's oldest sausage kitchen.

Würstl Toni (Alter Kornmarkt; dishes €2-3; ☺ till late) This simple sausage stand – and especially its *Knacker in der Semmel mit allem* (sausages in a bun with the works) – has cult status among night owls.

Dampfnudel Uli (☎ 532 97; Watmarkt 4; dishes €2-7.50; ☺ 10am-6pm Tue-Sun) Oldtimers pack into this rose-pink patrician tower dating from 1260 for the Regensburg speciality *Dampfnudel*: steamed yeast buns drowned in creamy vanilla custard (€5.40). Look for photos of famous visitors, including US Presidents Regan and Bush Snr amid the earthen beer mugs clut-tering the walls.

There's a **farmers market** (☺ 9am-4pm; ☺ daily) on Neupfarrplatz; otherwise try **Norma Super-market** (Hauptbahnhof), also open daily.

Drinking
BREWERIES & BEER GARDENS
All beer gardens are attached to year-round restaurants where no-nonsense dishes cost around €8 to €15.

Kneitinger (☎ 524 55; Arnulfsplatz 3; ☺ 9am-11pm) Students, professors and workers squeeze cheek-by-jowl at this quintessential Bavarian brewery-pub for hearty home cooking and delicious house brews. It's been in business since 1530. Ask here or at the tourist office about weekly brewery tours.

Spitalgarten (☎ 847 74; www.spitalgarten.de; St Katharinenplatz 1) Crossing the Danube on the Steinerne Brücke takes you to one of the oldest hospital breweries in Bavaria. The

---

'OUT' & ABOUT IN REGENSBURG

Regensburg has a small but lively gay and lesbian scene. Its lynchpin is the café-bar **Schierstatt** (☎ 870 0762; An der Schierstatt 1; ☯ 10am-1am), which also draws some hets. On Thursday night, Schierstatt is a warm-up stop for the legendary lesbigay party at **Scala** (☎ 522 93; Gesandtenstrasse 6, Pustetpassage; ☯ 11pm-3am). Keep tabs on the latest hotspots via the magazine *Just Different* and the website www.gay-regensburg.de (in German).

---

riverside beer garden has grand views of the city, and friendly service.

Bischofshof am Dom (☎ 584 60; Krautermarkt 3) Rounding out Regensburg's trio of breweries is this historic bishops' residence, with a stately walled beer garden.

Alte Linde (☎ 880 80; Müllerstrasse 1) Accessed via the romantic Steinerne Brücke; enjoy a mug of ale while taking in panoramic views of the Altstadt at this large, leafy beer garden on a Danube island.

BARS

Paletti (☎ 515 93; Gesandtenstrasse 6, Pustetpassage; ☯ 8am-1am Mon-Sat, 3pm-1am Sun) Soak up *la dolce vita*, Regensburg style, along with thimble-sized espressos or a chilled Pinot Grigio in this art-clad bar and its mural-covered courtyard.

Felix (☎ 590 59; Frölich-Türken-Strasse 6; ☯ 9am-1am Mon-Sat, 10am-1am Sun) Leaf through the lengthy drinks menu, including Baileys lattes and beers galore, beneath a chandelier made from twisted metal and shards of glass.

Also recommended:

Moritz (Untere Bachgasse 15; ☯ 7.30am-1am Mon-Thu, 7.30am-2am Fri & Sat) Funky tangerine-painted walls mix it with Gothic cross-vaulted ceilings and killer cocktails.

Oscar Bar (☎ 630 8455; Rote-Hahnen-Gasse 2) Chic and sleek with a crowd to match.

Cafebar (☎ 541 67; Gesandtenstrasse 14) Hole-in-the-wall hipster's hang-out with cracked Art Deco tiling, a marble bar and grappas that pack a punch.

Entertainment

Look for the local what's-on guide, *Logo* (in German), in cafés, bars and shops around town.

CINEMAS

Art-house cinemas with occasional screenings of movies in their original language (including English):

Film-Galerie (☎ 560 901; Bertoldstrasse 9) On the 6th floor of the Leerer Beutel cultural centre.

Garbo-Filmtheater (☎ 575 86; Weissgerbergraben 11)

Ostentor-Kino (☎ 791 974; Adolf-Schmetzer-Strasse 5)

CLUBS

Entry to clubs costs around €5 depending on the night – theme nights usually cost more but include a free drink. All generally spin chart music. Check out www.kult.de (in German) and click on locations/Regensburg.

The young and the beautiful regularly make for **Suzie Wong Lounge** (Obermünsterplatz; ☯ 11.30pm-late Tue-Sat), while an older, sophisticated crowd sips mai-tais and whiskey sours at **Domus** (A-Kolping-Strasse; ☯ midnight-5am Fri, Sat & prior to public holidays), in an ivy-covered medieval tower.

LIVE MUSIC

Jazzclub im Leeren Beutel (☎ 563 375; Bertoldstrasse 9) Catch smooth or swinging tunes from local and visiting talent.

Alte Mälzerei (☎ 788 8150; Galgenbergstrasse 20) Local and international bands, cabaret, spoken word, dance parties – the programme at this cultural centre is unpredictable, eclectic and classy.

Irish Harp (☎ 572 68; Brückstrasse 1) Regular live music (usually from 9pm from Monday to Saturday throughout summer, and sometimes spontaneous) packs out this high-spirited pub.

Theater Regensburg (☎ 507 2424; Bismarckplatz) The city's municipal theatre keeps the high-brow crowd entertained with a varied menu of opera, ballet, classical concerts and drama.

Regensburger Domspatzen The cathedral's famous boys' choir, known as the 'Cathedral Sparrows', sings at the 10am Sunday service in the Dom.

Shopping

In addition to pralines from Prinzess (opposite), unique souvenirs include natural brushes handmade by **Bürsten Ernst** (Glockengasse 10) since 1894, and hats handmade by master milliner Andreas Nuslan at **Hutkönig** (Domplatz).

Getting There & Away

Direct trains run from Regensburg to Munich (€21.80, 1½ hours), Nuremberg (€16.40, one hour), Passau (€23, 1½ hours) and Landshut (€10.60, 45 minutes).

Regensburg is approximately an hour's drive southeast of Nuremberg and northwest of Passau via the A3 autobahn. The A93 runs south to Munich.

Getting Around
Regensburg's compact Altstadt is easily explored on foot.

BICYCLE
Bikehaus (☎ 599 8808; Bahnhofstrasse 17 & 18; bikes per day €9.50) is a full-service outfit with bike sales, rental, repair, storage and cyclist staff happy to help you plan trips around the region. The main rental outlet (which also has a range of kids' bikes) is on the same side of the street as the Hauptbahnhof (Bahnhofstrasse 18) and is open from 10am to 1pm and 2pm to 7pm Tuesday to Sunday. Its sales outlet directly across the street (Bahnhofstrasse 17) rents a limited number of bikes (no kids' bikes), and is open from 10am to 2pm and 3pm to 7pm Wednesday to Monday.

BUS
The Altstadtbus loops frequently between the Hauptbahnhof and the Altstadt (per ride €0.50) daily except Sunday. Regular buses converge at the Albertstrasse stop, also just north of the train station. Single tickets cost €1.60 and day passes €3.30 on weekdays and €3 on weekends. Weekend passes are good for up to five people travelling together.

CAR & MOTORCYCLE
The Steinerne Brücke is closed to private vehicles. The main river crossings are via the Nibelungenbrücke and the Eiserne Brücke. Car parks in the Altstadt charge from €1.20 per hour and are well signposted. Parking is free at the Unterer Wöhrd lot on the northern bank near the Nibelungenbrücke, from where it's about a 10-minute walk to the Altstadt.

TAXI
For a taxi call ☎ 194 10 or ☎ 520 52.

AROUND REGENSBURG
Walhalla
Cantilevered onto the hillside, with sweeping views over the Danube from its wraparound porticoes, **Walhalla** (☎ 09403-961 680; adult/concession €4/3; ☉ 9am-5.45pm Apr-Sep, 9am-4.45pm Oct,

10am-11.45am & 1-3.45pm Nov-Mar) is modelled on the Parthenon in Athens, and dedicated to the giants of Germanic thought and deed. It was the brainchild of King Ludwig I and was designed by Leo von Klenze in 1842.

The temple's marble-lined interior contains 127 marble busts and 64 commemorative tablets of statesmen, scientists and artists. On rare occasions, the Bavarian government inducts a new worthy German to this illustrious circle. The most recent (in 2003) was Sophie Scholl, a member of *Die Weisse Rose* Nazi resistance group (see the boxed text, p95), whose abstract, snow-white likeness hasn't yet been yellowed by time like the more realistic depictions of fellow residents such as Beethoven, Brahms, Luther and Einstein. (If passing under their gaze doesn't leave you at least a little in awe, you're probably holidaying in the wrong country.)

For all its splendour, Walhalla doesn't get overly crowded – except after closing hours in summer, when Regensburg locals gather here after dark for impromptu barbeques and parties as the sun sets over the Danube and stars fill the sky.

Walhalla is about 10km east of Regensburg. The most scenic way to get here, in fine weather, is by boat. Cruises operated by **Personenschifffahrt Klinger** (☎ 0941-521 04; adult/under 14yr/student/family return €12/6.50/8.50/25; ☉ 10.30am & 2pm Apr-Oct) travel from Regensburg's Steinerne Brücke landing docks to those at Walhalla, from where it's a hefty 15-minute climb up 358 steps. Boat trips include a 1¼-hour stop at Walhalla (entrance to the interior costs extra). Access is easier arriving by road: drivers should follow the road to Donaustauf along the northern bank of the Danube. Bus 5 also makes the trip out here regularly from Regensburg's Hauptbahnhof.

Befreiungshalle
About 30km upstream from Regensburg awaits another monumental piece of architecture dreamed up by King Ludwig I, the grandiose **Befreiungshalle** (Hall of Liberation; ☎ 0941-682 070; Befreiungshallestrasse 3; adult/concession €3/2.50; ☉ 9am-6pm Fri-Wed, 9am-8pm Thu mid-Mar-Oct, 10am-4pm daily Nov–mid-Mar). This pale-yellow cylinder, perched above the Danube near Kelheim, serves to commemorate Napoleon's defeat in 1815. Inside, the ring of super-sized winged white marble sculptures of the Roman goddess Victoria is a real trip.

It's best reached via your own wheels on the B16.

Danube Gorge & Kloster Weltenburg

Carving through craggy cliffs and weathered rock formations, the **Danube Gorge** (Donaudurchbruch) is one of the most dramatic stretches of the river.

The only way to enjoy this natural spectacle is from the water. You can board one of the cruise boats leaving from the Danube landing docks in Kelheim from mid-March to October (one way/return €4.20/€7.40, bicycles one way/return €1.80/€3.60). Fit and experienced paddlers can rent a kayak or canoe from **Altmühltaler Erlebniswelt** (☎ 0179-500 7267; www .altmuehltaler-erlebniswelt.de, in German; per 3hr/weekend

€15/37) in Kloster Weltenburg; the company can pick it up in Kelheim for an additional per-kilometre charge.

At the end of the 40-minute cruise from Kelheim (20 minutes in the other direction), boats dock at **Kloster Weltenburg**, an ancient Benedictine abbey, which also operates the world's oldest monastic brewery (since 1050). Now state of the art, it makes several varieties, including a *Dunkles* and a delicious *Bockbier*. The **Klosterschenke** (☎ 09441-3682; Asamstrasse 32; 8am-7pm mid-Mar–Oct) is fronted by an idyllic chestnut-canopied beer garden that swarms with revellers on warm weekends and around holidays.

For spiritual sustenance, pop into the **Klosterkirche Weltenburg**, a magnificent rococo

---

DETOUR: STRAUBING

A stately city for most of the year, Straubing (population 44,500, elevation 331m) gives Munich's Oktoberfest a run for its money when it erupts into a beery roar for 11 days during August's **Gäubodenfest**. This epic drink-up began in 1812 as a social gathering for grain farmers, and more than a million merrymakers now pour into town each year. Despite the crowds, Gäubodenfest remains a traditional celebration that's infinitely less touristy than Munich's famous party.

Straubing also passionately celebrates its star-crossed lovers, Agnes and Albrecht. Agnes, a barber's daughter, had the gall to fall in love with and secretly wed the heir to the duchy of Bavaria, Albrecht. That didn't sit well with Albrecht's father, Duke Ernst I, who had her bumped off. Later haunted by remorse, the duke built a chapel, the **Agnes-Bernauer-Kapelle**, in the moss-covered churchyard of **Basilika St Peter** (Petersgasse), a 15-minute stroll east of the centre of town along the Danube. Agnes is also honoured during the quadrennial **Agnes-Bernauer-Festival** (next held in July 2011). Anytime, you can dig into the world-famous Agnes-Bernauer-Torte (a crunchy hazelnut and mocha cream cake) at **Cafe Krönner** (☎ 109 94; Theresienplatz 22; dishes €3-5.80; 8.15am-6.15pm Mon-Fri, 8am-6pm Sat), or its ice-cream sundae version, the Agnes-Bernauer-Becher.

Straubing offers plenty of cultural indulgence too. Its **Gäubodenmuseum** (☎ 974 110; Fraunhoferstrasse 9; adult/concession €2.50/1.50; 10am-4pm Tue-Sun) houses the Römerschatz, one of Germany's most important collections of Roman treasures; while the pride and joy of the late-Gothic hall church **Basilika St Jakob** (Pfarrplatz) is the brilliant stained-glass 'Moses window' designed by Albrecht Dürer. The latter is a few steps from Straubing's landmark, the **Stadtturm** – a 14th-century, 68m-high watchtower with a giant clock face. Opposite, you'll find the **tourist office** (☎ 944 307; www.straubing.de in German; Theresienplatz 20; 9am-5pm Mon-Fri, 9am-noon Sat), which stocks info on the city, including its exuberant festivals.

Straubing is situated about a third of the way from Regensburg to Passau, and makes a good stop en route between the two. If you want to stay, the family-run **Hotel-Restaurant Seethaler** (☎ 939 50; www.hotel-seethaler.de in German; Theresienplatz 25; s €63-69, d €93-99; P ⊠ 🖵) is a delightful place that dates back over 500 years and overlooks Straubing's pedestrianised main drag (locally referred to as Stadtplatz). The hotel's 1st-floor lobby is canopied by a heavy beamed Gothic ceiling, while rooms are bright, contemporary and wi-fi'd. At street level, its restaurant (main €9.80 to €14.80) cooks traditional treats like pork filets in cognac, and apple cake in beer sauce.

Trains connect Straubing directly with Regensburg (€7.90, 30 minutes) but coming from Passau (€12.40, one hour) requires a change in Plattling. From the Nuremberg–Passau A3 autobahn, drivers should take the Kirchroth exit. There's free parking at Grossparkplatz Am Hagen, south of Stadtplatz, from where it's a five-minute walk. The compact historic centre is easily strollable (or, during Gäubodenfest, staggerable).

church designed by the Asam brothers (see p41). Its most arresting feature is the high altar, which shows St George triumphant on horseback, with the slain dragon and rescued princess at his feet.

Coming from Regensburg, trains run hourly to Saal (30 minutes), and a bus meets the train and goes to Kelheim (10 minutes); the combined bus/train tickets cost €5.

PASSAU
☎ 0851 / pop 51,000 / elev 302m

Water has quite literally shaped the picturesque Austrian border town of Passau. Its Altstadt sits on a narrow peninsula that juts into the confluence of three rivers: the Danube, Inn and Ilz. The rivers brought wealth to Passau, which for centuries was an important trading centre, especially for salt, the so-called 'white gold'. Christianity, meanwhile, brought prestige as Passau evolved into the largest bishopric in the Roman Empire. The Altstadt remains largely as it was when the powerful prince-bishops built its winding lanes, tunnels and archways, graced by baroque architecture; but its western edge (around Nibelungenplatz) is getting a makeover in the shape of a new, globalised shopping centre slated for completion by the time of this book's publication.

Passau is a major river-cruise stop and is often deluged with day visitors. It is also the convergence of eight long-distance cycling routes, and a good jumping-off point for explorations into Austria and beyond.

Orientation
The Hauptbahnhof is about a 10-minute walk west of the heart of the Altstadt (around the Dom), where most sights, hotels and restaurants are located. The Veste Oberhaus leans out from a steep hillside on the Danube's northern bank.

Information
Banks proliferate throughout the city.
Buchhandlung Rupprecht (☎ 931 270; Ludwigstrasse 18) Maps, travel books, English-language novels.
Coffee Fellows (☎ 490 5883; Schrottgasse 12; internet access per hr €2.60; ⏲ 7am-midnight Mon-Fri, 9am-midnight Sat & Sun) Café-bar with internet access plus regular events from movie nights to jazz brunches.
Post office (Bahnhofstrasse 27)
Tourist office (☎ 955 980; www.passau.de) Altstadt (Rathausplatz 3; ⏲ 8.30am-6pm Mon-Fri, 9am-4pm Sat

& Sun Easter–mid-Oct, 8.30am-5pm Mon-Thu, 8.30am-4pm Fri mid-Oct–Easter); Hauptbahnhof (Bahnhofstrasse 36; ⏲ 9am-5pm Mon-Thu year-round, 9am-5pm Fri Easter–mid-Oct, 9am-4pm Fri mid-Oct–Easter)

Sights
VESTE OBERHAUS
A 13th-century defensive fortress, built by the prince-bishops, Veste Oberhaus towers over Passau with patriarchal pomp. Not surprisingly, views of the city and into Austria are superb from up here.

Inside the bastion is the **Oberhausmuseum** (☎ 493 3512; Veste Oberhaus 125; permanent collections adult/concession/family €5/4/10; ⏲ 9am-5pm Mon-Fri, 10am-6pm Sat, Sun & holidays mid-Mar–mid-Nov), a regional history museum where you can uncover the mysteries of medieval cathedral building, learn what it took to become a knight and explore Passau's period as a centre of the salt trade. Displays are labelled in English.

DOM ST STEPHAN
The green onion domes of Passau's **Dom St Stephan** (St Stephen's Cathedral; Domplatz; admission free; ⏲ 6.30am-at least 6pm) float serenely above the town's silhouette. There's been a church in this spot since the late 5th century, but what you see today is much younger thanks to the Great Fire of 1662, which ravaged much of the medieval town, including the ancient cathedral. The rebuilding job went to a team of Italians, notably the architect Carlo Lurago and the stucco master Giovanni Battista Carlone. The result is a bit like standing on a tier of a wedding cake, with multidimensional decorations in every direction, including frescoes inspired by a tapestry series by Rubens.

The lofty interior provides incredible acoustics for its pièce de résistance, the world's largest organ, above the main entrance, with four registers and an astonishing 17,974 pipes. Half-hour **organ recitals** take place at noon daily Monday to Saturday (adult/child €4/€2) and at 7.30pm on Thursday (adult/child €5/€3) from May to October and for a week around Christmas. Show up at least 30 minutes early to ensure a seat.

Outside on Domplatz stands a **statue of Maximilian I Joseph**, the first Bavarian king.

RESIDENZPLATZ
Pride of place on this showy square belongs to the 18th-century **Neue Bischöfliche Residenz** (New Bishop's Residence; Residenzplatz 8). Melchior

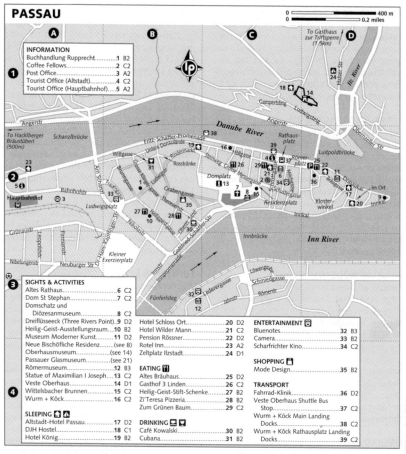

PASSAU

Hefele, a student of Balthasar Neumann, drafted the stucco-draped façade, as well as the rococo staircase, which winds towards a wonderfully over-the-top ceiling fresco entitled *The Gods of Olympus Protecting Immortal Passau*.

The bishops resided in these splendid digs until 1871. Today, the diocese administration occupies most of the rooms, but several have been set aside for the **Domschatz und Diözesanmuseum** (Cathedral Treasury & Museum; Residenzplatz 8; adult/child/family €2/1/2.50; 10am-4pm Mon-Sat May-Oct). The ecclesiastical finery – including monstrances, vestments, sculptures and paintings – exemplifies the wealth and power of the Church rulers. The museum is accessed from inside the Dom, except

during the organ concerts when entry is via Residenzplatz.

At the square's centre is the **Wittelsbacher Brunnen** (1903), a sprightly fountain depicting Mary (Bavaria's patron saint) surrounded by allegories of the three local rivers.

ALTES RATHAUS

A short walk north of Residenzplatz, via Schrottgasse, is Passau's **Rathaus** (Rathausplatz 2), a grand Gothic building topped by its 19th-century landmark painted tower. A carillon chimes several times daily (hours are listed on the wall, alongside historical flood-level markers).

The entrance on Schrottgasse takes you to the **Grosser Rathaussaal** (Great Assembly Room; adult/

concession €1.50/1; 10am-4pm Apr-Oct), where large-scale paintings by 19th-century local artist Ferdinand Wagner show scenes from Passau's history with melodramatic flourish. If it's not being used for a wedding or a meeting, also sneak into the adjacent 'small assembly room' for a peek at the ceiling fresco, which again features allegories of the three rivers.

PASSAUER GLASMUSEUM

Allow at least an hour to take in the warren of rooms filled with some 30,000 priceless pieces of glass and crystal from the baroque, classical, Art Nouveau and Art Deco periods at the **Passauer Glasmuseum** (Passau Glass Museum; 350 71; Am Rathausplatz; adult/concession €5/4; 1-5pm). Be sure to pick up a floor plan as it's easy to get lost. Kids accompanied by parents are free (perhaps in the hope that parents will keep a close eye on their charges, given the fragile collections).

MUSEUM MODERNER KUNST

Gothic architecture contrasts with cutting-edge 20th- and 21st-century artworks displayed during rotating exhibitions at the **Museum Moderner Kunst** (Museum of Modern Art; 383 8790; Bräugasse 17; adult/concession/family €5/3/10; 10am-6pm Tue-Sun). Some spotlight a single practitioner, including crowd pleasers such as Salvador Dalí or Gustav Klimt, while others focus on themes as varied as football (soccer) or women. The museum was set up by a resident of the Heilig-Geist-Stift-Schenke (see the boxed text, p208).

DREIFLÜSSECK

The tip of the Altstadt peninsula is known as the **Dreiflüsseck** (Three Rivers Point) and is the only place from which you can actually see the Danube, Ilz and Inn all at once (except from above, that is). Benches and a small patch of grass make it a peaceful place to take time out from sightseeing, and kids can burn off some energy on the playground equipment.

RÖMERMUSEUM

Roman Passau can be viewed from the ground up at the **Römermuseum** (Roman Museum; 347 69; Lederergasse 43; adult/concession €2/1; 10am-4pm Tue-Sun Mar–mid-Nov). Ruins from the Roman fort, the Kastell Boitro, which stood here from AD 250 to 400, are still in situ. The museum itself displays civilian and military artefacts unearthed here and elsewhere in Eastern Bavaria.

Tours

Passau's pastel-shaded buildings are at their prettiest when viewed from its surrounding waterways. Local operator **Wurm + Köck** (929 292; www.donauschiffahrt.com; Höllgasse 26) runs a smorgasbord of boat trips, including 45-minute trips around the Altstadt (tickets €7.50, at least once hourly 10am to 5pm March to October, 11am to 3pm November to February), and cruises to Linz, Austria (one way/return €22/25, bicycles free, at least once daily Tuesday to Sunday May to October), with an option to come back by bus or train. If you like to travel in style, the company also has a glitzy new 'crystal ship' decked out with 100,000 Swarovski crystals glittering on its staircases, light fittings and fountains, which takes a two-hour spin around the Danube Valley (tickets €11.80, at least two daily, early April to October). Confirm departure docks when you book.

Festivals & Events

A procession of locals dressed up in historical costumes kicks off the springtime beer festival, **Maidult** (www.passauer-dult.de), April to May; beer also flows at its autumn (September) counterpart, **Herbstdult**. The **Festspiele Europäische Wochen** (Festival 'European Weeks'; www.ew-passau .de, in German; tickets 752 020), from mid-June to late July, brings together top international talent for opera, concerts, readings, theatre, film and art. Events take place in and around Passau, Upper Austria and the Czech Republic. In December Passau's **Christmas Market** sets up in front of the cathedral; while the second Thursday and third Tuesday of December features a **Wood Market**, selling wooden toys, baskets and more made in the Bavarian forest, at stalls throughout the Altstadt.

Sleeping

BUDGET

Rotel Inn (951 60; www.rotel-inn.de; s/d €25/40; P) Geared for cyclists, 'rooms' at this 'cabin hotel' near the train station are literally capsules, with an inbuilt futon and phone for incoming (but not outgoing) calls. Breakfast and parking each cost €5 extra.

   Pension Rössner (931 350; www.pension-roessner .de; Bräugasse 19; s €35, d €45-60; P) This immaculate *Pension*, in a restored mansion near the tip of the peninsula, offers great value for money and a friendly, cosy ambience. Each room is uniquely decorated and many overlook the fortress. For the best views, book into the 'panorama suite' (€90), opening onto an enclosed balcony.

Other good budget bets:

Zeltplatz Ilzstadt (☎ 414 57; Halser Strasse 34; campsites per adult/under 18yr €7/6; **P**) Tent-only campground idyllically set on the Ilz River, 15 minutes' walk from the Altstadt. Catch bus 1, 2 or 4 to Kleiner Exerzierplatz-Ilzbrücke.

DJH hostel (☎ 493 780; www.passau.jugendherberge .de; Veste Oberhaus 125; dm incl breakfast & linen €18.55; ✗) Beautifully renovated hostel right in the Veste Oberhaus fortress. To get here, see p209.

MIDRANGE & TOP END

Most of Passau's higher-end hotels, including the standout places listed here, have on-site restaurants, with mains averaging €15 to €25.

Hotel Wilder Mann (☎ 350 71; www.wilder-mann .com, in German; Am Rathausplatz; s €50-60, d €80-140; ☐) Sharing space with the glass museum, this historic hotel boasts former guests ranging from Empress Elizabeth (Sisi) of Austria to Mikhail Gorbachev and Henry Kissinger. Trimmings such as carved bedsteads seek to recapture those heady days, while mod cons include wi-fi. Try for a peaceful garden-view room at the back.

Hotel König (☎ 3850; www.hotel-koenig.de; Untere Donaulände 1; s €59-90, d €85-140; **P** ✗) This riverside property puts you smack bang in the middle of the Altstadt. Timber-rich rooms – many of them enormous – spread out over two buildings and most come with views of the Danube and fortress, as well as wi-fi. The restaurant has a partly covered terrace.

Altstadt-Hotel Passau (☎ 3370; www.altstadt-hotel .de; Bräugasse 23-29; s €65-86, d €85-115; **P** ✗) On the northern side of the peninsula, this pretty hotel has a refined air of class and comfort, amenities including wi-fi, and a gastronomic restaurant cooking creative regional fare.

Hotel Schloss Ort (☎ 340 72; www.schlosshotel-passau .de, in German; Im Ort 11; s €68-88, d €97-136; **P**) Medieval palace walls conceal this boutique hotel, stylishly done out with polished timber floors and crisp white cotton sheets. Romantics should book a room with a wrought-iron, four-poster bed.

Eating

Gasthaus zur Triftsperre (☎ 511 62; Triftsperrstrasse 15; mains €5-13; ✆ 10am-midnight Tue-Sun Feb-Dec) It's an easy and enjoyable 3km cycle (or stroll) along the Ilz River to this earthy beer garden and restaurant. Regulars are drawn by the home-made cakes and fresh trout. If you don't feel like pedalling back, you could rent one of the rooms (single with shared bathroom €18 to €22, double with shared bathroom €36 to €44, single with private bathroom €28 to €32, double with private bathroom €45 to €60).

Zi'Teresa Pizzeria (☎ 2138; Theresienstrasse 26; pizza €5-8.50, mains €10-18; ✆ 11.30am-11.30pm; **V**) Theresienstrasse and its offshoots buzz with places to eat, drink and hang out, such as this hot spot serving outstanding thin-crust pizzas, tasty pastas and generous appetisers.

Zum Grünen Baum (☎ 356 35; Höllgasse 7; mains €6-13; ✆ 10am-1am; **V**) Eccentric design touches such as a 'cutlery chandelier' adorn this quirky restaurant, which serves organic beer and wine and excellent desserts (ask for the unlisted 'variety platter'). The toy-filled back room is a winner with families.

Altes Bräuhaus (☎ 490 5252; Bräugasse 5; mains €7.60-9.90; ✆ 11am-1am; **V**) Comfort food in this traditional dark timber dining room includes pork schnitzel and *Wammerl* (smoked pork belly with bacon and sauerkraut), but there are also a handful of vegetarian dishes like mushroom soup with bread dumplings.

Gasthof 3 Linden (☎ 756 8383; Steinweg 6; mains €8.45-14.75; ✆ 10am-1am; **V**) Gleaming modular timber furniture and geometric floors give Gasthof 3 Linden a sleek retro feel. The credo here is 'the Bavarian sausage is the beer's best friend', but meatless dishes include spinach pasta in Gorgonzola cream sauce, and salads (say if you don't want them swimming in vinaigrette). Good kids' menu, too. Try the house cocktail of cold champagne, Innstadt beer and fresh fruit.

ourpick Heilig-Geist-Stift-Schenke (☎ 2607; Heiliggeistgasse 4; mains €12.20-16.90; ✆ 10am-1am Thu-Tue) Not only does the 'Holy Spirit Foundation' have a succession of walnut-panelled rooms, a candlelit cellar (open from 6pm) and a vine-draped garden (reflecting its own wine; see the boxed text, p208), but its food is equally inspired. Specialities include *Spiessbraten* (marinated meat licked by a beechwood fire) and fish plucked live from the concrete trough. The garden's apricot tree produces the handmade jam incorporated in the *Marillenpalatschinke* (a rolled-up pancake) and fruit for the *Marillenknödel* (filled yeast dumplings), and the schnapps are also home made.

Farmers markets (Domplatz) are held outside the Dom every Tuesday and Friday morning, and at the bus station on Saturday morning.

Drinking

Cubana (☎ 490 9570; Rosstränke 9; ☻ Wed-Sun) Fans of fiery rhythms let their hair down at this lounge bar, particularly over cut-price cocktails during happy hour (7pm to 9pm Wednesday to Saturday, all night Sunday).

Café Kowalski (☎ 2487; Oberer Sand 1; dishes €5-9; ☻ 10am-1am Sun-Wed, 10am-3am Fri & Sat) Conversation flows as freely as the wine, beer and adjacent Inn River at this gregarious spot. If hunger strikes, snack on super-sized schnitzels and sandwiches.

Hacklberger Bräustüberl (☎ 583 82; Bräuhausplatz 7; mains €5-13; ☻ 9am-1am) A glass of *Zwickl bier*, this microbrewery's speciality, is best enjoyed in its parklike beer garden in summer – and soaked up with its updated traditional fare anytime.

Entertainment

Ask the tourist offices for a booklet (in German, but easy to navigate) that lists entertainment options city wide.

Camera (☎ 342 30; Am Ludwigsplatz; ☻ Thu-Mon) At this happening dance club a pretence-free crowd sweats it out on the dance floor, either to a DJ or the occasional live band (usually on Thursday).

Bluenotes (☎ 343 77; Lederergasse 50) Across the Inn River; live music is often performed at this sophisticated spot, which also mixes smooth cocktails.

Scharfrichter Kino (☎ 2655; Milchgasse 2) This lively cultural centre stages theatre and cabaret, including autumn's Passauer Kabarett-Tage (Passau Cabaret Days), a decades-old tradition of political satire that was sued and shut down by the establishment before the counterculture spurred its revival. It's best appreciated by German speakers with a knowledge of local political nuances and dialect.

Shopping

Wander along Höllgasse, the heart of Passau's little artists quarter, to find original art, homewares and jewellery. Nearby, fashion designer Silvia Ritcher can tailor make garments to order (usually in just a few days); otherwise you can pick up her designs off the rack at her shop, **Mode Design** (☎ 2492; Grabengasse 24), where you'll see her sewing in her open studio out the back.

Getting There & Away

Direct trains connect Passau with Munich (€28.30, 2¼ hours), Regensburg (€19.10, 1½ hours), Landshut (€18.70, 1¼ hours) and Nuremberg (€39, two hours). Change in Plattling for Zwiesel (€17.80, 1½ hours) and other Bavarian Forest towns.

Passau is just off the A3 autobahn from Nuremberg and Regensburg, which connects with the A92 to Munich near Deggendorf.

PASSAU'S HOLY SPIRIT

There may be no vineyards in this neck of the woods but – with a little divine intervention – the **Heilig-Geist-Stift-Schenke** (Holy Spirit Foundation; p207) has been producing its own wine for centuries.

Passau's most historic restaurant is actually part of a former Franciscan monastery. In 1358, a wealthy local family created a foundation here for the poor, where residents lived for free on the condition that they prayed for the family in the adjoining chapel. To fund the foundation, the family established vineyards in Krems (then also part of the Habsburg Empire, and now in Austria). Wine was given to residents with meals as a gesture of respect (providing they kept up their prayers, of course).

During WWII, Germans were not permitted to own land over the border, and the foundation risked losing its vineyards and, by extension, the foundation itself. However, in a display of the cross-cultural connections harking back to the Habsburg era, Austrians claimed the vineyards as their own, protecting and working them until the end of the war, when they safely returned them.

The foundation remains as a subsidised residence today. Prayers are no longer required, but its frescoed Gothic chapel still gets plenty of visitors. Now the **Heilig-Geist-Ausstellungsraum** (Holy Spirit Exhibition Centre; admission free; ☻ 10am-5pm during exhibitions), it regularly hosts experimental contemporary art and sculpture exhibitions; pop in to see what's on. Best of all, you can taste the **Stiftswein** (Foundation Wine; per glass €2.90) at the Heilig-Geist-Stift-Schenke. Amen.

DETOUR: 'POPETOWN'

Few people outside of Bavaria had heard of **Marktl am Inn** (☎ 08678; population 2700) before 19 April 2005, the day its native son Joseph Ratzinger (b 1927) became Pope Benedict XVI. To cope with the village's overnight status as a kind of 'popetown' for pilgrims and the plain curious, a state-of-the-art **tourist office** (☎ 748 820; www.markt-marktl.de; Marktplatz 1; ⏰ 9am-6pm May-Aug, 10am-5pm Sep-Apr) has been established on the main square, **Marktplatz**. Outside, a striking bronze **pillar** by sculptor Joseph Michael Neustifter commemorates Ratzinger's first homecoming as pontiff in 2006.

Marktl's main papal attraction is Ratzinger's **Geburthaus** (Birth House; ☎ 747 680; Marktplatz 11; adult/concession/under 12yr €3.50/2.50/free; ⏰ 2-6pm Tue-Fri, 10am-6pm Sat & Sun mid-Mar–Oct). This simple, pretty 1701-built Bavarian home where he lived for the first two years of his life has been turned into an excellent little museum. A video presentation and interpretive signs are in German, but the atmosphere and personal photos make it worthwhile for non-German speakers, and **guided tours** (tours €1; ⏰ 3pm) are usually offered in both English and German. The two-storey building has been modified for wheelchair access.

Across the square, you can view the pope's baptismal font in the light-filled **Pfarrkirche St Oswald** (Parish Church of St Oswald; Marktplatz 6), except during church services. The nearby **Heimatmuseum** (Local History Museum, ☎ 7341; Marktplatz 2; adult/child €2/1.50) guards a golden chalice and a skullcap used by Ratzinger in his private chapel in Rome, but opening hours are highly erratic – check with the tourist office.

A clutch of places have sprung up in the village where you can now eat a mitre-shaped cake or 'pope's pizza' and drink 'Papst-Bier' (Pope's Beer; it's almost expensive enough to make you wonder if it's brewed with holy water) and stock up on rosaries and religious board games. If you'd like to stay, there's a basic but pleasant hotel, **Gasthof-Pension-Hummel** (☎ 282; Hauptstrasse 34; s/d €38/55; Ⓟ). Call beforehand, as reception hours are erratic.

Marktl is signposted just off the B12 between Munich and Passau. Coming by train requires one or more changes from most destinations in Eastern Bavaria. When you exit the station, turn right onto Simbacher Strasse, then right onto Bahnhofstrasse, which leads into Marktplatz (about a 10-minute walk all up).

Getting Around

Central Passau is compact, so most sights are reachable on foot. The CityBus regularly connects the *Bahnhof* with the Altstadt (€0.80). Longer trips on Stadtwerke buses cost €1.50; day passes are €3.50.

The walk up the hill to Veste Oberhaus, via Luitpoldbrücke and Ludwigsteig path, takes about 30 minutes. From mid-March to October, a **shuttle bus** (one way/return €2.50/5; ⏰ 10am-5pm Mon-Fri, 10am-6pm Sat, Sun & holidays) operates half-hourly from Rathausplatz.

There are several public car parks near the Hauptbahnhof but only one in the Altstadt, at Römerplatz (per hour/day €1.10/10).

Fahrrad-Klinik (☎ 334 11; Bräugasse 10) rents out bikes from €11 per day. Bikes can also be rented from the train station for €12 per day.

BAVARIAN FOREST

As you near Bavaria's eastern edge, the altitude steadily climbs and the woods become as dark and thick as in the fairy tales. Together with the Bohemian Forest on the Czech side of the border, the Bayerischer Wald (Bavarian Forest) forms the largest continuous woodland area in Europe. Its meadows, moorland, mountains, raised bogs, streams and lakes are interspersed with little-disturbed valleys, and also embrace the wild and rugged **Nationalpark Bayerischer Wald** (Bavarian Forest National Park).

The abundance of timber as a heat source led to the birth of the local glass industry in the late 17th century. Glass is still produced here today, and all along the **Glasstrasse**, a 250km-long route connecting Neustadt an der Waldnaab with Passau, you can visit glassblowing studios, factories and shops.

The forest's main towns, Zwiesel (p211) and Bodenmais (p212), are both well set up for hiking and biking excursions, as well as skiing (although note that most hotels, restaurants and museums shut from November until the ski season starts in mid-December).

NATURE KNOWS BEST

You're hiking beneath a towering canopy of spruce when suddenly you arrive in a near-apocalyptic wasteland of skeletal, grey, leafless trees, some still standing, others rotting on the forest floor. What's going on here?

Welcome to the domain of the bark beetle, a voracious little scarab that has chewed through enormous swaths of the Nationalpark Bayerischer Wald. It's dubbed the 'book printer' for the squiggly lines created by the path of its feeding in the spruce, its sole diet. Over the centuries people have cleared the original mixed forest to fuel local ovens and glass smelters. Spruce was introduced because of its quick-yield growth, and the bark beetle couldn't have been more pleased. Since 'discovering' their new fecund habitat a decade or so ago, these critters have devoured upwards of 40 sq km of the park's trees, mostly in the higher elevations.

So what about fighting back? Well, this is a national park and the idea is to let nature take its course without human interference. This philosophy did not sit well with locals, who feared the beetles would kill not only the trees but also the tourism industry. Indeed, when the park was enlarged to the north in 1997 to encompass new villages, it actually became illegal in this area for residents and businesses *not* to eradicate the beetles to prevent them from spreading.

Meanwhile, in the rest of the park, nature is proving it has a way of tending to itself. Beneath the corpses of fallen spruce, an even greater variety of trees – fir, mountain ash, beech and other deciduous species – is slowly taking root as well. These slower-growing but hardier trees will restore the park's original 'mixed-forest' blend where the spread of arborial predators is held in check by the trees themselves. It's anticipated that in around 40 to 50 years time, this 'self-policing' forest will be as thriving and self-sustaining as it once was.

Downhill skiers head to the **Grosser Arber** (1456m), the highest mountain in the Bavarian Forest, situated 15km from Zwiesel and 14km from Bodenmais. With mostly easy to moderate runs (and a kickin' snowboard park), it's especially popular with families, although it has also hosted World Cup ski races. Ski passes cost €24 per day; other tickets are also available. Free buses from Zwiesel depart four times per day; hourly buses from Bodenmais cost €1.50 per ride. In summer, the mountain summit is a popular destination with hikers, who can follow a thrilling trail leading along a creek, across a gorge and past waterfalls. The easy alternative to get to the top is a gondola ride aboard the **Arber-Bergbahn** (☎ 09925-941 40; one way/return €7/9.50).

For travel around the Bavarian Forest, the best value is the Bayerwald-Ticket (adult/child accompanied by parents €6/free), a day pass good for unlimited travel on bus and rail (train travel is also covered by a Bayern ticket).

The region also makes a good jumping-off point for the Czech Republic – you can hike or bike over the border, and Prague is only three hours away by car or about five hours by train from Bayerisch Eisenstein (one way €18.80). Check passport and visa requirements with a Czech consulate before heading out.

Nationalpark Bayerischer Wald

A paradise for outdoor enthusiasts, the Nationalpark Bayerischer Wald was carved out in 1970 as Germany's first national park and expanded by one-third in 1997 to its current size of 243 sq km. The protected park, roamed by deer, wild boar, lynx, fox, otter and countless bird species, stretches from Bayerisch Eisenstein to Finsterau along the Czech border and seamlessly blends into the much larger Šumava National Park on the Czech side. On the German side, three main mountains – Rachel, Lusen and Grosser Falkenstein – soar to between 1300m and 1450m. Crisscrossing the park are hundreds of kilometres of hiking, biking and cross-country skiing trails.

INFORMATION

Hours for the park's two information centres vary depending on Bavarian school holidays, but they generally open from 9.30am to at least 4pm, and close during November.

Hans-Eisenmann-Haus (☎ 08558-961 50; www
.nationalpark-bayerischer-wald.de, in German;
Böhmstrasse 35, Neuschönau) Southern park information centre incorporating an activity schedule, children's discovery room and library.

Haus zur Wildnis (☎ 09922-500 20; www.nationalpark
-bayerischer-wald.de, in German; Ludwigsthal) Northern park information centre with excellent exhibits, such

as a topographical model of hiking trails, 3D films with forest 'scents', plus kids' activities and a café. Located a 15-minute signed walk through the forest from the train station at Ludwigsthal on the line to Baerisch Eisenstein (push the red button for the train to stop).

SIGHTS & ACTIVITIES

An easy way to commune with nature is strolling around the **Tierfreigelände** (animal preserve; admission free; 24hr), right by the parking lot at the Hans-Eisenmann-Haus. A 7km loop trail (suitable for wheelchairs and child strollers) takes you past large outdoor habitats; the best time to spot the wolves, lynxes, brown bears, red deer, owls and other species here is early morning and late afternoon.

Another popular trail (around four hours, round trip) goes from the DJH hostel to the **Lusen peak** (1373m), which has been eaten bare of its tree cover by the bark beetle but offers great views, sometimes as far as the Alps. For longer hikes, the rangers at the park's information centres are a fount of information and can provide maps.

Life-size exhibits at the outdoor museum **Freilichtmuseum Finsterau** (08557-960 60; Museumstrasse 51, Finsterau; adult/child/family €3.50/1.50/7.50; 9am-6pm May-Sep, 9am-4pm Oct, 11am-4pm Christmas-Apr) include historic farmhouses, a smithy and an old inn.

SLEEPING & EATING

Park offices and tourist offices can advise about camping options in the park, which are open year-round except November.

DJH Neuschönau-Waldhäuser (08553-6000; jhwaldhaeuser@djh-bayern.de; Herbergsweg 2, Neuschönau; dm incl breakfast & linen €15.20-24.20;) This is the only lodging option right in the heart of the national park and is an ideal base for outdoor explorations. It is closed at various times during the year, so call ahead.

Schwellhäusl (09925-460; mains €5-9; 10am-7.30pm) In the northern park, near Zwiesel, an easy half-hour walk along a brook leads to this old forest lodge next to a little lake where you can fortify yourself with a cool beer or a hearty meal amid mounted boar heads.

GETTING THERE & AROUND

From mid-May through to October, several roads within the national park are closed to private vehicles and served instead by the **Igel-Bus** (09920-5968; 1-/3-/7-day ticket €3.50/8.50/12). The natural gas–powered

buses operate on four routes, including one connecting the Grafenau train station with the Hans-Eisenmann-Haus, the DJH hostel and the Lusen hiking area (Lusen-Bus). The Rachel-Bus provides access to the park from Spiegelau, a stop on the Waldbahn from Zwiesel to Grafenau. The Bayerwald-Ticket is valid on all Igel-Bus lines.

Zwiesel

09922 / pop 10,500 / elev 585m

One of the area's bigger centres, Zwiesel is a great exploration base thanks to its train connections and down-to-earth ambience. Glass production is big business here, with a prestigious glass-making school right in the town.

INFORMATION

Naturpark Informationshaus (802 480; www .naturpark-bayer-wald.de; Infozentrum 3, along the B11; 9.30am-4.30pm Tue-Sun) Information and exhibits about the Naturpark Bayerischer Wald inside an experimental building that's completely energy self-sufficient.

Zwiesel tourist office (www.zwiesel-tourismus.de, in German) Town centre (840 523; Rathaus, Stadtplatz 27; 9am-5pm Mon-Fri, 10am-noon Sat Jul & Aug); Zwiesel-Süd (840 529; along the B11, near exit Zwiesel-Süd; 10am-1pm & 2-5pm Mon-Fri, 1-3pm Sat, 10am-noon Sun) Hours are longer in summer and shorter in November.

SIGHTS & ACTIVITIES

A jumble of 17 rooms take in the history of the forest, local customs and glass-making at the **Waldmuseum** (Forest Museum; 608 88; www .waldmuseum-zwiesel.de, in German; Stadtplatz 28; adult /concession €2/1; 9am-5pm Mon-Fri, 10am-noon & 2-6pm Sat & Sun mid-May–mid-Oct, 10am-noon & 2-5pm Mon-Fri, 10am-2pm Sat & Sun mid-Oct–mid-May). Quirkier exhibits include the transplanted contents of an old pharmacy.

To see glass-making in action, pop into the workshop at **Zwiesel Kristall** (formerly Schott-Zwiesel Glaswerke; 982 49; Dr-Schott-Strasse 35; 10am-3pm Mon-Fri). Glass-making is also on view at **Glashütte Theresienthal** (1030; Theresienthaler Strasse; factory admission free, museum adult/child €3/1.50; factory 9.30am-2.30pm Mon-Fri, museum 10am-2pm daily), which is around 2km north of town (accessible by bus) and has some stunning original 1920s designs for sale in its main shop, as well as second shop (open noon to 4.30pm Monday to Friday and 10am to 4pm Saturday) selling seconds, samples and discontinued series out the back. You'll also find lots of smaller studios throughout town.

The tourist office stocks route descriptions (some in English) for **hiking trails** that fan out from Zwiesel, including an easy and scenic 15km walk (around four hours one way) following the river to Bayerisch Eisenstein, from where you can catch a train back.

SLEEPING & EATING

Azur-Ferienpark Bayerischer Wald (☎ 802 595; www.azur-camping.de/zwiesel/zwiesel.html, in German; Waldesruhweg 34; per person €5-7.50, campsite €6; P) This convenient campground is about 500m north of the train station, near public pools and sports facilities.

Landhaus Karin (☎ 2187; www.schall-fewo.de, in German; Buschweg 24; d €46, apt €24-55; P) Run by a delightful young couple, this child- and pet-friendly property sits right on the edge of the forest and has modern rooms and apartments. Rates include admission to a local fitness centre. Buses stop right outside.

Hotel-Gasthof Kapfhammer (☎ 843 10; www .hotel-kapfhammer.de; Holzweberstrasse 6-10; s/d €41/72) British royalty has overnighted at this charming place, which nonetheless has a homey atmosphere and a good Bavarian restaurant (mains €8 to €15).

our pick **Hotel Zur Waldbahn** (☎ 3001; www.zur waldbahn.de, in German; Bahnhofplatz 2; s €58-62, d €80-96; P ☒ ☎) Opposite the *Bahnhof*, many of the rooms at this characteristic inn run by three generations of the same family open to balconies with views over the town. The breakfast buffet is an especially generous spread and even includes home-made jams. If you've treated yourself to Bavarian (potato) and Bohemian (bread) dumplings with wild forest mushrooms at the restaurant (meals €8 to €15; it's the best in town, and open to nonguests), you can work it off in the slate-and-glass pool, complete with soothing massage jets.

Cosy restaurants are dotted throughout the town centre.

GETTING THERE & AROUND

Zwiesel is reached by rail from Munich via Plattling (€35.20, 2½ hours), Regensburg (€19.60, two hours), Landshut (€19.40, two hours) and Passau (€17.80, 1½ hours); most trains continue to Bayerisch Eisenstein, with connections to Prague.

The Waldbahn regional train makes hourly trips between Zwiesel and Bodenmais (€2.80, 19 minutes) and two-hourly between Zwiesel and Grafenau (€6.20, 50 minutes). From Grafenau you can catch the Igel-Bus into the Nationalpark Bayerischer Wald; buses from Zwiesel to Falkenstein in the park depart every two hours.

Drivers coming from the A3 autobahn should get off at Deggendorf and follow the B11 to Zwiesel.

Zwiesel's tourist office has information about bike hire in the area.

Bodenmais
☎ 09924 / pop 3500 / elev 689m
About 15km northwest of Zwiesel, and a major tourist magnet, is the beautifully located town of Bodenmais.

INFORMATION

Tourist office (☎ 778 135; www.bodenmais.de, in German; Bahnhofstrasse 56; ☺ 8am-5pm Mon-Fri, 9am-1pm Sat, 9am-noon Sun) Adjacent to the train station on the main street.

SIGHTS & ACTIVITIES

A highlight – especially if you're travelling with kids – is **Silberberg** (☎ 7710; www.silber berghahn.de; Rechensöldenweg 8-10; mine tours adult/under 16yr/16-18yr/family €5.90/3.50/3.20/17.20; ☺ 45min tours hourly 10am-5pm), a disused mineral mine 2.6km from town inside Bodenmais' highest mountain (995m). Tours taking in some of its 20km of tunnels are in German; you can ask for an English leaflet. The tunnels stay a constant 5°C year-round, with 90% humidity, and as such, some sections are used for curative treatments. Outside on the mountain, various summer-time activities (prices vary) include a chairlift and a sled, as well as a kids' playground with an animal enclosure, while in winter you can ski here. From May to October, the mountain is served from town by a little **tourist train** (per ride €5; ☺ 9.30am-4pm); in winter it's served half-hourly by ski buses. The mountain's summit has swooping valley views.

There are 21km of groomed cross-country trails in the town itself but most people head about 5km east to the **Bretterschachten** area (served by ski bus every half-hour; €1 per ride), which offers the most reliable conditions on 65km of tracks.

SLEEPING & EATING

Sport-und Ferienpension Adam (☎ 902 270; www .sportpensionadam.de, in German; Hirtenweg 1; d €41, apt €36-45; P) With its free mountain-bike and cross-country-ski hire, this family-run chalet is tailor-made for sporting types. In addition to bright rooms, there's a guest kitchen and a sauna.

Neue Post (☎ 9580; www.hotel-neue-post.de; Kötztinger Strasse 25; s €38-63, d €72-132; **P** ✗) Just 200m from the train station, you can bliss out in the Nordic sauna or swim laps in the pool at this large, comfortable hotel, which also has a top-rated restaurant (mains €6.80 to €16.80; venison is a speciality) and an umbrella-shaded dining terrace.

Die Waidlerstub'n (☎ 822; Marktplatz; mains €5.50-15; **V**) Bodenmais' oldest restaurant has outdoor seating on the market square and an inspired menu of hearty specials and brimming salads.

SHOPPING

Waldglashütte Joska (☎ 7790; Am Moosbach 1) This, the largest of Joska's three Bondenmais outlets, is a little village of its own, with a huge kids' playground and its own café. In addition to its own glass, it wholesales glass from around the world.

Herrgottschnitzer von Bodenmais (☎ 393; Dreifaltigkeitsplatz 11) Hand-carved religious figurines are the speciality of this famous glass workshop.

GETTING THERE & AWAY

The Waldbahn regional train connects Zwiesel with Bodenmais (€2.70, 20 minutes) hourly. Bus 8645 goes from Bodenmais via the Grosser Arber to Bayerisch Eisenstein. Drivers should take the B11 to Zwiesel and then follow the signs to Bodenmais.

Frauenau

☎ 09926 / pop 3000 / elev 624m

The 'glass heart of the Bavarian Forest', Frauenau is home to the outstanding **Glasmuseum** (www.glasmuseum-frauenau.de, in German; Am Museumspark 1; adult/child/concession/family €5/2.50 /4.50/11; ☯ 9am-5pm Mon-Fri, 10am-4pm Sat, Sun & holidays). Exhibits are housed in a light-filled new glass-and-steel building that also contains the local **tourist office** (☎ 941 00; www.frauenau.de, in German; ☯ 9am-noon & 1.30-4pm Mon-Fri year-round, 9.30-11.30am Sat mid-May–mid-Oct). Inside you can trace 4000 years of glass history, starting with the ancient Egyptians and ending with modern glass art from around the world. Other sections look at the human side of the glass industry's history in the region, with issues such as working conditions.

Frauenau is also home to prestigious glass-blowing studios (with attached shops); the tourist office has information. Waldbahn trains run every two hours between Zweisel and Frauenau (in the direction of Grafenau); the Glasmuseum is a few metres from the train station.

LANDSHUT

☎ 0871 / pop 60,000 / elev 385m

The gabled, sugared-almond-coloured mansions and medieval castle in Landshut, about 70km northeast of Munich, are reminders of the city's golden age in the 14th and 15th centuries when it was the seat of the Bavaria-Landshut duchy under the so-called 'Rich Dukes'.

The city is beautifully sited on the Isar River, which splits into two arms – the Kleine Isar and the Grosse Isar – near the town centre. Nearly all major sights are concentrated on the main thoroughfare, the partly pedestrianised Altstadt, which in this case refers only to a street, not the entire historic district. Altstadt is paralleled by Neustadt, meaning 'new town', but also a single street. Just to make things more confusing, Neustadt is also within the historic district.

Information

Bücher Pustet (☎ 2001; Altstadt 28) Well-stocked bookshop.

Police (☎ 110, nonemergency 925 20)

Post office City Centre (Postplatz 395); Hauptbahnhof (Bahnhofsplatz 1a) The city-centre branch is next to the Heiliggeistkirche.

Sparkasse (Bischof-Sailer-Platz) English-enabled ATMs.

Tourist office (☎ 922 050; www.landshut.de, in German; Rathaus, Altstadt 315; ☯ 9am-5pm Mon-Fri, 9am-noon Sat) This branch's central location is handy.

Sights

ALTSTADT

Baroque-embellished Gothic town houses fringe both sides of Landshut's most beautiful street, which is bookended by two churches. The main procession of the Landshuter Hochzeit (see the boxed text, p215) comes through here, which is fitting since some of the buildings have historical connections to the actual event.

Hedwig, the bride, stayed at the **Grasberger Haus** (Altstadt 300) with its lovely vaulted foyer, while the most illustrious wedding guest, Emperor Friedrich III, shacked up in the

Pappenberger Haus (Altstadt 81), right opposite the **Rathaus** (Altstadt 315), Landshut's triple-gabled town hall. Here, in the **Prunksaal** (state hall; admission free; 2-3pm Mon-Fri), the royal couple took their first spin on the dance floor. Murals, added in the 19th century, capture scenes from the wedding. Today, the hall offers a baronial setting for concerts and official functions.

A few steps south is the magnificent **Stadtresidenz** (City Residence; ☎ 924 110; Altstadt 79; adult/under 18yr/senior €3/free/2; 9am-6pm Apr-Sep, 10am-4pm Oct-Mar, closed Mon), considered to be the first Renaissance palace north of the Alps. The arcaded courtyard leads to lavish rooms, including the **Italienischer Saal** (Italian Great Hall), with festive stucco and mythological frescoes.

Towards the southern end of Altstadt, one more mansion stands out: the **Alte Post** (Altstadt 28), which served as an assembly hall in the 16th century and later became a post office. The elaborately frescoed façade presents a who's who of Wittelsbach rulers.

BASILIKA ST MARTIN

Legend has it the plan was to build the Gothic **Basilika St Martin** (Kirchgasse; 8am-6pm Apr-Sep, 8am-5pm Oct-Mar) so high as to be able to peer right into the dinner pot of the duke residing in the hilltop Burg Trausnitz. To that end, the steeple soars 130m above the town, making it the world's tallest brick tower.

This crowning achievement of architect Hans von Burghausen has an equally dramatic interior. A Triumphal Cross (1495), hewn from a single tree trunk with a Jesus figure four times life size, dangles above the choir, while the second stained-glass window in the left aisle is a 20th-century sequence ostensibly depicting the life and martyrdom of St Castulus, but if you look closely you'll see that some of the saint's tormentors resemble Hitler, Goebbels and Göring, hence its nickname, 'Nazifenster'.

BURG TRAUSNITZ

Founded in 1204, the hilltop castle **Burg Trausnitz** (☎ 924 110; www.burg-trausnitz.de; adult/under 18yr €4/free, combination ticket with Cabinet €6/free; 9am-6pm Apr-Sep, 10am-4pm Oct-Mar) is considered the seat of the Wittelsbach dynasty and served as residence of the local dukes until 1503. Each fiddled with its appearance to bring it into line with the style of the day. From the late-Romanesque period stems the

Georgskapelle, a two-storey chapel later decorated with intricate Gothic sculptures. The Renaissance brought the **Narrentreppe** (Fools' Stairs), decked out with cheeky murals depicting commedia dell'arte scenes.

Wondrous collections of rarities, oddities and art amassed by inquisitive rulers (including Landshut's own Prince Wilhelm) during the Renaissance are on show at the castle's **Kunst-und Wunderkammer** (Cabinet of Art & Curiosities; adult/under 18yr €4/free, combination ticket with Cabinet €6/free; 9am-6pm Apr-Sep, 10am-4pm Oct-Mar); they include a stuffed Nile crocodile, a parrot-shaped clock and a cherry pit engraved with erotic scenes.

The castle is reached via a set of stairs nicknamed 'Ochsenklavier' (oxen piano), which veers off Alte Bergstrasse. Views of the town are stunning from up here, and the adjacent **Hofgarten** makes for a peaceful stroll.

Festivals & Events

Aside from the famous Landshuter Hochzeit (boxed text, opposite), the town also hosts the biennial **Landshuter Hofmusiktage** (☎ 922 050; www.landshuter-hofmusiktage.com, in German), a two-week festival of medieval, Renaissance and baroque music held every even-numbered year in July.

Sleeping

Campingplatz Landshut (☎ 533 66; fax 533 66; Breslauer Strasse 122; per campsite/tent/person €5.50/3/4.50; year-round) Campers can pitch up at this well-tended riverside campground.

DJH hostel (☎ 234 49; jugendherberge@landshut.de; Richard-Schirrmann-Weg 6; dm incl breakfast & linen €14.20-20.20; closed Christmas-early Jan; P) Housed in a cleverly modernised medieval building, Landshut's hostel is about halfway between Altstadt and Burg Trausnitz.

Hotel Goldene Sonne (☎ 925 30; www.goldenesonne.de; Neustadt 250; s €64-118, d €75-130; P) This lemon-yellow-painted property marries a long hospitality tradition with the latest amenities, including wi-fi, in colourful rooms. The restaurant (mains €8 to €14) is excellent (suckling pig is a speciality) and the beer garden is a great place for an ale.

Hotel-Gasthof Zur Insel (☎ 923 160; fax 9231 636; Badstrasse 16; s €65-75, d with shared bathroom €65-70, d with private bathroom €75-85; P) On the banks of a river island two blocks from Altstadt, Zur Insel's umbrella-lined waterfront beer garden/restaurant (mains €6.90 to €8.50, 9am to midnight) overflows with locals. Upstairs, its

---

LANDSHUTER HOCHZEIT

Every four years, Landshut locals really cut loose during the **Landshuter Hochzeit** (www.landshuter -hochzeit.de), when over 2000 of them dress in medieval costume to re-enact the grandiose 1475 wedding of Georg, son of Duke Ludwig the Rich, to Hedwig, daughter of the king of Poland.

By all accounts, the original event was a grandiose spectacle. The wedding ceremony at Basilika St Martin, attended by European royalty, was followed by a bridal procession along Altstadt cheered on by the townspeople. This kicked off a week-long free-for-all courtesy of the duke. The final gustatorial tally included some 320 oxen, 200,000 eggs, 2300 sheep, 11,500 geese, and rivers of beer and wine.

Today's festival isn't quite as lavish, but it's a good party nonetheless. Held over four weekends in July (plus some additional midweek events), it sees over 650,000 visitors roll up for jousting tournaments, dances, medieval music, markets and general merriment.

The next festivals are scheduled for 2009 and 2013. Tickets (available from the tourist office) need to be booked at least six months in advance, and range from €8 for concerts to €29 for jousting, and up to €50 for combined dinner-and-show events. See the website for more information.

---

19 guest rooms have French-washed walls, dark-timber furniture and dated but clean mottled-brown-tiled bathrooms. Kids are welcomed with open arms.

Eating

Dolce Vita (☎ 261 91; Neustadt 436, entrance Bischof-Sailer-Platz; mains €5.70-17.70; ☽ 9am-6pm Mon, 9am-midnight Tue-Sat, 10am-10pm Sun; **V**) Run by the friendly Ferrale family, 'the sweet life' is absolutely that, with a lively alfresco terrace and authentically prepared calamari, scampi and tiramisu. It's attached to a café-bar and gourmet deli that also stocks wine.

Zum Ainmiller (☎ 211 63; Altstadt 195; mains €7.80-12.30; ☽ Tue-Sun; ✗) If possible, make your way past the suit of armour to the historic cellar or out to the courtyard with castle views to dine on Bavarian specialities like boiled beef with horseradish sauce and fresh market veggies, or bubbling cheese *spätzle* (noodles) served in a sizzling pan, and finish off with cheese strudel with plum compote.

Blaue Stunde (☎ 258 73; Bischof-Sailer-Platz; mains €14.80-18.70; ☽ 8.30am-1am Mon-Sat, 9.30am-midnight Sun; **V**) International fusion dishes at this contemporary café-bar-restaurant include desserts like orange pannacotta with strawberry-rhubarb salad, or flambéed semolina blancmange. It also has great home-made cakes, and imported Belgian chocolates.

Fürstenhof (☎ 925 50; Stethaimerstrasse 3; mains €18-25; ☽ Mon-Sat) Chef Andre Greul managed to wrest a star from those notoriously finicky Michelin testers for his avant-garde interpretations of Franco-German cuisine. It's inside a romantic Art Nouveau villa that also incorporates a hotel (singles €75 to €100, doubles €100 to €120).

Getting There & Around

Landshut is directly connected by regional trains to Munich (€12.40, 45 minutes), Passau (€18.70, 1¼ hours) and Regensburg (€10.60, 45 minutes). The A92 runs right past the town, which is also at the crossroads of the B15 and B299.

The Hauptbahnhof is about 2km northwest of the historic district. Buses 1, 2, 3 and 6 connect the train station with the historic centre (single trips €1.60, day passes €3), or walk south on Luitpoldstrasse and across the Isar. Bikes can be rented from **Radl-Station am Bahnhof** (☎ 1438 153; Hauptbahnhof; per day €9; ☽ 8.30am-noon & 1.30-6pm Mon-Fri, 9am-1pm Sat). Parking is free for the first hour in the CCL shopping mall at Am Alten Viehmarkt (the so-named former 'cattle market'), near the northern end of Neustadt.

Nuremberg & Franconia

'I'm Franconian, not Bavarian!' you'll hear while travelling through this glorious sprawl of fairy-tale forests, farmland, and valleys meandering past limestone cliffs and caves. Sure enough, Franconia has distinct traditions, dialect and dress.

Franconia only became part of Bavaria in 1806, and the conservatism prevalent further south is tempered here by liberal, *very* laid-back tendencies. (When a Franconian casually says '*basstscho*' – 'it fits' – they're over the moon; conversely, devastation merely elicits a shrug and a nonchalant '*werd scho wida*' – 'it'll get better again'.)

While the people are uniquely Franconian, they share with the rest of Bavaria breathtaking countryside teeming with outdoor pursuits and countless romantic villages and castles. Fittingly, the northern half of the Romantic Road – from Würzburg to Dinkelsbühl – runs through this enchanted landscape; it's covered separately in the Romantic Road chapter (p252).

Franconia's cache of historic cities and towns includes baroque Bamberg, opera-going Bayreuth and its tour de force, Nuremberg. This former Free Imperial City has seen some of history's giddiest heights and grimmest depths: artisan Albrecht Dürer hailed from Nuremberg, but so did Hitler's Nazi rallies. Yet Nuremberg's darkest hours heralded the dawn of its current role as one of the world's leading proponents of human rights, and it remains a dynamic interchange for traditional and contemporary creativity.

Chances are you'll hear Franconians mention that their beer is the best in Bavaria or beyond. And after visiting some of Franconia's hundreds (yes, hundreds) of breweries, who couldn't agree?

HIGHLIGHTS

- Devouring Nuremberg's famous finger-sized sausages at its best sausage kitchen, **Bratwursthäusle** (boxed text, p225)
- Draining your camera batteries as you try to capture the sheer magnificence of World Heritage–listed **Bamberg** (p230)
- Hiking between small, family-run breweries surrounding the 'Swiss Franconian' village of **Aufsess** (p236)
- Pulling up at a pebbled beach for a picnic after paddling past craggy rock formations in a canoe through the **Naturpark Altmühltal** (p245)
- Scaring yourself stupid in the birth chamber of Frankenstein's monster, Ingolstadt's **Deutsches Medizinhistorisches Museum** (boxed text, p248)

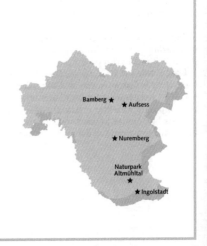

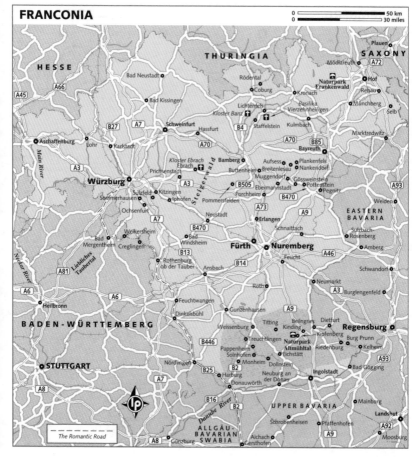

FRANCONIA

NUREMBERG
☎ 0911 / pop 500,000 / elev 289m

Bavaria's second-largest city, Nuremberg (Nürnberg), woos visitors with its wonderfully restored medieval Altstadt (old town), its grand castle and its magical Christkindlesmarkt (Christmas market). Thriving traditions also include sizzling *Nürnberger Bratwürste* (finger-sized sausages) and *Lebkuchen* – large, soft gingerbread cookies, traditionally eaten at Christmas time but available here year-round. Both within and beyond the high stone wall encircling the Altstadt is a wealth of major museums that shed light on Nuremberg's significant history.

Nuremberg's traditions are only part of its story: it's the powerhouse of numerous industries, including printing, plastics and toys, and it's home to hip clubs and a flurry of festivals.

History

For centuries Nuremberg was the unofficial capital of the Holy Roman Empire and the preferred residence of German kings. Thanks to the 'Golden Bull', a law passed in 1356 by Emperor Karl IV, every newly elected king or emperor was required to hold his first gathering of parliament in Nuremberg. From 1424 to 1800, the city was also the empire's 'treasure chest', guarding the crown jewels and many of today's priceless artworks. Especially in the 15th century, numerous artistic masters, Nuremberg local Albrecht Dürer foremost

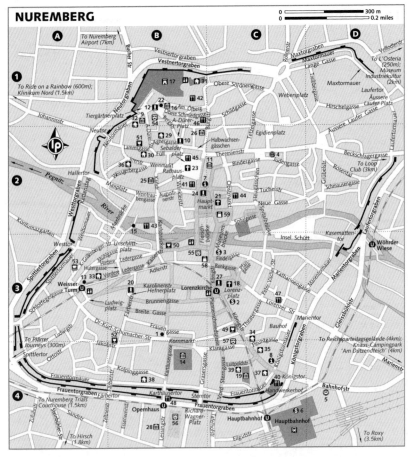

NUREMBERG

0 300 m
0 0.2 miles

among them, lived and worked here, leaving their legacy throughout the city.

Under Napoleon, the former Free Imperial City – already weakened and bankrupt by the Thirty Years' War – was absorbed into the Kingdom of Bavaria in 1806. The city's comeback occurred as a result of industrialisation, and a major milestone came in 1835 when Germany's first railway linked Nuremberg and the neighbouring city of Fürth.

In the 20th century, Nuremberg became linked with, and heavily burdened by, the National Socialists. After seizing power in 1933, Hitler selected Nuremberg as the site for his mass party rallies. In 1935, the infamous Nürnberger Gesetze (Nuremberg Laws), which stripped Jews of their German citizen-

ship in addition to other repressive measures, were also enacted in the city.

During WWII Allied bombing raids killed about 6000 people and destroyed about 90% of the Altstadt. Afterwards, numerous top Nazis were tried by an international military tribunal at the Nuremberg Trials. Painstaking rebuilding – using the original stone – saw the restoration of almost all main buildings, including the castle and three medieval churches.

Postwar, Nuremberg has transformed itself into the 'City of Human Rights', hosting, among other events, the Human Rights Conference and the Nuremberg International Human Rights Award; and receiving the Unesco Prize for Human Rights Education.

Orientation

Guarded by the landmark Kaiserburg (Imperial Castle), Nuremberg's Altstadt – home to most of the major sights – is enclosed by the reconstructed town wall. The placid Pegnitz River separates the quieter and statelier Sebalder Altstadt in the north from the southern Lorenzer Altstadt, which is a partly pedestrianised shopping precinct.

The Hauptbahnhof (central train station) is just outside the walls, southwest of the Altstadt. From here, Königstrasse, the main artery, runs north to Hauptmarkt, the main square.

The Reichsparteitagsgelände (Nazi Party Rally Grounds) is about 4km southeast of the Altstadt in Luitpoldhain, while the Nuremberg Trials courthouse is just west of the Altstadt.

Information

BOOKSHOPS
Buchhandlung Edelmann (☎ 992 060; Kornmarkt 8) English-language novels and a good selection of travel guides.

EMERGENCY
Klinikum Nord (☎ 3980; Prof-Ernst-Nathan Strasse 1) Hospital with 24-hour emergency room.

INTERNET ACCESS
Several internet cafés cum call shops in the basement of the Hauptbahnhof offer cheap online access.

Mir Internet Telecafé (☎ 2427 578; Innere Laufer Gasse 6; from per 15min €0.50; ⏰ 11am-11.30pm Mon-Sat, noon-10.30pm Sun)

MONEY
Commerzbank (Königstrasse 21)
HypoVereinsbank (Königstrasse 3)
Reisebank (Hauptbahnhof)

POST
Post office (Bahnhofplatz 1)

TOURIST INFORMATION
Tourist office (www.tourismus.nuernberg.de) Hauptmarkt (☎ 2336 135; Hauptmarkt 18; ⏰ 9am-6pm Mon-Sat, 10am-4pm Sun May-Oct, 9am-6pm Mon-Sat Nov & Jan-Apr, 10am-7pm daily during Christkindlesmarkt); Künstlerhaus (☎ 233 6131; Königstrasse 93; ⏰ 9am-7pm Mon-Sat year-round, plus 10am-4pm Sun during Christkindlesmarkt) Staff sell the Nürnberg + Fürth Card (€19), available to overnight visitors and good for two days of unlimited public transport and admission to most museums and attractions in both cities.

TRAVEL AGENCIES
Plärrer Journeys (☎ 929 760; Gostenhofer Hauptstrasse 27) A good general travel agency that also has a last-minute ticket desk at the airport.

Sights

Most of the city's major sights have family tickets available for sale – check at the ticket desk.

NUREMBERG & FRANCONIA

HAUPTMARKT

This bustling square in the heart of the Altstadt is the site of daily markets as well as the famous Christkindlesmarkt. At the eastern end is the ornate Gothic **Pfarrkirche Unsere Liebe Frau** (1350–58), also known as simply the Frauenkirche. The work of Prague cathedral builder Peter Parler, it's the oldest Gothic hall church in Bavaria and stands on the ground of Nuremberg's first synagogue. The western façade is beautifully ornamented and is where, every day at noon, crowds crane their necks to witness a spectacle called *Männleinlaufen*. It features seven figures, representing electoral princes, parading clockwise three times around Emperor Karl IV to chimed accompaniment. The scene commemorates the passage of the Golden Bull in 1356.

Rising from the square like a Gothic spire, the gargoyle-adorned, 19m-tall **Schöner Brunnen** (Beautiful Fountain) is a gilded replica of the 14th-century original, though it no longer spouts water. Look for the seamless golden ring in the ornate wrought-iron gate on the southwestern side. Local superstition has it that if you turn it three times, your wish will come true. (Be careful not to confuse it with the gold ring on the opposite side of the gate, which, it's claimed, will make you conceive – if you're female, of course.)

ALTES RATHAUS & ST SEBALDUSKIRCHE

Beneath the **Altes Rathaus** (old town hall; 1616–22), a hulk of a building with elegant Renaissance interiors, are the **Lochgefängnisse** (Medieval Dungeons; ☎ 231 2690; Rathausplatz; adult/under 14yr €3/1.50; ⏱ 20min tours half-hourly 10am-4.30pm Tue-Sun Apr-Oct, Mon-Fri Feb, daily during Christkindlesmarkt), consisting of 12 small cells and a torture chamber. Leaflets in languages other than German (€0.50) are free.

Opposite the Altes Rathaus is the 13th-century **St Sebalduskirche**, Nuremberg's oldest church, the exterior of which is replete with religious sculptures and symbols. Check out the ornate carvings over the Bridal Doorway to the north, showing the Wise and Foolish Virgins. Inside, the bronze shrine of **St Sebald** (Nuremberg's own saint) is a Gothic and Renaissance masterpiece that took its maker, Peter Vischer the Elder, and his two sons more than 11 years to complete. (Vischer is in it, too, sporting a skullcap.) Tours of the church's **tower** (adult/child €3/1.50) are by prior arrangement only.

STADTMUSEUM FEMBOHAUS

Offering an entertaining overview of the city's history, highlights of the **Stadtmuseum Fembohaus** (City Museum; ☎ 231 2595; Burgstrasse 15; adult/child €5/2.50; ⏱ 10am-5pm Tue-Fri, 10am-6pm Sat & Sun) include the restored historic rooms of this 16th-century merchant house. Also here, **Noricama** (adult/child €4/2; ⏱ 10am-5pm Tue-Fri, 10am-6pm Sat & Sun) takes you on a flashy Hollywoodesque multimedia journey (in German and English) through Nuremberg's history.

ALBRECHT-DÜRER-HAUS

Dürer, Germany's most famous Renaissance draughtsman, lived and worked at the **Albrecht Dürer Haus** (Albrecht Dürer House; ☎ 231 2568; Albrecht-Dürer-Strasse 39; adult/concession €5/2.50, with audioguide €12/8; ⏱ 10am-5pm Fri-Wed, 10am-8pm Thu) from 1509 until his death in 1528. After a multimedia show, there's an audioguided tour of the four-storey house, which is narrated by 'Agnes', Dürer's wife. Highlights are the hands-on demonstrations in the re-created studio and print shop on the 3rd floor and, in the attic, a gallery featuring copies and originals of Dürer's work.

Special tours led by an actress dressed as Agnes take place at 6pm Thursday, 3pm Saturday and 11am Sunday; there's an English-language tour at 2pm Saturday.

FELSENGÄNGE

Beneath the **Albrecht Dürer Monument** on Albrecht-Dürer-Platz are the chilly **Felsengänge** (Underground Cellars; ☎ 227 066; tours adult/concession €4.50/3.50; ⏱ tours 11am, 1pm, 3pm & 5pm). Departing from the brewery shop at Burgstrasse 19, tours descend to this four-storey subterranean warren dating from the 14th century, which once housed a brewery and a beer cellar. During

---

NUREMBERG'S BEST MUSEUMS IF YOU'RE A...

- Trainspotter: **Verkehrsmuseum** (p222)

- Kid: **Spielzeugmuseum** (opposite)

- Art aficionado: **Neues Museum** (p222)

- General history buff: **Germanisches Nationalmuseum** (opposite)

- WWII history buff: **Documentation-szentrum** (p222)

WWII, it served as an air-raid shelter. Tours take a minimum of three people. Take a jacket against the chill (and note there are no toilets).

TIERGÄRTNERPLATZ
Ringed by charming half-timbered houses, the eastern edge of **Tiergärtnerplatz** is graced by the beautiful **Pilatushaus**. Out the front is Jürgen Goertz's 1984 bronze sculpture **Der Hase – Hommage á Dürer** (The Hare – A Tribute to Dürer). This nod to Dürer's watercolour original called *Junger Feldhase* (1502) shows the dire results of tampering with nature.

During WWII, prescient officials moved key artworks to the **Historischer Kunstbunker** (Historical Art Shelter; ☎ 227 066; Obere Schmiedgasse 52; tours €4.50/3.50; ⏲ tours 3pm), a network of caves underneath the Kaiserburg, as early as 1940. This was technically a form of resistance, since Hitler forbade such 'defeatist' thinking. There's also a film of the bombing of Nuremberg. Tours depart from the brewery-shop at Burgstrasse 19. A minimum of three people is needed for tours.

KAISERBURG
Construction of Nuremberg's landmark, the immensely proportioned **Kaiserburg** (Imperial Castle; ☎ 200 9540; adult/concession incl museum €6/5, well & tower only €3/2; ⏲ 9am-6pm Apr-Sep, 10am-4pm Oct-Mar), began during the reign of Hohenstaufen King Konrad III in the 12th century and dragged on for about 400 years. The complex, for centuries the receptacle of the Holy Roman Empire's treasures, consists of three parts: the Kaiserburg and Stadtburg (the Emperor's Palace and City Fortress), as well as the Burggrafenburg (Count's Residence), which was largely destroyed in 1420. Wedged between its surviving towers are the Kaiserstallung (Royal Stables), which today house the DJH hostel.

The **Kaiserburg Museum** chronicles the history of the castle and provides a survey of medieval defence techniques. Other Tardislike sections open to visitors include the royal living quarters, and the Imperial and Knights' Halls, and the **Romanesque Doppelkapelle** (Twin Chapel). The latter poignantly illustrates medieval hierarchy: common folk sat in the dimly lit lower section, with the royals having entered up above directly from the palace.

Enjoy panoramic city views from atop the **Sinwellturm** (Sinwell Tower; 113 steps) or peer into the amazing 48m-deep **Tiefer Brunnen** (Deep Well) – guides lower a platter of candles so you can see its depth; it still yields drinking water.

The grassy knoll at the southeast corner of the **castle gardens** (open seasonally) is **Am Ölberg**, a favourite spot to sit and gaze out over the city's rooftops.

SPIELZEUGMUSEUM
Nuremberg has long been a centre of toy manufacturing, and the **Spielzeugmuseum** (Toy Museum; ☎ 231 3164; Karlstrasse 13-15; adult/concession €4/2; ⏲ 10am-5pm Tue-Fri, 10am-6pm Sat & Sun, plus 10am-5pm Mon during Christkindlesmarkt & 10am-8pm during Toy Fair) presents them in their infinite variety – from historical wooden and paper toys to toy trains, books and computer games. Kids and kids at heart will delight in the play area.

South of here across Karlsbrücke you'll come to a tiny island surrounded by a scenic stretch of the Pegnitz River. On the north bank is the covered wooden **Henkersteg** (Hangman's Bridge).

LUDWIGSPLATZ TO LORENZPLATZ
At the foot of the fortified **Weisser Turm** (White Tower; now the gateway to the U-Bahn station of the same name) stands the dramatic **Ehekarussell Brunnen** (Marriage Merry-Go-Round), a remarkable metallic fountain with six timeless interpretations of marriage based on a verse by medieval cobbler-poet Hans Sachs. Further east, another modern fountain, the **Peter-Henlein-Brunnen** on Hefnerplatz, is dedicated to the 16th-century tinkerer credited with making the first pocket watch.

The site of the Altstadt's other U-Bahn station, Lorenzplatz, is dominated by the **Lorenzkirche** (Gothic Church of St Lawrence), which is chock-full of artistic highlights. Check out the 15th-century tabernacle in the left aisle – the delicate carved strands wind up to the vaulted ceiling. Remarkable also are the stained glass (including a rose window 9m in diameter) and Veit Stoss' *Engelsgruss* (Annunciation), a wooden carving with life-size figures, suspended above the high altar.

North of the church, the **Tugendbrunnen** (1589) is a fountain featuring the seven Virtues with a figure of Justice looking on.

GERMANISCHES NATIONALMUSEUM
Spanning prehistory to the early 20th century the **Germanisches Nationalmuseum** (German National

Museum; ☎ 133 10; Kartäusergasse 1; adult/concession €6/4, free 6-9pm Wed; ◷ 10am-6pm Tue & Thu-Sun, 10am-9pm Wed) is the country's most important museum of German culture. It features works by German painters and sculptors, an archaeological collection, arms and armour, musical and scientific instruments and toys. Among its many highlights is Dürer's anatomically detailed *Hercules Slaying the Stymphalian Birds*. The research library has over 500,000 volumes and 1500 periodicals.

At the museum's entrance is the inspired **Way of Human Rights**, a symbolic row of 29 white concrete pillars (and one oak tree) bearing the 30 articles of the Universal Declaration of Human Rights. Each pillar is inscribed in German and, in succession, the language of peoples whose rights have been violated, with the oak representing languages not explicitly mentioned.

VERKEHRSMUSEUM

Nuremberg's **Verkehrsmuseum** (Transportation Museum; ☎ 01804-442 233; Lessingstrasse 6; adult/under 17yr €4/2; ◷ 10am-3pm Mon, 1-5pm Thu, 10am-5pm Sun) combines two major exhibits under one roof: the **Deutsche Bahn Museum** (German Railway Museum) and the **Museum für Kommunikation** (Museum of Telecommunications). The former explores the origins and history of Germany's legendary railway system; the latter showcases development in telecommunications, including historic telephones dating back over 100 years.

NEUES MUSEUM

Paralleling international developments in both contemporary art and design, the **Neues Museum** (New Museum; ☎ 240 200; entry via Klarissenplatz; adult/concession €4/3, Sun €1; ◷ 10am-8pm Tue-Fri, 10am-6pm Sat & Sun) presents paintings, sculpture, photography, video art and installations. Equally stunning is the building itself, with a dramatic 100m curved glass façade that, literally and figuratively, reflects the stone town wall opposite.

MUSEUM INDUSTRIEKULTUR

A former screw-manufacturing plant now houses the **Museum Industruriekultur** (Museum of Industrial Culture; ☎ 231 3875; Sulzbacker Strasse 62; adult/concession €5/2.50; ◷ 9am-5pm Tue-Fri, 10am-6pm Sat & Sun), with quirky exhibits such as talking washing machines, a fully functional 1920s cinema and a kids' fun learning lab with various vehicles to 'test drive'.

REICHSPARTEITAGSGELÄNDE

Nuremberg's role during the Third Reich is emblazoned in minds around the world through the black-and-white images of rapturous Nazi supporters thronging the city's flag-lined streets as bayonet-bearing troops salute their Führer.

The rallies at the **Reichsparteitagsgelände** (Nazi Party Rally Grounds) were part of an orchestrated propaganda campaign that began as early as 1927 to garner support for the NSDAP, which had a strong following in Nuremberg, in part because Hitler promised Franconians their own state separate to Bavaria. In 1933, the party planned a ridiculously large purpose-built complex in the southeastern Luitpoldhain suburb. Nazi leaders hoped to establish a metaphorical link between Nuremberg's illustrious past as *Reichstagstadt* (where parliament met during the Holy Roman Empire) and the Third Reich's new rally centre (the *Reichsparteitag*).

Most of the parades, rallies and events took place at the **Zeppelinfeld**, fronted by a 350m-long grandstand, the **Zeppelintribüne**. The grounds are bisected by the 60m-wide **Grosse Strasse** (Great Road), which culminates, 2km south, at the **Märzfeld** (March Field), planned as a military exercise ground. West of the Grosse Strasse was to have been the **Deutsches Stadion**, with a seating capacity of 400,000. Its construction never progressed beyond the initial excavation; the hole later filled with groundwater to become today's Silbersee lake.

Much of the actual Reichsparteitagsgelände was destroyed during 1945 bombing raids, but enough is left to sense the dimension and scale of this gargantuan complex. At the area's northwestern edge once stood the **Luitpoldarena**; designed for mass SS and SA parades, it's now a park. The half-built **Kongresshalle** (Congress Hall), meant to outdo Rome's Colosseum in both scale and style, is the largest remaining Nazi building.

Today the Kongresshalle's north wing houses the outstanding **Documentationszentrum** (Documentation Centre; ☎ 231 5666; Bayernstrasse 110; adult/concession €5/2.50; ◷ 9am-6pm Mon-Fri, 10am-6pm Sat & Sun). It puts the Nazi Party Rally Grounds into historical context, examining the causes, relationships and consequences of the Nazi terror regime. Early rooms focus on general background, but the most relevant to the city are Room 6, which details Nuremberg's specific role as the party's headquarters; Room 7, which screens a film showing architect Albert Speer's grand-scale designs for the complex; and Room 8, with a harrowing overview of how construction materials came from the concentration camps.

Nowadays the Zeppelintribüne grandstand hosts sporting events and concerts. Also here is the **Franken Stadion**, which hosted several World Cup football games in 2006.

Take tram 4 to Dutzendteich, or tram 9 to Luitpoldhain.

NUREMBERG TRIALS COURTHOUSE

Nazis were tried in 1945 to 1946 for crimes against peace and humanity in Schwurgerichtssaal 600 (Court Room 600) of what is today the **Landgericht Nürnberg-Fürth** (Nuremberg-Fürth Courthouse; ☎ 231 5421; Fürther Strasse 110, entry from Bärenschanzstrasse; adult/concession €2.50/1.25; ☽ tours hourly 1-4pm Sat & Sun). The Allies held the trials in Nuremberg for obvious symbolic reasons, in addition to the fact that there was (and still is) a secure underground tunnel between the courthouse and adjacent prison (though today it only has female prisoners).

The initial and most famous trial, conducted by international prosecutors, saw 24 people accused, of which 19 were convicted and sentenced. Following trials also resulted in the conviction, sentencing and execution of Nazi leaders and underlings until 1949. Hermann Göring, the Reich's field marshall, cheated the hangman by taking a cyanide capsule in his cell hours before his scheduled execution.

To get here you will need to take the U1 U-Bahn to Bärenschanze.

Tours

The tourist office runs 2½-hour English-language **walking tours** (adult/under 14yr incl admission to Kaiserburg €8/free; ☽ tours 1pm May-Oct & during Christkindlesmarkt) from the Hauptmarkt branch. It also operates 2½-hour **coach tours** (adult/under 12yr €11/5.50; ☽ tours 9.30am Apr-Oct & during Christkindlesmarkt) in English and German, taking in the city's major sights including the Reichsparteitagsgelände.

Festivals & Events

Every year, millions of visitors flock to Nuremberg's world-famous **Christkindlesmarkt** (☽ 9.30am-8pm Mon-Wed, 9.30am-9pm Thu-Sat, 10.30am-9pm Sun late Nov-24 Dec) to browse the stalls sell-ing toys, trinkets, gingerbread and sweets while warming up with sizzling *Bratwürste* (roast sausages) and gluhwein (sweet mulled wine). The most enchanting time to visit is after dark, when the brightly coloured lights create a fairy-tale spectacle. Adjoining the main market is the adorable children's **Kinderweihnacht**, with such delights as carousels, miniature train rides and child-size food portions.

Nuremburg's Altstadt also comes to life during several summer festivals. The **Bardentreffen** in early August is an open-air medieval music festival. But the summer festival highlight is the 12-day **Altstadtfest** in September when the entire old town is taken over by music and theatre, stalls selling speciality foods, craft stands and lots more. Auto-racing fans should check out the **Norisring Races**, a Formula Three race around the Zeppelintribüne in late June or early July.

Sleeping

Accommodation is tight during trade fairs and festivals (when rates can jump), but inexpensive accommodation in all price ranges is easily found at other times.

BUDGET

Knaus-Campingpark 'Am Dutzendteich' (☎ 981 2717; www.knauscamp.de, in German; Hans-Kalb-Strasse 56; campsite €12, per person/tent from €6/2.50) Campers can head to this well-equipped campground near the lakes in the Volkspark, southeast of the city. Take U-Bahn U1 to Messezentrum.

Lette 'm Sleep (☎ 992 8128; www.backpackers.de; Frauentormauer 42; dm €16-25, sheets €3, s/d incl linen from €30/49, apt with kitchen from €165; ☒ ▣) A backpacker favourite, this independent hostel is just five minutes' walk from the Hauptbahnhof, with a laundry, colourfully painted dorms and some groovy self-catering apartments. The retro-styled kitchen and velour-furnished common room are great areas to chill; internet (plus wi-fi), tea and coffee are free, and staff are wired into what's happening around town.

DJH Jugendgästehaus (☎ 230 9360; www.nuernberg.jugendherberge.de; Burg 2; B&B with linen €20.70-24.70; ☒ ▣) In the former castle stables, about 20 to 30 minutes' walk north of the Hauptbahnhof, this spotless, family-friendly hostel has 317 beds in bright, airy dorms as well as a piano and table tennis. There's a 1am curfew but no daytime lockout.

Probst-Garni Hotel (☎ 203 433; fax 205 9336; Luitpoldstrasse 9; s/d with shared bathroom €21/43, with private bathroom €56/70) Nuremberg's most reasonably priced *Pension* is a friendly place squeezed on the 3rd floor of a creaky but well-located building. Some singles are tiny, but other rooms are perfectly adequate. Rooms with private bathroom have TV.

MIDRANGE

our pick Hotel Elch (☎ 249 2980; www.hotel-elch.com; Irrerstrasse 9; s €52-85, d €69-110; ✕) Tucked up in the antiques quarter, this 14th-century, half-timbered house has morphed into this snug, romantic little 12-room hotel. A couple of rooms (Nos 2 and 7) have half-timbered walls and ceilings, too, and modern touches include contemporary art, glazed terracotta bathrooms and free wi-fi. The original, wood-beamed 'Schnitzelria' restaurant (mains €6.90 to €11) downstairs serves 49 different kinds of – you guessed it – schnitzel.

Garden Hotel (☎ 205 060; Vordere Ledergasse 12; www .gardenhotel-nuernberg.de; s €72-90, d €95-120; 🖵) Not as leafy as its name suggests, this mid-20th-century place in the central Altstadt nevertheless has lots of greenery, such as lime-green chiffon curtains in the guestrooms and '60s pistachio vinyl booths in its breakfast room, giving it a fresh, funky edge.

Burghotel (☎ 238 890; www.burghotel-nuernberg .de; Lammsgasse 3; s €78-122; d €95-185; 🖵 🐾) Immaculate rooms at this friendly hotel span small singles and doubles with '50s-style built-in timber furniture reminiscent of old-fashioned train carriages through to some much larger 'comfort' rooms under the eaves with spacious sitting areas, but all guests can use the basement heated swimming pool and sauna. Nearby parking can be arranged for €10 per 24 hours.

Hotel Victoria (☎ 240 50; www.hotelvictoria.de, in German; Königstrasse 80; s/d from €78/99; 🅿 ✕ 🖵) Blending the historic and the new (like Nuremberg itself), this chic hotel has cutting-edge interiors within a newly restored 1896-built structure. Through the corridors lined with black-and-white photographs, minimalist rooms incorporate streamlined contemporary blonde wood furniture, crisp white sheets and minibars. Public areas have free wi-fi, and some rooms have broadband. Parking costs €11.

Hotel Deutscher Kaiser (☎ 242 660; www.deut scher-kaiser-hotel.de; Königstrasse 55; s €87-99, d €106-125;

🅿 🖵) A grand sandstone staircase leads to ornately decorated rooms in this 1880s-built hotel. Bathrooms are equipped with bidets and there's a lavish hot and cold buffet breakfast, but the real gem is the elegant reading room with newspapers and magazines in German and English. Staff are professional and genuine. Parking (€10) is limited to just five spots, on a first-come, first-served basis.

TOP END

Hotel Drei Raben (☎ 274 380; www.hotel-drei-raben .de; Königstrasse 63; r €100-185; ✕ 🖵) The design of this original hotel builds upon the legend of the three ravens perched on the building's chimney stack, who tell stories from Nuremberg lore. Each of the 'mythology' rooms uses décor and art including sand-stone-sculpted bedheads and etched-glass bathroom doors to reflect a particular tale – from the life of Albrecht Dürer to the history of the local football club. Junior suites have claw-foot tubs. Barman David Davis creates cocktails and mixes them at your table in the bar from 9pm (nonguests welcome).

Agneshof (☎ 214 440; www.agneshof-nuernberg .de, in German; Agnesgasse 10; s €100-260, d €125-260; 🅿 ✕ 🖵) Peacefully situated in the antiques quarter near the St Sebalduskirche. The Agneshof's public areas have a sophisticated, artsy touch, as do the pared-down rooms, many of which come with balconies spilling over with geranium-filled window boxes in summer. There's a state-of-the-art wellness centre, and a pretty summer courtyard garden strewn with deckchairs. Parking (by reservation) costs €15 per day.

Dürer Hotel (☎ 214 6650; www.duererhotel-nuern berg.de; Neutormauer 32; s €110-138, d €155-200; 🅿 🖵) A stone's throw from the Albrecht-Dürer-Haus. Six rooms at this sprawling, family-run four-star hotel open to a courtyard garden, and all are equipped with amenities such as trouser presses and German-made Dermafit bath products. Wi-fi is available and guests can use the swimming pool at the nearby Burghotel. On-site parking costs €10 per day.

Eating
RESTAURANTS

Traditional Bavarian cooking is *big* in Nuremberg, but there are also plenty of international options. See the boxed text, opposite, for the low-down on the city's famous finger-sized sausages.

L'Osteria (☎ 558 283; Pirckheimer Strasse 116; mains €5.50-9, wine per glass €3; ☺ 11am-midnight Mon-Sat, 5pm-midnight Sun; **V**) It's worth heading out of the Aldstadt centre for what is easily the best pizza in town. Help yourself to the large bottles of wine on the tables and pay for what you drink. There's an enclosed latticed terrace in warm weather. Take Tram 9 from the Hauptbahnhof to the Wurzelbaurerstrasse stop.

Burgwächter (☎ 222 126; Am Ölberg 10; mains €5.90-13.80; **V**) In the shadow of the castle, this is a great place with a terraced beer garden and terrific city views. The prime steaks and grilled cuts will please carnivores but vegetarians aren't forgotten, with home-made Swabian filled pastas and other meatless Bavarian specialities (which, contrary to appearances, isn't an oxymoron).

Hütt'n (☎ 201 9881; Burgstrasse 19; mains €7.50-14.50; ☺ from 4pm Mon-Wed, approx Sep-Jun) Be prepared to queue for a table at this local haunt. The special here is the *ofenfrische Krustenbraten:* roast port with crackling, dumplings and sauerkraut salad. There's also a near-endless variety of schnapps.

Enchilada (☎ 244 8498; Obstmarkt 5; mains €8.90-15.90; **V**) Vegetarians (at least those who like spinach, which seems to dominate the meatless dishes) will rejoice at the taco platters, burritos and quesadillas served at this candle-lit place with lazy ceiling fans. Salads (served in a tortilla bowl) include 'Pacifico' with garlic shrimps topped with smoked salmon; for dessert try the 'Churros' – deep-fried dough strips with sugar and cinnamon, smothered in whipped cream and chocolate sauce.

Tucherbräu (☎ 204 609; Am Kartäusertor 1; mains €10.80-90) It's a bit on the pricey side, but the best reason to head into this rambling traditional restaurant – aside from its excellent Bavarian and handful of international dishes – is the countrified beer garden hidden out the back, which feels far from the hubbub of the city. Service is attentive and it's handily situated near the Hauptbahnhof.

CAFÉS & QUICK EATS

Good fast-food fare is found along Lorenzer Strasse; inside the Hauptbahnhof you'll also find some surprisingly healthy options amid the usual fast-food suspects.

Souptopia (☎ 240 6697; Lorenzer Strasse 27; soups €3-6; ☺ Mon-Sat; **V**) This place overflows with locals filling up on its steaming bowls of home-made

---

THE SPICE OF LIFE

Nuremberg's famous *Lebkucken* (gingerbread cookies) and its finger-sized *Bratwürste* (sausages), infused with marjoram, salt and pepper, originate from the city's key position at the intersection of spice-trading routes during the Middle Ages.

How the sausages came to be finger-sized is less certain, but the most commonly held theory is that they stem from dark medieval days when the city ensured its citizens had to be off the streets after dark, and hence all shops had to close. In order to feed hungry nocturnal citizens (and make a buck), shopkeepers made the sausages small enough to slide through the keyholes of their doors.

Proper Nuremberg *Bratwürste* should be made only from ham and/or pork shoulder (with a bit of bacon fat to hold them together), grilled on an open flame over beechwood at a constant, slow-burning temperature, and served in a traditional pewter dish.

ourpick **Bratwursthäusle** (☎ 227 695; Rathaus-Platz 1; mains €6.20-11; ☺ Mon-Sat) These *Bratwürste* traditions are passionately upheld here by fourth-generation sausage specialist Kai Behringer. Kai has his own butchery (his is the only sausage kitchen in Nuremberg to do so), which provides the sausages grilled in an island kitchen right in the centre of his main restaurant, with copper saucepans hanging overhead. All of the ingredients (such as cabbage for the sauerkraut) are locally farmed by Kai's friends and delivered fresh; at the end of each day, any uncooked sausages are canned fresh and sold in specialist food shops around town. You can dine in the timbered restaurant or on the terrace with views of the Sebalduskirche, Rathaus and Hauptmarkt, but if you're in a hurry, €1.80 will get you *drei im Weckla* (three sausages in a bun).

Kai has recently opened two other top-notch sausage kitchens in town: **Goldenes Posthorn** (☎ 225 153; Glöckleinsgasse 2, cnr Sebalder Platz; mains €6-12; **V**), housed in a 1498 former wine tavern; and **Bratwurstglöcklein** (☎ 227 625; Handwerkerhof; mains €6.20-11; ☺ Mon-Sat mid-Mar–Dec), inside Nuremberg's traditional craft market.

soups. Vegetarians and nonvegetarians will find plenty of choices; there are also sandwiches brimming with fresh ingredients.

Café am Trödelmarkt (☎ 208 877; Trödelmarkt 42; dishes €3.50-4.20; 🕙 9am-6pm Mon-Sat, 11am-6pm Sun; **V**) A gorgeous place on a sunny day, this multilevel waterfront café overlooks the covered Henkersteg bridge. It's especially popular for its continental breakfasts, and has fantastic cakes as well as good blackboard lunchtime specials between 11am and 2pm.

Drinking

Many of the best bars are in the pedestrian zone south of the Pegnitz. Virtually all serve food, and most open from around noon until midnight or later unless otherwise noted.

Barfüsser Kleines Brauhaus (☎ 204 242; Hallplatz 2) A staircase (and lift for wheelchair access) descends to a cavernous vaulted cellar of this brewery-pub filled with copper pipes direct from the brewery, framed old advertisements and tabletop *Eichenholzfässchen* (individual 5L oakwood kegs).

Treibhaus (☎ 223 041; Karl-Grillenberger-Strasse 28) This bustling café is a Nuremberg institution, popular with students, shoppers and anyone else in search of an unpretentious and convivial ambience. Inexpensive breakfasts are served until the evening, but the hot and cold snacks are also worth a try.

Sausalitos (☎ 200 4889; Färber Strasse 10) With its slick Santa Fe décor, this is the place where hipsters congregate for copious cocktails. It's at its most rocking during Margarita Happy Hour between 11pm and 2am Monday to Thursday.

Café Lucas (☎ 227 845; Kaiserstrasse 22) This two-storey café draws the designer set for convincing cocktails, snacks and a few choice larger meals; outdoors, wooden tables overlook the river.

Saigon Bar (☎ 244 8657; Lammsgasse 8; 🕙 from 10pm Thu-Sun) Do as Nurembergers do and make this your last stop after a night on the town. With a background beat of drum 'n bass, this essential late-night bar does a top-rate *caipirinha*, the Brazilian drink that's at least as popular in Bavaria as it is in Rio, made from smashed limes, brown sugar, crushed ice and white pitú rum.

Entertainment

Doppelpunkt, Nuremberg's popular free listings magazine for nightlife and cultural

fixtures, is in German only, but it's easy to navigate, as is its website, www.doppelpunkt .de. There's comprehensive information (in English) about gay and lesbian parties, clubs and events at www.nuernberg.gay-web.de.

LIVE MUSIC & NIGHTCLUBS

Stereo Deluxe (☎ 530 060; Klaragasse 8; admission from €5; 🕙 Thu-Sat) First a home-grown record label for modern urban sound, Deluxe is now also a hip café with a red strobe-lit club in the basement. Very cool.

Hirsch (☎ 429 414; Vogelweiherstrasse 66; admission €6-10; 🕙 7pm-2am Sun-Thu, 9pm-5am Fri & Sat) A converted factory, the Hirsch has live alternative music in two separate areas, as well as theme nights and a summer beer garden. DJs spin everything from drum 'n bass to acid jazz and '70s disco, and there are monthly Pink Hirsch gay parties.

Loop Club (☎ 686 767; Klingenhofstrasse 52; 🕙 10pm-4am Thu-Sat) With three dance areas and a languid chill-out zone with lounge music, this place attracts a slightly older crowd. Take the U-Bahn U2 to Herrnhütte, turn right and it's a five-minute walk. There's a Nightliner bus service back to town after the trains stop running.

Other recommendations:

Mach 1 (☎ 203 030; Kaiserstrasse 1-9; admission €4-6; 🕙 Thu-Sat) Legendary dance temple with top international DJs and an infamously strict door policy. Dress to impress.

Hausbrauerei Altstadthof (☎ 221 570; Bergstrasse 19; 🕙 Mon-Sat) Brew-pub where the basement cellar resonates with live folk, blues and rock.

CINEMAS

Roxy (☎ 488 40; Julius-Lossmann-Strasse 116) Specialises in English- and French-language first-run films – take the Worzeldorferstrasse-bound tram 8 and exit at the Südfriedhof stop.

THEATRE & CLASSICAL MUSIC

Altstadthof (☎ 244 9859; Bergstrasse 19) Tucked away in a complex that also includes a brew-pub and boutiques, this small independent theatre presents entertaining comedies (generally in German).

Staatstheater Nuremberg (☎ box office 231 3575; Richard-Wagner-Platz 2-10) Nuremberg's magnificent theatre complex consists of the Art Nouveau *Opernhaus* (opera house), the *Schauspielhaus* (drama theatre) and the *Kammerspiele* (chamber plays); the latter two also feature contemporary productions. The Nürnberger Philharmoniker also performs here.

Shopping

The northeastern Altstadt is home to some high-end antique shops; you'll find quirky jewellers' showrooms on the Trödelmarkt.

Some of Nuremberg's best traditional gingerbread cookies are made by **Lebkuchen Schmidt** (Plobenhofstrassee 6, Hauptmarkt), whose shop windows are piled high with decorative metal tins.

The Nuremberg branch of the Rothenburg-based Christmas-ornament emporium, **Käthe Wohlfahrt** (Königstrasse 8), gets especially busy during the Christkindlesmarkt.

Getting There & Away

Nuremberg airport (☎ 937 00) is 7km north of the city centre and is served by regional and international carriers, including discount carrier Air Berlin, and Air France and Lufthansa.

InterCity Express or InterCity trains run hourly to and from Frankfurt (€45, 2¼ hours) and Munich (€45, 1¾ hours). Regional trains travel hourly to Bamberg (€10.60, one hour) and Würzburg (€16.60, 1¼ hours) and every other hour to Regensburg (€16.40, one hour).

Several autobahns, including the Berlin–Munich A9, converge on Nuremberg, but only the north–south A73 joins B4, the ring road.

Getting Around

TO/FROM THE AIRPORT

Every second U-Bahn 2 (every few minutes between 5am and 12.30am) runs from the Hauptbahnhof to the airport in 12 minutes (look for the plane symbol on the front of the train). A taxi between the airport and central Nuremberg costs about €20.

BICYCLE

Ride on a Rainbow (☎ 397 337; Adam-Kraft-Strasse 55; per day from €10) hires out bikes of all sorts and offers good weekly deals.

PUBLIC TRANSPORT

Walking's the ticket in the Altstadt. Tickets on buses, trams and U-Bahn/S-Bahn cost €1.80. A day pass for one/two adults costs €3.60/€6.20; Saturday passes are valid all weekend.

TAXI

Call ☎ 194 10 for a taxi.

AROUND NUREMBERG

Radiating out from Nuremberg, the historic cities of Fürth, 9km to the north, and Ansbach, 50km southwest, both reward exploration. For a taste of medieval Franconia, head around 50km north of Nuremberg to the Kellerwald's ancient stone cellars and beer gardens deep in the forest of Forchheim (boxed text, below).

Travelling about 24km north of Nuremberg brings you to **Erlangen** (population 101,000, elevation 279m), a buzzing university and Siemens company town. Although there are few sights and activities as such for visitors, Erlangen's tree-lined boulevards, ivy-covered buildings and picnic-friendly gardens surrounding its Schloss make it a good spot to pull up for lunch. Around Pentecost the **Erlanger Bergkirchweih**, a 12-day folk and beer festival on the Burgberg, takes place with the city as backdrop. Erlangen is on the A73 autobahn (just north of the A3) and is served by rail from Nuremberg.

Nuremberg's tourist office has free maps of the surrounding region.

Fürth

☎ 0911 / pop 110,000 / elev 297m

Nuremberg might be only 9km away, but its neighbour, Fürth, is a spirited city with its

---

DETOUR: FORCHHEIM'S KELLERWALD

When JRR Tolkien opened his *Fellowship of the Ring* with a rousing hobbit birthday party in the mythical Shire, he quite possibly drew his inspiration from Franconia's 10-day **St Annafest** (St Anna Festival; ☎ 09191-714 338; www.annafest.eu, in German; ☯ late Jul-early Aug), held in the **Kellerwald** – 24 wooded beer gardens and medieval stone cellars in the forests of Forchheim.

Every year this ancient festival draws around half a million local revellers who feast on platters of *Bratwürste* and swig Franconian brews while carnival acts and bands perform into the night. Even if you're not here at festival time, many of the Kellerwald's beer gardens are open year-round; most from around 10am until midnight.

Forchheim is a well-signed half-hour drive from both Nuremberg and Bamberg.

own identity and history that extends back over 1000 years. Still, Fürth and Nuremberg have long been linked. As a result of their shared role as the site of Germany's first railway, Fürth lays claim to being the world's smallest city to have its own subway system (six stops as of December 2007), though its compact size means walking across town is often speedier than waiting for a train.

There are no fewer than 2000 heritage-listed buildings and architectural monuments in Fürth (the most per square kilometre in Bavaria), dating from late medieval times onwards. Fürth also once had the largest Jewish community in southern Germany; they settled here from 1528 on. During WWII many were forced to emigrate, including former US Secretary of State, Henry Kissinger, who was born here in 1923. Today, Yiddish culture is celebrated during the **International Klezmer Festival** in March. Fürth's **tourist office** (☎ 406 615; www.fuerth.de; Bahnhofplatz 2; ☻ 10am-6pm Mon-Fri, 10am-1pm Sat) has details, as well as information on the 11-day **Michaelis-Kirchweih**, a huge street carnival with rides, food and merriment, held in late September.

SIGHTS

A room for celebrating the Feast of Tabernacles and a ritual mikvah bath in the basement are highlights of the **Jewish Museum of Franconia** (☎ 770 577; Königstrasse 89; adult/concession €3/1.50; ☻ 10am-8pm Tue, 10am-5pm Wed-Sun).

Housed in the former headquarters of the Grundig electronics corporation, the **Rundfunkmuseum** (Radio Broadcasting Museum; ☎ 756 8110; Kurgartenstrasse 37; adult/concession €3/2; ☻ noon-5pm Tue-Fri, 10am-5pm Sat & Sun) takes you on a journey through 80 years of German radio and TV history. The 12 exhibit rooms chronicle events and milestones, from the first radio broadcast in Berlin in 1923 to the use of propaganda radio in WWII to the latest digital technology. Take U-Bahn U1 to Stadtgrenze, from where it's a 200m walk.

SLEEPING & EATING

Gustavstrasse is home to several good restaurants and cafés, particularly near the quaint square, Waagplatz.

Schwarzes Kreuz (☎ 740 910; www.schwarzes-kreuz -fuerth.de; Königstrasse 81; s €58-80, d €80-110; ℗ 🗶) Housed in a gracious 1620 building, this is the only privately owned and run hotel in Fürth to occupy truly atmospheric premises, but the 'Black Cross' doesn't take its elegant surroundings for granted. You can read on the decked 1st-floor terrace (blazing with red geraniums in summer), or in modernised rooms (some with floating floors), and there's a gourmet Franconian restaurant (mains €10 to €28.50) downstairs. Onsite parking is free.

Walhalla (☎ 772 266; Obstmarkt 3; mains €8.70-13.90; ☻ Fri-Wed Sep-Mar, Fri-Sun, Tue & Wed Apr-Aug) With its knick-knacks strewn through the dining room, heavy timber décor and delicious aromas of home cooking, this locals' favourite is like dining in your grandmother's living room, and the welcome is just as warm.

ENTERTAINMENT

Jazz has a strong following in Fürth; for information on venues and gigs, check the local listings magazines (see p226), which also cover Nuremberg; or ask at record shops such as **Da capo** (Karolinenstrasse 36), which has a good jazz section.

GETTING THERE & AWAY

The U1 runs from Nuremberg's Hauptbahnhof to Fürth several times hourly (€1.80, 15 minutes).

If you're driving from Nuremberg, take Fürtherstrasse west, which leads directly there.

Ansbach

☎ 0981 / pop 40,000 / elev 409m

Ansbach still preserves the graceful charm of the margravial residence it was for nearly 500 years, but its web of cobbled squares filled with open-air cafés (in summer, at least) make it a thriving contemporary city with a cosmopolitan flair.

Founded as a Benedictine monastery by St Gumbertus in 748, Ansbach came under the rule of the Hohenzollern clan in 1331, and they made it their residence in 1456. The palace and many of the statuesque town mansions lining the Altstadt's pedestrianised lanes date back to its cultural heyday in the early 18th century.

Ansbach's rococo heritage is celebrated each year in late June during the **Ansbacher Rococo Festival**; and – music to Bach-lovers' ears – it also hosts the biennial **International Bach Week**, held in late July in odd-numbered years. The **Kasper Hauser Festival** contemplates the 19th-century death in Ansbach of Kaspar Hauser, which remains an intriguing, unsolved crime story – see the boxed text, opposite.

ORIENTATION

The train and bus stations are about a 10-minute walk south of the Altstadt, near the southwestern edge of the Hofgarten (Palace Garden). Walking north on Bischof-Meiser-Strasse will take you straight to the Residenz Ansbach; the Altstadt is just west of here.

INFORMATION

Tourist office (☎ 512 43; www.ansbach.de; Johann-Sebastian-Bach-Platz 1; ☯ 9am-5pm Mon-Fri, 10am-1pm Sat May-Oct, 9am-12.30pm & 2-5pm Mon-Fri Nov-Apr)

Next to the Gumbertuskirche; books tickets for Ansbach's festivals.

SIGHTS

Residenz Ansbach

Starting out in the 14th century as a moated castle, the margraves' opulent palace, the **Residenz Ansbach** (☎ 953 8390; Promenade 27; adult/concession/under 18yr €4/3/free; ☯ tours hourly 9am-5pm Tue-Sun Apr-Sep, 10am-3pm daily Oct-Mar) had a Renaissance makeover before getting its baroque looks in the first half of the 18th century, thanks to Italian architect Gabriel de Gabrieli.

THE MYSTERIOUS LIFE & DEATH OF KASPAR HAUSER

Sixteen-year-old Kaspar Hauser first surfaced in dire physical condition – barely able to stand or see in direct sunlight – in the Nuremberg square, Unschlittplatz, on Whit Monday in 1828.

Repeatedly uttering the phrase 'I want to be a rider like my father', he was thought to be retarded and was held in a jail cell for two months, treated like a freak show. A local professor came to his rescue and within months the boy could speak, read and write, and he revealed that his past 12 years had been spent chained within a completely dark coffinlike cave. His 'keeper' had supplied food and water but had beaten him if he made any noise.

In October 1829, an unknown assassin attempted to murder Kaspar Hauser. For his safety, he was removed from the local professor's care and eventually ended up in Ansbach in November 1831. In Ansbach he became close to the town's head judge, Anselm von Feuerbach. It was Feuerbach who first publicly advanced the controversial theory that Kaspar was, in fact, the prince of Baden – who reportedly died at birth – and thus was the rightful heir to the contested Baden throne. Feuerbach may well have been onto something, for he suddenly dropped dead of suspected poisoning.

On 14 December 1833, Kaspar was lured into an Ansbach park with the promise that he would be told who his true parents were. There he was stabbed in the chest; he died three days later from his wounds.

Following more than 3000 books, over 14,000 articles and two feature films about the mystery, in 1996 the German news weekly *Der Spiegel* published the results of a DNA test suggesting that there were too many discrepancies to conclude that Kaspar was related to the House of Baden. That might well have been the end of it, but more twists were yet to come. In 2002, the public TV networks ZDF and Arte called for a second DNA test. Subsequently, hi-tech forensic tests have been carried out on sweat from his hat band, strands of his hair and blood-stained clothing. This battery of tests revealed numerous comparisons with members of the House of Baden. The tests also confirmed that all of the samples were from the same person, *except* the blood staining the underclothes he wore the day he was stabbed, which was found to be from another person (his killer perhaps?).

In September of even-numbered years, theories are debated during Ansbach's **Kaspar Hauser Festival**. Year-round you can visit the excellent **Markgrafenmuseum** (Margravial Museum; ☎ 977 5056; Kaspar-Hauser-Platz 1; adult/concession €2.50/1; ☯ 10am-5pm daily May-Sep, Tue-Sun Oct-Apr), where displays include Hauser's bloodstained undergarments and the letter he carried when he was first found in Nuremberg. Some German skills will be of help in understanding the exhibits.

In Platenstrasse, right in Ansbach's Altstadt, the pair of statues, **Kaspar-Hauser-Denkmal** (1981), shows him both as the scruffy kid he was at his discovery and as the dapper man about town at the end of his life. A **Memorial Stone** marks the spot of the attack in the Hofgarten, just east of the Orangerie. Hauser is buried in Ansbach's **Stadtfriedhof**, about 600m south of the Altstadt via Maximilianstrasse, where his tombstone reads: 'Here lies Kaspar Hauser, an enigma of his time, his birth unknown, his death a mystery'. For now, at least. Stay tuned.

Compulsory tours are in German only (but ask for an English-language pamphlet). Buy your tickets in the net-vaulted **Gothic Hall**, where you can peruse glass-encased porcelain and faïences. Over the next 50 or so minutes, you'll see 27 magnificently furnished rooms, including the **Festsaal** (Banquet Hall), with a ceiling fresco by Carlo Carlone; the **Kachelsaal** (Tile Hall), smothered in 2800 hand-painted tiles; and the dizzying **Spiegelkabinett** (Mirror Cabinet), decked out with precious Meissen porcelain.

East of the palace, across the Promenade, is the sprawling **Hofgarten**, where the architectural focus is the **Orangerie**.

Gumbertuskirche

Behind the altar of the three-towered **Gumbertuskirche** (Church of St Gumbertus; Johann-Sebastian-Bach-Platz), an inauspicious door leads through to the **Schwanenritterkapelle**, a late-Gothic chapel filled with elaborate epitaphs of members of the Order of the Swan. Below here, the **Fürstengruft** holds the sarcophagi of 25 Ansbach margraves. The adjacent Romanesque **crypt** (adult/child & concession €0.50/free; 🕑 10am-noon Sun year-round, plus 3-5pm Fri-Sun Apr-Oct) is the most ancient section of the church.

SLEEPING & EATING

Hotel Schwarzer Bock (☎ 421 240; www.schwarzerbock .com; Pfarrstrasse 31; s €45-65, d €80-100; Ⓟ ✗) A stuffed mountain goat greets you at the entrance to this epicentral, terracotta-coloured rococo mansion. Timber-floored rooms are charmingly old-fashioned, and there's a small fitness room. Kids are welcomed warmly both at the hotel and the creative Franconian restaurant (mains €8.50 to €14.50), which opens to a sunny beer garden.

Hotel Zum Lamm (☎ 969 9900; www.hotel-zum-lamm .de; Endressstrasse 23; s €55-70, d €78-102; Ⓟ ✗) Ask for one of the rustically furnished rooms at this friendly inn, which offers free parking and bike storage as well as cable TV, wi-fi and a traditional Bavarian restaurant (mains €7 to €15) favoured by locals.

Stadtcafé (☎ 7449; Martin-Luther-Platz 15; mains €5.90-11.90; 🕑 8am-11pm Mon-Thu, 8am-1am Fri & Sat, 10am-11pm Sun; ✗ Ⓥ) Some of the rough-around-the-edges charm has been lost at this re-sited Ansbach institution, but it still serves outstanding salads and pastas and remains a focal point for the town's social life. Now installed on the 1st floor (with great views of Martin-Luther-Platz from the pool tables), access is either via a little arcade off Platenstrasse on the western side, or off Uzstrasse on the eastern side. There's a table-filled terrace out the back in summer.

GETTING THERE & AWAY

Frequent trains connect Ansbach with Nuremberg's Hauptbahnhof (€10, 45 minutes). Ansbach is about 50km southwest of Nuremberg, at the juncture of the B13 and the B14, just north of the A6 autobahn.

BAMBERG

☎ 0951 / pop 70,000 / elev 240m

An architectural masterpiece of abundant historic buildings with an almost complete absence of modern eyesores, Bamberg's entire Altstadt is a Unesco World Heritage site. Bisected by rivers and canals, the city is magnificently sited on seven hills. As such it's known as the 'Franconian Rome', but its chic ambience is in some ways reminiscent of Paris' Left Bank. About 8000 students inject liveliness into the streets, pavement cafés, pubs and no fewer than 10 breweries producing the city's famous smoked beer.

History

Bamberg's name derives from the Babenberg dynasty, who built a castle in the 9th century in the spot now occupied by the cathedral. In 1002, Emperor Heinrich II (973–1024) took over the castle, founded a bishopric five years later and thus laid the groundwork for the next 800 years of Bamberg's history as seat of the ruling prince-bishops.

The city reached another heyday in the 18th century under Prince-Bishop Lothar Franz von Schönborn (1655–1729), who hired some of Europe's finest architects, including Balthasar Neumann and brothers Georg and Johann Dientzenhofer, to rid the town of its medieval look in favour of the more elegant and 'contemporary' baroque. Tax relief and other incentives were given to citizens willing to rebuild their homes; poorer folk simply plastered over the half-timbered façades. Many remain intact because Bamberg miraculously emerged from the WWII bombing raids with hardly a scratch.

Orientation

Two waterways traverse Bamberg: the Rhine-Main-Danube-Canal and Regnitz

River, paralleling it further south. The Hauptbahnhof is located about 2km from the central Altstadt. The city bus hub (ZOB) is on Promenadestrasse, just north of Schönleinsplatz.

Information

Citibank (Schönleinsplatz)

Collibri (☎ 208 580; Austrasse 14) The city's best bookshop.

Internet Telecafe (☎ 2975 717; Untere Königstrasse 19; from per hr €1.50; ☺ 9am-10pm Mon-Fri, 10am-10pm Sat, 12.30-10pm Sun) If it's full, you'll find several other internet cafés in the same street.

Klinikum Bamberg (☎ 5030; Burgerstrasse 80) Hospital with 24-hour emergency room.

Post office Altstadt (Promenadestrasse); Ludwigstrasse (Ludwigstrasse 25)

Tourist office (☎ 297 6200; www.bamberg.info; Geyerswörthstrasse 3; ☺ 9.30am-6pm Mon-Fri, 9.30am-2.30pm Sat year-round, plus 9.30am-2.30pm Sun Apr-Dec) Staff sell the Bamberg Card (€8.50), good for 48 hours of admission to most city attractions, use of local buses and an English audioguided tour.

Sights

SCHLOSS GEYERSWÖRTH

Originally the ancestral home of the patrician Geyer family; then Prince-Bishop Ernst von Mengersdorf (r 1583–91) took such a liking to its picturesque river setting that he acquired the grounds and mansion and replaced it with **Schloss Geyerswörth** (Geyerswörthplatz). It's his coat of arms that graces the portal to the inner courtyard. The tower can be climbed for free from 9am to 5pm Monday to Thursday and to 1pm on Friday. Ask for the keys at the adjacent tourist office.

ALTES RATHAUS

The small footbridge Geyerswörthsteg crosses the Regnitz just outside the Schloss. From here, you'll have the best views of the Gothic 1462 **Altes Rathaus** (Old Town Hall; Obere Brücke 1), which perches on a tiny artificial island between two bridges like a ship in dry dock. Look for the cherub's leg sticking out from the fresco on the east side.

For closer views, turning at the end of the Geyerswörthsteg then right again onto Obere Brücke brings you face to façade with the imposing tower, a baroque addition by Balthasar Neumann. It provides access to the precious porcelain and faïences – mostly from Strassbourg and Meissen – housed in the **Sammlung Ludwig Bamberg** (Ludwig Gallery, Bamberg; ☎ 871871; Obere Brücke 1; adult/concession €3.50/2.50; ☺ 9.30am-4.30pm Tue-Sun).

KLEIN VENEDIG

A row of diminutive, half-timbered cottages once inhabited by fishermen and their families comprises Bamberg's **Klein Venedig** (Little Venice), which clasps the Regnitz' east bank between Markusbrücke and Untere Brücke. The little homes balance on poles set right into the water and are fronted by tiny gardens and terraces.

Klein Venedig is well worth a stroll but looks at least as pretty from a distance, especially in summer when red geraniums spill from flower boxes. Good vantage points include the Untere Brücke near the Altes Rathaus, and Am Leinritt (boxed text, below).

BÖTTINGERHAUS & SCHLOSS CONCORDIA

Two of Bamberg's most beautiful baroque mansions are on the left bank in the southern

---

BAMBERG'S BEST STREETS TO WANDER

Bamberg has a lengthy must-see list of spectacular buildings and fascinating museums, but equally as rewarding is just wandering its atmosphere-steeped backstreets.

Karolinestrasse Meander past speciality shops selling small, unique gifts, southeast past antiquarian bookshops and antique shops.

Concordiastrasse With few cars and small, ancient houses, this peaceful spot transports you back to centuries gone by.

Eisgrube At Eisgrube 14 you'll see the round door that inspired ETA Hoffmann's apple-faced character, *Apfelweib* ('Apple Wife'), in his fairy tale *Der Goldene Topf* (The Golden Pot).

Am Leinritt Strolling along the southwestern bank of the Regnitz gives you postcard views of Klein Venedig (Little Venice).

Mühlwörth Following riverside Mühlwörth rewards you with views of Schloss Concordia and the cathedral towers, but if you continue along here, you'll reach the *Hainbad* (city park), a great place for a picnic, sunbathing or even a swim in the river (there are no lifeguards, but plenty of locals take to the water on hot days).

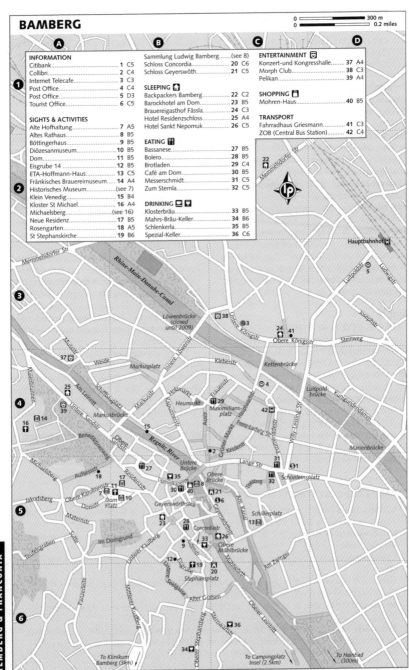

BAMBERG

INFORMATION	Sammlung Ludwig Bamberg......(see 8)	**ENTERTAINMENT**
Citibank............................... **1** C5	Schloss Concordia.................. **20** C6	Konzert-und Kongresshalle....... **37** A4
Collibri............................... **2** C4	Schloss Geyerswöth.............. **21** C5	Morph Club............................ **38** C3
Internet Telecafe................. **3** C3		Pelikan................................. **39** A4
Post Office.......................... **4** C4	**SLEEPING**	
Post Office.......................... **5** D3	Backpackers Bamberg............. **22** C2	**SHOPPING**
Tourist Office...................... **6** C5	Barockhotel am Dom.............. **23** B5	Mohren-Haus......................... **40** B5
	Brauereigasthof Fässla........... **24** C3	
SIGHTS & ACTIVITIES	Hotel Residenzschloss............ **25** A4	**TRANSPORT**
Alte Hofhaltung.................... **7** A5	Hotel Sankt Nepomuk............ **26** C5	Fahrradhaus Griesmann.......... **41** C3
Altes Rathaus....................... **8** B5		ZOB (Central Bus Station)........ **42** C4
Böttingerhaus....................... **9** B5	**EATING**	
Diözesanmuseum................. **10** B5	Bassanese............................. **27** B5	
Dom................................... **11** B5	Bolero.................................. **28** B5	
Eisgrube 14......................... **12** B5	Brotladen............................. **29** C4	
ETA-Hoffmann-Haus............ **13** C5	Café am Dom........................ **30** B5	
Fränkisches Brauereimuseum.. **14** A4	Messerschmidt....................... **31** C5	
Historisches Museum..........(see 7)	Zum Sternla.......................... **32** C5	
Klein Venedig...................... **15** B4		
Kloster St Michael............... **16** A4	**DRINKING**	
Michaelsberg....................(see 16)	Klosterbräu........................... **33** B5	
Neue Residenz..................... **17** B5	Mahrs-Bräu-Keller................. **34** B6	
Rosengarten........................ **18** A5	Schlenkerla........................... **35** B5	
St Stephanskirche................ **19** B6	Spezial-Keller....................... **36** C6	

Altstadt. Both are the former homes of wealthy privy councillor Ignaz Böttinger. The former, the 1713 **Böttingerhaus** (Judenstrasse 14), is a heavily ornamented grand Italian palazzo shoe-horned into narrow Judenstrasse. Its interior is closed to visitors, but it rewards a photo stop from outside.

After Böttinger's family of 14 outgrew the space three years later, he hired Johann Dietzenhofer to build the even grander **Schloss Concordia** (Concordiastrasse 28), a moated palace a short walk south of Böttingerhaus. It's now the home of the Künstlerhaus Villa Concordia, a state-sponsored artists' residence, and is open during events and exhibits – the tourist office can let you know what's on when.

ST STEPHANSKIRCHE

Much of Franconia is Protestant (whereas the rest of Bavaria is predominantly Catholic). Bamberg's main Protestant church, **St Stephanskirche** (Church of St Stephan; St Stephansplatz 4; 9am-5pm) was consecrated in 1020 by Pope Benedikt VIII and turned baroque in the 17th century at the hands of Giovanni Bonalino and Antonio Petrini.

ETA-HOFFMANN-HAUS

The 18th-century writer and composer Ernst Theodor Amadeus (ETA) Hoffmann (1776–1822) is best known for using the fantastical and supernatural to probe the complexity of human experience. Hoffmann came to Bamberg in 1808 as the local theatre's music director, but lost his job after a disastrous first performance. He nevertheless stayed in town until 1813, working as a tutor and writer. His former home, **ETA-Hoffmann-Haus** (Schillerplatz 26; adult/concession €2/1; 4-6pm Tue-Fri, 10am-noon Sat & Sun May-Oct), is now a small museum.

CATHEDRAL QUARTER

West of the Regnitz sprawls the former quarter of the prince-bishops, moored by the humungous hilltop Dom (cathedral) and dotted with various other religious buildings.

Dom

The quartet of spires of Bamberg's **Dom** (Cathedral; Domplatz; 9.30am-6pm Mon-Fri, 9.30-11.30am & 12.45-6pm Sat, 12.30-1.45pm & 2.45-6pm Sun May-Oct, 9.30am-5pm Mon-Sat, 12.30-1.45pm & 2.45-5pm Sun Nov-Apr) soars above the cityscape. Founded by Heinrich II in 1004, its current appearance dates to the early 13th century and is the outcome of a Romanesque-Gothic duel between church architects after the original and its immediate successor burnt down in the 12th century. The pillars have the original light hues of Franconian sandstone thanks to Ludwig I, who eradicated all postmedieval decoration in the early 19th century. From May to October free 30-minute organ concerts take place at noon on Saturday.

The interior contains superb and often intriguing works of art. In the north aisle, you'll spot the **Lächelnde Engel** (Smiling Angel), who smirkingly hands the martyr's crown to the headless St Denis.

In the west choir is the marble tomb of **Pope Clemens II**, the only papal burial place north of the Alps. Of the several altars, the **Bamberger Altar**, carved by Veit Stoss in 1523, is worth closer inspection. Because its central theme is the birth of Christ, it's also called the 'Christmas altar'.

However, the Dom's star attraction is the statue of the chivalric knight-king, the **Bamberger Reiter**. Nobody has a clue as to either the name of the artist or the young king on the steed. The canopy above the statue represents the heavenly Jerusalem, suggesting the mysterious figure may have been revered as a saint.

Diözesanmuseum

A door in the Dom's south aisle leads to the cloister and the former chapter house built by Balthasar Neumann in 1730, which is now home to the **Diözesanmuseum** (Cathedral Treasury; ☎ 502 316; Domplatz 5; adult/concession €3/2.50; 10am-5pm Tue-Sun). There's Gothic sculpture and objects from the Dom's former baroque decoration on the ground floor, but the real treasures await upstairs. Besides a bevy of sculpture and liturgical objects, there's a superb collection of 11th-century textiles, including Heinrich II's famous 'star-spangled' cloak with heavy gold embroidery.

Alte Hofhaltung

The Renaissance-style 1570 **Alte Hofhaltung** (Domplatz) is a former prince-bishops' palace, built on the site of an 11th-century fortress. Its prettiest section is the inner courtyard surrounded by half-timbered, balconied buildings, reached via the **Schöne Pforte** (Beautiful Gate; 1573). In summer, the Calderón Festival takes place in the courtyard.

The gabled Ratsstube (Council Chamber) is home of the **Historisches Museum** (Historical

Museum; ☎ 871 142; adult/concession €3/2; ☐ 9am-5pm Tue-Sun May-Oct), with an eclectic mix of art and historical exhibits.

Neue Residenz

Home to Bamberg's prince-bishops from 1703 until secularisation in 1802, the **Neue Residenz** (New Residence; ☎ 519 390; Domplatz 8; adult/concession €4/3; ☐ 9am-6pm Apr-Sep, 10am-4pm Oct-Mar) has some 40 stuccoed rooms stuffed with furniture and tapestries from the 17th and 18th centuries.

Under the same roof is the **Bayerische Staatsgalerie** (Bavarian State Gallery). Its strengths are in medieval, Renaissance and baroque paintings, with works by Anthony Van Dyck, Hans Baldung Grien and Cranach the Elder.

The Altstadt's sea of red rooftops spread out below the residence's small but exquisite baroque **Rosengarten** (Rose Garden).

Michaelsberg

A steep climb brings you to the top of **Michaelsberg** and the former Benedictine **Kloster St Michael** (1610), now a home for the elderly. The monastery church is a must-see for its baroque art and the meticulous depictions of nearly 600 medicinal plants and flowers on the vaulted ceiling (local legend has it that if you have a backache and crawl through the upright tomb in the middle of the church, you'll be cured forever). Splendid panoramas unfold from the garden terrace.

The ex-monastery's vaulted cellars are an atmospheric backdrop for the **Fränkisches Brauereimuseum** (Franconian Brewery Museum; ☎ 530 16; Michaelsberg 10f; adult/concession €2/1.50; ☐ 1-5pm Wed-Sun Apr-Oct). Exhibits show plaster(ed) dummies of monks, who began making beer here as early as 1122. There's plenty of historical equipment and documentation of the beer-making process.

Tours

Beer lovers can brewery hop and take in the city's sights en route on the **Brewery Trail** (ticket €24). The tourist office kits you out with a 36-page brochure with a map of the breweries, their history and detailed tasting notes for their brews, along with a stylish canvas day pack, vouchers for five half-litres of beer, and a proper ceramic stein.

Two-hour guided **walking tours** (adult/concession €5/3.50; ☐ tours 10.30am & 2pm Mon-Sat Apr-Oct, 2pm Mon-Sat, 11am Sun Nov-Mar) in German depart from the tourist office.

Festivals & Events

Kids will love the **street magician festival** held in Grüner Markt in mid-July.

Highlights of the **Sandkerwa**, held in the Alstadt in late August, include the *Fischerstechen*, a kind of boat jousting, and a big fireworks finale.

On the third weekend in October every year, the Altstadt turns into a **flea and antique market**.

In addition to the **Christmas market** on Maximiliansplatz, another favourite December tradition, especially with children, is following the **Bamberger Krippenweg**, an enchanting route of 34 nativity scenes set up in churches and museums throughout the city.

Sleeping

Campingplatz Insel (☎ 563 20; www.campinginsel.de; Am Campingplatz 1; adult €3, tent €3.50-7; ℗) The camping options are limited to this well-equipped place, which has high-grade bathroom amenities and is located in a riverside spot convenient to public transport. Take bus 18 from ZOB to Campingplatz.

Backpackers Bamberg (☎ 222 1718; www.backpackersbamberg.de; Memmelsdorfer Strasse 21; dm €16-19; ✗) Staying at this gem of a little eight-bed hostel, set within an old half-timbered house, is like having your own little pad in Bamberg. You can cook in the kitchen filled with restored antiques and dine in the cosy common room or on the rooftop terrace, before bedding down in brightly coloured, spotless dorms. It's a five-minute walk to the Hauptbahnhof, and a 10-minute walk to the Altstadt. Definitely book ahead.

Brauereigasthof Fässla (☎ 265 16; www.faessla.de; Obere Königstrasse 19-21; s/d €40/60; ℗) Rooms at this snug guesthouse are a mere staircase up from the pub and covered courtyard. Chairs at the on-site restaurant (mains €7 to €10, closed Sunday) are embossed with Fässla's cute coat of arms – a gnome rolling a giant beer barrel.

Barockhotel am Dom (☎ 540 31; www.barokhotel.de, in German; Vorderer Bach 4; s €62-67, d €89-93; ✗) In the Cathedral Quarter, this gracious place embodies Bamberg's baroque heritage. Peaceful rooms include TV and direct-dial phones, and there's a lift. Enjoy breakfast in the grand 14th-century cross-vaulted Gothic room.

Hotel Sankt Nepomuk (☎ 984 20; www.hotel-nepomuk.de; Obere Mühlbrücke 9; s €85, d €115-130; ℗) This is a classy yet family-friendly establishment in an A-frame-shaped former mill right on the Regnitz. It has a superb gourmet restaurant (mains €15 to €30), fully equipped rustic rooms and you can hire bicycles here.

Hotel Residenzschloss (☎ 609 10; www.residenzschloss.com; Untere Sandstrasse 32; s €134-154, d €169-189; P X ⬚) Opposite the concert hall, Bamberg's top hotel in a historic former hospital caters for deep-pocketed travellers but its rooms are truly palatial. Facilities include a Roman-style steam bath and whirlpool. (It's owned by Warsteiner, Germany's largest brewery, hence the piano bar's beverage of choice.)

Eating & Drinking

Local specialities include the *Fränkischer Sauerbraten* (beef, first marinated, then braised) and the *Bamberger Zwiebel* (stuffed onions cooked in beer sauce). The *Bamberger Hörnla*, usually just referred to as a *Bamberger*, is an ultrabuttery version of a croissant.

Bamberg's 10 breweries, together with another 81 in the region, collectively produce over 200 varieties, including *Rauchbier*, a dark-red ale infused with the smoke of smouldering beech wood, giving it a smooth bacony flavour (it tastes infinitely better than it sounds; vegetarians can rest assured there's no meat involved).

RESTAURANTS

Bolero (☎ 509 0290; Judenstrasse 7-9; tapas from €2.80, mains €7-20; ⓨ from 5pm) About 30 different tapas are the mainstay of this sprawling bodega. Rustic wooden tables and candlelight transport you straight to southern Spain, as does the beer garden's brio.

Zum Sternla (☎ 287 50; Lange Strasse 46; mains €6.90-11.50) Bamberg's oldest *Wirtshaus* (inn), Zum Sternla was established in 1380 and the camaraderie among its patrons has seemingly changed little in the intervening years. Bargain-priced staples include pork dishes, steaks, dumplings and sauerkraut, as well as specials, but it's a great, nontouristy place for traditional *Brotzeit* (snack), or just a pretzel and a beer.

Messerschmidtt (☎ 297 800; Lange Strasse 41; mains €12-29) In the birth house of plane engineer Willy Messerschmidtt, who also founded his first company here in 1923, is this stylish gourmet regional restaurant. It oozes old-world tradition with its dark wood, white-linen table settings and formal service. Above

the ornately moulded exterior is a charming alfresco terrace overlooking a pretty park. The attached wine tavern has a looser atmosphere, but the same prices.

BREWERIES

Bamberg's breweries are not just for drinking; they all serve food (mains cost €4 to €13).

Spezial-Keller (☎ 548 87; Sternwartstrasse; ⓨ Tue-Sun) Spezial-Keller's smoky *Rauchbier* (smoky ale) is superb. Coupled with great views of the Dom and the Altstadt from the city's best beer garden, this place is well worth at least one visit. Every year in November, crowds gather here to ring in *Bockbier* (malty beer) season.

Schlenkerla (☎ 560 60; Dominikanerstrasse 6; ⓨ Wed-Mon) Decked out with lamps fashioned from antlers, this 16th-century restaurant at the foot of the Dom is famous for its tasty Franconian specialities and its *Rauchbier*, served directly from the oak barrel.

Mahrs-Bräu-Keller (☎ 534 86; Oberer Stephansberg 36; ⓨ Tue-Sun) Wash down the house speciality – pizza cooked over beechwood in an outdoor stone oven – with Pilsner at this Art Deco cellar.

Klosterbräu (☎ 522 65; Obere Mühlbrücke 3; ⓨ Thu-Tue) This beautiful half-timbered brewery is Bamberg's oldest, with a young, fun crowd and friendly staff.

CAFÉS

Café am Dom (☎ 519 290; Ringleingasse 2; snacks €1.50-2.50; ⓨ 7am-6.30pm Mon-Wed, Fri & Sat, 1-6pm Sun) The best cakes in town are made and served at this appealing café, which also has a handful of guest rooms (doubles €80), and delicious pralines stamped with the insignia of the Bamberger Reiter.

Bassanese (☎ 509 568; Karolinestrasse 2; snacks €4-8; ⓨ to 7pm) Right in front of the Rathaus on the bridge, enjoy authentic Italian *gelato*, strudels and handmade chocolates in wicker chairs on the cobblestones while taking in the views.

QUICK EATS & SELF-CATERING

The daily local **produce market** (Grüner Markt) is a good place to stock up. On Saturday, head to the organic **Bauernmarkt** (farmers market; Promenade).

The owner of **Brotladen** (☎ 474 47; Fleischstrasse 3) drives to village bakeries all over the region early each morning to amass over 50 different types of bread.

Entertainment

The free magazines *Franky, Treff* and *Fränkische Nacht* (in German) are usually found in pubs, and list the latest in spots and events.

Pelikan (☎ 603 410; Untere Sandstrasse 45) Up there with the best, Pelikan is a candlelit place with occasional live music and a Thai-oriented menu (€3.50 to €14). In summer, head for the convivial beer garden in the inner courtyard.

Morph Club (☎ 423 0208; Siechenstrasse 7; ⏰ 11am-4pm) R&B, techno, rap and disco all get a workout at this high-octane nightclub.

Classical music lovers should try to catch a concert by the famous Bamberger Symphoniker orchestra, which usually plays in the modern **Konzert-und Kongresshalle** (☎ 964 7100; Mussstrasse 1), on the Regnitz north of the Altstadt.

Shopping

Owner-run shops and one-off fashion boutiques are dotted throughout the Altstadt, such as **Mohren-Haus** (Obere Brücke 14), a 13th-century former pharmacy that's now a fragrant tea shop selling loose-leaf teas. Also in and around the Altstadt are some 30 antique shops.

Getting There & Away

There are at least hourly Regional Express and RegionalBahn trains to and from Nuremberg (€9.40, RE/RB 45/60 minutes) and Würzburg (€14.20, one hour), as well as ICE trains every two hours from Munich (€44, three hours) and Berlin (€63, 4¼ hours). Bamberg is just south of A70 (Schweinfurt–Kulmbach–Bayreuth) and at the start of the A73 to Nuremberg.

Getting Around

Walking is the best option in town, but you can also hire bicycles at **Fahrradhaus Griesmann** (☎ 229 67; Obere Königstrasse 42; per day €7.50-9.50). The tourist office stocks bicycle-path maps of the vicinity.

Cars are a hassle in the city centre, so you're better off parking on the outskirts and walking or taking a bus (per trip €1.10). Several buses, including 1, 2 and 14, connect the train station with the **ZOB** (Promenadestrasse). Bus 10 goes from the ZOB to the Domplatz. Call ☎ 150 15 for a taxi.

AROUND BAMBERG

Blanketed by beech and oak forest, the rural area to the west and south of Bamberg is known as the **Steigerwald**. Much of it is a nature park, and prime hiking and cycling territory, but there are also a couple of cultural highlights: the horseshoe-shaped summer residence of Prince-Bishop Lothar Franz von Schönborn, **Schloss Weissenstein** (☎ 09548-981 80; Schlossplatz 1, Pommersfelden; admission & 30/60min tour €3/5, park entry €0.50; ⏰ 10am-5pm Apr-Oct), which is still owned by the current count of Schönborn; and an 18th-century former monastery-turned-prison, **Kloster Ebrach** (☎ 09553-266; adult/concession €2.50/1.25; ⏰ 10.30am & 2.30pm Apr-Oct), with guided tours usually led by prison guards, and an attached monastery church dating from 1134.

The Steigerwald is not well served by public transport. If you're not motorised, bicycles are your best bet for getting around.

FRÄNKISCHE SCHWEIZ

Refreshingly off the beaten track, the naturpark Fränkische Schweiz (Franconian Switzerland) – a triangular rural region wedged in between Bayreuth, Nuremberg and Bamberg – is named for its enchanting landscape rather than any geopolitical relationship with its namesake. Narrow valleys carved by sprightly streams and otherworldly rock formations contain more than a thousand mysterious caves, making the area an outdoor-lover's paradise.

Canoeing and kayaking (from May to September), hiking, biking and caving all give you a deeper appreciation of this area, which is also extremely popular year-round with rock climbers, who have more than 5000 routes to grapple with. Outdoors specialists **Aktivreisen** (☎ 09196-998 566; www.aktiv-reisen.com; Forchheimer Strasse 14, Muggendorf; ⏰ 8am-5.30pm daily May-Sep, 9am-4pm Mon-Fri or by appointment Oct-Apr) organise all these activities and more – contact them directly for prices, programmes and transport to and from your accommodation on request.

The Fränkische Schweiz is also a beer-lover's paradise. Over 70 breweries, mostly small, family-run operations, are sprinkled throughout the area. They include **Krug** (☎ 09202-535; www.krug-braeu.de, in German; Breitenlesau; snacks from €2.90; ⏰ 8am-midnight Tue-Sun) and **Brauerei Schroll** (☎ 09204-248; Nankendorf; snacks €2.60-4.40, warm dishes Sat & Sun €6-8; ⏰ 10am-10pm Wed-Mon). If that wasn't impressive enough, the pint-sized Fränkische Schweiz village of **Aufsess** (population 1500, elevation 414m) holds the world record for the greatest number of breweries per capita (four; one for about every 375 residents), as well as the record for the world's smallest brewery, **Kathi Bräu** (☎ 09198-277; Hechenhof 1), where locals have their own mugs behind the bar. Aufsess' four breweries are linked by a **beer hiking trail**, taking you on a 14km loop through gently undulating countryside. Set off from **Brauerei Reichold** (☎ 09204-271; www.reichold.de, in German; Hochstahl 24; s/d €35/56), where the restaurant (meals from €10, open Wednesday to Sunday) uses generations-old recipes for dishes such as fantastic fresh chicken schnitzel. The owners will give you a trail map, a survival certificate if you make it all the way around, and, if you're keen, directions to another six breweries that can be added as part of a wider trail.

The B470 is the main route through the Fränkische Schweiz, but public transport is limited – check www.bahn.de for bus connections and schedules. Your own wheels, however, give you the freedom to unearth countless medieval castles perched on craggy hilltops and storybook-pretty villages of half-timbered gingerbread houses. Among them, standouts include the picture-perfect village of **Pottenstein** (population 5500, elevation 368m), home to glittering caves and caverns; **Gössweinstein** (population 1500, elevation 500m), crowned by a colossal, honey-coloured basilica designed by Balthasar Neumann; and **Buttenheim** (population 3417, elevation 273m), the birthplace of Löb (Levi) Strauss. His childhood home houses the faded-blue-shuttered **Levi-Strauss Museum** (☎ 09545-442 602; Marktstrasse 33; adult/child €2.60/1.30; 1-6pm Tue & Thu, 11am-3pm

Sat & Sun Mar-Oct, 2-5pm Tue & Thu, 11am-3pm Sat & Sun Nov-Feb), giving you a surprisingly uncommercial overview of the life of the jeans creator and the production of his 'waist overalls'. Buttenheim also has its own train station, with direct trains to and from Nuremberg (€7.90, 50 minutes) and Bamberg (€2.90, 12 minutes).

The best base for exploring this invigorating area is the independent hostel **Factory 41** (☎ 09204-918 905; www.factory41.de; Hauptstrasse 41, Plankenfels; dm incl linen & breakfast €19, s/d €30/50; P). It occupies a fabulously renovated former ceramics factory, with industrial stainless-steel fittings, a whiz-bang island kitchen and orange-toned common room warmed by a wood fire. Dorms and private rooms are state of the art. Mountain bikes can be rented for €10 per day, and the owners are a fount of info on experiencing both the area's great outdoors and great beer.

Less than five minutes' walk from Factory 41 is the earthy traditional restaurant, **Goldenes Lamm** (☎ 09204-257; Hauptstrasse 9; mains €6-8; Wed-Mon), dishing up enormous portions of Franconian cuisine.

A central **information office** (☎ 09194-797 779; www.fraenkische-schweiz.com; Oberes Tor 1, Ebermannstadt; 8am-4.30pm Mon-Thu, 8am-noon Fri) can provide information on the Fränkische Schweiz region.

BAYREUTH
☎ 0921 / pop 73,000 / elev 345m

Quiet for most of the year, the elegant, cobbled streets of Bayreuth (*by*-roit) teem each summer with musicians, singers and opera pilgrims.

FRANCONIANS' TOP FIVE BEER-DRINKING TIPS

Chances are you'll be sampling at least some of Franconia's superb brews, so it helps to know the local etiquette. The following tips from well-practised Franconian beer drinkers will help you get started.

Cheers (Part I) It's customary to clink glasses, accompanied by a heartfelt *prost!* (cheers!) or *zum wohl!* (to your health!) each time someone at the table gets a fresh beer, even if it's out of synch with yours.

Cheers (Part II) You've probably already heard, but it's worth repeating that it's essential to look each person in the eye while clinking, or risk seven years of bad sex. Franconians take this *very* seriously and will be perturbed if you don't do it. (Well, seven years is a long time…)

Cheers (Part III) After clinking (the bottom of the glass or bottle, not the top), bang your beer on the table before taking a sip.

Refills If you're drinking from traditional opaque steins, staff can't tell when you're finished; lay your mug sideways on the table so they know to bring you another.

Last Drinks At traditional Franconian guesthouses and breweries, while your drinking companions are still finishing their beers, ask for an equalising *Schnitt* – a half-serve of tap beer for half-price (you'll almost always end up being given more).

Bayreuth's glory days arrived in 1735 when Wilhelmine, sister of King Frederick the Great of Prussia, married Margrave Friedrich. Wilhelmine invited Europe's leading artists, poets, composers and architects to court. As a result, the city became home to some superb rococo and baroque architecture.

Richard Wagner arrived on the scene in 1872, and his presence attracted philosopher Friedrich Nietzsche as well as composers Franz Liszt and Anton Bruckner. In 1876 Wagner founded his eponymous opera festival, and he and Bayreuth have been as intimately linked as Tristan and Isolde ever since.

Orientation

The Hauptbahnhof is five to 10 minutes' walk north of the historic, cobbled centre. Head south on Bahnhofstrasse to Luitpoldplatz and on to the pedestrianised Maximilianstrasse, the main drag, also known as Markt. The central bus station (ZOB) is one block north of Markt at the junction of Schulstrasse, Kanalstrasse and Hohenzollernring. Several key sights are outside the town centre, including the Eremitage (6km east) and the Festspielhaus (1.5km north).

Information

Tourist office (☎ 885 88; www.bayreuth.de; Luitpoldplatz 9; ☯ 9am-6pm Mon-Fri, 9.30am-1pm Sat year-round, plus 10am-2pm Sun May-Oct) Staff sell the three-day Bayreuth Card (€11.50), which covers unlimited trips on city buses, entry to several museums and a guided city walking tour (opposite).

Sights
TOWN CENTRE

The stunning baroque Markgräfliches Opernhaus (Margravial Opera House; ☎ 759 6922; Opernstrasse 14; adult/concession/under 18yr €5/4/free; ☯ 9am-6pm Apr-Sep, 10am-4pm Oct-Mar, closed rehearsal & performance days) initially attracted Wagner to Bayreuth. Designed between 1744 and 1748 by Giuseppe Galli Bibiena and his son Carlo, it remained Germany's largest opera house until 1871. Yet Wagner deemed the place too quaint for his 'serious' work, and conducted here just once. In May or June the house hosts a festival of opera and ballet, the Fränkische Festwoche.

South of here is Wilhelmine's Neues Schloss (New Palace; ☎ 759 690; Ludwigstrasse 21; adult/concession/under 18yr €4/free/3; ☯ 9am-6pm Apr-Sep, 10am-4pm Oct-Mar), the margravial residence after 1753. On the ground floor is a collection of porcelain made in Bayreuth in the 18th century. Behind the palace sprawls the vast, leafy Hofgarten (admission free; ☯ 24hr).

To learn more about the man behind the myth, visit Haus Wahnfried, the composer's former home on the northern edge of Hofgarten, which now contains the Richard Wagner Museum (☎ 757 2816; Richard-Wagner-Strasse 48; adult/concession Sep-Jun €4/2, Jul-Aug €4.50/3; ☯ 9am-5pm Fri-Mon & Wed, 9am-8pm Tue & Thu Apr-Oct, 10am-5pm daily Nov-Mar). Wagner built the mansion with cash provided by King Ludwig II. Inside is an undynamic, if comprehensive, chronological exhibit about Wagner's life, with glass cases crammed with documents, photographs, clothing, coins, porcelain and personal effects. Unless you're a Wagner fan or at least a German speaker, it's hard to fully appreciate this museum. The composer is buried in the garden, as is his wife, Cosima, and their dog, Russ.

The composer and virtuoso Franz Liszt (1811–86) was one of the seminal figures of classical music in 19th-century Europe, and was also the father of Cosima, Wagner's wife. Within earshot of Haus Wahnfried is the house where he died, now the Franz-Liszt-Museum (☎ 516 6488; Wahnfriedstrasse 9; adult/concession €1.60/0.50; ☯ 10am-noon & 2-5pm Sep-Jun, 10am-5pm Jul & Aug). On view are a sparkling grand piano, his death mask, correspondence and portraits.

OUTSIDE THE TOWN CENTRE

North of the Hauptbahnhof, the Festspielhaus (☎ 787 80; Festspielhügel 1-2; adult/concession €5/4), built in 1872, was also constructed with Ludwig II's backing. The acoustics of the place are truly amazing as its builders took the body density of a packed house into account. Access varies depending on rehearsals and concerts; check with the tourist office or the Festspielhaus for tour times. To get here, take bus 5 to Am Festspielhaus.

About 6km east of the centre is the Eremitage, a lush park surrounding the Altes Schloss (☎ 759 6937; Eremitage; adult/concession/under 18yr €3/2/free; ☯ 9am-6pm Apr-Sep, 10am-4pm early–mid Oct, closed mid-Oct–Mar), Friedrich and Wilhelmine's summer residence. Also here is the Eremitage's Neues Schloss (not to be confused with the Schloss of the same name in town), which is anchored by a mosaic Sun Temple topped by a gilded Apollo sculpture. Gracing the Neues Schloss are the grottoes, where the fountains start gushing on the hour between 10am and 5pm from May to mid-October (10 minutes later in the Lower Grotto). The Orangerie's winter-garden café makes a peaceful spot for a break. Take bus 2 or 3 from Markt (about 20 minutes).

A one-hour guided tour (in German) plumbs the sweet-smelling depths of **Maisel's Brauerei-und-Büttnerei-Museum** (☎ 401 234; Kulmbacher Strasse 40; tours adult/concession €4/2; ⏰ tours 2pm Mon-Sat), northwest of the town centre. Beer was brewed at this 2400-sq-m, 19th-century plant until the 1970s (the plant is now housed in modern premises next door), and today the *Guinness Book of World Records* lists it as the world's most comprehensive beer museum, covering all aspects of the brewing process including barrel making, old advertising posters and over 4500 beer mugs. Tours wrap up with a foaming glass of *Weissbier* (wheat beer).

Germany's first garden-design museum sprawls around the magnificent rococo palace, **Schloss Fantaisie** (☎ 7314 0011; Bamberger Strasse 3; adult/concession €3/2.50; ⏰ 9am-6pm Tue-Sun Apr-Sep, 10am-4pm Tue-Sun early–mid Oct, closed mid-Oct–Mar), about 5km west of Bayreuth.

Tours

Guided **city walking tours** (adult/student €5.50/3) depart from the tourist office at 10.30am daily from May to October, and 10.30am on Saturday from November to April.

Festivals & Events

The **Richard Wagner Festival** (www.festspiele.de, in German) runs for 30 days from late July to August, with each performance attended by an audience of 1900. Ticket demand is insane – the waiting time is around nine years! Applying for tickets is a highly complicated business – your best bet is to contact Bayreuth's tourist office for advice, including possibilities for scoring last-minute tickets.

Ticketholders face another endurance test. The opening notes of some operas ring out in the afternoon so people can get home by midnight. Adding to that, the seats are hard wood, ventilation is poor and there's no air-conditioning. But hang in there: on blisteringly hot days, water is sprayed on the roof during the interval!

Sleeping

Accommodation is as rare as hen's teeth during the Richard Wagner Festival (during which time prices often jump); book *way* ahead.

Gasthof Hirsch (☎ 267 14; ap.kambach@t-online.de; St Georgen Strasse 6; dm/d €22/44) This charming guesthouse is the best budget option in Bayreuth, with delightfully furnished rooms in doubles or a three-bed dorm with its own piano. Bathrooms are shared, but there are hot- and cold-water basins in all rooms, home-made apple-and-mint, cinnamon or Calvados jam at breakfast, and parking out the front. Rates drop by €2 per person for stays of more than three days.

Hotel Goldener Hirsch (☎ 230 46; goldener.hirsch@bayreuth-online.de; Bahnhofstrasse 13; s €59-75, d €79-85; P ✗ ▣) The black-and-white photos in the foyer of this very friendly, forest-green hotel tell the story of the building's history dating back to 1753. Public areas have a 1970s flair, but rooms are spacious, and some have bathtubs. It's well positioned close to the train station; parking's free.

Hotel Goldener Anker (☎ 650 51; www.anker-bayreuth.de; Opernstrasse 6; s €68-128, d €98-218; P ✗) Service is impeccable at this refined hotel; it's been owned by the same family since the 16th century, but now incorporates mod cons, including wi-fi. It's just a few steps from the opera house in the pedestrian area, but there's vehicle access to the hotel's on-site parking (€12 per day).

The surrounding countryside shelters some grand sleeping options, such as the former hunting lodge **Jagdschloss Thiergarten** (www.schlosshotel-thiergarten.de), 6km southeast of Bayreuth; the tourist office has a list.

Eating & Drinking

Hansl's Wood Oven Pizzeria (☎ 543 44; Friedrichstrasse 15; small/large pizzas from €3.10/4.60; V) Bayreuth's best pizza is found at this little hole in the wall. Choose your own ingredients from the check-list menu, and top your pizza off with the free spiced chilli olive oil. In summer, long outdoor tables ease the squeezed-to-capacity crowd inside.

Kraftraum (☎ 800 2515; Sophienstrasse 16; mains €4.20-7.90, weekend brunch €11; ⏰ 8am-1am; V) This vegetarian restaurant has plenty to tempt the most committed carnivores, including jacket potatoes, soups and huge salads (including a 'hobbit salad'). Brunch – a smorgasbord of muesli, stewed apple, pancakes, antipasto platters, salmon, cheese and loads more, served on Saturday and Sunday – has a devoted local following.

Oskar (☎ 516 0553; Maximilianstrasse 33; mains €7.60-13.60; ⏰ 11.30am-2pm & 6-11.30pm) In the old town hall (later a police station), this flowing Bavarian beer hall–style place bustles from morning to night. Sit in the busy bar, a cosy, hops-decorated room, or the winter garden. Dumplings, the house speciality, dominate the menu. Of course, you can just head here for a beer.

Engin's Ponte (☎ 8710-503; Opernstrasse 24-26; mains €9.70-11.90; ☺ 8am-late; **V**) German-Italian fusion fare is dished up in the semi-industrial surrounds of this stylish new place with contemporary art on the walls and a great canal-side location. Great rum cocktails, too.

Miamiam Glouglou (☎ 656 66; Von-Römer-Strasse 28; mains €10.60-20.20) Bypass the brightly lit modern room with big-screen TVs and head for the candlelit rustic room for classic French bistro cuisine, such as grilled steak with Roquefort cheese, chicken in mustard sauce, and crêpes.

Other recommended drinking spots:

Odeon Café (☎ 150 1010; Alexanderstrasse 7; ☺ 6pm-late) L-shaped place with a dark-timbered bar and hardcover cocktail list some 60 pages long.

Underground (☎ 633 47; Von-Römer-Strasse 15) Decked out with London tube logos and pictures of the Queen, yes, this bar-café has a gay clientele, though the crowd's usually as mixed as the cocktails.

Movida (☎ 162 7658; Himmelkronstrasse 1; ☺ 10am-late Mon-Sat, 2pm-late Sun) Ultrahip new hang-out 2.5km northwest of the city centre within a spaceshiplike former

---

DETOUR: 'LITTLE BERLIN'

Imagine you live in a quiet village of around 55 residents – a close-knit existence where you're surrounded by friends and family. Then imagine that a 2m-high fence is erected overnight out the front of your house, cutting you off from them and the western half of your village. Armed soldiers brutally threaten you when you try to wave to them, but this soon becomes impossible anyway: the fence is rapidly followed by a 700m-long concrete wall, then by splinter mines along another metal latticed fence, wired to a 24-hour command centre. Your family has to wait an average of six weeks for permission for what was once a two-minute walk to visit you; you're not allowed to visit their side of the village at all.

For the villagers of Mödlareuth (aka Little Berlin), including brothers still living only 20m from each other, this was their fate for 24 years beginning in 1966.

How the little village's division came about is an accident of geography. After WWI, new state boundaries meant one half of the village now belonged to the state of Thuringia and the other to the state of Bavaria, but both were part of a united Germany and village life continued harmoniously. Hitler's downfall, however, saw the Thuringian half of the village become East German territory behind the 'Iron Curtain'. Suddenly, as happened in Berlin, families and neighbours a few streets apart were effectively on opposite sides of the world – a reality that was especially stark here given Mödlareuth's tiny size.

On 10 November 1989, a Trabi (East German two-stroke Trabant car) spotted on the western side of Mödlareuth was the villagers' first-hand confirmation of the wall's historic fall in Berlin the day before – though the mine-ridden 'death strip' dividing the village meant people had to travel to the checkpoint 60km away just to cross the street. It was another month before the first pedestrian access reopened, and it wasn't until the wall was razed on 17 June 1990 that residents were once more able to drive through their village.

Today, the **Deutsch-Deutsches Museum** (German-German Museum; ☎ 09295-1334; Mödlareuth 13; adult/concession €2/1 incl film; ☺ 9am-6pm Tue-Sun Mar-Oct, 9am-5pm Tue-Sun Nov-Feb, by arrangement Mon year-round) has preserved sections of the wall and presents rotating exhibits, such as escape craft and personal possessions salvaged from ill-fated attempts to cross the border. Yet despite the village's traumatic history, the museum showcases the triumph of human spirit. During Mödlareuth's division and its aftermath, the museum's local founder, the filmmaker and photographer Arndt Schaffner, recorded and curated footage, photographs, personal accounts and possessions. His poignant film (screened at the museum in English, German and French) traces the history of the village, whose teensy population before, during and after its division has remained static.

Mödlareuth is 66km northwest of Bayreuth. Driving from Bayreuth, follow the A9 north for 46km, then the A72 east for 9.5km. Take the Hof/Töpen exit and follow the signs to Töpen (3km). In the centre of Töpen, turn right onto Mödlareutherstrasse and follow it for another 3km. When you see the helicopter and the tank, you're there.

furniture store, with cool grooves, tented booths, a cigar bar, and a slick menu of 'fashion salads' and sushi.

Getting There & Around

Bayreuth is a stop on the ICE train line from Dresden to Nuremberg. Regional trains to Nuremberg also depart hourly (€14.20, one hour). Getting to Bamberg requires a change in Lichtenfels (€18.20, 1½ hours). There are two exits to Bayreuth off the A9, which bring you to the eastern side of town.

AROUND BAYREUTH
Kulmbach
☎ 09221 / pop 30,000 / elev 306m

Home to four large and several smaller breweries, Kulmbach is a mecca for beer lovers, particularly for its *Eisbock* (iced beer). Frost transforms the alcohol into a kind of molasses, making it one of the strongest beers in the world. *Eisbock* is available only from November to March, but if you're here in late July or early August, you'll find plenty of beer flowing during the rollicking beer festival, **Kulmbacher Bierfest**.

Kulmbach's **tourist office** (☎ 958 80; www.kulmbach.de, in German; Sutte 2; 🕑 9am-5.30pm Mon, Tue & Thu, 9am-4pm Wed, 9am-5pm Fri, plus 10am-noon Sat Mar-Oct) has free walking-tour maps in English.

For an overview of the local brewing history, stop by the **Bayerisches Brauereimuseum** (Bavarian Brewery Museum; ☎ 805 14; Hofer Strasse 20; adult/concession €4.50/4; 🕑 10am-5pm Tue-Fri, 9am-5pm Sat & Sun Apr-Oct, 10am-5pm Tue-Sun Nov-Mar).

Behind the foreboding bastions of the exquisite medieval fortress, the **Plassenburg** (☎ 947 505; adult/concession €4/3; 🕑 9am-6pm Apr-Oct, 10am-4pm Nov-Mar), is the arcaded Renaissance Schöner Hof (Beautiful Courtyard), also the setting for summer concerts. Inside, the fortress contains several museums, the highlight being the **Deutsche Zinnfigurenmuseum** (German Tin Figurine Museum). With 300,000 of the objects it's the world's largest of its kind, including about 170 dioramas re-creating historical or mythological scenes. A **shuttle bus** (adult/child return €2.20/1) travels here every half-hour.

Drivers should take the B85 to Kulmbach, 30km northwest of Bayreuth From Bayreuth, a few regional trains make direct trips (€6.40, 40 minutes).

Kronach & the Frankenwald
☎ 09261 / pop 20,000 / elev 307m

Medieval Kronach, embraced by a fortified wall and crowned by a fortress, is the gateway to the **Naturpark Frankenwald**. This dense forest of deep valleys carved by rivers and creeks is not only ideal terrain for hiking and other outdoor pursuits, it also supplies as many as a million Christmas trees for German homes each year.

Information on both the town and the Frankenwald is available at Kronach's **tourist office** (☎ 972 36; www.kronach.de; Marktplatz 5; 🕑 10am-5pm Mon-Fri, 10am-2pm Sat May-Sep, 10am-4pm Mon-Fri Oct-Apr).

Start your explorations in the old town centre, here called the *Obere Stadt* (upper town). Navigate the narrow alleys lined with half-timbered houses, eventually coming to the Gothic **Pfarrkirche St Johannes** for a look at its north portal topped with an emotive stone sculpture of St John the Baptist (1498). Then head up to the never-conquered **Festung Rosenberg** (☎ 604 10; adult/concession incl entrance to Fränkische Galerie €3.50/2; 🕑 9.30am-5.30pm Tue-Sun Mar-Oct, 10am-4pm Tue-Sun Nov-Feb), one of the largest fortresses in Germany. It's accessed by an early-baroque gate built in 1662 by Antonio Petrini. Entry incorporates a tour (in German), the highlight of which is descending to the maze of dungeons.

Entry prices to the complex increase slightly when there's a feature exhibition at the onsite **Fränkische Galerie** (☎ 604 10; adult/concession €2.50/1, incl Festung Rosenberg €3.50/2; 🕑 9.30am-5.30pm Mar-Oct, 10am-4pm Nov-Feb), where you can admire sculpture and altar paintings by Franconian artists working between the 13th and the 16th centuries, including works by Tilmann Riemenschneider and the Dürer disciple Hans von Kulmbach.

Kronach is about 45km northwest of Bayreuth (22km north of Kulmbach) and 33km east of Coburg. Regional trains to and from Bayreuth require a change in Hochstadt (€12.40, 1¾ hours); to and from Coburg, you must change in Lichtenfels (€7.90, one hour). Take the B85 if you're driving.

COBURG
☎ 09561 / pop 41,700 / elev 297m

Lorded over by Veste Coburg, one of Germany's finest medieval fortresses, Coburg has a blue-blooded pedigree. In 1857, Albert of Saxe-Coburg-Gotha took vows with his first cousin Queen Victoria, thereby founding the present British royal family (who quietly adopted the name of Windsor during WWI). Today, a statue of Prince Albert anchors Coburg's grand main square, Markt.

Flanking the square is the ornate **Stadthaus** (Town House), a Renaissance edifice with a trio of stepped gables, red trim and a pretty oriel; and the baroque, blue-and-gold-trimmed **Rathaus**.

Stately and refined for most of the year, Coburg explodes during the three-day **Samba Festival** in mid-July, which draws around 80 bands, 3000 dancers and up to 250,000 revellers.

Information

Tourist office (☎ 741 80; www.coburg-tourist.de; Herrngasse 4; ⏰ 9am-6.30pm Mon-Fri, 9am-1pm Sat Apr-Oct, 9am-5pm Mon-Fri, 9am-1pm Sat Nov-Mar) Just off Markt. Staff have info about a single ticket to seven museums in the area plus three days' bus travel and a guided city tour in German for €9.50.

Sights

VESTE COBURG

Enthroned above town in a triple ring of fortified walls, the **Veste Coburg** is a storybook medieval fortress that safeguards the **Kunst Sammlungen** (Gallery; ☎ 8790; adult/child €3.30/1.80; ⏰ 9.30am-5pm Tue-Sun Apr-Oct, 1-4pm Tue-Sun Nov-Mar). Besides works by such star painters as Rembrandt, Dürer and Cranach the Elder, its vast collection also encompasses 350,000 copper etchings and some fancifully decorated sledges and carriages. As you enter the gallery building, look out for the original Napoleonic copper cannon, inscribed with the signature 'N'.

In 1530, Protestant reformer Martin Luther, under imperial ban, sought refuge at the fortress for about half a year; his former quarters are also a highlight. Audioguides cost €1.50, as do entertaining kids' audioguides (German only).

The **Veste-Express** (one way/return €2/3; ⏰ Apr-Oct), a tourist train, makes the trip to the fortress every 30 minutes. Bus 8 goes uphill year-round from Herrngasse near the Markt (€1.25 each way). Alternatively the walk up the steepish path takes about 30 minutes.

SCHLOSS EHRENBURG

In 1547, Coburg's dukes moved into a new residence, right in town, the **Schloss Ehrenburg** (☎ 767 57; Schlossplatz; tours adult/concession/under 18yr €4/3/free, incl Schloss Rosenau €6/5/free; ⏰ 9am-5pm Tue-Sun Apr-Sep, 10am-3pm Tue-Sun Oct-Mar). Albert spent his childhood here and Queen Victoria stayed in a room with Germany's first flushing toi-

let (1860). The most splendid room is the **Riesensaal** (Hall of Giants), where the baroque ceiling is supported by 28 statues of Atlas. Tours are in German only.

COBURGER PUPPENMUSEUM

Spanning 33 rooms, the delightfully old-fashioned **Coburger Puppenmuseum** (Coburg Doll Museum; ☎ 741 80; Rückerstrasse 2/3; adult/child €2/1.50; ⏰ 10am-4pm Tue-Sun Apr-Oct, noon-4pm Tue-Sun Nov-Mar) brings together literally thousands of dolls and dolls' houses dating from 1800 to 1956.

Sleeping & Eating

The 30cm-long Coburg sausage is a local speciality; pick one up from the rolling kitchens on the Markt (€1.50).

Romantik Hotel Goldene Traube (☎ 8760; www.goldenetraube.com; Am Viktoriabrunnen 2; s €85-110, d €118-159; **P**) Owner Bernd Glauben is the president of the German Sommelier's union, and you can taste and buy over 400 different wines in this charming hotel's little wine bar. The wines can also be tasted at the hotel's casual restaurant, Weinstübla (mains €6.50 to €11.50, open 5pm to midnight Monday to Friday), draped with (artificial) vines, and its truly sublime gourmet restaurant, Meer & Mehr (mains €22.50 to €24.50, menus €34 to €62, closed Sunday lunch). Both restaurants are open to nonguests. Many rooms are a vision of pink and rose, while others are splashed with bright Mediterranean yellows and oranges. It's right in the Altstadt; garaged parking costs €6 but open-air, off-street parking is free.

München Hofbräu (☎ 234 923; Kleine Johannisgasse 8; mains €5.10-20) Friendly staff at this traditional timber-lined restaurant will guide you through a menu specialising in curry-spiced sausages and infinite pork dishes. There's a play area for kids with books, pencils, toys and games.

Goldenes Kreuz (☎ 513 407; Herrngasse 1; mains €9.80-18.90) Candles, hidden alcoves and stained-glass windows make this newly opened restaurant-bar a romantic spot for Franconian fare.

Some other recommendations for drinking and dining include the following.

Ratskeller (☎ 924 00; Markt 1; mains €7-20) Elegant setting with padded red-leather seating within Coburg's spectacular town hall, serving good regional dishes from Thuringia and Franconia.

Café Prinz Albert (☎ 945 20; Ketschengasse 27; dishes €2.50-5; ⏰ to 6.30pm) Great for coffee and cake or the Prince Albert breakfast – a crosscultural marriage of sausages, eggs and Bamberger croissants.

Getting There & Away

Direct trains travel from Bamberg (€9.60, 45 minutes) and Nuremberg (€18.70, 1¾ hours) every other hour. There are also regular services between Coburg, Bayreuth and Kronach; trips to Kulmbach require a change in Lichtenfels.

Coburg is on the A73.

AROUND COBURG
Rödental

☎ 09563 / pop 14,000 / elev 306m

The village of Rödental, about 6km northeast of Coburg, is known for its palace, and as the home of the Goebel factory, makers of the world-famous Hummel ceramic figurines.

Schloss Rosenau (☎ 308 413; Rosenau 1; adult/concession/under 18yr €4/3/free, incl Schloss Ehrenhof €6/5/free; ✆ 9am-5pm Apr-Sep, 10am-3pm Oct-Mar) is the birthplace of Prince Albert (1819) and a favourite palace of his wife Queen Victoria. It's medieval at its core, but Albert's father, Ernst I, had it revamped in neo-Gothic style. A highlight is the ornate Marmorsaal (Marble Hall) on the ground floor. The Orangerie in the romantic English garden contains the renowned **Museum für Moderne Glas** (Museum of Modern Glass; ☎ 1606; admission €1; ✆ 10am-1pm & 1.30-5pm Tue-Sun Apr-Oct, 1-4pm Tue-Sun Nov-Mar); a stunning new extension to the museum should be open by the time you're reading this.

The Goebel family has been manufacturing porcelain figurines since 1871, including the Hummelfiguren: cutesy statuettes with names such as 'Apple Tree Boy' or 'Goose Girl' that grace the cabinets of millions of collectors worldwide. Each design was created by a nun named Maria Innocentia, who trained at the Munich Academy of Fine Arts. Local production is decreasing (in 1995 the factory had 1000 workers; today it has 200), so it's best to call ahead to confirm opening hours for the company-run **Information Centre** (☎ 09503-923 03; Coburger Strasse 7; admission free) to get an overview of the art of porcelain-making, observe artists at work and peruse collector's items.

Bus 8312 make several trips a day from Coburg's *Bahnhof* to Rödental. It stops at the Goebel factory, from where it's a 700m walk to the Schloss. Drivers should head for Neustädter Strasse and follow the signs.

Basilika Vierzehnheiligen

The ornate, gilded 18th-century pilgrimage church **Basilika Vierzehnheiligen** (☎ 09571-950 80; Vierzehnheiligen 2; admission by donation; ✆ 6.30am-7pm Apr-Oct, 7.30am-dusk Nov-Mar) stands in the spot where, in 1445, a young shepherd reported having recurring visions of the infant Jesus flanked by the 14 Nothelfer (Holy Helpers). The shepherd reported the 'little ones' asking for a chapel to be built here so that they might have a place from which to work their miracles. Lo and behold, miracles did happen and the chapel was consecrated in 1448. When in 1741 the original church was close to collapse, the local abbot commissioned Balthasar Neumann to build a new one. Inside, attention focuses on the amazing freestanding altar, supposedly placed right on the spot of the initial apparition. The work of stucco artists Johann Michael and Franz Xaver Feichtmayr of Wessobrunn, it's studded with statues of the 14 saints with one of the infant Jesus balancing up on top.

Around the back, grab a table in the sprawling beer garden of the **Alte Klosterbrauerei** (☎ 09571-3488; ✆ 10am-8pm) for a half-litre of the bracing *Nothelfertrunk* beer. Stay long enough and you may glimpse the nun in habit who lugs in cases for refilling.

Regional trains connect Coburg with the station at Lichtenfels (€4.80, 22 minutes), from where taxis wait to bring you to Vierzehnheiligen (about €5). Vierzehnheiligen is near Staffelstein and Lichtenfels, just off the B173, about 25km south of Coburg.

NATURPARK ALTMÜHLTAL

A kaleidoscope of juniper-strewn hillsides in summer, blazing with red, yellow and brown leaves in autumn, and blanketed in snow in the winter months, the Naturpark Altmühltal (Altmühl Valley Nature Park) straddles the border between Franconia and Upper Bavaria. Meandering through its little valleys is the Altmühl River, a gentle stream that morphs into the mighty Rhein-Main-Donau-Kanal (Rhine-Main-Danube-Canal) near Beilngries, before emptying into the Danube at Kelheim. It's a region largely undiscovered by international travellers, who make up only 5% of all tourists here. The earliest 'visitors' were the Romans; their empire's northern boundary, the Limes, ran right through today's park – see the boxed text, p246.

The town of Eichstätt is the park's main gateway for excursions. Razed by the Swedes during the Thirty Years' War (1618–48), it was rebuilt by Italian architects, notably

Gabriel de Gabrieli, who imbued it with a Mediterranean flair.

Well-marked hiking and cycling trails traverse the park, but the most peaceful way to explore is canoeing along its willow-fringed waterways.

Orientation

The park sprawls over 2900 sq km west of Regensburg, south of the A6 autobahn, east of Gunzenhausen and north of Ingolstadt. The A9 runs right through it north–south.

Eichstätt is somewhat south of the park's centre and home to the central information centre. Other larger towns include Gunzenhausen, Treuchtlingen, Weissenburg and Pappenheim west of Eichstätt, and Beilngries, Riedenburg and Kelheim to Eichstätt's east.

Information

Staff at the excellent **Informationszentrum Naturpark Altmühltal** (Altmühltal Nature Park Information Centre; ☎ 08421-987 60; www.naturpark-altmuehltal.de, in German; Notre Dame 1, Eichstätt; ☺ 9am-5pm Mon-Sat, 10am-5pm Sun Easter-Oct, 9am-noon & 2-4pm Mon-Thu, 10am-noon Fri Nov-Easter) can put together an entire itinerary for free and send you (for face value) maps and charts of the area and information on bike, boat and car hire. The information centre is housed in an ex-monastery, and hosts contemporary art exhibitions in the stunningly frescoed former church. Upstairs are exhibits about the park's wildlife and habitats, while out the back, its garden's plants and ponds recreate the park's landscapes.

Information is also available from local tourist offices in towns throughout the park.

Sights
EICHSTÄTT

Back in 908 BC, Eichstätt's town bishops first got the rights to build fortifications, hold markets and mint their own coins. The town continues to be shaped by Catholicism, and is home to Germany's only Catholic university.

An enormous stained-glass window by Hans Holbein the Elder graces Eichstätt's central **Dom**. Its Pappenheimer Altar (1489–97), carved from sandstone, depicts a pilgrimage from Pappenheim to Jerusalem. Look out for the seated statue of St Willibald, the town's first bishop.

Behind the Dom is the baroque **Residenz** (Residenzplatz; admission €1; ☺ tours 11am & 3pm Mon-Thu,

11am Fri, 10.15am, 11am, 11.45am, 2pm, 2.45pm & 3.30pm Sat & Sun Apr-Oct), built between 1725 and 1736. It's a Gabrieli building and former prince-bishops' palace with a stunning main staircase and a hall of mirrors. In the square is a golden statue of the Madonna atop a 19m-high column.

The **Markt**, a baroque square north of the Dom, is the heart of the partly pedestrianised Altstadt. About 300m northwest of here, on Westenstrasse, is the **Kloster St Walburg**, the burial site of Willibald's sister, Walburga. Every year between mid-October and late February, water oozes from Walburga's relics and drips down into a catchment. The nuns bottle diluted versions of this *Walburgisöl* (Walburga oil) and give it away to the faithful. Climb the stairs to the upper chapel, adorned with pilgrims' handmade thank yous – some very recent – to the saint.

Looming over the town centre is the hilltop castle of **Willibaldsburg** (1355–1725), home to the **Jura-Museum** (Jurassic Museum; ☎ 08421-4730; Burgstrasse 19; adult/concession/under 16yr both museums €4/3/free; ☺ 9am-6pm Tue-Sun Apr-Sep, 10am-4pm Tue-Sun Nov-Mar), which is great even if fossils usually don't quicken your pulse. Highlights are a locally found archaeopteryx and aquariums with living specimens of the same animal species that were fossilised eons ago. Also here is the **Museum of Pre-History & Early History**, where the 6000-year-old mammoth skeleton has to be seen to be believed.

Near the castle's car park, the **Bastionsgarten** (admission free; ☺ 9am-6pm Apr-Sep), a garden built onto the ramparts, is probably better known as the 'Garden at Eichstätt' (there's a hefty coffee-table book of the same name, with copper plates of the original plantings). The garden was first established by the scientifically minded and status-craving Prince-Bishop Johann Konrad von Gemmingen in the early 17th century and featured rare-for-the-times specimens, such as tulips.

Looking across the valley, you'll see the **limestone quarry** (adult/concession €2/1, chisel & hammer hire per day €1.50; ☺ 9.30am-6pm), where you can dig for fossils (kids will especially love it). Drive up or take a bus from Domplatz (return €2, 10 minutes). Buses run Monday to Friday only and times are irregular – check with the tourist office. Otherwise, a 4km hiking trail leads from the town centre, which is part of a 9km loop trail.

Eichstätt's local **tourist office** (☎ 08421-600 1400; www.eichstaett.info, in German; Domplatz 8; ☺ 9am-

6pm Mon-Sat, 10am-1pm Sun Apr-Oct, 10am-noon & 2-4pm Mon-Thu, 10am-noon Fri Nov-Mar), next to the Dom, runs 1½-hour **walking tours** in German (€3) from April to October at 1.30pm Saturday (also Monday and Wednesday at 1.30pm in July and August), as well as evening walks at 8.30pm from May to mid-September and 7.30pm from mid-September to October.

RIEDENBURG

Riedenburg is the main town along the canalised stretch of the Altmühl. It's known as the 'Three-Castle-Town', but two of the three, Tachenstein and Rabenstein, are all but ruins. Only **Burg Rosenburg** (☎ 09442-2752; adult/under 15yr €6/3; 🕙 9am-5pm Tue-Sun Mar-Oct, falconry shows 11am & 3pm Tue-Sun) still presides over the town. Originally it was the dream castle of a medieval minstrel who also happened to be a falconer. Today, a falconer continues the tradition with a flock of not only falcons, but also eagles, vultures and other birds of prey. Admission covers entry to the castle museum and birds of prey exhibits as well as scheduled falconry shows.

BURG PRUNN

Framed by woodland, the turrets and towers of **Burg Prunn** (☎ 09442-3323; adult/concession/under 16yr €4/2/free; 🕙 9am-6pm Tue-Sun Apr-Oct, 10am-4pm Tue-Sun Nov-Mar) stand sentinel on a rocky bluff above the canal. This quintessential medieval castle is a magnificent sight from below, perhaps even more impressive than from close-up. In 1569, Wiguläus Hundt, a local researcher, happened upon a hand-written copy of the medieval *Nibelungen* song, which became known as the 'Prunner Codex' and is now in the Bavarian State Library in Munich. The epic inspired Wagner's *Nibelungen* opera cycle.

Activities

The Informationszentrum Naturpark Altmühltal has a full list of hire outlets for boats and bikes.

CANOEING & KAYAKING

The slow-moving Altmühl wends for about 150km, with lots of little dams along the way, as well as a couple of fun pseudo rapids about 10km northwest of Dollnstein. (Signs near the rapids warn of impending doom, but locals say that if you heed the warning to stay to the right, you'll be pretty safe.)

The main boating season is from May to September, at which time it's a good idea

to book boats and accommodation in advance. During hot summers, the water level in the Altmühl can sometimes sink too low for navigation, so check in advance with the tourist office. Always pack sunblock and insect repellent.

Several companies offer (unguided) packages, including the boat, transfer back to the embarkation point and, for overnight tours, luggage transfer and lodging. The two main outfitters are **San-Aktiv Tours** (☎ 09831-4936; www.san-aktiv-tours.com; Bühringer Strasse 11, Gunzenhausen) and **Natour** (☎ 09141-922929; www.natour.de, in German; Gänswirtshaus 12, Weissenburg). You can also hire one- and two-person canoes from numerous companies all along the river. Single-person kayaks start at about €15, while canoes for two or three people start at around €30. For an additional fee, staff will haul you and the boats to or from your embarkation point (sample fees include Eichstätt–Solnhofen €25 for the first boat, then €3 for each additional boat). Besides San-Aktiv Tours and Natour, other companies include **Franken-Boot** (☎ 09142-4645; www.frankenboot.de; Treuchtlingen), **Lemming Tours** (☎ 09145-235; www.lemmingtours.de; Solnhofen) and **Bootsverleih Otto Rehm** (☎ 08422-987654; www.rehm-r.de; Dollnstein). Or try **Fahrradgarage** (☎ 08421-2110; www.fahrradgarage.de, in German; Herzoggasse 3, Eichstätt), run by friendly, English-speaking Frank Warmuth.

CYCLING

With around 800km of trails – most of them away from traffic – the Altmühltal is ideal for leisurely cycling. Advance room reservations are a good idea from June to August, especially on weekends, when trails can get crowded.

The 166km-long **Altmühltal Radweg**, from Gunzenhausen to Kelheim, largely parallels the Altmühl. Lose the crowds by venturing into the serene side valleys. The park's newest cycling trail is the **Limes-Radweg** (p246).

Fahrradgarage (above) hires out bicycles for €8 per day. Staff will bring the bikes to you or transport you and the bikes to anywhere in the park for an additional fee.

Most hire companies will also store bicycles; Fahrradgarage charges €0.60/€2 per hour/day.

HIKING

Spring and autumn are the best times for hiking along the park's 3000km of way-marked trails, including over a dozen long-distance routes. The most scenic is the **Altmühltal-Panoramaweg**

THE LIMES

One of the most recent additions to Bavaria's bevy of Unesco-listed sites is its portion of **the Limes** – the Romans' northern overland boundary. (The continuation of the boundary, the Danube, is referred to in German as the *Nasse Limes* – the Wet Limes.)

The Limes (*lee*-mas) is not an in-your-face World Heritage site like Bamberg's ensemble of baroque buildings. Instead, these Roman remains can be hard to spot: the Informationszentrum Naturpark Altmühltal sells topographical maps marking the more prominent ruins, but most still take a bit of unearthing.

In the Naturpark Altmühltal's mid-east, the township of Kipfenberg has a significant section of the Roman wall, as well as a rebuilt watchtower. A new museum, the **Römer und Bajuwaren Museum** (Roman & Ancient Bavarian Museum; Burg Kipfenberg; adult/child/family €3/1.50/7; ⏰ 10am-4pm Apr-May & Sep-Oct, 10am-6pm Jun-Aug, 10am-4pm Sat & Sun Nov-Mar), has been set up here with archaeological exhibits. Interpretive signs are in German, but it's still a lot of fun for non-German speakers, especially kids, as you get to try on Roman helmets and clothes. Any adult actually arriving here dressed in Roman clothing (togas et al) gets in for half-price.

You can follow in the Romans' footsteps on the 120km-long **Limesweg** (Limes hiking trail), from Gunzenhausen to Bad Gögging, which is marked with yellow-and-green signs. Cyclists can set out on the **Limes-Radweg** (Limes cycling trail), which shadows the Limes for 97km through the park. Contact the park office or local tourist offices, including the Kipfenberg **tourist office** (☎ 08465-941 040; www.kipfenberg.de, in German; Marktplatz 2; ⏰ 9am-noon & 2-6pm Mon-Thu, 9am-noon & 4-6pm Fri & Sat May-Sep, 9am-noon Mon-Fri Oct-Apr), for details.

---

from Gunzenhausen to Kelheim, which traverses 200 elevated kilometres that take in some spectacular views. The main trail's markers are yellow, while its numerous loop trails are marked in blue. Also slicing through the park is the new (old) long-distance walking trail, the Limesweg (see above).

ROCK CLIMBING

The Jurassic limestone mountains in the Altmühltal have long exerted their challenge on rock hounds. You'll find rocks suitable for climbing around Dollnstein, throughout the park, with degrees of difficulty ranging from III to X (XI being the toughest).

Sport IN (☎ 0841-472 23; Jesuitenstrasse 17, Ingolstadt) offers a set programme of rock-climbing excursions and can create customised tours.

Tours

Between April and October, several companies run boat trips along the Rhine-Main-Danube-Canal from Kelheim to Riedenburg (around two hours one way), with stops in Essing and Prunn; try **Personenschiffahrt** (☎ 09441-5858; www.schiffahrt-kelheim.de, in German; one way/return to Riedenburg €7/11.90). Some boats continue on to Beilngries and Berching (about another two hours), where you can catch a shuttle bus (operated by the boat companies) back to Kelheim. Note that boats leave from the Altmühl landing docks in Kelheim, not the Danube landing docks.

You can also start your journey in Berching or Beilngries, but there are far fewer departures. Check schedules with the **Beilngries tourist office** (☎ 08641-8435; www.beilngries.de, in German; Hauptstrasse 14; ⏰ 9am-noon & 2-7pm Mon-Fri, 9am-noon & 3-7pm Sat, 10am-noon Sun May–mid-Oct, 9am-noon & 2-4pm Mon-Thu, 9am-noon Fri mid-Oct–Apr).

For tours from Kelheim through the Danube Gorge and to Kloster Weltenburg, see p203.

Sleeping & Eating

Hotels, *Pensionen*, guesthouses and hostels abound in villages and towns throughout the park. Staff at the Informationszentrum Naturpark Altmühltal can help you find accommodation park-wide, although they don't reserve rooms.

EICHSTÄTT

Camping Daum (☎ 908 147; near Pickheimer Brücke; per campsite €7; **P**) This all-seasons campsite is on the northern bank of the Altmühl River, about 1km east of the town centre. It's closed around late August or early September during the 10-day oompah-pah-ing Volksfest (Eichstätt's 'Oktoberfest'), which takes place right next door. Motorised campervans are permitted, but towed caravans aren't.

Kloster St Walburg (☎ 988 70; www.bistum-eichsta ett.de/abtei-st-walburg, in German; Marienhaus; s/d €34/56; P ⊠) Airy, contemporary rooms inside this functioning abbey feature framed paper-cuts and other artworks by the nuns (who are also the receptionists), and some attic rooms have views of Eichstätt's crumbling town walls. Breakfast by candlelight is served in a vaulted cellar, and there's a communal TV lounge (instead of in-room TVs), as well as a self-catering kitchen.

Fuchs (☎ 08421-6789; Ostenstrasse 8; s €38-45, d €68-76; P ⊠) Above a luscious confectionery and cake shop (cakes from €2), this spick-and-span place has welcome underfloor heating in the bathrooms on frosty mornings, while in summer you can breakfast in the sunny courtyard before launching your boat on the nearby ramp (the hotel also offers boat storage).

Gasthof Sonne (☎ 08421-6791; www.sonne-eichs taett.de, in German; Buchtal 17; s €39-45, d €58-70; P ⊠) Most of Sonne's generously sized, warmly carpeted rooms open onto slatted wooden balconies. The friendly owners also cook up regional fare at the respected onsite restaurant (meals €10 to €15).

Wirtshaus Zum Gutmann (☎ 904 716; Am Graben 36; mains €5-12; ☼ 6pm-late Tue-Sun) Rock, folk and other genres regularly take to the stage at this atmospheric inn, which serves a great selection of salads, curry sausages, schnitzel and dumplings with spinach and cheese. Be sure to try the famous Titting wheat beer.

Café im Paradeis (☎ 08421-3313; Markt 9; mains €10.50-19.80) Recharge with a nourishing home-made meal – or just a delicious 'chococcino' (creamy chocolate cappuccino) – surrounded by antiques in the cosy back room or outside on the trendy terrace.

A clutch of cafés and park benches cluster around the Herzogsteg, the little footbridge crossing the river in town. Pick up sausages of every conceivable sort at **Metzgerei Schneider** (☎ 909 80; Marktplatz 14). **Markets** (Marktplatz) take place on Wednesday and Saturday mornings.

ELSEWHERE IN NATURPARK ALTMÜHLTAL
Camping is allowed only in designated areas along the river for €3 per tent; individual travellers don't need reservations. Large groups should reserve at the park information office.

Gasthof Stirzer (☎ 08464-8658; www.stirzer.de; Haupstrasse 45, Dietfurt; s €24, d €54-60; P) Prices are disproportionately cheap at this converted farm/brewery (restaurant mains €8 to €15) in the park's northeast because although each of the 20 guestrooms in the 500-year-old building has its own bathroom, it's not always on the same floor as your room. Envirofriendly renovations include hypoallergenic materials, and the organic menu features nettle soup as well as lamb as part of the park's push to reintroduce sheep to maintain the naturally grazed landscape.

Gasthof Xaver Bösl (☎ 08423-247; www.boesl-titting .de; Marktstrasse 25, Titting; s/d €30/58; P) It's not fancy, but this small tangerine-coloured guesthouse in the park's mid-north has a sauna and lovely terrace. The charming owner makes sausages that he sells in his own *Metzgerei* (butchery) and serves at the onsite restaurant (mains €6 to €10).

Hotel Die Gams (☎ 08461-6100; www.hotel-gams .de, in German; Hauptstrasse 16, Beilngries; s €54-84, d €78-98) This is a classy place with flowing rooms, some of which have whirlpool spas in bathrooms big enough to be guestrooms themselves. The restaurant (mains €7.80 to €19.80) turns out impressive German and international cuisine.

Schloss Arnsberg (☎ 08465-3154; www.schloss-arns berg.de; Kipfenberg-Arnsberg; s/d €55/88; P) Six kilometres from Kipfenberg, this historic castle's perch atop a sheer rockface gives it birds-eye valley views. Rooms are regally proportioned, and the restaurant (mains €9.80 to €15.60) has top-notch regional cuisine.

Getting There & Away
There's a train service hourly or better between Ingolstadt and Eichstätt (€4.80, 20 minutes). Nuremberg–Munich trains also stop in the park at Kinding, from where bus 9232 travels to Eichstätt (45 minutes).

Bus 9226 takes about 1½ hours from Beilngries to Ingolstadt.

Getting Around
BUS
The FreizeitBus Altmühltal–Donautal operates from mid-April to October; buses are equipped to transport bicycles. All-day tickets cost €9.50 for passengers with bicycles, €6.50 for passengers without, or €21.50 per family with bikes, €16 without.

Route FzB1 runs from Regensburg to Kelheim and then to Riedenburg on weekends and holidays only. Route FzB2 travels between Treuchtlingen, Eichstätt, Beilngries,

Dietfurt and Riedenburg with all-day service on weekends and holidays and restricted service on weekdays. Bus 9232 connects Beilngries with Eichstätt several times daily and takes 45 minutes.

TRAIN
Eichstätt has two train stations. Mainline trains stop at the *Bahnhof*, 5km from the town centre, from where connecting diesel trains shuttle to the Stadtbahnhof (town train station; located near the town centre). Be sure you get the correct train when departing from the *Bahnhof*, as there are no departure boards and trains are labelled with both directions. Ask someone before you board, or you could end up visiting more of the park than you bargained for.

Trains run between Eichstätt *Bahnhof* and Treuchtlingen hourly or more (€4.80, 25 minutes); there are also regular services between and Treuchtlingen and Gunzenhausen. RE trains from Munich that travel through Eichstätt *Bahnhof* also stop in Dollnstein, Solnhofen and Pappenheim. Some require a change in Ingolstadt.

INGOLSTADT
☎ 0841 / pop 122,422 / elev 374m
Strolling through Ingolstadt's medieval centre, where wagons rattled over cobblestone, it's easy to forget its surrounding modern industry, including the oil refineries that power the sleek autos manufactured here at Audi's headquarters. Instead, the Altstadt makes a suitably atmospheric setting for the chilling monster in *Frankenstein,* who was born here (in the author's imagination, at least), but its streets are also crammed with contemporary museums and lively cafés.

Situated in Upper Bavaria (so yes, its residents aren't Franconian, but Bavarian), Ingolstadt is an ideal gateway to the Naturpark Altmühltal, which unfurls to the north.

Orientation
The Hauptbahnhof is 2.5km southeast of the Altstadt; buses 10, 11, 15 and 16 make the trip every few minutes. The Danube flows south of the Altstadt, while the Audi factory is about 2km north of the city centre.

Information
Das @ Café (Sauerstrasse 2; per hr €1.75; ⏰ 10am-8pm Mon-Sat) Internet café just off Rathausplatz.
Dresdner Bank (Rathausplatz 3)
Post office Altstadt (Am Stein 8; ⏰ 8.30am-6pm Mon-Fri, 9am-1pm Sat); Hauptbahnhof (⏰ 8.30am-6pm Mon-Fri, 9am-12.30pm Sat)
Tourist office (www.ingolstadt-tourismus.de; ⏰ 8am-5.30pm Mon-Fri, 9.30am-2pm Sat & Sun Apr-Oct, 9am-5pm Mon-Fri, 10am-2pm Sat Nov-Mar); Altstadt (☎ 305 3030; Rathausplatz 2); Hauptbahnhof (☎ 305 3005; Elisabethstrasse 3),

---

FRANKENSTEIN'S BABY

Mary Shelley's *Frankenstein*, published in 1818, set a creepy precedent for monster fantasies. Contrary to popular misconception, the novel's eponymous character is not the monster but the young scientist, Viktor Frankenstein, who travels to Ingolstadt to study medicine. Frankenstein becomes obsessed with the idea of creating a human being, shopping for parts at the local cemetery. His resulting creature then sets out to destroy its maker.

Shelley chose Ingolstadt because it was home to a prominent university and medical faculty, where professors and their students carried out experiments on corpses and dead tissue. Today their lab houses the ghoulish **Deutsches Medizinhistorisches Museum** (German Museum of Medical History; ☎ 305 1860; Anatomiestrasse 18/20; adult/under 16yr €3/free; ⏰ 10am-noon & 2-5pm Tue-Sun). The museum's ground floor eases you in with birthing chairs, enema syringes and lancets for blood-letting. Upstairs things get closer to the bone with displays of human skeletons, preserved musculature and organs, foetuses of conjoined twins, a pregnant uterus and a cyclops. Pack a strong stomach for the visit.

If you're still game, you can follow a character dressed as the good doctor on **Dr Frankenstein's Murder & Mystery Tour** (☎ 9519 9961; www.frankenstein.in, in German; 70min tour €8; ⏰ 9.30pm May-Jul, 9pm Aug-Oct, dates vary). The walking tours (accommodating up to 10 people only) are in German; due to the spooky twists and turns – such as various other characters who lurk in hidden passageways and leap out from the shadows – children under 14 aren't allowed. Tickets need to be booked in advance through the tourist office.

INDUSTRIAL ART

Concrete and steel may usually put function over form, but two mould-breaking museums prove they can also be surprisingly expressive contemporary art materials. At the **Museum für Konkrete Kunst** (Museum of Concrete Art; ☎ 305 1871; Tränktorstrasse 6-8; adult/child €3/1.50; ☻ 10am-5pm Tue-Sun) you can take time out from the abstract art and installations in its sculpture garden. The **Lechner Museum** (☎ 305 2250; Esplanade 9; adult/concession/under 16yr €3/1.50/free; ☻ 11am-6pm Thu-Sun) is housed in a light-flooded glass-and-steel former Audi workshop and showcases the sculptures of Alf Lechner and various other artists working with steel.

Both museums are located in Ingolstadt's Altstadt.

Sights

The tourist office has a detailed list of Ingolstadt's varied museums. For anyone with a fascination for horror, the most macabre is the Deutsches Medizinhistorisches Museum (boxed text, opposite).

ASAMKIRCHE MARIA DE VICTORIA

The Altstadt's crown jewel is the **Asamkirche Maria de Victoria** (☎ 175 18; Neubaustrasse 11/2; adult/child €2/1.50; ☻ 9am-noon & 1-5pm Tue-Sun Mar-Oct, 10am-noon & 1-4pm Tue-Sun Nov-Mar), a baroque masterpiece designed by brothers Cosmas Damian and Egid Quirin Asam between 1732 and 1736.

The church's mesmerising trompe l'oeil ceiling, painted in just six weeks in 1735, is the world's largest fresco on a flat surface. Visual illusions abound: stand on the little circle in the diamond tile near the door and look over your left shoulder at the archer with the flaming red turban – wherever you walk, the arrow points right at you. The fresco's Horn of Plenty, Moses' staff and the treasure chest also appear to dramatically alter as you move around the room.

Before leaving, ask the museum staff to let you into the side chamber for a look at the **Lepanto Monstrance**, a gold and silver depiction of the Battle of Lepanto (1571).

BAYERISCHES ARMEE MUSEUM & REDUIT TILLY

Fresh from a trip to wealth-laden France in 1418, Ludwig the Bearded borrowed heavily from Gallic design to create the Neues Schloss – an ostentatious 'new palace' of Gothic net vaulting and individually carved doorways. Today it guards the **Bayerisches Armee Museum** (Bavarian Military Museum; ☎ 937 70; Paradeplatz 4; adult/concession/under 18yr €3.50/3/free; ☻ 8.45am-5pm Tue-Sun). Exhibits include armaments from the 14th century to WWII and a wonderful collection of 17,000 tin soldiers.

Across the river, part two of the museum is housed in the **Reduit Tilly** (adult/concession/under 18yr €3.50/3/free; ☻ 8.45am-5pm Tue-Sun), named for the Thirty Years' War general. Exhibits here pivot around Germany's involvement in WWI.

A combination ticket for both branches of the museum costs €4.50 (€3.50 concession, under 18s free).

AUDI MUSEUM MOBILE & FACTORY

Car nuts won't want to miss the hi-tech **Audi Museum Mobile** (☎ 375 75; Ettinger Strasse 40; adult/under 18yr €2/1, tour €4/2; ☻ 9am-6pm). Three gleaming floors chronicle Audi's history from its humble beginnings in 1899 into the future via some 50 cars and 20 motorbikes, and newfangled prototypes gliding past on an open lift. One-hour tours (in German) depart twice hourly.

To go behind the scenes of the manufacturing process, you can take a two-hour tour of the adjacent **Audi factory** (tour €6; ☻ 9am-2pm Mon-Fri, production days only). English tours take place at 12.30pm; advance bookings are essential.

Audi's snazzy premises make a striking backdrop for **jazz concerts** held here several times a month year-round, with major artists performing additional dates from September to May – contact the museum for dates and bookings.

To get here, take bus 11 or 44.

LIEBFRAUENMÜNSTER

Founded by Duke Ludwig the Bearded in 1425 and built up over the next 100 years, the most distinctive exterior feature of this Gothic hall **church** is the pair of square towers that flank the main entrance. Inside, the soaring ceiling vaults' strands of delicate stonework sensuously intertwine into geometric filigree patterns – somehow the whole thing seems completely organic. Look out for the brilliant stained-glass windows and the high altar (1560) by Hans Mielich.

DETOUR: NEUBURG AN DER DONAU

A picturesque half-day trip from Ingolstadt, **Neuburg an der Donau** (☎ 08431, population 27,951, elevation 400m) hugs the banks of the Danube 22km to the west. Magnificent Renaissance and baroque buildings cluster in its *Obere Stadt* (upper town), atop a little hill through the terracotta **Oberes Tor**, a 16th-century town gate flanked by stocky, cylindrical twin towers.

The *Obere Stadt* is as pretty as a film set, but refreshingly deserted even on weekdays in high summer, and time seems to slide by here in slow-mo. Its set piece is the 'Newcastle', which inspired the town's name. This Italianate **Residenzschloss** was built between 1530 and 1545 by Count Ott-heinrich. In 1665, Elector Philipp Wilhelm added the baroque eastern wing, topped off by the dove-white round towers that give the palace its distinctive silhouette. The palace courtyard is flanked by double arcades, with prized sgraffito (inscribed decorative patterns). Off the courtyard, the airy **Schloss-museum** (Palace Museum; ☎ 8897; Residenzstrasse A2; adult/concession/under 16yr €5/4/free; ☷ 9am-6pm Tue-Sun Apr-Sep, 10am-4pm Tue-Sun Oct-Mar) has well-organised sections on prehistory as well as Neuburg's glory days as a royal residence. Highlights include the Schlosskapelle, Germany's oldest Protestant church (1543), the new Flemish Gallery and the garden's fantastical grottoes studded with white Danube shells, but there's a host of other visual treats in store. The Schloss is wheelchair accessible.

Heading a few steps west of the Schloss on Amalienstrasse brings you to the exquisite **Karlsplatz**, graced by ancient linden trees and meticulously restored historic buildings, including the copper

---

KREUZTOR

The Gothic **Kreuztor** (1385) was one of the four main gates into the city until the 19th century and its red-brick fairy-tale outline is now the emblem of Ingolstadt. This and the main gate within the Neues Schloss are all that remain of the city gates, but the former fortifications, now flats, still encircle the city.

STADTMUSEUM & TOY MUSEUM

Ingolstadt's sprawling **Stadtmuseum** (City Museum; ☎ 305 1885; Auf der Schanz 45; adult/child €3/1.50; ☷ 9am-5pm Tue-Fri, 10am-5pm Sat & Sun) houses oodles of ancient artefacts dating back to the Celts, but the cutest exhibits are found in the on-site **Toy Museum**, with antique and contemporary toys – from an adorable mechanical brown bear on red wheels through to gaming consoles. If you're here on the first or third Sunday of the month, you can also watch two vintage model railways in action from 1.30pm to 4.30pm.

Sleeping

Azur Campingplatz Auwaldsee (☎ 961 1616; www .azur-camping.de/ingolstadt; tent €4.50-6, person €5.50-7, car €6-8, family camping package €28; **P**) About 3km southeast of the city centre, this huge forested campground rents rowing and sailing boats to potter about on the lake here, and also has a shop and restaurant. The infrequent bus 60 goes this way; a taxi from the city centre will cost about €10.

Hotel Anker (☎ 300 05; www.hotel-restaurant-anker .de, in German; Tränktorstrasse 1; s €54, d €84-88) Bright, modern rooms with cable TV and friendly service make this family-run hotel a good-value choice in the Altstadt. The typical German restaurant (meals €5 to €13) attracts a loyal local following.

Hotel Adler (☎ 351 07; www.hotel-adler-ingolstadt .de; Theresienstrasse 22; s €68-72, d €95; **P**) It doesn't get more central than this wonderfully down-to-earth 500-year-old hotel right on Theresienstrasse, where solid timber ceilings in the rooms (some nonsmoking) blend with new carpets and freestanding heavy wooden wardrobes. Eggs are cooked to order at break-fast, wi-fi is available and parking costs just €2 per day.

Hotel Rappensberger (☎ 31 40; www.rappensberger .de; Harderstrasse 3; s €115-125, d €155; **P**) This stylish Altstadt hotel has well-designed modern rooms (including a number of smart 'business' rooms with large desks and free wi-fi) done out in lemon and lime, with all-glass showers, marble vanities and gummi bears on the pillows.

Sophisticated spots outside the town centre:

Hotel Ammerland (☎ 953 450; www.hotel-ammerland .de; Ziegeleistrasse 64; s €69-99, d €75-125; **P** ✗ ▣) Colourfully decorated hotel, about 4km north of the Altstadt, with some themed rooms such as 'Golfing', 'Africa' and 'Matisse', and an amazing in-house bar.

Kult Hotel (☎ 951 00; www.kult-hotel.de, in Ger-man; Theodor-Heussstrasse 25; s €95-185, d €120-220; **P** ✗ ▣) Cube-like designer hotel around 3km northeast of the Altstadt, with clean lines, chrome fixtures and natural fabrics.

cupola of the late-Renaissance **Hofkirche** (1607–8). The church dwarfs the square's comparatively modest **Rathaus** (1609), while the yellow-and-pink **Provinzialbibliothek** houses a historical library and has a wonderful baroque festival hall upstairs, which can only be seen on guided tours (in German); tours cost €1.50 and are usually held at 2.30pm Wednesday, May to October.

After strolling around town, quench your thirst with a glass of hand-picked German wines at **Vivat** (☎ 648 113; Amalienstrasse A61; wine per glass from €3.20, dishes €2.60-5.70; ☻ 2pm-late Tue-Fri, 11am-late Sat & Sun), either on its street-side terrace, or in the cool stone cellars done out with polished stone floors, crimson-, cream- and black-vinyl chairs, and contemporary art. For a full-blown meal, try **Gasthaus Zur Blauen Traube** (☎ 8392; www.zur-blauen-traube.de; Amalienstrasse 49; mains €5-12.90), a Bavarian-as-it-gets inn with fare heavier than its hefty dark-timber furnishings. Neuburg's **tourist office** (☎ 552 41; www.neuburg-donau.de, in German; Ottheinrichplatz A118, Obere Stadt; ☻ 9am-6pm Mon-Fri, 10am-noon & 2-5pm Sat & Sun May-Oct, 9am-noon & 2-4pm Mon-Thu, 9am-noon Fri Nov-Apr) can help if you want to stay.

Regional trains connect Neuburg with Ingolstadt (€3.50, 15 minutes, hourly). The B16 runs right past town and connects with the B13, which leads north to Ingolstadt.

The *Bahnhof* is about 1km south of the *Obere Stadt* and Danube. Bus 3 loops between the station, the *Obere Stadt* and the centre of Neuburg's modern town, Spitalplatz, at 30-minute intervals (€1 per ride).

Eating & Drinking

Pedestrianised Dollstrasse and Theresienstrasse are packed with places to eat and drink. The world's oldest health and safety regulation, Germany's Beer Purity Law of 1516, was issued in Ingolstadt; it's still borne out today by a mug of smooth Herrnbräu, Nordbräu or Ingobräu.

Zum Daniel (☎ 352 72; Roseneckstrasse 1; mains €5.50-12.90; ☻ Tue-Sun) Lined with black-and-white photos, with scrubbed timber floors, Ingolstadt's oldest pub dates back to 1472 and drips with character and tradition. Locals swear by Daniel's pork roast, but all of the Bavarian fare here is first-rate.

Swept Away (☎ 931 1679; Donaustrasse 14; mains €7-15; ☻ 5.30pm-1am Sun-Thu, 7pm-3am Fri & Sat; Ⓥ) A rarity in Bavaria; vegetarians will definitely be swept away by the purely veggie world menu at this quirky bamboo-clad place featuring over 500 cocktails as well as live bands.

Weissbräuhaus (☎ 328 90; Dollstrasse 3; Brotzeit €5-8, mains €9-15.50) Delicious *Weissbräupfändl* (pork filet with sizzling home-made Spätzle noodles dusted with cinnamon) are among the Bavarian favourites at this traditional beer hall. If the weather's behaving, take a seat at blue-and-white checked tables in the split-level fountained garden out the back.

Restaurant Antalya (☎ 330 48; Dollstrasse 6; mains €9-14.20; ☻ 11.30am-3pm & 5pm-1am) If you like your Turkish food served on plates with silverware rather than wrapped in paper, take a seat at the white-clothed tables of this elegant place turning out aromatic dishes like lamb with peppers and rice amid woven wall hangings and Middle Eastern artefacts.

Stock up on fresh produce and baked goods at the lively **markets** (Theaterplatz; ☻ 7am-1pm Wed & Sat).

Some hip cafés:

Café Reitschule (☎ 931 2870; Mauthstrasse 8) Dominated by a huge bar, some incongruous palm trees and a lively young crowd.

Le Café (☎ 322 61; Schrannenstrasse 1; ☻ 7.30am-1am Mon-Wed, 7.30am-2am Thu & Fri, 9am-2am Sat & Sun) Landmark cranberry-coloured café-bar with a good-time vibe day or night.

Getting There & Around

Direct trains connect Ingolstadt with Nuremberg (€27, 30 minutes), Munich (€14.20, one hour) and Regensburg (€12.40, one hour). Ingolstadt has an efficient bus network: single journeys cost €1.80 (free if you have a Bayern Ticket), but better value is a 'guest ticket' (€3.50) for seven days' travel, available from the tourist office. By car, take the Ingolstadt exit off the A9.

Romantic Road

Winding from Würzburg's vineyard-ribboned hills to Füssen at the foot of the Alps, the Romantic Road strings together an enchanting collection of villages, cities and castles. But this fabled road is more than just one long photo opportunity.

The 350km-long road cuts through a cultural and historical cross-section of southern Germany; it traverses Franconia and a wedge of Baden-Württemberg in the north, and Bavarian Swabia and the Allgäu in the south. Along the way, you can get a completely different perspective by scaling medieval towers and town walls. For a greater challenge, there are hiking and cycling versions of the entire Romantic Road route.

Spring brings the area's beer gardens to life and kicks off a jam-packed programme of festivals and concerts that extend throughout the summer. Cooler weather has its own allure: open fires, misty valleys and few, if any, crowds. Sure, visitor numbers pick up during the Christmas markets, but so does the area's *Gemütlichkeit* (cosiness). Lingering at fairy-lit, snow-covered stalls selling nutcrackers, tree ornaments and hand-carved wooden toys, while sipping a steaming mug of gluhwein (mulled wine with sugar and spice), makes December perhaps the most magical time of all to visit.

No matter what time of year you're here, the road proper is only a starting point. Venturing off on spontaneous side trips lets you experience the road's true serendipity (and serendipity, after all, is the essence of every great romance).

HIGHLIGHTS

- Glimpsing Ludwig II's fantasy palace, **Schloss Neuschwanstein** (p283), rise through the mountain mist like a dreamy mirage

- Catching an organ recital in the ethereal basilica dominating the pastoral village of **Ottobeuren** (boxed text, p280)

- Sniffing, sipping and stocking up on superb white wines in and around vibrant **Würzburg** (p258)

- Dining alfresco on freshly caught fish on the harbourside promenade of Lake Constance's charming island, **Lindau** (p286)

- Piecing together Augsburg's still-thriving artistic and industrial traditions at the **Maximilianmuseum** (p273)

Getting Around

In 1950, the Romantic Road became one of Germany's first tourist routes and remains its most popular today. Although billed as a single 'road', it's actually a series of interlinking roads connecting Würzbug and Füssen via 25 key villages, towns and cities, along with an additional handful of castles and churches signposted just off the main route.

Most people travel the Romantic Road from north to south, which is how we've covered it in this book, but it works just as well the other way round.

Trains serve most (but not all) of the route's major stops. There are also local buses year-round for places not reached by train, but these can be tedious, slow and complicated. For convenience and flexibility, the ideal way to explore the Romantic Road in depth is by car. Brown-and-white 'Romantische Strasse' signs are posted along the length of the route. However, if you're driving, take note of road numbers and upcoming towns listed throughout this chapter, as signs are few and far between in some stretches.

With its gentle gradients and ever-changing scenery, the Romantic Road also makes an ideal bike trip, with its own signposted **Romantic Road cycling route**, mainly away from traffic. Tourist offices stock detailed cycling advice, including lists of 'bicycle-friendly' hotels and information about public-storage facilities.

Hikers can tackle the **Romantic Road long distance hiking route**, which leads mostly through meadows, fields and forests, as well as through each township en route. Allow three weeks to hike the full route at a brisk pace, or four if you plan to sightsee along the way.

A good first stop is the info-packed English-language website www.romanticroad .de. See also p22 for a recommended week-long driving itinerary.

TOURS

From April to October the **Deutsche Touring Europabus** (☎ 069-790 3230; www.romanticroadcoach .de), often referred to as the Romantic Road bus, runs one coach daily in each direction between Frankfurt and Munich, passing through most Romantic Road towns and villages along the way. However, check routes and pickup/drop-off points with Deutsche Touring, as changes to the route were in the works at the time of writing, with several towns currently served by the bus mooted to be bypassed.

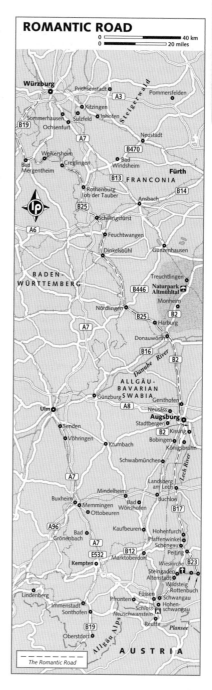

ROMANTIC ROAD

Deutsche Touring Europabuses leave at 8am daily from the Hauptbahnhof in Frankfurt and 8.15am from the Starnberger *Bahnhof* in Munich and take about 13 hours to complete the route nonstop. Breaking your journey as often as you like is allowed, but plan your stops carefully as you'll have to wait a full day for the next bus to come around. You can buy a ticket for the entire distance or for shorter segments between any of the stops, but always reserve ahead as buses often don't stop if there are no disembarkations.

Europabus tickets are available online at the Deutsche Touring website (www.deutsche-touring.de), railway stations and **EurAide** (p76) at the Munich Hauptbahnhof; it's also possible to pay directly on the bus. Tickets for the entire Frankfurt–Munich route one way /return cost €98.80/138.40. Sample segment fares include Würzburg–Rothenburg €13.80/€19.30 and Rothenburg–Füssen €47.50/€64; prices and durations for all segments are posted on the website. Eurail and German Rail pass-holders get a 60% discount; InterRail pass-holders, seniors and children aged four to 12 pay half-price; students and those under 26 years qualify for 10% off (though there are no discounts for Bahn-Card holders).

Bicycle transportation on the Europabus must be reserved at least three days before you're intending to travel by calling ☎ 069-7903 230. The cost is €3 for journeys with one to four stops, and €15 for over 15 stops.

ROMANCE ON THE RAILS

With a bit of planning, you can take a charming train trip along the **Romantic Railway** (☎ 9083-340; www.bayerisches-eisenbahnmuseum.de), an otherwise-disused line connecting Nördlingen, Dinkelsbühl and Feuchtwangen. Two kinds of services run each summer. Steam trains only run once or twice a month between April and September, with an additional journey in December. On Sundays from mid-June to early September, a cherry-red 'railbus' travels along the same track. One-way/return tickets for either cost €16/24 per adult and €8/16 per child for either the steam train or the railbus, but booking ahead is essential. Tourist offices in the three towns can also provide information.

Deutsche Touring can also assist with route planning and accommodation.

For a fun, far more personal tour, Rothenburg-based **TooT Tours** (☎ 07958-311; www .toot-tours.com) can create customised itineraries based on your interests for one to seven people year-round (an especially good option from November to March when the Europabus doesn't run). TooT's bilingual local guides provide in-depth historical and contemporary background. Start and end points are flexible, and it can also arrange accommodation for multiday trips to fit your budget.

WÜRZBURG

☎ 0931 / pop 130,000 / elev 182m

Straddling the Main River, Würzburg is the northern gateway to the Romantic Road. The vineyards surrounding the city attest to its status as the capital of Fränkisches Weinland (Franconian Wine Country), meaning that unlike the rest of Bavaria, here beer takes a backseat to wine.

Throughout Würzburg, you'll repeatedly come across the work of two men who have shaped its legacy: artisan and former city mayor Tilman Riemenschneider; and architect Balthasar Neumann, the main brain behind the Residenz, the city's landmark palace.

Würzburg was decimated in WWII when firebombs flattened over 90% of the city centre. The damage was so comprehensive that authorities initially planned to leave the ruins as a life-size reminder of the horrors of war. But Würzburg's citizens valiantly rebuilt their city, and the overall recovery is remarkable. Today Würzburg is a spirited university hub (more than one-fifth of its population is made up of students) spilling over with cafés, bars and clubs.

History

Würzburg was a Franconian duchy when, in 686, three roving Irish missionaries – Kilian, Totnan and Kolonat – passed through and proposed that Duke Gosbert convert to Christianity… and ditch his wife. Gosbert was purportedly mulling it over when his wife had the three bumped off in 689. When the murders were discovered decades later, the three martyrs became saints, and Würzburg became a pilgrimage city and, in 742, a bishopric, which it would remain for the next 1060 years.

Würzburg's golden age arrived with the election of three artistically inclined prince-bishops from the House of Schönborn; the Residenz was built on their shift. Napoleon finally put an end to ecclesiastic rule in 1802; 14 years later, Würzburg became part of Bavaria.

In 1887, Alois Alzheimer took his medical degree here at the 1582-established Julius-Maximilian Universität. It remains a prestigious university, specialising in medicine, biochemistry and technology.

Orientation

Würzburg's Altstadt is, not coincidentally, shaped something like a bishop's hat. Duplicating this bishop's-hat shape in an outer layer is the leafy Ringpark.

Kaiserstrasse, running south from the train station into the Altstadt, is the main shopping strip. The Main River forms the western boundary of the Altstadt and the fortress is found on the west bank. Alte Mainbrücke, a 15th-century stone footbridge, is the most scenic route across the river. The Residenz is located on the Altstadt's eastern edge. At the northern end of the Altstadt is the Hauptbahnhof and the central bus station is just west of here.

Information

Internet cafés regularly open, close and move, but you'll find at least a couple along Sanderstrasse, charging €1 to €2 per hour.

After-hours emergencies (☎ 192 22)

Deutsche Bank (Juliuspromenade 66)

Hugendubel (☎ 354 040; Schmalzmarkt 12) Bookshop with a good stock of English-language novels and travel guides.

Juliusspital (☎ 3930; Juliuspromenade 19) Hospital with emergency services.

Post offices Altstadt (Paradeplatz); Bahnhof (Bahnhofs-platz 2) Telephone and fax services available.

Postbank (Bahnhofplatz 2)

Sparkasse (Barbarossaplatz) Bank

Tourist office (☎ 372 398; www.wuerzburg.de; Marktplatz; 🕐 10am-6pm Mon-Fri, 10am-2pm Sat May-Oct, 10am-6pm Mon-Fri, 10am-2pm Sat Apr & Nov-Dec, 10am-4pm Mon-Fri, 10am-1pm Sat Jan-Mar) In the baroque Falkenhaus.

Sights

RESIDENZ

The Unesco-listed **Residenz** (☎ 355 170; Balthasar-Neumann-Promenade; adult/concession €5/4; 🕐 9am-6pm Apr-Oct, 10am-4pm Oct-Mar, guided English tours 11am & 3pm) is one Germany's most important and beautiful baroque palaces.

Johann Philipp Franz von Schönborn, unhappy with his old-fashioned digs up in Marienberg Fortress, hired a young architect Balthasar Neumann to build a new palace in town. Construction started in 1720; it took almost 60 years before the interior was completed. In WWII, only the central section escaped unharmed; the rest required extensive restoration.

In 1750, the ceiling above Neumann's brilliant **Grand Staircase**, a single central set of steps that splits and zigzags up to the 1st floor, was topped by what still is the world's largest fresco, by Tiepolo. It allegorically depicts the four then-known continents (Europe, Africa, America and Asia).

The ice-white stucco of the **Weisser Saal** (White Hall) is a soothing interlude before entering the **Kaisersaal** (Imperial Hall), canopied by yet another impressive Tiepolo fresco. Renovations at the time of research were expected to wrap up by early 2009. Other meticulously restored staterooms include the gilded stucco **Spiegelkabinett** (Mirror Hall), covered with a unique mirrorlike glass painted with figural, floral and animal motifs that make you feel as if you're standing inside a Fabergé egg.

Some sections of the south wing can only be seen on guided tours (included in the entry fee), but you're free to explore the north wing on your own – turn left in the Kaisersaal. North-wing highlights include the velveteen-draped bed where Napoleon I slept in 1812.

Hofkirche & Hofgarten

In the residence's south wing, the **Hofkirche** (Court Church; admission free) is another Neumann and Tiepolo co-production. Its marble columns, gold leaf and profusion of angels match the Residenz in its splendour and proportions. Hours vary here; check with the information desk or tourist office.

Behind the Residenz, the **Hofgarten** (admission free; 🕐 dawn-dusk) has whimsical sculptures of children, mostly by court sculptor Peter Wagner. Concerts, festivals and special events take place here during the warmer months. Enter through intricate wrought-iron gates into the French- and English-style gardens, partly built on the old baroque bastions.

ROMANTIC ROAD

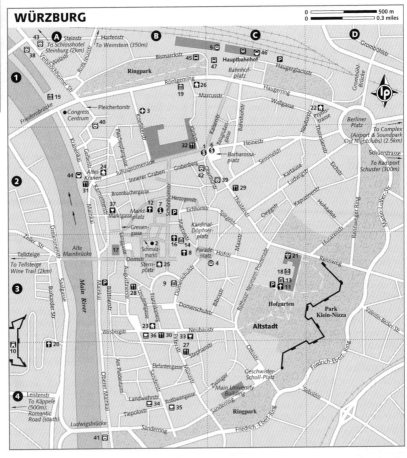

WÜRZBURG

Martin-von-Wagner Museum

The extensive private collection of King Ludwig I's painter, sculptor and art procurer, Martin von Wagner (1777–1858), forms the basis of the **Martin-von-Wagner Museum** (☎ 312 288; Residenzplatz 2, enter next to the Hofkirche; admission free).

Within the museum, the **Antikensammlung** (Antiquities Collection; ☽ 2-5pm Tue-Sat) focuses on Greek, Roman and Egyptian ceramics, vases, figurines and marble sculptures from 1500 BC to AD 300. The **Gemäldegalerie** (Art Gallery; ☽ 9.30am-12.30pm Tue-Sat) has primarily German, Dutch and Italian paintings from the 15th to the 19th centuries, including works by Tiepolo. Finally, the **Graphische Sammlung** (Graphics Collection; ☽ 4-6pm Tue & Thu)

consists of drawings, copperplate etchings and woodcuts, including some by Albrecht Dürer.

Staatlicher Hofkeller Würzburg

Atmospherically housed in the cellar of the Residenz is a winery owned and run by the Bavarian government, **Staatlicher Hofkeller Würzburg** (☎ 305 0931; Residenzplatz 3; hourly tours €6; ☽ 10-5pm Sat, 10-4pm Sun Mar–mid-Dec). It produces some exceptional wines; tours conclude with a tasting.

RATHAUS & GRAFENECKART

Adjoining the **Rathaus**, the 1659-built **Grafeneckart** (Domstrasse; admission free; ☽ 8am-11pm) houses a scale model of the WWII bombing, which starkly depicts the extent of the damage to the city following the night of 16 March 1945, when 5000 citizens lost their lives. Viewing it before you climb up to the fortress overlooking the city gives you an appreciation of Würzburg's astonishing recovery.

DOM ST KILIAN & AROUND
Würzburg's Romanesque **Dom St Kilian** (St Kilian's Cathedral; 10am-5pm Mon-Sat, 1-6pm Sun Easter-Oct, 10am-noon & 2.5pm Mon-Sat, 1-6pm Sun Nov-Easter) was built between 1040 and 1237, although numerous alterations have added Gothic, Renaissance and baroque elements. The row of elaborate pillar-mounted tombstones was hewn from red marble by Tilman Riemenschneider. Attached to the north transept is the festive Balthasar Neumann–designed **Schönbornkapelle**, the final resting place of the Schönborn bishops.

Modern and contemporary art sits alongside works by Romantic, Gothic and baroque masters at the **Museum am Dom** (3866 5600; admission €4, incl Domschatz €5; 10am-7pm Tue-Sun Apr-Oct, 10am-5pm Tue-Sun Nov-Mar).

Abutting the Dom, the **Neumünster** (321 1830; 7am-6pm) is an 11th-century Romanesque church built on the site of the martyrdom of Sts Kilian, Kolonat and Totnan, who lie buried in its crypt. The north exit leads to the peaceful **Lusamgärtlein** cloister, sheltering the grave of the medieval minstrel Walther von der Vogelweide.

One block south of the Dom, a Neumann-designed town house harbours the **Domschatz**

(Cathedral Treasury; 3866 5600; Plattnerstrasse; adult/concession €2.50/1.75, incl Museum am Dom €5; 2-5pm Tue-Sun). Displays of ministerial garments, golden and bejewelled liturgical items and bishops' insignia are accompanied by spiritual music and intimate spotlighting.

MARIENKAPELLE
Balthasar Neumann is buried in the late-Gothic **Marienkapelle** (321 1830; Marktplatz; 8am-6.30pm), built between 1377 and 1481, alongside numerous Franconian knights and burghers. Among them is Konrad von Schaumberg (died in 1499), for whom Riemenschneider designed the tombstone. The prolific sculptor produced the sandstone figures of Adam and Eve above the entrance portal.

RÖNTGEN MUSEUM GEDÄCHTNISSTÄTTE
Nobel Prize–winner Wilhelm Conrad Röntgen discovered the X-ray in 1895; his laboratory forms the heart of the **Röntgen Museum Gedächtnisstätte** (351 1103; Röntgenring 8; admission free; 8am-4pm Mon-Thu, 8am-3pm Fri). Illuminating multimedia displays chart the emergence of the X-ray process.

MUSEUM IM KULTURSPEICHER
An old riverside granary is the home of the **Museum im Kulturspeicher** (Museum in the Cultural Memory; 322 250; Veitshöchheimer Strasse 5; adult/concession €3/2; 11am-7pm Wed, 11am-9pm Thu, 11am-6pm Fri-Sun), which incorporates Würzburg's **Municipal Gallery**, with regional art from the

19th to the 21st centuries; and the **Sammlung Ruppert**, a collection of post-1945 European sculpture, paintings and photographs.

FESTUNG MARIENBERG

Panoramic views over the city's red rooftops and vine-covered hills extend from **Festung Marienberg** (Marienberg Fortress), which has presided over Würzburg since the city's prince-bishops commenced its construction in 1201; they governed from here until 1719. At night floodlights dramatically illuminate the hulking structure, which has only been penetrated once, by Swedish troops in the Thirty Years' War, in 1631. In summer, the gently sloping lawns are strewn with picnickers.

The prince-bishops' pompous lifestyle is on show in the residential wing at the **Fürstenbaumuseum** (☎ 355 1753; adult/concession €4/3; ⏱ 9am-6pm Tue-Sun Apr-Oct), the highlight of which is a huge tapestry showing the entire family of Julius Echter von Mespelbrunn. The city's history is laid out in the upper-level exhibition rooms.

A striking collection of Tilman Riemenschneider sculptures take pride of place in the **Mainfränkisches Museum** (☎ 205 940; Festung Marienberg; adult/concession €3/1.50; ⏱ 10am-5pm Tue-Sun Apr-Oct, 10am-4pm Tue-Sun Nov-Mar). In another section, porcelain, glass, furniture and other such objects illustrate life during the baroque and rococo eras; from the same period are the sketches and drawings by Neumann and Tiepolo.

The fortress is a 30-minute walk up the hill from the Alte Mainbrücke via the **Tellsteige trail**, which is part of the 4km-long **Weinwanderweg** (wine hiking trail) through the vineyards around Marienberg.

ST BURKHARD & KÄPPELE

On your way up to the fortress, you'll pass **St Burkhard** (☎ 424 12; ⏱ 8am-6pm Apr-Oct, 8am-4.30pm Nov-Mar), a Romanesque basilica with a Gothic extension. Treasures include a Madonna by Riemenschneider and a 14th-century relief depicting the Crucifixion.

Further south, in a prime location atop the Nikolausberg, the **Käppele** (☎ 726 70; ⏱ 8am-7pm), built in 1752, is a triple onion-domed pilgrimage church designed by Neumann. The Stations of the Cross featuring life-size figures by Peter Wagner lead up to the church. The outside terrace is a great spot for photographs of the Marienberg and the city beyond.

Tours

The tourist office runs 90-minute English-language **city walks** (tours €6; ⏱ 1pm Sat May-Oct, plus 6.30pm Sun-Fri mid-Jun–mid-Sep).

See opposite and p256 for winery tours.

Festivals & Events

The **Africa Festival** (☎ 150 60; www.africafestival .org; ⏱ early May or Jun) is held on the meadows northwest of the river at Mainwiesen, complete with markets, food stalls and, if it rains, lots of mud. It's a 15-minute walk from the Hauptbahnhof, or take tram 2 or 4 to Talavera and follow the drums.

Also held here for 10 days during June is the **Umsonst & Draussen** (☎ 883 521; www.umsonst -und-draussen.de, in German), a huge free live-music festival held over two stages with local and international bands.

Every May, the weekend-long **Weindorf** (Wine Village; ☎ 728 57; www.weindorfwuerzburg.de, in German) sets up on Marktplatz.

The Residenz courtyard and garden provide a sublime setting for classical music during the **Würzburger Mozartfest** (☎ 372 336; ⏱ early Jun-early Jul).

Sleeping

The tourist office can provide lists of camp-sites within striking distance of the city.

Babelfish Hostel (☎ 304 0430; www.babelfish-hostel .de; Prymstrasse 3; dm €16-18; Ⓟ ⌧ ▯) This green-powered, independent hostel is operated by two fun-loving locals. Facilities include spotless dorms, a chilled commonroom/kitchen, free wi-fi and bike rental (per day €5), and it has quirky touches like multicoloured flowers suspended from the shower ceilings. It's a hop, skip and a jump from the train station; enter via Haugerring. Parking's free.

Pension Spehnkuch (☎ 547 52; www.pension-spehn kuch.de; Röntgenring 7; s €31-33, d €56-60) Up a narrow flight of stairs, this little *Pension* 100m from the train station has zero frills, but rooms are clean and the English-speaking staff welcoming, making it popular with budget-minded travellers. Breakfast is served in a sunny room with a balcony.

Hotel Zum Winzermännle (☎ 541 56; www.winzer maennle.de; Domstrasse 32; s €56-70, d €86-100, f €105-130; ▯) This former winery in the city's pedestrianised heart was rebuilt in its original style after the war as a guesthouse by the same charming family. In addition to cavernous rooms there are some self-catering apartments (€120 to €160).

Hotel Residence (☎ 535 46; www.wuerzburg-hotel.de; Juliuspromenade 1; s €60-85, d €80-120; P) Framed by dormer windows, the Residence is no Residenz, but it does have warmly decorated, elegant rooms near the river and the congress centre, and it's within strolling distance of the city's main sights.

Schlosshotel Steinburg (☎ 970 20; www.steinburg.com; Auf dem Steinberg; s €105, d €142-185; P X ⊠) A perfect first (or last) stop on the Romantic Road, this former palace amid the vineyards has two terraces affording magical views over the city. Individually designed rooms are appropriately gorgeous, and there's a Romanesque indoor pool and sauna.

Hotel Rebstock (☎ 309 30; www.rebstock.com; Neubaustrasse 7; s €109-147, d €187-200; P X ⊠ 💻) Don't be misled by the Best Western sign out the front: Würzburg's top hotel, in a meticulously restored rococo town house, has unique, stylishly furnished rooms, impeccable service and a great Altstadt location below the fortress. Extras include free newspapers and rental bikes.

Eating & Drinking

Würzburg has a smorgasbord of places to eat and drink, from cheap, cheerful student hang-outs (especially along Neubaustrasse and Sanderstrasse) to gourmet restaurants attached to world-class wineries.

Excellent bakeries can be found sprinkled along Semmelstrasse (*Semmel*, appropriately enough, is the Bavarian word for bread rolls).

If you're here around September to mid-October, be sure to try *Bremser* – sweet, *very* alcoholic juice from early-harvested grapes, available in bars and restaurants around town; traditionally served with *Zwiebelkuchen* (onion cake).

RESTAURANTS

Le Clochard Bistro (☎ 129 07; Neubaustrasse 20; dishes €4.20-7.90; V) Warmed by an open fireplace, this cosy crêperie does authentic Breton *galettes* (savoury buckwheat crêpes) and sugar-dusted sweet crêpes, and also has a good selection of salads and pastas.

Auflauf (☎ 571 343; Peterplatz 5; mains €7.90-9.50; V) At this always-busy, unpretentious place with blue-and-white décor and timber tables, you can order gratins and the signature *Aufläufe* (casseroles) à la carte or create your own from a checklist of ingredients.

Backöfele (☎ 590 59; Ursulinergasse 2; mains €8.90-18.40) Begin a memorable meal at this cobble-floored, candlelit restaurant with *Fränkische Mostsuppe* (frothy Franconian wine soup with cinnamon croutons) and follow up with Backöfele's innovative twists on traditional game, steak and fish dishes. Bookings are recommended.

WINERY-RESTAURANTS

Franconia's superb wines – mostly whites – are bottled in the distinctive Bocksbeutel, a flattened teardrop-shaped flagon. You can sample some of the area's finest at the 1773 **Alter Kranen** (Old Crane; Kranenkai 1) beer garden and attached restaurant, **Weingasthof am Alten Kranen** (☎ 601 30; mains €9.80-15.90).

Other historic wineries that offer top-end dining at on-site restaurants include **Weingut Juliusspital** (☎ 393 1406; Juliuspromenade 19), **Bürgerspital Weingut** (☎ 350 3403; Theaterstrasse 19) and Michelin-starred fare right in the vineyards at the northern edge of town, at Weingut am Stein's restaurant, **Weinstein** (☎ 286 901; Mittlerer Steinbergweg 5; ✆ from 5pm Mon-Sat).

Vineyards also stretch across the surrounding countryside, see the boxed text, p260.

Drinking

MUCK (☎ 465 1144; Sanderstrasse 29; dishes €2.40-5.50) One of the earliest openers in town (officially 8am but often 7am), this easygoing hang-out does a mean breakfast including a mammoth, refillable pot of coffee. You can while away the day playing board games; by night it morphs into something of a house party.

Uni-Café (☎ 156 70; Neubaustrasse 2; snacks €3-7) Hugely popular café set over two levels, with a student-priced, daily changing set menu and buzzy bar.

Gehrings (☎ 525 45; Neubaustrasse 24; mains €4.20-5.90; V) Live music often plays at this wonderfully local, owner-run pub, where Würzburgers of all ages tuck into fantastic Franconian potato-based dishes, such as *Rösti* – fried potato cakes with toppings like sheep's cheese and broccoli.

Kult (☎ 531 43; Landwehrstrasse 10; mains €5.50-8.50; ✆ 9am-1am Mon-Fri, 10am-1am Sat & Sun; V) Old washing machine and dryer drums have been turned into light fittings at this student-house–like café that draws an alternative crowd for its organic food, steaming mugs of Ovaltine and good beer. By day, regulars strum guitars; nighttime sees DJs spinning cool grooves.

DETOUR: FRÄNKISCHES WEINLAND

Würzburg is at the centre of the Fränkisches Weinland (Franconian Wine Country), which is roughly hemmed in by three low mountain ranges: the Spessart to the west, the Rhön to the north and the Steigerwald to the east. Strolling among the vineyards and sampling the crops of local wine estates is a perfect way to whet your palate for a romantic roadtrip.

Wineries in Würzburg offer tours and tastings, and you can also take a 4km-long wine hiking trail through the vineyards around Würzburg's Marienberg Fortress. But if you have an afternoon to spare, it's well worth a spin through the surrounding countryside, where the Main River meanders past picturesque villages seemingly lifted from a Grimm brothers' fairy tale.

Highlights include **Sommerhausen** (population 1700), on the B13, about 15km south of Würzburg, where the cobbled streets lead right into the vineyards, where around a dozen estates offer tastings. Artists continue to fall in love with this walled town; you can see their work exhibited in its little local galleries.

About 24km southeast of Würzburg and 3km south of Kitzingen (the wine country's administrative centre) on the B8, follow the signs to sleepy little **Sulzfeld** (population 1250), which feels far removed from the hubbub of modern life. Hugging a bank of the Main, it hasn't grown much beyond the perimeter of its preserved medieval wall, which runs for 900m and is fortified by 18 towers. To soak up Sulzfeld's wines, try its famous *Meterbratwurst:* 100cm of sausage curled up like a pretzel. You'll find it at inns around town; with salad, the whole thing usually costs around €12.

Iphofen (population 4500), east of the Main on the B8, about 30km southeast of Würzburg, has preserved a medieval flair largely because of its nearly intact towered and gated town wall. Some of the best Franconian wines are produced nearby, including the famous Julius-Echter-Berg.

On the western edge of the Steigerwald forest, half-timbered and baroque houses line the little lanes of **Prichsenstadt** (population 3200), which is imbued with a dreamy, unspoilt quality untouched by tourism. Prichsenstadt is about 40km east of Würzburg on the B286 just north of the A3. The most atmospheric way to enter is via the twin-turreted western gate.

Comprehensive information, including wineries that can be visited seasonally, is most easily picked up at Würzburg's tourist office, which also has details of some really charming places to stay throughout the wine country.

Public transportation to the Fränkisches Weinland is an option if you're travelling to a single village from Würzburg, but connections between most villages are limited or nonexistent.

Zum Stachel (☎ 527 70; www.weinhaus-stachel.de; Gressengasse 1; ☺ Mon-Sat) There's a restaurant at this 15th-century watering hole (a favourite haunt of Tilman Riemenschneider, among others), but better yet is to just enjoy a drink on one of its stone balconies overlooking the *Romeo and Juliet*–like Renaissance courtyard.

Entertainment

Frizz (http://wuerzburg.bewegungsmelder .de, in German) is the town's monthly listing magazine, available free at pubs and cafés.

From May to mid-October, a public beach (with trucked-in sand), with bars and restaurants, sets up along the river at the **Stadtstrand** (City Beach; ☺ 11am-11pm weather permitting).

Standard (☎ 511 40; Oberthuerstrasse 11a) Soulful jazz spins beneath a corrugated-iron ceiling and stainless-steel fans, while bands and DJs play a couple of times or more a week in a second, dimly lit downstairs bar.

Pleicherhof (☎ 465 2510; www.pleicherhof.de; Pleichertorstrasse 30; ☺ café from 11.30am Tue-Sun, beer garden from noon Tue-Sun, club 11.30pm-late Wed, Fri & Sat) The best night to hit this disco in an old cellar is Wednesday, when funk and soul hit the decks; there are also occasional live bands.

Serious party animals should head to the **complex** (Gattingerstrasse 17; ☺ Tue, Wed, Fri & Sat) in eastern Würzburg. Dance temples here include **Airport** (☎ 237 71), which throbs with a mix of techno, house, blackbeat and disco; and **Soundpark Ost** (☎ 230 80), which has two rooms for dancing to a wild mix of musical styles and a third for resting eardrums. Take bus 26 from the central bus station.

Also recommended:

Omnibus (☎ 561 21; Theaterstrasse 10) Würzburg's best bet for live funk, blues, soul and old-time rock 'n' roll.

Das Boot (☎ 593 53; Veitshöchheimer Strasse 14;
🕑 Mon & Thu-Sat) Permanently moored party boat and
a Würzburg institution, with a Thai restaurant, English bar
and Machine Room dance area on board.
Zauberberg (☎ 329 2680; www.zauberberg.info;
Veitshöchheimer Strasse 20; 🕑 Thu-Sat) Nightclub
beloved by locals for its summer beer garden, regular
reggae nights and Moroccan tent chill-out area serving
mint tea.

Getting There & Away

Frequent trains serve Bamberg (€16.40, one
hour), Nuremberg (€16.60, 1¼ hours) and
Rothenburg ob der Tauber (€10.60, 1¼ hours),
with a change in Steinach.

The Romantic Road Europabus stops just
around the corner from the Hauptbahnhof
on Bismarckstrasse.

Car-hire agencies at the Hauptbahnhof
include **Europcar** (☎ 120 60; Bahnhofsplatz 5).

Getting Around

Würzburg is easily seen on foot, but there's a
good network of buses and trams; tickets cost
€2. Call ☎ 194 10 for a taxi.

Bicycle-hire outlets include **Radsport Schuster**
(☎ 123 38; Raiffeisenstrasse 3; 🕑 9am-6.30pm Mon-Fri,
9am-2pm Sat, 9am-8pm Sun Mar-Aug, 9am-6.30pm Mon-Fri,
9am-2pm Sat Sep-Feb), which charges around €10
per day.

WEIKERSHEIM

☎ 07934 / pop 7555 / elev 227m

Tranquil Weikersheim is the ancestral home
and former residence of the counts and
princes of Hohenlohe, a Franconian dynasty
from the 12th century. Its restored Marktplatz
is home to the **tourist office** (☎ 102; www.weiker
sheim.de, in German; 🕑 9am-5.30pm Mon-Fri).

Footsteps from here, announcing its presence with a crest-festooned gate and onion-
domed church steeple, **Schloss Weikersheim**
(☎ 992 950; adult/child €5/2.50; 🕑 9am-6pm Apr-Oct,
10am-noon & 1.30-4.30pm Nov-Mar) is filled with 16th-
and 18th-century furniture, and backed by an
even more impressive symmetrical baroque
garden. Since the last of the local Hohenlohes
died childless in the 18th century, the palace
has pretty much remained frozen in time.
Highlights of the one-hour tour include the
Chinesisches Spiegelkabinett (Chinese Mirror
Cabinet) and the **Rittersaal** (Knights' Hall).
This grand banqueting hall pays homage to
the family's favourite pastime, the hunt, with
a menagerie of stucco animals – deer, boar
and a badly proportioned elephant (the artist
had never seen one in real life) inhabiting the
walls. The palace's upper-storey windows look
out over the gardens, including the whimsical
Zwergengallerie (Gnome Gallery). The castle
can only be seen by guided tour in German,

TOP STOPS ON THE ROMANTIC ROAD FOR...

Revelling in romance
Rothenburg (p264) Watch the sun set over the Tauber Valley from the gardens outside the twin-turreted medieval gate of the road's most romantic town.

Simply revelling
Würzburg (opposite) If cosy tables for two and charming inns leave you cold, head to the hip student city of
Würzburg for hot clubs, bars and live music venues, as well as chilled cafés.

Embracing the great outdoors
Füssen & Schwangau (p285) Options to get your pulse rate up in this Alpine area include sailing, windsurfing,
skiing, snowboarding, hang-gliding, hiking and some great bike trails.

Keeping kids out of mischief
Augsburg (boxed text, p278) Not only does it have an active nightlife for adults, Augsburg also has a host of
activities to entertain little visitors – from its interactive puppet museum to its zoo and Planetarium.

Losing the crowds
Weikersheim (above) The Romantic Road's crowds don't reach Oktoberfest proportions, but still, if you didn't
come to Bavaria to hang out with international tourists, head for spots where locals take visiting friends, such as
Weikersheim's rambling palace.

but ask to be lent an English-language leaflet. Tours commence on the hour.

For a cosy meal in a 15th-century house of hewn stone and timber, head 100m south of Marktplatz to **Die Bastion** (☎ 8872; Mühlstrasse 14; mains €8.50-14.50; ❤ Thu-Tue), where friendly owners dish up delicious regional cuisine in tune with the seasons.

The Europabus stops on Marktplatz, but Weikersheim is otherwise best reached with your own wheels. It sits 41km south of Würzburg just off the B19.

CREGLINGEN
☎ 07933 / pop 5000 / elev 270m
A little-known Romantic Road gem, the **Hergottskirche** (Church of Our Lord; ☎ 508; Kirchplatz 2; adult/child €2/1; ❤ 9.15am-6.30pm May-Oct, 9.15am-5.30pm Apr, noon-4pm Tue-Sun Dec & Feb-Mar, closed Jan) in the pretty village of Creglingen is home to Tilman Riemenschneider's late-15th-century masterpiece, the filigreed, unpainted Marienaltar. Some of the finest work is in the altar's predella (bottom portion), where Riemenschneider himself is purportedly the central figure in the group on the right.

Across the street from the church is the **Fingerhutmuseum** (Thimble Museum; ☎ 370; Kohlesmühle; adult/child & concession €1.50/1; ❤ 10am-12.30pm & 2-5pm Tue-Sun Apr-Oct, 1-4pm Nov-late Dec & Mar, closed late Dec-Feb). To avoid being considered working class, aristocratic women wanted thimbles that would be considered jewellery rather than tools, and pieces of art among the

ROMANTIC ROAD ALTERNATIVES
Maybe you've travelled this road before, or maybe you're so smitten you're looking for even more trail magic. The following routes cross paths with the Romantic Road.
Castle Road (Burgenstrasse; www.burgenstrasse.de) Travels from Mannheim to Prague past 70 castles and palaces, including stops in Bamberg and Nuremberg. From May to September, Deutsche Touring (p253) runs one coach daily in each direction between Mannheim and Nuremberg via Rothenburg ob der Tauber.
Sisi's Road (Sisistrasse; www.regio-augsburg.de/sisistrasse) Spans four countries (Germany, Austria, Italy and Hungary) following the footsteps of Empress Elisabeth (Sisi) of Austria. Within Bavaria, the road connects Augsburg, Neuschwanstein and Sisi's birthplace, Munich.

3000-strong collection of these diminutive sewing aids here include thimbles made of gold, silver or hand-painted fine porcelain. You can also peek into the attached workshop, where thimbles are made today for collectors worldwide.

The church and Fingerhutmuseum are about 600m south of the village centre, where the intimate **Jüdisches Museum** (Jewish Museum; ☎ 7010; Badgasse 3; admission by donation; ❤ 2-5pm Sun or year-round by appointment) uses English labelling and multimedia displays to interpret Jewish life within the district and after members of its community left Creglingen.

Within in a medieval tower that forms part of the old town wall is the **Lindleinturm-Museum** (☎ 7237; Stadtgraben 12; admission free; ❤ 10am-noon Fri, 10am-noon & 2-5pm Sat & Sun Easter-Oct & year-round by appointment), the tiny home of crotchety Margarete Böttiger. She lived here from 1927 until her death in 1995 without central heating or hot water, and with only felines for company, which is why locals called it 'Katzenturm' (Cat Tower).

The friendly **tourist office** (☎ 631; www.creglingen.de; Bad Mergentheimer Strasse 14; ❤ 9am-noon & 1-5pm Mon Fri) can help with finding a place to stay, including a couple of **apartments** (d €30, additional person €5) within the town wall towers; and a **shepherd's cottage** in the surrounding countryside. Hours can vary.

Creglingen is just 13km west of Weikersheim and 20km northwest of Rothenburg ob der Tauber via scenic, well-signposted back roads, but public transport to or from either town is pretty much nonexistent. At the time of writing, the Europabus continues to pass through Creglingen, allowing you to prearrange a pick-up or drop-off. However, this may change in coming years; contact Creglingen's tourist office or Deutsche Touring (p253) for updates.

ROTHENBURG OB DER TAUBER
☎ 09861 / pop 12,700 / elev 425m
With its web of cobbled lanes hugged by higgledy-piggledy houses, towered walls and traditional wrought-iron shop signs, Rothenburg ob der Tauber (above the Tauber River) is almost impossibly charming. In summer and during the Christmas season especially, day-trippers (an estimated two million each year) fill Rothenburg's narrow streets, but since the entire Altstadt is a picture-perfect 'sight', visitors disperse all over town, making

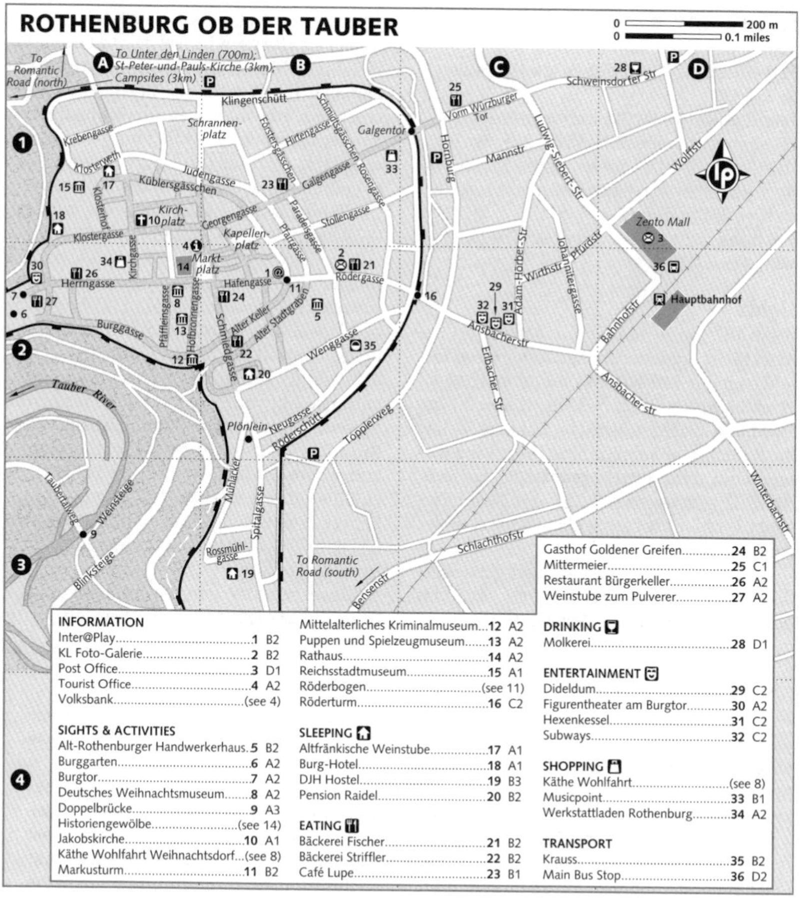
ROTHENBURG OB DER TAUBER
0 200 m
0 0.1 miles
To Unter den Linden (700m); St-Peter-und-Pauls-Kirche (3km); Campsites (3km)
To Romantic Road (north)
To Romantic Road (south)
Klingenschütt
Schrannenplatz
Galgentor
Vorm Würzburger Tor
Schweinsdorfer Str
Mannstr
Ludwig-Siebert-Str
Wolfstr
Zento Mall
Hauptbahnhof
Bahnhofstr
Ansbacherstr
Erlbacher Str
Adam-Hörber-Str
Johannitergasse
Wirthstr
Pfarrstr
Marktplatz
Kirchplatz
Kapellenplatz
Judengasse
Klostergasse
Herrngasse
Hafengasse
Burggasse
Schmiedgasse
Alter Keller
Alter Stadtgraben
Wenggasse
Rödergasse
Tauber River
Plönlein
Neugasse
Röderschütt
Topplerweg
Mühlacker
Spitalgasse
Rossmühlgasse
Weinsteige
Taubertalweg
Blinksteige
Schlachthofstr
Bensenstr
Winterbachstr
INFORMATION
Inter@Play 1 B2
KL Foto-Galerie 2 B2
Post Office 3 D1
Tourist Office 4 A2
Volksbank (see 4)
SIGHTS & ACTIVITIES
Alt-Rothenburger Handwerkerhaus 5 B2
Burggarten 6 A2
Burgtor 7 A2
Deutsches Weihnachtsmuseum 8 A2
Doppelbrücke 9 A3
Historiengewölbe (see 14)
Jakobskirche 10 A1
Käthe Wohlfahrt Weihnachtsdorf (see 8)
Markusturm 11 B2
Mittelalterliches Kriminalmuseum 12 A2
Puppen und Spielzeugmuseum 13 A2
Rathaus 14 A2
Reichsstadtmuseum 15 A1
Röderbogen (see 11)
Röderturm 16 C2
SLEEPING
Altfränkische Weinstube 17 A1
Burg-Hotel 18 A1
DJH Hostel 19 B3
Pension Raidel 20 B2
EATING
Bäckerei Fischer 21 B2
Bäckerei Striffler 22 B2
Café Lupe 23 B1
Gasthof Goldener Greifen 24 B2
Mittermeier 25 C1
Restaurant Bürgerkeller 26 A2
Weinstube zum Pulverer 27 A2
DRINKING
Molkerei 28 D1
ENTERTAINMENT
Dideldum 29 C2
Figurentheater am Burgtor 30 A2
Hexenkessel 31 C2
Subways 32 C2
SHOPPING
Käthe Wohlfahrt (see 8)
Musicpoint 33 B1
Werkstattladen Rothenburg 34 A2
TRANSPORT
Krauss 35 B2
Main Bus Stop 36 D2

it possible to find peaceful spots far from the crowds. Even so, the town is at its most romantic when the yellow lamplight casts its spell long after the last tour buses have left.

History

Rothenburg's recorded history starts with the 10th-century construction of a castle at the southern end of what is now the Spital quarter. In the 12th century, the town was brought under the control of the Hohenstaufen dynasty, which built another castle and fortifications. In 1274, Rothenburg became a Free Imperial City, and managed to survive the Peasants' War and the Thirty Years' War (1618–48), before being absorbed into Bavaria in 1802. During WWII, a charmed American general prevented a second wave of bombings, and today it remains one of the world's most exquisitely preserved medieval towns.

Orientation

Rothenburg is surrounded by an intact 3.5km-long town wall of which 2.5km are walkable. The main shopping drag is Schmiedgasse, which runs south from the central square, Marktplatz, to the Plönlein, a fork in the road anchored by an ochre-yellow half-timbered cottage and fountain that has become Rothenburg's unofficial emblem.

Information

Inter@Play (☎ 933 5599; Milchmarkt 3; per hr €3; 🕒 8am-2am) Internet access.

KL Foto-Galerie (☎ 862 66; Rödergasse 11) Basic photo services.

Post office (Zentro Mall, Bahnhofstrasse 15) Opposite the *Bahnhof.*

Tourist office (☎ 404 800, 24hr room referral hotline 194 12; www.rothenburg.de; Marktplatz 2; ☻ 9am-6pm Mon-Fri, 10am-3pm Sat & Sun Apr-Oct, 9am-5pm Mon-Fri, 10am-1pm Sat Nov-Mar) There are information leaflets in the foyer, which is always open.

Volksbank (Marktplatz) Just to the right of the tourist office, with an ATM.

Sights

From the top of the Gothic **Rathaus** on the Marktplatz, majestic Tauber Valley views unfold from the **Rathausturm** (Town Hall Tower; ☎ 404 39; adult/concession €1.50; ☻ 9.30am-12.30pm & 1-5pm Apr-Oct, noon-3pm Dec), reached by 220 steps. Below the Rathaus, the subterranean prison and torture room at the **Historiengewölbe** (Historical Vaults; ☎ 867 51; adult/concession €2/1.50; ☻ 9.30am-5.30pm Apr-Oct, 1-4pm Dec) are creepy enough to get under your skin.

Glorious 14th-century stained-glass windows frame the **Jakobskirche** (Gothic Church of St Jacob; ☎ 700 620; Klostergasse 15; adult/under 18yr €2/0.50; ☻ 9am-5.15pm Apr-Oct, 10am-5pm Dec, 10am-noon & 2-4pm Nov & Jan-Mar), but its real *pièce de résistance* is Tilman Riemenschneider's carved **Heilig Blut Altar** (Sacred Blood Altar). The gilded cross above the main scene depicting the Last Supper incorporates Rothenburg's treasured reliquary: a capsule made of rock crystal said to contain three drops of Christ's blood.

Highlights of the **Reichsstadtmuseum** (Imperial City Museum; ☎ 939 043; Klosterhof 5; adult/under 18yr €3/2; ☻ 10am-5pm Apr-Oct, 1-4pm Nov-Mar), housed in a former Dominican convent, include the superb *Rothenburger Passion* (1494), a cycle of 12 panels by Martinus Schwarz, and the oldest convent kitchen in Germany, as well as weapons and armour. Outside the main entrance (on your right as you're facing the museum), you'll see a spinning barrel, where the nuns distributed bread to the poor – and where women would leave babies they couldn't afford to keep. For a serene break between sightseeing, head to the **Klostergarten** (☻ 10am-5pm Apr-Oct) behind the museum (enter from Klosterhof).

More serenity can be enjoyed in the beautiful **Burggarten** (Castle Garden), with

---

ETERNAL CHRISTMAS

Rothenburg is exceptionally enchanting during the **Christmas market** (Marktplatz; ☻ Dec), when the brightly coloured stalls twinkle between the Rathaus and St Jakobskirche. But even if you're not travelling at Christmas time, it's easy to feel you are.

Year-round, German Christmas customs through the ages are on show at the **Deutsches Weihnachtmuseum** (German Christmas Museum; ☎ 409 365; Herrngasse 1; adult/under 18yr €4/2; ☻ 10am-5.30pm Easter–mid-Jan, 10am-5.30pm Sat & Sun mid-Jan–Easter), where you'll learn, for example, that Christmas-tree baubles were inspired by the apples in Adam and Eve's Garden of Eden (signs are in English and German). The museum sits within the cavernous Christmas emporium **Käthe Wohlfahrt Weihnachtsdorf** (☎ 4090; Herrngasse 1), which sells a truly mind-boggling assortment of decorations, ornaments and quality Christmassy souvenirs.

Christmas wouldn't be Christmas without dolls and toys, and collector Katharina Engels has assembled an amazing range at the **Puppen und Spielzeugmuseum** (Doll & Toy Museum; ☎ 7330; Hofbronnengasse 13; adult/under 18yr €4/1.50; ☻ 9.30am-6pm Mar-Dec, 11am-5pm Jan & Feb). Teddy bears and wooden toys, carousels and marionette theatres, tin figurines and infinite dolls made of porcelain, paper, wood and wax, along with dolls houses, doll tea services, doll shops and more are traditionally displayed in glass cases.

Christmas is also, ideally, white. Rothenburg's enticing bakery windows are piled high year-round with mountains of the town's pastry speciality, *Schneeballen* (snowballs) – dough ribbons loosely shaped into balls then deep-fried and dipped in cinnamon or powdered sugar. (Local tip: don't bite into one or you'll be wearing a small avalanche; instead smash it inside its paper bag and eat it in pieces.) Locals also advise to buy from a bakery, not (surprisingly enough) a shop specialising solely in snowballs, as quality varies dramatically. **Bäckerei Striffler** (Untere Schmiedegasse 1) makes the best; **Bäckerei Fischer** (Rödergasse 13) is also a local favourite. Kitchenware shops in the Altstadt also sell *Schneeballeneisen* (around €15) – long metal pincherlike contraptions for making your own snowballs at home.

panoramic views over the Tauber Valley. To get to the park, you'll pass through the twin-turreted **Burgtor** (Castle Gate). Look up to see the ghoulish mask on the façade; would-be attackers of the city were repelled by hot pitch poured through its mouth.

East along Burggasse, you can also see the **Doppelbrücke**, a double-decker bridge ideal for watching the fireworks displays during the Reichsstadt-Festtage. Also visible is the head of a trail that leads down the valley and over to the pretty **St-Peter-und-Pauls-Kirche** in Detwang, which contains another stunning Riemenschneider altar.

In addition to containing gruesome tools of torture and execution, the **Mittelalterliches Kriminalmuseum** (Medieval Crime Museum; ☎ 5359; Burggasse 3; adult/under 18yr €3.80/2.20; ☾ 9.30am-6pm Apr-Oct, 2-4pm Nov & Jan-Feb, 10am-4pm Mar & Dec) documents (in English and German) famous criminal cases and legal proceedings in the Middle Ages, including witch trials.

East of Marktplatz on Hafengasse leads you past the begging-to-be-photographed ensemble of the **Markusturm** (Marcus Tower) and the **Röderbogen** (Röder Arch).

Hidden down a little alley is the **Alt-Rothenburger Handwerkerhaus** (Old Rothenburg's Artisans House; ☎ 942 80; Alter Stadtgraben 26; adult/child €2.50/0.50; ☾ 11am-5pm Mon-Fri, 10am-5pm Sat & Sun Easter-Oct, 2-4pm Nov-early Jan), where numerous artisans – including coopers, weavers, cobblers and potters – have had their workshops during the house's 700-plus-year existence.

Tours

The tourist office runs 90-minute English-language **walking tours** (adult/12-18yr/under 12yr €6/3/free; ☾ 2pm Apr-Oct); there's no minimum number of participants. **Private walking tours** (☎ 07958-570) in English or German are also available. An atmospheric walking tour of the Altstadt is conducted every evening by the **Nachtwächter** (Night Watchman walking tours; tours adult/12-18yr/under 12yr €6/3/free; ☾ tours English 8pm Apr-Dec, German 9.30pm Apr-Dec), dressed in traditional long black robes and toting a *Hellebarde* – a combined spear, hook and axe, which holds its candle-lantern. Walking tours depart from outside the Rathaus.

Horse-drawn carriage rides start at about €5 per person for 30 minutes. You'll find them in the Altstadt, usually on Schrannenplatz or Marktplatz.

For yet more romance, you can drift silently over the woods and valleys (and if conditions

are right, Rothenburg's Altstadt) at sunrise or sunset in a hot air balloon operated by **Happy Ballooning** (☎ 878 88; www.happy-ballooning .de; per person 60-90min balloon ride €180; ☾ by reservation, weather permitting).

Festivals & Events

Rothenburg's **Christmas market** (boxed text, opposite) is one of Germany's most magical.

Throughout the year, numerous festivities revolve around the tale of the Meistertrunk (see the boxed text, p266); while colourfully dressed couples dance during the **Historischer Schäfertanz** (Historical Shepherds' Dance; Marktplatz; ☾ Apr & Oct).

Sleeping

For such a charming town, Rothenburg has surprisingly good-value accommodation. Plans for a new independent hostel are in the works – check with the tourist office or www .backpackernetwork.de for updates.

In the village of Detwang, about 1.5km below the Altstadt, are two campsites: the **Campingplatz Tauber-Idyll** (☎ 3177; www.rothen burg.de/tauberidyll, in German; Detwang 28; per tent/person €5.50/4.75; ☾ Easter-late Oct) and **Campingplatz Tauber-Romantik** (☎ 6191; www.camping-tauberromantik.de; Detwang 39; per tent/person €5/5; ☾ Easter-late Oct), both situated in a riverside nature preserve.

DJH hostel (☎ 941 60; www.djh.de, in German; Mühlacker 1; dm €17-19; ☒ 🖳) Rothenburg's HI hostel occupies a vast former horse-powered mill and hospital, but it's frequently booked out by rambunctious school groups.

Pension Raidel (☎ 3115; www.romanticroad.com /raidel; Wenggasse 3; s/d with shared bathroom €24/49, with private bathroom €39/59; ℗) Right in the Altstadt, this atmosphere-laden half-timbered inn has 500-year-old exposed beams studded with wooden nails, and musical instruments for guests to play. Rooms without their own bathroom have basins and the cosy breakfast room has an original copper boiler.

Altfränkische Weinstube (☎ 6404; www.roman ticroad.com/altfraenkische-weinstube; Klosterhof 7; s €55, d €60-69; ☒) Tucked away in a quiet side street near the Reichsstadtmuseum, most guest-rooms at this historic inn have four-poster and/or canopied beds, while the candlelit restaurant (mains €6.50 to €17.80) serves up good-value regional fare and great wines. The two-decades-old English Conversation Club – an ever-changing group of English-speaking visitors and locals headed by its

---

DRINK & YE SHALL BE FREE

The year is 1631. The raging Thirty Years' War – pitching Catholics against Protestants – has reached the gates of Rothenburg ob der Tauber. Catholic General Tilly and 60,000 of his troops have besieged the Protestant market town, and the town dignitaries are sentenced to death. And that's pretty much where history ends and the legend of Meistertrunk begins. So the tale goes, Rothenburg's town council tries to sate Tilly's blood lust by proffering a 3.25L mug of wine. Tilly then challenges the men to down the wine in one gulp. The mayor accepts – and succeeds – thereby saving the town. Or, so they say…

Of course, it's pretty much accepted that Tilly was really placated with hard cash. Nevertheless, in 1881, local poet Adam Hörber couldn't resist turning the tale into a play, which is performed during the **Reichsstadt Festtage** (Imperial City Festival) in early September; and during the **Rothenburger Herbst**, a harvest celebration in October. It's also the highlight of the **Historisches Festspiel 'Der Meistertrunk'** (Historic Meistertrunk Festival) each year on Whitsuntide (mid-May to early June), which also features parades, dances and a medieval market. The story is also reenacted by the clock figures on the tourist office building several times daily. The huge tankard that inspired the legend is displayed at the **Reichsstadtmuseum** (p264).

---

charismatic founder 'Hermann the German' – meets here on Wednesday nights; everyone is welcome.

Burg-Hotel (☎ 948 90; www.burghotel.rothenburg.de; Klostergasse 1-3; s €90-110, d €100-170; (P) (X) (▢)) Each of the 15 elegantly furnished guestrooms at this boutique hotel built into the town walls has its own private sitting area. The lower floors shelter a decadent spa (€10 per person for exclusive use) with tanning beds, saunas and rainforest showers, and a cellar with a Steinway piano; while phenomenal valley views unfurl from the breakfast room and stone terrace. Wi-fi's free; garaged parking costs €7.50

Eating

Weinstube zum Pulverer (☎ 976 182; Herrngasse 31; dishes €2.80-8; 🕑 Wed-Mon) The ornately carved timber chairs in this ancient wine bar are works of art. Its simple but filling dishes, like soup in a bowl made of bread, gourmet sandwiches and cakes, are equally artistic.

Café Lupe (☎ 875 117; Galgengasse 13; dishes €3.30-7.90; 🕑 2-6pm Mon-Sat) Locals escape the tourist crowds at this unpretentious, French-washed café, which serves a good variety of breakfast options and light meals, such as filled baguettes, as well as excellent coffee.

Gasthof Goldener Greifen (☎ 2281; Obere Schmiedgasse 5; menus €9.60-14.20, mains €6.80-15.80; 🕑 closed Sun evening) Classic regional fare focussing on schnitzel, sausages and especially pork (fried, roasted, breaded et al) is dished up in this homey restaurant in the heart of the Altstadt. There are also comfy rooms upstairs (doubles €60 to €82).

Restaurant Bürgerkeller (☎ 2126; Herrngasse 24; mains €7.80-13.50; 🕑 Thu-Tue; (V)) Down a short flight of steps in a frescoed 16th-century cellar, this hidden spot serves local, seasonal produce, such as autumn mushrooms and spring asparagus as part of classic Franconian mains, as well as delicious warm apple strudel with vanilla ice cream and real whipped cream.

Mittermeier (☎ 945 40; www.mittermeier.rothenburg .de; Vorm Würzburger Tor; mains €22-26; (P) (X)) Artistic chefs at this classy establishment just outside the Würzburger gate create Michelin-starred cuisine, such as a Tauber Forest saddle of venison with chanterelles, mango sauerkraut and handmade potato noodles, using locally harvested, seasonal produce. The 400-strong wine list is among the best in Franconia. It also runs a programme of cooking courses – check the website for dates and prices. Rooms are available (single/double/suite from €63/70/170).

Drinking

There's no shortage of leafy beer gardens and cosy inns for a drink; wander through Rothenburg's cobbled back lanes to uncover your own favourites. Listings in the Sleeping and Eating sections are also good spots for a drink.

Unter den Linden (☎ 5909; Kurze Steige 1; 🕑 10am-10pm Easter-Oct) Idyllically situated on the banks of the Tauber, this wonderful beer garden set around an old saw mill has honest-to-goodness snacks and meals (€5 to €8), such as home-made bread with butter and fresh-cut chives. Live music frequently plays, and there's a cosy stone hall with an open fire, an outdoor kids' play area and a tepee bonfire when the autumn leaves start to fall.

Molkerei (☎ 933 310; www.molkerei.rothenburg.de, in German; Schweinsdorfer Strasse 25b; 5pm-midnight Mon-Thu, 3pm-2am Fri & Sat, 10am-midnight Sun) Updated industrial décor and cavernous open-plan spaces attract the young and hip at this re-incarnated old dairy with cow-painted bath-rooms and aluminium ceiling pipes. There are regular DJ parties, and the kitchen churns out great pizzas, pastas and steaks (around €7 to €9) for the herds.

Entertainment

our pick Figurentheater am Burgtor (☎ 3333; www .figurentheater-rothenburg.com; Herrngasse 38; adult/child af-ternoon show €6/4, evening show €10/7) This delightful little puppet theatre is operated by two actor brothers who make all the puppets and sets, and write the scripts. Children's fairy tales (in German) play at 4pm daily, lasting around 45 minutes. At 8pm a political satire puppet show for adults takes place in German (around 80 minutes), while at 9.45pm there's a puppet show for adults in English (30 minutes). All shows require a minimum audience of four people. The theatre's at the base of the Burgtor, inside which the puppets and sets are made.

Hexenkessel (Witches' Cauldron; ☎ 3686; www.th-hex enkessel.de, in German; Ansbacherstrasse 1; 9pm-4.30am Thu-Sat) has been throwing dance parties since the disco era. In the same wedge of town, known by locals as the Bermuda Triangle, are several other late-night bars, including the laid-back **Dideldum** (☎ 936 9369; Ansbacherstrasse 15e; 8pm-2am Wed-Mon) and the slicked-up, subter-ranean **Subways** (☎ 9369 563; www.bistro-bar-subways .de, in German; Ansbacherstrasse; 8am-1am Wed, Thu & Sun, 9pm-4am Fri & Sat).

Shopping

Christmas trimmings abound throughout town – see the boxed text, p264. Handmade items, including wooden toys, are made in the area by people with disabilities and sold at **Werkstattladen Rothenburg** (Kirchgasse 1).

Musicpoint (Galgengasse 48) Has a fantastic array of hard-to-find CDs as well as musical instruments.

Getting There & Away

Rothenburg is on a branch line to Steinach, with hourly trains from 5am to 8pm. From Steinach there's frequent direct train service with Würzburg (€9.60, 1¼ hours), and con-nections to other Franconian and Romantic Road towns. The Europabus stops at the *Bahnhof*, and also at Schrannenplatz.

Rothenburg has its own exit off the A7 between Würzburg and Ulm.

Coming from Creglingen, cyclists can fol-low the 'Liebliches Taubertal' bicycle track through the Tauber Valley; or the 'Altmühl' track from the Altmühltal Naturpark. Less known, but also well signposted, is the 'Aischtal' bicycle track, which wends here from Bamberg.

Getting Around

Rothenburg's Altstadt is closed to nonresident vehicles from 11am to 4pm and 7pm to 9am Monday to Friday and all day on weekends; hotel guests are exempt. Galgentor is the only gate that's always open.

There are five car parks just outside the northern, northeastern and southeastern walls. Of these, P5 and the lower part of P4 (both in the northeast) are free, while the upper part of P4 costs €5 all day; the others are more expensive. For a taxi call ☎ 7227.

Some hotels rent bikes, or try **Krauss** (☎ 3495; Wenggasse 42; per half/full day €4/8; 9am-6pm Tue-Fri, 9am-1pm Sat Mar-Oct, 1-6pm Tue-Fri, 9am-1pm Sat Nov-Feb).

SCHILLINGFÜRST

☎ 09868 / pop 2840 / elev 516m

Against the dramatic backdrop of Schilling-fürst's square-cut, hilltop castle, **Bayerischer Jagdfalkenhof** (☎ 222; Schloss Schillingfürst, Am Wall; adult/under 16yr €7/4; flight shows 11am & 3pm Mar-Oct, plus additional show 5pm May-Aug), prehistoric-like eagles, falcons, hawks and vultures respond to a series of signals to land directly on their trainer's hands during flight shows. A **museum** unravels the baroque castle's religious ties.

THE GREAT DIVIDE

Just a few hundred metres south of the Schillingfürst exit on the Romantic Road (here the B25) you'll cross the **European Water Divide**, marked with a green sign by the roadside. Every single drop of rain that falls south of here flows into the Danube to the Black Sea; every drop that falls north flows to the Rhine and ultimately the North Sea.

From Rothenburg, take the B25 south for 10km, then follow the signs to your left.

FEUCHTWANGEN

☎ 09852 / pop 12,700 / elev 450m

Romantic roadtrippers often bypass Feuchtwangen (literally 'wet cheeks'), but it rewards a stop to check out the Marktplatz's half-timbered and step-gabled town houses, anchored by the **Röhrenbrunnen** (1727) fountain; you'll also find the **tourist office** (☎ 904 55; Marktplatz 1; 9am-6.30pm Mon-Fri, 1-5pm Sat & Sun May-Sep, 9am-5pm Mon-Fri Oct-Apr) here.

East of the Markt, the excellent **Frankenmuseum's** (☎ 2575; Museumstrasse 19; adult/child/family €21/0.50/5; 10am-5pm Wed-Sun May-Sep, 2-5pm Mar-Apr & Oct-Dec) baroque to late-19th-century rooms will again provide glimpses of the times, while others contain naive folk art and precious faïences.

The Europabus stops at the *Busbahnhof*, the main bus station. The *Busbahnhof* is also served year-round by buses to and from Ansbach (p228), 40 minutes to the north, or Dinkelsbuhl, 20 minutes south. A limited number of scheduled trips by the Romantic Railway (boxed text, p254) travel between Nördlingen, Dinkelsbühl and Feuchtwangen. Feuchtwangen is on the B25.

DINKELSBÜHL

☎ 09851 / pop 11,700 / elev 442m

Dinkelsbühl's colourfully painted half-timbered houses and narrow, cobbled lanes huddle within its fortified town wall. Gracing the wall are four historic gates and 18 towers.

Dinkelsbühl traces its roots to a royal residence founded by Carolingian kings in the 8th century. Located at the intersection of two major trade routes, it rose to prominence in the Middle Ages as a centre of textile manufacturing. Dinkelsbühl escaped destruction both during the Thirty Years' War and WWII, leaving its Altstadt virtually intact to this day.

Artists inspired by the quaint Altstadt came here in the late 19th century, using the Weisses Ross hotel as a base to exchange ideas; and the town remains a thriving artists' community of sculptors, painters and designers. Studios, galleries and shops continue to set up in nooks and crannies around town.

Orientation & Information

The Altstadt is five minutes' walk west of the *Busbahnhof*, via Wörnitzer Tor, beneath which flows the Wörnitzer River. Next door to the *Busbahnhof* you'll find the post office and police station; there's also a pretty view of the town's red rooftops and towers from here.

The **tourist office** (☎ 902 40; www.dinkelsbuehl.de; Marktplatz; 9am-6pm Mon-Fri, 10am-1pm & 2-4pm Sat, 10am-noon Sun May-Oct, 10am-1pm & 2-5pm Mon-Fri, 10am-noon Sat Nov-Apr) is located on Marktplatz, also known as Weinmarkt, opposite the Münster St Georg; enter via Segringer Strasse.

Sights & Activities

Within the walls, **Weinmarkt**, the main square, is lined by a row of picture-perfect Renaissance mansions. The step-gabled and turreted **Ratsherrntrinkstube** on the corner, which once hosted Emperor Karl V and King Gustav Adolf of Sweden, is now home to the tourist office.

Dinkelsbühl is particularly romantic after dark: look for a little box on the north wall of the **Schranne**, a former granary just north of the tourist office; after 11pm two €2 coins will illuminate the town's major medieval landmarks for one hour.

Standing sentry over Weinmarkt is **Münster St Georg** (9am-noon & 2-7pm Jun-Sep, 9am-noon & 2-5pm Oct-May) one of the purest late-Gothic hall churches in southern Germany. It is filled with treasures such as the **Sebastiansaltar** (1520), donated by the archers' guild, which depicts the martyrdom of St Sebastian (he was shot full of arrows). Look at the upper section of the last window in the right aisle to see the **'Pretzl Window'** that was donated by the bakers' guild.

The **Historisches Museum's** (☎ 3293; Altrathausplatz; adult/concession €3/1; 10am-4pm Tue-Sun) residence in the town's historic Rathaus provides an atmospheric backdrop for its collections interpreting Dinkelsbühl's history. Confirm opening hours with the tourist office.

At the other end of the spectrum, the **Museum of the 3rd Dimension** (☎ 6336; Nördlinger Tor; adult/concession/under 12yr €8/6/5.50; 10am-6pm Apr-Oct, 11am-4pm Sat & Sun Nov-Mar), just outside the western town gate, is probably the first dedicated entirely to simulating acid trips. Inside are three floors of holographic images, stereoscopes and attention-grabbing 3-D imagery (especially in the nude section on the 3rd floor).

Ask the tourist office for information on **Nordic walking** in the area.

Tours

One-hour **walking tours** (tours €3; ☺ 2.30pm & 8.30pm Apr-Oct, 2.30pm Sat & Sun Nov-Mar) in German depart from the Münster St Georg. A **night watchman** in medieval garb takes visitors on a free German tour at 9pm daily from April to October (Saturday only November to March).

From Easter to October (weather permitting), you can clip-clop around town for 40 minutes of leisurely sightseeing aboard a **horse-drawn carriage** (adult/child/family €6/3/15).

The tourist office sells **walking-tour maps** (map €0.30) plotting a course around the town's sights.

Festivals & Events

In mid-July, Dinkelsbühl celebrates the 10-day **Kinderzeche** (Children's Festival), commemorating how, in the Thirty Years' War, the town's children persuaded the invading Swedish troops to spare the town from devastation. The Kinderzeche festivities include a pageant, reenactments, music and other entertainment.

Autumn heralds the **fish harvest** with festivities celebrating the town's locally caught carp, pike-perch, tench and trout.

Sleeping

DCC-Campingplatz Romantische Strasse (☎ 7817; www.campingpark-dinkelsbuehl.de; Kobelsmühle 2; per tent €8.70, if arriving by bike €6.15, per person €4.10; **P**) This year-round campsite lies on a lake about 300m northeast of Wörnitzer Tor. Lake swimming and fishing aside, there's also an exercise circuit, tennis courts, minigolf and a kids' playground.

Goldenes Lamm (☎ 2267; www.goldenes.de; Lange Gasse 26-28; s €35-48, d €60-70; **P** ✗) An ancient wooden staircase leads up to Goldenes Lamm's renovated rooms, which are topped by a rooftop garden deck strewn with sun-lounges. The attached restaurant (mains €4.90 to €16.80, closed Wednesday October to May) and beer garden are local favourites.

Weisses Ross (☎ 579 890; www.weisses-ross.de, in German; Staingasse 12; s €46-63, d €68-99) A gathering place for influential artists since 1888, the ancient building and stables housing this charming hotel look like they could tumble down at any moment, which only adds to the *Gemütlichkeit* within its immaculate, comfortable rooms and gourmet restaurant (mains €7 to €14.80).

Eating & Drinking

Nightlife per se is limited but café terraces spilling over with drinkers and diners give Dinkelsbühl's Altstadt the feel of an outdoor party throughout the warmer months.

Delicious local specialities include freshwater fish, Hesselberg lamb and *Schneckennudel* buns (rolled with almonds, citrus peel, cinnamon, currants and raisins).

Tee-Café Tee-Laden (☎ 589 820; Turmgasse 13; snacks & sweets from €0.80; ☺ 9am-6.30pm Mon-Sat) This wonderful little shop-café blends Dinkelsbühl's traditions with emerging artistic trends. Take a seat at its smart white-leather booths or on the terrace for a high tea (€7.50) of fresh scones and fruity marmalade. It also has a tantalising array of handmade chocolates and sells local pottery as well as canisters of dozens of varieties of teas.

Weib's Brauhaus (☎ 579 490; Untere Schmiedgasse 13; mains €3.80-12.30; ☺ 11am-1am Thu-Mon, 6pm-1am Wed; **V**) A female brewmaster presides over the copper vats at this sage-green half-timbered restaurant-pub, which has a good-time vibe thanks to its friendly crowd of regulars. Many dishes are made with the house brew, including the popular *Weib's Töpfle* ('woman's pot'; €10.20) of pork medallions and deep-fried mashed potato.

our pick Deutsches Haus (☎ 6058; Weinmarkt 3; menu €16.90, mains €10.90-15.90; **V**) If you look at this historic building from the Rothenburg gate at the north of the street, its central windows appear straight, but when standing directly in front you'll see this is an illusion created by its 13th-century architects, and the façade is actually off kilter. The mahogany-panelled interior is a wonderfully formal setting for traditionally prepared game and fish (the house specialities). Vegetarian dishes like panfried potato and carrot with mushroom-cream sauce are limited in number but not in quality. Should you not feel like moving afterwards, head upstairs to its four-star rooms (doubles €99 to €125).

Getting There & Around

Other than a handful of scheduled trips by the Romantic Railway (boxed text, p254), Dinkelsbühl is not served by trains. Regional buses to Rothenburg (one hour) and Nördlingen (40 minutes) stop at the Busbahnhof; the tourist office has updated schedules or within Germany you can call ☎ 0800-1507 090. Bus travel is included in a

Bayern ticket. The Europabus stops right in the Altstadt at Schweinemarkt.

The tourist office hires out bicycles for €5 per day or €25 per week. From Easter to October, the Altstadt is closed to vehicles from 1pm to 6pm Sunday.

Dinkelsbühl is on the B25.

NÖRDLINGEN

☎ 09081 / pop 20,000 / elev 433m

On the ground, Nördlingen looks like your average charming medieval town, with a tangled Altstadt of colourful, half-timbered buildings, and a refreshingly down-to-earth, workaday air. But viewed from above (from the Daniel Tower, for example), Nördlingen is extraordinary.

The town is almost perfectly circular, thanks to its intact 14th-century town walls, which are punctuated by 16 towers and two bastions as well as five gates. You can circumnavigate along the sentry walk of the covered town wall, and climb up at any of the gates: Baldinger Tor, Löpsinger Tor, Deininger Tor, Reimlinger Tor or Berger Tor, located at the end of the streets bearing their names.

Not only is Nördlingen circular, but it lies within the flattened Ries Basin, a huge crater (some 25km in diameter) that was created more than 15 million years ago by a massive meteorite, meaning it actually resembles a dish. The crater is marked by road signs on the Romantic Road.

Orientation

The *Bahnhof* is about a 15-minute walk southeast of the Altstadt. The St Georgskirche on Markt sits at Nördlingen's centre, from where five main roads radiate towards the town gates. The little Eger River traverses the northern Altstadt, separating the Gerberviertel (Tanner's Quarter), home to both the Stadtmuseum and the Ries Crater Museum, from the rest of the Altstadt.

Information

Tourist office (☎ 841 16; www.noerdlingen.de, in German; Marktplatz 2; ☾ 9am-6pm Mon-Thu, 9am-4.30pm Fri, 9.30am-1pm Sat Easter- Oct plus 9am-1pm Sun May-Sep, 9am-5pm Mon-Thu, 9am-3.30pm Fri Nov-Easter)

Sights

In the town centre, the immense late-Gothic **St Georgskirche** (Church of St George) got its baroque mantle in the 18th century. To truly

appreciate Nördlingen's circular shape and the dished-out crater in which it lies, scramble up the 350 steps of the church's 90m-tall **Daniel Tower** (adult/under 15yr €2/1.40; ☾ 9am-8pm Apr-Oct, 9am-5.30pm Nov-Mar). The guard, who actually lives up here, sounds out the watch every half-hour from 10pm to midnight.

The Ries crater was used by US astronauts training for the first moon landing. Among the displays at the **Ries Crater Museum** (☎ 273 8220; Eugene-Shoemaker-Platz 1; adult/student/child €4/2/1.50; ☾ 10am-noon & 1.30-4.30pm Tue-Sun) is a genuine moon rock (well, if you believe they put a man on the moon…), which is on permanent loan from NASA. The modern museum is set in an ancient barn, and explores the formation of meteorites and the effects of such violent collisions on Earth. Fossils and other geological displays also shed light on the mystery of meteors.

Costumes and displays on local history are displayed in the **Stadtmuseum** (☎ 273 8230; Vordere Gerbergasse 1; adult/child €3/1.50; ☾ 1.30-4.30pm Tue-Sun approx Apr-Oct, exact dates change each year); while a fascinating exhibition on the history of the town walls and fortification system is on show at the **Stadtmauermuseum** (☎ 9180; Löpsinger Torturm; adult/concession €1.50/0.50; ☾ 10am-4.30pm Apr-Oct).

Old trains retire gracefully to the **Bayerisches Eisenbahnmuseum** (Bavarian Railway Museum; ☎ 340; www.bayerisches-eisenbahnmuseum.de; Am Hohen Weg 6a; adult/child €4/2; ☾ noon-4pm Tue-Sat, 10am-5pm Sun May-Sep, noon-4pm Sat, 10am-5pm Sun Oct-Mar), a disused engine depot adjacent to Nördlingen's *Bahnhof* (entry is from the far side of the tracks on Am Hohen Weg only). Trainspotters will delight at the museum's locomotives and carriages in various states of repair; check opening hours ahead as they can vary.

Tours

Guided **walking tours** (in German; adult/under 12yr €3/free) depart from the tourist office at 2pm from Easter to October, and also at 8.30pm from mid-May to mid-September.

Festivals & Events

The 10-day **Nördlinger Pfingstmesse**, held at Whitsuntide/Pentecost (dates vary), is the town's biggest party with beer tents, food stalls and entertainment taking over the Altstadt.

Sleeping & Eating

Hotel Altreuter (☎ 4319; hotel-café-altreuter@nordschwaben.de; Marktplatz 11; s €35-45, d €48-64; ⓟ) Kids warmly welcomed at this epicentral hotel, though you may have a hard time getting them past the delectable sweet shop and café (snacks €5 to €6.60) that forms the entrance/reception. Airy, whitewashed rooms have light wood furniture and the hotel has its own garage, but you'll also find a public parking area in front of the hotel.

Kaiserhof Hotel Sonne (☎ 5067; www.kaiserhof -hotel-sonne.de, in German; Marktplatz 3; s €55-65, d €75-120; P ✗) Right on the main square, Nördlingen's top digs have hosted a procession of emperors and their entourages since 1405. Rooms mix modern comforts with traditional charm, and there's an atmospheric regional restaurant (meals €5.50 to €18).

Café Radlos (☎ 5040; www.café-radlos.de, in German; Löpsinger Strasse 8; snacks €2.80-7.80, mains €8.80-12.80; ☽ 10am-1am Thu-Tue; ☐ V) More than just a place to tuck into tasty Bavarian dishes, Radlos has cherry-red walls that showcase local art and photographic exhibits. Kids have their own toy-filled corner, while you while away the hours with board games, catch regular live bands, or soak up the sunshine in the beer garden.

La Fontana (☎ 211 021; Bei den Kornschrannen 2; mains around €8; ☽ Tue-Sun; V) Housed in an enormous ochre-red barn dating from 1602; take a seat on the mezzanine to dine on Mediterranean fare, including good-value pizzas and pastas. No need to ask if the ingredients are fresh – under the same raked roof is a **market hall** laden with farm-fresh meats, cheeses, breads and produce.

Getting There & Around

Trains leave hourly to Donauwörth (€4.80, 30 minutes), with connections to Augsburg and Munich. The Europabus stops at the Rathaus, as do regional buses to Dinkelsbühl and Feuchtwangen.

Nördlingen is on the B25. There are free car parks at all five city gates; some time restrictions apply.

HARBURG
☎ 09080 / pop 5800

Looming over the Wörnitz River, the medieval covered parapets, towers, turrets, keep and red-tiled roofs of the 12th-century **Schloss Harburg** (☎ 968 60; adult/under 18yr €5/3; ☽ tours in German hourly 10am-4pm Tue-Sun Apr-Oct, closed Nov-Mar) are so perfectly intact they almost seem like a film set; even more so up close. Tours evoke

the ghosts that are said to still lurk in the castle. There are English tours at 10am on Wednesday and Sunday; otherwise you can buy an English leaflet (€0.50).

From the castle, the walk to Harburg's cute half-timbered **Altstadt** takes about 10 minutes, slightly more the other way when you're climbing uphill. For a fabulous panorama of the village and the castle, head to the **Stone Bridge** (1702) spanning the Wörnitz. The **tourist office** (☎ 969 90; www.stadt-harburg-schwaben.de, in German; Schlossstrasse; ☽ 8am-noon Mon, Wed & Fri, 2-4pm Tue, 4-6pm Thu) is at the Rathaus.

A handful of guesthouses are squeezed into the Altstadt's miniature streets, but the most romantic place to eat and/or sleep is within the soaring stone walls of historic Schloss Harburg at the **Fürstliche Burgschenke** (☎ 1504; www.burgschenke-harburg.de, in German; d €75-95; P). Charming rooms – including a honeymoon suite with a sunken bedroom canopied in soft satin – are hidden high in the towers with unfolding valley views, and all come with private bathroom, TV and telephone. Down the winding red-carpeted staircase, the regional fare and friendly service at the elegant restaurant (mains €7.70 to €16.80, closes 6pm Sunday and all day Monday) are first-rate.

The Europabus stops in the village but not at the castle. Train services run to and from Nördlingen (€3.50, 19 minutes), about 15km northwest. Harburg's train station is about a 15-minute walk to the Altstadt (so about a 30-minute walk up to the castle). Local **buses** (☎ 0906-217 27) connect Harburg with Donauwörth.

Harburg is on the B25.

DONAUWÖRTH
☎ 0906 / pop 18,287 / elev 403m

Idyllically sited at the confluence of the Danube and Wörnitz Rivers, Donauwörth rose from its humble beginnings as a fishing village in the 5th century to its zenith as a Free Imperial City in 1301. Three medieval gates and five town wall towers still guard it today, and faithful rebuilding after WWII destroyed 75% of the medieval town has meant that steep-roofed town houses in a rainbow of colours still line its main street, Reichsstrasse.

Reichsstrasse is about a 10-minute walk north of the train station: turn right onto Bahnhofstrasse and cross the bridge onto the little river island, Ried Island. The **tourist office** (☎ 789 151; www.donauwoerth.de, in German; Rathausgasse 1;

9am-noon & 1-6pm Mon-Fri, 3-6pm Sat & Sun May-Sep, 9am-noon & 1-5pm Mon-Thu, 9am-1pm Fri Oct-Apr) is across from the other side of the island, at the bottom of Reichsstrasse.

Over 5600 people from the town work at Eurocopter, an immense commercial and military helicopter manufacturing plant that accounts for the choppers you'll see (and hear) overhead.

Sights

Donauwörth's landmark is the **Rathaus**, begun in 1236 and altered through the centuries. The carillon on the ornamented step gable plays (at 11am and 4pm daily) a composition by local legend Werner Egk (1901–83) from his opera *Die Zaubergeige* (The Magic Violin).

A few steps northeast of the Rathaus, through the **Ochsentörl** town gate, is the **Promenade**, a flower-festooned linear park and cycleway shaded by trees, through which runs a little canal. The park leads past the ruined fortress, the **Mangoldfelsen**, to one of Germany's oldest disused railway tunnels, which you can enter as a shortcut to the northwestern part of town.

From the Rathaus, Reichsstrasse heads west to the 15th-century **Liebfrauenkirche**, a Gothic three-nave church with original frescoes and a sloping floor that drops 120cm. Swabia's largest church bell (6550kg) hangs in the belfry. On Saturdays, Sundays and public holidays from May to September, you can climb the 56m-high church tower up 250 steps to the wraparound balcony at the top (adult/child €1/0.50). If weather conditions are right, you can make out the Alps in the distance.

Reichsstrasse changes its name to Heilig-Kreuz-Strasse, at the end of which stands its namesake, the **Heilig-Kreuz-Kirche** (1717–20), a soaring baroque confection by Josef Schmuzer. The faithful have flocked here for centuries to worship a chip of wood said to come from the Holy Cross.

In a former Capuchin monastery, the delightful **Käthe-Kruse-Puppenmuseum** (Doll Museum; ☎ 789 170; Pflegstrasse 21a; adult/concession €2.50/1.50; 11am-5pm Tue-Sun May-Sep, 2-5pm Tue-Sun Apr & Oct, 2-5pm Wed, Sat & Sun Nov-Mar plus 2-5pm daily 25 Dec-6 Jan) is every little girl's fantasy; it's filled with dolls and doll houses by world-renowned designer Käthe Kruse (1883–1968).

Sleeping & Eating

Hotel Drei Kronen (☎ 706 170; www.hotel3kronen.com, in German; Bahnhofstrasse 25; s/d from €65/104; P X 🖳)

One block from the train station, the pink-hued 'Three Crowns' has comfortable contemporary rooms and a lamp-lit restaurant (mains €10 to €13.50), as well as a summer beer garden with live accordions swaying along with patrons' steins.

Café Engel (☎ 34 81; Reichsstrasse 10; mains €5.60-8.40; 8.30am-6pm Mon & Wed-Sat, 10am-6pm Sun) Inside Donauwörth's oldest building, dating from the 13th century, you'll find an old-fashioned café on the 1st floor serving Bavarian dishes like pork schnitzel. At street level, Engel sells handmade chocolates like *Donauwörther Nüsse* (nut-filled chocolates) and sweets such as the brightly coloured *Donaukiesel* ('Danube stones', named for the smooth, round *Kiesel* stones from the riverbed).

Café Rafaello (☎ 999 9266; Fischerplatz 1; mains €9.20-19; V) Beneath the twin-turreted Rider Tor gate, on Ried Island, this trendy Italian eatery with a loftlike interior specialises in seafood, such as scampi, calamari and mussels in white wine, and also has gigantic gourmet salads and elaborate desserts.

So the jokes go in Bavaria, the initials DON on Donauwörth locals' car number-plates stand for *Dorf ohne Nachtleben* ('village without nightlife'). What action there is (a handful of bars) can be found on **Hindenburg-Strasse**, the main thoroughfare through little Ried Island.

Getting There & Away

There's a direct hourly train service to Nördlingen (€4.80, 30 minutes) via Harburg, and hourly or better trains to Augsburg (€4.80, 30 minutes). The Europabus stops at the Liebfrauenkirche. Donauwörth is at the crossroads of the B2, the B16 and the B25.

AUGSBURG

☎ 0821 / pop 275,000 / elev 489m

The largest city along the Romantic Road (and Bavaria's third largest), Augsburg has been shaped by the Romans, by medieval artisans, bankers and traders and, in more recent times, by industry and technology. Traces of all these phases are evident throughout its cobbled streets today and are interpreted in its cache of museums, all of which are housed in historic buildings.

As the administrative centre of Swabia the wheels of business and commerce turn in Augsburg year-round, but the best time to visit is in summer, when its grand squares and canal-woven backstreets spill over with *joie de vivre*.

History

Founded in 15 BC by the Romans as an Imperial military camp called Augusta Vindelicorum, Augsburg grew to be the capital of the then-province of Raetia.

A bishopric from the 8th century, Augsburg became a Free Imperial City in 1316. The city prospered in the Middle Ages as a major trading centre (mostly gold, silver and copper) and financial and banking hub. During the Renaissance, the self-made Jakob Fugger 'The Rich', in particular, amassed untold wealth, though his strong sense of social responsibility saw him establish one of the world's first social-welfare estates, the Fuggerei, which still operates today. Fugger and Kaiser Maximilian had a symbiotic relationship, with Maximilian providing the power, and Fugger the cash.

In 1518 Martin Luther was summoned to Augsburg to disavow his writings. Following his unequivocal refusal, in 1530 the reformers presented the *Confessio Augustana*, a summary of the Protestant doctrine, to Karl V, which led to the recognition of the Lutheran faith as equal to the Catholic in 1555 in what went down in history as the Peace of Augsburg.

The city was subsumed into the Bavarian kingdom in 1805, which saw it lose its status as an artistic capital to Munich. Its renewal from the scars of the Thirty Years' War came with industrialisation: in 1897 Rudolf Diesel invented the diesel engine here, and the ME163 built by the Messerschmidt factory was the most advanced fighter plane in WWII. Consequently, Augsburg received a severe drubbing by Allied bombers, but its recovery has resulted in a reinvigorated city and cultural scene.

Orientation

The Hauptbahnhof is at the western end of Bahnhofstrasse, which intersects with Fuggerstrasse at the Königsplatz, the city's main bus transfer point. Parallel to Fuggerstrasse two blocks east is the city's main drag, Maximilianstrasse, which leads to Rathausplatz, the main square.

Information

Buchhandlung Rieger & Kranzfelder (☎ 517 880; Fugger Stadtpalast, Maximilianstrasse 36) Stocks English-language books.

Citibank (Bahnhofstrasse 2)

Easy Internet Café (☎ 508 1878; Bahnhofstrasse 29; per hr €1.50-2.10; ◷ 7am-midnight Mon-Fri, 8am-midnight Sat, 10am-midnight Sun) Rates fluctuate during the day.

HypoVereinsbank (Bahnhofstrasse 11)

Post office Next to the Hauptbahnhof.

Rotes Kreuz (Red Cross; ☎ 192 22) Call for a doctor or ambulance.

Tourist office (☎ 502 070; www.augsburg-tourismus .de; Maximilianstrasse 57; ◷ 9am-6pm Mon-Fri, 10am-4pm Sat, 10am-2pm Sun Apr-Oct, 9am-4pm Mon-Fri, 10am-2pm Sat Nov-Mar, extended hours during Dec) Reserves rooms free by phone; a €2 room booking fee applies for bookings made in person.

Venzentinum (☎ 316 70; Franziskonergasse 12) Hospital.

Sights & Activities

RATHAUSPLATZ & AROUND

The heart of Augsburg's Altstadt, this large, pedestrianised square is anchored by the **Augustusbrunnen**, a fountain honouring the Roman emperor; its four figures represent the Lech River and the Wertach, Singold and Brunnenbach Brooks.

Rising above the square are the twin onion-domed spires of the Renaissance **Rathaus** (town hall), built by Elias Holl from 1615 to 1620 and crowned by a 4m-tall pinecone, the city's emblem (also an ancient fertility symbol). Upstairs is the **Goldener Saal** (Golden Hall; ☎ 324 9196; Rathausplatz; adult/student/under 10yr €2/1/free; ◷ 10am-6pm), a huge banquet hall with an amazing gilded and frescoed coffered ceiling.

For panoramic views over Rathausplatz and the city, climb to the top of the **Perlachturm** (Perlach Tower; ☎ 502 070; Rathausplatz; adult/concession €1/0.50; ◷ 10am-6pm daily May-Oct, 3-6pm Fri-Sun Dec), a former guard tower, and also an Elias Holl creation.

One block west of Rathhausplatz is the spectacularly renovated **Maximilianmuseum** (☎ 324 4102; Philippine-Welser-Strasse 24; adult/child €3.50/2; ◷ 10am-9pm Tue, 10am-5pm Wed-Sun), occupying two patrician town houses joined by a statue-studded courtyard covered by a glass-and-steel roof. Highlights include a fabulous collection of Elias Holl's original wooden models for his architectural creations, and a collection of gold and silver coins that can be viewed through sliding magnifying glass panels. Opening to the courtyard is a chic café, where kids won't want to miss turning

AUGSBURG

0   500 m
0   0.3 miles

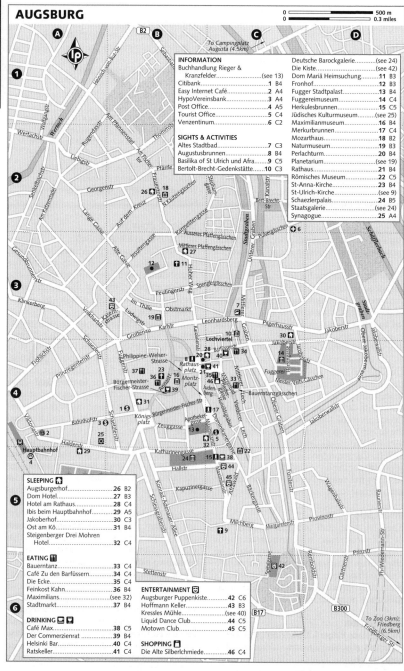

the pages of the 'magic book' that brings Augsburg's history to life.

DOM DISTRICT

Augsburg's cathedral, the **Dom Mariä Heimsuchung**, has its origins in the 10th century but was 'Gothicised' and enlarged in the 14th and 15th centuries. The star treasures here are the so-called 'Prophets' Windows'. Depicting David, Daniel, Jonah, Hosea and Moses, they are among the oldest figurative stained-glass windows in Germany, dating from the 12th century. Look out for four paintings by Hans Holbein the Elder, including one of Jesus' circumcision.

The building west of the Dom is the **Fronhof**, the former bishop's palace. In the predecessor of the current 1743 building, the *Confessio Augustana* was proclaimed in 1530. It's a superb setting for its annual **classical concert series** (☎ 309 84; www.konzerte-im-fronhof.de, in German) in July.

Allow an hour to take in an audioguided tour (in English) of the **Mozarthaus** (☎ 324 3894; Frauentorstrasse 30; adult/concession €3.50/2 incl audioguide; ☑ 10am-9pm Tue, 10am-5pm Wed-Sun), the house where Leopold Mozart – Wolfgang Amadeus' father, who was also his music teacher and creator of the acclaimed 'violin technique' – was born in 1719.

ST-ANNA-KIRCHE

Founded as a Carmelite monastery in 1321, **St-Anna-Kirche** (Church of St Anny; ☎ 392 92; Im Annahof 2, off Annastrasse; ☑ 10am-noon Tue-Sat, 3-5pm Tue-Sun) hosted Martin Luther during his stay in 1518. His rooms have been turned into the **Lutherstiege**, a small museum about the Reformation. There's a portrait of Luther by Lucas Cranach the Elder in the eastern choir, while at the opposite end is the **Fuggerkapelle**, the chapel where Jakob Fugger and his brothers are buried. Also pop into the lavishly frescoed **Goldschmiedekapelle** (Goldsmiths' Chapel; 1420).

MAXIMILIANSTRASSE

Rathausplatz marks the northern end of Maximilianstrasse, a grand boulevard named for Kaiser Maximilian (1459–1519), which is lined by patrician mansions and graced with two impressive fountains. The **Merkurbrunnen** (1599), at the intersection with Bürgermeister-Fischer-Strasse, is by Dutch artist Adriaen de Vries and features the god Mercury as a sym-

bol of trade. Further south, near Hallstrasse, is the **Herkulesbrunnen** (1602), also by de Vries, which shows Hercules fighting the seven-headed Hydra, representing Augsburg's commercial importance.

In between the two fountains, at No 36-38, is the restored **Fugger Stadtpalast** (1515), the palatial town house and 'corporate' headquarters of Jakob Fugger. It embraces the **Damenhof** (Ladies' Court), a gorgeous inner courtyard arcaded in Italian Renaissance style. Outside is the spot where Luther famously stood his ground in 1518.

In 1765 local banker Liebert von Liebenhofen commissioned an ebullient rococo palace, the **Schaezlerpalais** (☎ 324 4117; Maximilianstrasse 46; adult/concession €7/5.50; ☑ 10am-5pm Tue-Sun). Designed by Carl Albert von Lespilliez, today the palace houses two museums (covered by a single admission fee). The **Deutsche Barockgalerie** (German Baroque Gallery) offers an exhaustive survey of German 17th- and 18th-century artists, very few of whom are household names. In the attached deconsecrated church is the **Staatsgalerie** (Bavarian State Gallery), which has mostly Augsburg-related works by Old Masters, including a portrait of Jakob Fugger by Albrecht Dürer, and a couple more works by Hans Holbein the Elder painted around 1500 (look closely and you'll see the sky-blue-and-white checks of the Bavarian flag on the trousers of the Bavarian provocateurs, highlighting the fierce rivalry between Augsburg and Bavaria, giving you an idea of the tensions to be overcome when Augsburg was absorbed into the Bavarian state).

Another onion-domed tower, belonging to the late-Gothic **Basilika of St Ulrich and Afra** (☑ 8am-6pm Mon-Tue & Thu-Sun, 8am-10.30am & 3-6pm Wed), crowns the southern end of Maximilianstrasse. The adjacent **St-Ulrich-Kirche** (☑ 10.30am-4.30pm May-Sep) was a preaching hall of the basilica's Benedictine abbey and has been a Lutheran church since 1524. Its peaceful coexistence with its Catholic neighbour has long symbolised Augsburg's religious tolerance.

LECHVIERTEL

Rushing canals stemming from the Lech River traverse the mostly pedestrianised Lechviertel district (sometimes referred to as Jakobviertel). Playwright and poet Bertolt Brecht was born here, and his house has been

---

BRECHT: AUGSBURG'S BREAKAWAY SON

Throughout his life, Bertolt Brecht (1898–1956) and his native Augsburg did not see eye-to-eye. Augsburg was then a straight-laced bourgeois community wary of Brecht's Marxism, while he disdained its conservative attitudes. At the age of 20, he abandoned the city to study medicine in Munich, where he also began to write. His first play to reach the stage – *Trommeln in der Nacht* (Drums in the Night) – quickly made Brecht a household name in the theatre world.

Drawn to Berlin, a cultural hotbed throughout the 1920s, the black-leather-jacket-wearing, cigar-chomping Brecht went on to develop his theory of 'epic theatre', which compels audiences to detach emotionally from the characters and to view the action critically and intellectually. His biggest success was *Die Dreigroschenoper* (The Threepenny Opera; 1928), featuring the catchy 'Mack the Knife'.

Brecht went into exile during the Nazi years, surfaced in Hollywood as a scriptwriter, then left the USA under the scrutiny of the McCarthy-era witch hunts. In 1949 he unsettled Augsburgers again by choosing to live in communist East Berlin, where he founded the Berliner Ensemble theatre company with his wife, Helene Weigel; he remained there until his death.

The first time one of his plays was performed in his home town wasn't until 1982. But Augsburg now embraces its breakaway son. Under the banner Augsburg Brecht Connected (ABC), it hosts the three-day **Brecht Festival** in July, with performances of his plays, readings and contemporary poems written with hallmark Brecht style (and substance), and 'Brecht on the Decks' DJ parties.

Year-round you can visit the **Bertolt-Brecht-Gedenkstätte** (Brecht Birthhouse; ☎ 324 2779; Am Rain 7; adult/concession €3.50/2; ۩ 10am-9pm Tue, 10am-5pm Wed-Sun), a converted former tile factory where he lived for the first two years of his life before moving across town. Among the displays are old theatre posters and a great series of life-size chronological photos, as well as the bedroom of his mother (about whom he said 'I loved her in my way but she wanted to be loved in her own'). Information panels are in German, but you can buy a detailed English guide to its permanent exhibits (€5), which makes a unique memento of this now-open-minded city in which Brecht would surely feel at home.

---

turned into a memorial museum (see the boxed text, above).

Even if you don't plan to get wet, it's worth a peek inside the **Altes Stadtbad** (☎ 324 9779; Leonhardsberg 15; day ticket adult/concession €4/2.40), a stunning Art Nouveau covered swimming pool with ornamental tiles and stained-glass windows. Check with the tourist office as opening hours vary; it's generally closed during summer.

RÖMISCHES MUSEUM

Military weapons, sarcophagi, gold coins and tombstones are among the relics of Roman Augsburg at the **Römisches Museum** (Roman Museum; ☎ 324 4134; Dominikanergasse 15; adult/concession €3.50/2; ۩ 10am-9pm Tue, 10am-5pm Wed-Sun), housed inside a former 16th-century monastery church.

FUGGEREI

The legacy of Jakob Fugger 'The Rich' lives on at Augsburg's Catholic welfare settlement, the **Fuggerei** (☎ 450 8019; btwn Jakobstrasse & Meister-Veits-Gässchen; adult/child €2/1 incl Fuggereimuseum; ۩ 9am-8pm Apr-Oct, 9am-6pm Nov-Mar), which is the oldest of its kind in existence.

Around 200 people live here today and their rent remains frozen at 1 Rhenish guilder (now €0.88) per *year*, plus utilities and three daily prayers. Bemused residents wave to you as you wander through the car-free lanes of this gated community flanked by its 52 pin-neat houses (containing 140 apartments) and little gardens.

To see how residents lived before running water and central heating, one of the apartments now houses the **Fuggereimuseum**. Interpretive panels are in German but you can ask for an information leaflet in English.

SYNAGOGUE

Augsburg's beautiful Art Nouveau synagogue (1914–17) was devastated in 1938, but reopened in 1985 and now contains the **Jüdisches Kulturmuseum** (Museum of Jewish Culture; ☎ 513 658; Halderstrasse 8; adult/concession €2/1.50; ۩ 9am-8pm Wed, 9am-4pm Thu-Fri, 10am-5pm Sun). The permanent exhibit documents Jewish life in the region and explains traditions, rituals and customs from the 17th to the 19th centuries.

Tours

A great way to absorb Augsburg's history is on a two-hour guided **walking tour** (adult/concession €7/5; ☺ 2pm daily Apr-Oct, 2pm Sat Nov-Mar) run by the tourist office. Tours, in English and German, depart from the Rathaus.

Festivals & Events

Mozart's music fills Augsburg during the **Deutsches Mozartfest** (German Mozart Festival; www .deutsche-mozart-gesellschaft.de), which is held in May every three years; the next are in 2009 and 2012. The **Augsburger Mozartfest** (Augsburg Mozart Festival; www.mozartstadt.de) takes place in the years between the German Mozart festivals.

Swabia's biggest party, the **Plärrer** (www.plaer rer-volksfest.de, in German) sees beer flowing and bands playing around Easter and again in late August/early September.

See the boxed text, opposite, for details about the Brecht Festival.

Sleeping

BUDGET

Campingplatz Augusta (☎ 707 575; www.caravaning park.de, in German; Mühlhauser Strasse 54b; 2 adults, tent & car €18, motel s/d €32/38; **P**) This year-round campsite with a restaurant, kids' playground and handful of motel rooms is on a swimming lake, some 7km from the city centre. Take bus 23 to the terminus, from where it's a 2km walk.

Jakoberhof (☎ 510 030; www.jakoberhof.de; Jakober- strasse 41; s with shared/private bathroom from €26/74, d with shared/private bathroom from €39/99; **P** ✗) This friendly *Pension* spans a collection of three buildings near the Fuggerei. It also has family rooms, a decent Bavarian restaurant (mains €8, closed November to March) and free parking and bike storage. Take tram 1 or bus 22 or 23.

Ibis beim Hauptbahnhof (☎ 501 60; www.ibisho tel.com; Halderstrasse 25; r €55-65; **P** 🛍) OK, it's a chain so obviously don't expect *Gemütlichkeit*. But if you forego the optional €9.50 breakfast per person, this place, a stone's throw from the train station, is one of the best deals in town, with decent-sized rooms, a bar and wi- fi (which, bizarrely, is only accessible from 6pm to 9am; it costs €7.95 for those hours). Room rates are around 10% cheaper if you book online.

MIDRANGE

Ost am Kö (☎ 502 040; www.ostamkoe.de; Fuggerstrasse 4-6; s €59-109, d €78-140; **P** ✗ 🛍) Behind a boxy, pale-tangerine 1960s façade awaits this uberfriendly, uberefficient hotel with lots of personal touches and a bountiful buffet breakfast. It's on a busy street, but windows are soundproofed.

Hotel am Rathaus (☎ 346 490; www.hotel-am -rathaus-augsburg.de, in German; Am Hinteren Perlachberg 1; s €60-90, d €90-120; **P** ✗ 🖵) As central at it gets, footsteps from Rathausplatz and Maximilianstrasse, this boutique hotel has fresh neutral décor and a sunny little breakfast room. Ask about its weekend specials.

Dom Hotel (☎ 343 930; www.domhotel-augsburg.de; Frauentorstrasse 8; s €70-105, d €90-140; **P** ✗ 🛍) If the walls could talk. Martin Luther hid in the garden of this former residence of Bavarian duke Provost Johann, before his escape from the Catholic Cardinal Cajetan. Now a chic hotel with fabulous views of the cathedral steeples, its contemporary rooms have cut- ting-edge, minimalist décor.

Augsburgerhof (☎ 343 050; www.augsburger-hof .de; Auf dem Kreuz 2; s €85-105, d €92-130; **P** ✗ 🖵) Framed by window boxes blazing with ge- raniums in summer, higher-priced rooms at this 'Romantikhotel' open onto its pretty courtyard, but all are thoughtfully furnished and have cable TV and telephone, and there's an outstanding restaurant on site.

TOP END

Steigenberger Drei Mohren Hotel (☎ 503 60; www .augsburg.steigenberger.de, in German; Maximilianstrasse 40; s €105-208, d €131-276; **P** ✗ 🛏 🖵) A proud Leopold Mozart stayed here with his prodi- gious kids in 1766 and it remains Augsburg's oldest and grandest hotel. Regal rooms come with marble bathrooms and original art. You can dine in-house on French-influenced fare at Bistro 3M, or have a gastronomic extrava- ganza at Maximilians (closed dinner Sunday), which swings during Sunday's jazz brunch.

Eating

Café Zu den Barfüssern (☎ 450 4966; Barfüsserstrasse 10; snacks €1-4.50; ☺ 11am-6pm Mon-Sat) Follow a short flight of steps down from the street through a covered passageway to uncover this pretty place on a little canal. Run by a team of handicapped staff, for whom it provides work opportunities as part of a community project, it serves delectable home-made cakes and pastries.

Feinkost Kahn (☎ 312 031; Annastrasse 16; mains €6.90-9.90; ☺ 8am-7pm Mon-Wed, 8am-8pm Fri & Sun,

8am-6pm Sat) Next to the Annastrasse entrance of the Stadtmarkt, Feinkost Kahn's interior is a cross between a gourmet food emporium and a spaceship, with a curved white modular mezzanine and booths. The cured meats, sauces and olive oils on display are incorporated into its meals, which are top-notch value for money; and if you like them, you can buy them to take with you.

Bauerntanz (☎ 153 644; Bauerntanzgässchen 1; mains €8.90-14.20; ☺ 11.30am-11.30pm Mon, 11am-11.30pm Tue-Sun) Framed by lace curtains, this dark-timber place with copper lamps serves big portions of creative Swabian and Bavarian food (*spätzle*, veal medallions and more *spätzle*) using choice ingredients. There's outdoor seating in fine weather.

Die Ecke (☎ 510 600; Elias-Holl-Platz 2; lunch menu €16, lunch mains €14-16, dinner menu €59, dinner mains €13-28; ☺ 11am-2pm & 5.30pm-1am) Augsburgers celebrate special occasions at 'The Corner', an elegant dining room with silver plates, white-clothed tables and duck-shaped china terrines, which specialises in cooking deer in creative ways. To whet your appetite, start your meal with the delicious apple soup.

Dozens of stalls and stand-up eateries serve everything from Asian to Bavarian to delicious Greek dips and *dolmades* (rice rolled up in vine leaves) at Augsburg's snacker's fantasy, the **Stadtmarkt** (City Market; btwn Fuggerstrasse & Annastrasse; ☺ 7am-6pm Mon-Fri, 7am-2pm Sat; Ⓥ).

You'll find lots of bakeries in and around Bahnhofstrasse, and delightful cafés along Maximilianstrassse.

Drinking

Helsinki Bar (☎ 372 90; Barfüsserstrasse 4) The Nordic blonde-wood furnishings and suspended table lighting consistently attract a cool crowd to this sophisticated bar, which shares space with the Kressles Mühle cultural centre.

Café Max (☎ 154 700; Maximilianstrasse 67) Artists and students congregate at this atmospheric café over giant breakfasts, while out the back, the sky-lit bar, Atrium, mixes some of the city's best cocktails.

Der Commerzienrat (☎ 157 766; Bürgermeister-Fischer-Strasse 12; ☺ 11am-1am Mon-Sat) This hole-in-the-wall, Art Deco–style bar opens to a split-level seating area and serves good coffee as well as punchy beer cocktails to a mixed straight and gay crowd.

Ratskeller (☎ 3198 8238; Rathausplatz 2) Augsburg's hippest new hang-out is the reconfigured, multilevel Ratskeller. Ambiently lit corners, ante-rooms and mezzanines are strewn with comfy lounges, and there's a wide terrace out the back. Ratskeller's kitchen also has a strong local following, especially for its *Schweinebraten* – roast pork with dumplings and red-cabbage sauerkraut (€8.60).

Entertainment

Kressles Mühle (☎ 362 15; www.kresslesmuehle.de, in German; Barfüsserstrasse 4) Behind Helsinki Bar, this cultural centre housed in an ivy-covered 13th-century flourmill is a lynchpin of the city's creative community, with a schedule that ranges from poetry slams to stand-up comedy, meditative gonging and folk dancing.

AUGSBURG FOR CHILDREN

Augsburg has a great range of activities to keep little visitors busy.

Modern and classic fairy tales – *Aladdin* to *Rumpelstiltsken* to *The Little Prince* – play at the **Augsburger Puppenkiste** (Augsburg Puppet Box; ☎ 450 3450; Spitalgasse 15; afternoon show €7.80-9.80, evening show €14.50-19.80; ☺ 3pm & 7.30pm Wed & Sat, 2pm & 4pm Sun). The stars on strings are so endearing and the sets so elaborate that even non-German speakers (and non-kids) will enjoy a show. It's often sold out; make advance reservations or check with the tourist office for remaining tickets. Kids will also adore the adjoining museum, **Die Kiste** (☎ 450 3450; adult/under 12yr/family €4.20/2.70/10.80; ☺ 10am-7pm Tue-Sun, last entry 6pm), which takes you on a journey through the marionettes' 50-plus-year career on stage, TV and film, and also has a painting corner and little movie 'cabins'.

Also in central Augsburg, the **Naturmuseum** (☎ 324 6740; Ludwigstrasse 2; adult/student/under 10yr 3.50/2/free; ☺ 10am-9pm Tue, 10am-5pm Tue-Sun) has animal skeletons and exhibits on apes and butterflies, while budding astronomers can stargaze at the adjacent **Planetarium** (☎ 324 6740; www.s-planetarium.de, in German; adult/family €4.50/10; ☺ varies).

Heading 3km southeast of town on Friedberger Strasse brings you to Augsburg's **zoo** (☎ 567 1490; adult €5-7, under 15yr €2.50-3.50). Take bus 32 (marked 'Zoo') from Königsplatz.

Hoffmann Keller (Kasernstrasse 2) Informal jam sessions and gigs by local acts regularly take to the small stage down the far end of this elongated, atmosphere-charged venue.

Clubs where you can shake it include **Liquid Dance Club** (☎ 518 815; www.liquid-club.de; Maximilianstrasse 71; ✆ 10pm-late Fri, 11pm-late Sat), a UV-lit vaulted space spinning hip-hop, house, R&B and electro, and **Motown Club** (☎ 508 3033; www.motownclub.de; Afrawald 4; ✆ 10pm-3am Tue, 9pm-3am Wed, 10pm-5am Thu-Sat). Cover charges and drinks specials vary depending on the night; keep tabs on what's happening via the websites.

The tourist office keeps daily programmes for Augsburg's handful of arthouse cinemas, as well as details of what's showing at various open-air film screenings in summer.

See the boxed text, opposite, for entertainment options for kids.

Shopping

The quaint, narrow street Pfladergasse is lined with artisan shops such as jewellery shop **Die Alte Silberlchmiede** (The Old Silversmith; ☎ 389 45; Pfladergasse 10), which occupies a 13th-century house and courtyard. It's usually possible to pop inside its workshops to watch original designs being handcrafted.

Getting There & Away

Augsburg is just south off the A8. The northbound B2 and the southbound B17 are part of the Romantic Road.

Regional trains connect Augsburg and Munich at least hourly (€10.60, 50 minutes), with faster and pricier InterCity Express (ICE) and InterCity (IC) trains passing through as well. Regional Express (RE) trains depart every other hour to Füssen (€16.60, two hours) and to Lindau (€26, three hours). The Europabus stops at the Hauptbahnhof and the Rathaus.

The **Lufthansa Airport Bus** (☎ 0981 3152; one way/return €15/24) runs between Augsburg's Hauptbahnhof and the Munich airport three times daily in each direction (70 minutes).

Getting Around

Most rides within town on the bus and tram network cost €1; longer trips to the outlying suburbs are €2. A 24-hour ticket costs €6.20 and is good for up to two adults and six children travelling together.

The tourist office rents bikes from €10 per day.

SOUTH OF AUGSBURG

South of Augsburg, the Romantic Road enters its least scenic stretch, although there are a few spots to break your journey. Note that the Romantic Road changes route numbers several times in this sector.

From Augsburg, a spur road spirits you 6.5km east to **Friedberg**, a medieval town founded in 1204, with a charming fountained central square. From here, retrace your route back to Augsburg to join the southbound B17.

Sign-spotters may want to take a quick detour to **Kissing**, 13km southeast of Augsburg. It's by no means as romantic as it sounds – though first mentioned in 1050, these days it's essentially a commuter town of 11,500 inhabitants, surrounded by suburban sprawl. There's no tourist office (which makes sense, since there's little to see), but Kissing's town signs provide an apt photo opp. To fuel yourself for the onward journey, **Restaurant Rosenhof** (☎ 08233-7369 999; Rosenstrasse 23, Kissing; mains €6.20-10.90; ✆ 11am-2pm & 5.30-11pm Sun-Mon & Wed-Fri, 5.30-11pm Sat; V) has good salads, pastas and pork dishes, and a friendly atmosphere.

About 42km south of Augsburg on the B17 is historic **Landsberg am Lech**, founded by Heinrich der Löwe (Henry the Lion) in 1160. It possesses an especially appealing Marktplatz ringed by stately buildings, including the impressive Rathaus. Its awesome façade (1720) is the work of Dominikus Zimmermann, who moonlighted as the town's mayor from 1749 to 1754 while creating the Johanniskirche (1752). Also worth a look is the parish church Maria Himmelfahrt (1458–88), famous for its luminous stained-glass windows.

To Landsberg's south, the route cuts through the **Pfaffenwinkel** (Clerics' Corner), which has the greatest density of churches and monasteries anywhere in Germany (which is really saying something). After the tranquil gateway town of **Hohenfurch**, the B17 travels to **Schongau**, which preserves a largely intact medieval appearance. Sights include the town wall, the Gothic *Ballenhaus* (festival hall) and the baroque Maria Himmelfahrt church (1753), where the choir stucco bears the distinctive Zimmermann touch.

In Altenstadt, about 2km west of Schongau, the Romanesque **Basilika St Michael** (1220) has great frescoes, a delicate baptismal font and a 3.5m-high crucifix from around 1200, which is revered as the 'Great God of Altenstadt'.

DETOUR: OTTOBEUREN & KNEIPP-LAND

Cradled by pre-Alpine mountains, **Ottobeuren** (☎ 08332, population 8095, elevation 660m) rewards a 45-minute or so drive west of the Romantic Road, both for its awe-inspiring basilica and abbey, and its legacy as the home town of Sebastian Kneipp, the father of modern holistic therapy.

Appearing from a distance like a celestial mirage, Ottobeuren's Benedictine abbey and basilica, **Benediktinerabtei Ottobeuren**, stretches nearly half a kilometre from its main church portal to the utility buildings. The abbey was founded in 764, and still has about two dozen active friars today. Its **basilica** (admission incl tours & concerts by donation; ✆ 8am-6pm, 30min tours 2pm Sat late Feb-late Nov, organ recitals 4pm Sat late Feb-late Nov), tinged with rose, pistachio and gold, was built between 1737 and 1766. Inside is a rococo explosion of gilded altars, delicate stucco, multicoloured frescoes, marble pillars and a cacophony of angels. In the former abbot's residence, exhibits in the **Benediktinerabtei Museum** (☎ 7980; admission €2.50; ✆ 10am-noon & 2-5pm Mon-Fri Apr-Oct, 2-4pm Mon-Fri Nov-Mar, 10am-noon & 2-4pm Sat & Sun year-round) include an old pharmacy and baroque theatre displays. Peek into the ballroom-sized library with 15,000 volumes, and check out the majestic **Kaisersaal** (Imperial Hall), the site of the annual **Ottobeurer Konzerte** (✆ May-Sep; tickets €15 to €35) classical concert series. Check with Ottobeuren's **tourist office** (☎ 921 950; www.ottobeuren .de, in German; Marktplatz 14; ✆ 9am-noon & 2-5pm Mon-Thu, 9am-noon & 2-4pm Fri), right at the foot of the basilica, for ticket availability. The abbey's **Kloster-Café** (☎ 925 929; snacks from €2; ✆ 10am-5.30pm, closed Thu Nov-Apr) serves sinfully rich cakes. More cafés, plus restaurants and guest houses, cluster around Marktplatz.

Ottobeuren's crystal-clear waters, pristine air, sunshine and fertile farmland inspired the teachings of its own 'herb priest' or 'water doctor', Sebastian Kneipp (1821–97). The son of an impoverished Allgäu weaver, Kneipp was born in the little hamlet of Stephansried, 3km from Ottobeuren's village centre. During his theological studies he contracted tuberculosis, but he chanced upon

---

The B17 winds from Schongau a further 4.5km south to **Peiting**, then continues southeast on the B23 to **Rottenbuch** in the Ammertal (Ammer Valley). Rottenbuch is dominated by an 11th-century Augustinian monastery whose church got its baroque outfit courtesy of Franz Xaver Schmädl and Josef Schmuzer (stucco), and Matthäus Günther (frescoes). Hiking trails lead from the depth of Ammer Gorge back up to elevations reaching 900m. Rottenbuch's **tourist office** (☎ 08867-1464; www.rottenbuch.de, in German; Klosterhof 36, Rottenbuch; ✆ 9am-noon Mon-Fri Jan-Oct) has maps and directions.

From here, the B23 travels west through **Wildsteig** before rejoining the B17 in **Steingaden**, where one of the route's highlights awaits: the Wieskirche.

WIESKIRCHE

About a million art lovers and spiritual pilgrims flock annually to the magnum opus of brothers Dominikus and Johann Baptist Zimmermann, the **Wieskirche** (☎ 8862-932 930; www.wieskirche.de; Steingaden; admission by donation; ✆ 8am-7pm Apr-Oct, 8am-5pm Nov-Mar, phones staffed 8am-noon & 1-5pm Mon-Thu, 8am-noon Fri).

Now a Unesco World Heritage site, the Wieskirche has gleaming white pillars topped by capital stones that look like leaping flames against the white, gold and pastel stucco, while the vaulted ceiling fresco celebrates Christ's Resurrection as he is carried on a rainbow. But the central object of worship is the rather unassuming statue of the **Scourged Saviour**, now part of the high altar. Originally used in a Good Friday procession in 1730, the statue ended up with a local innkeeper. Then, on 14 June 1738, during evening prayers, tears suddenly began weeping from the statue's eyes. Over the next few years, so many pilgrims poured into the town that the local abbot commissioned the church to house it.

Visitors are asked not to tour through during services, though you're welcome to attend a full service, provided you're seated.

The Europabus makes a 30-minute stop at the Wieskirche on its south–north route (Munich–Frankfurt), but only drops off and picks up on its north–south route (Frankfurt–Munich). Local bus 73 connects the church with Füssen's bus station, next to the train station.

a booklet about the curative properties of fresh water. He regularly immersed himself in the icy Danube and, his health improving, he began curate work in the region, becoming not just a spiritual healer, but a physical one.

Kneipp's cures are founded on five pillars: hydrotherapy; exercise therapy; nutrition therapy using wholefoods; phytotherapy (medicinal herbs); and regulative therapy ('orderliness' in one's life). Authorities were suspicious of these avant-garde philosophies, hauling Kneipp into court in 1860 and 1866 under the Charlatan Act (both cases were dismissed). Ironically today, state ministries regulate the right of establishments offering treatments to carry the Kneipp name, and the area encompassing Ottobeuren has been named **Kneipp-land** (Kneipp Country).

You can take a Kneipp cure at Ottobeuren's rambling, wood-panelled **Hotel St Ulrich** (☎ 923 520; www.kneipp-und-kur.de, in German; Bannwaldweg 10; s €45-54, d €72-86; ☻ approx Feb-Nov; P ✗ ♨). Contact the hotel for spa treatment prices and packages; the restaurant (mains €15) can arrange 'Kneipp diet' menus for guests and nonguests, but you'll need to book ahead.

Sprinkled along Ottobeuren's footpaths are Kneipp **tread baths** and **arm basins**; the tourist office has a map showing their locations.

To embrace Kneipp's pillar of active physical movement, and take in some glorious country-side, the **Kneipp Cycle Route** (☎ 08261-995 375; www.unterallgaeu.de) is a 56km-long loop linking Ottobeuren with Bad Wörishofen and Bad Grönenbach. Details about the Allgäu's Kneipp cures and spas are also available at www.allgaeu.de. Bikes can be rented from **Anna's Bike Shop** (☎ 1234; Markt-Rottenbacherstrasse 8; per day from €6; ☻ 3-7pm Mon, Tue, Thu & Fri, 9am-1pm Sat).

Ottobeuren is about 11km southeast of the nearest large town, Memmingen, and 63km west of the Romantic Road village Landsberg am Lech. Bus 955 travels several times daily to Ottobeuren from Memmingen's central bus station (€2.65, 17 minutes), from where there are train connections to Augsburg. From Landsberg, the quickest route is to follow the A69 west for 49km, then turn right onto the B18/E54 for 2km, from where signs lead to Ottobeuren.

FÜSSEN & SCHWANGAU

☎ 08362 / pop 17,700 / elev 800m

Nestled at the foot of the Alps, Schwangau and Füssen form two anchors of the area known as Königswinkel (King's Nook). The king in question, Bavaria's beloved Ludwig II, built his fantasy castle Schloss Neuschwanstein here. This, as well as his ancestral holiday home, the palace Schloss Hohenschwangau, are actually in the tiny village of Hohenschwangau, the third 'corner' in this triangle, and are still owned by the royal family of Bavaria.

Ludwig's Schloss Linderhof (p143) is about 45km northeast of here. A good way to see it is on a scenic circular driving trip from Füssen via Reutte in Austria (14km south of Füssen), the Plansee lake (10km east of Reutte) and the Wieskirche (30km north of Füssen). Although this loop is only 120km all up, allow half a day for stops – and for navigating the twisting Alpine roads.

Orientation

The Königswinkel's only *Bahnhof* is in Füssen's northern Altstadt, a five-minute walk from the tourist office. The Lech River traverses the town and flows into the Forggensee. Schwangau is

about 4km east of Füssen via the B17 (Romantic Road), which, in town, is called Münchener Strasse. Hohenschwangau village is more or less in between and south of the two, about 5km from Füssen and 3km from Schwangau. Füssen is the bigger town with better infrastructure. Buses 73 and 78 connect all three.

Information

Füssen tourist office (☎ 938 50; www.fuessen.de; Kaiser-Maximilian-Platz 1; ☻ 8.30am-6.30pm Mon-Fri, 10am-2pm Sat & Sun Jun-Sep, 8.30am-6pm Mon-Fri, 10am-2pm Sat & Sun Apr-May & Oct, 8.30am-5pm Mon-Fri, 10am-2pm Sat Nov-Mar) Efficient office about three minutes' walk west of the *Bahnhof*, with a water sculpture of rotating pillars out the front.

Schwangau tourist office (☎ 819 80; www.schwan gau.de, in German; Münchener Strasse 2; ☻ 8am-6pm Mon-Fri, 8.30am-12.30pm Sat, 10am-noon Sun Jul-Sep, 8am-12.30pm & 1.30-5pm Mon-Fri, 9am-noon Sat, 10am-noon Sun Oct-Jun)

Sights & Activities

Most people, of course, head here for the castles, but Füssen's Altstadt also has some intriguing sights, while the mountains and lakes, such as the Alpsee, offer water and snow sports.

FÜSSEN & SCHWANGAU

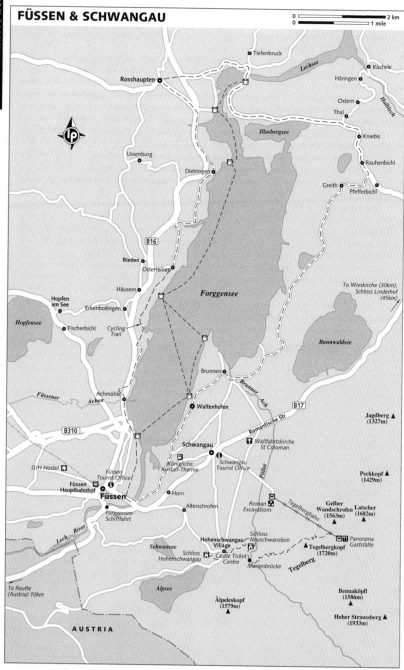

0 — 2 km
0 — 1 mile

Tiefenbruck

Lechsee

Küchele

Häringen

Rosshaupten

Ostern

Thal

Kniebis

Illasbergsee

Rauhenbichl

Ussenburg

Dietringen

Greith

Pfefferbichl

B16

Rieden

Osterreinen

Häusern

Forggensee

Hopfen am See

Erkenboilingen

To Wieskirche (30km);
Schloss Linderhof
(45km)

Hopfensee

Fischerbichl

Cycling Trail

Bannwaldsee

Füssener Achen

Achmühle

Brunnen

Branner Ach

B17

Jagdberg (1327m)

B310

Waltenhofen

Romantische Str

Pechkopf (1429m)

DJH Hostel

Schwangau

Wallfahrtskirche St Coloman

Königliche Kristall-Therme

Schwangau Tourist Office

Füssen Tourist Office

Füssen Hauptbahnhof

Füssen

Horn

Pöllat

Roman Excavations

Tegelbergbahn

Gelber Wandschrofen (1563m)

Latscher (1682m)

Forggensee-Schifffahrt

Alterschrofen

Panorama Gaststätte

Lech River

To Reutte (Austria) 10km

Schwansee

Hohenschwangau Village

Schloss Neuschwanstein

Schloss Hohenschwangau

Castle Ticket Centre

Marienbrücke

Tegelbergkopf (1720m)

Tegelberg

Bennaköpfl (1586m)

Alpsee

Älpeleskopf (1579m)

Hoher Straussberg (1933m)

AUSTRIA

AN UPHILL BATTLE?

Schloss Neuschwanstein inspired Disneyland's signature citadel, Sleeping Beauty's Castle, but ironically Disneyland itself has inspired what Neuschwanstein and the Königswinkel have become today. Around 1.3 million annual visitors churn through on tours simultaneously rotating through the rooms.

If Neuschwanstein is 'Fantasy Land', then Alpenseestrasse in Hohenschwangau, where the ticket centre is located, is 'Main Street Bavaria'. Hohenschwangau basically exists to cater for castle visitors, and positively teems with cafés and souvenir shops selling Bavarian souvenirs (steins et al). The only thing missing is mouse ears.

The foundation administered by Ludwig's ancestors operates several local hotels and recently unveiled plans for a new theatre, a visitor centre, and, most controversially, a cable car ferrying tourists directly from Hohenschwangau village up the steep mountainside to Neuschwanstein. Locals are emphatically against destroying the forested slopes to make way for it (and against the area becoming any more Disney-fied in general); and at the time of research, the council had flatly rejected the proposal. On top of that, Schloss Neuschwanstein (unlike Schloss Hohenschwangau) is owned by the state of Bavaria, and even if it should get past the council, to date the state has said it would override any such move – watch this space.

Even in the absence of a cable car, tourism is in full force, but don't let the theme-park atmosphere deter you. There are some beautiful Alpine walks in the area, the lakes are dazzling and, in any case, the hurdy-gurdy of it all is actually fun. And while there are now Disney castles everywhere from Paris to Japan, there's only one Schloss Neuschwanstein.

SCHLOSS NEUSCHWANSTEIN

King Ludwig II envisaged his dream palace **Schloss Neuschwanstein** (☎ 930 830; adult/concession €9/8, incl Schloss Hohenschwangau €17/15; ☼ tickets on sale 8am-5pm Apr-Sep, 9am-3pm Oct-Mar) as a giant stage that would allow him to live out the Germanic mythology immortalised in the operas of his idol, Richard Wagner. To that end, a theatre designer rather than an architect laid out the initial blueprint.

Construction began in 1869, and the grey-white granite edifice was an anachronism from the start; by the time Ludwig died in 1886, the first high-rises had pierced New York's skyline. Despite his love of the medieval look, however, Ludwig's hi-tech instalments included a hot-air heating system and running water. Tragically, the king was able to enjoy only about 170 days in his dream palace, which was never completed.

Murals depicting scenes from the opera *Tannhäuser* adorn the castle's centrepiece, the lavish **Sängersaal** (Minstrels' Hall). Although it wasn't used during Ludwig's time, concerts are now held here every September (tickets start at €25 and are available from February each year through the Schwangau tourist office).

Ludwig's *Tristan und Isolde*–themed **bedroom** is dominated by a huge bed crowned with intricately carved Gothic cathedral-like spires, with a small stained-glass chapel alcove. Other completed sections include an **artificial grotto** (another allusion to *Tannhäuser*); the **living room**, with murals incorporating more than 100 swans (Schwangau means 'land of swans', and the bird has long been a symbol of the royal family); and the Byzantine **Thronsaal** (Throne Room), which remained throneless: Ludwig ordered it shortly before his death but it was never delivered. The painting on the wall opposite the throne platform depicts another castle dreamed up by Ludwig that was never built.

Brand-new additions inside the castle include a **multimedia room** showing a film about Ludwig's life (included in castle entry; a monitor outside shows the language it's being screened in); and a contemporary **café** (cakes €2.40-2.70). There are, of course, gift shops here, too.

The castle is around a 45-minute uphill walk from Hohenschwangau village. **Horse-drawn carriages** (€5 up to castle, €2.50 down; ☼ year-round) depart from outside Hotel Müller on Alpenseestrasse a few doors uphill from the ticket centre, but these are only slightly faster. Note, too, that there's still a steep eight-minute walk from where the carriages drop you up to the castle entrance.

Inside the castle, tours involve scaling 365 steps. Travellers with disabilities can book a special **wheelchair-accessible castle tour** on a Wednesday using the otherwise off-limits elevator – contact the ticket office for

---

BUYING CASTLE TICKETS

Each of the castles can only be seen on 35-minute guided tours (in German or English; handsets for other languages are available). Tickets for either castle must be purchased from the **ticket centre** (☎ 930 830; www.ticket-center-hohenschwangau.de; Alpenseestrasse 12, Hohenschwangau). A Royal Ticket lets you visit both castles (on the same day only), visiting Schloss Hohenschwangau first, followed by Schloss Neuschwanstein. Entry is free for children under 18 years, but a ticket is still required.

You can reserve tickets up to the close of business the day prior to your visit, either by phone, by email or online. You'll need a major credit card to guarantee your booking, but you may cancel as late as two hours before your preassigned tour time. A nonrefundable booking fee of €1.80 per castle ticket applies (€3.20 per Royal Ticket). Be sure to arrive at the ticket centre at least an hour before your tour time for Neuschwanstein (30 minutes prior for Hohenschwangau tours) to collect your ticket. There's a separate queue for reserved tickets.

Without a reservation, in high summer you'll need to queue at the ticket centre by 8.30am or even earlier to ensure you get a ticket.

Your ticket lists your tour number and time. Wait by the castle entrance close to the time indicated on your ticket until the digital display shows your tour number. Then put your ticket into the turnstile and join the lane marked with your tour number.

Castle tickets are only good for the assigned tour time, so it's important to allow enough time to get there. It takes about 45 minutes to walk between Neuschwanstein and Hohenschwangau castles via a signed walking trail. If you plan to take horse-drawn carriages between both castles, you'll need to return to Alpenseestrasse in Hohenschwangau village and change there.

EurAide (p76) runs day tours from Munich to Neuschwanstein and Linderhof (p143) daily from April to about October and less frequently during the rest of the year.

---

seasonal tour times. Those with tickets for the wheelchair-accessible tour are allowed to drive right up to the castle.

See the boxed text on above for information on purchasing tickets.

MARIENBRÜCKE
Spanning the spectacular Pöllat Gorge over a waterfall, the **Marienbrücke** (Mary's Bridge) offers the quintessential postcard view of Neuschwanstein framed by wooded hills. The castle is a steep 15-minute walk from here (not suitable for wheelchairs or prams). Trails lead down below the bridge, where you'll find some peaceful picnic spots.

Minibuses (€1.80 up to bridge, €1 down; ☙ year-round) depart from outside Hotel Lisl on Alpenseestrasse in Hohenschwangau village (diagonally opposite Hotel Müller).

SCHLOSS HOHENSCHWANGAU
Ludwig spent his childhood holidays at sun-yellow **Schloss Hohenschwangau** (☎ 930 830; adult/concession €9/8, incl Schloss Neuschwanstein €17/15; ☙ tickets on sale 8am-5.30pm Apr-Sep, 9am-3.30pm Oct-Mar). It was originally built in the 12th century by Schwangau knights, but Ludwig's father, Max II, had the ruin reconstructed in neo-

Gothic fashion in the 1830s. There's a cosier, much less ostentatious feel here than at Neuschwanstein, though Ludwig's eccentric taste is still evident, as in the stars he had painted on his bedroom ceiling.

It was here that Ludwig first met Wagner, and in the **Hohenstaufensaal** (High Baptism Hall) you'll see the maple piano where the composer entertained the king.

Schloss Hohenschwangau is not suitable for travellers with impaired mobility.

Horse-drawn carriages (€3.50 up to castle, €1.50 down; ☙ year-round except in snow or icy conditions) are less frequent than those to Schloss Neuschwanstein, and take about 15 minutes to reach the castle (it's about 20 minutes on foot). The carriages depart from the castle ticket centre on Alpenseestrasse in Hohenschwangau village.

See boxed text above for ticket information.

ALTSTADT FÜSSEN
Füssen has a distinct resort feel, with multilingual street and hotel signs, and upmarket designer boutiques, but there are some architectural treasures here, too. The town is also famous for its lute- and violin-making traditions – the tourist office has details of **workshops** that can be visited.

The Altstadt's tangle of lanes is lorded over by the **Hohe Schloss**, a late-Gothic former summer residence of the bishops of Augsburg. In the inner courtyard you'll do a double take before realising that the gables, oriels and even windows are merely illusionary, painted in 1499. The courtyard also has some great contemporary steel sculptures. In its north wing, the **Staatsgalerie im Hohen Schloss** (Hohen Schloss Art Gallery; ☎ 903 164; Magnusplatz 10; adult/concession incl Städtische Gemäldegalerie €2.50/2; ☼ 11am-5pm Tue-Sun Apr-Oct, 1-4pm Fri-Sun Nov-Mar) houses late-Gothic and Renaissance paintings and sculpture by Swabian and Franconian artists. One floor below is the **Städtische Gemäldegalerie** (Municipal Art Gallery), where the emphasis is on 19th-century artists, mostly from Bavaria. Behind the Schloss is the leafy **Baumgarten** (Tree Garden), from where you can walk down to the river's walking path/cycleway.

Nearby, the former **Benediktinerkloster St Mang** (Benedictine Abbey of St Mang) traces its history back to an 8th-century missionary, Magnus, who founded a monk's cell here. Within the abbey, the **Museum Füssen** (☎ 903 145; Lechhalde 3; adult/under 14yr/concession €2.50/free/2; ☼ 11am-5pm Tue-Sun Apr-Oct, 1-4pm Fri-Sun Nov-Mar) provides access to the abbey's festive baroque rooms and the **St Anna Kapelle** (830), where the haunting highlight is the **Füssener Totentanz**, a pictorial representation of the Dance of Death cycle from 1602, created during the dark days of the black plague. The abbey's Romanesque cloister hosts free **concerts** featuring traditional Bavarian bands from 7pm to 8pm every Sunday during July and August.

TEGELBERGBAHN

Breathtaking 360-degree views of the Alps and gem-coloured lakes unfurl from the top of the Tegelberg (1720m), reached by **cable car** (Tegelbergbahn; ☎ 983 60; one way/return €9.50/16; ☼ 8.30am-5pm Jul-Oct, 9am-5pm Nov-Jun). The last ascent/descent is 20 minutes before closing. From here, it's a wonderful hike down to the castles (follow the signs to Königsschlösser) in about two to three hours. Call ahead for a weather report (☎ 810 10), as fog can close in rapidly. The cable car is sometimes closed for maintenance in November or December.

The mountain station is also a launch point for hang-gliders and parasailers. In winter, a day's **skiing** or **snowboarding** (☎ 808 7852) here costs around €22.50, plus gear hire; various passes are available.

The valley station is about 2km southeast of Schwangau and served by bus 73 and 78 from both the Schwangau village centre and the Füssen train station.

FORGGENSEE

Glimmering an unearthly, opaque jade-green, the Forggensee is actually a reservoir created in the 1950s from the bed of the Lech River and is now a popular watersports centre, with activities including swimming, sailing, boating, and windsurfing. A 40km-long bike trail hugs its shore, the paved sections of which are great for in-line skating.

You can catch a ride on boats operated by **Forggensee-Schifffahrt** (☎ 921 363; Lechhalde 3, Füssen; adult €6-8.50, under 14yr €3.50). Tickets are sold onboard; check with the tourist offices about current cruise schedules and where to hire sporting equipment.

KÖNIGLICHE KRISTALL-THERME

Views of the illuminated castles make the **Königliche Kristall-Therme** (☎ 819 630; Am Kurpark, Schwangau; admission 4hr/all day €12.20/15.80; ☼ 9am-10pm Sun-Thu, 9am-11pm Fri & Sat) a sensational spot for a swim, hydro-massage, meditation or sauna. Some nights (usually Tuesday and Friday) are for nudists only.

Sleeping

There's no shortage of places to sleep in the area, including some luxurious lakeside campgrounds – the tourist offices have lists.

DJH hostel (☎ 7754; www.djh.de; Mariahilferstrasse 5, Füssen; dm €17.50-19; ☼ closed mid-Nov–late Dec; Ⓟ ✗) This well-maintained hostel is a five- to 10-minute walk west of the train station; breakfast and linen are included.

Pension Kössler (☎ 7304; www.pension-koessler.de, in German; Kemptener Strasse 42, Füssen; s €30-33, d €60-66; Ⓟ) Trailing flowers from its balconies in summer, this pretty chalet offers perennially outstanding value. Guest rooms come with private bathroom, balcony (or terrace), TV and telephone, and you can unwind in the sunny garden.

Altstadt Hotel zum Hechten (☎ 916 00; www.hotel-hechten.com; Ritterstrasse 6, Füssen; s €47-57, d €84-90; Ⓟ) Set around a quiet inner courtyard, this child-friendly place is one of Füssen's oldest Altstadt hotels, with rustic public areas and bright, modern guest rooms.

Hotel Sonne (☎ 9080; www.hotel-sonne.de; Reichenstrasse 37, Füssen; s €68-111, d €95-142; Ⓟ ✗ 🖳)

DETOUR: LINDAU, LAKE CONSTANCE

Some 100km southwest of Füssen, **Lindau** (☎ 08382, population 24,500, elevation 400m) is well off the Romantic Road, but is one of Bavaria's jewels, and makes an ideal stopover to or from the Black Forest.

Lindau occupies the only snippet of Bavarian shore on Lake Constance, which it shares with Baden-Württemberg as well as Austria and Switzerland. Lindau's historic Altstadt lies on a petite island (reached by a causeway) and exudes old-world wealth and romance. Ringed by Alpine peaks, its deep-blue harbour is something straight off a chocolate box.

Strolling around this charming island gives you an insight into its history; it started as a 9th-century nunnery and blossomed into a prosperous trading route stop. In the early 13th century it became a Free Imperial City through until 1802, and part of Bavaria in 1805. But the influence that stands out most today derives from its 10-year French occupation after WWII. The French founded a casino in 1950, and a swanky new incarnation (on the site of the original) is just before the bridge to the island.

You can hire a *Stadthörer*, a self-guided audio tour (in English or German) with commentary on about 15 island sites for €7.50 from Lindau's **tourist office** (☎ 260 030; www.lindau.de; Ludwigstrasse 68; ◷ 9am-1pm & 2-7pm Mon-Fri, 2-7pm Sat & Sun May-Sep, 9am-1pm & 2-5pm Mon-Fri Oct-Apr), situated opposite the *Bahnhof*. Footsteps away from here is Lindau's little harbour, which is guarded by a **lighthouse** (adult/child €1.60/0.50; ◷ 10am-6pm Easter-Oct, depending on the weather), which can be climbed, and a **pillar** topped by the Bavarian lion. Both date to the middle of the 19th century, making them historic youngsters compared to the 13th-century former lighthouse/town fortification, the **Mangturm**.

Lindau is a paradise for **sailing** and **windsurfing**; the tourist office has a list of outfits offering equipment hire and instruction. You can hire **row boats** and **paddle boats** at several spots along the northern shore in season. **Weisse Flotte** (☎ 275 8410; ticket office cnr Bahnhofplatz & Seepromenade) runs round-trip boat tours (€7.50, one hour) several times daily from Lindau harbour to Bregenz (Austria) and the mouth of the Rhine. **Bodensee Schiffsbetriebe** (BSB; ☎ 275 8410; www.bsb-online

---

One of the colourful buildings lining Füssen's Altstadt, this tangerine-painted hotel has been given a stunning contemporary makeover inside, with gleaming rooms and bathrooms, but it still retains a friendly, down-to-earth atmosphere. Wheelchair access is possible.

Eggensberger (☎ 910 30; www.eggensberger.de, in German; Enzenbergstrasse 5, Hopfen am See; r €128-244; P ⊗ �ⓢ) In the little hamlet of Hopfen am See, a couple of blocks back from the lake, this 'bio' hotel with restaurant (meals €21) is run by four brothers and has a host of spa treatments at its wellness centre as well as soothing rooms. It's also possible to stay at the adjacent farm set in meadows grazed by cows producing the restaurant's milk and cheese, and roamed by chickens providing its eggs – contact directly for availability.

Eating

Escape the tourist crush at the following locals' favourites.

Pizzeria San Marco (☎ 813 39; Füssener Strasse 6, Schwangau; mains €5-10) A convivial crowd congregates at this rustic Italian-style place,

which serves up better-than-average pizzas and pastas.

Zur Schloss-Eule (☎ 0170-758 2937; Magnusplatz 6, Füssen; dishes €5.10-7.20; ◷ 11am-6pm Wed-Sat, 1-6pm Sun; Ⓥ) This wonderful little hole in the wall serves all-organic fare, including vegan-friendly, gluten-free buckwheat crêpes, soy cappuccinos and Fair Trade coffee.

Ritterstub'n (☎ 7759; Ritter-Strasse 4, Füssen; menu €14.50, mains from €6.50; ◷ closed lunch Mon) The speciality of this historic restaurant is *Brätknödelsuppe* – finely minced calf meat moulded into egg-and-flour dumplings in a clear soup. It also has good local lake fish.

Aquila (☎ 6253; Brotmarkt 9, Füssen; mains €8.90-12.50; ◷ closed Wed mid-Sep–mid-Jun) With ancient wooden floorboards and traditional Tyrolean décor, this cosy spot has delicious local specialities, like spit-roasted meats, pork in beer sauce, and trout in almond butter with parsley potatoes.

Getting There & Away

Direct regional trains to and from Augsburg (€16.40, two hours) depart every two hours, with trains every other hour requiring a change

.com) operates a year-round scheduled boat service between lake communities, including Bregenz (€4.20, 22 minutes) in Austria.

Swimming is possible around the lake, including several public pools. The largest of these (with some cool waterslides) is the **Strandbad Eichwald** (☎ 5539; adult/child €3/2); check with the tourist office for seasonal hours. Just nearby, the ecocampsite **Park-Camping Lindau am See** (☎ 722 36; www.park-camping.de; Fraunhoferstrasse 20; per person €5.50-6.50, tent €2.50, car €2.70-3; ⊗ closed mid-Nov–mid-Mar; Ⓟ ▯) has a beach, grocery store and restaurant, and rents bikes from €7 to €14 per day.

ourpick **Hotel Schreier** (☎ 944 484; www.hotel-schreier.de; Fäbergasse 2; s €75-90, d €115-160; Ⓟ ✗) Grand hotels garland the lake, but tucked in among them, this family-run place is a little-known treat with nine boutique rooms named after a flavour of ice cream served at its ice-cream shop-café below. 'Vanilla' has a sunlounge-strewn terrace overlooking the lake, as does 'Cappuccino', one floor up ('Strawberry' and 'Cherry' have balconies). There are only three parking spots, so reserve ahead if you're driving.

Lakeside dining spots include local hang-out **Nana** (☎ 934 70; Bahnhofplatz 1; mains €14.90-24.90; ⊗ 9am-late Apr-Oct, 5pm-late Nov-Mar; Ⓥ), with a Mediterranean menu (couscous salad, mozzarella plates and fish platters) and live music most nights. Carving through the centre of the island, Lindau's cobbled main street, **Maximilianstrasse**, is lined with elegant cafés, restaurants and crêperies.

Direct trains connect Lindau with Augsburg (€26, three hours) several times daily.

The Altstadt is largely car free; at the island's northwest edge, the parking lot P5 charges €5 all day, as does P3, just to the left of the bridge on the mainland.

Bikes can be rented from **Unger's Fahrradverleih** (☎ 943 688; Inselgraben 14; per day €8-15; ⊗ 9am-1pm & 3-6pm Mon-Fri, 9am-1pm Sat & Sun). Buses 1 and 2 serving the mainland run every half-hour. All buses converge at the central bus station (ZUP), about 800m north of the bridge on the mainland.

Lindau is on the B31 and also connected to Munich by the A96.

in Buchloe. There are also regular services to and from Munich (€20.80, two hours), with a change in Buchloe or Kaufbeuren.

The Europabus stops at the tourist office in Schwangau, in Hohenschwangau village and at Füssen *Bahnhof*, its southern terminus.

Several roads lead to the Königswinkel: the A7 from Memmingen and Kempten, the B16 from Kaufbeuren and the B17 (Romantic Road) from Augsburg/Munich.

Getting Around

Local bus 78 connects the castles, Füssen, Schwangau and the Tegelbergbahn, while bus 56 runs to the lake at Hopfen am See. There's a **taxi** (☎ 7700) rank at the *Bahnhof*.

In Füssen you can rent bikes at **Ski Sport Luggi** (☎ 342; Bahnhof; per day €8-10; ⊗ 9am-6pm Mon-Sat, 9am-11am Sun); staff can also bring bikes to your hotel. **Mayr** (☎ 814 58; Mitteldorf 3) in Schwangau charges similar rates.

The Black Forest

Deep, dark and as delicious as its famous cherry cake, the Black Forest serves up some of Germany's most beautiful scenery. Enigmatic when blanketed in early-morning mist, this mother of all forests weaves a patchwork of wrinkled valleys and fir trees, rolling highlands and glacial lakes. Here natural highs reach from the gurgling Brigach to the thundering Todtnauer waterfall and the Kaiserstuhl's tumbling vineyards. Take this storybook setting and fill it with heavy-lidded farmhouses, mooing cows and earthy locals to get the picture.

To the north, the swish spa town of Baden-Baden beckons with its therapeutic Roman baths, grand casino and classical villas; down south, the vibrant university city of Freiburg exudes a laid-back vibe in the cobblestone lanes leading to its flame-red Gothic cathedral. In between are gems like Villingen, a medieval town dwarfed by ring walls and chunky towers; the Kinzigtal villages of Schiltach and Gengenbach lined with half-timbered houses; and the totally cuckoo town of Triberg – a clockwork shrine to German punctuality.

Locals counteract their weakness for creamy gateaux with active pursuits. In 1864 they coined the concept of taking a walk in the woods by establishing the Schwarzwaldverein, Germany's first walking club. Since then they've developed an extensive network of hiking and cycling trails through the forest. The Black Forest comprises two mammoth nature reserves: Naturpark Schwarzwald Mitte/Nord in the north and Naturpark Südschwarzwald in the south. So whether you want to zip around hairpin bends or drift in cool lakes, cross-country ski through woodlands or snowshoe around the highest peak, Feldberg, the Black Forest is the original green giant with its clean air and vast natural playground.

HIGHLIGHTS

- Treading the cobbles in **Freiburg** (opposite) to glimpse the blushing Gothic minster
- Swishing through twinkling woodlands on a pair of cross-country skis at **Martinskapelle** (p298)
- Devouring Black Forest cake and hearing cuckoos call in **Triberg** (p297)
- Drifting away Roman-style in the thermal waters of **Baden-Baden** (p304)
- Wandering through the higgledy-piggledy streets of **Schiltach** (p308), lined with half-timbered houses

Baden-Baden ★

Schiltach ★

★ Triberg

Martinskapelle ★

★ Freiburg

SOUTHERN BLACK FOREST

FREIBURG

☎ 0761 / pop 213,000

Take gorgeous Black Forest scenery, mix in a medieval Altstadt, sprinkle with 20,000 students and add a liberal dash of cool – *et voilà!* – you have Freiburg. This southern charmer has cobbles for strolling, bars for drinking and the easy-going attitude of a university city. Lined with half-timbered houses in sweetshop shades, its narrow alleyways lead to the Münster's filigree spires.

In summer Freiburg exudes Mediterranean flair when its alfresco cafés and beer gardens hum with folk catching the rays in Germany's warmest city. The eco-conscious locals have shrewdly tapped into that natural energy source and Freiburg now generates nearly as much solar power as the whole of Britain.

Freiburg bursts into life in summer with the mammoth three-week **Zelt-Musik Festival**, held in June or July. The line-up features theatre and cabaret performances, concerts, parties and kids' activities. For details, visit the website www.zmf.de. During advent Freiburg's **Weihnachtsmarkt** (Christmas market) adds festive sparkle to the Rathausplatz with spicy gluhwein (mulled wine), craft stalls and carousels.

Orientation

The Altstadt's focal point is the intersection of Kaiser-Joseph-Strasse, the centre's main north–south artery, with east–west Bertoldstrasse. About 600m west is the Hauptbahnhof and bus station, which define the western edge of the Altstadt. The Dreisam River runs along the Altstadt's southern edge.

Information

Buchhandlung Rombach (☎ 4500 2400; Bertoldstrasse 10) Stocks English titles.

Call Shop Freiburg (Talstrasse 1; per hr €2; ☉ 9am-11pm Mon-Sat, 11am-10pm Sun) Cheap internet access and discount calls.

Police station (Rotteckring)

Post office (Eisenbahnstrasse 58-62)

Tee-Online (Grünwälderstrasse 19; per hr €3.50; ☉ 9am-9pm Mon-Thu, 9am-8pm Fri & Sat, 10am-7pm Sun) Hip café with internet access, wi-fi and free tea.

Tourist office (☎ 388 1880; www.freiburg.de; Rathausplatz 2-4; ☉ 8am-8pm Mon-Fri, 9.30am-5pm Sat

& 10am-noon Sun Jun-Sep; 8am-6pm Mon-Fri, 9.30am-2.30pm Sat, 10am-noon Sun Oct-May) Well stocked with 1:50,000-scale cycling maps (€4.50 to €10) and the useful booklet *Freiburg – Official Guide* (€4).

Sights

The **Museumticket** (€4), valid for one day, gets you into all five of Freiburg's municipal museums (www.museen.freiburg.de in German).

MÜNSTER

Freiburg's 11th-century **Münster** (☉ 10am-5pm Mon-Sat, 1pm-7.30pm Sun) is the monster of all minsters, a red-sandstone giant that looms above the half-timbered façades framing the square. Its riot of punctured spires and gargoyles flush scarlet in the dusk light.

The **main portal** is adorned with sculptures depicting scenes from the Old and New Testaments – spy allegorical figures such as Voluptuousness (the one with snakes on her back) and Satan himself. Nearby are medieval wall markings used to ensure that merchandise (eg loaves of bread) were of the requisite size.

Square at the base, the sturdy **tower** becomes an octagon higher up and is crowned by a filigreed 116m-high spire. Ascend the **tower** (adult/student €1.50/1; ☉ 9.30am-5pm Mon-Sat, 1-5pm Sun & holidays) for an excellent view of the church's intricate construction; on clear days you can spy the Vosges Mountains in France.

Inside the Münster, the kaleidoscopic **stained-glass windows** dazzle. Many were financed by various guilds – in the bottom panels look for a pretzel, scissors and other symbols of medieval trades. The **high altar** features a masterful triptych of the coronation of the Virgin Mary by Hans Baldung, best viewed on a **guided tour** (€2; ☉ at 2pm).

SOUTH OF THE MÜNSTER

Facing the Münster's south side is the arcaded brick-red **Historisches Kaufhaus**, a 16th-century merchants' hall. The coats of arms on the oriels and the four figures above the balcony symbolise Freiburg's allegiance to the House of Habsburg.

The sculptor Christian Wentzinger built a baroque town house east of the Kaufhaus in 1761. Inside is a wrought-iron staircase that guides the eye to an elaborate ceiling fresco. Nowadays, it shelters the **Museum für Stadtgeschichte** (Municipal History Museum; ☎ 201 2515; Münsterplatz 30; adult/concession €2/1; ☉ 10am-5pm Tue-Sun), spelling out in artefacts Freiburg's eventful past.

THE BLACK FOREST

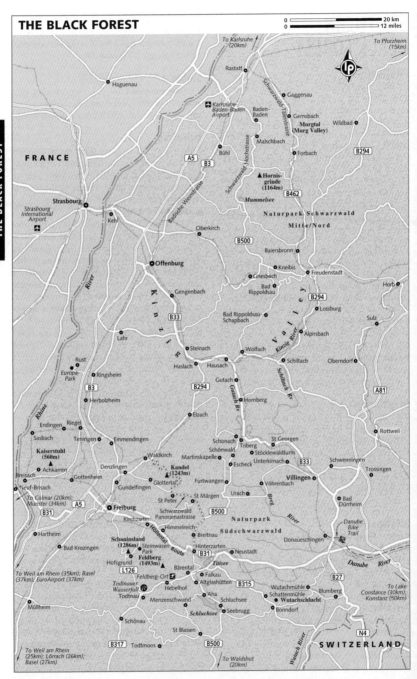

THE BLACK FOREST

Housed in a former monastery, the **Augustinermuseum** (☎ 201 2531; Augustinerplatz 1; free entry; ⊙ 10am-5pm Tue-Sun) showcases paintings by Baldung, Matthias Grünewald and Cranach. Its rich collection of medieval stained glass ranks among Germany's finest.

Stepping south, the **Museum für Neue Kunst** (Museum of Modern Art; ☎ 201 2581; Marienstrasse 10; adult/concession €2/1; ⊙ 10am-5pm Tue-Sun) leaps back into the 20th century with expressionist and abstract art, including expressive works by Oskar Kokoschka and Otto Dix.

Trace the little canal west through the former fishing quarter of **Fischerau** to **Martinstor** (Kaiser-Joseph-Strasse), one of Freiburg's two surviving town gates. Edging north along Kaiser-Joseph-Strasse brings you to the trickling **Bertoldsbrunnen** fountain, which marks where the city's thoroughfares have crossed since it was founded in 1091.

A block east of the Museum für Neue Kunst is the muralled, 13th-century **Schwabentor**, a massive city gate with tram tracks running under its arches. Trails nearby wind up to the forested **Schlossberg**, which dominates the town and is topped by the ice-cream cone–shaped **Aussichtsturm** (lookout tower); scale it for far-reaching views.

WESTERN ALTSTADT

Freiburg locals hang out by the fountain in chestnut-shaded Rathausplatz. On its western side, note the red-sandstone **Neues Rathaus** (New City Hall), comprising two Renaissance town houses that flank an arcaded section leading to a cobblestone courtyard. The tower contains a carillon, played at noon daily.

Linked to the Neues Rathaus by an over-the-street pedestrian bridge is the step-gabled **Altes Rathaus** (Old City Hall; 1559), which houses the tourist office. Freiburg's oldest town hall, the 13th-century **Gerichtslaube**, is slightly west along Turmstrasse.

The medieval **Martinskirche**, once part of a Franciscan monastery, demands attention on the northern side of Rathausplatz. Severely damaged in WWII, it was rebuilt in the ascetic style typical of this mendicant order. Across the street on Franziskanerstrasse is its architectural antithesis, the marvellously extravagant **Haus zum Walfisch** (House of the Whale), whose late-Gothic oriel is garnished with two impish gargoyles.

In a delightful park further west, sits the neo-Gothic Colombischlössle villa, housing the **Museum für Ur- und Frühgeschichte** (Museum of Pre- & Early History; ☎ 201 2571; www.museen.freiburg.de in German; Rotteckring 5; adult/concession €2/1; ⊙ 10am-5pm Tue-Sun). Climb the cast-iron staircase to reach an eclectic bunch of archaeological exhibits from the Stone Age to Roman times.

Tours

Freiburg Kultour (☎ 290 7447; www.freiburg-kultour.com; Rathausplatz 2-4), based in the tourist office, offers 1½- to two-hour **walking tours** (adult/child 12-18yr €7/6; ⊙ 10.30am Mon-Fri & 10am Sat Apr-Oct, 10am Sat & 10.30am Sun Nov-Mar) of the Altstadt and Münster in German and English.

Velotaxi (☎ 0172-768 4370; ⊙ mid-Apr–Oct) charges €6.50 for a 15-minute, two-person spin of the Altstadt in a rain-protected pedicab. Order by phone or look for one at Rathausplatz or Münsterplatz.

Sleeping

The tourist office can help with a hotel booking for €3 and hands out a brochure listing good-value private rooms.

Hirzberg Camping (☎ 350 54; www.freiburg-camping.de; Kartäuserstrasse 99; campsites per adult/tent €6/3.50; ⊙ year-round; P ⊡) Pitch a tent at this serene woodland campsite 1.5km east of Schwabentor. It has cooking facilities and rents out tents, caravans and bikes. Take tram 1 to Stadthalle, walk north and cross the river.

our pick **Black Forest Hostel** (☎ 881 7870; www.blackforest-hostel.de; Kartäuserstrasse 33; dm €13-21, s €28, d €46; ✕ ⊡) Freiburg's funkiest budget digs are five minutes' stroll from the centre. Overlooking vineyards, this former factory has been lovingly revamped as a hostel where

THE BLACK FOREST

FREIBURG BENEATH YOUR FEET

As you stroll around Freiburg's mostly pedestrianised Altstadt, be sure to look down at the pavement for the cheerful mosaics found in front of many shops. A diamond marks a jewellery shop, a cow is for a butcher, a pretzel for a baker and so on.

Keep an eye out for the Bächle, the permanently flowing rivulets that run along many footpaths. Originally part of an elaborate system to deliver nonpotable water, these literal 'tourist traps' now provide welcome relief for hot feet on sweltering summer days. It's said that if you fall into one you'll marry a Freiburger or a Freiburgerin.

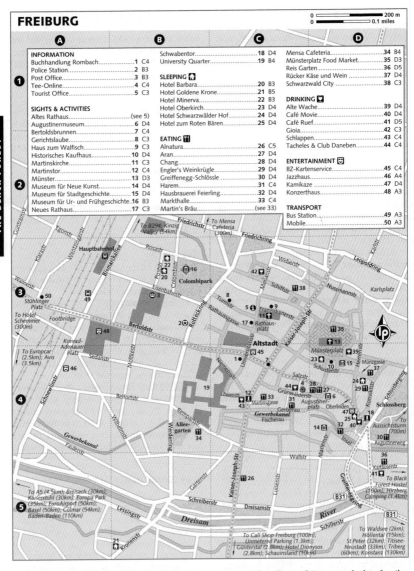

FREIBURG

backpackers can cook up a storm in the kitchen, play pool or strum guitars in the lounge. Dorms are comfy and the stainless-steel showers are like something out of a sci-fi movie. Bike hire costs €5 per day.

Hotel Dionysos (☎ 293 53; www.hoteldionysos.de in German; Hirschstrasse 2, Günterstal; s/d with washbasin €28/40, d with shower €45) South of the Altstadt in the

streamside village of Günterstal, this family-run hotel has spotless rooms and a Greek restaurant. It's an easy trundle on tram line 4.

Hotel Goldene Krone (☎ 137 6083; www.hotelpension -goldene-krone.de; Mattenstrasse 2a; s/d €45/65; **P** ❑) Surrounding a courtyard, the contemporary, parquet-floored rooms here offer superb value. It's 10 minutes' amble from the centre.

Hotel Schwarzwälder Hof (☎ 380 30; www .schwarzwaelder-hof.eu; Herrenstrasse 43; s €45-60, d €75-95; ☒ ▯) This bijou hotel has an unrivalled style-for-euro ratio. A wrought-iron staircase sweeps up to snazzy rooms that are temples to chalk whites and chocolate browns. Some have postcard views of the Altstadt.

Hotel Barbara (☎ 296 250; www.hotel-barbara.de; Poststrasse 4; s €69-89, d €89-119; ▯) Tucked down a quiet street, this town house oozes Art Nouveau charm with its high ceilings and twisting staircase. The pastel-hued rooms offer old-style comfort, but bathrooms are a bit pokey. Try the home-made jams at breakfast.

Hotel Minerva (☎ 386 490; www.minerva-freiburg.de in German; Poststrasse 8; s €75-90, d €95-125; ℙ ☒ ▯) All curvaceous windows and polished wood, this Art Nouveau charmer is five minutes' trudge from the Altstadt. The convivial rooms are painted in sunny shades and feature free wi-fi. The sauna is another big plus.

Hotel Oberkirch (☎ 202 6868; www.hotel-oberkirch .de; Münsterplatz 22; s €95-118, d €139-161; ℙ) Wake up to Münster views at this green-shuttered hotel. It's as though Laura Ashley has been let loose in the country-style rooms with floral wallpaper and half-canopies over the beds. Oberkirch has an intoxicating 250-year history; during a fire in WWII the hotelier doused the blaze with wine from his cellar.

Hotel zum Roten Bären (☎ 387 870; www.roter -baeren.de; Oberlinden 12; s €108-130, d €136-169; ℙ ▯) Billed as Germany's oldest guesthouse, this bubblegum-pink hotel near Schwabentor dates to 1120. Though the vaulted cellar is medieval, rooms are modern with sleek wood furnishings.

Eating

As a university city, Freiburg has plenty of cheap eats, especially around Martinstor and Konviktstrasse. Cafés and restaurants fringe Münsterplatz and the cobbled lanes fanning out from the square.

Aran (☎ 290 9664; Salzstrasse 28; light meals €2-5; ☯ 8.30am-11pm Mon-Thu, to midnight Fri & Sat, 9.30am-11pm Sun; ⓥ) This organic café has a terrace facing Augustinerplatz that's perfect for chilling. Locals pile in for fresh juices, chunky soups and sandwiches like tuna-artichoke and cashew-chilli.

Mensa cafeterias (mains €3-5; ☯ 11.30am-2pm & 5.20-7.30pm Mon-Fri); Stefan-Meier-Strasse 28 (on the campus at the northern end of Hebelstrasse; ☯ may be closed for dinner during holiday periods); Rempartstrasse 18 (☯ also 11.30am-1.30pm Sat) If you can produce student ID, a world of salad buffets and other filling fodder will open before you at these locations.

Markthalle (Martinsgasse 235; light meals €3-6; ☯ 8am-7pm) A food court whose Mexican, Italian, Indian, Korean and French counters offer fast, tasty lunches.

Reis Garten (☎ 208 8819; Kartäuserstrasse 3; mains €5-12; ☯ 11.30am-11.30pm Mon-Fri, 12pm-11.30pm Sat, 2-11.30pm Sun) Centred on a pretty courtyard, this Chinese den rustles up the usual suspects, from chop suey to crispy duck. Lunch is particularly good value (€3.90).

Harem (☎ 225 33; Gerberau 7c; mains €6-9; ☯ 11.30am-midnight Mon-Sat) Harem spices up the Altstadt with Turkish specialities such as crisp *börek* (filled pastries). All meals cost €5.90 from 11.30am to 4pm. Don't miss the original city walls out back.

Chang (☎ 137 9684; Grünwälderstrasse 21; mains €6-9.50; ☯ 12pm-11pm Sun-Thu, to midnight Fri & Sat) Gold walls and tables inlaid with teak carvings define this sleek Thai restaurant, where a few euro buys you a curry or *pad thai* (stir-fried noodles).

Hausbrauerei Feierling (☎ 243 480; Gerberau 46; mains €6-12; ☯ 11am-midnight, to 1am Fri & Sat; ⓥ) Starring one of Freiburg's best beer gardens, this brewpub serves great vegetarian options and humungous schnitzels with *Brägele* (chipped potatoes). If you drink one too many, take care not to fall in the stream or you may become dinner for the open-jawed *Krokodil*.

Martin's Bräu (☎ 387 0018; Fressgässle 1; mains €7-14; ☯ 11am-midnight, to 2am Fri & Sat) Copper vats gleam at this microbrewery down the alley from Martinstor, serving home-brewed beers. Chefs in the show kitchen whip up carnivorous fare including ox tongue salad and half-metre-long bratwursts. Free wi-fi is available.

Englers Weinkrügle (☎ 383 115; Konviktstrasse 12; mains €7.60-13.50; ☯ 11am-2pm & 5.30-9.30pm Tue-Sun) A warm, woody Baden-style *Weinstube* (wine tavern) with wisteria growing out front and regional flavours on the menu. The trout in various guises (for instance with Riesling or almond-butter sauce) is delicious.

Greiffenegg-Schlössle (☎ 327 28; Schlossbergring 3; mains €19-28; ☯ 11am-midnight) Perched above Freiburg, this posh villa whets appetites with dishes such as pike-perch and lamb in a pepper-feta crust. The terrace and chestnut-shaded beer garden are great for watching the sun set over the city's red rooftops.

Self-caterers can stock up on picnic treats at the following places:

Alnatura (Kaiser-Joseph-Strasse 261; ⊙ 9am-8pm Mon-Fri, 9am-6pm Sat) Organic supermarket.

Münsterplatz food market (⊙ until 1pm Mon-Fri, to 1.30pm Sat) Stalls are particularly numerous and varied on Saturday. On a per-calorie basis, the least expensive meals in town are the wurst-in-a-bun (€2), topped with fried onions (a Freiburg tradition), sold here.

Rücker Käse und Wein (Münzgasse 1; ⊙ 9am-6.30pm Mon-Fri, 9am-3pm Sat) For local wine, ham and cheese.

Schwarzwald City (Schiffstrasse 5; ⊙ 10am-7pm Mon-Fri, 10am-6pm Sat) Central shopping mall with a supermarket, bakery, juice bar & free wi-fi.

Drinking

Freiburg boasts the liveliest after-dark scene in the Black Forest; the spectrum covers everything from down-at-heel pubs to chichi wine bars and rollicking clubs.

Schlappen (☎ 334 94; Löwenstrasse 2; ⊙ 11am-1am Mon-Thu, 11am-3am Fri & Sat, 3pm-1am Sun) With its jazz-themed back room and poster-plastered walls, this relaxed watering hole is a perennial favourite. Light meals –such as *Flammkuchen* (Alsatian-style pizza) – are on offer and you can try 10 different types of absinthe (€3). Check out the wacky men's urinal: step closer to the man in the mirror and watch the water flow…

Alte Wache (☎ 202 870; Münsterplatz 38; ⊙ 10am) Right on the square, this 18th-century guardhouse serves local Müller-Thurgau and Pinot Noir wines at the tasting tables. If they whet your appetite, order the Münsterteller (€6) to nibble on cheese and olives.

Café Movie (☎ 382 210; Oberlinden 22; ⊙ 11am-2am Mon-Thu & Sun, to 3am Fri & Sat) Bob Marley and Che Guevara beam down from the walls at this moody pub. The landlord loves reggae grooves and big-screen sports – you'll find both in equal measures here.

Gioia (☎ 137 5588; Unterlinden 3; ⊙ 9am-midnight Mon-Fri, to 1am Sat & Sun) Maroon-green chessboard walls and leopard-print chairs jazz up Gioia, a relaxed Italian bar for an espresso or *caipirinha*. Take a seat beside the fountain on the patio.

Tacheles & Club Daneben (☎ 319 6669; www .tacheles-freiburg.de; Grünwälderstrasse 17; ⊙ 11am-2am Mon-Thu, 11am-5am Fri & Sat; 11am-1am Sun) Freiburg nights don't get much wilder than Tacheles. They begin with enormous schnitzels (€6.90) in the courtyard and move swiftly on to dangerously cheap drinking sessions at the bar. At 11pm partygoers shuffle over to cavelike Club Daneben for booty-shaking beneath the glitter balls.

Café Ruef (☎ 336 63; Kartäuserstrasse 2; ⊙ 6am-midnight) This mellow student den is stuffed with well-worn armchairs and friendly faces – most fixed on the *Fussball*. Ruef has a split personality: by day it's a bakery with tasty pies (around €2) and by night a pub with occasional live music.

Entertainment

Get the free listings monthly, *Freiburg Aktuell*, at hotels and the tourist office.

TICKETS

BZ-Kartenservice (☎ 01805-556 656; www.badische -zeitung.de in German; Bertoldstrasse 7; ⊙ 9am-7pm Mon-Fri, 9am-4pm Sat) Click on 'Termine' for events tickets.

LIVE MUSIC

Jazzhaus (☎ 349 73; www.jazzhaus.de; Schnewlinstrasse 1) Under the brick arches of a wine cellar, this venue hosts first-rate jazz, rock and hip-hop concerts (€10 to €30) at 8pm at least three nights a week (see the website for details). It morphs into a club (admission around €6) from 11pm to 3am on Friday and Saturday nights.

Waldsee (☎ 736 88; www.waldsee-freiburg.de; Waldseestrasse 84; ⊙ 11am-2am Mon-Thu, 11am-3am Fri & Sat, 10am-1am Sun) Nestled by a lake in the forest, Waldsee stages events from jazz sessions to club nights (admission roughly €5). Check the website for the full line-up. It's 30 minutes' walk from the centre

Konzerthaus (☎ 388 1552; www.konzerthaus.freiburg .de in German; Konrad-Adenauer-Platz 1) A hulking modern concert hall that doubles as a cultural events centre. Keep an eye out for the tornado sculptures out front.

CLUBS

Kamikaze (www.klubkamikaze.de; Oberlinden 8; ⊙ 10pm-late Wed-Sat) Freiburg's hippest club, Kamikaze is a cavelike haunt with exposed brick and plump sofas. DJs spin everything from electro to drum'n'bass, with live music every other week. Try the kamikaze bomber – an explosive mix of Jägermeister, apricot brandy and cranberry juice.

Getting There & Around

AIR

Freiburg shares **EuroAirport** (www.euroairport .com) with Basel (Switzerland) and Mulhouse (France). Destinations include London and Luton with EasyJet.

BUS

The **Airport Bus** (☎ 500 500; www.freiburger-reise dienst.de in German) goes from Freiburg's bus station to EuroAirport (€18, 55 minutes, 15 times daily).

SüdbadenBus (www.suedbadenbus.de, in German) and **RVF** (☎ 01805-77 99 66; www.rvf.de, in German) run to towns and villages throughout the southern Black Forest. Single tickets for one/two/three zones cost €2/3.40/4.80 (40% less for children age six to 14); a 24-hour Regio24 ticket costs €5/10/10 for one person and €8/16/16 for two to five people.

From Freiburg, bus 1066 travels at 4pm on weekdays to Haslach, Hausach and Schiltach (2¼ hours) in the Kinzig Valley. See the town listings in the Southern Black Forest for other bus options to/from Freiburg.

Bus and tram travel within Freiburg (www .vag-freiburg.de) is charged at the one-zone rate. Buy tickets from the vending machines or from the driver and validate upon boarding.

CAR & MOTORCYCLE

The Frankfurt-Basel A5 passes west of Freiburg. The scenic B31 leads east through the Höllental to Lake Constance. The B294 goes north into the Black Forest.

Car-hire agencies include **Europcar** (☎ 515 100; Löracherstrasse 10) and **Avis** (☎ 197 19; St-Georgener-Strasse 7).

About 1.5km south of Martinstor, there's unmetered parking on some side streets (eg Türkenlouisstrasse). To get there from the Altstadt drive south on Günterstalstrasse (the southern continuation of Kaiser-Joseph-Strasse).

TRAIN

Freiburg is on a major north–south rail corridor with frequent departures for destinations such as Basel (€13.40 to €20.80, 45 to 65 minutes) and Baden-Baden (€16.60 to

€25, 45 to 80 minutes). Freiburg is also the western terminus of the Höllentalbahn to Donaueschingen via Titisee-Neustadt (€4.80, 38 minutes, twice an hour). There's a local connection to Breisach (€4.80, 26 minutes, at least hourly).

BICYCLE

Bike paths run along the Dreisam River, leading westward to Breisach and then into France.

Mobile (☎ 292 7998; www.mobile-freiburg.com in German; Wentzingerstrasse 15; 3hr/day/week €5/12.50/50, under 17yr half price; ☯ 24hr) across the bridge from the Hauptbahnhof, rents bikes and sells cycling maps (€6.80).

AROUND FREIBURG
Schauinsland

A ride on the 3.6km **Schauinslandbahn** (cable car; adult/child 6-14yr/student return €11.50/7/10.50, one-way €8/5/7.50; ☯ 9am-5pm, to 6pm Jul-Sep) to the 1286m **Schauinsland peak** (www.bergwelt-schauinsland.de in German) is a speedy way to reach the Black Forest highlands from Freiburg. The lookout tower affords tremendous vistas of the Rhine Valley and Alps. Aside from walking and cross-country skiing, Schauinsland beckons thrillseekers with an 8km off-road **scooter track.** The bone-shaking experience costs €23, including cable car access and equipment hire. To get to the lift from town, take tram 4 to Günterstal and then bus 21 to Talstation.

One of the slickest hotels in this neck of the woods is **Halde** (☎ 07602-944 70; www.halde.com; Oberried-Hofsgrund; s €124-136, d €186-208; ⓟ ⌨ ☻). The hilltop hideaway is the place to curl up by an open fire or drift in a mare's milk bath in the spa. In the wood-panelled restaurant (mains €12.50 to €25) Martin Hegar presents local flavours, from fresh trout to wild boar, with panache. He cooks with mainly locally sourced, organic produce.

THE BLACK FOREST

FREE RIDE

In most parts of the Black Forest your hotel or guesthouse will issue you with the excellent Schwarzwald-Gästekarte (Guest Card) for discounts – or freebies – on museums, ski lifts, events and attractions. Versions of the card with the Konus symbol (showing a bus, a train and a tram) entitle you to free use of public transport throughout Black Forest.

Almost all tourist offices in the Black Forest sell the three-day **SchwarzwaldCard** (adult/child 4-11yr/family €28/18/90, incl 1 day at Europa-Park €50/40/167) for admission to around 150 attractions in the Black Forest, including museums, ski lifts, boat trips, spas and swimming pools. Details on both cards are available at www.blackforest-tourism.com.

MOVE YOUR ASS

A novel way to explore the woodlands and valleys is to rent a donkey for the day. **Eselwanderungen im Schwarzwald** (☎ 0761-7075 171; www.eselwanderungen.de; Dobelpeterhof, Kirchzarten Neuhäuser; from €50 per day; ☒ weekends & summer holidays) hires beasts of burden who obligingly lug the heavy packs, leaving walkers free to enjoy the wonderful scenery of the Southern Black Forest. Kids in tow? There's nothing like a meek mule with impeccable eco credentials to motivate the little 'uns to walk – and like it. The owners will even help arrange donkey-friendly accommodation if you want to extend your hike in the hills.

Steinwasen Park

This woodsy **family park** (☎ 07602-944 680; www.steinwasen-park.de; Steinwasen 1, Oberried; adult/child 4-11yr €18/15; ☒ 10am-5pm late Mar–mid-May & mid-Sep–mid-Nov) is alive with Black Forest and Alpine critters. A forest trail weaves past animal-friendly enclosures home to wild boar, ibex and burrowing marmots. The biggest draw is one of the world's longest hanging bridges, stretching 218m above the valley. Not to be outdone by its rival, Europa-Park, Steinwasen has introduced whizzy rides such as Gletscherblitz and River Splash.

Todtnauer Wasserfall

Heading south on the Freiburg–Feldberg road, you'll glimpse the roaring Todtnauer Wasserfall. While the 97m falls are not as high as those in Triberg (opposite), they're every bit as spectacular – tumbling down sheer rock faces and illuminating the velvety hills with their brilliance. Hike the zigzagging 9km trail to Aftersteg for views over the cataract. Take care on paths in winter when the falls often freeze solid. The waterfall car park is on the L126.

WEST OF FREIBURG
Breisach
☎ 07667 / pop 14,000

Bang in the heart of wine country, Breisach is where the Black Forest, Germany, says *bonjour* to Alsace, France. The quaint town is separated from its Gallic neighbours by the Rhine, but they unite in their passion for a good bottle of plonk. Strolling the cobbled streets past candy-coloured houses, you'd never guess 85% of the town was flattened in WWII, so successful has been the reconstruction. Vauban's star-shaped French fortress-town of **Neuf-Brisach** (New Breisach) sits 4km west of Breisach; both towns are candidates for Unesco World Heritage status.

The Romanesque and Gothic **St Stephansmünster** towers over the centre. Inside there's a faded fresco cycle, *The Last Judgment* (1491) by Martin Schongauer, a delicate Gothic rood loft and a magnificent **high altar triptych** (1526) carved from linden wood. From the shady square, the Schänzletreppe leads down to **Gutgesellentor**, the town gate where scandalous Pope John XXIII was caught fleeing the Council of Constance in 1415.

Briesach's centre proper is between Gutgesellentor and Markplatz. Visit the **tourist office** (☎ 940 155; www.breisach.de; Marktplatz 16; ☒ 9am-5pm Mon-Fri & 10am-1pm Sat Apr-Dec, also 1-4pm Sun May-Oct, 9am-12.30pm & 1.30-5pm Mon-Fri Jan-Mar) for accommodation options, details on local vintners and well-stuffed picnic hampers (€15). On the last weekend in August, locals celebrate the grape with fervour at the **Breisach Wine Festival**. The event kicks off with the coronation of the *Weinprinzessin* (wine princess) and moves onto wine tasting, brass bands and fireworks on the banks of the Rhine. For more details, see www.weinfest-breisach.de.

Breisach is an excellent base for **cycling**; the plentiful options include crossing the Rhine to the delightful French town of Colmar, or pedalling through terraced vineyards to Freiburg. Hire your own set of wheels from **Funbike** (☎ 7733; Metzgergasse 1; 1/3 days €10/27; ☒ 9am-noon & 6-7pm Apr-Oct) opposite the tourist office.

Boat excursions are possible along the Rhine and are run by **BFS** (☎ 942 010; www.bfs-info.de in German; Rheinuferstrasse; ☒ Apr-Sep); the dock is 500m southwest of the tourist office.

DJH hostel (☎ 7665; www.jugendherberge-breisach.de; Rheinuferstrasse 12; dm 1st/subsequent night €24.30/21; ☒) Hugging the banks of the Rhine, this riverfront hostel's superb facilities include a barbecue hut and volleyball court. There's a campsite and swimming pool next door.

You'll find a handful of restaurants and cafés between Gutgesellentor and the tourist office, plus a **Minimal supermarket** (Bahnhofstrasse; ☒ 8am-8pm Mon-Sat) opposite the train station.

Breisach's train station is on Bahnhofstrasse, 500m southeast of Marktplatz; it serves Freiburg (€4.80, 27 minutes, at least hourly) and towns in the Kaisterstuhl. Buses go to Colmar, 22km west.

Kaiserstuhl

Rising between the Black Forest and French Vosges, the low-lying volcanic hills of Kaiserstuhl in the Upper Rhine Valley produce highly quaffable wines including *Spätburgunder* (Pinot Noir) and *Grauburgunder* (Pinot Gris).

The wines owe their quality to a unique microclimate (the warmest and sunniest in Germany) and the fertile loess (clay and silt) soil that retains heat at night and is ideal nurturing terrain for **vines**. Wildlife enthusiasts should have their binoculars handy to spot lizards, praying mantids and European bee-eaters.

Breisach tourist office has details on cellar tours, wine tastings, bike paths like the 55km **Kaisterstuhltour** circuit; and walking trails such as the 15km **Winzerweg** (Wine Growers' Trail) from Achkarren to Riegel.

The **Kaiserstuhlbahn** rail loop goes all the way around the Kaisterstuhl. Stops (where you may have to change trains) include Sasbach, Endingen, Riegel and Gottenheim.

Europa-Park

Germany's largest **theme park** (☎ 01805-776 688; www.europapark.de; adult/child 4-14yr €30/26.50; ☯ 9am-6pm early Apr-early Nov & early Dec-early Jan, later in peak season), 35km north of Freiburg near Rust, is Europe in miniature. Get soaked fjord-rafting in Scandinavia before nipping across to England to race at Silverstone, or Greece to unravel the mysteries of Atlantis. Aside from white-knuckle thrills, Welt der Kinder amuses tots with labyrinths and Viking ships. When Mickey waltzed off to Paris, Europa-Park even got their own mousy mascot, Euromaus.

Shuttle buses (hourly in the morning) link Ringsheim train station, on the Freiburg–Offenburg line, with the park. By car, take the A5 to Herbolzheim (exit 58).

NORTHEAST OF FREIBURG
St Peter
☎ 07660 / pop 2500

The folk of St Peter, on the southern slopes of Mt Kandel (1243m), are deeply committed to age-old traditions. On religious holidays villagers still proudly sport their colourful, handmade *Trachten* (folkloric costumes).

The most outstanding landmark is the **former Benedictine abbey**, a rococo jewel designed by Peter Thumb of Vorarlberg. Many

of the period's top artists collaborated on the sumptuous interior of the twin-towered red-sandstone **church** (guided tours €6; ☯ open daily, tours 11am Tue, 2.30pm Thu, 11.30am Sun), including Joseph Anton Feuchtmayer, who fashioned the gilded statues of Zähringer dukes. Tours (in German) take you inside the monastery complex.

The **tourist office** (☎ 910 224; www.st-peter-schwarzwald.de in German; Klosterhof 11; ☯ 9am-noon & 2-5pm Mon-Fri Easter-Oct, 10am-noon Sat Jul & Aug, 9am-noon Mon-Fri, 2-5pm during school holidays Nov-Easter) is under the archway leading to the **Klosterhof** (abbey courtyard). A nearby information panel shows room availability.

By public transport, the best way to get from Freiburg to St Peter is to take the train to Kirchzarten (13 minutes, two or three an hour) and then bus 7216 (24 minutes, two or three an hour).

St Peter is on the **Schwarzwald Panoramastrasse** (Black Forest Panorama Rd; www.schwarzwald-panorama strasse.de), a 50km-long scenic route from Waldkirch (26km northeast of Freiburg) to Hinterzarten (5km west of Titisee) with dreamy mountain views.

Triberg
☎ 07722 / pop 5400

Heir to the Black Forest cake recipe, nesting ground of the world's biggest cuckoos and spring of Germany's highest waterfall – Triberg is a torrent of Schwarzwald superlatives and tourist kitsch. In bleak winters past, it was here that forest folk huddled in snowbound farmhouses and carved clocks that would drive the world dotty; and here that in 1884 the waterfall was harnessed to power the country's first electric street lamps. Josef Keller's original recipe for the cake that appears on every sweet trolley can now be found in Café Schäfer (p298).

ORIENTATION & INFORMATION

Triberg's main drag is the B500 running parallel to the Gutach River. The town's focal point is the Marktplatz, a steep 1.2km uphill from the *Bahnhof*.

Post office On Marktplatz next to the Rathaus.
Tourist office (☎ 866 490; www.triberg.de in German; Wallfahrtstrasse 4; ☯ 10am-5pm) Inside the Schwarzwald-Museum, 50m uphill from the river.

SIGHTS & ACTIVITIES

Niagara they ain't, but Germany's highest **falls** (☎ 2724; adult/child 8-16yr/family €2.50/0.90/5.60;

THE BLACK FOREST

Mar-early Nov & 25-30 Dec) exude their own wild romanticism. Fed by the Gutach River, they plunge 163m in seven cascades bordered by mossy rocks. On the nature trail through the wooded gorge, you'll come across tribes of overfed red squirrels after the bags of nuts sold at the entrance (€0.50).

Triberg is the undisputed cuckoo-clock capital. Two timepieces claim the title of *welt-grösste Kuckucksuhr* (world's largest cuckoo clock), giving rise to the battle of the birds, with Triberg in one corner and Schonach in the other. Triberg's underdog **World's Biggest Cuckoo Clock**, complete with gear-driven innards, is 1km up the hill in Schonach, inside a snug little **chalet** (☎ 4689; Untertalstrasse 28; adult/child €1.20/0.60; 9am-6pm). Its commercially savvy **rival** (☎ 962 20; www.uhren-park.de; Schonachbach 27; admission €1.50; 9am-6pm Mon-Sat, 10am-6pm Sun Easter-Oct), listed in *Guinness*, is at the other end of town on the B33 between Triberg and Hornberg.

Every hour people gather for the free spectacle at the **House of 1000 Clocks** (☎ 963 00; Hauptstrasse 79; 9am-5pm Sat, 10am-5pm Sun), where a glockenspiel bashes out classical melodies and the cuckoo greets his fans with a croaky squawk. Be sure to glimpse the trendy clocks inside, which eschew the cuckoo in favour of sheep, monkeys and even a chest-thumping Tarzan. The latest quartz models are equipped with a sensor that puts the cuckoo to sleep when the lights are off. Peace at last!

SLEEPING & EATING

DJH hostel (☎ 4110; www.jugendherberge-triberg.de; Rohrbacher Strasse 35; dm 1st/subsequent night €21.30/18.10;) On a scenic wooded ridge, Triberg's well-kept hostel is a steep 3km trudge from the Hauptbahnhof or 1200m uphill from Marktplatz.

Kukucksnest (☎ 869 487; Wallfahrtstrasse 15; d €50;) Below is the shop of master wood-carver Gerald Burger, above is the beautiful nest he has carved for his guests, featuring blonde-wood rooms with flat-screen TVs. The *Wurzelsepp* (faces carved into fir tree roots) by the entrance supposedly ward off evil spirits.

our pick Parkhotel Wehrle (☎ 860 20; www.parkhotel -wehrle.de; Hauptstrasse 51; d €129-149;) A haven of style in Triberg's sea of kitsch, even well-travelled Hemingway waxed lyrical about his stay at this 400-year-old hotel. Rooms fuse Biedermeier elegance with contemporary

flourishes like bevelled glass and sexy transparent shower stalls. The spa is something else with a starlit ice chamber, whirlpools and a kidney-shaped pool playing underwater music. Soothing treatments range from hot chocolate facials to rose-petal baths.

Café Schäfer (☎ 44 65; www.café-schaefer-triberg.de; Hauptstrasse 33; coffee & cake €4-6; 9am-6pm Mon-Fri, 8am-6pm Sat, 11am-6pm Sun, closed Wed) The Black Forest cake here is the real deal and Claus Schäfer (p184) has the original recipe to prove it. The aroma draws you to the glass counter showcasing the masterpiece: layers of moist sponge, fresh cream and sour cherries, with a mere suggestion of Kirsch (cherry brandy) and heavenly dusting of chocolate.

GETTING THERE & AROUND

The Schwarzwaldbahn railway line loops southeast to Konstanz (€20.10, 1½ hours), and northwest to Offenburg (€9.60, 40 minutes, hourly).

Bus 7150 travels north through the Gutach and Kinzig valleys to Offenburg; bus 7265 heads south to Villingen via St Georgen (one hour). Buses operate between the *Bahnhof* and Marktplatz, and to the nearby town of Schonach, about once an hour (€1.65).

Stöcklewaldturm

Triberg waterfall is the trailhead for a glorious 6.5km walk to Stöcklewaldturm (1070m). A steady hike through deep-green spruce forest and pastures brings you to this 19th-century **lookout tower**, where it's worth climbing 127 steps (entry €0.50) for 360° views stretching from the Swabian Alb to the Alps when the weather is fine. Footpaths head off in all directions from the summit, where a café provides light refreshments. The car park on the K5727 is a 10-minute stroll from the tower.

Martinskapelle

Named after a tiny chapel at the head of the Bregtal valley, Martinskapelle is one the Black Forest's best-kept secrets. A road curves steeply to the 1100m peak, past hip-roofed farmhouses that cling to forested slopes. A superb year-round walk is the 4km trail to **Brendturm** (1149m), commanding sweeping views across the Black Forest to Feldberg, the Vosges and Alps. Thoroughly doused in snow most winters, this is where clued-up locals come to cross-country ski on waymarked *Loipen*, including a 2km floodlit track.

After a vigorous hike in the woods, **Höhengasthaus Kolmenhof** (☎ 07723-931 00; An der Donauquelle; mains €8.80-14.90; ⏱ 11.30am-7.30pm Sat-Thu) is a cosy spot for a gluhwein and home cooking. Franz and Karin rustle up delicious fresh trout with cranberry sauce. Don't miss the spring of the **Breg** in their backyard; it's hard to believe this mere trickle of a stream is the source of the mighty Danube. The owners won an award for green initiatives, including cooking with local produce (the trout is fresh from their pond) and generating electricity using solar power.

Bus 7270 runs roughly hourly from Triberg Marktplatz to Escheck (€1.65, 23 minutes); from here it's a 4.5km trudge up to Martinskapelle. If you're driving, take the B500 from Triberg following signs to Schwarzenbach, Weissenbach and the K5730 to Martinskapelle.

Villingen-Schwenningen
☎ 07721 / pop 37,231

The spitting image of Freiburg on a smaller scale, Villingen recalls its medieval origins in the cobbled Altstadt, where merchants' houses huddle around the glowing Münster. Locals nickname it Städtle (little town), but they clearly think big during February's Fasnet celebrations (boxed text, below) when parades bring a stampede of jangling *Narros* to the streets.

Villingen's younger twin is Schwenningen, but while the towns are often mentioned in the same breath, each has its own flavour and history: Villingen once belonged to the Grand Duchy of Baden, while Schwenningen was part of the duchy of Württemberg – conflicting allegiances that apparently can't be reconciled.

ORIENTATION & INFORMATION
Surrounded by a ring road, Villingen's Altstadt is crisscrossed by mostly pedestrianised streets: north–south Obere Strasse and Niedere Strasse; and east–west Bickenstrasse and Rietstrasse. The *Bahnhof* and bus station are east of the ring on Bahnhofstrasse. Schwenningen's centre is 5km east.

Post office (Bahnhofstrasse 6, Villingen)
Villingen tourist office (☎ 822 340; www.tourism us-vs.de; Rietgasse 2; ⏱ 9am-5pm Mon-Sat, 11am-5pm Sun) In the Franziskaner Museum.

SIGHTS & ACTIVITIES
Villingen's **Altstadt** is a flashback to the Middle Ages with its preserved medieval walls, gates and cobblestones. The real crowd-puller is the red-sandstone **Münster** with striking disparate spires: one overlaid with coloured tiles, the other spiky and festooned with gargoyles. The Romanesque portals with *haut-relief* doors depict dramatic biblical scenes.

A saunter around **Münsterplatz** takes in the step-gabled **Altes Rathaus** and Klaus Ringwald's **Münsterbrunnen**, a bronze fountain portraying characters that have shaped Villingen's past; look out for a drowned rat at the base. The square hums with activity on market days (Wednesday and Saturday) when stalls are piled high with local goods.

Sidling up to Riettor and occupying a former Franciscan monastery, the **Franziskaner Museum** (☎ 822 351; Rietgasse 2; adult/concession €3/2; ⏱ 1-5pm Tue-Sat, 11am-5pm Sun & holidays) is a romp through the town's art and culture. The collection shifts from 18th-century cuckoo clocks to Celtic artefacts unearthed at **Magdalenenberg**, 30 minutes' walk south of the centre. Dating to 616

NARRI-NARRO!

If getting stuffed with straw, kidnapped by witches and showered with bonbons sounds like your idea of fun, you'll love **Villinger Fasnet** (www.narrozunft.de). In the bleak midwinter, this pre-Lenten celebration is a feast of all things forbidden before 40 days of fasting. Dubbed the fifth season, the 500-year-old Alemannic festivity runs from Epiphany to Ash Wednesday. The highlight is the final week of partying and parades, where folk don handcarved masks that give them the anonymity to misbehave. Everyone is welcome – dress up, it's tradition! – but don't call it carnival unless you want to be banished to the tower like Romäus.

Shrove Tuesday is the big event when all Fasnet characters take to the cobbled streets of the Altstadt for a four-hour procession. Look out for the jesterlike *Narro* who jumps to the jangle of bells, the *Butzesel* donkey who sweeps the streets with a fir branch to the crack of whips, the *Wuescht* whose trousers are filled with straw, the crinkly *Morbili* with a basket full of pralines and the feline *Kater Miau*. The whole shebang is rounded out with the ritual burning of the straw at midnight on Münsterplatz.

BC, the site is one of the largest Hallstatt burial chambers ever discovered in Central Europe and is shaded by a 1000-year-old oak tree.

Behind the Franziskaner, the **Spitalgarten** is a peaceful pocket of greenery flanked by the original city walls. Here your gaze is drawn to the **Romäusturm**, a lofty 13th-century thieves' tower where the giant of Villingen, Romäus, looms large.

When the sun shines, the tree-fringed **Kneippbad** (Lido; ☎ 534 41; Am Kneippbad 1; adult/child €3.30/2.20; ♡ 6.30am-8pm Mon-Fri, 8am-8pm Sat & Sun Jun-Aug) northwest of the Altstadt draws families to its outdoor pools, slides and volleyball courts.

Villingen is the starting point for some wonderful Black Forest **walks**, including the 12km hike to Unterkirnach. The woodland trail shadows the Brigach River upstream past **Feldner Mühle** watermill, where pony rides (€0.50), a playground and animals – including emus – amuse kids. Cross the car park at Kirnacher *Bahnhof* to reach a Roman path, where wagon tracks are still visible. This brings you to **Salvest**, a serene picnic spot where deer roam. From nearby Ackerloch Grillschopf, retrace your steps to Villingen or take the bus from Unterkirnach (€2.65, 17 minutes).

SLEEPING & EATING

The compact Altstadt is dotted with restaurants and cafés, but the best sleeping options are northwest of the centre around the Kurgarten.

Haus Bächle (☎ 597 29; Am Kneippbad 5; s/d €13/24; P ✗) This half-timbered house overlooks the flowery Kurgarten. The tidy rooms are an absolute bargain and the Kneippbad is next door for early-morning swims.

Rindenmühle (☎ 886 80; www.rindenmuehle.de; Am Kneippbad 9; s €67, d €89-94; P ▣) A few paces from Bächle, this converted watermill houses one of Villingen's smartest hotels. The spacious rooms in muted tones have wi-fi. In the kitchen, Martin Weisser creates award-winning flavours using home-grown organic produce, including chicken, geese and herbs plucked fresh from his garden.

Ackerloch Grillschopf (☎ 54 421; Unteres Ackerloch; snacks €3-8; ♡ 11.30am-midnight) Perched on a hill with valley views, this rustic barn doubles as a butcher selling home-smoked Black Forest ham (animals are reared in stress-free conditions) prepared without artificial additives or preservatives. After a long hike, whiffs of suckling pig roasting on a spit might tempt you in

for *Haxen* (pork knuckles). Choose snacks at the counter and grill 'em at the barbecue.

Don Antonio (☎ 506 084; Färberstrasse 18; mains €10.50-14.50; ♡ 6pm-midnight) This vibrant Spanish haunt has a party vibe. Flamenco plays, candles flicker and groups huddle around huge plates of tapas (€15) in the cavelike alcoves.

our pick Osteria & Enoteca de' Messeri (☎ 216 40; www.osteriademesseri.de; Gerberstrasse 3; lunch €10, dinner €30; ♡ 12pm-2.30pm, 6.30-10.30pm, closed Mon lunch, Sun) Fabio Vallini is Villingen's Italian master chef, whipping up Tuscan specialities with passion and prowess. Enter the Enoteca to see him kindling the fire, rolling pasta and shaving parmesan into paper-thin curls. The seasonal menu might include gnocchi with (handpicked) porcini or pigeon in truffle cream. The ivy-draped courtyard is popular in summer and kids are always welcomed as part of *la familia*.

DRINKING

For wall-to-wall bars, look no further than Färberstrasse.

Zampolli (☎ 328 65; Rietstrasse 33; coffee €2-4 ♡ 9.30am-11pm Mon-Sat, 10.30am-11pm Sun, closed Dec-Jan) This buzzing gelateria by day is also a relaxed bar with a terrace facing Riettor by night. Ice cream is made Italian-style with fresh cream and fruit, and the espresso is the best in town.

Gasthaus Ott (☎ 288 44; www.ott-vs.de; Färberstrasse 36; ♡ 11am-1am Mon-Thu, 11am-3am Fri & Sat, 2pm-1am Sun) Packed at weekends, this lively pub is a Färberstrasse favourite with its laid-back vibe, good beer and grotto-style cubby holes.

GETTING THERE & AROUND

Villingen's *Bahnhof* sits on the scenic Schwarzwaldbahn railway line from Konstanz and Donaueschingen to Triberg and Offenburg. Change in Donaueschingen to get to Freiburg.

From Villingen, bus 7265 makes regular trips north to Triberg via St Georgen. Frequent buses (for example line 1) link Villingen with Schwenningen.

Villingen-Schwenningen is just west of the A81 Stuttgart–Singen motorway and is also crossed by the B33 to Triberg and the B27 to Rottweil.

SOUTHEAST OF FREIBURG
Titisee-Neustadt
☎ 07651 / pop 12,000

Titisee is a cheerful summertime playground with a name that makes English-speaking visitors giggle. The ice-age lake is naturally the star attraction; ringed by forest it shimmers bottle-green or petrol-blue depending on the angle and time of day.

The entrance to the village is firmly tourist territory with souvenir shops galore, but if you follow the flowery 6km waterfront promenade, **Seestrasse**, you'll leave the crowds behind to discover sheltered bays ideal for swimming and picnicking. For giddy views, head up to 1192m **Hochfirst** tower, which overlooks Titisee from the east.

A relaxed way to appreciate the lake is from the relative quiet of a **rowing boat**. Competition is hot with a number of companies vying for custom along the lakefront; expect to pay around €6 per hour.

The Titisee area is popular for **Nordic walking**, which – for the uninitiated – is like cross-country skiing without the skis. Its main purpose is to exercise the upper body.

The town also bills itself as a *Bikerparadies* (that's a paradise for cyclists, not for Hell's Angels) with **cycling** paths and routes heading in every direction.

When snow falls, Titisee is a fine base for **cross-country skiing**. Its hills and woodlands are crisscrossed by *Loipen* (tracks), ranging from a 1km novice trail to a 14km route venturing deep into the forest. There's even a 3km floodlit track for swishing through the snow under the stars. A map outside the tourist office pinpoints cross-country and Nordic walking trails in the area.

The **tourist office** (☎ 980 40; www.titisee-neustadt .de; Strandbadstrasse 4; ⏱ 9am-6pm Mon-Fri, 10am-1pm Sat, Sun & holidays May-Oct, 9am-noon & 1.30-5pm Mon-Fri Nov-Apr), 500m southwest of the station, can make bookings and stocks walking and cycling maps.

SLEEPING & EATING

Titisee-Neustadt and its surrounds have tons of hotels, *Pensionen* (guesthouses) and campsites to pick from; better deals are slightly away from the main drag.

DJH hostel (☎ 238; www.jugendherberge-titisee -veltishof.de; Bruderhalde 27; dm 1st/subsequent night €18.70/15.40; ✗) Housed in a rambling farmhouse at the lake's western tip, this hostel has great facilities, including a barbecue area and toboggan rental. It's 30 minutes' walk from the station or a five-minute ride on bus 7300.

Bergseeblick (☎ 82 57; www.bergseeblick-titisee.de; Erlenweg 3; s €24-30, d 48-58; P) This family-run

chalet near the church offers quiet rooms with floral fabrics and plenty of pine. The fabulously kitsch collection of gnomes next door features Snow White and her Seven Dwarfs.

Alemannenhof (☎ 911 80; www.hotel-aleman nenhof.de; Hinterzarten am Titisee; s €77-129, d €112-168; P ❑ ☑) Lakefront Alemannenhof blends rustic charm with modern comfort in rooms that open onto balconies facing Titisee. A pool and private beach are other perks. Savour treats like rabbit in lavender sauce on the restaurant's lantern-lit terrace.

Seebachstueble (☎ 82 31; Seebachstrasse 43; mains €8-25; ⏱ lunch & dinner) Markus Ketterer's seasonal flavours might include milk-fed lamb on apricot-ginger sauce or rump steak with Thai prawns, using locally sourced produce. Kids love the ice cream from a local farm.

Picnickers should try **Gutscher** (cnr Strandbadstrasse & Seestrasse; ⏱ daily) for local specialities including ham, cheese, schnapps and bread loaves the size of car tyres.

GETTING THERE & AROUND

Rail routes include the Höllentalbahn to Freiburg and Donaueschingen (twice an hour; stops at both Titisee and Neustadt); and the Dreiseenbahn to Feldberg and Schluchsee (hourly; stops at Titisee).

From Titisee train station, bus 7257 serves Schluchsee (three or four times a day) and bus 7300 Feldberg-Bärental (15 minutes; seven Monday to Saturday, three on Sunday and holidays). Bus 7257 connects Titisee with Neustadt every hour.

Bikes (and in winter, ski equipment) can be hired from **Ski-Hirt** (☎ 922 80; Titiseestrasse 26, Neustadt), which can also supply details on local cycling options.

Feldberg
☎ 07655 / pop 1800

At 1493m Feldberg is the highest mountain in the Black Forest – no surprise, then, that it's the region's premier downhill skiing area. The actual mountaintop is treeless and not particularly attractive, looking very much like a monk's tonsured skull, but on clear days the view southward towards the Alps is stunning.

Feldberg is also the name given to a cluster of five villages, of which **Altglashütten** is the hub. Its Rathaus houses the **tourist office** (☎ 8019; www.feldberg-schwarzwald.de in German; Kirchgasse 1; ⏱ 8.30am-5.30pm Mon-Fri, also 10am-noon

Sat in summer, 10am-noon Sun Jul & Aug), which rents Nordic walking poles for €3 per day.

Situated around 2km north is the postcard-perfect **Bärental**, where traditional Black Forest farmhouses snuggle against the hillsides. East of Bärental in the Haslach Valley is **Falkau**, a family-friendly resort with a pretty waterfall. **Windgfällweiher**, a pristine lake for swimming or picnicking, lies 1km southeast of Altglashütten.

Just 9km west of Altglashütten is **Feldberg-Ort**, in the heart of the 42-sq-km nature preserve that covers much of the mountain. The **tourist office** (☎ 07676-933 630; Dr-Pilet-Spur 4, Feldberg; ⏲ 10am-5pm Tue-Sun) is in the Haus der Natur, which offers information and maps on the Feldberg area, and rents sports equipment. Most ski lifts are here, including the panoramic **Feldbergbahn chairlift** (one-way/return €5.60/7.20) to the **Bismarckdenkmal** (Bismarck monument).

ACTIVITIES

The Feldberg area is great for **hiking**. The most rewarding trail is the 12km **Feldberg-Steig** from Haus der Natur to Feldberg summit, where views stretch from Zugspitze to Mont Blanc when the weather is fine. As much of Feldberg is a nature reserve, you may well spot rare wildflowers or animals such as mountain hens, deer and chamois.

Feldberg ski area (adult/child under 15yr per day €25/13, from 1pm €17.50/9) comprises 28 lifts accessible with the same ticket. Four groomed cross-country trails are also available. If you want to hire skis, look for signs reading 'Skiverleih'; a reliable choice is **Skiverleih Schubnell** (☎ 560; www.skiverleih-feldberg.de in German; Bärentaler Strasse 1, Altglashütten).

If stomping through deep powder appeals, check out Feldberg's **snowshoeing** routes, which include the scenic 3km Seebuck-Trail and the more challenging 9km Gipfel-Trail. The Haus der Natur rents lightweight snowshoes for €10/5 per day for adults/children.

SLEEPING

The tourist office hands out the *Hüttenverzeichnis* listing huts and *Pensionen* offering reasonably priced beds.

Jugendherberge Hebelhof (☎ 07676-221; www.jugendherberge.de; Passhöhe 14; dm 1st/subsequent night €20.10/16.90; ✗) Close to Feldberg-Ort, this chalet-style hostel has spick-and-span dorms, plus a ski room and volleyball court. It's served by bus 7300 from Bärental train station to Hebelhof (15 minutes, hourly).

Sonneck Hotel (☎ 211; www.sonneck-feldberg.de; Schwarzenbachweg 5, Altglashütten; d €72-76; ℗) This revamped hotel opposite the tourist office offers light-filled, immaculate rooms with balconies. The wood-panelled restaurant (mains €8 to €15) rolls out hearty fare like *Wurstsalat* (sausage salad).

GETTING THERE & AWAY

Bärental and Altglashütten are stops on the Dreiseenbahn, linking Titisee with Seebrugg (Schluchsee). From the train station in Bärental, bus 7300 makes trips at least hourly to Feldberg-Ort.

From late December until the end of the season shuttle buses, run by Feldberg SBG, link Feldberg and Titisee with the ski lifts (free with a lift ticket or *Gästekarte*).

If you're driving, take the B31 (Freiburg–Donaueschingen) to Titisee, then the B317. To get to Altglashütten, head down the B500 from Bärental.

Schluchsee
☎ 07656 / pop 2600

The hilltop town of Schluchsee tumbles down to the Black Forest's biggest lake. It's popular for outdoor activities, especially swimming, windsurfing and hiking. Accessible by bike or on foot, the western shore's secluded bays attract local naturists, so don't be surprised if you come across the odd skinny-dipper!

Next to the Rathaus, the **tourist office** (☎ 7732; www.schluchsee.de; Haus des Gastes, Fischbacher Strasse 7; ⏲ 8am-6pm Mon-Thu, 9am-6pm Fri, also 10am-noon Sat Jul, 10am-noon Sat & Sun Aug & holiday weekends) has stacks of information on activities and accommodation, plus free wi-fi.

Great fun for all the family is the lakefront lido, **Aqua Fun Strandbad** (Strandbadstrasse; adult/student/child €3.80/2.50/1.50; ⏲ 9am-7pm late May–mid-Sep) with its heated pool, as well as sandy beach, volleyball court, waterslides and an adventure playground.

T Toth (☎ 9230; www.seerundfahrten.de in German; round trip €6, less for single stops) runs a boat service around the Schluchsee, with stops in Aha, the dam (Staumauer), Seebrugg and Schluchsee Strandbad (hourly from 11am to 5pm May to late October). You can hop on and off as you please; the round trip takes one hour.

SLEEPING & EATING

Schluchsee is a less developed town than Titisee, but there are some good-value

Pensionen (the tourist office has a list). The '70s-style hotels around Kirchplatz have seen better days.

DJH hostel (☎ 329; www.jugendherberge-schluchsee -wolfsgrund.de; Im Wolfsgrund 28; dm 1st/subsequent night €18.70/15.40; ☒) On a peninsula jutting into Schluchsee, this charming hostel is a 10-minute walk west along the lakefront from the train station. Facilities include table tennis and a barbecue area.

There's a supermarket, **Isele Markt** (Kirchplatz 2; ☺ 8am-12.30pm & 2.30-6.30pm Mon-Fri, 8am-1pm Sat), across the square from the church.

GETTING THERE & AROUND
The hourly Dreiseenbahn train travels to Feldberg and Titisee. Bus 7257 links Schluchsee with Neustadt and Titisee train stations (three or four times a day).

Wutachschlucht
Jagged, near-vertical rock faces dwarf everything beneath them along the wild Wutach-schlucht (Wutach Gorge). The **Wutach** ('angry river' in loose translation) rises almost at the summit of the Feldberg and flows into the Rhine near Waldshut, on the Swiss frontier. This microclimate harbours an extraordinary variety of wild orchids and ferns, as well as rare birds from treecreepers to kingfishers, and countless species of butterflies, beetles and lizards.

The **tourist office** (☎ 07703-7607; www.bonndorf.de in German; Martinstrasse 5; ☺ 9am-noon & 2-6pm Mon-Fri, 10am-noon Sat May-Oct, 9am-noon & 2-5pm Mon-Fri except Wed afternoon Nov-Apr) in Bonndorf, 15km east of Schluchsee, has hiking information, maps and a list of places to stay.

To appreciate the Wutachschlucht in all of its splendour, hike 13km through the canyon from **Schattenmühle** to **Wutachmühle** (or the other way round). If you have the energy, you can add the romantic, 2.5km-long **Lotenbach-Klamm** (Lotenbach Glen) to your tour. May to September is the best time to tackle the walk and it's worth carrying supplies as there's very little between the trailheads.

Bus 7258 runs between Bonndorf and Neustadt train station (40 minutes, hourly Monday to Saturday, every two hours Sunday). Bus 7344 links Bonndorf to Schattenmühle and Wutachmühle (every hour or two Monday to Friday during school times).

NORTHERN BLACK FOREST

BADEN-BADEN
☎ 07221 / pop 54,800
Queen Victoria and Victoria Beckham, Bismarck and Brahms, they all came to Baden-Baden – the royal, the rich and the moneyed wannabees – to take the therapeutic waters or fritter away their fortunes in the casino. Today Baden-Baden is the grande dame of German spas, ageing but still elegant with its *belle époque* townscape of palatial villas and tree-lined avenues. It's free to stroll the city's glorious gardens and even the top spas don't require deep pockets (at one of them, pockets are banned entirely!).

Baden-Baden matches the fanfare of Ascot – fancy hats and all – with its **Grand Festival Week** held at the Iffezheim racecourse in late August. This highlight on the horse-racing calendar welcomes some of the world's top jockeys to the track. A glamorous prize-giving ball rounds out the event. For more details, visit the website www.iffezheim.de.

Orientation
Baden-Baden's core is Leopoldsplatz, surrounded by pedestrianised shopping streets. Most sights – including Lichtentaler Allee, on the west bank of the Oosbach River – are within easy walking distance. The *Bahnhof* is in the suburb of Oos, 4km northwest of the centre, with the bus station out the front.

Information
Branch tourist office (Kaiserallee 3; ☺ 10am-5pm Mon-Sat, 2-5pm Sun) In the Trinkhalle. Sells events tickets.
Internet Café (Lange Strasse 54; per hr €2; ☺ 10am-10pm) Internet access at the northern edge of the pedestrianised centre.
Main tourist office (☎ 275 200; www.baden-baden .com; Schwarzwaldstrasse 52; ☺ 9am-6pm Mon-Sat, 9am-1pm Sun) Situated 2km northwest of the town centre. If you're driving from the northwest (from the A5) it's on the way into town. Sells events tickets.
Post office (Lange Strasse 44) Inside Kaufhaus Wagener.

Sights
KURHAUS & CASINO
In the heart of Baden-Baden, the **Kurhaus** (☎ 353-202; www.kurhaus-baden-baden.de in German; Kaiserallee 1) towers above a manicured garden. Corinthian columns and a frieze of mythical

griffins grace its monumental façade. An alley of chestnut trees, flanked by two rows of boutiques, links the Kurhaus with Kaiserallee.

Inside is the opulent 19th-century **casino** (☎ 302 40; www.casino-baden-baden.de; admission €3; 2pm-2am Sun-Thu, 2pm-3am Fri & Sat), which seeks to emulate – indeed, outdo – the splendour of France's famed chateaux. Marlene Dietrich called it 'the most beautiful casino in the world'. Men must wear a jacket and tie, rentable for €8 and €3 respectively. If you just want to gawp at the lavish interior, consider a **guided tour** (€4), every half-hour from 9.30am (10am from October to March) until 12pm daily.

In the park north of the Kurhaus stands the **Trinkhalle** (Pump Room; Kaiserallee 3), housing a branch of the tourist office, with a 90m-long portico decorated with frescoes of local myths. To feel ten years younger, nip inside for a free glass of curative mineral water from a tap (10am to 2am, and until 3am Friday and Saturday) linked to the springs below. The café sells plastic cups for €0.20.

LICHTENTALER ALLEE

The gateway to Lichtentaler Allee is **Baden-Baden Theater**, a neobaroque confection whose frilly interior resembles the Opéra-Garnier in Paris. From here the elegant promenade shadows the sprightly Oosbach from Goetheplatz to Kloster Lichtenthal 3km south. Even today, the fragrant boulevard conjures up visions of 19th-century aristocrats and artists taking languid strolls.

The nearby sky-lit **Kunsthalle** (State Art Gallery; ☎ 300 763; Lichtentaler Allee 8a; adult/concession €5/4; 11am-6pm Tue-Sun, 11am-8pm Wed) showcases rotating exhibitions of contemporary art in neoclassical surrounds.

Linked to the Kunsthalle by a glass bridge is **Museum Frieder Burda** (☎ 398 980; www.museum-frieder-burda.de; Lichtentaler Allee 8b; adult/student €8/6; 11am-6pm Tue-Sun), an architecturally innovative edifice designed by Richard Meier. The star collection of modern and contemporary art includes the revered brushwork of Pollock, Warhol and Picasso.

About 1km south is the **Gönneranlage**, a rose garden ablaze with more than 400 varieties that thrive in the local microclimate, said to be Mediterranean. Said to be almost Siberian is the **Russische Kirche** (Russian Church; Maria-Victoria-Strasse; admission €0.50; 10am-6pm) slightly to the east. Built in the Byzantine style in 1882, it is topped with a brilliantly golden onion dome.

Lichtentaler Allee concludes at the **Kloster Lichtenthal**, a Cistercian abbey founded in 1245, with an **abbey church** (daily) where generations of the margraves of Baden lie buried.

Activities
SPAS

Revisit Roman times with a long soak in the sublime 19th-century **Friedrichsbad** (☎ 275 920; www.roemisch-irisches-bad.de; Römerplatz 1; 9am-10pm, last admission 7pm). With its cupola, mosaic tiles and circular pool ringed by columns, the bathhouse is the vision of a neo-Renaissance palace. The **Roman-Irish Bath** (admission €21, incl soap-and-brush massage €29) consists of timed hot and cold showers, saunas and steam rooms that leave you feeling scrubbed, lubed and loose as a goose. No clothing is allowed so leave your modesty at the reception.

Catapulting you back to the 21st century, the glass-fronted **Caracalla-Therme** (☎ 275 940;

QUIET RETREATS

Baden-Baden is synonymous with casinos and spas, but its quieter corners are every bit as lovely. A vine-enveloped staircase twists up from Marktplatz to **Neues Schloss**, the former residence of the margraves of Baden-Baden, offering fabulous views of the Black Forest's undulating hills.

A snippet of Italy, **Florentinerberg** (Florentine Hill) is where the Romans used to cool off after taking the thermal waters; check out the ruins of the original baths at the foot of the hill. The serene botanic gardens here nurture wisteria, cypress trees and fragrant orange and lemon groves.

Paradies on Annaberg is an oasis of calm. Framed by grand villas, the Italianate gardens are the perfect spot to unwind beside dancing fountains and waterfalls on lawns that afford far-reaching vistas of Baden-Baden. Bus 205 to Friedrichshöhe runs nearby.

Around 15 minutes' walk north of the centre is **Altes Schloss**. Dating to 1102, this crumbling castle is the place to act out fairy-tale fantasies with its winding staircases and dungeons. Perched high above the city, it offers a superb panorama of Baden-Baden, the Black Forest and Rhine Valley. Seek out Rüdiger Oppermann's wind harp.

www.caracalla.de; Römerplatz 11; 2/3/4hr €13/15/17; ⊙ 8am-10pm, last admission 8pm) shelters pools, grottos, whirlpools, water massages and a surge channel. The sauna complex fires imaginations with experiences from a rustic sizzle in a log-cabin to an all-glass steam temple. Bathing suits must be worn everywhere except in the upstairs sauna; towels can be rented.

HIKING

Baden-Baden is a marvellous place to get out and stride. Favourite walking destinations include the **Altes Schloss**, 2.5km north of the centre; **Geroldsauer waterfalls**, 6km south of Leopoldsplatz; and the **Yburg castle ruin**, in the wine country southwest of town. A more ambitious but worthwhile hike is the 40km circular **Panoramaweg**, which twists up into the hills and takes in waterfalls, orchards and woodlands; the vistas over Baden-Baden from Malschbach are fabulous.

A **Standseilbahn** (cable car; ☎ 2770; www.stadt werke-baden-baden.de in German; adult/child 6-15yr one-way €2/1.30, return €4/2; ⊙ 10am-10pm Apr-Dec) whisks you to the 668m-high summit of **Mt Merkur**, east of the centre, where marked trails lead off in all directions. To get there take bus 204 or 205 from Leopoldsplatz.

Sleeping

Baden-Baden is chock-a-block with plush hotels but there aren't many bargains. The tourist office has a room-reservation service; a 10% fee is deducted from the cost of the room.

DJH hostel (☎ 522 23; www.jugendherberge-baden -baden.de; Hardbergstrasse 34; dm 1st/subsequent night €18.70/15.40; ✕) Situated 2.5km northwest of the centre, this hostel won't bowl you over with charm, but it's passable if you're on a tight budget. Take bus 201 to Grosse Dollenstrasse and walk 750m up the hill from the church.

Hotel am Markt (☎ 270 40; www.hotel-am-markt -baden.de; Marktplatz 18; s €30-47 d €60-80; P ✕ 🖳) This peach-fronted hotel next to the Stiftskirche is a real find. Its 23 rooms are homey and bathrooms squeaky-clean. Free internet access is a bonus.

Rathausglöckel (☎ 906 10; www.rathausgloeckel.de; Steinstrasse 7; d €65-95; 🖳) Down the hill from the Stiftskirche, this family-run hotel occupies a 16th-century town house. The recently renovated rooms (some with rooftop views) are dressed in muted tones with pine furniture.

Am Friedrichsbad (☎ 396 340; www.hotel-am -friedrichsbad.de; Gernsbacher Strasse 31; s/d €99/129;

P ✕) This classic 1920s building facing Friedrichsbad houses spacious rooms, decorated with prints of the Jewish ghetto in Prague, the owner's hometown.

Steigenberger Badischer Hof (☎ 93 40; www .badischer-hof.steigenberger.com; Lange Strasse 47; s €125-159, d €188-260; P ✕ 🖳 🐾) Perfect for splashing out, with swanky quarters, attentive staff and droves of bathrobed guests shuffling to the spa. In some rooms you can choose between mineral water and tap water – in your bathtub, that is.

Eating & Drinking

Most restaurants huddle in the pedestrianised stretch around Leopoldsplatz. Baden-Baden's nightlife is low-key, but you'll find a few beer gardens and wine bars for a quiet drink.

Monte Christo (☎ 393 434; Eichstrasse 5; tapas €3.60-8.80; ⊙ 5pm-1am Mon-Sat) This Spanish tapas bar is a winning combination of friendly service, fair prices and tasty morsels from spicy chorizo to thick wedges of tortilla.

Jensens (☎ 397 900; Sophienstrasse 45; light meals €5-8; ⊙ from 10.30am) Opposite Caracalla-Therme, this bistro has a hip feel with its pepper-red walls, wood floors and jazzy tunes. Enjoy a beer or crisp *Flammkuchen* (around €6) on the patio. Wi-fi is available.

Aumatt (☎ 337 55; Aumattstrasse 36a; mains €7.50-15; ⊙ 11.30am-1am) Families flock to this riverside beer garden for its playground, sandpit and kids' meals (€3.50). Fondue and schnitzel staples top the menu.

Leo's (☎ 380 81; Luisenstrasse 8-10; mains €9.50-21.50; ⊙ 8am-2am) Smack in the centre, Leo's is a trendy bistro and wine bar that rolls out creative pasta dishes and large salads. The terrace is a crowd-magnet in summer.

La Provence (☎ 255 50; Schlossstrasse 20; mains €13.50-21.50; ⊙ noon-11pm, to 1am Fri & Sat) Housed in the Neues Schloss wine cellar, the vaulted ceilings, Art Nouveau mirrors and French sense of humour at La Provence complement the cuisine – think garlicky snails and duck breast in lavender-honey sauce.

Entertainment

Ensconced in an historic railway station, the **Festspielhaus** (☎ 301 3101; www.festspielhaus.de; Beim Alten Bahnhof 2, Robert-Schumann-Platz) presents a superb repertoire of classical concerts, opera and ballet.

The much-celebrated **Baden-Badener Philharmonie** (☎ 932 791; www.philharmonie.baden-baden.de;

Solms-Strasse 1) frequently performs in the Kurhaus.

Getting There & Away

Karlsruhe–Baden-Baden airport (Baden Airpark; www .badenairpark.de), 15km west of town, serves destinations including London, Rome and Dublin by Ryanair.

Baden-Baden is close to the A5 (Frankfurt–Basel autobahn) and is the northern starting point of the Schwarzwald-Hochstrasse (opposite), which follows the B500.

Baden-Baden is on a major north–south rail corridor. Destinations with twice-hourly runs include Freiburg (€16.60 to €25, 45 to 80 minutes) and Karlsruhe (€5, more by IC or ICE, 15 to 20 minutes). Buses depart from stands next to the *Bahnhof*.

Getting Around
BUS

Stadtwerke Baden-Baden (☎ 27 71; www.stadtwerke -baden-baden.de) run local buses that cost €1.50 for a one-zone single ticket, €2 for a two-zone ticket and €4.50 for a 24-hour pass valid for three zones.

Bus 201 (every 10 minutes) links the *Bahnhof* with Leopoldsplatz. Bus 205 links the *Bahnhof* with the airport from Monday to Friday.

CAR & MOTORCYCLE

The centre is mostly pedestrianised, so it's best to park and walk. Michaelstunnel on the D500 diverts traffic away from the centre, ducking underground west of the Festspielhaus and surfacing south of the Russische Kirche. There is a free parking lot north of the centre on Schlossstrasse, close to the Neues Schloss.

FREUDENSTADT
☎ 07441 / pop 23,000

This spa town was the brainchild of Duke Friedrich I of Württemberg, who decided to build a new capital in 1599. Together with his favourite architect, Heinrich Schickardt, he scoured Bologna and Rome for inspiration and came back with plans for a town laid out like a spider web. Freudenstadt's main artery is its gigantic Marktplatz, Germany's largest, measuring 216m by 219m.

Orientation & Information

Freudenstadt's focal point is the Marktplatz on the B28. The town has two train stations:

the Stadtbahnhof, five minutes' walk north of Marktplatz, and the Hauptbahnhof, 2km southeast of Marktplatz. The central bus station is outside the Stadtbahnhof.

ATMs There are several on the Marktplatz.

Post office (Marktplatz 64)

Tourist office (☎ 8640; www.freudenstadt.de; Marktplatz 64; ☑ 9am-6pm Mon-Fri, 10am-2pm Sat, Sun & holidays May-Oct; 10am-5pm Mon-Fri, 10am-1pm Sat, 11am-1pm Sun & holidays Nov-Apr) Has an internet terminal (per 5/60min €0.50/6). Hotel reservations are free.

Sights & Activities

The **Marktplatz** is really too huge to feel like a square, chopped into three chunks by a T-junction of heavily trafficked roads. The central vein is flanked by Italianate arcades giving weatherproof access to dozens of shops.

The immense red-sandstone **Stadtkirche** (☑ 10am-5pm) is a potpourri of styles, with Gothic windows, Renaissance portals and baroque towers. The two **naves** are at right angles to each other – yet another unusual design by the geometrically minded duke. Of note inside is a Cluniac-style **baptismal font** with intricate animal ornamentations.

Locals unwind in the pools, steam rooms and salt grottos at the glass-fronted **Panorama-Bad** (☎ 921 300; www.panorama-bad.de in German; Ludwig-Jahn-Strasse 60; adult/child 6-17yr all day €8/6.50; ☑ 9am-10pm Mon-Sat, 9am-8pm Sun & holidays).

The undulating hills and fir woodlands of the northern Black Forest offer myriad **hiking** opportunities. The town is a base for scenic trails such as the 12km uphill trudge to Kniebis on the Schwarzwald-Hochstrasse, where there are far-reaching views over the Kinzig Valley. The tourist office provides details and maps.

When the weather warms, Freudenstadt is a magnet for **mountain bikers**. Favourite routes include the 85km route through the Kinzigtal looping from Freudenstadt to Kehl, which zips through unspoilt forest and half-timbered villages like Schiltach and Gengenbach. Equally popular is the 60km Murgtal tour, taking in lakes and streams en route to Rastatt. Both valleys have dedicated bike trails and it's possible to return to Freudenstadt by train.

Sleeping & Eating

The tourist office provides details on *Pensionen* and farmhouses in the region (expect to pay €20 to €30 per person). Numerous cafés with alfresco seating fringe the square, but Freudenstadt falls quiet after dark.

Camping Langenwald (☎ 2862; www.camping-langenwald.de; Strasburger Strasse 167; campsites per adult/child/tent/car €6/3.50/5/3; ☯ Easter-1 Nov; P ▣) With a solar-heated pool and nature trail, this leafy site has impeccable eco credentials. Other pluses include the volleyball court and playground. It's served by bus 12 to Kniebis.

DJH hostel (☎ 7720; www.jugendherberge.de; Eugen-Nägele-Strasse 69; dm 1st/subsequent nights €18.70/15.40; ✗) This decent hostel, 1km northeast of the Stadtbahnhof, offers spartan but clean dorms. Facilities include cross-country ski rental. Take bus 15 from the Hauptbahnhof.

Hotel Adler (☎ 915 20; www.adler-fds.de; Forststrasse 15-17; s €34-48, d €58-82; P ✗ ▣) A few paces from Marktplatz, this family-run hotel has bright, comfy rooms. Chill in the garden or make a free cuppa in the TV lounge.

Hotel Schwanen (☎ 915 50; www.schwanen-freudenstadt.de in German; Forststrasse 6; s €38-47, d 80-88; P ✗) Don't be fooled by the '70s-style wallpaper at reception – rooms have recently been spruced up with modern trimmings and wi-fi.

Turmbräu (☎ 905 121; www.turmbraeu.de in German; Marktplatz 64; mains €7-16; ☯ 10am-1am, to 3am Fri & Sat) This lively microbrewery doubles as a beer garden. Pull up a chair in ye-olde barn to munch *Maultaschen* (Swabian ravioli)

and guzzle Turmbräu brews – a 5L barrel costs €12.50.

The **restaurant** (mains €7 -12) at Hotel Schwanen serves filling *Riesenpfannkuchen* (giant pancakes), while Hotel Adler's **restaurant** (mains €7-18) is famed for its yummy *Spätzle* (egg noodles with cheese) and blueberry wine.

Getting There & Away

Trains on the Ortenau rail line, serving Offenburg and Strasbourg, depart hourly from the Hauptbahnhof. The 24-hour Europass offers the best value, covering one adult and two children for €9.20. The hourly Murgtalbahn goes to Karlsruhe (€14.20, 1½ hours) from the Stadtbahnhof and Hauptbahnhof.

Freudenstadt marks the southern end of the Schwarzwald-Hochstrasse and is also a terminus of the stunning Schwarzwald-Tälerstrasse (below), which runs from Rastatt via Alpirsbach.

Getting Around

Freudenstadt's **bus network** (☎ 07443-247 340; www.vgf-info.de in German) comprises five local routes (A, B, C, D and 15); single tickets cost €1.40. Local and regional buses link the Hauptbahnhof to Marktplatz.

TOP FIVE SCENIC DRIVES IN THE BLACK FOREST

More than just pretty drives, many of these routes focus on a theme, such as Franco-German friendship, wine growing and clock-making. Local tourist offices provide details and brochures.

- **Schwarzwald-Hochstrasse** (Black Forest Hwy) Following the B500, this connects Baden-Baden with Freudenstadt, 60km to the south. It affords expansive views of the Upper Rhine Valley and, further west, the Vosges Mountains in Alsace (France) and skirts a number of lakes, including the emerald-green Mummelsee. From May to October you can travel by bus twice a day.

- **Badische Weinstrasse** (Baden Wine Rd) A wine quaffer's delight. From Baden-Baden south to Lörrach, this 160km route zips through the red-wine vineyards of Ortenau, the Pinot Noir of Kaiserstuhl and Tuniberg, and the white-wine vines of Markgräflerland.

- **Schwarzwald-Tälerstrasse** (Black Forest Valley Rd) Twists 100km from Rastatt to Freudenstadt. It appeals to vista vultures with its steep valleys (the Murgtal and Kinzig), punctuated by thick woodlands, granite cliffs and gin-clear streams. High points include Gernsbach's half-timbered houses, Forbach's beautifully preserved wooden bridge and freshly tapped beer in Alpirsbach.

- **Deutsche Uhrenstrasse** (German Clock Rd) A 320km-long loop starting in Villingen-Schwenningen that revolves around the story of clock-making in the Black Forest. Stops include the cuckoo capitals of Triberg and Furtwangen.

- **Grüne Strasse** (Green Rd) Links the Black Forest with the Rhine Valley and the Vosges Mountains in France. Popular with hikers and cyclists, this 160km route takes you through Kirchzarten, Freiburg, Breisach, Neuf-Brisach, Colmar and Munster.

THE BLACK FOREST

There's bike rental at **Intersport Glaser** (☎ 918 590; Katharinenstrasse 8; bike rental per day €14-20), 200m north of Marktplatz.

KINZIG VALLEY

The horseshoe-shaped Kinzig Valley begins south of Freudenstadt and traces the Kinzig River south to Schiltach, west to Haslach and north to Offenburg. Carving a path through orchards and densely wooded hills, the valley is a real Black Forest beauty, filled with enchanting half-timbered villages. Warm air from the Rhine Valley makes this an extremely fertile area: in spring the valley is awash with pink-and-white almond and cherry blossom, while in autumn the terraced vineyards turn a riot of gold and crimson.

Getting There & Away

Bus 7160 shuttles between Offenburg and Gutach. The B294 follows the Kinzig from Freudenstadt to Haslach, from where the B33 leads north to Offenburg. If you're going south, pick up the B33 to Triberg and beyond in Hausach.

The hourly Kinzigtal rail line links Freudenstadt's Hauptbahnhof with Offenburg, stopping in Alpirsbach, Schiltach, Hausach, Haslach and Gengenbach. From Hausach, trains go southeast to Triberg, Villingen and Donaueschingen, where you can change for Konstanz.

Alpirsbach

☎ 07444 / pop 7000

Legend has it Alpirsbach is named after a clumsy cleric who, when a glass of beer slipped from his hand and rolled into the river, exclaimed: *All Bier ist in den Bach!* (All the beer is in the stream!). Today Alpirsbacher Klosterbräu is indeed brewed from pure spring water. Guided tours of the **brewery** (€6; ☒ tours at 2.30pm), next to the Klosterkirche, are in German, though guides may speak English. Beer tasting is thrown in for the price of a ticket.

The **tourist office** (☎ 951 6281; www.alpirsbach.de; Hauptstrasse 20) next to the train station can supply hiking maps and, for cyclists, information on the 84km Kinzigtalradweg from Offenburg to Lossburg.

Across the way from the brewery is **Schau-Confiserie Heinzelmann** (☎ 1599; Krähenbadstrasse 3; ☒ 9am-12pm & 2-6pm Tue-Fri, 9am-12pm Sat), where you can see chocolates being made and sample scrummy beer-filled pralines.

Once the centrepiece of a Benedictine monastery, the 11th-century **Klosterkirche St Benedict** (☎ 951 6281; www.schloesser-und-gaerten .de; Freudenstädterstrasse; adult/student €3/2.30; ☒ 10am-4.30pm mid-Mar–mid-Apr; 10am-5.30pm mid-Apr–1 Nov; 1.30-3.30pm Wed, Sat & Sun 2 Nov–mid-Mar) has a wood-beamed, unadorned interior. Stroll the Gothic **cloister** around midday to see its red-sandstone façade blush. The monk cells in the **Dormitorium** have been lovingly restored; be sure to glimpse the enormous tooth and tusk of a woolly mammoth near the exit.

Schiltach

☎ 07836 / pop 4000

Schiltach meets most people's vision of a picture-book Black Forest village with its steep wooded hillsides, façades bursting with scarlet geraniums and row upon row of half-timbered houses. One of the greatest pleasures here is wandering the Altstadt's warren of cobbled lanes, pausing to gaze up at the former homes of tanners, merchants and raft builders.

INFORMATION

The **tourist office** (☎ 5850; www.schiltach.de; Marktplatz 6; ☒ 9am-noon & 2-5pm Mon-Fri, 10am-noon Sat) in the Rathaus can help find accommodation and offers free internet access. There's an **ATM** just below Marktplatz.

SIGHTS & ACTIVITIES

The main hub is the triangular **Marktplatz**, built on a steep slope, where the step-gabled **Rathaus** is embellished with murals illustrating the town's history. It's worth climbing above the village for views over the red rooftops to the surrounding hills. Look out for plaques representing medieval trades and sloping roofs with open attics, where tanners used to hang their skins to dry.

Museum am Markt (☎ 5875; Marktplatz 13; free entry; ☒ 11am-4pm Apr-Oct) is crammed with everything from antique spinning wheels to Biedermeier costumes. Highlights include the cobbler's workshop and an interactive display recounting the tale of the devilish Teufel von Schiltach.

Because Schiltach is at the confluence of the **Kinzig** and **Schiltach Rivers**, logging was big business here until the 19th century and huge rafts were built to ship timber as far as the Netherlands. The willow-fringed banks now attract grey herons and kids who come to splash in the shallow water when the sun's out.

The riverfront **Schüttesäge Museum** (☎ 5850; Hauptstrasse 1; entry free; ☽ 11am-5pm Tue-Sun Apr-Oct) focuses on Schiltach's rafting tradition with reconstructed workshops, a watermill generating hydroelectric power for many homes in the area and touchy-feely exhibits for kids, from different kinds of bark to forest animals.

SLEEPING & EATING

Schiltach has some first-rate places to stay and eat; most cluster around the Altstadt.

Campingplatz Schiltach (☎ 7289; www.camping platz-schiltach.de; Bahnhofstrasse 6; campsites per adult/child/tent/car €4/2/3.50/2.50; **P**) The cheery Brede family run this green campsite on the bonnie banks of the Kinzig. It has excellent recycling facilities and plenty of information on getting around by public transport. Little 'uns can let off steam in the playground and sandpit.

Gasthof Sonne (☎ 957 570; Marktplatz 3; www.son neschiltach.de; s €42.50-50, d €72-80; **▯**) Choosing a room is an adventure at this half-timbered guesthouse. Is it to be a romantic rose-tinged nest or a knight's chamber complete with shining armour?

Weysses Rössle (☎ 387; www.weysses-roessle.de; Schenkenzeller Strasse 42; s/d €47/68; **P ▯**) Rosemarie and Ulrich continue the tradition of 19 generations in this 16th-century inn. Countrified rooms decorated with rosewood and floral fabrics also feature snazzy bathrooms and wi-fi. Its restaurant uses locally sourced, organic fare.

Great-grandparents peer down from the walls in the beamed **restaurant** (mains €10-21) at Weysses Rössle, which serves dishes like Baden snail soup and dark beer roast. Gasthof Sonne's **restaurant** (mains €8.50 -14.50) also tempts, with Swabian specialities like *Katzagschroi* (beef, onions and fried potatoes); the name refers to the cat's whine when it finds no leftovers in the kitchen.

Gutach
☎ 07831 / pop 2300

A 4km detour south of the Kinzig Valley is the **Schwarzwälder Freilichtmuseum** (Black Forest Open-Air Museum; ☎ 93 560; www.vogtsbauernhof.org; adult//student/child/family €6/5/3/13; ☽ 9am-6pm early Apr–early Nov, to 8pm Aug). Centred on the Vogtsbauernhof, a self-contained farmstead that has stood here since 1612, this reconstructed farming hamlet is a fascinating insight into Black Forest traditions, architecture and crafts. The other farmhouses have been moved from their original locations and authentically recreated with

LOO WITH A VIEW

Super-sized cuckoos and giant gateaux, whatever next? How about the world's biggest loo. Drive a couple of minutes south of Gutach on the B33 and there – drum roll please – is the super bog. The brainchild of design guru Philippe Starck, the 12m-high ceramic toilet is the centrepiece of the **Duravit Design Centre** (☎ 07833-700; www.duravit.de; Werderstrasse 36, Hornberg; ☽ 7.30am-7pm Mon-Fri, 12-4pm Sat). It's the last word in toilet humour and can be visited without spending a penny. Take a stroll around the bowl for sweeping views across the Black Forest.

thatched half-hipped roofs, darkwood panelling and heavy beams. You'll explore barns filled with wagons and horn sleds, atmospheric *Stuben* (parlours), *Rauchküchen* (kitchens for smoking fish and meat) and pantries for storing sauerkraut and potatoes. A highlight is the **Hippenseppenhof** (1599) with its eye-catching crucifix, chapel and massive hipped roof constructed from 400 trees. Regular demonstrations range from sheep sheering to basket weaving and butter making.

Ten minutes' walk down the valley is the year-round **Schwarzwald Rodelbahn** (☎ 965 580; www.schwarzwaldrodelbahn.de; Singersbach 4; adult/child €2.50/2; ☽ 9am-8pm Apr-Oct, 9am-5pm Nov-Mar). The self-controlled bobs are heaps of fun and pretty fast if you lay off the breaks.

Haslach
☎ 07832 / pop 7000

Back in the Kinzig Valley, Haslach's 17th-century Capuchin monastery shelters the **Schwarzwälder Trachtenmuseum** (Black Forest Costume Museum; ☎ 706 172; admission €2; ☽ 9am-5pm Tue-Sat, 10am-5pm Sun & holidays Apr–mid-Oct; 9am-noon & 1-5pm Tue-Fri mid-Oct–Dec & Feb-Mar), a must-see for fans of flamboyant headwear. Elaborate creations include the Bollenhut, a straw bonnet topped with woollen pompons – red for unmarried women, black for married – and the Schäppel, a fragile-looking crown made from hundreds of beads and weighing up to 5kg.

GENGENBACH
☎ 07803 / pop 11,200

Düsseldorf? Nein! That famous scene with greedy Augustus Gloop in *Charlie and the*

Chocolate Factory was actually filmed here, though the caption would have you believe it was in a city found 400km north. But you can see why the producers fell for this wine-growing town, 11km south of Offenburg, with its cobbled alleyways, medieval towers and charming half-timbered houses swathed in vines.

INFORMATION

The **tourist office** (☎ 930 143; www.stadt-gengenbach .de; Im Winzerhof; ☻ 9am-12.30pm & 1.30-5pm Mon-Fri Sep-Jun, no midday closure Jul & Aug, also open 10am-noon Sat May-Oct), in the courtyard across from Hauptstrasse 21, rents out bicycles. Three-speed bikes cost €5.50 and mountain bikes are €9.50 per day.

SIGHTS & ACTIVITIES

The best way to explore Gengenbach is to wander its narrow lanes. Head down to the **Stadtkirche**, with its slender baroque tower, or to the 18th-century **Rathaus**, an imposing pink-and-cream confection between the town's two tower-topped gates. Just off Hauptstrasse, **Engelgasse** is pure fairy-tale stuff with its uneven cobblestones, colourful flower boxes and immaculate collection of half-timbered houses.

Dominating the triangular **Marktplatz** is a fountain with a statue of a knight, a symbol of the village's medieval status as a Free Imperial City. The **Narrenmuseum** (☎ 5749; Niggelturm, Hauptstrasse; admission €2; ☻ 2-5pm Wed & Sat, 10am-noon & 2-5pm Sun Apr-Oct) exhibits costumes and masks worn during **Fasend** (held seven weeks before Easter). Climb to the seventh floor for sweeping vistas over the Kinzig Valley.

The **Weinlehrpfad** trail leads from the Altstadt to terraced vineyards with views as far as Strasbourg when the weather is fine. The gentle walk takes around an hour to complete; maps and information are available at the tourist office. The free, lantern-lit **Nachtwächterrundgang** (night watchman tour) starts at the Rathaus on Wednesdays and Saturdays at 10pm from May to July, and 9pm from August to October.

FESTIVALS & EVENTS

At Christmas time, the Rathaus morphs into one of world's biggest **advent calendars**

GREAT BLACK FOREST ESCAPES   *Kerry Walker*

▪ **Unterroturachhof** (☎ 07657-754; www.schwarzwaldruhe.de; Urach; apt €28; P) The smiley Bärmann family run this creaking 17th-century farmhouse set in a serene valley. Its name is sure to get your tongue in a twist, so get practising as it's not unusual to have to ask for directions. A narrow, bumpy lane leads up from Urach (look for signs at Zur Sägemühle bakery) to this gorgeous Black Forest hideaway. If you're seeking an authentic on-the-farm experience, the modestly priced apartments here are ideal. In summer, you can even fish your own trout from the pond and grill it on a barbecue under the stars.

▪ **Weinhaus St Remigius** (☎ 07664-593 89; www.weinhaus-remigius.de; Gündlingerstrasse 7; Breisach-Niederrimsingen; apt €45-65; P) Explore the Black Forest wine country by staying overnight at this traditional *Winzerhaus* (wine grower's house), 10km south of Breisach. As well as offering access to hiking and cycling trails through Kaiserstuhl, the family-run winery shelters a tasting room for quaffing home-grown wines and schnapps. The bright, modern apartment easily accommodates families. There's enough space to park your bikes or enjoy a barbecue in the courtyard.

▪ **Kirchlebauernhof** (☎ 07602-247; www.kirchlehof.de; Hofsgrund; apt €30-45; P) With dreamy views to Feldberg on one side and Schauinsland on the other, this beautiful farmhouse overlooks the chapel in Hofsgrund, 15 minutes' drive from Freiberg. Kids love the resident cows and the Lorenz family's two Bernese mountain dogs. Light streams into the rustic pinewood apartments featuring fully equipped kitchens and balconies. Perched at 1060m, the farm is a great base for walking in summer and cross-country skiing at Schauinsland in winter.

Got some tips about the Black Forest that you'd love to share with Lonely Planet readers? Create your own Bluelist and upload it onto our website – www.lonelyplanet.com.

(blu.list) *v.* to recommend a travel experience. www.lonelyplanet.com/bluelist

BLUELIST.

(Marktplatz; ☺ calendar doors open 6pm 30 Nov-23 Dec). Its 24 windows open one 'door' at a time to reveal festive scenes painted by acclaimed artists such as French illustrator Tomi Ungerer. The fantastical calendar can be admired until Epiphany (6th January) and is complemented by a Christmas market from 13th to 23rd December.

SLEEPING & EATING

The Marktplatz and Hauptstrasse are lined with cafés and *Weinstuben* where you can drink in the Altstadt atmosphere.

Schloss Ortenberg (☎ 0781-317 49; www.jugendher berge-schloss-ortenberg.de; Burgweg 21; dm €19.70-22.70; P 🖳) If you've ever dreamed of spending a night at Hogwarts, this wistful 12th-century castle won't disappoint. The dining hall gleams with polished wood and a staircase sweeps up to dorms with wonderful Kinzig Valley views. Schimmelturm offers a 360° panorama of vineyards, the Rhine Valley and not-so-distant Strasbourg Cathedral. Bus 7134 runs to Ortenberger Hof, 500m from the hostel.

Winzer & Obsthof Roser (☎ 3723; www.winzerhof -roser.de; Einachstrasse 15; d €42-56, apt €38-55; P) This family-run vineyard is a quiet retreat 10 minutes' walk from the Altstadt. Light floods the country-style rooms and apartments with chunky pine and sunny paint jobs. Sample home-grown wine and schnapps on the patio.

Winzerstüble (☎ 3636; Hauptstrasse 18; Flammkuchen €6.50-9; ☺ from 10am) In the cobbled courtyard next to the tourist office, this wine tavern serves local produce and wine. Visitors can sample light, crisp *Flammkuchen* with Müller-Thurgau and Riesling wines. The wine tasting at 6.30pm every Friday costs €9.50.

Directory

CONTENTS

ACCOMMODATION

Bavaria and the Black Forest offer all types of places to unpack your suitcase, from hostels, campgrounds and family hotels to chains, business hotels and luxury resorts. Reservations are a good idea between June and September, around major holidays (p316) and festivals (p20) and, in business-oriented cities, during trade shows.

This book lists accommodation as budget, midrange and top end; prices are for doubles with private bathrooms, breakfast and VAT. Places we consider extra-special have been identified with ourpick .

Some regional variations notwithstanding, budget stays will have you checking in at hostels, *Pensionen* or simple family hotels charging €80 or less. Midrange accommodation generally offers the best value for money.

PRACTICALITIES

- The Monday edition of *Süddeutsche Zeitung* has a *New York Times* supplement, but the *International Herald Tribune* is also available, especially in cities.

- *Der Spiegel* and *Focus* magazines are popular German newsweeklies, which, along with the *Economist, Time* and *Newsweek,* are sold at train stations and major newsstands.

- Radio stations are regional with most featuring a mix of news, talk and music.

- Electrical supply is 220V AC, 50 Hz.

- Germany uses the metric system (see the conversion chart on the inside front cover).

- For women's clothing sizes, a German size 36 equals size 6 in the US and size 10 in the UK, then it increases in increments of two, making size 38 a US 8 and UK 12.

Expect to pay between €80 and €150 for a clean, comfortable, decent-sized double with at least a modicum of style, a private bathroom, cable TV and direct-dial telephone. Communal saunas and basic fitness facilities are quite common as well.

Top-end places start at €150 and offer deluxe amenities, perhaps a scenic location, special décor or historical ambience. Many also have pools, saunas, business centres or other upmarket facilities.

Properties with designated nonsmoking rooms are on the rise and identified with ⊠ in this book. By contrast, rooms with air-con are rare; properties that do have at least some air-con are denoted with ❄ .

Many tourist office and hotel websites let you check for room availability and make reservations. Staff can also help you in person or, if you arrive after office hours, post vacancies in the window or a display case. You'll also see electronic reservation boards that connect you directly to local properties for free, but these don't work reliably.

Online booking services include www .venere.com and www.hotel.de. For last-minute bargains, check www.hrs.com.

Camping

Campsites are generally well maintained but may get jammed in summer. The core season runs from May to September with only a few remaining open year-round. There are usually separate charges per person (between €3 and €6), tent (€2.50 to €8) and car (€2 to €4), and additional fees for hot showers, resort tax, electricity and sewage disposal. A Camping Card International (p315) may yield some savings.

The *ADAC Camping & Caravanning Führer,* available in bookshops, is a comprehensive camping guide, in German. Other handy sources include www.alanrogers.com and www.eurocampings.de.

Farm Stays

A holiday on a working farm is a big hit with kids who love interacting with their favourite barnyard animals and helping with everyday chores. Accommodation ranges from bare-bones rooms with shared facilities to fully furnished holiday flats. Minimum stays of three days are common. For details, check www.landtourismus.de or www.bauernhofur laub.com (in German).

Hostels

Bavaria has a growing crop of indie hostels, but thus far the only outpost in the Black Forest is in Freiburg. Geared toward backpackers, these hostels attract a convivial, international crowd to mixed dorms and private rooms. No two hostels are alike but typical facilities include communal kitchens, lockers, internet access, laundry and a common room for chilling. Many have private rooms for couples or solo travellers. For details, see the destination chapters or go to www.backpackernetwork .de. Online booking systems include www .gomio.com, www.hostelworld.com, www .hostels.com and www.hostels.net.

Hostelling International–affiliated hostels are run by the **Deutsches Jugendherbergswerk** (DJH; www.jugendherberge.de, in German) and cater primarily to German school groups and families. Most have recently been modernised but can't quite shake that institutional feel. Rates in gender-segregated dorms or in family rooms range from €13 to €25 per person, including linen and breakfast. People over 27 are charged an extra €3 or €4. In Bavaria, if space is tight, priority is given to people under 27, except for those travelling as a family.

Unless you're a member of your home country's HI association, you either need to buy a Hostelling International Card for €15.50 (valid for one year) or six individual stamps costing €3.10 per night. Both are available at any DJH hostel.

For DJH reservations, contact the hostel directly by phone, fax or email; only a few are set up for online bookings.

Hotels

Hotels range from small family-run establishments to comfortable mid-sized properties to luxurious international chains. Those serving only breakfast are called Hotel Garni. This being Germany, you can generally expect even budget abodes to be spotlessly clean, comfortable and well run.

In most older, privately run hotels rooms may vary dramatically in terms of size, décor and amenities. The cheapest share bathroom facilities, while others may come with a shower cubicle installed but no private toilet; only pricier ones have ensuite bathrooms. If possible, ask to see several rooms before committing.

Pensions, Inns & Private Rooms

Pensionen (guesthouses) and *Gasthöfe* or *Gasthäuser* (inns) are smaller, less formal and cheaper than hotels; the latter two usually have a restaurant. Expect clean rooms but only minimal amenities – maybe a radio, sometimes a small TV, almost never a phone. Facilities may be shared. What rooms lack in amenities, though, they often make up for in charm and authenticity.

Privatzimmer (essentially guest rooms in private homes) are ubiquitous and great for catching a glimpse into how locals live, although privacy seekers may find these places a

---

THE 'CURSE' OF THE KUR

Nearly every resort in Bavaria or the Black Forest levies a *Kurtaxe* (resort tax) on its overnight visitors. This is a fee ranging from €0.50 to €3.50 per person per night, which is added to your hotel bill. The money is used to subsidise visitor-oriented events such as concerts and lectures, and sometimes free public transport as well.

> **BOOK YOUR STAY ONLINE**
>
> For more accommodation reviews and rec-
> ommendations by Lonely Planet authors,
> check out the online booking service at
> www.lonelyplanet.com/hotels. You'll find
> the true, insider lowdown on the best places
> to stay. Reviews are thorough and independ-
> ent. Best of all, you can book online.

bit too intimate. Tourist offices list rooms available, or look around for *Zimmer Frei* (rooms
available) signs in house or shop windows. Per
person prices range from €13 to €35.

Rental Accommodation
Renting a *Ferienwohnung* (furnished flat)
for a week or longer is a sensible option for
self-caterers, families and small groups. Stays
under a week usually incur a surcharge, and
there's almost always a 'cleaning fee' payable
at the end.

ACTIVITIES
No matter what kind of activity gets you
off that couch, you'll be able to pursue it in
Bavaria and the Black Forest, a region of lakes
and rivers, mountains and forests. Wherever
you go, you'll find outfitters and local operators eager to gear you up. Flip the page to
the Black Forest & Bavaria Outdoors chapter
(p56) for an overview of active pursuits that
beckon, and to the Walking in the Bavarian
Alps chapter (p61) for hiking tips.

BUSINESS HOURS
Shops are permitted to be open until 8pm
Monday to Saturday but – except for a few in
the big city centres – most lock up at 6pm or
6.30pm (1pm or 2pm on Saturday). Stock up
on basic supplies (albeit at inflated prices) at
train stations and petrol stations after hours
and on Sunday. Many bakeries open for a few
hours on Sundays.

Banks do business from 8.30am to 4pm
Monday to Friday (sometimes 6pm Thursday).
Outside city centres, shops and businesses
usually observe a two- to three-hour lunch
break. And speaking of lunch, it's generally
served between 11.30am and 2pm, while
dinner feedings are from 5.30pm to 9.30pm.
Many restaurants observe a *Ruhetag* (day of
rest), usually Monday or Tuesday. Major variations to the above are listed in reviews.

Pubs and bars pour drinks from around
6pm, unless they serve food in which case
they're also open during the day. Big-city clubs
don't really get going before 11pm or midnight and often keep buzzing until sunrise.

Museums usually take Monday off but stay
open late one evening a week.

Always call ahead to confirm the hours if
you've got your eye on a particular place.

CHILDREN
Practicalities
Bavaria is a very family-friendly destination
and most places are happy to cater for kids,
whether with smaller dinner portions, a highchair, special attention on a tour, making up a
special bed or giving them a little extra attention. That said, amenities and services specifically geared to children are rare.

Overall, children enjoy lots of discounts
for everything from museum admissions to
bus fares and tour tickets, although the cut-
off age can be anything from six to 18. Many
hotels and hostels have rooms with three or
four beds or large doubles with a sofa bed or
sofa chair. Some properties, especially those in
the countryside, don't charge extra for small
children staying in their parents' room if they
don't require extra bedding. In vehicles, children's safety seats are compulsory and available for rent from car-hire companies.

Breast-feeding in public is practised, especially in the cities, although most women are
discreet about it. If you need a babysitter, ask
staff at your hotel for a referral. For more tips
and tricks, consult Lonely Planet's *Travel with
Children* or have a look at www.travelwith
yourkids.com or www.flyingwithkids.com.
Also see Eating with Kids (p47).

Sights & Activities
It's easy to keep kids entertained no matter
where you travel in Bavaria. The great outdoors, of course, yield endless possibilities.
A day spent swimming, bicycling, walking or
otherwise engaging in physical activity is sure
to send the little ones quickly off to dream-
land. Farm holidays (p313) are an excellent
way for city kids to get a full nature immersion. Bavaria's legend-shrouded castles, including the medieval Schloss Harburg (p271)
and the fantastic Schloss Neuschwanstein
(p283), are sure to fuel the imagination of
many a Harry Potter fan. Older kids get a kick
out of Hollywood magic made in Germany

at the Bavaria Filmstadt theme park (p104) in Munich.

Even in the cities possibilities for keeping kids entertained abound. Take them to parks, playgrounds, public pools, zoos or such kid-friendly museums as the Deutsches Museum (p101) in Munich or the Spielzeugmuseum (Toy Museum; p221) in Nuremberg. For more Munich-specific ideas, see p107; for Augsburg see p278.

CLIMATE CHARTS

For general advice on climate and when to travel in Bavaria and the Black Forest, see p16. The climate charts below provide a snapshot of local weather patterns.

CUSTOMS

Most articles that you take to Germany for your personal use may be imported free of duty and tax. The following allowances

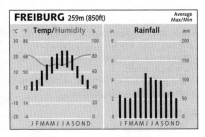

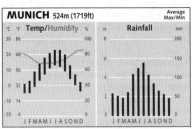

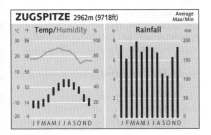

apply to duty-free goods purchased in a non-European Union country. In addition, you can bring in other products up to a value of €175.

Alcohol 1L of strong liquor or 2L of less than 22% alcohol by volume and 2L of wine (if over age 17)

Coffee and tea 500g of coffee or 200g of coffee extracts and 100g of tea or 40g of tea extracts (if over age 15)

Perfume 50g of perfume or scent and 0.25L of eau de toilette

Tobacco 200 cigarettes or 100 cigarillos or 50 cigars or 250g of loose tobacco (if over age 17)

DANGERS & ANNOYANCES

Bavaria has a very low crime rate and is a remarkably safe place to live and travel in. Of course you should still take all the usual precautions, such as locking hotel rooms and cars, not leaving valuables unattended, as well as keeping an eye out for pickpockets in crowds and not taking midnight strolls in city parks.

In Munich and the Bavarian Alps, the *Föhn* (a warm, dry wind) is a local weather-related annoyance most common in autumn. It seems to give some people headaches or make them cranky but also brings exquisitely clear views of the mountains.

DISCOUNT CARDS

If you're a full-time student, the **International Student Identity Card** (ISIC; www.isic.org) is your ticket to savings on air fares, travel insurance and many local attractions. For nonstudents under 26, the International Youth Travel Card (IYTC) or the **Euro<26 Youth Card** (www.euro26 .org) grant similar savings and benefits. All are issued by student unions, hostelling organisations and youth-oriented travel agencies.

Discounts are also widely available for seniors, children, families and the disabled, although no special cards are needed. In some cases you may be asked to show ID to prove your age.

Some cities offer Welcome Cards entitling visitors to discounts on museums, sights and tours, plus unlimited trips on local public transport. They can be good value if you plan on taking advantage of most of the benefits and don't qualify for any of the standard discounts.

Frequent campers can save up to 25% in camping fees with the **Camping Card International** (www.campingcardinternational.com). It's available from your local camping or motoring associations and also includes third-party liability insurance while on campgrounds.

DIRECTORY

'NO SMOKING' COMES TO GERMANY

Germans love their cars, their beer and their cigarettes. About one in four help keep the tobacco industry in business and even higher prices and new antismoking legislation are unlikely to change that. On 1 January 2008, the toughest nonsmoking laws within Germany went into effect in Bavaria. Smoking is a complete no-no in all schools, hospitals, airports and other public facilities, as well as in cafés, restaurants, bars, clubs and even beer tents (yes, a smokefree Oktoberfest).

The adjacent state of Baden-Württemberg, which encompasses the Black Forest, is a bit more relaxed. Since August 2007, smoking in public buildings is generally *Verboten* (forbidden), but facilities may provide separate, enclosed rooms for lighting up. The same is true of bars and restaurants. Lighting up in clubs is *Verboten,* but beer gardens, street cafés and beer festivals are still OK.

EMBASSIES & CONSULATES

Most foreign embassies are in Berlin but many countries, including the following, have consular offices in Munich. Where they don't, we've listed the nearest office. For other foreign missions in Germany as well as German missions around the world, see www.auswaertiges-amt.de.

Australia (☎ 069-905 580; fax 9055 8119; Grüneburgweg 58-62, Frankfurt-am-Main)

Canada (Map pp82-3; ☎ 089-219 9570; munic@international.gc.ca; Tal 29, Munich)

China (Map p80; ☎ 089-1730 1611, fax 089-1730 1619; Romanstrasse 107, Munich)

France (Map pp82-3; ☎ 089-419 4110, fax 4194 1141; Heimeranstrasse 10, Munich)

Ireland (off Map p85; ☎ 089-2080 5990, fax 2080 5989; Denninger Strasse 15, Munich)

Italy (Map pp82-3; ☎ 089-4180 0303 144; italconsul.monaco@t-online.de; Möhlstrasse 3, Munich)

Japan (Map p85; ☎ 089-417 6040; info-pr@japangk-munich.de; Karl-Scharnagl-Ring 7, Munich)

Netherlands (Map p81; ☎ 089-206 026 710; www.niederlandeweb.de; Nymphenburger Str 20a, Munich)

New Zealand (☎ 030-206 210; nzembassy.berlin@t-online.de; Friedrichstrasse 60, Berlin)

UK (Map p85; ☎ 089-211 090, fax 2110 9144; Bürkleinstrasse 10, Munich) Also for Australian nationals during Oktoberfest.

USA (Map p81; ☎ 089-288 80, fax 283 047; Königinstrasse 5, Munich)

FOOD

Eating recommendations in this guide match all tastes and travel budgets. Budget eateries include takeaways, delis, cafés, snack bars, markets and basic restaurants where main courses cost less than €10. At midrange establishments you usually get tablecloths, full menus, beer and wine lists, and mains ranging from €10 to €20. Top-end places tend to be full gourmet affairs, with expert service and mains from €20. Places with a good selection for vegetarians are denoted Ⓥ. For more on cuisine and eating customs, see p44.

GAY & LESBIAN TRAVELLERS

Homosexuality is legal in Bavaria and the Black Forest, but the scene, even in Munich, is tiny compared to, say, Berlin or Cologne. Nuremberg, Regensburg and Freiburg are a little more relaxed as well, but in rural areas gays and lesbians tend to keep a low profile. There are websites aplenty but most are in German only. Try www.gayscape.com, www.justbegay.de, www.gay-web.de or, for women, www.lesarion.de.

See p124 for an overview of the Munich scene and p201 for Regensburg.

HOLIDAYS

Germans are huge fans of minivacations built around public holiday periods and Bavaria and the Black Forest are favourite getaway destinations, so expect heavy crowds on the roads and everywhere you go. Businesses and offices are closed on these public holidays.

Neujahrstag (New Year's Day) 1 January

Heilige Drei Könige (Epiphany) 6 January

Ostern (Easter) March/April – Good Friday, Easter Sunday and Easter Monday

Maifeiertag (Labour Day) 1 May

Christi Himmelfahrt (Ascension Day) 40 days after Easter

Pfingsten (Whitsun/Pentecost) mid-May to mid-June – Whit Sunday and Whit Monday

Fronleichnam (Corpus Christi) 10 days after Pentecost

Mariä Himmelfahrt (Assumption Day, Bavaria only) 15 August

Tag der Deutschen Einheit (Day of German Unity) 3 October

Allerheiligen (All Saints Day) 1 November

Weihnachtstag (Christmas Day) 25 December

Weihnachtstag (Boxing/St Stephen's Day) 26 December

INSURANCE

No matter how long or short your trip, make sure you have adequate travel insurance covering you for medical expenses, luggage theft or loss, and against cancellations or delays of your travel arrangements. Check your existing insurance policies at home (medical, renters, homeowners etc), since some policiesmay already provide worldwide coverage. Details about medical insurance are on p329. For information about what kind of coverage you need while driving in southern Germany, see p326.

Worldwide travel insurance is available at www.lonelyplanet.com/travel_services. You can buy, extend and claim online anytime – even if you're already on the road.

INTERNET ACCESS

Internet cafés are listed throughout the destination chapters, but most have about the lifespan of a fruit fly, so please forgive us if our listings are outdated and ask staff at your hotel for a recommendation. Public libraries offer free terminals and sometimes wi-fi access, but downsides may include time limits, reservation requirements and queues. Internet access is also available at slightly seedy telephone call shops, which cluster near train stations.

In hotels and hostels, high-speed access and wi-fi (W-LAN in German) are common; only in older properties will they resort to dial-up. Lodging properties offering internet terminals for their guests are identified with 🖳 . The availability of wi-fi is also indicated with each review. There may be a fee for either service.

Some cafés and pubs offer wi-fi access, sometimes at no charge with purchase. Check the directories at www.jiwire.com or www.hotspot-locations.com and see www.kropla.com. Useful trip-planning websites are listed on p19.

THE LEGAL AGE FOR...

- Drinking beer or wine: 14
- Being served beer or wine in a pub: 16
- Buying cigarettes: 18
- Driving a car: 18
- Sexual consent: 14 (with restrictions)*
- Voting in an election: 18

* Travellers may be subject to the laws of their own country in regard to sexual relations.

LEGAL MATTERS

By law, you must carry photo identification such as your passport, national identity card or driving licence. The permissible blood-alcohol limit is 0.05%; drivers caught exceeding this amount are subject to stiff fines, a confiscated licence and even jail time. For general road rules, see p327.

If you are arrested, you have the right to make a phone call and are presumed innocent until proven guilty. If you don't know a lawyer, contact your nearest consulate (opposite) for a referral.

MAPS

Most tourist offices distribute free (but often very basic) city maps, but for driving around Bavaria and the Black Forest you'll need a detailed road map or atlas such as those published by Falkplan, Freytag & Berndt, RV Verlag or ADAC. Look for them at bookshops, tourist offices, newsagents and petrol stations. Find downloadable maps and driving directions at www.viamichelin.de, www.maps .google.de and www.stadtplandienst.de.

MONEY

Euros come in seven notes (five, 10, 20, 50, 100, 200 and 500 euros) and eight coins (one and two euro coins, and one, two, five, 10, 20 and 50 cent coins). At the time of writing, the euro was at an all-time high against the US dollar, although minor fluctuations are common. See the exchange-rate table on the inside front cover for some guidelines.

Exchange money at airports, some banks and currency exchange offices, such as Reisebank, American Express and TravelEx. In rural areas, such facilities are rare, so make sure you have plenty of cash. For an overview of what things cost, see p19.

ATMs

ATMs linked to international networks such as Cirrus, Plus, Star and Maestro are ubiquitous, accessible 24/7 and the easiest and quickest way to obtain cash. Check with your bank or credit-card company about fees.

Credit Cards

Germany is a cash-based society and it's best not to assume that you'll be able to use credit cards – inquire first. Even so, a piece of plastic can be vital in emergencies and occasionally also useful for phone or internet bookings.

DIRECTORY

Avoid getting cash on your credit card via ATMs since fees are steep and you'll be charged interest immediately (in other words, there's no grace period as with purchases). Report lost or stolen cards to the following:

American Express (☎ 01805-840 840)
MasterCard (☎ 0800-819 1040)
Visa (☎ 0800-811 8440)

Tipping
Restaurant bills always include a *Bedienung* (service charge) but unless service was abhorrent most people add about 5% or 10%. At hotels, porters get about €1 per bag and it's also nice to leave some cash for the room cleaners. Tip bartenders about 5% per drink and taxi drivers around 10%.

Travellers Cheques
Travellers cheques are becoming increasingly obsolete in the age of network-linked ATMs. It doesn't help that German businesses generally don't accept them, even if denominated in euros, and banks charge exorbitant fees for cashing them (currency exchange offices are usually better). American Express offices cash Amex cheques free of charge.

POST
Main post offices, which are often near train stations, are usually open from 8am to 6pm Monday to Friday and till 2pm on Saturday. Expect suburban and rural branches to be closed at lunchtime and after 5pm or 5.30pm weekdays and noon on Saturday.

Mailing standard-sized postcards within Germany and the EU costs €0.65; a 20g letter is €0.70 and a 50g letter €1. Postcards to North America and Australasia cost €1, a 20g airmail letter costs €1.70 and a 50g airmail letter costs €2. A surcharge applies to oversized envelopes. For full details see www.deutsche-post.de.

Letters sent within Germany take one to two days for delivery; those addressed to destinations within Europe or to North America take four to six days and those to Australasia five to seven days.

SHOPPING
Bavaria is a fun place to shop with a big selection of everyday and unique items. Regional products include traditional Bavarian dirndls, lederhosen and Loden jackets. Beer mugs are the classic souvenir, no matter whether made of glass or stoneware, plain or deco-rated, with or without pewter lid. The choices are endless.

Good-quality woodcarvings are widely available in the Alpine regions (Oberammergau's are especially famous). Fans of the fragile can pick up exquisite china made by the Nymphenburger Porzellan Manufaktur or beautiful vases, bowls or ornaments handmade by glass artisans in the Bavarian Forest.

Famous toy brands include stuffed animals by Steiff and collectable Käthe Kruse dolls. At Christmas markets you can stock up on tree ornaments, nutcrackers and other decorations. The main wine regions are near Würzburg in Franconia and around Freiburg in the Baden area.

The Black Forest is the birthplace of German clock making and not only of the cuckoo variety. Precision instruments such as microscopes and binoculars are also a speciality. Cutlery is first-rate, with Wüsthof and JA Henckels being leading brands.

Bargaining almost never occurs, except at flea markets.

SOLO TRAVELLERS
Southern Germans are generally friendly but can be rather reserved and aren't likely to initiate a conversation with strangers. This shouldn't stop you from approaching them, though, since most will quite happily respond and even be extra helpful once they find out you're a traveller. Young people especially speak at least some English and many are keen to practise it.

For more on the subject, check out the website of the nonprofit **Connecting: Solo Travel Network** (www.cstn.org).

TELEPHONE & FAX
Fax
Faxes can be sent from and received at most hotels, photocopy shops and internet cafés.

Mobile Phones
Mobile phones operate on GSM 900/1800. If your home country uses a different standard, you'll need a multiband GSM phone in Germany. If you have an unlocked multiband phone, a prepaid rechargeable SIM card from a German telecom provider might work out cheaper than using your own network. Cards are available at any telecommunications store (eg T-Online, Vodafone, E-Plus or O2) and give you a local number with-

out signing a contract. These places also sell prepaid GSM900/1800 phones, including some airtime, starting at €30. Recharge airtime by buying scratch-off cards sold at newsagents, supermarkets, petrol stations and general stores.

Calls made to a mobile phone are more expensive than those to a landline, but incoming calls are free.

Phone Codes

German phone numbers consist of an area code, which starts with 0, and the local number. Area codes can be up to six numbers and local numbers up to nine digits long. If dialling from a landline within the same city, you don't need to dial the area code. If using a mobile, you must dial it.

If calling Germany from abroad, first dial your country's international access code, then 49 (Germany's country code), the area code (dropping the initial 0) and the local number. Germany's international access code is ☎ 00.

Deutsche Telekom directory assistance (☎ 118 37 for an English-speaking operator) charges a ridiculous €1.39 per minute for numbers within Germany and €1.99 for numbers outside Germany (☎ 118 34). Get the same information for free at www.telefonbuch.de. A much cheaper provider is the fully automated **Telix** (☎ 118 10), which charges €0.39 per minute.

Numbers starting with ☎ 0800 are tollfree but numbers starting with 0190 or 900 are charged at exorbitant rates. Direct-dialled calls made from hotel rooms are also usually charged at a premium.

If you have access to a private phone, you can benefit from cheaper rates by using a call-by-call access code (eg ☎ 01016 or 010090). Rates are published in the daily newspapers or online at www.billigertelefonieren.de.

Telephone call shops may also offer competitive calling rates but often charge steep connection fees. Always make sure you understand the charges involved.

With a high-speed internet connection, you can talk for free via **Skype** (www.skype.com), or use their SkypeOut service, which allows you to call landlines from your computer.

Phonecards

Most public payphones only work with Deutsche Telecom (DT) phonecards, available in denominations of €5, €10 and €20 from DT stores, post offices, newsagents and tourist offices.

For long-distance and international calls, prepaid calling cards issued by other providers tend to offer better rates. Look for them at newsagents and telephone call shops. There may be a connection fee. Most cards work with payphones with a surcharge.

TIME

Clocks in Germany are set to central European time (GMT/UTC plus one hour). Daylight-saving time kicks in at 2am on the last Sunday in March and ends on the last Sunday in October. The use of the 24-hour clock (eg where 6.30pm is 18.30) is common. See the World Time Zones map on p358 for an overview.

TOURIST INFORMATION

Tourist offices are listed throughout this book under Information. Good websites for your pretrip research are www.bayern.by and www.germany-tourism.de.

Each region also operates its own tourist office:

Black Forest Tourism Office (☎ 0761-896 460; www.schwarzwald-tourismus.info; mail@schwarzwald-tourismus.info)
Eastern Bavarian Tourism Association (☎ 0941-585 390; www.ostbayern-tourismus.de, in German; info@ostbayern-tourismus.de)
Franconian Tourism Association (☎ 0911-941 510; www.frankentourismus.org, in German; info@frankentourismus.de)
Tourism Association Allgäu-Bavarian Swabia (☎ 01805-127 000; www.bavarian-alps.info or www.allgaeu.de; info@allgaeu.de)
Upper Bavarian Tourism Association (☎ 089-829 2180; www.oberbayern-tourismus.de; touristinfo@oberbayern.de)

TOURS

For information on touring the Romantic Road, see p253.

Bicycle & Walking Tours

Active types might want to consider a self-guided tour, where rates typically include bicycle rental, lodging and luggage transfer between hotels. The Romantic Road and King Ludwig's castles are popular destinations.
Bents Tour (in the UK ☎ 01568 780 800; www.bentstours.com)
Euro Bike & Walking (in the US ☎ 800-321-6060; www.eurobike.com)

DIRECTORY

Sherpa Expeditions (in the UK ☎ 020-8577 2717; www.sherpa-walking-holidays.co.uk)

River Cruises

Cruising the Danube, the Rhine and the Rhine–Main–Danube Canal aboard a 'floating hotel' is a relaxing way of touring around southern Germany. The following US-based companies offer all-inclusive tours with English-speaking guides:

Amadeus Waterways (☎ 800-626-0126; www.amadeuswaterways.com)

Uniworld (☎ 800-733-7820; www.uniworld.com)

Viking (☎ 800-304-9616; www.vikingrivercruises.us)

Skiing Holidays

A number of operators offer package tours to Garmisch-Partenkirchen, which has the largest skiing area in Germany and the most reliable snow conditions.

Adventure on Skis (in the US ☎ 800-628-9655, 413-568-2855; www.advonskis.com)

Ski.com (in the US ☎ 800-778-8589; www.ski.com)

TRAVELLERS WITH DISABILITIES

Overall, southern Germany caters well for the needs of the *Behinderte* (disabled), especially the wheelchair-bound. You'll find access ramps and/or lifts in many public buildings, including train stations, museums, theatres and cinemas. In historic towns, though, cobble-stoned streets make getting around quite cumbersome. Newer hotels have lifts and rooms with extra-wide doors and spacious bathrooms. Nearly all trains are accessible, and local buses and U-Bahns are becoming increasingly so as well. Seeing-eye dogs are allowed on all forms of public transport.

Many local and regional tourism offices have special brochures for people with disabilities, although usually in German. Good general resources include the following.

Deutsche Bahn Mobility Service Center (☎ 01805-512 512, per min €0.12; www.bahn.de; ☒ 8am-8pm Mon-Fri, 8am-2pm Sat) Live train-access information and help with route planning. The website has useful information in English.

German National Tourism Office (www.germany-tourism.de) Has an entire section (under Travel Tips) about barrier-free travel in Germany.

Munich for Physically Challenged Tourists (www.munich.de, then type 'disabled' in the search box) Excellent and comprehensive brochure put together by the Munich tourist office and downloadable for free. Also publishes a separate PDF file assessing 21 Munich hotels in terms of needs of the disabled.

Natko (☎ 06131-250 410; www.natko.de, in German) Central clearing house for inquiries about travelling in Germany as a disabled person.

VISAS

Most EU nationals only need their national identity card or passport to enter, stay and work in Germany. Citizens of Australia, Canada, Israel, Japan, New Zealand, Poland, Switzerland and the US are among those countries that need only a valid passport (no visa) if entering as tourists for up to three months within a six-month period. Passports should be valid for at least another four months from the planned date of departure from Germany.

Nationals from other countries need a so-called Schengen Visa, named after the 1995 Schengen Agreement that abolished passport controls between Austria, Belgium, Denmark, Finland, France, Germany, Iceland, Italy, Greece, Luxembourg, Netherlands, Norway, Portugal, Spain and Sweden. The Agreement was expanded on 21 December 2007 to include the Czech Republic, Estonia, Hungary, Latvia, Lithuania, Malta, Poland, Slovakia and Slovenia. Switzerland is expected to join in late 2008. For full details, see www.auswaertiges-amt.de or check with a German consulate in your country.

WOMEN TRAVELLERS

Bavaria and the Black Forest are safe to travel in, even for solo women. It's quite normal to split dinner bills, even on dates, or for a woman to start talking to a man. Going alone to cafés and restaurants is perfectly acceptable, even at night. In bars and nightclubs, solo women are likely to attract some attention, but if you don't want company, most men will respect a firm 'no thank you'. If you feel threatened, protesting loudly will often make the offender slink away with embarrassment or spur others to come to your defence.

Good online resources include **Journeywoman** (www.journeywoman.com) and **Her Own Way** (www.voyage.gc.ca, follow the Publications link). The latter is published by the Canadian government, but contains lots of good general advice.

If assaulted call the **police** (☎ 110) or contact a women's centre first. Note that hotlines are not staffed around the clock.

Aschaffenburg ☎ 06021-247 28

Freiburg ☎ 0761-285 8585

Munich ☎ 089-763 737

Nuremberg ☎ 0911-284 400

Regensburg ☎ 0941-241 71

Transport

CONTENTS

GETTING THERE & AWAY

Flights, tours and rail tickets can all be booked online at www.lonelyplanet.com /travel_services.

ENTERING THE COUNTRY

Entering Germany is usually a straightforward procedure. Citizens of most Western countries don't need a visa, but other nationals may need to obtain what is called a Schengen Visa. If arriving in Germany from any of the 24 Schengen countries, such as Austria or Italy, you no longer have to go through passport and customs checks, no matter your nationality. For a list of Schengen countries and an overview of passport and visa requirements, see opposite.

AIR
Airports

Southern Germany is served by numerous airports. The main hub, of course, is **Flughafen München** (Munich International Airport; MUC; ☎ 089-975 00; www.munich-airport.de), although most transcontinental flights actually land at **Frankfurt Airport** (FRA; ☎ 01805-372 4636; www.frankfurt-airport.de), which is closer to northern Bavaria, including the Romantic Road.

Budget airlines generally fly to smaller airports. The most convenient for the north-

---

THINGS CHANGE...

The information in this chapter is particularly vulnerable to change. Check directly with the airline or a travel agent to make sure you understand how a fare (and ticket you may buy) works and be aware of the security requirements for international travel. Shop carefully. The details given in this chapter should be regarded as pointers and are not a substitute for your own careful, up-to-date research.

---

ern Black Forest is **Karlsruhe-Baden-Baden** (FKB; ☎ 07229-662 000; www.badenairpark.de), while Freiburg and the southern Black Forest are closer to the **EuroAirport Basel-Mulhouse-Freiburg** (BSL; ☎ +41-61-325 3111 in Switzerland; www.euroairport.com). Another option is **Friedrichshafen** (FDH; ☎ 07541-284 01; www.fly-away.de), positioned on Lake Constance between Bavaria and the Black Forest. The main airport in Franconia is **Nuremberg** (NUE; ☎ 0911-937 00; www.airport-nuernberg.de). Despite the name, **Frankfurt-Hahn** (HHN; ☎ 06543-509 200; www.hahn-airport.de) is nowhere near Frankfurt proper but about 110km northwest of the city on the Moselle River – not too convenient for southern Germany! For Eastern Bavaria or the Bavarian Alps, **Salzburg Airport** (SZG; ☎ +43-662-8580-251; www.salzburg-airport.com) is also convenient.

For details about individual airports, including 'getting to and from' information, see the destination chapters.

Airlines

The main airline serving Germany, **Lufthansa** (LH; ☎ 01803-803 803; www.lufthansa.de), operates a huge network of domestic and international flights and has one of the world's best safety records. Other major national carriers and budget airlines are listed below along with their telephone numbers in Germany for reservations, flight changes etc. For contact details in your home country, see the airline's website.

Air Berlin (AB; ☎ 01805-737 800; www.airberlin.com)
Air Canada (AC; ☎ 01805-0247 226; www.aircanada.ca)
Air France (AF; ☎ 01805-830 830; www.airfrance.com)
Air New Zealand (NZ; ☎ 0800-5494 5494; www.airnz.co.nz)

CLIMATE CHANGE & TRAVEL

Climate change is a serious threat to the ecosystems that humans rely upon, and air travel is the fastest-growing contributor to the problem. Lonely Planet regards travel, overall, as a global benefit, but believes we all have a responsibility to limit our personal impact on global warming.

Flying & Climate Change

Pretty much every form of motor travel generates CO_2 (the main cause of human-induced climate change) but planes are far and away the worst offenders, not just because of the sheer distances they allow us to travel, but because they release greenhouse gases high into the atmosphere. The statistics are frightening: two people taking a return flight between Europe and the US will contribute as much to climate change as an average household's gas and electricity consumption over a whole year.

Carbon Offset Schemes

Climatecare.org and other websites use 'carbon calculators' that allow jetsetters to offset the greenhouse gases they are responsible for with contributions to energy-saving projects and other climate-friendly initiatives in the developing world – including projects in India, Honduras, Kazakhstan and Uganda.

Lonely Planet, together with Rough Guides and other concerned partners in the travel industry, supports the carbon offset scheme run by climatecare.org. Lonely Planet offsets all of its staff and author travel.

For more information check out our website: lonelyplanet.com.

Alitalia (AZ; ☎ 01805-074 747; www.alitalia.com)
American Airlines (AA; ☎ 0180-324 2324; www.aa.com)
British Airways (BA; ☎ 01805-266 522; www.britishairways.com)
Condor (DE; ☎ 01805-707 202; www.condor.com)
Delta Air Lines (DL; ☎ 0180-333 7880; www.delta.com)
easyJet (EZY/EZS; ☎ 01805-029 292; www.easyjet.com)
El Al (LY; ☎ 089-210 6920; www.elal.co.il)
Germania Express (ST; ☎ 01805-737 100; www.gexx.com)
Germanwings (4U; ☎ 0900-191 9100, per min €0.99; www.germanwings.com)
Iberia (IB; ☎ 01803-000 613; www.iberia.com)
LTU (LT; ☎ 0211-941-8888; www.ltu.de)
Qantas Airways (QF; ☎ 01805-250 620; www.qantas.com.au)
Ryanair (FR; ☎ 0900-1160 500, per min €0.62; www.ryanair.com)
Scandinavian Airlines/SAS (SK; ☎ 01803-234 023; www.scandinavian.net)
Singapore Airlines (SQ; ☎ 069-719 5200; www.singaporeair.com)
TuiFly (X3; ☎ 01805 757510; www.tuifly.com)
United Airlines (UA; ☎ 069-5007 0387; www.united.com)

Tickets

Everybody loves a bargain and timing is key when it comes to snapping up cheap air fares. You can generally save a bundle by booking early, travelling midweek (Tuesday to Thursday) or flying in the late evening or early morning.

Your best friend in ferreting out deals is the internet. Start by checking fares at www.expedia.com, www.travelocity.com and www.orbitz.com, then run the same flight request through meta-search engines such as www.sidestep.com, www.opodo.com or www.kayak.com. If you're not tied to particular travel dates, use the flexible-date search tool to find the lowest fares or consult www.itasoftware.com.

Many airlines now guarantee the lowest fares on their own websites, so check these out as well. To get the skinny on which low-cost airlines fly where, go to www.whichbudget.com and then book tickets on the airline website.

Australia & New Zealand

The dominant carriers to central Europe are Qantas, British Airways and Singapore Airlines. Flights here go either via Asia or the Middle East, with possible stopovers in such cities as Singapore or Bahrain, or across Canada or the US. For the latter, possible stopovers are Honolulu, Los Angeles or Vancouver. Round-the-world (RTW) tickets may work out to be cheaper than return fares.

Canada

Lufthansa and Air Canada fly to Frankfurt and Munich from all major Canadian airports. Some flights may involve a stopover in a Canadian or European airport.

Continental Europe

Lufthansa and other carriers connect major European cities with Frankfurt and Munich. Budget airline Ryanair flies to Karlsruhe-Baden-Baden, EuroAirport Basel-Mulhouse-Freiburg, Friedrichshafen, Salzburg and Frankfurt-Hahn from all over Europe, while easyJet serves EuroAirport Basel-Mulhouse-Freiburg and Munich. Air Berlin has flights from lots of European cities to Munich, Frankfurt, Salzburg, Nuremberg, Friedrichshafen and Karlsruhe-Baden-Baden. German-based TuiFly flies to Karlsruhe-Baden-Baden, Nuremberg and Munich. Munich is also served by Germania Express and Germanwings from Moscow, St Petersburg, Helsinki and Stockholm.

Other Parts of Germany

Unless you're travelling to Bavaria or the Black Forest from northern Germany, say Hamburg or Berlin, planes are only marginally faster than trains if you factor in the time it takes to travel to and from the airports. Lufthansa, Air Berlin, Germania Express, TuiFly and Germanwings are among the airlines flying domestically.

UK & Ireland

About a dozen airlines fly to southern Germany from practically every airport in the UK and Ireland. Lufthansa and British Airways are the main national carriers but prices are usually lower on Ryanair, easyJet, TuiFly and Air Berlin.

USA

Lufthansa and all major US carriers operate flights from nearly every big US city to Frankfurt and Munich. In addition, German carriers LTU and Condor operate seasonal (ie summer) flights from select US cities (Condor flies from Anchorage and Fairbanks to Frankfurt, for instance). Good fares may also be available from such Asia-based airlines as Air India and Singapore Airlines.

Fares are lowest from early November to mid-December and then again from mid-January to Easter, gradually rising in the following months and peaking in July and August.

LAND
Border Crossings

Germany is bordered (anticlockwise) by Denmark, the Netherlands, Belgium, Luxembourg, France, Switzerland, Austria, the Czech Republic and Poland. The Schengen Agreement (p320) abolished passport and customs formalities between Germany and all bordering countries.

Bus

Although slower and less comfortable, buses have their use if you wish to avoid flying altogether, have missed out on those superlow air fares, are travelling at short notice or live in an area poorly served by air or train.

Eurolines (www.eurolines.com) is the umbrella organisation of 32 European coach operators connecting 500 destinations across Europe. Its website has links to each national company's site, with detailed fare and route information, promotional offers, contact numbers and, in many cases, an online booking system. Children ages four to 12 pay half price, while teens, students and seniors get 10% off regular fares. In Germany, Eurolines is represented by **Deutsche Touring** (www.touring.de).

If Bavaria and the Black Forest are part of your European-wide itinerary, a **Eurolines Pass** (www.eurolines-pass.com) may be your ticket to savings. It allows for unlimited travel between 35 European cities within a 15- or 30-day period. During peak travel (mid-June to mid-September) it costs €329/439 for those over 26 and €279/359 for travellers under 26. Lower prices apply during the rest of the year. The pass is available online and from travel agents.

Backpacker-geared **Busabout** (☎ in the UK +44-20 7950 1661; www.busabout.com) is a hop-on hop-off service that runs coaches along three interlocking European loops between May and October. Stops include Munich and Salzburg. Loops can be combined. In Munich, for instance, the northern loop intersects with the southern loop to Italy. Trips on one loop cost €459, on two loops €799 and on three €969. Check the website for the lowdown or to buy a pass.

Car & Motorcycle

When bringing your own vehicle to Germany, you need a valid driving licence, your car registration certificate and proof of insurance. Foreign cars must display a nationality sticker unless they have official Euro-plates. You also need to carry a warning (hazard) triangle and a first-aid kit. For road rules and other driving-related information see p327.

Coming from the UK, the fastest way to the continent is via the **Eurotunnel** (☎ 08705-353 535 in the UK, 01805-000 248 in Germany; www.eurotunnel .com). These shuttle trains whisk cars, motorbikes, bicycles and coaches from Folkestone through the Channel Tunnel to Coquelles (near Calais, France) in about 35 minutes. From there, you can be in Munich in about nine or 10 hours and in Freiburg in six or seven hours. Shuttles run daily around the clock, with several departures hourly during peak periods. Fares are calculated per vehicle, including all passengers, and depend on such factors as time of day, season and length of stay. Expect to pay between €49 and €80 for a standard one-way ticket. The website and travel agents have full details.

Train

Long-distance trains connecting major German cities with those in other countries are called EuroCity (EC) trains. Seat reservations are highly recommended, especially during the peak summer season and around major holidays (p316).

Linking the UK with continental Europe, the **Eurostar** (www.eurostar.com) takes less than three hours from London-St Pancras to Paris, where you can get the brand-new TGV Est Européen high-speed line to Munich taking another 6¼ hours. Trains reach speeds of up to 320kph and have ultracomfy carriages designed by Christian Lacroix. Special 'family areas' have tables that convert into game boards and seats that can be tipped up so kids have space to play.

There are also direct overnight trains to Munich from Amsterdam, Copenhagen, Belgrade, Budapest, Bucharest, Florence, Milan, Prague, Rome, Venice and Vienna. Freiburg has overnight links with Amsterdam and Copenhagen.

For details, see Rail Europe (p328) or check with a travel agent.

LAKE

The Romanshorn–Friedrichshafen ferry provides the quickest way across Lake Constance between Switzerland and Germany. From Friedrichshafen, you can be in either Freiburg or Munich in roughly two hours driving time. Ferries operated by **SBS Schifffahrt** (☎ in Switzerland +41-71-466-7888; www.sbsag.ch) take 40 minutes and charge €6.80 per person. Bicycles are €4.30, cars start at €15.50.

SEA

There are no longer any direct ferry services between Germany and the UK, but you can just as easily go via Holland, Belgium or France and drive or train it from there. Check www.cross-channel-ferries-france.co.uk for all your options.

GETTING AROUND

Getting around Bavaria and the Black Forest is most efficient by car or by train. Regional bus services fill the gaps in areas not well served by the rail network.

AIR

Although it is possible to fly, say, from Frankfurt to Munich or Salzburg, the time and cost involved don't make air travel a sensible way to get around southern Germany.

BICYCLE

Bicycling is allowed on all roads and highways but not on the autobahns (motorways). Cyclists must follow the same rules of the road as vehicles. Helmets are not compulsory, not even for children, but wearing one is still a good idea.

Bicycles may be taken on most trains but require a separate *Fahrradkarte* (bicycle ticket). These cost €9 on long-distance trains (IC, EC, NZ reservations required) and €4.50 on regional trains (IRE, RB, RE and S-Bahn, valid all day). Bicycles are not allowed on high-speed ICE trains. There is no charge at all on some trains; for specifics inquire at a local station or call the Deutsche Bahn (DB) on the **DB Radfahrer-Hotline** (bicycle hotline; ☎ 01805-151 415). Free lines are also listed in DB's complimentary *Bahn & Bike* brochure (in German), as are the almost 250 stations throughout the country where you can hire bikes for between €3 and €13. All the information is also on www.bahn.de.

Many regional companies use buses with special bike racks. Bicycles are also allowed on practically all lake and river boats.

For additional cycling information, including bicycle hire, see p56.

BUS

Basically, wherever there is a train, take it. Buses are generally slower, less dependable and more polluting than trains, but in some rural areas they may be your only public transport option. This is especially true of the Bavarian Forest and the Black Forest, sections of the

ROAD DISTANCES (KM)

	Aschaffenburg	Augsburg	Bamberg	Bayreuth	Lindau	Munich (München)	Nuremberg (Nürnberg)	Passau	Regensburg	Rothenburg ob der Tauber
Augsburg	320									
Bamberg	174	235								
Bayreuth	238	238	71							
Lindau	376	157	367	371						
Munich (München)	354	70	230	233	178					
Nuremberg (Nürnberg)	185	170	62	84	296	166				
Passau	400	244	276	278	369	192	222			
Regensburg	284	177	162	162	300	123	104	120		
Rothenburg ob der Tauber	143	183	150	180	238	243	106	311	196	
Würzburg	80	251	96	160	301	279	110	324	209	67

Alpine foothills and the Alpine region. Separate bus companies, each with its own tariffs and schedules, operate in the different regions.

In cities, buses generally converge at the *Busbahnhof* or *Zentraler Omnibus Bahnhof/ ZOB* (central bus station), often near the Hauptbahnhof (main train station). The frequency of service varies from 'rarely' to 'constantly'. Commuter-geared routes offer limited or no service in the evenings and on weekends, so keep this in mind or risk finding yourself stuck in a remote place on a Saturday night. Always ask about special fare deals, such as day or weekly passes or tourist tickets.

Europabus

Europabus coach services is run by **Deutsche Touring** (www.touring.de) and geared towards individual travellers on three routes within southern Germany.

Romantische Strasse (Romantic Road) The most popular route operates between Würzburg and Füssen from April to October. There are links to Würzburg from Frankfurt and to Füssen from Munich. See p253 for full details.

Burgenstrasse (Castle Road) Dozens of castles and palaces line this route from Mannheim to Nuremberg via Rothenburg ob der Tauber and Ansbach; buses run from May to September.

Strassbourg-Reutlingen Year-round service from Strassbourg, France to Reutlingen via the Black Forest and such towns as Freudenstadt and Tübingen.

There's one coach in either direction daily. It's possible to change between the Romantic Road and the Burgenstrasse routes in Rothenburg ob der Tauber. Tickets can be purchased by phone or online and are available either for the entire distance or for segments between any of the stops. Various discounts are available. See p253 in the Romantic Road chapter for further details.

CAR & MOTORCYCLE

German roads are excellent and motoring around can be a lot of fun. Autobahns are supplemented by an extensive network of *Bundesstrassen* (secondary 'B' roads, highways, country roads). No tolls are charged on public roads.

If your car doesn't have a navigation system, a good map or road atlas is essential, especially when negotiating country roads. Navigating in Germany is not done by the points of the compass. That is to say that you'll find no signs saying 'north' or 'west'. Rather, you'll see signs pointing you in the direction of a city, so you'd best have that map right in your lap to stay oriented. Maps cost a few euros and are sold at bookstores, train stations, airports and petrol stations. The best are published by Freytag & Berndt, ADAC, Falk and Euro Map. Free maps available from tourist offices or rental agencies are generally inadequate.

Note that distances may appear short, but traffic can be heavy and there are countless things to do and see en route, so don't aim to cover too much ground per day. Traffic reports on the radio (in German) usually follow the on-the-hour news summary. Up-to-the-minute travel and road-construction information in English is available online at www.bayerninfo.de.

Seat belts are mandatory for all passengers and there's a €30 fine per person if you get caught not wearing one. Children need a child seat if under four years old and a seat cushion if under 12; children may not ride in the front until age 13. Motorcyclists must wear helmets. Using hand-held mobile phones while driving is very much *Verboten* (forbidden).

Along each autobahn, you'll find elaborate service areas every 40km to 60km with petrol stations, toilet facilities and restaurants; some are open 24 hours. In between are *Rastplätze* (rest stops), which usually have picnic tables and toilet facilities.

Automobile Associations

Germany's main motoring organisation, the **Allgemeiner Deutscher Automobil-Club** (ADAC; ☎ 0180-222 2222 for roadside assistance, ☎ 222 222 if calling from mobile phone; www.adac.de, in German) has offices in all major cities and many smaller ones. Its roadside assistance is also available to members of its affiliates, including British AA, American AAA and Canadian CAA.

Driving Licence

Drivers need a valid driving licence. International Driving Permits (IDP) are not compulsory but having one may help Germans make sense of your home licence (always carry that one too) and may simplify the car or motorcycle hire process. IDPs are inexpensive, valid for one year and issued by your local automobile association – bring a passport photo and your home licence.

Fuel & Spare Parts

Petrol stations, which are mostly self-service, are generally ubiquitous except in sparsely populated rural areas. Petrol is sold in litres. In January 2008 the average cost for mid-grade fuel was around €1.40 per litre; for up-to-date prices see www.clever-tanken.de (in German).

Finding spare parts should not be a problem, especially in the cities, although availability of course depends on the age and model of your car. Be sure to have some sort of roadside emergency assistance plan (left) in case your car breaks down.

Hire

As anywhere, rates for car hire vary quite considerably by model, pick-up date and location, but you should be able to get an economy-size vehicle from about €35 per day, plus insurance and taxes. Expect surcharges for car hire originating at airports and train stations, and for additional drivers and one-way hire. Child or infant safety seats are usually available for about €5 per day and should be reserved at the time of booking.

To hire your own wheels you generally need to be at least 25 years old with a valid driving licence as well as a major credit card. Some companies hire out to drivers between the ages of 21 and 24 for an additional charge (about €12 to €20 per day). Younger people or those without a credit card are often out of luck, although some local outfits may accept cash or travellers cheque deposits. Taking your car into an Eastern European country, such as the Czech Republic or Poland, is often a no-no, so check in advance if that's where you're planning to head.

All the main international companies maintain branches at airports, major train stations and in the towns. Companies include **Avis** (☎ 01805-217 702; www.avis.com), **Europcar** (☎ 01805-8000; www.europcar.com), **Hertz** (☎ 01805-333 535; www.hertz.com) and Sixt or **Budget** (☎ 01805-244 388; www.budget.com), each with offices or affiliates from Aschaffenburg to Zwiesel.

Prebooked and prepaid packages, arranged in your home country, usually work out cheaper than on-the-spot hire. The same is true of fly-drive packages. Check for deals with online agencies (eg www.expedia.com) or your travel agent.

Insurance

German law requires that all registered vehicles carry third-party liability insurance.

You could get seriously screwed by driving uninsured or even underinsured. Germans are very fussy about their cars, and even nudging someone's bumper when jostling out of a tight parking space may well result in you having to foot the bill for an entire new one.

When hiring a vehicle, make sure your contract includes adequate liability insurance at the very minimum. Car-hire agencies almost never include insurance that covers damage to the vehicle itself, called Collision Damage Waiver (CDW) or Loss Damage Waiver (LDW). It's optional, but driving without one is not recommended. Some credit card companies cover CDW and LDW for a certain period if you charge the entire cost to your card. Always confirm with your card issuer what coverage it provides in Germany.

Road Rules

Driving is on the right-hand side of the road and standard international signs are in use. If you're unfamiliar with these, pick up a pamphlet at your local motoring organisation. Obey the road rules carefully: speed and red-light cameras are common and notices are sent to the car's registration address, wherever that may be. If you're renting a car, the police will obtain your home address from the rental agency and mail the notice to you. There's also a long list of other finable actions, including using abusive language or gestures and running out of petrol on the autobahn.

Speed limits are 50km/h on city streets and 100km/h on highways and country roads unless otherwise posted. And yes, it's true, there are sections of autobahns where there's no speed limit! Always keep an eye out for signs indicating that slower speeds must be observed or risk getting ticketed. And remember, the higher the speed, the higher the emissions.

Drivers unaccustomed to the high speeds on autobahns should be extra careful when passing another vehicle. It takes only seconds for a car in the rear-view mirror to close in at 200km/h. Pass as quickly as possible, then quickly return to the right lane. Ignore those annoying drivers who flash their headlights or tailgate you to make you drive faster and get out of the way. It's an illegal practice anyway, as is passing on the right.

If you break down, pull over to the side of the road immediately and set up your warning triangle about 100m behind the car. Emergency call boxes are spaced about 2km

apart or, if you have a mobile phone, call the ADAC roadside assistance at ☎ 222 222 and wait for assistance.

The highest permissible blood-alcohol level for drivers is 0.05%, which for most people equates to roughly one glass of wine or two small beers.

Pedestrians at crossings have the absolute right of way over all motor vehicles. Always watch out for bicyclists when turning right; they too have the right of way. Right turns at a red light are only legal if there's also a green arrow pointing to the right.

Note that some garages and parking lots close at night and charge an overnight fee.

HITCHING & RIDE-SHARE

Trampen (hitching) is never entirely safe and, frankly, we don't recommend it. That said, in some remote parts of Bavaria and the Black Forest – such as sections of the Alpine foothills and the Bavarian Forest – that are poorly served by public transport, you will occasionally see people thumbing for a ride. Remember that it's safer to travel in pairs and be sure to let someone know where you're planning to go.

A safer and more predictable form of traveling is ride-shares, where you travel as a passenger in exchange for some petrol money. Most arrangements are now made via online ride-boards at www.mitfahrzentrale.de, www.mitfahrgelegenheit.de (in German) or www.drive2day.de. You can advertise a ride yourself or link up with a driver going to your destination.

LOCAL TRANSPORT

Most towns have efficient public transport systems. Bigger cities, such as Munich and Nuremberg, integrate buses, trams, and U-Bahn (underground) and S-Bahn (suburban) trains into a single network.

Fares are either determined by zones or time travelled, or sometimes by both. *Streifenkarten* (multiticket strips) or *Tageskarten* (day passes) generally offer better value than single-ride tickets. Sometimes tickets must be stamped upon boarding in order to be valid. Fines are levied if you're caught without a valid ticket. For details, see the Getting Around entries in the destination chapters.

Taxis are metered and charged at a base rate (flag fall) plus a per-kilometre fee. These are fixed but vary across cities. Some charge extra for bulky luggage or night-time rides. Rarely can you flag down a taxi. Rather, you board at a taxi rank or order one by phone (numbers are listed throughout this book or look them up under *Taxiruf* in the phonebook).

TRAIN

Germany's rail system is operated almost entirely by **Deutsche Bahn** (DB; ☎ reservations & information 118 61, toll-free automated timetable 0800-150 7090; www.bahn.de) with an 'alphabet soup' of train types serving just about every corner of the country. Long-distance trains are either called ICE (InterCity Express), which travel at speeds of up to 280km/h, or the only slightly slower IC (InterCity) or EC (EuroCity) trains. Both run at hourly or bi-hourly intervals. Regional service is provided by the IRE (InterRegio Express), the RB (RegionalBahn), the SE (StadtExpress) and the S-Bahn.

Many train stations have a *Reisezentrum* (travel centre) where staff sell tickets and can help you plan an itinerary (ask for an English-speaking agent). Smaller stations may only have a few ticket windows or no staff at all. In this case, you must buy tickets from vending machines. These are also plentiful at staffed stations and convenient if you don't want to queue at a ticket counter. English instructions are normally provided. Both agents and machines accept major credit cards. Tickets sold onboard (cash only) incur a service fee (€3 to €8) unless the station where you boarded was unstaffed or had a broken vending machine. Tickets are also available online up to 10 minutes before departure but need to be printed out.

Most train stations have coin-operated lockers charging from €0.50 to €4 for 24 hours. *Gepäckaufbewahrung* (left-luggage offices) charge similar rates.

See p324 for more details on taking your bicycle on the train.

Classes

German trains have 1st- and 2nd-class cars, both of them modern and comfortable. Seating is either in compartments of up to six people or in open-plan carriages with panoramic windows. Trains and stations are now completely nonsmoking. ICE, IC and EC trains are fully air-conditioned and have a restaurant or self-service bistro.

Costs

Standard, non-discounted train tickets tend to be quite expensive, but promotions, discount tickets and special offers become available all the time. Check the website or ask at the train station.

Permanent rail deals include the Bayern-Ticket and the Baden-Württemberg-Ticket. For €27 up to five passengers travelling together get unlimited rides within either state from 9am until 3am of the following day from Monday to Friday. On weekends the ticket is valid from midnight until 3am the following day. It's good for 2nd-class travel on all IRE, SE, RB and S-Bahn trains, as well as all public buses, trams and U-Bahns. Solo travellers can get the Bayern-Ticket Single for €19 or the Baden-Württemberg-Ticket Single for €18. Finally, there's the Bayern-Ticket Nacht that allows up to five night owls to travel from 6pm to 6am (7am on weekends and holiday), also for €19. There's a €2 surcharge for tickets bought from agents instead of vending machines.

Reservations

Seat reservations for long-distance travel are highly recommended, especially on a Friday or Sunday afternoon, around holidays or in summer. They can be made up to 10 minutes before departure by phone, online or at ticket counters. The cost is €3.50 per person or €7 for groups of up to five people; if bought online the cost drops to €1.50 and €3, respectively.

Train Passes

If residing permanently outside Europe, you qualify for the German Rail Pass, which entitles you to unlimited 1st- or 2nd-class travel for four to 10 days within a one-month period. Sample prices for four/seven/10 days of travel are €219/309/399 in 1st class and €169/229/289 in 2nd class (half-price for children ages six to 11). The pass is valid on all trains within Germany, plus Salzburg and Basel as well as some river services, and entitles you to discounts on the Europabus along the Romantic Road, Castle Road and Bayerische Zugspitzbahn. The German Rail Youth Pass for people between 12 and 25 and the German Rail Twin Pass for two adults travelling together are variations on the scheme. If Bavaria is part of a wider European itinerary, look into a **Eurail Pass** (www.eurail.com).

In the US, Canada and the UK, a great resource for rail passes is **Rail Europe** (www.rail europe.com; US ☎ 877-382-7245; Canada ☎ 800-361-7245; UK ☎ 08705-371 371), a major agency specialising in train travel around Europe. The website also lists affiliated agents in other countries, including Australia, New Zealand and Japan.

Health

CONTENTS

BEFORE YOU GO

While Germany has excellent health care, prevention is the key to staying healthy while abroad. Planning before departure, particularly for pre-existing illnesses, will be beneficial. Bring medications in their original, labelled, containers. A signed and dated letter from your physician describing your conditions and medications, including generic names, is a good idea. If carrying syringes or needles, be sure to have a physician's letter documenting their medical necessity. Carry a spare pair of contact lenses and glasses, and take your optical prescription with you.

INSURANCE

If you're an EU citizen, an E111 form, available from health centres or, in the UK, post offices, covers you for most medical care. E111 will not cover you for nonemergencies, or emergency repatriation. Citizens from other countries should find out if there is a reciprocal arrangement for free medical care between their country and Germany. If you do need health insurance, make sure you get a policy that covers you for the worst possible case, such as an accident requiring an emergency flight home. Find out in advance if your insurance plan will make payments directly to providers or reimburse you later for overseas health expenditures.

RECOMMENDED VACCINATIONS

No jabs are required to travel to Germany. The World Health Organization (WHO), however, recommends that all travellers should be covered for diphtheria, tetanus, measles, mumps, rubella and polio, regardless of their destination.

IN TRANSIT

DEEP VEIN THROMBOSIS (DVT)

Blood clots may form in the legs during flights, chiefly because of prolonged immobility. The longer the flight, the greater the risk. The chief symptom of DVT is swelling or pain of the foot, ankle or calf, usually but not always on just one side. When a blood clot travels to the lungs, it may cause chest pain and difficulty breathing. Travellers with any of these symptoms should immediately seek medical attention.

To prevent the development of DVT on long flights walk about the cabin, contract the leg muscles while sitting, drink plenty of fluids and avoid alcohol and tobacco (before or between flights; the flight itself will be nonsmoking).

JET LAG & MOTION SICKNESS

To avoid jet lag (common when crossing more than five time zones) try to drink plenty of nonalchoholic fluids and eat light meals. Upon arrival, get exposure to natural sunlight and readjust your schedule (for meals, sleep etc) as soon as possible.

The first choices for treating motion sickness are usually antihistamines such as dimenhydrinate (Dramamine) and meclizine (Antivert, Bonine). A herbal alternative is ginger.

IN MUNICH, BAVARIA & THE BLACK FOREST

AVAILABILITY & COST OF HEALTH CARE

Excellent health care is readily available and for minor illnesses such as colds pharmacists can provide advice and sell over-the-counter medication. They can also advise when more specialised help is required and point you in the right direction.

TRAVELLER'S DIARRHOEA

If you develop diarrhoea, be sure to drink plenty of fluids, preferably in the form of an oral rehydration solution such as Dioralyte. If diarrhoea is bloody, persists for more than 72 hours or is accompanied by fever, shaking, chills or severe abdominal pain you should seek medical attention.

ENVIRONMENTAL HAZARDS
Heatstroke

Heat exhaustion occurs as a result of excessive fluid loss with inadequate replacement of fluids and salt. Symptoms include headache, dizziness and tiredness. Dehydration is already happening by the time you feel thirsty – aim to drink sufficient water to produce pale, diluted urine. To treat heat exhaustion drink water and/or fruit juice, and cool the body with cold water and fans.

Hypothermia

Hypothermia occurs when the body loses heat faster than it can produce it. As ever, proper preparation will reduce the risks of getting it. Even on a hot day in the mountains, the weather can change rapidly, so carry waterproof garments, warm layers and a hat, and leave details of your route with a responsible person.

Hypothermia starts with shivering, loss of judgment and clumsiness. Unless rewarming occurs, the sufferer deteriorates into apathy, confusion and coma. Prevent further heat loss by seeking shelter, warm dry clothing, hot sweet drinks and shared bodily warmth.

SEXUAL HEALTH

Emergency contraception is available with a doctor's prescription in Germany. It is most effective if taken within 24 hours of unprotected sex. Condoms are readily available throughout Germany.

TRAVELLING WITH CHILDREN

Make sure children are up-to-date with routine vaccinations, and discuss possible travel vaccines well before departure as some vaccines are not suitable for children under one year old.

MEDICAL CHECKLIST

All the following are readily available in Germany. If you are hiking out of town, these items may come in handy.

- acetaminophen, paracetamol, or aspirin
- acetazolamide (Diamox; for altitude sickness)
- adhesive or paper tape
- antibacterial ointment (for cuts and abrasions)
- antibiotics
- antidiarrhoeal drugs (eg loperamide)
- antihistamines (for hay fever and allergic reactions)
- anti-inflammatory drugs (eg ibuprofen)
- bandages, gauze, gauze rolls
- DEET-containing insect repellent for the skin
- oral rehydration salts
- pocketknife
- pyrethrin-containing insect spray for clothing, tents and bed nets
- scissors, safety pins, tweezers
- steroid cream or cortisone (for poison ivy and other allergic rashes)
- sun block
- thermometer

If your child has been vomiting or has diarrhoea, lost fluid and salts must be replaced. It may be helpful to take rehydration powders with water that has been boiled.

WOMEN'S HEALTH

Emotional stress, exhaustion and travelling through different time zones can all contribute to an upset in the menstrual pattern.

If using oral contraceptives, remember some antibiotics, diarrhoea and vomiting can stop the pill from working. Time zones, gastrointestinal upsets and antibiotics do not affect injectable contraception.

Travelling during pregnancy is usually possible but always consult your doctor before planning your trip. The riskiest times for travel are during the first 12 weeks of pregnancy and after 30 weeks.

Language

CONTENTS

German belongs to the Indo-European language group and is spoken by more than 100 million people in countries throughout the world, including Austria and part of Switzerland. Regional dialects still thrive throughout Germany, especially in Cologne, rural Bavaria, Swabia and parts of Saxony. The Sorb minority in eastern Germany has its own language. In northern Germany it is common to hear Plattdeutsch (Low German) and Frisian spoken. Both are distant relatives of English, and the fact that many German words survive in the English vocabulary today makes things a lot easier for native English speakers.

All German school children learn a foreign language – usually English – which means most can speak it to a certain degree.

The words and phrases included in this language guide should help you through the most common travel situations. For language that will be of help when dining see p48. If you're keen to delve a little further into the language, pick up a copy of Lonely Planet's *German Phrasebook*.

GRAMMAR

German grammar can be a nightmare for English speakers. Nouns come in three genders: masculine, feminine and neuter. The corresponding forms of the definite article ('the' in English) are *der*, *die* and *das*, with the universal plural form, *die*. Nouns and articles will alter according to complex grammatical rules relating to the noun's function within a phrase – known as 'case'. In German there are four cases: nominative, accusative, dative and genitive. We haven't allowed for all possible permutations of case in this language guide – it's simply too complex to cover here. However, bad German is better than no German at all, so even if you muddle your cases, you'll find that you'll still be understood – and your efforts will be appreciated regardless.

If you've noticed that written German seems to be full of capital letters, the reason is that German nouns always begin with a capital letter.

PRONUNCIATION

The pronunciation of words and phrases throughout this chapter is based on High German, which is understood throughout the country.

Regional Variation

The German dialect spoken around Munich only differs from High German in pronunciation. In the Munich dialect, when the pairs of letters **p/b**, **k/g**, and **t/d** occur at the start of the word, there's no audible difference between them. In the sentences *Ich backe* (I bake) and *Ich packe* (I pack), the **p** and **b** are pronounced the same, sounding like a combination of both letters. Also, the combinations **st** and **sp** are pronounced 'sht' and 'shp', so the girl's name Astrid would be pronounced 'ashtrid'.

Vowels

German Example	Pronunciation Guide
hat	**a** (eg the 'u' in 'run')
habe	**ah** (eg 'father')
mein	**ai** (eg 'aisle')
Bär	**air** (eg 'hair', with no 'r' sound)
Boot	**aw** (eg 'saw')
leben	**ay** (eg 'say')
Bett/Männer/kaufen	**e** (eg 'bed')
fliegen	**ee** (eg 'thief')
schön	**er** (eg 'her', with no 'r' sound)
mit	**i** (eg 'bit')
Koffer	**o** (eg 'pot')

LANGUAGE

Leute/Häuser	**oy** (eg 'toy')
Schuhe	**oo** (eg 'moon')
Haus	**ow** (eg 'how')
züruck	**ü** ('ee' said with rounded lips)
unter	**u** (eg 'put')

Consonants

The only two tricky consonant sounds in German are **ch** and **r**. All other consonants are pronounced much the same as their English counterparts (except **sch**, which is always as the 'sh' in 'shoe').

The **ch** sound is generally like the 'ch' in the Scottish *loch* – like a hiss from the back of the throat. When **ch** occurs after the vowels **e** and **i** it's more like 'sh', produced with the tongue more forward in the mouth. In this book we've simplified things by using the one symbol **kh** for both sounds.

The **r** sound is different from English, and it isn't rolled like in Italian or Spanish. It's pronounced at the back of the throat, almost like saying 'g' as in 'get' with some friction – a bit like gargling.

Word Stress

As a general rule, word stress in German mostly falls on the first syllable. In the pronunciation guides in the following words and phrases, the stressed syllable is shown in italics.

ACCOMMODATION

Where's a ...?

Wo ist ...?	vaw ist ...
bed and breakfast	
eine Pension	*ai*·ne pahng·*zyawn*
campsite	
ein Campingplatz	ain *kem*·ping·plats
guesthouse	
eine Pension	*ai*·ne pahng·*zyawn*
hotel	
ein Hotel	ain ho·*tel*
youth hostel	
eine Jugendherberge	*ai*·ne *yoo*·gent·her·ber·ge

What's the address?

Wie ist die Adresse?	vee ist dee a·*dre*·se

I'd like to book a room, please.

Ich möchte bitte ein	ikh *merkh*·te *bi*·te ain
Zimmer reservieren.	*tsi*·mer re·zer·vee·ren

For (three) nights/weeks.

Für (drei) Nächte/	für (drai) *nekh*·te/
Wochen.	*vo*·khen

Do you have a ... room?

Haben Sie ein ...?	*hah*·ben zee ain ...
single	
Einzelzimmer	*ain*·tsel·tsi·mer
double	
Doppelzimmer mit	*do*·pel·tsi·mer mit
einem Doppelbett	*ai*·nem *do*·pel·bet
twin	
Doppelzimmer mit zwei	*do*·pel·tsi·mer mit tsvai
Einzelbetten	*ain*·tsel·be·ten

How much is it per ...?

Wie viel kostet es pro ...?	vee feel *kos*·tet es praw ...
night	
Nacht	nakht
person	
Person	per·*zawn*

May I see it?

Kann ich es sehen?	kan ikh es *zay*·en

Can I get another room?

Kann ich noch ein	kan ikh nokh ain
Zimmer bekommen?	*tsi*·mer be·*ko*·men

It's fine. I'll take it.

Es ist gut, ich nehme es.	es ist goot ikh *nay*·me es

I'm leaving now.

Ich reise jetzt ab.	ikh *rai*·ze yetst ap

CONVERSATION & ESSENTIALS

German uses polite and informal forms for 'you' (*Sie* and *Du* respectively). When addressing people you don't know well always use the polite form (though younger people will be less inclined to expect it). In this language guide we use the polite form unless indicated by 'inf' (informal) in brackets.

If you need to ask for assistance from a stranger, remember to always introduce your request with a simple *Entschuldigung* (Excuse me, ...).

Hello.	*Grüss Gott.*	grüs got
Hi.	*Hallo.*	ha·lo/ha·*law*
Good ...	*Guten ...*	*goo*·ten ...
day	*Tag*	tahk
morning	*Morgen*	*mor*·gen
afternoon	*Tag*	tahk
evening	*Abend*	*ah*·bent

Goodbye.		
Auf Wiedersehen.		owf *vee*·der·zay·en
See you later.		
Bis später.		bis *shpay*·ter
Bye.		
Tschüss/Tschau.		chüs/chow

How are you?
  Wie geht es Ihnen?   vee gayt es *ee*·nen
  Wie geht es dir? (inf) vee gayt es deer
Fine.
  Danke, gut.   *dang*·ke goot
And you?
  Und Ihnen?   unt *ee*·nen
  Und dir? (inf)   unt deer
What's your name?
  Wie ist Ihr Name? vee ist eer *nah*·me
  Wie heisst du? (inf) vee haist doo
My name is ...
  Mein Name ist .../ main *nah*·me ist .../
  Ich heisse ...   ikh *hai*·se ...
Yes.
  Ja.   yah
No.
  Nein.   nain
Please.
  Bitte.   *bi*·te
Thank you (very much).
  Danke/Vielen Dank. *dang*·ke/*fee*·len dangk
You're welcome.
  Bitte (sehr).   *bi*·te (zair)
Excuse me, ... (before asking for help or directions)
  Entschuldigung, ... ent·*shul*·di·gung ...
Sorry.
  Entschuldigung. ent·*shul*·di·gung

DIRECTIONS
Could you help me, please?
  Können Sie mir bitte helfen?
  ker·nen zee meer *bi*·te *hel*·fen
Where's (a bank)?
  Wo ist (eine Bank)?
  vaw ist (*ai*·ne bangk)
I'm looking for (the cathedral).
  Ich suche (den Dom).
  ikh *zoo*·khe (dayn dawm)
Which way's (a public toilet)?
  In welcher Richtung ist eine öffentliche toilette?
  in *vel*·kher *rikh*·tung ist (*ai*·ne *er*·fent·li·khe to·a·*le*·te)
How far is it?
  Wie weit ist es?
  vee *vait* ist es
Can you show me (on the map)?
  Können Sie es mir (auf der Karte) zeigen?
  ker·nen zee es meer (owf dair *kar*·te) *tsai*·gen

near	*nahe*	*nah*·e
far away	*weit weg*	vait vek
here	*hier*	heer
there	*dort*	dort
straight ahead	*geradeaus*	ge·rah·de·*ows*

north	*Norden*	*nor*·den
south	*Süden*	*zü*·den
east	*Osten*	*os*·ten
west	*Westen*	*ves*·ten

Turn ...
Biegen Sie ... ab. *bee*·gen zee ... ap
  left/right
  links/rechts   lingks/rekhts
  at the next corner
  an der nächsten Ecke an dair *naykhs*·ten e·ke
  at the traffic lights
  bei der Ampel   bai dair *am*·pel

EMERGENCIES
Help!
  Hilfe!   *hil*·fe
It's an emergency!
  Es ist ein Notfall! es ist ain *nawt*·fal
Call the police!
  Rufen Sie die Polizei! *roo*·fen zee dee po·li·*tsai*
Call a doctor!
  Rufen Sie einen Arzt! *roo*·fen zee *ai*·nen artst
Call an ambulance!
  Rufen Sie einen *roo*·fen zee *ai*·nen
   Krankenwagen! *krang*·ken·vah·gen
Leave me alone!
  Lassen Sie mich in Ruhe! *la*·sen zee mikh in *roo*·e
Go away!
  Gehen Sie weg! *gay*·en zee vek
I'm lost.
  Ich habe mich verirrt. ikh *hah*·be mikh fer·*irt*

HEALTH
Where's the nearest ...?
Wo ist der/die/das nächste ...? (m/f/n)
vaw ist dair/dee/das *naykhs*·te ...
  chemist
  Apotheke (f) a·po·*tay*·ke

dentist
Zahnarzt/	tsahn·artst/
Zahnärztin (m/f)	tsahn·erts·tin

doctor
Arzt/Ärztin (m/f)	artst/erts·tin

hospital
Krankenhaus (n)	krang·ken·hows

I need a doctor (who speaks English).
Ich brauche einen Arzt (der Englisch spricht).
ikh brow·khe ai·nen artst (dair eng·lish shprikht)

I'm allergic to ...
Ich bin allergisch gegen ... ikh bin a·lair·gish gay·gen ...

antibiotics
Antibiotika   an·ti·bi·aw·ti·ka

aspirin
Aspirin   as·pi·reen

penicillin
Penizillin   pe·ni·tsi·leen

I'm sick.
Ich bin krank.
ikh bin krangk

LANGUAGE DIFFICULTIES

Do you speak English?
Sprechen Sie Englisch?
shpre·khen zee eng·lish

Does anyone here speak English?
Spricht hier jemand Englisch?
shprikht heer yay·mant eng·lish

I (don't) understand.
Ich verstehe (nicht).
ikh fer·shtay·e (nikht)

Could you please write it down?
Könnten Sie das bitte aufschreiben?
kern·ten zee das bi·te owf·shrai·ben

NUMBERS

1	ains	aints
2	zwei	tsvai
3	drei	drai
4	vier	feer
5	fünf	fünf
6	sechs	zeks
7	sieben	zee·ben
8	acht	akht
9	neun	noyn
10	zehn	tsayn
11	elf	elf
12	zwölf	zverlf
13	dreizehn	drai·tsayn
14	vierzehn	feer·tsayn
15	fünfzehn	fünf·tsayn
16	sechzehn	zeks·tsayn
17	siebzehn	zeep·tsayn
18	achtzehn	akh·tsayn
19	neunzehn	noyn·tsayn
20	zwanzig	tsvan·tsikh
21	einundzwanzig	ain·unt·tsvan·tsikh
22	zweiundzwanzig	tsvai·unt·tsvan·tsikh
30	dreizig	drai·tsikh
31	einunddreizig	ain·und·drai·tsikh
40	vierzig	feer·tsikh
50	fünfzig	fünf·tsikh
60	sechzig	zekh·tsikh
70	siebzig	zeep·tsikh
80	achtzig	akh·tsikh
90	neunzig	noyn·tsikh
100	hundert	hun·dert
1000	tausend	tow·sent
2000	zwei tausend	tsvai tow·sent

SHOPPING & SERVICES

I'm looking for ...
Ich suche ...
ikh zoo·khe ...

Where's the (nearest) ...?
Wo ist der/die/das (nächste) ...? (m/f/n)
vaw ist dair/dee/das (naykhs·te) ...

How much (is this)?
Wie viel (kostet das)?
vee feel (kos·tet das)

I'm just looking.
Ich schaue mich nur um.
ikh show·e mikh noor um

Can you write down the price?
Können Sie den Preis aufschreiben?
ker·nen zee dayn prais owf·shrai·ben

I'd like to ...
Ich möchte ...   ikh merkh·te ...

change money (cash)
Geld umtauschen   gelt um·tow·shen

cash a cheque
einen Scheck einlösen   ai·nen shek ain·ler·zen

change some travellers cheques
Reisechecks einlösen   rai·ze·sheks ain·ler·zen

Do you accept ...?
Nehmen Sie ...?   nay·men zee ...

credit cards
Kreditkarten   kre·deet·kar·ten

travellers cheques
Reisechecks   rai·ze·sheks

What time does it open/close?
Wann macht er/sie/es auf/zu? (m/f/n)
van makht air/zee/es owf/tsoo

I want to buy a phonecard.
Ich möchte eine Telefonkarte kaufen.
ikh *merkh*·te *ai*·ne te·le·*fawn*·kar·te *kow*·fen
Where's the local internet cafe?
Wo ist hier ein Internet-Café?
vaw ist heer ain *in*·ter·net·ka·fay

an ATM	*ein Geldautomat*	ain *gelt*·ow·to·maht
an exchange	*eine Geldwechsel-*	*ai*·ne *gelt*·vek·sel·
office	*stube*	shtoo·be
a bank	*eine Bank*	*ai*·ne bangk
the ... embassy	*die ... Botschaft*	dee *bot*·shaft
the hospital	*das Krankenhaus*	das *krang*·ken·hows
the market	*der Markt*	dair markt
the police	*die Polizei*	dee po·li·*tsai*
the post office	*das Postamt*	das *post*·amt
a public phone	*ein öffentliches*	ain er·*fent*·li·khes
	Telefon	te·le·*fawn*
a public toilet	*eine öffentliche*	ain er·*fent*·li·khe
	Toilette	to·a·*le*·te

I'd like to ...
Ich möchte ...   ikh *merkh*·te ...
  get internet access
  Internetzugang haben   *in*·ter·net·tsoo·gang *hah*·ben
  check my email
  meine E-Mails checken   *mai*·ne ee·mayls *che*·ken

TIME & DATES
What time is it?
Wie spät ist es?   vee shpayt ist es
It's (one) o'clock.
Es ist (ein) Uhr.   es ist (ain) oor
Twenty past one.
Zwanzig nach eins.   tsvan·tsikh nahkh ains
Half past one.
Halb zwei. ('half two') halp tsvai
Quarter to one.
Viertel vor eins.   *fir*·tel fawr ains
am
  morgens/vormittags   *mor*·gens/*fawr*·mi·tahks
pm
  nachmittags/abends   *nahkh*·mi·tahks/*ah*·bents

now	*jetzt*	yetst
today	*heute*	*hoy*·te
tonight	*heute Abend*	*hoy*·te *ah*·bent
tomorrow	*morgen*	*mor*·gen

Monday	*Montag*	*mawn*·tahk
Tuesday	*Dienstag*	*deens*·tahk
Wednesday	*Mittwoch*	*mit*·vokh
Thursday	*Donnerstag*	*do*·ners·tahk
Friday	*Freitag*	*frai*·tahk
Saturday	*Samstag*	*zams*·tahk
Sunday	*Sonntag*	*zon*·tahk

January	*Januar*	*yan*·u·ahr
February	*Februar*	*fay*·bru·ahr
March	*März*	merts
April	*April*	a·*pril*
May	*Mai*	mai
June	*Juni*	*yoo*·ni
July	*Juli*	*yoo*·li
August	*August*	ow·*gust*
September	*September*	zep·*tem*·ber
October	*Oktober*	ok·*taw*·ber
November	*November*	no·*vem*·ber
December	*Dezember*	de·*tsem*·ber

TRANSPORT
Public Transport
What time does the ... leave?
Wann fährt ... ab?   van fairt ... ap

bus	*der Bus*	dair bus
train	*der Zug*	dair tsook
first	*erste*	*ers*·te
last	*letzte*	*lets*·te
next	*nächste*	*naykhs*·te

Where's the nearest metro station?
Wo ist der nächste U-Bahnhof?
vaw ist dair *naykhs*·te oo·bahn·hawf
Which (bus) goes to ...?
Welcher Bus fährt ...?
vel·kher bus fairt ...

metro		
U-Bahn		*oo*·bahn
(metro) station		
(U-)Bahnhof		*(oo)*·bahn·hawf
tram		
Strassenbahn		*shtrah*·sen·bahn
tram stop		
Strassenbahnhalte-		*shtrah*·sen·bahn·*hal*·te·
stelle		*shte*·le
urban railway		
S-Bahn		*es*·bahn

A ... ticket to (Munich).
Einen ... nach (München).   *ai*·nen ... nahkh (moon·*khyen*)
  one-way
  einfache Fahrkarte   ain·fa·khe *fahr*·kar·te
  return
  Rückfahrkarte   *rük*·fahr·kar·te

Is this seat free?
Ist dieser Platz frei?   ist *dee*·zer plats frai
Do I need to change trains?
Muss ich umsteigen?   mus ikh *um*·shtai·gen
Are you free? (taxi)
Sind Sie frei?   zint zee frai

How much is it to ...?
Was kostet es bis ...?   vas *kos*·tet es bis ...
Please take me to (this address).
Bitte bringen Sie mich   *bi*·te *bring*·en zee mikh
zu (dieser Adresse).   tsoo (*dee*·zer a·*dre*·se)

Private Transport
Where can I hire a ...?
Wo kann ich ... mieten?   vaw kan ikh ... *mee*·ten
I'd like to hire a/an ...
Ich möchte ... mieten.   ikh *merkh*·te ... *mee*·ten
  bicycle
  ein Fahrrad   ain *fahr*·raht
  car
  ein Auto   ain *ow*·to
  motorbike
  ein Motorrad   ain *maw*·tor·raht

ROAD SIGNS

Gefahr	Danger
Einfahrt Verboten	No Entry
Einbahnstrasse	One-Way
Einfahrt	Entrance
Ausfahrt	Exit
Ausfahrt Freihalten	Keep Clear
Parkverbot	No Parking
Mautstelle	Toll
Radweg	Cycle Path

---

diesel
Diesel   *dee*·zel
LPG
Autogas   *ow*·to·gahs
petrol (gas)
Benzin   ben·*tseen*

Where's a petrol station?
Wo ist eine Tankstelle?
vaw ist *ai*·ne *tangk*·shte·le
Does this road go to ...?
Führt diese Strasse nach ...?
fürt *dee*·ze *shtrah*·se nahkh ...

(How long) Can I park here?
(Wie lange) Kann ich hier parken?
(vee *lang*·e) kan ikh heer *par*·ken
Where do I pay?
Wo muss ich bezahlen?
vaw mus ikh be·*tsah*·len
I need a mechanic.
Ich brauche einen Mechaniker.
ikh *brow*·khe *ai*·nen me·*khah*·ni·ker
I've run out of petrol.
Ich habe kein Benzin mehr.
ikh *hah*·be kain ben·*tseen* mair

TRAVEL WITH CHILDREN
I need a ...
Ich brauche ...   ikh *brow*·khe ...
Is there a/an ...?
Gibt es ...?   gipt es ...
  baby change room
  einen Wickelraum   *ai*·nen *vi*·kel·rowm
  baby seat
  einen Babysitz   *ai*·nen *bay*·bi·zits
  booster seat
  einen Kindersitz   *ai*·nen *kin*·der·zits
  child-minding service
  einen Babysitter-Service   *ai*·nen *bay*·bi·si·ter·*ser*·vis
  highchair
  einen Kinderstuhl   *ai*·nen *kin*·der·shtool
  infant formula (milk)
  Trockenmilch für   *tro*·ken·milkh für
  Säuglinge   *soyg*·ling·e
  potty
  ein Kindertöpfchen   ain *kin*·der·terpf·khen
  stroller
  einen Kinderwagen   *ai*·nen *kin*·der·vah·gen

Do you mind if I breastfeed here?
Kann ich meinem Kind hier die Brust geben?
kan ikh *mai*·nem kint heer dee brust *gay*·ben
Are children allowed?
Sind Kinder erlaubt?
zint *kin*·der er·*lowpt*

Also available from Lonely Planet:
German Phrasebook

Glossary

(pl) indicates plural

Abtei – abbey
ADAC – Allgemeiner Deutscher Automobil Club (German Automobile Association)
Allee – avenue
Altstadt – old town
Apotheke – pharmacy
Ärzt – doctor
Ausgang – exit

Bad – spa, bath
Bahnhof – train station
Basilika – basilica
Bedienung – service; service charge
Behinderte – disabled person
Berg – mountain
Bibliothek – library
Biergarten – beer garden
Bierkeller – cellar pub
Brauerei – brewery
Brotzeit – literally 'bread time', typically an afternoon snack featuring bread with cold cuts, cheeses or sausages
Brücke – bridge
Brunnen – fountain, well
Burg – castle
Busbahnhof – bus station

CDU – Christian Democratic Union
Christkindlmarkt – Christmas food and craft market; sometimes spelt *Christkindlesmarkt*; see also *Weihnachtsmarkt*
CSU – Christian Social Union; Bavarian offshoot of *CDU*

DB – Deutsche Bahn (German national railway)
Denkmal – memorial
Deutsche Reich – German empire; refers to the period 1871–1918
DJH – Deutsches Jugendherbergswerk (German youth hostel association)
Dom – cathedral
Dorf – village

Eingang – entrance

Fahrrad – bicycle
Fasching – pre-Lenten carnival
Fasnet – pre-Lenten carnival in Black Forest
Ferienwohnung, **Ferienwohnungen** (pl) – holiday flat or apartment

Fest – festival
Flohmarkt – flea market
Flughafen – airport
Föhn – an intense autumn wind in the Alpine foothills
Franken – 'Franks', Germanic people influential in Europe between the 3rd and 8th centuries

Krankenhaus – hospital
Kunst – art
Kurfürst – prince-elector
Kurhaus – literally 'spa house', but usually a spa town's central building, used for social gatherings and events
Kurort – spa resort
Kurtaxe – resort tax
Kurverwaltung – spa resort administration
Kurzentrum – spa centre

Land, **Länder** (pl) – state
Landtag – state parliament

Markgraf – margrave; German nobleman ranking above a count
Markt – market; often used instead of *Marktplatz*
Marktplatz – marketplace or square; often abbreviated to *Markt*
Mass – 1L tankard or stein of beer
Meistersinger – literally 'master singer'; highest level in medieval troubadour guilds
Mensa – university cafeteria
Milchcafé – coffee with milk
Münster – minster, large church, cathedral

Nord – north
Notdienst – emergency service
NSDAP – National Socialist German Workers' Party, Nazi party

Ost – east

Pension, **Pensionen** (pl) – inexpensive boarding house
Pfarrkirche – parish church
Platz – square
Postamt – post office

Radwandern – bicycle touring
Rathaus – town hall
Ratskeller – town hall restaurant
Reisezentrum – travel centre in train or bus stations
Ruhetag – 'rest day'; closing day at a shop or restaurant

Saal, Säle (pl) – hall, room
Sammlung – collection
S-Bahn – *Schnellbahn*; suburban-metropolitan trains
Schatzkammer – treasury
Schifffahrt – shipping, navigation
Schloss – palace
Schnellimbiss – fast-food stall or restaurants
See – lake
Seilbahn – cable car
Speisekarte – menu
Stadt – city, town
Stadtbad, Stadtbäder (pl) – public pool
Staudamm, Staumauer – dam
Strasse – street; often abbreviated to Str
Süd – south

Tal – valley
Tor – gate
Tracht, Trachten (pl) – folkloric outfit
Turm – tower

U-Bahn – underground (subway) train

Verboten – forbidden
Viertel – quarter, district
Volksmusik – folk music

Wald – forest
Wasserfall – waterfall
Weg – way, path
Weihnachtsmarkt – Christmas market; see also *Christkindlmarkt*
Weingut – wine-growing estate
Weinstube – traditional wine bar or tavern
West – west
Wiese – meadow

Zahnradbahn – cog-wheel railway
Zeitung – newspaper
Zimmer Frei – room available (for accommodation purposes)

The Authors

ANDREA SCHULTE-PEEVERS
Coordinating Author

Andrea will forever cherish the memory of waking up to the smell of hops from the brewery opposite the Munich garret she rented while writing this book. She's logged countless miles travelling in nearly 60 countries on five continents and carries her dog-eared passport like a badge of honour. Born and raised in Germany and educated in London and at UCLA, Andrea has built a career on writing about her native country for almost two decades. She's authored or contributed to about 40 Lonely Planet titles, including the first two editions of this book and all five editions of the Germany country guide.

CATHERINE LE NEVEZ
Regensburg, Eastern Bavaria & the Bavarian Forest; Nuremberg & Franconia; Romantic Road

Catherine's wanderlust began when she road-tripped across Europe, including Germany, aged four. She's been hitting the road ever since, completing her Doctorate of Creative Arts in Writing, Masters in Professional Writing, postgrad qualifications in Editing and Publishing, and numerous Lonely Planet guidebooks along the way.

Despite finding herself skidding down snowy mountainous backroads and scaling the steps of Walhalla in a searing heatwave, Catherine falls for Bavaria more every time…not only because of its beer – though that's reason enough! – but above all because of its fun, kind-hearted people.

KERRY WALKER
Walking in the Bavarian Alps, Salzburg, The Black Forest

Born in Essex, Kerry bid Blighty farewell after completing a languages degree in 2000. With a 1968 caravan, empty pockets and her crazy German boyfriend, Andy, she spent four years globetrotting from China to Patagonia. A lifelong fan of cuckoo clocks (there's one above her desk), cake and wilderness, she settled in the Black Forest and can be found hiking the hills, snowshoeing and mushroom-picking when not on her travels. True to her surname, she jumped at the chance to leg it up the Bavarian Alps for this edition. Her travel writing includes Lonely Planet *Austria*, city guides to Vienna, Geneva and Strasbourg, plus scores of online guides for Whatsonwhen.

Behind the Scenes

THIS BOOK

This 3rd edition of *Munich, Bavaria & the Black Forest* was researched and written by Andrea Schulte-Peevers, Catherine Le Nevez and Kerry Walker. The 2nd edition (titled *Munich & Bavaria)* was written by Andrea and Catherine, with Jeremy Gray. Andrea wrote the 1st edition of this book (then entitled *Bavaria*). Andrea coordinated this edition, which was commissioned out of Lonely Planet's London office and produced by the following:

Commissioning Editors Fiona Buchan, Fayette Fox & Korina Miller
Coordinating Editor Amy Thomas
Coordinating Cartographer Anita Banh
Coordinating Layout Designer Wibowo Rusli
Managing Editors Bruce Evans & Imogen Bannister
Managing Cartographer Mark Griffiths
Managing Layout Designer Adam McCrow
Assisting Editors David Andrew, David Carroll, Kate James, Kristin Odijk & Stephanie Ong
Assisting Cartographers Amanda Sierp, Barbara Benson & Sam Sayer
Cover Designer Pepi Bluck
Project Manager Sarah Sloane
Language Content Coordinator Quentin Frayne

Thanks to Ryan Evans, Lisa Knights, Naomi Parker, Trent Paton, Dianne Schallmeiner & Celia Wood

THANKS
ANDREA SCHULTE-PEEVERS

Big fat thanks to Fayette Fox, Amy Thomas and Mark Griffiths for being so patient and understanding, and basically saving my sanity. Same goes to my heart-throb husband David, the world's best dishwasher…and so much more. Jennifer Bligh and Gerhard Maier get heaps of gratitude for opening eyes, ears and doors, and for riding to the rescue at the last minute. A heartfelt thank you to Nizar, Sasha, Oskar, Karim and the entire Meininger crew for being such wonderful hosts. Victoria Larson deserves another gold medal for her kind support. Finally, a special nod also to Georg and Gaby Overs, Helga Mannhardt, Dave O'Neill and Antje Sievers.

CATHERINE LE NEVEZ

It was a joy returning to Bavaria – and Franconia! – for this book. *Vielen Dank* to all the wonderful locals, tourism professionals and fellow travellers who offered insights, assistance and good times along the way. In particular, thanks once again to (Saint) Dirk and Ralph in Fränkische Schweiz; Holger, Marco, Louisa-Verena and Hannah-Lilith in Würzburg; and Harry and Daniel in Rothenburg. Special thanks to Georg Schroll for the interview. *Danke* also to Korina Miller for the gig, as well as Fayette Fox, Mark Griffiths, co-authors Andrea and

---

THE LONELY PLANET STORY

Fresh from an epic journey across Europe, Asia and Australia in 1972, Tony and Maureen Wheeler sat at their kitchen table stapling together notes. The first Lonely Planet guidebook, *Across Asia on the Cheap*, was born.

Travellers snapped up the guides. Inspired by their success, the Wheelers began publishing books to Southeast Asia, India and beyond. Demand was prodigious, and the Wheelers expanded the business rapidly to keep up. Over the years, Lonely Planet extended its coverage to every country and into the virtual world via lonelyplanet.com and the Thorn Tree message board.

As Lonely Planet became a globally loved brand, Tony and Maureen received several offers for the company. But it wasn't until 2007 that they found a partner whom they trusted to remain true to the company's principles of travelling widely, treading lightly and giving sustainably. In October of that year, BBC Worldwide acquired a 75% share in the company, pledging to uphold Lonely Planet's commitment to independent travel, trustworthy advice and editorial independence.

Today, Lonely Planet has offices in Melbourne, London and Oakland, with over 500 staff members and 300 authors. Tony and Maureen are still actively involved with Lonely Planet. They're travelling more often than ever, and they're devoting their spare time to charitable projects. And the company is still driven by the philosophy of *Across Asia on the Cheap*: 'All you've got to do is decide to go and the hardest part is over. So go!'

Kerry, and everyone at Lonely Planet. As ever, *merci surtout* to my family.

KERRY WALKER
A great big thank you to my boyfriend, travel companion and Black Forest kid, Andy Christiani, for his tireless enthusiasm, support and insider tips. Fellow authors Andrea and Catherine were a pleasure to work with. Enormous thanks also to the tourism professionals who made the road to research silky smooth, particularly the teams in Gengenbach, Alpirsbach, Freiburg, Baden-Baden and Titisee. A heartfelt *Dankeschön* to the folk I met on the road who shared their fascinating stories, especially Claus Schäfer for his pearls of wisdom on Black Forest cake–baking and Tom Herzog-Singer in Villingen. Thanks also to the Statistisches Landesamt Baden-Württemberg, Stuttgart, for their help.

OUR READERS
Many thanks to the travellers who used the last edition and wrote to us with helpful hints, useful advice and interesting anecdotes:
Gianluca Agrati, Graeme Baker, David Bligh, Andrew Brown, Diane Caulkett, Ann Clark, Rachel Clarke, Marg Gelilander, Melanie Habersetzer, Andrew Lang, Gavin Moodie, Erdmute Oehmke, Anna Poller, Simon Smith, Sara Venturi, Gordon Woods

ACKNOWLEDGMENTS
Many thanks to the following for the use of their content:
Globe on title page ©Mountain High Maps 1993 Digital Wisdom, Inc.
Internal photographs p6 Werner Dieterich /Alamy; p7 Chris Fredriksson/Alamy; p8 Elvele Images /Alamy; p9 Vario Images GmbH Co KG/Alamy; p10 Jon Arnold Images Ltd/Alamy; p181 Ludger Vorfeld /Alamy; p182 Mediacolor's/Alamy; p183, p186 Pat Behnke/Alamy; p183 Louise Murray/Alamy; p187

SEND US YOUR FEEDBACK
We love to hear from travellers – your comments keep us on our toes and help make our books better. Our well-travelled team reads every word on what you loved or loathed about this book. Although we cannot reply individually to postal submissions, we always guarantee that your feedback goes straight to the appropriate authors, in time for the next edition. Each person who sends us information is thanked in the next edition – and the most useful submissions are rewarded with a free book.

To send us your updates – and find out about Lonely Planet events, newsletters and travel news – visit our award-winning website: **www.lonelyplanet.com/contact**.

Note: we may edit, reproduce and incorporate your comments in Lonely Planet products such as guidebooks, websites and digital products, so let us know if you don't want your comments reproduced or your name acknowledged. For a copy of our privacy policy visit www.lonelyplanet.com/privacy.

LOOK Die Bildagentur der Fotografen GmbH/Alamy. All other photographs by Lonely Planet Images, and by Dennis Johnson p5; David Peevers p7 (#1), p10 (#1); Grant Dixon p9 (#1); Martin Moos p11, p12.

Munich transport map p86 Schnellbahn Netzplan © 2007 Münchner Verkehrs- und Tarifverbund GmbH (MVV).

All images are the copyright of the photographers unless otherwise indicated. Many of the images in this guide are available for licensing from Lonely Planet Images: www.lonelyplanet images.com.

Index

000 Map pages
000 Photograph pages

GreenDex

Everyone's going green these days. Germany as a whole, and Bavaria in particular, are leading the way in many areas, from investing heavily in renewable energy sources to widespread recycling, bike-path networks and organic farming. But how do you know which businesses are actually ecofriendly and which are simply jumping on the eco/sustainable bandwagon?

The following sights, activities, eating, accommodation and transport choices have been selected by Lonely Planet authors because they demonstrate a commitment to sustainability. We've selected restaurants and hotels that serve up organic food or support local producers. Attractions are listed because they're involved in conservation or environmental education.

For more tips about travelling sustainably in the region, turn to the Getting Started chapter on p16. If you think we've missed anywhere out, or if you disagree with our choices, email us at talk2us@lonelyplanet.com.au and set us straight for next time. For more information about sustainable tourism and Lonely Planet, see www.lonelyplanet.com/responsibletravel.

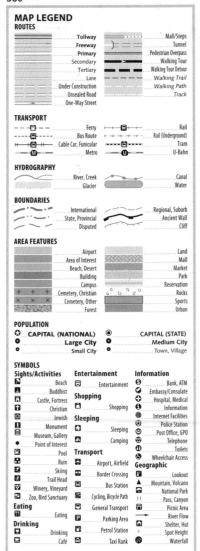

MAP LEGEND

ROUTES

Tollway	Mall/Steps
Freeway	Tunnel
Primary	Pedestrian Overpass
Secondary	Walking Tour
Tertiary	Walking Tour Detour
Lane	Walking Trail
Under Construction	Walking Path
Unsealed Road	Track
One-Way Street	

TRANSPORT

Ferry	Rail
Bus Route	Rail (Underground)
Cable Car, Funicular	Tram
Metro	U-Bahn

HYDROGRAPHY

River, Creek	Canal
Glacier	Water

BOUNDARIES

International	Regional, Suburb
State, Provincial	Ancient Wall
Disputed	Cliff

AREA FEATURES

Airport	Land
Area of Interest	Mall
Beach, Desert	Market
Building	Park
Campus	Reservation
Cemetery, Christian	Rocks
Cemetery, Other	Sports
Forest	Urban

POPULATION

CAPITAL (NATIONAL)	CAPITAL (STATE)
Large City	Medium City
Small City	Town, Village

SYMBOLS

Sights/Activities	Entertainment	Information
Beach	Entertainment	Bank, ATM
Buddhist	**Shopping**	Embassy/Consulate
Castle, Fortress	Shopping	Hospital, Medical
Christian	**Sleeping**	Information
Jewish	Sleeping	Internet Facilities
Monument	Camping	Police Station
Museum, Gallery	**Transport**	Post Office, GPO
Point of Interest	Airport, Airfield	Telephone
Pool	Border Crossing	Toilets
Ruin	Bus Station	Wheelchair Access
Skiing	Cycling, Bicycle Path	**Geographic**
Trail Head	General Transport	Lookout
Winery, Vineyard	Parking Area	Mountain, Volcano
Zoo, Bird Sanctuary	Petrol Station	National Park
Eating	Taxi Rank	Pass, Canyon
Eating		Picnic Area
Drinking		River Flow
Drinking		Shelter, Hut
Café		Spot Height
		Waterfall

LONELY PLANET OFFICES

Australia
Head Office
Locked Bag 1, Footscray, Victoria 3011
☎ 03 8379 8000, fax 03 8379 8111
talk2us@lonelyplanet.com.au

USA
150 Linden St, Oakland, CA 94607
☎ 510 893 8555, toll free 800 275 8555
fax 510 893 8572
info@lonelyplanet.com

UK
2nd Floor, 186 City Road,
London EC1V 2NT
☎ 020 7106 2100, fax 020 7106 2101
go@lonelyplanet.co.uk

Published by Lonely Planet Publications Pty Ltd
ABN 36 005 607 983

© Lonely Planet Publications Pty Ltd 2008

© photographers as indicated 2008

Cover photograph: Christmas near Mittenwald, Bavarian Alps; Alamy.
Many of the images in this guide are available for licensing from
Lonely Planet Images: www.lonelyplanetimages.com.

Although the authors and Lonely Planet have taken
all reasonable care in preparing this book, we make
no warranty about the accuracy or completeness of
its content and, to the maximum extent permitted,
disclaim all liability arising from its use.

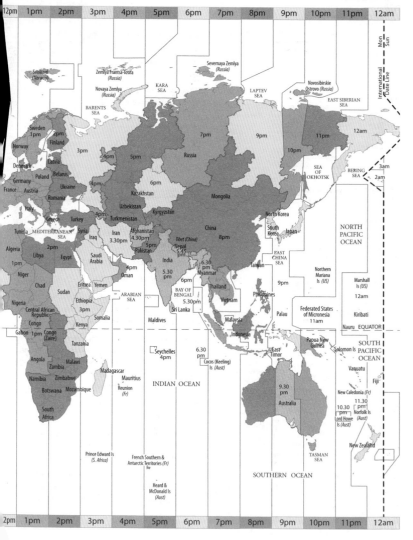